A Bibliography of British Business Histories

FRANCIS GOODALL

with an introduction by
Geoffrey Jones, Jonathan Liebenau, David Jeremy and
Richard Davenport-Hines

of the Business History Unit,
London School of Economics

Gower
Aldershot · Brookfield USA · Hong Kong · Singapore · Sydney

Published by
Gower Publishing Company Limited,
Gower House, Croft Road, Aldershot, Hants. GU11 3HR,
England

Gower Publishing Company,
Old Post Road, Brookfield, Vermont 05036
United States of America.

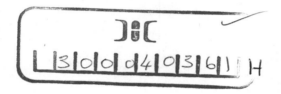

ISBN 0-566-05307-1

Printed and bound in Great Britain by
Biddles Limited, Guildford and King's Lynn

A BIBLIOGRAPHY OF BRITISH BUSINESS HISTORIES

Contents

1 Introduction

The nature of business history

The scale of economic activity ranges between international regions and individual households, but whatever the scale of activities, wealth is generated, institutions have to be organised, markets are manipulated, and goods and services are supplied. The history of micro economic units, companies and their groupings, and industrial sectors, is crucial to understanding the actual practice of capitalist commerce. Business history aims to describe, analyse, and extract from this analysis the working of commercial organisations. By looking at the structure and development of companies, concomitant changes in productive capacities, and the activities of entrepreneurs and managers, business historians build up a picture of the changing world of commerce.

Business history has long fitted uneasily within traditional academic structures.[1] In Britain interest in business history was formalised in 1934 when the Business Archives Council (BAC) was established by a group of academics and businessmen. Business history was already an expanding field, with histories of firms and industries for cotton (Daniels, Unwin, Wadsworth & Mann), wool (Heaton), iron and steel (Ashton), coal (Ashton and Sykes) and copper (Hamilton).[2] At Harvard a Business History Society had already been formed in 1926 at the Business School's Baker Library by N. S. B. Gras, A. H. Cole and others. The Business Archives Council in Britain largely confined itself to listing locations of company records, stifled in its earliest aspirations by the outbreak of war. Since 1945 the BAC has continued its valuable work in registering business records, has started to build up a library, and organised an annual conference attended by business historians and archivists. Over the past decade it has stimulated business history by sponsoring several publications and by offering an annual book prize endowed by Professor John Wadsworth.(3)

In the universities, however, business history became marginalised from economic history, which concentrates on topics such as national economies, policy analysis, and large scale trade. Consequently business historians have often looked to other disciplines. In some countries, such as the United States, these have been located at business schools or within large corporations. In Britain, where fewer congenial homes have been found, most business historians work in the economic history departments of universities and polytechnics. Since 1959 recent research has been reported in *Business History*, the main academic journal, initially edited by Professor Francis Hyde and his colleagues in the Economic History Department at Liverpool University. Unlike the United States, Japan and Germany, there is no business history society, and there are only two specialised centres for research in this area: the Business History Unit at the London School of Economics (LSE) and the Economic History Department and University Archives at the University of Glasgow. The former was launched in 1979 and is essentially a research centre headed by Leslie Hannah, the first professor of business history in the LSE and in the UK. The University of Glasgow's initiative began in 1960 when Peter Payne (now professor of economic history at the University of Aberdeen) started to collect business archives from firms in the west of Scotland which were casualties of industrial decline. These archives spawned a number of case studies including Peter Payne's prize-winning *Colvilles*, Tony Slaven's "John Brown's between the Wars" (*Business History*) and John Hume and Michael Moss's *Beardmores*.(4) More recently the economic historians and the archivists at Glasgow University have joined to promote an historical computing programme which is producing results with implications for the debate about wealth creation in modern Britain.(5) Although there are relatively few specialist centres of business history in Britain, a large quantity of work by British business historians addressing central themes of business history has been produced, as this bibliography demonstrates.

These themes relate to industries or industrial groups, individuals or types of key actors, or topics which span industries or people. Two organising themes which have been of particular influence are strategy and structure. Understanding business strategy or the character of business decisions, like efforts to increase efficiency and forward planning, are a key bridge between business history and other approaches to studying business. Similarly, analysing the structure of companies by looking into management and organisational matters bears direct relations to business decision making. It is no accident that Professor A D Chandler's book, *Strategy and Structure*, which was published in 1962 and dealt with the evolution of management structures in large American corporations, has become a seminal work for business historians in all countries.(6)

2

Another group of topics attracting attention among business historians includes marketing, finance, and personnel relations. Marketing studies, only recently considered for businesses outside retail trade, are increasingly recognised as relevant not only to Britain's late-twentieth century service economy but as a means to understanding why otherwise similar organisations performed quite differently in shared competitive situations. The study of finance addresses questions of the flow of money to support industry as well as history of financial institutions; the study of personnel relations brings business history together with the history of industrial relations, organised labour and work practices. Entrepreneurship and innovation are two further themes which assess the dynamics, motivations, incentives and technical character of business. Other issues include government/industry relations and nationalised industries which raise questions about utilities as businesses, key sectors of production, regulation and control. The books in the Gower business history series, of which this bibliography forms a part, confront many of these themes.[7]

These apparently diverse subjects are held together by approach and methodology. To begin with, this is an approach from the point of view of the company. Typically questions are posed asking what conditions of practice led to certain decisions, what kinds of choices conditions allowed, what factors were taken into consideration. When we analyse how a corporation grew we need to consider more than the fact of growth, but also have to understand what circumstances gave rise to development.

Because questions are posed in this way there is usually a distinction between the work of recent business historians and historians of companies whose goals are more limited. This bibliography includes references to both, but the distinction will become clear as users delve into the texts. Then it becomes apparent that business history is distinct from company chronologies, and that the central concerns of business historians are different from those whose interest is company genealogy: the best 'academic' company histories - such as D C Coleman's magisterial three volume history of Courtaulds - place the experience of their firms in a wider context.[8]

Business history is an international subject, more popular in industrialised countries and most well regarded in the leading industrialised societies: Germany, Japan and the United States. Japan is particularly active in this discipline, and its 300 university lectureships in business history provide a striking contrast with the handful of academic posts in Britain - at Glasgow, Nottingham and the London School of Economics - devoted to the subject. The strength of British business history is based on the wealth of information available about the history of hundreds of British firms, their significance in the development of manufacturing since the industrial revolution, and the depth of interest in history traditionally found in Britain. Equally, British cases have been used extensively by foreign historians, as is also evident in this bibliography. The relatively poor performance of British industry since the late nineteenth century, and its disastrous withering since the early 1970s, and especially since 1979, has provided additional interest in the British experience for students of business failure - and for those who hope that the United Kingdom's failure may yet be reversed.

New directions

In recent years a number of distinct research trends have emerged, and numerous subsidiary uses have been found for business history. The establishment of the Business History Unit has helped to focus interest in developing the new research trends. Academic work in business history has moved from predominantly glossy public relations accounts of heroic company development towards broad integration into the mainstream of historical scholarship. The place of business within developing economies, its relationship with society in general, and the way industry displaced agriculture in many countries are the larger questions in which these enquiries fit.

Academic business historians have been strongly influenced by the schema proposed by Chandler and applied to the growth of large managerially-run businesses in the United States. He described how the introduction of hierarchical forms of organisation could control large multidivisional companies and administer not only static business but also dynamic corporations. These alterations in corporate structure allowed for growth, increased power, and the opportunity to plan for change. Out of these capabilities emerged a conscious effort to develop business strategies. The elaboration of these themes in Chandler's *The Visible Hand* [9]
provided a clear challenge to British and other business historians to assess the development of business outside the United States.
Numerous differences were found. Britain was shown to retain smaller, family-controlled units far longer than the United States, and to avoid capital investment and professionalisation of managerial functions. Other differences stem from different capital markets and governmental policies towards trade and industry. It has emerged that British multinationals grew in different countries, and with different organisational forms, than their American equivalents. But of even greater significance were the social differences which emerged when entrepreneurship and cultural incentives for industrial success were examined. [10] It is now evident that many models of business development formulated on the basis of American experience apply only partially, if at all, to Britain and elsewhere in Europe.

It seems clear that internationally comparative research projects represent one of the most promising avenues for future research. Fundamental answers to the key questions concerning the generally poor performance of British business in the twentieth century are only likely to be found by looking at the performance of business in other countries.

Comparative research on the evolution of labour management policies in Britain, the United States and Japan, on innovation in British, German and American science-based industries, and on the differences between countries in the development of their multinational and financial institutions, is already yielding important new insights.(11) Comparative business history was one of the themes pursued at a special session on business history at the 1986 British Economic History Society meeting at Cheltenham. As one of the papers at this session observed, the United Kingdom, with its diversity of business experience between England, Scotland, Wales and Ireland presents many opportunities for comparative work even within its own national boundaries.(12)

Other practitioners of business history have had more narrow objectives in view. They have used the history of a firm to celebrate it, to advertise or present an image of an enterprise which has both well-founded stability and dynamism. Some companies have regarded business histories as tools to discover more about themselves in other ways. The sense of corporate identity is often strong, sometimes too strong for managers to manoeuvre around. Writing company history often helps to explain the genesis and character of institutional identities. A well-written analysis of this type might even be a useful management tool, as has been found by some American companies.

There have long been other fields which have looked to the history of business for information and supplementary material. Local historians have done so frequently, using methodologies of business historians and occasionally themselves writing company histories. Similarly, biographers make use of business history, although until recently the area of business biography was almost non-existent except where it has been linked to other themes, such as business and religious groups or business and philanthropy. However, the publication of some outstanding monographs in this area , and the appearance of the five-volume *Dictionary of Business Biography*, has done much to revive business biography.(13)

Methodology of business history

Business historians have been eclectic in their methods, using public, private and official sources. Some writers have done valuable statistical analyses. The use of oral history has recently become fashionable, as evidenced by the publication of several company histories which have relied extensively on interviews.(14) However, most business history research has continued to be archivally based. Business archives are notoriously difficult to find and use.(15) Partly this is because they are often guarded with proprietary interest but they also tend to be disregarded. To some degree, they are composed of useless ephemera. However, advertisements and summary progress reports, graphics and memoranda are all of potential value. Often these have been discarded, creating problems of documentation. Sometimes, when such material is found, it is impossible to reconstruct its context, or discern its completeness. There is a full range of all historical methodologies represented in this bibliography, contradicting the notion that there is 'a business history methodology' at all. But the similarity is always on the concentration on a company or group of companies, and usually archival sources of local origin.

Certain methodological problems continue to plague business historians. What grounds are there for comparability? How many case studies convincingly make a case? What groups can be legitimately brought together to generalise beyond those specifically studied? When can a group of local studies be used to make national conclusions? There are no easy answers to these methodological quandaries, but increasingly careful studies are being undertaken which indicate widening horizons.

The utility of this bibliography

There are numerous ways in which this bibliography is uniquely useful. By its comprehensiveness and its industrial classification it allows for industry-wide coverage. Not only can an historian retrieve references to studies of one company , but groups of companies, and even industrial classes can be gathered. This provides a quick and easy way of assessing the depth of writing in any particular area, and is especially useful in constructing comparisons of industrial groups. Such comparisons are especially useful when cross-national analyses are wanted. Furthermore, not only can the sources be identified by industrial area, they can also be grouped thematically. So broader studies and issue-orientated approaches are quickly apparent.

This bibliography also forms a teaching tool of great potential. There are flourishing business history courses at many universities and polytechnics, such as the London School of Economics and Ealing College of Higher Education, and we hope that the students on such courses will find this work of value, especially if they are researching dissertations in specialist areas. Moreover since industrial and therefore regional groups are easily retrievable, special reading lists for local history, industrial archaeology, and economic history can be quickly constructed.

Business history in Britain remains a subject in which there is too much detail and too few overviews, where heroic generalisations are rare and well-meaning but inconsequential case studies plentiful. Our feeling, however, is that business history is on the verge of a breakthrough, and that in its wide-ranging concerns it can help to revive and reinvigorate the currently demoralised subject of history. Our hope is that this bibliography will not only facilitate the study of business history, but it will suggest new ideas about possible research topics.

Footnotes

(1)   For earlier critical bibliographies of business history see Roy Church, 'Business History in Britain', *Journal of European Economic History* 5 (1976); Leslie Hannah, 'New Issues in British Business History', *Business History Review* 57 (1983); Anthony Slaven, 'The Uses of Business Records: Some Research Trends in British Business History', *Business Archives* 50 (1984).

(2)   T. S. Ashton, *Iron and Steel in the Industrial Revolution* (Manchester, 1924); T. S. Ashton and J. Sykes, *The Coal Industry of the Eighteenth Century* (Manchester, 1929); G. W. Daniels, *The Early English Cotton Industry* (Manchester, 1920); H. Hamilton, *The English Brass and Copper Industries to 1800* (London, 1926); G. Unwin, *Samuel Oldknow and the Arkwrights* (Manchester, 1924); A. P. Wadsworth and J.de L. Mann, *The Cotton Trade and Industrial Lancashire 1600-1780* (Manchester, 1931).

(3)   For an account of the history of the Business Archives Council see Peter Mathias in *Business Archives* 50 (1984).

(4)   Peter L. Payne, *Studies in Scottish Business History* (London, 1967); Peter L. Payne, *Colvilles and the Scottish Steel Industry* (Oxford, 1979); Anthony Slaven, 'A Shipyard in Depression: John Brown's of Clydebank 1919-1938', *Business History* 19 (1977); John Hume and Michael Moss, *Beardmore: The History of a Scottish Industrial Giant* (London, 1979).

(5)   Michael Moss, 'Business History at the University of Glasgow', *Business History Newsletter* 11 (1985); Michael Moss and John Hume, 'Listing the Wealthy in Scotland', *Bulletin of the Institute of Historical Research* (1986).

(6)   Alfred D. Chandler, *Strategy and Structure: Chapters in the History of the Industrial Enterprise* (Cambridge, Mass., 1962).

(7)   Geoffrey Jones (ed.), *British Multinationals: Origins, Management and Performance* (1986); R. P. T. Davenport-Hines (ed.), *Markets and Bagmen* (1986); Jonathan Liebenau (ed.), *The Challenge of New Technology* (1987); David J. Jeremy (ed.), *Business and Religion* (1987); J.-J. van Helten (ed.), *Essays in British Finance* (1987). Future volumes will include studies of government-industry relations and business strategies.

(8)   D. C. Coleman, *Courtaulds: An Economic and Social History*, 3 vols. (Oxford, 1969, 1980). Other academic company histories which adroitly place their subjects within a wider social or political context include Barry Supple, *The Royal Exchange Assurance 1720-1970* (Cambridge, 1970); Clive Trebilcock, *Phoenix Assurance and the Development of British Insurance 1782-1870* (Cambridge, 1985); Charles Wilson, *First with the News: The History of W. H. Smith 1792-1972* (London, 1985); and on a charming but more modest scale, Asa Briggs, *Wine for Sale: Victoria Wine and the Liquor Trade 1860-1984* (London, 1985).

(9)   Alfred D. Chandler, *The Visible Hand: The Managerial Revolution in American Business* (Cambridge, Mass., 1977).

(10) A useful introduction to the comparison of American and European business experience is provided by the essays in Alfred D. Chandler and Herman Daems (eds.), *Managerial Hierarchies* (Cambridge, Mass.,1982). This theme is also pursued, in the case of multinationals, by Peter Hertner and Geoffrey Jones (eds.), *Multinationals: Theory and History* (Aldershot, 1986).

(11) See Howard F. Gospel and C. R. Littler, *Managerial Strategies and Industrial Relations* (London, 1983) and e.g. Jonathan Liebenau (ed.), *The Challenge of New Technology: Innovation in British Business* (Aldershot, 1987). For a comparative insight on multinationals see A. Teichova and P. L. Cottrell (eds.), *International Business and Central Europe 1918-1939* (Leicester, 1983). On financial institutions see, for example, W. P. Kennedy and Ranald Michie, 'The London and New York Stock Exchanges 1850-1914', *Journal of Economic History* XLVI (1986). For a comparative study of business education, see Robert R. Locke, *The End of the Practical Man: Entrepreneurship and Higher Education in Germany, France and Great Britain, 1880-1940* (London, 1984).

(12) Charles W. Munn, 'The Development of Joint-Stock Business in the British Isles in the Nineteenth Century: A Comparative Approach'; paper presented at the 1986 Economic History Conference. For another exercise in comparative history, see Jonathan S. Boswell, *Business Policies in the Making: Three Steel Companies Compared* (London, 1983).

(13) David J. Jeremy and Christine Shaw (eds.), *Dictionary of Business Biography*, 5 vols. (London, 1984-86). An early attempt to revive the art of business biography was the Europa Library of Business Biography, edited by Neil McKendrick. Studies by R. J. Overy of *William Morris* (London, 1976), Clive Trebilcock of *The Vickers Brothers* (London, 1977), and R. A. Church of *Herbert Austin* (London, 1979) made useful contributions before the series collapsed. A more recent and substantial business biography was R. P. T. Davenport-Hines, *Dudley Docker: The Life and Times of a Trade Warrior* (Cambridge, 1984). The latter author has also edited *Speculators and Patriots: Essays in Business Biography* (London, 1986) treating the themes of speculation and patriotism discernable in the careers of seven entrepreneurs - financiers, industrialists, mineowners and a newspaper proprietor between 1880-1925. For one of the worst examples of this genre, see Jacques Attali, *Un Homme d'Influence: Sir Siegmund G. Warburg, 1902-82* (Paris, 1986).

(14) See, for example, histories of STC by Peter Young, *The Power of Speech* (London, 1983) and the two-volume history of The British Bank of the Middle East by Geoffrey Jones, *Banking and Empire in Iran* and *Banking and Oil* (Cambridge, 1986). For other fine examples see the 'Oral History Symposium' in F. H. H. King (ed.), *Eastern Banking: Essays in the History of the Hongkong and Shanghai Banking Corporation* (London, 1983). An essay written almost entirely from oral sources is Stanley Chapman, 'Hogg

Robinson: The Rise of a Lloyd's Broker' in Oliver M. Westall (ed.), *The Historian and the Business of Insurance* (Manchester, 1984).

(15) Tracing business archives has been appreciably eased by the publication, under the auspices of the Business Archives Council, of Lesley Richmond and Bridget Stockford, *Company Archives: The Survey of the Records of 1000 of the First Registered Companies in England and Wales* (Aldershot, 1986) and L. S. Pressnell and M. J. Orbell (eds.), *A Guide to the Historical Records of British Banking* (London, 1985).

2 Preface and user's guide

Preface

Students of business history are faced with a range of problems in their search for material. They will be concerned about the nature of material available, its scope and its quality. The value of any material may well depend upon the perspective of the researcher and whether the topic is approached from the direction of economic history, industrial archaeology, managerial structures and performance or a consideration of the political and sociological framework within which business operates. The frame of interest may be the history of a particular firm and its predecessors or a sector of business activity; it may be confined to a narrow field or seek to develop inter-firm comparisons within the United Kingdom or world-wide. The study of an individual firm as it grows (or declines) may provide valuable insights into trends in the economy as a whole and may suggest many tantalising questions on the nature of entrepreneurship, the role of competition or combination, methods of measuring success and so on.

The framework adopted for this bibliography, if it is to accommodate such a wide range of potential research, must provide easy accessibility to a wide range of material categorised both by the nature of business activity and the name of the firm, both fully cross-referenced to the main Author Index. This has been done so users are free to select any convenient point of entry - author, firm or type of business and are led forward systematically; as they follow their interest, other linkages and possibilities will open up an enormous body of research material.

The bibliography contains a very wide range of material relating to United Kingdom companies of the 19th and 20th centuries, including some whose main sphere of operations was overseas but were U K based; some foreign-owned firms with a large direct investment in the U K economy, e.g. Ford, are also included. No criterion on firm size has been adopted; there are histories of small family concerns as well as of multinationals.

The quality of the material is extremely variable. Some of the company histories are very slight indeed, offering perhaps a eulogy with a few dates and indications of profitability, a few statistics but no analysis or assessment of the company's performance relative to its competitors or the economy as a whole. Many such histories, particularly the older ones, were compiled to mark a jubilee or centenary and for circulation to customers and friends, rather than for general publication. No apology is necessary for the inclusion of such works, as they may provide the only information extant relating to particular firms or types of business activity.

One example is a book by 'Lesser Columbus' who made a series of visits to firms in his native Bristol around 1892 and describes factory processes in a variety of trades; of the companies he visited, Fry, Robinson and Wills at least are still operating though not necessarily under the same names. Another similar volume, *Fortunes made in Business* (Sampson Low 1884, 3 vols), provides a wealth of information, if uncritically. This genre survived between the wars as evidenced by books such as W H Beable's *Romance of Great Business* (Heath Cranton 1926, 2 vols) and Bridges and Tiltman *Kings of Commerce* (Harrap 1928). These all make interesting reading and may provide information not recorded elsewhere. Other perspectives on business history and the activities of businessmen are provided by books such as the *Whitehall Diary* of Thomas Jones for the political perspective, or O'Hagan's *Leaves from my Life* giving a financier's view.

Company histories written largely for their public relations value are still being produced, but because of the involvement of business historians and professional researchers, the average quality of recent works shows a sharp improvement. Many such books now include a note of the source material utilised and sometimes a full bibliography; such additional detail is noted in this volume.

Current developments in business history research are fully discussed in the introduction. Modern thematic work has been included together with older style company histories, theses for research degrees and journal articles. The detailed references to source material in recent work will enable researchers to follow up their own interests.

Some company histories are available only in typescript, lodged in a local library or held by the firm itself. A few such items have been found and included, but there are probably many more waiting to be uncovered. The researcher should approach the company concerned and also district and county libraries to establish what material is available. Even the catalogues of the British Library include much material relating to individual companies which is not listed here; technical brochures, annual reports and general publicity material were deemed to fall outside the scope of a listing of business histories even though they may be of interest to the specialist. Slight pamphlets, reports of the company's war efforts, press cuttings and entries from local directories were excluded. Similarly no attempt has been made to identify or assess archive material held by companies or lodged in a record office. The Business Archives Council can provide invaluable assistance here.

The bibliography was compiled from many sources. The first step was to examine the substantial collections of the Business Archives Council, the British Library of Political and Economic Science at the London School of Economics and the Library of the University of Bristol; listings were prepared of material which might be included. Volumes that appeared to reflect an interest in economic rather than business/company history were set aside. Selection of items for inclusion proved a difficult task and many first-rate books and articles fell outside the compiler's personal and pragmatic criteria and have unfortunately been omitted.

An approach was made by letter to the librarians of county and district councils who gave a magnificent response, many providing detailed lists of books in their collections; these responses have been incorporated and have enabled the inclusion of much material whose existence would not otherwise have been suspected. Further titles were noted during a verification of the various lists against entries in the British Library catalogue. A search in journals such as *Business History* and *Economic History Review* was very profitable. Newly available is the *Dictionary of Business Biography* (eds David J Jeremy and Christine Shaw, 5 vols Butterworth 1984-86) whose compilation has been one of the major early tasks of the Business History Unit of the London School of Economics. This provides a wealth of suggestions for further research. It is of particular interest as a number of unusual sources, including many from the period before 1914, are cited. Some of these will be eulogies following the style of Samuel Smiles but others provide fascinating insights. Today's instant journalism may provide similar help for future researchers. The late Professor S G Checkland acted as project co-ordinator for the *Dictionary of Scottish Business Biography* (eds Charles W Munn & Anthony Slaven, Aberdeen University Press) which will be available shortly; this will provide another fruitful source of material for the business historian.

There are a number of other potential sources of information on individual companies or business sectors which may be relevant. This preface is followed by a listing of other bibliographies. Walford in that listing gives details of bibliographies compiled for individual counties, which may well include details of local economic activity. There are many specialised libraries, eg those of the learned institutions and of trade associations which may be of assistance. Government reports such as those of the Monopolies and Restrictive Practices Commission and Board of Trade inquiries under the Companies Act may provide details not available elsewhere as may the reports of the Committee of Public Accounts. Two books by Edwards and Townsend are cited; these draw on a series of seminars at the London School of Economics extending over many years when senior executives presented reports on their businesses. Many of these are on general management topics but some provide statistical and historical data on individual firms. Many but by no means all of the items listed have been examined by the author who recognises their varied quality. He would welcome details of material he has overlooked (and errors which he may have made) and will add these to his master file so that by periodical updating this listing will be as comprehensive and useful as possible.

It was decided to incorporate an analysis of titles by the nature of the business; the Standard Industrial Classification (SIC) of the Central Statistical Office provides a readily accessible, detailed and systematic analysis of current business activity; the 1980 revision has been used. Designed for Government Statistical Service purposes, it allocates industrial activity into main divisions:-

0   Agriculture, Forestry and Fishing
1   Energy and Water Supply Industries
2   Extraction of Minerals and Ores other than Fuels; Manufacture of Metals, Mineral Products and Chemicals
3   Metal Goods, Engineering and Vehicles Industries
4   Other Manufacturing Industries
5   Construction
6   Distribution, Hotels and Catering, Repairs
7   Transport and Communication
8   Banking, Finance, Insurance, Business Services and Leasing
9   Other Services

Within these divisions, further subdivisions into two digit classes and three digit groups add to the precision of the scheme, e.g.

250   Chemical Industry
251   Basic Industrial Chemicals
255   Paint, Varnishes and Printing Ink
256   Specialised Chemical Products mainly for Industrial and Agricultural Purposes
257   Pharmaceutical Products
258   Soap and Toilet Preparations
259   Specialised Chemical Products mainly for Household and Office Use

The three digit groups are further refined by a fourth, and in some cases, a fifth digit; for the purposes of this bibliography only the three digit grouping has been used.

Where the general nature of a business is known but its precise nature is unclear or where it straddles several adjacent three-digit groups, the

14

class number is used, eg 250 Chemical Industry. Even then, the very precision of the classification ensures that it does not easily accommodate conglomerates or holding companies.

It is noteworthy that certain trades are much more prone to prepare company histories than others. There is a substantial over-representation of printers and publishers, insurance companies and co-operative societies. Other sectors, particularly the high-technology and service industries are severely under-represented. It is hoped that this imbalance will be corrected in due course.

User's Guide

The main listing of entries, the <u>Author Index</u>, is arranged alphabetically in the following format:-

Author:
    Title:
    Publisher: **Contents:**
    Name(s) of Firm:
    Standard Industrial Classification(s):   **Source Library:**

Following this are two further listings, each cross-referenced by author i) the <u>Company Index</u>, listing companies by name and ii) using the SIC to bring together all companies in the same line of business, the <u>Industrial Classification Index</u>.

Each Author Index entry has provision for citing two company names but occasionally additional names have been included in the Company Index; the cross-reference leads back to the Author Index. Consideration was given to attempting to cite the current names of companies still in existence; this was quickly abandoned as serving no useful purpose, quite apart from the practical difficulties. As an example, the car company renamed (in mid 1986) the Rover Group has for much of the post-war period had Leyland as a part of its name; in this case the style of 'British Leyland' has been adopted. The independent pre-war companies are however cited as the 'Austin Motor Co' and 'Morris Motors' as well as the old 'Rover Co'. A check in the Industrial Classification Index will locate all references to car makers.

Each entry in the Author Index may generate up to five SIC references in the Industrial Classification Index, which are each cross-referenced to the same Author Index entry. This will ensure that companies with a wide spread of activities can be located by any one of their SIC references and through the Author Index can be linked to other companies active in similar spheres of business.

The following detailed points apply to the Author Index:-

(i) In citing authors, no honours or titles have been shown. Where no author is credited, the name of the firm is given in lieu of an author.

(ii) The place (if not London) and date of publication is shown; where the book is privately produced, the publisher is identified as 'the firm' to include partnerships and private as well as public companies. Where the author is also the publisher, this is indicated.

(iii) An indication of content is given by the number of pages and whether the book is illustrated or indexed. If the author has identified details of his source material, this is indicated by 'sources'; this might range from a full-scale bibliography with footnotes to a sentence or two referring to the use of company records or archives, company accounts etc. The date of publication and authorship may suggest the potential value of such source material.

(iv) Firms are generally identified by their name at the time of writing of their history; no attempt has been made to update this other than to provide some degree of consistency in the Company Index. If required, a search in current or past editions of the *Stock Exchange Official Year Book* (Macmillan) or *Who Owns Whom* (Dun & Bradstreet) might be productive. Some histories deal with a business sector rather than individual firms; in such cases the Firm Index will show eg Brewing Industry.

(v) Where the nature of the business described appears to have no direct parallel in the SIC, the nearest contemporary equivalent is adopted. For trading companies, holding companies and UK-based firms whose main sphere of activity is overseas, group 839 for 'Central Offices not Allocable Elsewhere' is used, if possible with a rather more specific indicator.

(vi) The source library code indicates a positive location of the material. Where a book appears in the British Library catalogue, the code is asterisked(*) to suggest, at least for recent books, that it may be fairly widely available. Books in the library of the Business Archives Council are also specifically identified (§). In the absence of one or other of these indicators, another positive location is given based on the information from librarians. Where no location is shown, the titles have been culled from other sources, eg a citation in the Dictionary of Business Biography or a publisher's catalogue. Researchers are reminded that access to material is not necessarily freely available; the British Library is restricted to authorised readers; the Business Archives Council welcomes enquiries but a prior appointment is essential.

Acknowledgements

The author would like to thank the many people and organisations he consulted and in particular the librarians whose collections he visited and those who took enormous trouble to prepare lists of their business history collections and sent details in response to his request.

The work was made possible by a Social Science Small Grant from the Nuffield Foundation. The author would like to thank the Foundation for its support. He also gratefully acknowledges the assistance and encouragement of his colleagues at the Business History Unit, particularly Dr Geoffrey Jones, then Acting Director of the Unit and joint grantholder with Dr Jonathan Liebenau, Dr David Jeremy who introduced him to the Unit and Dr Richard Davenport-Hines. These four made up a steering committee for the project, made many helpful contributions during its progress and kindly contributed an introduction to the finished work. All errors are the sole responsibility of the author.

The classification of firms by type of business follows that in the Central Statistical Office's Standard Industrial Classification Revised 1980 (HMSO, ISBN 0 11 620150 9) and the three-digit summary of the full published classification appears with the permission of The Controller of Her Majesty's Stationery Office.

Standard Industrial Classification

0   Agriculture, Forestry and Fishing
010   Agriculture and Horticulture
020   Forestry
030   Fishing

100   Energy and Water Supply Industries
111   Coal Extraction and Manufacture of Solid Fuels
120   Coke Ovens
130   Extraction of Mineral Oil and Gas
140   Mineral Oil Processing
152   Nuclear Fuel Production
161   Production and Distribution of Electricity
162   Public Gas Supply
163   Production and Distibution of Other Forms of Energy
170   Water Supply Industry

200   Extraction of Minerals and Ores other than Fuels: Manufacture of Metals, Mineral Products and Chemicals
210   Extraction and Preparation of Metalliferous Ores
220   Metal Manufacturing
221   Iron and Steel Industry
222   Steel Tubes
223   Drawing, Cold Rolling and Cold Forming of Steel
224   Non-Ferrous Metals Industry

230   Extraction of Minerals, not elsewhere specified
231   Extraction of Stone, Clay, Sand and Gravel
233   Salt Extraction and Refining
239   Extraction of Other Minerals not elsewhere specified

240   Manufacture of Non-Metallic Mineral Products
241   Structural Clay Products
242   Cement, Lime and Plaster
243   Building Products of Concrete, Cement or Plaster
244   Asbestos Goods
245   Working of Stone and other Non-Metallic Minerals not elsewhere specified
246   Abrasive Products
247   Glass and Glassware
248   Refractory and Ceramic Goods

250   Chemical Industry
251   Basic Industrial Chemicals
255   Paints, Varnishes and Printing Ink
256   Specialised Chemical Products mainly for Industrial and Agricultural Purposes
257   Pharmaceutical Products
258   Soap and Toilet Preparations
259   Specialised Chemical Products mainly for Household and Office Use

260 Production of Man-Made Fibres

300 Metal Goods, Engineering and Vehicles Industries
310 Manufacture of Metal Products not elsewhere specified
311 Foundries
312 Forging, Pressing and Stamping
313 Bolts, Nuts etc., Springs, Non-Precision Chains, Metals Treatment
314 Metal Doors, Windows etc.
316 Hand Tools and Finished Metal Goods

320 Mechanical Engineering
320 Industrial Plant and Steelwork
321 Agricultural Machinery and Tractors
322 Metal-Working Machine Tools and Engineers' Tools
323 Textile Machinery
324 Machinery for the Food, Chemical and related industries: Process Engineering Contractors
325 Mining Machinery, Construction and Mechanical Handling Equipment
326 Mechanical Power Transmission Equipment
327 Machinery for the Printing, Paper, Wood, Leather, Rubber, Glass and related industries, Laundry & Dry Cleaning Machinery
328 Other Machinery and Mechanical Equipment
329 Ordnance, Small Arms and Ammunition

330 Manufacture of Office Machinery and Data Processing Equipment

340 Electrical and Electronic Engineering
341 Insulated Wires and Cables
342 Basic Electrical Equipment
343 Electrical Equipment for Industrial Use, and Batteries and Accumulators
344 Telecommunication Equipment, Electrical Measuring Equipment, Electronic Capital Goods and Passive Electronic Components
345 Other Electronic Equipment
346 Domestic-Type Electric Appliances
347 Electric Lamps and other Electric Lighting Equipment
348 Electrical Equipment Installation

350 Manufacture of Motor Vehicles and Parts Thereof
351 Motor Vehicles and Their Engines
352 Motor Vehicle Bodies, Trailers and Caravans
353 Motor Vehicle Parts

360 Manufacture of Other Transport Equipment
361 Shipbuilding and Repairing
362 Railway and Tramway Vehicles
363 Cycles and Motor Cycles
364 Aerospace Equipment Manufacturing and Repairing
365 Other Vehicles

370 Instrument Engineering
371 Measuring, Checking and Precision Instruments and Apparatus

372 Medical and Surgical Equipment and Orthopaedic Appliances
373 Optical Precision Instruments and Photographic Equipment
374 Clocks, Watches and other Timing Devices

400 Other Manufacturing Industries

410/420 Food, Drink and Tobacco Manufacturing Industries
411 Organic Oils and Fats (Other than Crude Animal Fats)
412 Slaughtering of Animals and Production of Meat and By-Products
413 Preparation of Milk and Milk Products
414 Processing of Fruit and Vegetables
415 Fish Processing
416 Grain Milling
418 Starch
419 Bread, Biscuits and Flour Confectionery
420 Sugar and Sugar By-Products
421 Ice Cream, Cocoa, Chocolate and Sugar Confectionery
422 Animal Feeding Stuffs
423 Miscellaneous Foods
424 Spirit Distilling and Compounding
426 Wines, Cider and Perry
427 Brewing and Malting
428 Soft Drinks
429 Tobacco Industry

430 Textile Industry
431 Woollen and Worsted Industry
432 Cotton and Silk Industries
433 Throwing, Texturing etc of Continuous Filament Yarn
434 Spinning and Weaving of Flax, Hemp and Ramie
435 Jute and Polypropylene Yarns and Fabrics
436 Hosiery and other Knitted Goods
437 Textile Finishing
438 Carpets and other Textile Floor Coverings
439 Miscellaneous Textiles

440 Manufacture of Leather and Leather Goods
441 Leather (Tanning and Dressing) and Fellmongery
442 Leather Goods

450 Footwear and Clothing Industries
451 Footwear
453 Clothing, Hats and Gloves
455 Household Textiles and other Made-Up Textiles
456 Fur Goods

460 Timber and Wooden Furniture Industries
461 Sawmilling, Planing etc of Wood
462 Manufacture of Semi-Finished Wood Products and Further Processing
and Treatment of Wood
463 Builders' Carpentry and Joinery
464 Wooden Containers
465 Other Wooden Articles (except Furniture)
466 Articles of Cork and Plaiting Materials, Brushes and Brooms

467 Wooden and Upholstered Furniture and Shop and Office Fittings

470 Manufacture of Paper and Paper Products, Printing and Publishing
471 Pulp, Paper and Board
472 Conversion of Paper and Board
475 Printing and Publishing

480 Processing of Rubber and Plastics
481 Rubber Products
482 Retreading and Specialist Repairing of Rubber Tyres
483 Processing of Plastics

490 Other Manufacturing Industries
491 Jewellery and Coins
492 Musical Instruments
493 Photographic and Cinematographic Processing Laboratories
494 Toys and Sports Goods
495 Miscellaneous Manufacturing Industries

500 Construction: General Construction and Demolition Work
501 Construction and Repair of Buildings
502 Civil Engineering
503 Installation of Fixtures and Fittings
504 Building Completion Work

600 Distribution, Hotels and Catering; Repairs

610 Wholesale Distribution
611 Wholesale Distribution of Agricultural Raw Materials, Live Animals, Textile Raw Materials and Semi-Manufactures
612 Wholesale Distribution of Fuels, Ores, Metals and Industrial Materials
613 Wholesale Distribution of Timber and Building Materials
614 Wholesale Distribution of Machinery, Industrial Equipment and Vehicles
615 Wholesale Distribution of Household Goods, Hardware and Ironmongery
616 Wholesale Distribution of Textiles, Clothing, Footwear and Leather Goods
617 Wholesale Distribution of Food, Drink and Tobacco
618 Wholesale Distribution of Pharmaceutical, Medical and other Chemists' Goods
619 Other Wholesale Distribution including General Wholesalers

620 Dealing in Scrap and Waste Materials
621 Dealing in Scrap Metals
622 Dealing in other Scrap Materials, or General Dealers

630 Commission Agents

640/650 Retail Distribution
641 Food Retailing
642 Confectioners, Tobacconists and Newsagents; Off-Licences
643 Dispensing and other Chemists

645 Retail Distribution of Clothing
646 Retail Distribution of Footwear and Leather Goods
647 Retail Distribution of Furnishing Fabrics and Household Textiles
648 Retail Distribution of Household Goods, Hardware and Ironmongery
651 Retail Distribution of Motor Vehicles and Parts
652 Filling Stations (Motor Fuel and Lubricants)
653 Retail Distribution of Books, Stationery and Office Supplies
654 Other Specialised Retail Distribution (Non-Food)
656 Mixed Retail Businesses

660 Hotels and Catering
661 Restaurants, Snack Bars, Cafes and other Eating Places
662 Public Houses and Bars
663 Night Clubs and Licenced Clubs
664 Canteens and Messes
665 Hotel Trade
667 Other Tourist or Short-Stay Accommodation

670 Repair of Consumer Goods and Vehicles
671 Repair and Servicing of Motor Vehicles
672 Repair of Footwear and Leather Goods
673 Repair of other Consumer Goods

700 Transport and Communication
710 Railways
721 Scheduled Road Passenger Transport and Urban Railways
722 Other Road Passenger Transport
723 Road Haulage
726 Transport not elsewhere specified
740 Sea Transport
750 Air Transport
761 Supporting Services to Inland Transport
763 Supporting Services to Sea Transport
764 Supporting Services to Air Transport
770 Miscellaneous Transport Services and Storage not elsewhere specified

790 Postal Services and Telecommunications

800 Banking, Finance, Insurance, Business Services and Leasing
810 Banking and Finance
814 Banking and Bill-Discounting
815 Other Financial Institutions
820 Insurance
831 Activities Auxiliary to Banking and Finance
832 Activities Auxiliary to Insurance
834 House and Estate Agents
835 Legal Services
836 Accountants, Auditors, Tax Experts
837 Profesional and Technical Services not elsewhere specified
838 Advertising
839 Business Services (Including Central Offices not Allocable Elsewhere)
841 Hiring Out Agricultural and Horticultural Equipment
842 Hiring Out Construction Machinery and Equipment
843 Hiring Out Office Machinery and Furniture

846 Hiring Out Consumer Goods
848 Hiring Out Transport Equipment
849 Hiring Out Other Movables

850 Owning and Dealing in Real Estate

900 Other Services
911 National and Local Government Services not elsewhere specified
912 Justice
913 Police
914 Fire Services
915 National Defence
919 Social Security
921 Refuse Disposal, Sanitation and Similar Services
923 Cleaning Services

930 Education
931 Higher Education
932 School Education (Nursery, Primary and Secondary)
933 Education not elsewhere specified and Vocational Training
936 Driving and Flying Schools
940 Research and Development

950 Medical and other Health Services
951 Hospitals, Nursing Homes etc
952 Other Medical Care Institutions
953 Medical Practices
954 Dental Practices
955 Agency and Private Midwives, Nurses etc
956 Veterinary Practices and Animal Hospitals

960 Other Services Provided to the General Public
961 Social Welfare, Charitable and Community Services
963 Trade Unions, Business and Professional Associations
966 Religious Organisations and Similar Associations
969 Tourist Offices and other Community Services
971 Film Production, Distribution and Exhibition
974 Radio and Television Services, Theatres etc
976 Authors, Music Composers and other Own Account Artists not elsewhere specified
977 Libraries, Museums, Art Galleries etc
979 Sport and other Recreational Services
981 Laundries and Dry Cleaners
982 Hairdressing and Beauty Parlours
989 Personal Services not elsewhere specified

990 Domestic Services

000 Diplomatic Representation, International Organisations, Allied Armed Forces

Bibliographies

Armstrong, John
Directory of Corporate Archives

Business Archives Council 1985   59pp

Bellamy, Joyce Margaret
Yorkshire Business Histories: A Bibliography

Bradford U P, Crosby Lockwood 1970 457pp

Benson, J; Neville, Robert G & Thompson, C H
Bibliography of the British Coal Industry

Oxford: O U P 1981   760pp

Business History Society of Japan
Union Catalog on Enterprise Histories and Biographies of Businessmen in the World outside of Japan
Tokyo: Yushodo Booksellers 1979   582pp

Chaloner, W H & Richardson, R C
A Bibliography of British Economic and Social History

Manchester: M U P 1984   208pp

Cockerell, H A L & Green, Edwin
The British Insurance Business 1547-1970: An Introduction & Guide to Historical Records in the U K
Heinemann 1976   142pp

Daniells, Lorna M
Studies in Enterprise: American and Canadian Company Histories and Biographies of Businessmen
Boston: Baker Library, Harvard 1957 169pp

Directors
Directory of Directors

Thomas Skinner Directories

Foster, Janet & Sheppard, Julia
British Archives: A Guide to Archive Resources in the United Kingdom
Macmillan 1982   533pp

Frone, Peggy M
Business History Collection: A Checklist

Dallas: Dallas Public Library   236pp

Glamorgan
> *The Economic History of Industrial Glamorgan*

> Cardiff: Glamorgan County Hist 1980

Greenwood, John
> *The Industrial Archaeology and Industrial History of Northern England: A Bibliography*
> Cranfield: author 1985   300pp index

Hadfield, Charles
> *Sources for the History of British Canals*

> Journal of Transport History   vol II no 2 1955

Hazzlewood, John William
> *House Journals*

> Vista Books 1963   115pp illus

Historical Manuscripts
> *Company Index compiled by the Royal Commission on Historical Manuscripts*
> Commission

Historical Manuscripts Commission
> *Accessions to Repositories and Reports Added to the National Register of Archives*
> HMSO

Horrocks, Sidney
> *Lancashire Business Histories: A Contribution towards a Lancashire Bibliography, vol 3*
> Manchester: 1971   116pp

Hudson, Patricia
> *The West Riding Wool Textile Industry: A Catalogue of Business Records from the 16th to the 20th Century*
> Edington, Wilts: Pasold 1975   560pp index

Jarvis, Rupert C
> *Sources for the History of Ports*

> Journal of Transport History   vol III no 2 1957

Jarvis, Rupert C
> *Sources for the History of Ships and Shipping*

> Journal of Transport History   vol III no 4 1958

Jeremy, David J & Shaw, Christine (eds)
> *Dictionary of Business Biography*

> Butterworth 1984-86   5 vols

Johnson, L C
Historical Records of the British Transport Commission
Journal of Transport History   vol I no 2 1953

Jones, Charles A
Bibliography of British-Based Foreign Industries

Boston, Mass: G K Hall & Co

Knight, R J B (ed)
Guide to the Manuscripts in the National Maritime Museum vol 2 (incl business records of 50 companies)
Mansell 1980   216pp illus index source

Larson, Henrietta M
Guide to Business History: Materials for the Study of American Business History & Suggestions for their Use
Cambridge, Mass: Harvard U P 1948   xxvi 1181pp

Lee, Charles E
Sources of Business History

Journal of Transport History   vol II no 3 1956

Leeds City Library
List of Sources of Business and Industrial History in the Archives Dept of Leeds City Library
Leeds City Library 1971   14pp

Lowe, Jane
A Guide to Sources in the History of the Cycle and Motor Industries in Coventry 1880-1939
Coventry: Coventry Polytechnic 1982 108pp

Lowe, Jane
Register of Business Records of Coventry and Related Areas
Coventry: Lanchester Poly 1977   174pp

Marsh, Arthur & Ryan, Victoria
Historical Directory of Trade Unions

Aldershot: Gower 1980-84   2 vols

Marwick, W H
A Bibliography of Scottish Business History

see Payne, Peter L (ed) 1967

Marwick, W H
A Bibliography of Scottish Economic History during the Last Decade 1963-70
Economic History Review   2nd ser vol XXIV no 3 1ⁱ

Mathias, Peter & Pearsall, A W H (eds)
   Shipping: A Survey of Historical Records

      Newton Abbot: David & Charles 1971 162pp
Morgan
   Morgan's British Trade Journal   (with a series of short company histories ca1870-1890)
      *
Ottley, George
   A Bibliography of British Railway History

      HMSO 1983   683pp index sources
Ottley, George
   Guide to the Transport History Collection in Leicester University Library
      Leicester: L U P 1981   31pp
Payne, Peter L
   The Early Scottish Limited Companies 1856-1895: An Historical and Analytical Survey
      Edinburgh: Scottish Academic 1980 140pp index sources
Pressnell, Leslie S & Orbell, M John
   A Guide to the Historical Records of British Banking

      Aldershot: Gower 1985   156pp index
Rath, T
   Business Records in the Public Record Office in the Age of the Industrial Revolution
      Business History   vol XVII no 2 1975
Richmond, Lesley & Stockford, Bridget
   Company Archives: A Survey of the Records of 1000 of the First Registered Companies in England & Wales
      Aldershot: Gower 1985
Ritchie, L A
   Modern British Shipbuilding: A Guide to Historical Records: Maritime Monographs and Reports no 48
      National Maritime Museum 1980   72pp index
Room, Adrian
   Directory of Trade Name Origins

      Routledge & Kegan Paul 1982   217pp sources
Rowe, David John
   Northern Business Histories: A Bibliography

      Library Association 1979   191pp

Rowe, David John
The Economy of the North East in the Nineteenth Century: A Survey with Records Published since 1945
Beamish: Open Air Museum 1973   28pp sources

Royal Statistical Society
Reviews of U K Statistical Sources: Royal Statistical Society and Economic & Social Research Council
Pergamon 1973-86   18 vols

Sheffield City Libraries
Catalogue of Business and Industrial Records

Sheffield City Libraries 1968   40pp

Slaven, A & Munn, C W (eds)
Scottish Dictionary of Business Biography

Aberdeen U P forthcoming

Stock Exchange
Stock Exchange Official Year Book

Macmillan

Walford
Walford's Guide to Reference Material

Library Association 4th ed 1982   3 vols

Wardle, D B
Sources for the History of Railways at the Public Record Office
Journal of Transport History   vol II no 4 1956

Wilcox, Michael
The Confederation of British Industry Predecessor Archive
Coventry: U Warwick 1984   51pp

Libraries

*	British Library, Great Russell Street, London WC1B 3DG
§	Business Archives Council, 185 Tower Bridge Road, London SE1 2UF
AIRDRPL	Monklands District Council; Airdrie Library, Wellwynd, Airdrie ML6 0AG
AVONPL	County of Avon; County Reference Library, College Green, Bristol BS1 5TL
BCRL	Buckinghamshire County Council; County Library, County Hall, Aylesbury, Bucks HP20 1UU
BCROB	Button Collection, Robinson College, Grange Road, Cambridge
BERKSPL	Royal County of Berkshire; Reading Central Library, Abbey Square, Reading, Berks RG1 3BQ
BLPES	British Library of Political & Economic Science, 10 Portugal Street, London WC2A 2HD - and Business History Unit
BMGHMPL	City of Birmingham Reference Library, Chamberlain Square, Birmingham B3 3HQ
BOLTNPL	Bolton Metropolitan Borough, Bolton Reference Library, Le Mans Crescent, Bolton BL1 1SE
BORDRPL	Borders Regional Council, Library, St. Mary's Mill, Selkirk TD7 5EW
BRENTPL	London Borough of Brent, Grange Museum, Neasden Lane, London NW10 1QB
BROMPL	London Borough of Bromley, Central Library, Bromley BR1 1EX
BURYPL	Metropolitan Borough of Bury; Textile Hall, Manchester Road, Bury, Lancashire BL9 0DR
CAMBSPL	Cambridgeshire Libraries, Peterborough Divisional Headquarters, Broadway, Peterborough PE1 1RX
CAMDNPL	London Borough of Camden, Holborn Library, 32-38 Theobald's Road, London WC1X 8PA
CHELTPL	Gloucestershire County Council; Cheltenham Library, Clarence Street, Cheltenham GL50 3JT
CLKMNPL	Clackmannan District Council; District Library, 17 Mar Street, Alloa FK10 1HT
CLWYDPL	Clwyd County Council; Library & Museum Service, County Civic Centre, Mold CH7 6NW
CORKPL	Cork City Library, Grand Parade, Cork, Eire
CROYPL	London Borough of Croydon; Central Library, Katharine Street, Croydon CR9 1ET

DERBYPL   Derbyshire County Council; County Librarian, County Offices,
          Matlock, Derbyshire DE4 3AG
DEVONPL   Devon County Library, Central Devon Area; Central Library,
          Castle Street, Exeter EX4 3PQ
DMBTNPL   Dumbarton District Libraries, Dumbarton Public Library,
          Strathleven Place, Dumbarton G82 4AJ
DNCSRPL   Doncaster Metropolitan Borough Council; Central Library,
          Waterdale, Doncaster, South Yorkshire DN1 3JE
DNDEEPL   City of Dundee District Council; Central Library, The
          Wellgate, Dundee DD1 1DB
DRHMPL   Durham County Council; County Librarian, County Hall,
          Durham DH1 5TY
DTI   Department of Trade and Industry, 1 Victoria Street, London
          SW1 0ET
DTPL   Dorset County Library, Colliton Park, Dorchester DT1 1XJ

DUDLYPL   Dudley Metropolitan Borough, Dudley Library, 46a High
          Street, Dudley, West Midlands DY1 1PN
DYFEDPL   Dyfed County Council, Public Library, St Peter's Street,
          Carmarthen, Dyfed SA31 1LN
EALNGPL   London Borough of Ealing; Library, 103 Ealing Broadway
          Centre, London W5 5JY
EDNBRPL   City of Edinburgh District Council, Central Library, George
          IV Bridge, Edinburgh EH1 1EG
EKLBRPL   East Kilbride District Council; Central Library, Olympia
          Building, Alexandra Arcade, East Kilbride G74 1LX
ELECC   Electricity Council; Library, 30 Millbank, London SW1

ELOTHPL   East Lothian District Council; Library, Lodge Street,
          Haddington EH41 3DX
ENFLDPL   London Borough of Enfield; Central Library, Cecil Road,
          Enfield, Middx EN2 6TW
ESSEXPL   Essex County Council; Colchester Central Library, Trinity
          Square, Colchester CO1 1JB
ESUSXPL   East Sussex County Library, 44 St Anne's Crescent, Lewes,
          East Sussex BN7 1SQ
GHL   Guildhall Library, Aldermanbury, London EC2P 2EJ

GLROHL   Greater London Record Office and History Library, 40
          Northampton Road, London EC1R 0HB
GLSGWPL   City of Glasgow District Council, The Mitchell Library, North
          Street, Glasgow G3 7DN
GWYNPL   Gwynedd County Council; Aberconwy Area Library, Mostyn
          Street, Llandudno LL30 2RS
HACKPL   London Borough of Hackney; Rose Lipman Library, De Beauvoir
          Road, London N1 5SQ

HDSFDPL	Kirklees Metropolitan Council; Central Library, Princess Alexandra Walk, Huddersfield, West Yorkshire HD1 2SU
HERTSPL	Hertfordshire County Council; Library Service, County Hall, Hertford SG13 8EJ
HIST	Historical Association, 59A Kennington Park Road, London SE11 4JH
HISTAD	History of Advertising Trust
HLFXPL	Calderdale Libraries, Central Library, Northgate House, Northgate, Halifax HX1 1UN
HMFULPL	London Borough of Hammersmith & Fulham; Central Library, Shepherds Bush Road, London W6 7AT
HMLTNPL	Hamilton District Council; District Library Headquarters, 98 Cadzow Street, Hamilton ML3 6HQ
HULLPL	Humberside County Council; Central Library, Albion Street, Hull HU1 3TF
ICIVILE	Institution of Civil Engineers, 1-7 Great George Street, London SW1P 3AA
IELECE	Institution of Electrical Engineers, Savoy Place, London WC2R 0BL
IGASE	Institution of Gas Engineers, 17 Grosvenor Crescent, Kondon SW1X 7ES
IHISTR	Institute of Historical Research, Senate House, London WC1E 7HU
ILFDPL	Redbridge Central Library, Oakfield Road, Ilford, Essex IG1 1EA
IMECHE	Institution of Mechanical Engineers, 1 Birdcage Walk, London SW1H 9JJ
INVRNPL	Highland Regional Council; Central Library Services, 31A Harbour Road, Inverness IV1 1UA
ISLTNPL	London Borough of Islington; Finsbury Reference Library, 245 St. John Street, London EC1V 4NB
KCLDYPL	Kirkcaldy District Council; Library, East Fergus Place, Kirkcaldy, Fife
KENSPL	Royal Borough of Kensington and Chelsea; Central Library, Phillimore Walk, London W8 7RX
KYLEPL	Kyle and Carrick District Library and Museum Services, Carnegie Library, 12 Main Street, Ayr KA8 8ED
LEEDSPL	Leeds City Council; Central Library, Municipal Buildings, Leeds LS1 3AB
LEICSPL	Leicestershire Studies Libraries, Information Centre, Bishop Street, Leicester LE1 6AA
LPOOLPL	Brown Picton and Hornby Library, William Brown Street, Liverpool L3 8EW
MACCPL	Cheshire County Council, Cheshire County Library, Park Green, Macclesfield, Cheshire SK11 6TW

MERTNPL   London Borough of Merton, Library, Crown House, London
Road, Morden, Surrey SM4 5DX

MGLAMPL   Mid Glamorgan County Council, County Library, Coed Parc,
Park Street, Bridgend CF31 4BA

MLOTHPL   Midlothian District Council, Library, 7 Station Road, Roslin,
Midlothian EH25 9PF

MMC   Monopolies & Mergers Commission Library, New Court, 48
Carey Street, London WC2A 2JT

MNCHRPL   City of Manchester, Central Library, St. Peter's Square,
Manchester M2 5PD

MRC   Modern Records Centre, University of Warwick Library,
Coventry CV4 7AL

MRTDFPL   Merthyr Tydfil Borough Council, Central Library, High Street,
Merthyr Tydfil, Mid Glamorgan CF47 8AF

MTHWLPL   Motherwell District Council, PO Box 14, Civic Centre,
Motherwell ML1 1TW

NEELBPL   North-Eastern Education and Library Board, Area Library,
Demesne Avenue, Ballymena, Co. Antrim BT43 7BG

NESLS   North East of Scotland Library Service, 14 Crown Terrace,
Aberdeen AB9 2BH

NHPTNPL   Northamptonshire County Council, Central Library, Abington
Street, Northampton NN1 2BA

NRFLKPL   Norfolk County Council, Central Library, Bethel Street,
Norwich NR2 1NJ

NRMYORK   National Railway Museum, Leeman Road, York YO2 4XJ

NWCSLPL   Central Library, Princess Square, Newcastle upon Tyne NE99
1MC

OFT   Office of Fair Trading Library, Field House, Breams
Buildings, London EC4A 1PP

OLDHMPL   Oldham Metropolitan Borough, Central Library, Union Street,
Oldham OL1 1DN

OXFDPL   Oxfordshire County Council, Central Library, Westgate,
Oxford OX1 1DJ

PRO   Public Record Office, Ruskin Avenue, Kew, Richmond TW9
4DU

PRTDNPL   Southern Education and Library Service, Local History
Department, 113 Church Street, Portadown, N Ireland

RAeS   Royal Aeronautical Society, 4 Hamilton Place, London

RCHMAN   Royal Commission on Historical Manuscripts, Quality House,
Quality Court, Chancery Lane, London WC2A 1HP

RCHMDPL   London Borough of Richmond upon Thames, Central Library,
Little Green, Richmond, Surrey TW9 1QL

RHISTS   Royal Historical Society, University College, London

RNFRWPL   Renfrew District Council, Central Library, High Street,
          Paisley PA1 2BB
ROMFDPL   London Borough of Havering, Central Library, St. Edward's
          Way, Romford RM1 3AR
ROTHMPL   Rotherham Metropolitan Borough Council, Brian O'Malley
          Central Library and Arts Centre, Rotherham S65 1JH
SALFDPL   City of Salford Local History Library, Peel Park, Salford M5
          4WU
SANDWPL   Metropolitan Borough of Sandwell, Central Library, High
          Street, West Bromwich, West Midlands B70 8DZ
SciMus   Library of the Science Museum, Exhibition Road, South
          Kensington, London SW7 5NH
SEELBPL   South-Eastern Education and Library Board, Windmill Hill,
          Ballynahinch, Co. Down BT24 8DH
SGLAMPL   County of South Glamorgan, Central Library, The Hayes,
          Cardiff CF1 2QU
SHEFFPL   Central Library, Surrey Street, Sheffield S1 1XZ

SKLVNPL   Strathkelvin District Council, William Patrick Library,
          Camphill Avenue, Kirkintilloch
SKPTPL   Stockport Central Library, Wellington Road South, Stockport
          SK1 3RS
SOLHLPL   Solihull Metropolitan District Council, Central Library,
          Homer Road, Solihull, West Midlands B91 3RG
SOMPL   Somerset Local History Library, Taunton

STLDPL   Shetland Islands Council, Shetland Library, Lower Hillhead,
          Lerwick ZE1 0EL
STYNEPL   Borough of South Tyneside, Central Library, Prince Georg
          Square, South Shields NE33 2PE
SWKPL   London Borough of Southwark, Local Studies Library, 211
          Borough High Street, London SE1 1JA
TAMESPL   Tameside Metropolitan Borough, Local Studies Library,
          Trinity Street, Stalybridge, Cheshire SK15 2BN
UBRIS   University of Bristol Library, Tyndall Avenue, Bristol BS8
          1TJ
URDNG   University of Reading Library

WALSLPL   Walsall Metropolitan Borough, Central Library, Lichfield
          Street, Walsall, West Midlands WS1 1TR
WANDSPL   Wandsworth Council, Battersea District Library, Lavender
          Hill, London SW11 1JB
WARRPL   Cheshire County Council, Warrington Library, Museum Street,
          Warrington, Cheshire WA1 1JB
WIGANPL   Wigan Metropolitan borough Council, Reference Library,
          Rodney Street, Wigan WN1 1DQ

WILTSPL   Wiltshire County Council, Library, Bythesea Road, Trowbridge BA14 8BS

WKFLDPL   Wakefield Metropolitan Borough Council, Library Headquarters, Balne Lane, Wakefield WF2 0DQ

WLOTHPL   West Lothian District Council, Disrict Library Headquarters, Wellpark, Marjoribanks Street, Bathgate EH48 1AN

WMNSTPL   City of Westminster, Marylebone Library, Marylebone Road, London NW1 5PS

WNCHRPL   Hampshire County Library Headquarters, 81 North Walls, Winchester SO23 8BY

Abbreviations

...	Words omitted
Agric	Agricultural
Antiq	Antiquarian
Arch	Archaeological
Assoc	Association, Associated
Berks	Berkshire
Bldg	Building
Brit	British
Bros	Brothers
Bull	Bulletin
Bus	Business
C	Council
C W S	Co-operative Wholesale Society
ca	circa
Ches	Cheshire
Co	Company
Co-op	Co-operative
Comp	Compiler
Corp	Corporation
Dept	Department
Dip	Diploma
Disc	Discussion
Dist	District
Div	Division
E	East, Eastern
Econ	Economic
Ed	Editor
Eng	Engineer, Engineering
Est	Established
F L A	Fellow of the Library Association
Found	Foundation
Gen	General
H M S O	Her Majesty's Stationery Office
Herts	Hertfordshire
Hist	History, Historical
I o W	Isle of Wight
incl	Including
Ind	Industry, Industrial
Ins	Insurance
Inst	Institute
J	Journal
L	London
Lancs	Lancashire

Leics	Leicestershire
Lib	Library
Lincs	Lincolnshire
Loc	Local
Ltd	Limited
Maint	Maintenance
Mem	Memorial
Mfr	Manufacturer, Manufacturing
Middx	Middlesex
N	North, Northern
N Abbot	Newton Abbot
Nat	Natural, National
nd	No Date
no	Number
Notts	Nottinghamshire
P	Press
Polit	Political
Poly	Polytechnic
Pres	Preservation
Publ	Publisher, Publication
Reg	Regional
repr	Reprinted, Reproduced
Res	Research
Rly	Railway
S	South, Southern
Sch	School
Scot	Scottish
Ser	Series
Soc	Society
Soc Stud	Social Studies
Staffs	Staffordshire
tr	Translated
UD	Urban District
UK	United Kingdom
UP	University Press
vol	Volume
W	West, Western
Wilts	Wiltshire
Yorks	Yorkshire

3   Author index

Aberdare Cables
>   *Aberdare Cables Limited 21st Anniversary: Paper Insulated Cables 1937-1958*
>   Aberdare: the firm 1958   31pp illus
>   Aberdare Cables
>   341   * §

Aberdeen Savings Bank
>   *Aberdeen Savings Bank: Its History from 1815 to 1965*
>
>   Aberdeen: A U P 1967   123pp illus
>   Aberdeen Savings Bank
>   814   ABRDNPL

Abrahart, Edward Noah
>   *The Clayton Aniline Company Limited 1876-1976*
>
>   Manchester: the firm 1976   95pp illus
>   Clayton Aniline Co
>   251   UBRIS

Accles & Pollock
>   *1899-1974: The First Seventy-Five Years of Achievement*
>
>   Oldbury: the firm 1974   22pp illus
>   Accles & Pollock
>   222   224   SANDWPL

Accles & Pollock
>   *Have You a Trumpet Handy? Jubilee Brochure 1899-1949*
>
>   the firm 1949   90pp illus
>   Accles & Pollock
>   222   224   UBRIS

Acres, W Marston
>   *The Bank of England from Within: 1694-1900*
>
>   Oxford U P 1931   2 vols illus index sources
>   Bank of England
>   814   * §

Acrow
>   *Acrow: The Success Story of Achievement through Team Spirit: 40 Years On 1936-1975*
>   the firm 1975   105pp illus
>   Acrow
>   325   §

Acrow
>   *Twenty-Eight Years of Progress 1936-1964*
>
>   the firm 1964   95pp illus
>   Acrow
>   325   TAMESPL

Adam, Alastair T
>   *Bruntons 1876-1962*
>
>   Musselburgh: the firm 1962   77pp illus
>   Brunton (Musselburgh)
>   223   ELOTHPL

40

Adam, Helen Pearl
British Leather: A Record of Achievement

Batsford 1946   82pp illus
Leather Industry
440   *

Adam, James S
A Fell Fine Baker: The Story of United Biscuits

Hutchinson Benham 1974   164pp illus index sources
United Biscuits
419   ABRDNPL

Adams, A R
Good Company: The Story of the Guided Weapons Division of British Aircraft Corporation
Stevenage: the firm 1976   220pp illus
British Aircraft Corporation
364   RAeS

Adams, John
The House of Kitcat: A Story of Bookbinding 1798-1948

Bere Regis: the firm 1948   64pp illus
Kitcat, G & J
475   §

Adams, Percy Walter Lewis
A History of the Adams Family of North Staffordshire and ...the Development of the Potteries
St. Catharine Press 1914   417pp illus
Adams, William
248   *

Adamsez
Adamsez: Jobs Down the Drain

West End Resource Centre 1980   8pp
Adamsez
248

Adburgham, Alison
Liberty's: A Biography of a Shop

Allen & Unwin 1975   160pp illus index
Liberty & Co
437   645   647   *

Adburgham, Alison
Shops and Shopping 1800-1914

Allen & Unwin 1964   xx 304pp illus index sources
Shops and Shopping
656   *

Addis, John Philip
The Crawshay Dynasty: A Study in Industrial Organisation and Development 1765-1867
Cardiff: Wales U P 1957   184pp illus index sources
Crawshay   GKN
111   221   *

Addis, John Philip
The Heavy Iron and Steel Industry in South Wales 1870-1950

Wales(Aberystwyth) PhD 1957
S Wales Iron & Steel
221

Aerialite
Aerialite Story 1932-1957: Twenty Five Years of Progress

Stalybridge: the firm 1957   60pp illus
Aerialite   Delta Cables
341   TAMESPL

Agnew, Geoffrey
Agnew's 1817-1967

the firm 1967   90pp illus
Agnew's
977   *

Ahvenainen, Jorma
The History of Star Paper

Jyväskylä: J U P 1976   106pp illus index sources
Star Paper Mill
471   §

Airey, Angela & John
The Bainbridges of Newcastle: A Family History 1679-1976

Newcastle: A & J Airey 1979   192pp illus
Bainbridges of Newcastle
656   *

Aiton & Co
Fifty Years of Progress 1900-1950

Derby: the firm 1958   48pp illus
Aiton & Co (Derby)
243   320   328   GHL

Alberts, Robert Carman
The Good Provider: H J Heinz and his 57 Varieties

Barker 1974   297pp illus index sources
Heinz, H J
410   *

Albright & Wilson
Albright & Wilson: Survey of a Chemical Group

the firm 1961   72pp
Albright & Wilson
251   *

Aldcroft, Derek Howard
Britain's Internal Airways: The Pioneer Stage of the 1930s

Business History   vol VI no 2 1964
Internal Airways
750

42

Aldcroft, Derek Howard
British Transport since 1914: An Economic History

Newton Abbot: David & Charles 1975 336pp illus sources

700   * §

Aldcroft, Derek Howard
Studies in British Transport History 1870-1970

Newton Abbot: David & Charles 1974 vi 309pp index sources

700   * §

Alderman, Geoffrey
The Railway Interest

Leicester: L U P 1973   344pp index sources
Railway Interest
710   815   *

Alderson, Frederick
The Comic Postcard in English Life

Newton Abbot: David & Charles 1970 112pp illus index
Bamforth & Co
475   *

Alderson, J W & Ogden, A E
Halifax Equitable Benefit Building Society Jubilee 1871-1921

Halifax: the firm 1921   148pp illus
Halifax Equitable Benefit Bldg Soc
815   HLFXPL

Aldington, Lord (Toby Low)
Grindlays 1828-1978

the firm 1978   161pp illus
Grindlay's Bank
814   *

Alexander, Kenneth J W & Jenkins, Carson L
Fairfields: A Study of Industrial Change

Allen Lane-Penguin 1970   285pp index
Fairfield Shipbuilding
320   361   *

Alexanders
Alexanders the Great

Edinburgh: the firm 1947   60pp illus
Alexanders
614   651   EDNBRPL

Alford, Bernard W E & Barker, Theodore C
A History of the Carpenters' Company

Allen & Unwin 1968   271pp illus
Carpenters' Company
465   *

Alford, Bernard William Ernest
Business Enterprise and the Growth of the Commercial Letterpress Printing Industry 1850-1914
Business History   vol VII no 1 1965
Letterpress Printing
475

Alford, Bernard William Ernest
Penny Cigarettes, Oligopoly and Entrepreneurship in the U K Tobacco Industry in the Late 19th Century
see Supple, Barry (ed) 1977
Tobacco Industry
429

Alford, Bernard William Ernest
The Flint and Bottle Glass Industry in the Early Nineteenth Century: A Case Study of a Bristol Firm
Business History   vol X no 1 1968
Ricketts, Henry & Co
247

Alford, Bernard William Ernest
W D & H O Wills and the Development of the U K Tobacco Industry 1786-1965
Methuen 1973   500pp illus index sources
Wills, W D & H O   Imperial Tobacco
429   *

Alford, L G C
Ruston & Hornsby Limited of Lincoln

Ruston & Hornsby
321   BLPES

Alford, L G C
The Development of Industrial Lincoln

1950
Lincoln Industries
                                         BLPES

Allan, Charles M
Bullionfield: Death of a Paper Mill, A Study of Redundancy

Gartocham: Famedram 1973   28pp
Watson's of Bullionfield   Associated Paper Mills
471   DNDEEPL

Allan, Mea
Tom's Weeds: The Story of Rochford's and their House Plants

Faber 1970   220pp illus index
Rochford's Nurseries
10   * §

Allen, Cecil John
A Century of Scientific Instrument Making 1853-1953

the firm 1953   63pp illus
Stanley, W F & Co
370   371   * §

Allen, Cecil John
The Great Eastern Railway

    Ian Allan 1955   221pp illus index
    Great Eastern Railway
    710   * §

Allen, Cecil John
The London & North Eastern Railway

    Ian Allan 1966   228pp illus index
    London & North Eastern Railway
    710   *

Allen, G C & Donnithorne, A G
Western Enterprise in Far Eastern Economic Development:
China and Japan
    Allen & Unwin 1954   291pp sources
    Far Eastern Econ Development
    630   770   839   *

Allen, George C & Donnithorne, Audrey G
Western Enterprise in Indonesia and Malaya: A Study in
Economic Development
    Allen & Unwin 1957   321pp
    Guthries
    630   770   839   *

Allen, George Cyril
Industrial Policy and Comparative Industrial Performance:
Britain and Japan
    see Marriner, Sheila (ed) 1978

Allen, George Cyril
The Industrial Development of Birmingham and the Black
Country 1860-1927
    Allen & Unwin, 1929   479pp index sources
    Birmingham & the Black Country
    111   220   300   *

Allen, Herbert Warner
Number Three Saint James's Street: A History of Berry's, the
Wine Merchants
    Chatto & Windus 1950   269pp illus
    Berry Bros & Rudd
    617   642   *

Allen, John R (ed)
Crombies of Grandholm and Cothal 1805-1960: Records of an
Aberdeenshire Enterprise
    Aberdeen: Central Press nd   139pp
    Crombie Knowles & Co
    431   ABRDNPL

Allen, Philip
Background to Aristoc 1919-1957: An Essay on the Fine Gauge
Full Fashioned Hosiery industry
    Nottingham: the firm 1957   31pp illus
    Aristoc
    436   §

Allen, Thomas
The First One Hundred Years of Thomas Allen Ltd

the firm 1954   63pp illus
Allen, Thomas
723   *

Allen, Walter Gore
John Heathcoat and his Heritage

Christopher Johnson 1958   222pp illus index
Heathcoat
430   *

Allen, Walter Gore
We the Undersigned...A History of the Royal London Mutual
Insurance Society Ltd and its Times 1861-1961
Newman Neame 1961   87pp illus
Royal London Mutual Ins Soc
820   * §

Allen, William Edward David
David Allens: The History of a Family Firm   1857-1957

John Murray 1957   322pp illus sources
David Allen Theatre Co   Allen, David
475   974   * §

Alliance Assurance
Alliance Assurance Co 1824-1924

the firm 1924   119pp illus
Alliance Assurance
820   §

Alliance Box Co
Packaging through Half a Century: A Short History

the firm 1950   24pp
Alliance Box Co
483   WARRPL

Allied Breweries
Allied's World

Southampton: Millbrook 1971   24pp
Allied Breweries
427   WARRPL

Allingham, E C
A Romance of the Rostrum: Being the Business Life of Henry
Stevens
1924   333pp
Stevens' Auction Rooms
839   GHL

Allman, A H
Williams Deacon's 1771-1970

Manchester: the firm 1971   180pp illus index
Williams Deacon's Bank   Manchester & Salford Bank
814   BOLTNPL

Allman, Geoff
  One Hundred Years of Key Making

  Wolverhampton: the firm 1982 48pp illus
  Hough, Arthur & Sons
  316   §
Alloa Co-operative Society
  Alloa Co-operative Society Ltd 1862-1912: A Historical
  Survey on the Occasion of the Society's Jubilee
  Alloa: the firm 1912   133pp illus
  Alloa Co-operative Society Forth Valley Co-op
  656   CLKMNPL
Aluminium Corporation
  Aluminium Corporation Ltd: Company History

  Dolgarrog: the firm 1983
  Aluminium Corporation
  224   GWYNPL
Aluminium Corporation
  Golden Jubilee: Aluminium Corporation Ltd 1909-1959

  Dolgarrog: the firm 1959
  Aluminium Corporation
  224   GWYNPL
Amalgamated Cotton Mills Trust
  Concerning Cotton: A Brief Account...of the Amalgamated
  Cotton Mills Trust Ltd and its Component Companies
  Manchester: the firm 1920   152pp illus
  Amalgamated Cotton Mills Trust Horrockses, Crewdson & Co
  432   *
Anderson, B L
  Institutional Investment before the First World War: The Union
  Marine Insurance Company 1897-1915
  see Marriner, Sheila (ed) 1978
  Union Marine Insurance Co
  820
Anderson, Donald
  Blundell's Collieries: The Progress of the Business

  Trans Hist Soc Lancs & Ches vol 116 1964, 48pp illus
  Pemberton Colliery Co   Blundells Collieries
  111   120   WIGANPL
Anderson, Donald
  The Orrell Coalfield 1740-1850

  Buxton: Moorland Publishing 1975 208pp illus sources
  Blundells Collieries
  111   120   *
Anderson, Donald with Lane, Jane
  Mines and Miners of South Lancashire

  Ashton-in-Makerfield: author 1981
  Blundells Collieries
  111   120

Anderson, James Gibson
The Birthplace and Genesis of Life Assurance

Frederick Muller 1937 93pp
Equitable Life Assurance
820 *

Anderson, James Lawson
The Story of the Commercial Bank of Scotland Limited during its Hundred Years from 1810 to 1910
Edinburgh: the firm 1910 113pp illus
Commercial Bank of Scotland
814 *

Anderson, John L
History of the House of Dewar

DCL Gazette Apr 1929-Jan 1930
Dewar, John & Sons
424

Anderson, John Richard Lane
East of Suez: A Study of Britain's Greatest Trading Enterprise

Hodder & Stoughton 1969 288pp illus index sources
B P
130 140 251 612 652 *

Anderson, Roy
White Star

Prescot: T Stephenson 1964 236pp illus index sources
White Star Line Oceanic Steam Navigation Co
740 * §

Anderson, Roy Claude
A History of Crosville Motor Services

Newton Abbot: David & Charles 1981 192pp illus index sources
Crosville Motor Services
721 * §

Anderson, Roy Claude
A History of the Llandudno and Colwyn Bay Electric Railway Ltd
Exeter: Quail Map Co 1968 26pp illus
Llandudno & Colwyn Bay Rly
710 *

Anderson, Roy Claude
A History of the Midland Red

Newton Abbot: David & Charles 1984 192pp
Midland Red British Electric Traction
721 *

Andrews, Allen
Tate & Lyle: A Record of the Activities of the Tate & Lyle Group
the firm 1965 88pp illus
Tate & Lyle
420

Andrews, G R & M
The Story of Wortley Ironworks: A Record of its History & Traditions and Eight Centuries of Yorkshire Iron-Making
1975   97pp illus index
Wortley Ironworks
221   SHEFFPL
Andrews, H H
Electricity in Transport over Sixty Years' Experience: English Electric Co 1883-1950
the firm 1951   183pp illus
English Electric   Siemens Brothers & Co
340   343   700   *
Andrews, Philip W S & Brunner, Elizabeth
Capital Development in Steel: A Study of the United Steel Companies
Oxford: Basil Blackwell 1951   374pp illus index sources
United Steel
221   222   *
Andrews, Philip W S & Brunner, Elizabeth
The Eagle Ironworks, Oxford: The Story of W Lucy and Company Limited
Mills & Boon 1965   64pp illus
Lucy, W & Co
320   342   §
Andrews, Philip W S & Brunner, Elizabeth
The Life of Lord Nuffield: A Study in Enterprise and Benevolence
Oxford: Basil Blackwell 1955   xvi 356pp illus index sources
Morris Motors
351   * §
Andrews, Sydney; Burls, John (ed)
Nine Generations: A History of the Andrews Family, Millers of Comber
Belfast: the firm 1958   170pp illus
Andrews, Isaac & Sons
416   434   *
Andrews, W Linton & Taylor, H A
Lords and Laborers of the Press: Men Who Fashioned the Modern British Newspaper
Southern Illinois U P 1970
Newspaper Industry
475
Anglo-South American Bank
The Anglo-South American Bank: A Record of Expansion; The Bradford Branch
the firm 1921   63pp
Anglo-South American Bank
814   839   *
Angus, George & Co
House of Angus: Being a Record of Progress throughout Six Reigns 1790-1935
Newcastle-upon-Tyne: the firm 1935 31pp
Angus, George & Co
256   328   432   *

Ansell, Walter
The Centenary Story of the Cheltenham & Gloucester Building Society 1850-1950
Cheltenham: the firm 1950   46pp illus
Cheltenham & Gloucester Bldg Soc
815   *

Antrobus, Hinson Allan
A History of the Assam Company 1839-1953

Edinburgh: the firm 1957   xv 501pp illus index sources
Assam Company
423   839   * §

Antrobus, Hinson Allan
A History of the Jorehaut Tea Company Ltd. 1859-1946

Tea & Rubber Mail 1946   368pp illus index
Jorehaut Tea Co
423   839   * §

Archdale
Archdale Machine Tools 1868-1948

the firm 1948   100pp illus
Archdale, James
322   BLPES

Archer, J F
A History of Staley, Radford & Co Ltd 1875-1975

the firm 1975   374pp illus
Staley, Radford & Co
740   UBRIS

Arlott, John
The Snuff Shop

Michael Joseph 1974   61pp illus
Fribourg & Treyer
642   *

Armitage, F
Lewis Berger & Sons: A New History

typescript ca1968   28pp
Berger, Lewis & Sons
255   HACKPL

Armitage, G W
A History of Cockhedge Mill 1802-1938

typescript nd   108pp
Cockhedge Mill
432   WARRPL

Armstrong, Arthur C
Bouverie Street to Bowling Green Lane: Fifty-Five Years of Specialized Publishing 1891-1946
Hodder & Stoughton 1946   224pp illus index
Temple Press
475   *

Armstrong, J W
100 Years of Manufacturing in Lincoln

1949
Lincoln Industries
BLPES

Armstrong, John
Hooley and the Bovril Company

Business History   vol XXVIII no 1 1986
Bovril
423   831

Armstrong, Warren
The Collins Story

Robert Hale 1957   192pp illus index
Collins Line
740   *

Army & Navy Stores
Yesterday's Shopping: The 1907 Army & Navy Stores Catalogue
- a facsimile
Newton Abbot: David & Charles 1969 1282pp illus
Army & Navy Co-operative Soc
656   *

Arnold, E J & Son
A Service to Education: The Story of the Growth of E J Arnold
& Son of Leeds
Leeds: the firm ca1963   64pp illus
Arnold, E J & Son
475   UBRIS

Arnold, H
Boiler-Making a Hundred Years Ago: The Early History of
William Arnold and Son (Huddersfield) Ltd.
Huddersfield Examiner   16pp
Arnold, William & Son
316   SHEFFPL

Arnold, Ralph Crispian Marshall
Orange Street & Brickhole Lane

Hart-Davis 1963   190pp
Constable & Co
475   *

Arrol, Sir William & Co
Sir William Arrol & Company Limited 1909-1950

Glasgow: the firm 1950   30pp illus
Arrol, Sir William & Co
320   325   502   UBRIS

Arthur, Maurice C B
The Radcliffe Paper Mill Co Ltd, Johnson Street, Radcliffe:
No.1 Mill, History prior to 1913
typescript 1969
Radcliffe Paper Mill Co
471   BURYPL

51

Arthur, William
The Succesful Merchant: Sketches of the Life of Mr. Samuel Budgett
Hamilton Andrews 1852   392pp
Budgett, Samuel
619   656   * §

Artizans
Artizans Centenary 1867-1967

the firm 1967   67pp illus
Artizans' & General Properties Co
850   *

Ashlee, Peter C
Tusks and Tortoiseshell: The Early Development of the British Plastics Industry...British Xylonite Company Ltd 1877-1920
Nottingham BA 1982
British Xylonite Co   Xylonite Group
251   483   HACKPL

Ashley, William James (ed)
British Industries

Longman 1903
British Industries
*

Ashmead, John
The Wings of the Phoenix

the firm 1954   142pp illus
Phoenix Assurance
820

Ashton Bros
Making for a New Age at Ashtons

Hyde: the firm 1961   18pp illus
Ashton Bros & Co   Courtaulds
432   *

Ashton, Thomas Southcliffe
An Eighteenth Century Industrialist: Peter Stubs of Warrington 1756-1806
Manchester: M U P 1939   156pp illus index
Stubs, Peter
316   *

Ashworth and Parker
Fifty Years of Progress: The Story of Ashworth and Parker

nd
Ashworth and Parker
320   BURYPL

Ashworth, A H
A Century of Progress: The Story of the House of Sheldon 1840-1940
Leeds: the firm nd   40pp illus
Sheldons
838   UBRIS

Ashworth, George
Ramsbottom Industrial and Provident Society Ltd Centenary 1858-1958
nd
Ramsbottom Ind Provident Soc
656   BURYPL

Ashworth, Herbert
The Building Society Story

Franey 1980   252pp illus index
Building Societies
815   *

Ashworth, William
The History of the British Coal Industry; vol 5: The Nationalised Industry 1946-1982
Oxford: O U P 1986   800pp illus index sources
Coal Industry
111

Associated Owners of City Properties
1904-1964: A Sixty Years Retrospect

ca1964
Assoc Owners of City Properties
850   GHL

Associated Portland Cement
Associated Portland Cement 1900-1950

the firm 1950   36pp illus
Associated Portland Cement   Blue Circle
242   §

Atherton, F W
History of the House of Buchanan

the firm 1931   39pp illus
Buchanan, James & Co
424   UBRIS

Atkins of Hinckley
Atkins of Hinckley 1722-1972

Hinckley: the firm ca1972   52pp illus
Atkins of Hinckley
436   LEICSPL

Atkins, Peter J
The Milk Trade of London ca1790-1914

Cambridge PhD 1977
Milk Trade of London
617   641

Atkinson, Glen
The Canal Duke's Collieries, Worsley 1760-1900

Swinton: Richardson 1982   52pp illus
Blundell's Collieries   Boardman, W & Co
111   *

Attenborough, John
A Living Memory: Hodder & Stoughton, Publishers 1865-1975

Hodder & Stoughton 1975   287pp illus index sources
Hodder & Stoughton
475   *

Atterbury, Paul
The Story of Minton from 1793 to the Present Day

the firm 1978
Minton
248

Atterton, David
Fifty Years of Development in Materials Technology

the firm 1982   64pp illus
Foseco Minsep
248   §

Atthill, Robin
The History of Clare's

Wells: Clares Carlton Ltd 1978   34pp illus
Clares Carlton
370   430   475   SOMPL

Austen-Leigh, Richard Leigh
The Story of a Printing House: Being a Short Account of the Strahans and Spottiswoodes
1912   62pp illus
Spottiswoode
475

Austin Motor Co
Austin Golden Jubilee: Our First Fifty Years: Longbridge 1905-1955
Longbridge: the firm 1955   88pp illus
Austin Motor Co
351   §

Austin Motor Co
Austin: 50 Years of Car Progress

Longbridge: the firm 1955   36pp illus
Austin Motor Co
351   MRC

Austin, F Earle
The Webster Saga: Being the Story of Enterprise and of a Family Business in London 1853-1953
the firm 1953   30pp
Webster, W J
465   648   976   GHL

Austin, James
100 Years of Progress 1850-1950

Hyde 1950   56pp illus
Austin, James & Sons(Dewsbury)
612   HDSFDPL

Austin, John & Ford, Malcolm
Steel Town: Dronfield and Wilson Cammell 1873-1883

    Sheffield: Scarsdale 1983   112pp illus sources
    Wilson Cammell
    221   *

Austin, P E
History of the Crittall Company

    typescript nd
    Crittall Manufacturing Co
    314

Aveling-Barford
The Origin and Development of Aveling-Barford Ltd

    Grantham: the firm ca1951   40pp illus
    Aveling-Barford Group
    325   §

Avery, David
Not on Queen Victoria's Birthday: The Story of the Rio Tinto Mines
    Collins 1974   464pp illus index sources
    Rio Tinto
    210   839   * §

Avery, W & T
W & T Avery, Ltd., Soho Foundry, Birmingham: A Record of its History and Scope
    the firm 1948   30pp illus
    Avery, W & T   Soho Foundry
    311   328   MRC

Avon Industrial Polymers
In Pursuit of Excellence: Avon 1885-1985

    Melksham: the firm 1985   26pp illus
    Avon Rubber Co
    251   481   483   §

Avon Rubber
A Romance of Rubber: The Avon Tyre and Rubber Works 1886-1927
    the firm 1927
    Avon Rubber Co
    481

Avro
Fifty Years Nearer the Sky: The Story of Avro

    the firm 1958   pamphlet
    Avro
    364   §

Ayer, Jules
A Century of Finance 1804-1904: The London House of Rothschild
    Neely 1905   135pp
    Rothschild
    814   GHL

Ayerst, David George Ogilvy
Guardian: Biography of a Newspaper

Collins 1971   702pp illus index sources
Guardian
475   * §

BEAMA
The BEAMA Book: A History and Survey

the firm 1926
British Electrical & Allied Mfr
963

B E T:
B E T: The Sixth Decade

the firm 1956
British Electric Traction
721   839

B P B
The History of B P B Industries

the firm 1973
British Plaster Board Industries
500   613   §

Bache, Mary
Salter: The Story of a Family Firm 1760-1960

West Bromwich: the firm 1960   95pp illus
Salter, Geo & Co
328   * §

Bacon, R K
The Life of Sir Enoch Hill: The Romance of the Modern Building
Society
Ivor Nicholson & Watson 1934   159pp
Halifax Building Society
815   *

Baglehole, K C
A Century of Service. A Brief History of Cable & Wireless Ltd.
1868-1968
the firm 1969   54pp illus index
Cable & Wireless
790   * §

Bailey, E H
Baileys of Matlock: 100 Years of Trading in Derbyshire
1866-1966
Matlock: the firm 1967   14pp illus
Baileys of Matlock
416   DERBYPL

Bailey, L A
On this Slender Thread a Life May Depend: An Authorised
History of Ethicon Limited, Edinburgh
Edinburgh: the firm 1977   ix 134pp illus
· Ethicon
257   *

Bain, Patrick
A History of A W Bain & Sons

the firm 1976
Bain, A W & Sons
832

Baines, Frank
The History of John Mowlem

typescript nd
Mowlem, John & Co
501   DTPL

Baker, Alfred
The Life of Sir Isaac Pitman

Sir Isaac Pitman 1908
Pitman, Isaac & Sons
475   *

Baker, Allan C & Civil, Thomas D A
Bagnalls of Stafford, Locomotive Builders and Railway Engineers 1875-1972
Lingfield: Oakwood Press 1973   265pp illus
Bagnall, W G   English Electric-A E I Traction
328   362   *

Baker, Henry
The 'Steel' Bakers of Rotherham: Being a Brief History of the Family & Business of Baker and Bessemer Ltd
the firm 1960   29pp
Baker and Bessemer
221   362   ROTHMPL

Baker, John Clifford Yorke
The Metropolitan Railway

South Godstone: Oakwood 1951   76pp illus
Metropolitan Railway   London Transport
710   721   *

Baker, Katherine
Nurdin & Peacock Ltd.: A History 1810-1977

Raynes Park: the firm 1979   74pp illus
Nurdin & Peacock
617   *

Baker, Peter Shaw
The Acorn that Grew into an Oak: The Story of a Business

the firm 1948   36pp illus
Potter & Clarke
427   618   643   *

Baker, W J
A History of the Marconi Company

Methuen 1970   414pp illus
Marconi
340   *

Balfour, Arthur
Arthur Balfour & Co. Ltd: A Centenary 1865-1965

Nottingham: the firm 1967   80pp
Balfour, Arthur
221   SHEFFPL

Balfour, Beatty & Co
Balfour, Beatty: 50 Years to 1959

the firm 1959   78pp
Balfour, Beatty & Co
500   *

Balfour, John Patrick Douglas
The Kindred Spirit: A History of Gin and the House of Booth

Newman Neame 1959   93pp illus
Booth's Distilleries
424   *

Ball, John D
McCorquodale & Company: The History of a Printing Firm

1970
McCorquodale & Co
475

Ball, Mia
The Worshipful Company of Brewers: A Short History

Hutchinson Benham 1977   143pp illus index sources
Brewers' Company
427   *

Ballantyne
The Ballantyne Press and its Founders 1796-1908

Edinburgh: Ballantyne, Hanson 1909   191pp illus
Ballantyne, Hanson
475   *

Ballin, H H
The Organisation of Electricity Supply in Great Britain

Electrical Press 1946   323pp index sources
Electricity Supply
161   *

Balmforth, Owen
Huddersfield Industrial Society Ltd: Jubilee History 1860-1910
Manchester: Co-op Printing 1910   256pp illus
Huddersfield Industrial Soc
656   HDSFDPL

Balston, Thomas
James Whatman, Father and Son

Methuen 1957   xi 170pp illus index
Whatman, J   Hollingsworth & Balston
471   * §

Balston, Thomas
William Balston, Papermaker 1759-1849

    Methuen 1954   xii 172pp illus index sources
    Balston, W & R Ltd
    471   * §

Bamberger, Louis
Louis Bamberger: Memories of Sixty Years in the Timber and Pianoforte Trades
    Sampson Low 1930   270pp illus
    Bambergers
    492   613   *

Bamfords
A Short History of Bamfords Ltd., 1871-1971

    Uttoxeter: the firm 1971   20pp
    Bamfords
    321   325

Bampton, D
Bamptons 1933-1973: A History in the Evolution of the Coachbuilding and Repairing Industry
    Swindon: the firm 1979   64pp illus index
    Bampton
    352   671   WILTSPL

Banbury, Lawrence G
A History of Cablemaking at Helsby Factory

    the firm 1980   32pp
    B I C C
    341   WARRPL

Banbury, P
Shipbuilders on the Thames & Medway

    Newton Abbot: David & Charles 1971 336pp illus
    Shipbuilders, Thames & Medway
    361   *

Bank Line
Seventy Years of Adventurous Trading: The Story of the Bank Line 1885-1955
    Liverpool: Shipping Telegraph 1956   136pp
    Bank Line
    740   §

Bankers, Institute of
The First Fifty Years of the Institute of Bankers 1879-1929

    Blades East & Blades 1929   69pp illus
    Institute of Bankers
    963   *

Banks, Howard
The Rise and Fall of Freddie Laker

    Faber 1982   155pp
    Laker Airways
    750   * §

Banthrone of Newton
>*The story of Banthrone of Newton 1600-1950*

>1950   28pp illus
>Banthrone of Newton
>424   427   KCLDYPL

Barber, Derek
>*Humberts into the Eighties: A History of Humberts, Chartered Surveyors 1842-1980*
>the firm 1980   xxviii 103pp illus
>Humberts
>834   837   §

Barber, L H
>*Clarks of Street 1825-1950*

>Street: the firm 1950   177pp illus
>Clark, C & J
>451   *

Barclay & Fry
>*Barclay & Fry 1799-1949*

>1949   16pp
>Barclay & Fry
>472   GHL

Barclay, Curle
>*The Development of Shipbuilding on the Upper Reaches of the Clyde: Messrs Barclay, Curle & Co Ltd*
>1911
>Barclay, Curle
>361

Barclay, John B
>*A Pot of Paint: One Hundred Years of Rolland Decorators Limited*
>Edinburgh: the firm 1975   48pp illus
>Rolland Decorators
>504   EDNBRPL

Barclay, John Francis
>*Arthur & Company Limited Glasgow: One Hundred Years of Textile Distribution*
>Glasgow: the firm 1953   xiii 172pp illus index
>Arthur, J F & Co
>616   * §

Barclay, Perkins
>*Anchor Magazine: Barclay's Brewery Serves Five Generations 1781-1931*
>the firm nd   112pp illus
>Barclay, Perkins & Co
>427   662   BLPES

Barclay, Perkins
>*Barclay, Perkins & Co Ltd; Guest Book: The History of a Famous Brewery 1781-1910*
>the firm 1910   48pp illus
>Barclay, Perkins & Co
>427   662   SWKPL

Barclay, Perkins
Barclay, Perkins' Brewery: A History and a Guide

the firm 1910   47pp illus
Barclay, Perkins & Co
427   662   SWKPL

Barclay, Perkins
Three Centuries: The Story of our Ancient Brewery

the firm 1951   28pp illus
Barclay, Perkins & Co
427   662   * §

Barclays Bank
Barclays Bank Ltd, Goslings Branch 1650-1950

the firm 1950   46pp illus
Barclays Bank
814   §

Barclays Bank (DC&O)
A Banking Centenary: Barclays Bank - Dominion, Colonial and Overseas 1836-1936
the firm 1938   270pp illus index
Barclays Bank (DC&O)
814   * §

Bardens, Dennis
Everything in Leather: The Story of Barrow, Hepburn & Gale Ltd

the firm 1948   89pp illus
Barrow, Hepburn & Gale
441   GLROHL

Barfield, T J
Scott Built a Dynamo: The Story of the First Eighty Years of Laurence, Scott & Electromotors
Norwich: the firm nd   76pp illus
Laurence, Scott & Electromotors
342   343   IELECE

Barford & Perkins
Memoir of J G Barford, J P: A Short History of Queen Street Ironworks and its Products
Peterborough: the firm 1924   39pp illus
Barford & Perkins
321   CAMBSPL

Barford, Edward
Reminiscences of a Lance-Corporal of Industry

Elm Tree Books 1972   182pp illus
Aveling-Barford Group   Perkins Engine Co
325   *

Barker & Co
Barker & Co, Coachbuilders: From Chariot to Car

the firm 1930   74pp illus
Barker & Co
352   §

Barker, Theodore C & Harris, John R
A Merseyside Town in the Industrial Revolution: St. Helens 1750-1900
Liverpool: L U P 1954   508pp illus
Pilkington Brothers   Coal Industry
111   247   *

Barker, Theodore C & Robbins, R Michael
A History of London Transport: Passenger Travel and the Development of the Metropolis
Allen & Unwin 1963-74   2vols illus index sources
London Transport
721   *

Barker, Theodore Cardwell
Lord Salisbury: Chairman of the Great Eastern Railway 1868-1872
see Marriner, Sheila (ed) 1978
Great Eastern Railway
710

Barker, Theodore Cardwell
Pilkington Brothers and the Glass Industry

Allen & Unwin 1960   296pp illus index sources
Pilkington Brothers
247   * §

Barker, Theodore Cardwell
Pilkington: The Reluctant Multinational

see Jones, Geoffrey (ed) 1986
Pilkington Brothers
247

Barker, Theodore Cardwell
The Glassmakers: Pilkington: The Rise of an International Company 1826-1976
Weidenfeld & Nicolson 1977   xxxi 557pp illus index sources
Pilkington Brothers
247   *

Barker, Theodore Cardwell
The Transport Contractors of Rye: John Jempson & Son: A Chapter in the History of British Road Haulage
Athlone 1982   88pp illus index sources
Jempson, John & Son
723   * §

Barlow, Ronald
Kebroyd Land and Milnes: Through Four and a Half Centuries

author 1956   88pp illus
Blackburn & Sutcliffe   Kebroyd Land and Milnes
437   UBRIS

Barman, Christian
The Man Who Built London Transport: A Biography of Frank Pick

Newton Abbot: David & Charles 1979 287pp illus index
London Transport
721   *

Barnaby, Kenneth Cloves
100 Years of Specialised Shipbuilding and Engineering: John I Thornycroft Centenary 1964
Hutchinson 1964   263pp illus index
Thornycroft, John I
351   361   * §
Barnard, Alfred
The Noted Breweries of Great Britain & Ireland

Sir J Causton & Sons 1889-91   4 vol illus
Brewing Industry
427   *
Barnard, Alfred
The Whisky Distilleries of the United Kingdom (repr)

Newton Abbot: David & Charles 1969 457pp illus
Whisky Distilleries
424   *
Barnard, R W
A Century of Service: The Story of the Prudential 1848-1948

the firm 1948   139pp illus
Prudential Assurance
820   * §
Barnards
Barnards: A Retrospect

Norwich: the firm 1911   13pp illus
Barnards
311   NRFLKPL
Barnes, Christopher Henry George Bartlett
Bristol Aircraft since 1910

Putnam 1964   415pp illus sources
Bristol Aeroplane Co
750   *
Barnes, Christopher Henry George Bartlett
Handley Page Aircraft since 1907

Putnam 1976   viii 664pp illus index
Handley Page
364   *
Barnes, Eric George
The Rise of the Midland Railway 1844-74 ; The Midland Main Line 1875-1922
Allen & Unwin 1966-69   2 vols illus index sources
Midland Railway
710   *
Barnsley Brewery Co
The Barnsley Brewery Co Ltd

the firm 1958
Barnsley Brewery Co   Courage & Co
427

Barrett, W & Co
The Romance of Barretts

Northampton: the firm ca1940   16pp illus
Barrett, W & Co
451   NHPTNPL

Barrie, Derek Stiven Maxwelton
The Barry Railway

Lingfield: Oakwood Press 1978
Barry Railway
710   *

Barrie, Derek Stiven Maxwelton
The Rhymney Railway

Lingfield: Oakwood Press 1952   46pp sources
Rhymney Railway
710   *

Barrow's Stores
Barrow's: A Store Record 1824-1949

Birmingham: the firm 1949   43pp illus
Barrow's Stores
617   641   §

Bartlett, James Neville
Alexander Pirie & Sons of Aberdeen and the Expansion of the British Paper Industry ca1860-1914
Business History   vol XXII no 1 1980
Pirie, Alexander & Sons
471

Bartlett, James Neville
Carpeting the Millions: The Growth of Britain's Carpet Industry

Edinburgh: John Donald 1978   xiii 296pp illus index sources
Stoddard, A F & Co
438   *

Bartlett, James Neville
The Mechanisation of the Kidderminster Carpet Industry

Business History   vol XI no 1 1967
Kidderminster Carpet Industry
438

Bartlett, P
The South Staffordshire Railway Company in the Black Country

typescript 1967   7pp
South Staffordshire Railway Co
710   SANDWPL

Barton, William & Sons
William Barton & Sons Limited: One Hundred and Fiftieth Anniversary 1802-1952
Edinburgh: the firm 1952   37pp illus
Barton, William & Sons
503   EDNBRPL

Bartrum, Harvey & Co
A Century of Progress 1845-1945

1945   25pp
Bartrum, Harvey & Co
616   GHL

Barty-King, Hugh
Eyes Right: The Story of Dollond & Aitchison, Opticians 1750-1985
Quiller Press 1986   264pp illus index sources
Dollond & Aitchison
373   654   §

Barty-King, Hugh
Food for Man and Beast: The Story of the London Corn Trade, Cattle Food Trade and Grain & Feed Trade Associations
Hutchinson Benham 1978   108pp illus index
London Corn Trade Assn
963   * §

Barty-King, Hugh
Girdle Round the Earth: The Story of Cable & Wireless and its Predecessors to Mark the Group's Jubilee 1929-1979
Heinemann 1979   xvi 413pp illus index sources
Cable & Wireless
790   * §

Barty-King, Hugh
Light Up The World: The Story of Leonard Dale and Dale Electric 1935-1985
Quiller Press 1985   144pp illus index
Dale Electric Group
342   §

Barty-King, Hugh
New Flame: How Gas Changed the Commercial, Domestic and Industrial Life of Britain 1813-1984
Graphmitre 1984   262pp illus sources
Gas Industry
162   §

Barty-King, Hugh
Scratch a Surveyor...Drivers Jonas, 1725-1975

Heinemann 1975   xiv 273pp illus index sources
Drivers Jonas
834   * §

Barty-King, Hugh
The AA: A History of the First 75 Years of the Automobile Association 1905-1980
Basingstoke: the firm 1980   319pp illus index sources
Automobile Association
969   * §

Barty-King, Hugh
The Baltic Exchange: The History of a Unique Market

Hutchinson Benham 1977   xx 431pp illus index sources
Baltic Exchange
831   * §

Basnett, Lois
The History of the Bolton and Leigh Railway based on the Hulton Papers (1824-1828)
Trans Lancs Ches Antiq Soc   vol 62 1950-51
Bolton and Leigh Railway Co
710   WIGANPL

Bass, Hugh G
Boyd's of Castle Buildings, Lisburn: A Short History of an Old Family Firm
Lisburn: the firm 1977   40pp illus
Boyd, Alexander & Co
645   SEELBPL

Bastin, R
Cunard and the Liverpool Emigrant Traffic 1860-1900

Liverpool MA 1971
Cunard
740

Baston, Christopher
The History of the Bryan Donkin Co Ltd 1803-1973

College of Education study 1973   49pp illus sources
Donkin, Bryan & Co
221   320   DERBYPL

Batchelors Foods
Just the Job

Newman Neame 1963   51pp
Batchelors Foods
414   415   *

Batchelors Peas
Batchelors Peas Ltd: 38 Years of Progress

the firm nd   31pp
Batchelors Peas
414   SHEFFPL

Bateman, G C
G C Bateman, Optician, Oxford

the firm 1937   20pp
Bateman, G C
654   OXFDPL

Battison, George
Wishaw Co-operative Society Ltd: A Record of its Struggles, Progress and Success from its Inception in 1889
Glasgow: Scottish C W S 1939   141pp illus
Wishaw Co-operative Soc
656   MTHWLPL

Baume & Co
A Hundred Years of Time: The Story of Baume and Company, Watchmakers
the firm 1949   28pp illus
Baume & Co
374   *

Baumer, Edward
The Early Days of the Sun Life Office 1710-1910

Sir Joseph Causton 1910   71pp illus
Sun Insurance
820   * §

Baxendale, W H
Sowerby Bridge Industrial Society Jubilee Celebration April 1910: Historical Sketch
Manchester: C W S 1910   134pp illus
Sowerby Bridge Industrial Soc
656   HLFXPL

Baxter, Payne and Lepper
Baxter, Payne and Lepper 1760-1985: A Chronicle of the Period 1760-1985
Bromley: the firm 1985   60pp illus
Baxter, Payne and Lepper
834   §

Beable, William Henry
Romance of Great Businesses

Heath Cranton 1926   2 vols

                                         *

Beable, William Henry
The History of Christy's: The History of Hats

the firm ca1930
Christy & Co
453   SKPTPL

Beale, J Bennett
As I Remember It

the firm 1967
Beales
656

Beale, Samuel R
The Crown Iron Works Being the History of L Sterne & Co Ltd 1874-1949
Glasgow; G U P 1951   85pp illus
Sterne, L & Co Ltd
221   328   §

Bean, David
Thomas Reed, the First 200 Years: A Brief History 1782-1982

the firm ca1982   64pp illus
Reed, Thomas
475   BLPES

Beardmore, J
Milestones along the Iron Highway

1951   48pp
Rownson, Drew & Clydesdale
648   GHL

Beaton, Kendall
Enterprise in Oil: A History of Shell in the United States

New York: Appleton-Century 1957   815pp illus index sources
Shell   Royal Dutch/Shell
130   140   612   652   *

Beaumont, Philip
History of the Moira Collieries

Derby: Bemrose 1919   130pp illus
Moira Colliery Co
111   *

Beaumont, Richard
Purdey's: The Guns and the Family

Newton Abbot: David & Charles   248pp illus index
Purdey, James & Sons
329   §

Beaven, J & T
A Proud Record of Specialists in Fine Leathers

Holt: the firm 1970   16pp illus
Beaven, J & T
440   WILTSPL

Beaven, J & T
*A Proud Record: A Brief Survey of the Activities of J & T
Beaven Ltd*
Holt: the firm 1948   24pp illus
Beaven, J & T
440   WILTSPL

Beaver, Patrick
*A Pedlar's Legacy: The Origins and History of Empire Stores
1831-1981*
Henry Melland 1981   127pp illus
Empire Stores
656   * §

Beaver, Patrick
Addis 1780-1980: All About the House

Publications for Companies 1980   55pp illus
Addis
466   * §

Beaver, Patrick
INITIAL: 1928-1978: The Story of the Initial Group

Publications for Companies 1978   vi 65pp illus
Initial Services
981   §

Beaver, Patrick
Readson Ltd. 1932-1982

Henry Melland 1983   64pp illus
Readson
323   430   453   *

Beaver, Patrick
Sunderland Marine Mutual Insurance: The First Hundred Years 1882-1982
Publications for Companies 1982   vii 56pp illus
Sunderland Marine
820   §

Beaver, Patrick
The Alsford Tradition: A Century of Quality Timber 1882-1982

Henry Melland 1982   100pp illus
Alsford, J
613   * §

Beaver, Patrick
The Match Makers: The Story of Bryant & May

Henry Melland 1985   128pp illus index
Bryant & May
256   §

Beaver, Patrick
Yes! We Have Some: The story of Fyffes

Publications for Companies nd   133pp illus index
Fyffes   Elders & Fyffes
617   *

Beckinsale, Robert Percy
The Trowbridge Woollen Industry as illustrated by the Stock Books of John and Thomas Clark 1804-1824
Wilts Arch & Nat Hist Soc 1951   249pp
Clark, John & Thomas
431   *

Beckles, N I
The Development of the Port and Trade of Dundee 1815-1967

Dundee PhD 1968
Dundee Port & Trade
763

Bedford, John
John Bedford & Sons Ltd 150th Anniversary 1792-1942

Sheffield: the firm 1942   55pp illus
Bedford, John & Sons
221   SHEFFPL

Beer, Edwin John
The Beginning of Rayon - and Corrigenda and Supplement (publ 1968, 36pp)
Paignton: Phoebe Beer 1962   206pp illus
Rayon
432   *

Begg, Cousland
Note It in a Book: The Story of Begg, Cousland & Co. of Glasgow 1854-1954
Harley 1958   56pp illus
Begg, Cousland
223   *

Behrend, Arthur
Portrait of a Family Firm: Bahr, Behrend & Co. 1793-1945

Liverpool: the firm 1970   205pp illus
Bahr, Behrend
770   * §

Behrend, George
Luxury Trains: From Orient Express to the T G V

New York: Vendome 1982   232pp illus
Luxury Trains
710   *

Behrend, George
Pullman in Europe

Ian Allan 1962   360pp illus
Pullman
710   *

Behrend, George
The History of Wagons-Lits 1875-1955

Modern Transport Publishing 1959   32pp illus
Wagons-Lits
710   *

Behrens
Sir Jacob Behrens, 1806-1889

Percy Lund, Humphries ca1925   100pp illus
Behrens, Jacob
616   *

Belfast Harbour Commissioners
Belfast Harbour Commissioners Centenary 1847-1947

Belfast: the firm 1947   58pp illus
Belfast Harbour Commissioners
763   §

Bell, David
Hebble Remembered

Norwich: Becknell 1983   32pp illus
Hebble Motor Services
721   *

Bell, Robert
Twenty Five Years of the North Eastern Railway Company 1898-1922
Railway Gazette 1951
North Eastern Railway
710

Bell, Roy Frederick
Gordon & Gotch, London: The Story of the Gordon & Gotch Century 1853-1953
the firm 1953   viii 152pp illus
Gordon & Gotch
475   653   * §

Bellamy, Joyce Margaret
A Hull Shipbuilding Firm: The History of C & W Earle and Earle's Shipbuilding and Engineering Company Ltd
Business History   vol VI no 1 1963
Earle, C & W   Earle's Shipbuilding & Engineering Co
320   361

Bellamy, Joyce Margaret
A Hundred Years of Pharmacy in Hull

Hull: Chemists' Association 1969   17pp
Hull Chemists
643   *

Bellamy, Joyce Margaret
Cotton Manufacture in Kingston upon Hull

Business History   vol IV no 2 1962
Hull Flax & Cotton Mill Co   Kingston Cotton Mill Co
432   434

Belling and Lee
Golden Jubilee 1922-1972

Enfield: the firm 1972   20pp illus
Belling & Lee
345   *

Belling and Lee
Silver Jubilee 1922-1947: A Brief History of the Firm's First Twenty Five Years
Enfield: the firm 1948   24pp
Belling & Lee
345   *

Bellman, Charles Harold
Bricks and Mortals: A Study of the Building Society Movement and..the Abbey National Building Society 1849-1949
Hutchinson 1949   228pp illus index sources
Abbey National
815   * §

Bellman, Charles Harold
The Thrifty Three Millions: A Study of the Building Society Movement and ...the Abbey Road Society
the firm 1935   357pp illus
Abbey Road Soc
815   *

Bemrose, Henry Howe
The House of Bemrose 1826-1926

Derby: Bemrose 1926   160pp illus
Bemrose & Sons
475   *

Benefit Footwear
Benefit Footwear 1847-1947

Leeds: the firm 1947   31pp illus
Benefit Footwear
451   §

Benfield & Loxley
Benfield & Loxley Ltd 1876-1976

Oxford: the firm 1976   27pp illus
Benfield & Loxley
501   OXFDPL

Benfield & Loxley
Benfield & Loxley Ltd: Builders, Oxford

Cheltenham: Ed J Burrows 1968   60pp illus
Benfield & Loxley
501   *

Benham, Maura
The Story of Tiptree Jam: The First Hundred Years 1885-1985

Tiptree: the firm 1985   56pp illus index sources
Wilkin & Sons
414   ESSEXPL

Benham, Stanley J
Under Five Generations: The Story of Benham & Sons Ltd

the firm 1937   51pp illus
Benham & Sons
316   *

Bennett, Opie
Case for Celebration: A Short History of Bennett, Opie 1880-1955
1955   19pp
Bennett, Opie
641   GHL

Bennett, Richard
Battersea Works 1856-1956

the firm 1956   67pp illus
Morgan Crucible Co
248   *

Bennett, Richard
Smith and Nephew 1856-1956: A Record of Service to Surgery and Medicine
the firm 1956   45pp illus
Smith & Nephew
257   618   §

Bennett, Richard
The Story of Bovril

the firm 1953   34pp illus
Bovril
423   BCROB

Bennett, Richard & Leavey, J A
A History of Smith and Nephew 1856-1981

the firm 1981   76pp
Smith & Nephew
257   618

Bennetts Dairies and Farms
Bennetts Dairies and Farms 50th Anniversary

Berrows Newspapers 1979   8pp illus
Bennetts Dairies & Farms
10   HWORCPL

Bennison, Brian R
The Economic and Social Origins of the Northern Clubs'
Federation Brewery: Early 20th Century Co-op. Brewing
Newcastle on Tyne Polytechnic 1985 79pp
Northern Clubs' Fed Brewery
427   §

Bentall, Rowan
My Store of Memories

W H Allen 1974   x 298pp illus
Bentalls of Kingston
656   * §

Bentley, Isaac
Isaac Bentley and Company Centenary 1868-1968

the firm nd   pamphlet
Bentley, Isaac & Co
140   SALFDPL

Bentley, Richard
Thomas Bentley 1730-1780 of Liverpool, Etruria and London

1927   96pp
Wedgwood & Bentley
248   *

Benwell Community Project
Adamsez: The Story of a Factory Closure

Benwell Community Project 1980   71pp sources
Adamsez
248   UBRIS

Benzie and Miller
Through the Years with Benzie and Miller Ltd, Fraserburgh
1887-1937
                              20pp illus
Benzie & Miller
656   NESLS

Beresford, M W
Prometheus Insured: The Sun Life Agency in Leeds during
Urbanisation 1716-1826
Economic History Review   2nd ser vol XXXV no1 1982
Sun Life Agency in Leeds
820

Berger, Thomas B
A Century and a Half of the House of Berger 1760-1910

Waterlow 1910   108pp illus
Berger, Lewis & Sons
255   *

Bertrams
>*Within a Mile of Edinburgh Town: The History of Bertrams*
>*Limited   1821-1955*
>Edinburgh: the firm 1955   40pp illus
>Bertrams
>322   327   *

Berwick Salmon Fisheries Company
>*A Salmon Saga: The Story of the Berwick Salmon Fisheries*
>*Company Limited 1856-1956*
>the firm 1956
>Berwick Salmon Fisheries Co
>30

Besant, Arthur Digby
>*1824-1924 Our Centenary: Being the History of the Clerical,*
>*Medical & General Life Assurance Society*
>Bristol: the firm 1924   x 342pp illus index
>Clerical, Medical & General Life
>820   * §

Bessbrook
>*60 years of Progress   1904-1964*
>
>Armagh: Fane Valley Co-op 1964   32pp illus
>Bessbrook Spinning Co
>434   PRTDNPL

Bessbrook
>*Bessbrook: A Record of Industry in a Northern Ireland Village*
>*Community and of a Scocial Experiment 1845-1945*
>Bessbrook: the firm 1945   64pp illus
>Bessbrook Spinning Co
>434   PRTDNPL

Best, Robert Dudley
>*Brass Chandelier: A Biography of R H Best of Birmingham*
>
>Allen & Unwin 1940   251pp illus index
>Best & Hobson
>316   *

Besterman, Theodore (ed)
>*The Publishing Firm of Cadell & Davies: Select Correspondence*
>*and Accounts   1793-1836*
>Oxford U P 1938   xxxv 189pp sources
>Cadell & Davies
>475   653   * §

Bevington, Vaizey and Foster
>*Bevington, Vaizey and Foster*
>
>1954   83pp
>Bevington, Vaizey and Foster
>832   GHL

Bexfield, Harold
>*A Short History of Sheffield Cutlery and the House of*
>*Wostenholm*
>Sheffield: Loxley Bros 1945   40pp illus
>Wostenholm, George & Son
>316   *

Beynon, Huw
Working for Ford

Harmondsworth: Penguin 1973   336pp index sources
Ford Motor
351   *

Beynon, Huw & Wainwright, Hilary
The Workers' Report on Vickers

Pluto 1979   208pp illus index
Vickers
329   361   364   *

Bezzant, Norman
Out of the Rock...

Heinemann 1980   xii 244pp illus index sources
Bath & Portland Group
231   242   * §

Bibby Line
Bibby Line 1807-1957

Liverpool: the firm 1957   64pp illus
Bibby Line
740   *

Bibby Line
From Sail to Oil: The Progress of the Bibby Line

Liverpool: Ports & Cities Publ 1927 33pp
Bibby Line
740   *

Bibby, J & Sons
The Bibby Story

Liverpool: the firm 1950   62pp illus
Bibby, J & Sons
411   422   *

Bibby, John B
The Bibbys of Conder Mill and their Descendants

Liverpool: author 1979
Bibby, J & Sons
411   422   LPOOLPL

Bibby, John B & Bibby, Charles L
A Miller's Tale: A History of J Bibby & Sons Ltd., Liverpool

Liverpool: the firm 1978   xi 218pp illus
Bibby, J & Sons
411   422   * §

Bidwell, William Henry
Annals of an East Anglian Bank

Norwich: Goose 1900   viii 411pp illus index
Gurney & Co   Barclays Bank
814   * §

Bignold, Charles Robert
Five Generations of the Bignold Family 1761-1947 and their Connection with the Norwich Union
Batsford 1948   319pp illus
Norwich Union
820   *

Billington, W D
The Nightingales to Bolton Turnpike Trust 1763-1877

typescript 1976   111pp illus sources
Nightingales to Bolton Turnpike   Doffcocker Turnpike
502   BOLTNPL

Bilsland Brothers
Fifty Years in the Baking Trade 1872-1922: Bilsland Brothers Ltd, Hydepark Bakery, Glasgow
Glasgow: the firm 1923   24pp illus
Bilsland Brothers
419   UBRIS

Binfield, Clyde
Business Paternalism and the Congregational Ideal

see Jeremy, D J (ed) 1987

Birch, L
Truman Hanbury Buxton & Co

Burton-on-Trent: the firm 1957   96pp illus
Truman Hanbury Buxton
427   §

Birch, Wm. & Sons
Birch Builds 1874-1974

York: nd   16pp
Birch, Wm & Sons
501   MRC

Bird, Anthony C & Hutton-Stott, Francis H
Lanchester Motor Cars

Cassell 1965   240pp illus
Lanchester Motor Co   B S A
351   *

Bird, Ernie A
Murex: The History of a Company and its People

Rainham: the firm 1980   80pp illus
Murex   British Oxygen Co
210   * §

Bird, Leslie
History of Bird Ltd

typescript nd   58pp
Bird   Johnson Group Cleaners
981   §

Birkhead, E
> *The Beginnings of British Civil Air Transport 1919-24*

> Leicester MA 1959
> Civil Air Transport
> 750

Birkin, Guy
> *Birkin Group 1962-1982*

> Nottingham: the firm 1983   16pp illus
> Birkin Group
> 439   DERBYPL

Birmingham Aluminium Casting Co
> *The Birmal Story: Written for the 50th Anniversary of the*
> *Birmingham Aluminium Casting (1903) Co Ltd*
> the firm 1953   20pp illus
> Birmingham Aluminium Casting
> 311   SANDWPL

Birmingham Co-operative Society
> *History of the Birmingham Co-operative Society Limited*
> *1881-1931*
> Birmingham: the firm 1931   234pp illus
> Birmingham Co-operative Society
> 656   *

Birmingham Small Arms Co
> *B S A Group News: Centenary Issue, June 7, 1961*

> the firm 1961   78pp illus
> B S A
> 329   351   363   SOLHLPL

Birmingham Small Arms Co
> *The History of the Birmingham Small Arms Company*
> *1861-1973*
> typescript   3 vols
> B S A
> 329   363   SOLHLPL

Birtles, Philip J
> *Planemakers 3: de Havilland*

> Janes 1984   160pp illus
> de Havilland
> 364   *

Black, Michael H
> *Cambridge University Press 1584-1984*

> Cambridge: C U P 1984   xvii 343pp illus index
> Cambridge University Press
> 475   * §

Black, Mona S
> *The Life and Work of Thomas Robinson Ferens 1847-1930*

> dissertation; Dip.Soc.Stud, Hull 1974
> Reckitt & Sons
> 259   418

Blackburn
The Blackburn Story 1909-1959

Brough: the firm 1960   40pp illus
Blackburn & General Aircraft
364   *

Blacker, Ken
London's Buses: The Independent Era 1922-1934: Country
Independents 1919-1939
St.Albans: H J Publications 1977   2 vols illus index
Buses in London
721   *

Blackie, Agnes Anna Coventry
Blackie & Son Ltd 1809-1959: A Short History of the Firm

Glasgow: Blackie & Son 1959   64pp illus
Blackie & Son
475   * §

Blackman, Janet
The Food Supply of an Industrial Town: A Study of Sheffield's
Public Markets 1780-1900
Business History   vol V no2 1963
Sheffield's Public Markets
617

Blagden, Cyprian
Fire More Than Water: Notes for the Story of a Ship

Longmans, Green 1949   42pp illus
Longman
475   * §

Blagden, Cyprian
The Stationers' Company: A History 1403-1959

Allen & Unwin 1960   321pp illus
Stationers' Company
475   653   *

Blair, Matthew
The Paisley Shawl and the Men who Produced it

Paisley: A Gardner 1904   84pp illus index
Clark   Coats, Paton & Baldwin
431   432   *

Blair, Matthew
The Paisley Thread Industry and the Men who Created and
Developed it
Paisley: A Gardner 1907   206pp illus index
Clark   Coats, Paton & Baldwin
431   432   *

Blake, David (ed)
Chronicles of the Firm of Widnell and Trollope, Chartered
Quantity Surveyors: Volume One 1852-1919
the firm 1974   24pp
Widnell & Trollope
837   §

Blake, George
'The Gourock'

Glasgow: the firm 1963   200pp illus
Gourock Ropework Co
439   *

Blake, George
B I Centenary 1856-1956

Collins 1956   272pp illus index
British India Steam Navigation Co P & O
740   *

Blake, George
Gellatly's 1862-1962: A Short History of the Firm

Blackie & Son 1962   178pp illus index
Gellatly, Hankey & Co
740   770   839   *

Blake, George
Lloyd's Register of Shipping 1760-1960

the firm 1960   194pp illus index
Lloyd's Register of Shipping
837   * §

Blake, George
The Ben Line: The History of Wm. Thomson & Co of Leith and Edinburgh 1825-1955
Nelson 1956   ix 222pp illus index
Thomson, Wm & Co   Ben Line Steamers
361   740   * §

Blake, George
The Romance of the Airdrie Savings Bank: Centenary Souvenir

Airdrie: Baird & Hamilton 1935   67pp illus
Airdrie Savings Bank
814   AIRDRPL

Blake, Robert Norman William
Esto Perpetua: The Norwich Union Life Insurance Society: An Account of 150 Years of Progress
Newman Neame 1958   117pp illus
Norwich Union
820   * §

Bland, Leslie
Fired with Enthusiasm: A History of King and Hutchings

manuscript nd   99pp
King & Hutchings
475   HILLPL

Blandford, Thomas & Newell, George
History of the Leicester Co-operative Hosiery Manufacturing Society Ltd
Leicester: Co-op Printing Soc 1898   116pp illus
Leicester Co-op Hosiery
436   LEICSPL

Blantyre Co-operative Society
History of Blantyre Co-operative Society Ltd

    the firm ca1934   68pp illus
    Blantyre Co-operative Soc
    656   MTHWLPL

Blatchford, Montagu J
History of the Halifax Industrial Society Limited for Fifty Years 1851-1901
    Halifax: the firm 1900   224pp illus
    Halifax Industrial Soc
    656   HLFXPL

Blaxill, Edwin Alec
These Hundred Years, 1838 to 1938: Blaxill & Co Ltd

    the firm 1938   32pp illus
    Blaxill & Co
    465   648   ESSEXPL

Bloom, John
It's No Sin to Make a Profit

    W H Allen 1971   251pp illus
    Rolls Razor   Colston
    346   *

Blum, Fred H
Work and Community: The Scott Bader Commonwealth and the Quest for a New Social Order
    Routledge & Kegan Paul 1968   392pp index
    Scott Bader and Co
    251   *

Blundell, Spence & Co
The Blundell Book 1811-1951: A Short History

    Hull: the firm 1951   76pp illus
    Blundell, Spence & Co
    255   GHL

Blunsden, John
The Power to Win

    Motor Racing Publications 1983   232pp illus
    Cosworth Engineering Co
    351   NHPTNPL

Blyth, Henry Edward
Through the Eye of a Needle: The Story of the English Sewing Cotton Company
    Manchester: the firm 1947   111pp illus
    English Sewing Cotton Co
    432   * §

Boase, Charles William
A Century of Banking in Dundee (Being the Annual Balance Sheets of the Dundee Banking Co from 1764 to 1864)
    Dundee: J P Mathew 1864   16 + 101(double) + 27pp
    Dundee Banking Co   Royal Bank of Scotland
    814   *

Boatmens' Building Society
Ballot or Sale? A Peep into the Past

typescript nd 12pp
Boatmens' Building Society
815 WMNSTPL

Boddy, Martin
The Building Societies

Macmillan 1980 176pp
Building Societies
815 *

Bolckow, Vaughan & Co
Thomas & Gilchrist 1879-1929 Bolckow & Vaughan

Middlesbrough: the firm 1929 31pp illus
Bolckow, Vaughan & Co
221 *

Bolitho, Henry Hector
*A Batsford Century: The Record of a Hundred Years of
Publishing and Bookselling 1843-1943*
Batsford 1943 148pp illus index
Batsford
475 653 * §

Bolitho, Henry Hector
Alfred Mond, First Lord Melchett

Martin Secker 1933 391pp illus
I C I Brunner, Mond
250 *

Bolitho, Henry Hector
James Lyle Mackay, First Earl of Inchcape

John Murray 1936 264pp illus
Inchcape P & O
740 770 839 *

Bolitho, Henry Hector & Peel, Derek
The Drummonds of Charing Cross

Allen & Unwin 1967 232pp illus ind sources
Drummonds
814 * §

Bolsover Colliery Co
The Bolsover Colliery Company Limited 1889-1939

the firm 1939 36pp
Bolsover Colliery Co
111 *

Bolton County Borough Transport Department
Bolton Corporation Transport Diamond Jubilee 1900-1960

Bolton: the firm 1960 31pp illus
Bolton Corporation Transport
721 BOLTNPL

Bolton Environmental Education Project
Horwich: A Century of Railway Works

Bolton Environmental Education 1985 54pp illus sources
Horwich Railway Works   Lancashire & Yorkshire Railway
362   710   BOLTNPL

Bonavia, Michael Robert
*A History of the L N E R :- The First Years 1923-33;   The Age
of the Streamliners 1934-39;   The Last Years 1939-48*
Allen & Unwin 1982   3 vols illus index
London & North Eastern Railway
710   *

Bonavia, Michael Robert
British Rail: The First 25 Years

Newton Abbot: David & Charles 1981 239pp illus index sources
British Rail
710   *

Bonavia, Michael Robert
Railway Policy Between the Wars

Manchester: M U P 1981   x 156pp index sources
Railways
710   *

Bonavia, Michael Robert
The Birth of British Rail

Allen & Unwin 1979   110pp illus index sources
British Rail
710   *

Bonavia, Michael Robert
The Four Great Railways

Newton Abbot: David & Charles 1980 223pp sources
Great Western Railway   London & North Eastern Railway
710   §

Bonavia, Michael Robert
The Organisation of British Railways

Shepperton: Ian Allan 1971   192pp
Railways
710   *

Bonavia, Michael Robert
The Twilight of British Rail?

Newton Abbot: David & Charles 1985 207pp illus
British Rail
710   *

Bonsor, Noel Reginald Pixell
*North Atlantic Seaway: The Passenger Services Linking the Old
World with the New*
Prescot: T Stephenson & Sons 1955   639pp illus
Atlantic Passenger Services
740   *

Bonsor, Noel Reginald Pixell
South Atlantic Seaway: The Passenger Lines and Liners from Europe to Brazil, Uruguay and Argentina
Brookside 1983   xxii 525pp illus
Atlantic Passenger Services
740   *

Booth, John
The "Old Vic" : A Century of Theatrical History 1816-1916

Stead 1917   72pp
Old Vic
974   *

Bootham Engineers
Bootham Engineers Ltd York 1831-1981

York: William Sessions 1982
Bootham Engineers
320

Boothman, J
The Sun Mill Company, Chadderton

Northern Mill Soc.Flywheel July 1985 24pp
Sun Mill Co
432   OLDHMPL

Borax Holdings
The Borax Story 1899-1953

the firm 1953   286pp illus
Borax Holdings
239   839   §

Borthwick, Alastair
The History of Smith & Wellstood Ltd, Ironfounders 1854-1954

Bonnybridge, Stirling: the firm 1954 89pp illus
Smith & Wellstood
311   316   §

Borthwick, Alastair
Yarrow & Company Limited: The First Hundred Years 1865-1965

Glasgow: the firm 1965   135pp illus index
Yarrow
320   361   * §

Bosley, P B
The Manchester and Milford Haven Railway 1860-1906: Promotion, Construction and Operation...
Wales(St David's, Lampeter) MA 1978
Manchester & Milford Haven Rly
710

Boswell, James (ed)
J S 100: The Story of Sainsbury's

the firm 1969   96pp illus
Sainsbury, J
641   656   GLROHL

Boswell, Jonathan S
Business Policies in the Making: Three Steel Companies Compared
Allen & Unwin 1983   241pp index sources
Dorman Long   United Steel
220   BLPES

Boswell, Jonathan S
Hope, Inefficiency or Public Duty? The United Steel Companies and West Cumberland 1918-1939
Business History   vol XXII no 1 1980
United Steel
221

Boulton & Paul
The Leaf and the Tree: The Story of Boulton and Paul 1797-1947: A Story of Expansion 1947-1962
Norwich: the firm 1947/1962   2 vols illus
Boulton & Paul
364   461   463   * §

Bourlet, James & Sons
Bourlet: Picture Restorers

1959   52pp
Bourlet, James & Sons
976   GHL

Bourne-Paterson, R A
The Imperial Continental Gas Association in the Twentieth Century 1901-1933
typescript 1970   206pp sources
Imperial Continental Gas
162   839   UBRIS

Bowbelski, Margaret
The Royal Small Arms Factory, Enfield

Enfield: Edmonton Hist Soc 1977   26pp illus
Royal Small Arms, Enfield
329   ENFLDPL

Bowden, Gregory Houston
The Story of the Raleigh Cycle

W H Allen 1975   216pp illus index
Raleigh Industries   Tube Investments
363   *

Bowen, Frank Charles
A Hundred Years of Towage: A History of Messrs William Watkins Ltd 1833-1933
Gravesend & Dartford Reporter 1933 215pp illus
Watkins, William
763   *

Bowen, Frank Charles
Seventy Years of Houstons

Nautical Magazine   vol 163 Mar 1950
Houston
740

Bowen, Frank Charles
    The Flag of the Southern Cross: The History of Shaw Savill &
    Albion Co Ltd 1858-1939
    Liverpool: the firm 1939   122pp illus index
    Shaw Savill & Albion Co
    740   *

Bowley, Marian
    The British Building Industry: Four Studies in Response and
    Resistance to Change
    Cambridge: C U P 1966
    Building
    500   *

Bowman, A I
    Kirkintilloch Shipbuilding

    Bishopbriggs: Strathkelvin 1983   83pp illus sources
    Hay, J & J   McGregor, Peter & Sons
    361   *

Bowmans (Warrington)
    Progress in Chemicals: The Story of Bowmans and Widnes
    1905-1955
    the firm 1955   17pp
    Bowmans (Warrington)
    251   WARRPL

Bowring
    Bowring- Building

    Galitzine Chant Russell 1966   48pp illus
    Bowring, C T & Co
    832   BLPES

Boyce, G H
    The Growth and Dissolution of a Large-scale Business
    Enterprise: The Furness Interests 1892-1919
    London PhD 1984
    Furness Interests
    111   210   221

Boyd, James Ian Craig
    The Festiniog Railway

    Lingfield: Oakwood Press 1960-61   2 vols illus
    Festiniog Railway
    710   *

Boyd, W
    The Story of the Wallsend Slipway and Engineering Co Ltd
    1891-1897

    Wallsend Slipway and Eng Co
    361   763

Boydell, Thomas
    The Jubilee History of the Leigh Friendly Co-operative Society
    Ltd 1857-1907
    Manchester: Co-op Printing Soc 1907 323pp illus
    Leigh Friendly Co-operative Soc
    656   *

Boyle, Emily
> *The Economic Development of the Irish Linen Industry*
> *1825-1913*
> Queen's University, Belfast PhD 1979
> Irish Linen
> 434

Boyson, Rhodes
> *The Ashworth Cotton Enterprise: The Rise & Fall of a Family*
> *Firm 1818-1880*
> Oxford: Clarendon 1970   285pp illus index sources
> Ashworth
> 432   *

Boyson, Rhodes
> *The Ashworth Cotton Factories and the Life of Henry Ashworth*
> *(1794-1830)*
> London PhD 1967
> Ashworth
> 432

Brace, Harold Witty
> *History of Seed Crushing in Great Britain*
>
> Land Books 1960   172pp illus
> British Oil & Cake Mills   Hull Stearine & Warehousing Co
> 411   *

Bradbury Wilkinson
> *Over a Century of Security Printing*
>
> New Malden: the firm   32pp illus
> Bradbury Wilkinson
> 475   MERTNPL

Braddon, Russell Reading
> *Roy Thomson of Fleet St.*
>
> Collins 1965   396pp illus index sources
> Thomson Organisation
> 475   *

Bradford Dyers' Association Ltd
> *Bradford Dyers' Association Ltd*
>
> typescript 1950 held by the firm
> Bradford Dyers' Association
> 431

Bradley, D
> *Fletcher and Stewart Ltd: A Business History with special*
> *reference to the Firm's Role in the World Sugar Industry*
> Nottingham MPhil 1972   304pp microfilm
> Fletcher & Stewart
> 420   DERBYPL

Bradley, Edwin H
> *Building on a Name: The History of Edwin H Bradley & Sons Ltd.*
>
> the firm 1983   75pp illus
> Bradley, Edwin H
> 500   WILTSPL

Bradley, Kenneth Granville
Copper Venture: The Discovery and Development Of Roan Antelope and Mufulira
the firm 1952   112pp illus index
Roan Antelope
210   839   *

Bradshaw, J B
The Country Miller: His Place in the Economy

Driffield: the firm 1951   24pp illus
Bradshaw & Co
416   §

Brailsford, Michael
Lee Steel 1874-1974

Sheffield: the firm 1974   48pp illus
Lee Steel
221

Brain, Jennifer
S A Brain & Co: The Cardiff Brewery 1882-1982

Cardiff: the firm 1982   28pp illus
Brain, S A & Co
427   §

Braithwaite, David
Building in the Blood: The Story of Dove Brothers of Islington 1781-1981
Geoffrey Cave 1981   160pp illus index sources
Dove Brothers
500   * §

Braithwaite, David
Savage of King's Lynn: Inventor of Machines and Merry-Go-Rounds
Cambridge: Patrick Stephens 1975   136pp illus index sources
Savages
321   *

Brampton Brewery
Brampton Brewery Co Ltd Souvenir Brochure

the firm 1922
Brampton Brewery Co
427   DERBYPL

Bramsen, Bo & Wain, Kathleen
The Hambros 1779-1979

Michael Joseph 1979   457pp illus index sources
Hambro's Bank
814   * §

Bramwell, A G
The Nelstrop Family in History: 1661-1900

typescript 1976   195pp
Nelstrop, Wm & Co
416   SKPTPL

Brandon, Ruth
    A Capitalist Romance: Singer and the Sewing Machine

    Barrie & Jenkins 1977   xiii 244pp illus index sources
    Singer Sewing Machines
    328   * §

Braund, Harold Ernest Wilton
    Calling to Mind: Being Some Account of the First Hundred Years
    (1870-1970) of Steel Brothers and Company Limited
    Oxford: Pergamon 1975   151pp illus index sources
    Steel Brothers & Co
    839   *

Brearley, C B E
    A History of the Association of British Chemical
    Manufacturers 1916-1967

    British Chemical Mfrs Assoc
    250   BLPES

Brearley, Harry
    Knotted String: Autobiography of a Steel Maker

    Longman 1941   198pp
    Brearley, Harry
    221   *

Brennan, John
    History of the Bradford Property Trust Limited 1928-1978

    the firm 1978   viii 55pp index
    Bradford Property Trust
    850   *

Brereton, Austin
    A Walk Down Bond Street: The Centenary Souvenir of the House
    of Ashton and Mitchell 1820-1920
    Selwyn & Blount 1920   24pp illus
    Ashton & Mitchell
    770   *

Breton, Norton
    History of Henckel, du Buisson & Company 1697 to 1947

    the firm 1948   43pp illus
    Henckel, du Buisson & Co
    839   §

Bretton, R
    Crossleys of Dean Clough

    Trans Halifax Antiq Soc   vol 1-3 1950-2
    Crossley, John & Sons
    438

Brewer, Roy
    1776-1876 Raithby Lawrence 1876-1976

    Leicester: the firm 1976   90pp illus
    de Montfort Press
    475   StBRD

Brewer, Roy
Friedheim: A Century of Service 1884-1984

the firm 1984   66pp illus
Friedheim, Oscar
          *

Brico
The History of Brico 1909-1959

1959   39pp illus
Brico
320   COVNPL

Bridge Foundry
Notes on the Bridge Foundry

typescript 1950
Bridge Foundry
311   WARRPL

Bridges, T C & Tiltman, H H
Kings of Commerce

Harrap 1928
          *

Bridges, Tom
A Short History of Chiltern Motor Holdings Ltd, formerly City Motor Co (Oxford) Ltd
the firm 1976   iii 40pp
Chiltern Motor Holdings   City Motor Co (Oxford)
614   651   *

Brierly, E
Clogs

typescript 1980   60pp illus sources
Tommy Lees, Tyldesley   Walkley, F (Clogs), Huddersfield
451   465   BOLTNPL

Briggs, Asa
Essays in the History of Publishing in Celebration of the 250th Anniversary of the House of Longman 1724-1974
Longman 1974   468pp illus index sources
Longman
475   BCROB

Briggs, Asa
Friends of the People: The Centenary History of Lewis's

Batsford 1956   242pp illus index sources
Lewis's
656   * §

Briggs, Asa
Marks & Spencer 1884-1984

Octopus 1984   128pp illus index
Marks & Spencer
645   656   *

Briggs, Asa
The B B C: The First Fifty Years

Oxford: O U P 1985   xvi 439pp illus index sources
British Broadcasting Corp
974   *

Briggs, Asa
The History of Broadcasting in the United Kingdom

Oxford U P 1961-79   4 vols illus index sources
British Broadcasting Corp
974   *

Briggs, Asa
Wine for Sale: Victoria Wine and the Liquor Trade 1860-1984

Batsford 1985   199pp illus index sources
Victoria Wine
642   * §

Briggs, Donald H C
A Merchant, a Banker and the Coal Trade, 1693-1971

1971
Briggs, Henry
111

Briggs, George
Jubilee History of the York Equitable Industrial Society Ltd

Manchester: C W S 1909   280pp illus
York Equitable Industrial Society
656   UBRIS

Briggs, J H Y
The Radical Saints of Shelton: The Ridgway Family, Methodist Pottery Manufacturers
see Jeremy, D J (ed) 1987
Ridgway
248

Briggs, K M
Henry Briggs Son & Company Limited, Adapted from some Historical Notes
ca1935
Briggs, Henry
111

Bright, Edward B & Charles
The Life Story of Sir Charles Tilson Bright, Civil Engineer

Constable 1908   478pp
Atlantic Telegraph Co
790   837   *

Bristol Brewery Georges and Co
144 Years of Brewing 1788-1932

Bristol: the firm 1938   99pp illus
Bristol Brewery Georges & Co
427   UBRIS

Bristol Commercial Vehicles
The First Fifty Years: The Story of the Birth and Development of Bristol Vehicles 1913-1963
Bristol: the firm nd   16pp illus
Bristol Commercial Vehicles
351   ABRDNPL

Bristow, Philip
The Mansfield Brew

Ringwood: Navigator 1966   188pp illus
Mansfield Brewery Co
427   662   *

British Aluminium
The History of the British Aluminium Company Limited 1894-1955
the firm 1955   78pp illus
British Aluminium
224   §

British and Foreign Marine Insurance
The British and Foreign Marine Insurance Company Limited 1863-1963
Liverpool: the firm 1963   104pp illus
British & Foreign Marine Ins
820   §

British Enkalon
British Enkalon: various pamphlets

illus
British Enkalon
260   NEELBPL

British Gas Light Co
A Short History of the Company 1824-1924

the firm 1924   52pp
British Gas Light Co
162   §

British Industrial Plastics
Growth of a Group: A History of the B I P Group 1895-1949

the firm 1949   46pp illus
British Industrial Plastics   B I P
251   *

British Land Company
1856-1956: The Centenary of the British Land Company Limited

the firm 1956
British Land Co
850

British Leyland; Radiators Division
A Brief History of Osberton Radiators 1919-1969

the firm ca1969   10pp
Osberton Radiators   British Leyland
353   OXFDPL

British Linen Bank
The British Linen Bank 1746-1946

1946   23pp
British Linen Bank
814   GHL

British Petroleum
Our Industry; An Introduction to the Petroleum Industry for the use of Members of the Staff
the firm 1958 (3rd. ed.)   472pp illus index
B P
130   140   251   612   652   * §

British Steel
Full Circle: The Story of Steelmaking on Deeside

Shotton: the firm 1980   16pp illus
British Steel   Summers, John & Sons
221   §

British Steel
Shotton in the 70s

Shotton: the firm ca1975
British Steel   Summers, John & Sons
221   CLWYDPL

British United Shoe Machinery Co
The Works and Products of the British United Shoe Machinery Co
Leicester: the firm ca1937   84pp illus
British United Shoe Machinery Co
327   LEICSPL

British Xylonite Co
Xylonite Group: Seventy Five Years 1877-1952

the firm 1952   40pp illus
British Xylonite Co   Xylonite Group
251   483   §

Briton Brush Co
Briton Brush Co: History of the Firm

Norwich: the firm 1933   16pp illus
Briton Brush Co
465   466   §

Britton, George Bryant & Sons
G B Britton & Sons: Cobblers' Tale: The End of the Tale

Bristol: Abson Press 1958/77   2 vols
Britton, G B & Sons   Ward White Group
451   *

Broadbent and Turner
Broadbent and Turner Ltd: The First Fifty Years: A Mass Observation Report
Mass Observation 1953
Broadbent and Turner
453   648   839   WARRPL

Broadbent, L H
The Avery Business 1730-1918

Birmingham: the firm 1949   86pp illus sources
Avery, W & T
328   *

Broadbent, Thomas
Thomas Broadbent and Sons Ltd 1864-1964

Huddersfield: the firm 1964   36pp illus
Broadbent, Thomas and Sons
320   HDSFDPL

Broadbridge, Seymour Albert
Studies in Railway Expansion and the Capital Market in England 1825-1873
Cass 1970   215pp illus sources
Railway Capital
710   815   *

Broadbridge, Seymour Albert
The Finances of the Lancashire and Yorkshire Railway 1835-1873
London PhD 1957
Lancashire & Yorkshire Railway
710   NRMYORK

Broadley, Alexander Meyrick
Garrard's 1721-1911: Crown Jewellers and Goldsmiths during Six Reigns and in Three Centuries
Stanley Paul 1912   182pp illus
Garrard's
491   654   * §

Brockhouse, J & Co
Constant Endeavour: A Record of Achievement

West Bromwich: the firm ca1945   58pp illus
Brockhouse, J & Co
223   311   312   320   353   SANDWPL

Brocklehurst
Brocklehurst-Whiston: The Story of its Activities

Macclesfield: the firm nd   64pp illus
Brocklehurst-Whiston
432   BLPES

Brogan, Colm
James Finlay & Company Limited, Manufacturers and East India Merchants 1750-1950
Glasgow: the firm 1951   276pp illus index
Finlay, James & Co
839   *

Brooke, Alan J
The Fancy Weavers and the Nortons

Huddersfield: typescript 1980   30pp
Norton, Joseph   West, Clayton
431   HDSFDPL

Brooke, D

The Origins and Development of Four Constituent Lines of the North Eastern Railway 1824-54

Hull MA 1961

North Eastern Railway

710

Brooke, D

The Struggle between Hull and the North Eastern Railway 1854-80

Journal of Transport History   new ser vol I no 4 1972

North Eastern Railway

710

Brooke, Edward Henry

Chronology of the Tinplate Works of Great Britain

Cardiff: William Lewis 1949   241pp

Tinplate Works

221   *

Brooke, Edward Henry

Monograph on the Tinplate Works in Great Britain

Swansea: E Davies 1932   143pp

Tinplate Works

221   *

Brookes, K P

Development of Manchester Airport 1919-64

Manchester MA 1965

Manchester Airport

764

Brooks, Brian

Charles Dickens Ltd 1923-1973

Cheltenham: the firm 1973   20pp illus

Dickens, Charles   Laxon, E and Co

467   617   642   CHELTPL

Brooks, William Collin

Grayson's of Liverpool: A History of Grayson, Rollo and Clover Docks

Liverpool: H Young 1956   96pp

Grayson, Rollo and Clover Docks

763

Brooks, William Collin

The First Hundred Million: A History of the Woolwich Equitable Building Society

the firm 1954   56pp

Woolwich Equitable Building Soc

815   * §

Brooks, William Collin

The First Hundred Years of the Woolwich Equitable Building Society

the firm 1947   208pp illus index

Woolwich Equitable Building Soc

815   * §

Brooks, William Collin
The History of Johnson & Phillips: A Romance of Seventy Five Years
the firm 1950   xi 212pp illus index
Johnson & Phillips
341   * §

Broomhead, Leslie James
The Great Oak: A Story of the Yorkshire Bank

Leeds: the firm 1981   100pp illus
Yorkshire Bank
814   §

Brough, Joseph
Wrought Iron: The End of an Era at Atlas Forge, Bolton

Bolton Council 1981   55pp illus
Walmsley, Thomas & Sons   Atlas Forge
311   312   BOLTNPL

Brown & Tawse Group
Brown & Tawse 1881-1957

Dundee: the firm 1957   40pp illus
Brown & Tawse Group
221   222   612   UBRIS

Brown Bayleys
Brown Bayleys 1871-1971: A Centenary

Sheffield; the firm 1971
Brown Bayleys
221

Brown, Antony
British Marine Mutual Insurance Association: B M M 1876-1976

Publications for Companies 1976
British Marine Mutual Insurance
820

Brown, Antony
Cuthbert Heath: Maker of the Modern Lloyd's of London

Newton Abbot: David & Charles 1980 220pp illus index sources
Lloyd's of London   Heath, C E & Co
820   * §

Brown, Antony
Hazard Unlimited: The Story of Lloyd's of London

P Davies 1978   xi 226pp illus index
Lloyd's of London
837   *

Brown, Charles
Origins and Progress of Horrockses, Crewdson & Co

Preston: Preston Guardian 1925
Horrockses, Crewdson & Co
432

Brown, John
John Brown & Company Ltd 1864-1924

the firm 1924
Brown, John
221   361
Brown, John Crosby
One Hundred Years of Merchant Banking: A History of Brown Brothers & Co; Brown, Shipley & Co
1909   374pp
Brown, Shipley & Co
814   §
Brown, John Falcon
Guinness and Hops

the firm 1980   xv 264pp index
Guinness
427   *
Brown, Muff & Co
Brown, Muff & Co Ltd: Rule Book

the firm 1934   84pp
Brown, Muff & Co
656   UBRIS
Brown, Muff & Co
The Bromuff Story: A Brief Chronicle of 150 Years of Progress 1814-1964
Bradford: the firm nd   32pp illus
Brown, Muff & Co
656   §
Brown, Stewart J
Alexander Buses

Swindon/Ratho: Fleetline 1984   96pp illus
Alexander, W & Sons
721   DNDEEPL
Brown, Stewart J
N B C: Antecedents and Formation

Ian Allan 1983   128pp
Tilling, Thomas   British Electric Traction
721   *
Brown, William Henry
A Century of Co-operation at Sheerness: Being a Chronicle of the Oldest Co-operative Society...in the United Kingdom
Manchester: C W S ca1920   101pp illus
Sheerness Economical Society
656   *
Brown, William Henry
A Century of London Co-operation   *(Also many other titles by this author on Co-operative Societies not listed here)*
the firm 1928   179pp illus
London Co-operative Society
656   *

Browne, B C
The History of the New R & W Hawthorn

1914
Hawthorn Leslie
361

Browne, Eric Gore
Glyns 1753-1953: Six Generations in Lombard Street

1953   266pp
Glyn Mills & Co
814   GHL

Browne, Eric Gore
The History of the House of Glyn Mills & Co

the firm 1933   197pp illus
Glyn Mills & Co
814   * §

Bruce, Alexander Balmain
The Life of William Denny, Shipbuilder, Dumbarton

Hodder & Stoughton 1888   xvi 479pp
Denny, William & Bros
361   *

Bruce, George
Kimberley Ale: The Story of Hardys & Hansons 1832-1982

Henry Melland 1982   128pp illus
Hardys & Hansons
427   662   * §

Bruce, George
Poland's at Lloyd's

Henry Melland 1979   160pp illus
Poland, John & Co
820   * §

Bruce, George
The Trentham Story

the firm 1978   192pp illus
Trenthams
500   §

Bruce-Gardyne, Jock
Meriden: Odyssey of a Lame Duck: Government Intervention in the Motor Cycle Industry...The Way the Money Goes
Centre for Policy Studies 1978   67pp
Meriden   Triumph Motor Cycles
363   *

Brunner, Elizabeth
Holiday Making and the Holiday Trades

Oxford: O U P 1945   65pp
Holidays
667   *

Brunner, Mond
     The First Fifty Years of Brunner, Mond & Co 1873-1923

       Northwich: the firm 1923   xi 106pp illus
       Brunner, Mond & Co   I C I
       251   §

Bryan, M A
     The Grassmoor Colliery Company 1880-1910

       dissertation BA Hons 1963   106pp illus
       Grassmoor Colliery Co
       111   DERBYPL

Bryant & May
     Making Matches 1861-1961 and other pamphlets

       Newman Neame 1961   27pp illus
       Bryant & May
       256   * §

Bryant, Arthur Wynne Morgan
     Liquid History: To Commorate Fifty Years of the Port of London Authority 1909-1959
       the firm 1960   xvi 84pp illus index
       Port of London
       763   *

Bryant, Arthur Wynne Morgan
     One Hundred Years under the Southern Cross

       ca1958   24pp
       Shaw Savill & Albion Co
       740   GHL

Bryer, R A, Brignall, T J & Maunders, A R
     Accounting for British Steel: A Financial Analysis of the Failure of the...Corporation 1967-80 and Who Was to Blame
       Aldershot: Gower 1982   xv 303pp illus index sources
       British Steel Corporation
       221

Brymbo
     The Story of Brymbo

       Brymbo: the firm 1959   51pp illus
       Brymbo Steel Works
       221   CLWYDPL

Buchan, Andrew
     Rhymney Beers: Famous over 100 Years

       the firm 1978   32pp illus
       Buchan's Breweries
       427   MGLAMPL

Buchanan, D J
     The JAP Story 1895-1951

       the firm 1951   48pp illus
       Prestwich, J A & Co
       363   *

Buck, Anne
> *Thomas Lester: His Lace and the East Midlands Industry 1820-1905*
> Bedford: Ruth Bean 1981   x 108pp illus index sources
> Lester, Thomas
> 439   *

Buckley, Francis
> *Old London Glasshouses*
>
> Stevens & Sons 1915   42pp
> Glasshouses
> 247   SWKPL

Buist, H Massac
> *Rolls-Royce Memories: A Coming-of-Age Souvenir*
>
> 1926   95pp illus
> Rolls-Royce
> 351   §

Bulleid, Henry Anthony Vaughan
> *The Aspinall Era*
>
> Ian Allan 1967   viii 270pp illus index
> Lancashire & Yorkshire Railway
> 710   *

Bulloch, John
> *The Pynours: Historical Notes on an Ancient Aberdeen Craft*
>
> Aberdeen: Edmond & Spark 1887   88pp
> Shore Porters' Soc of Aberdeen
> 763   *

Bulloch, Robert
> *A Century of Economic Striving: A History of the...Larkhall Victualling Society (Est.1821)*
> Glasgow: Scottish CWS 1922   200pp illus
> Larkhall Victualling Society
> 656   HMLTNPL

Bulmer, Edward F
> *Early Days of Cider Making - facsimile of 1937 edition published to mark Golden Jubilee of H P Bulmer & Co*
> Hereford: Museum of Cider 1980   30pp illus
> Bulmer, H P & Co
> 426   §

Burgess, Clare et al
> *Carrs: The Family and the Enterprise*
>
> typescript 1971
> Carr's Milling Industries
> 416

Burlingham, H
> *A Merchant Business through Six Reigns*
>
> Evesham: the firm 1934   20pp
> Burlingham, H
> 611   §

Burman, Thomas
Short History of Burman & Sons Ltd

the firm 1944
Burman & Sons
353

Burn, Duncan Lyall
The Economic History of Steelmaking 1867-1939: A Study in Competition
Cambridge: C U P 1940   x 548pp
Steel Industry
221   *

Burn, Duncan Lyall
The Steel Industry 1939-1959: A Study in Competition and Planning
Cambridge: C U P 1961   xvi 728pp illus
Steel Industry
221   *

Burnand, I B
The Gresham House Estate Co Ltd 1857-1957

1957   15pp
Gresham House Estate Co
850   GHL

Burnett, John
The Baking Industry in the Nineteenth Century

Business History   vol V no 2 1963
Baking Industry
419

Burnham, Lord (Lawson, Edward Frederick)
Peterborough Court: The Story of the Daily Telegraph

Cassell 1955   x 225pp illus
Daily Telegraph   Amalgamated Press
475   * §

Burnham, Thomas H & Hoskins, George O
Iron and Steel in Britain 1870-1930

Allen & Unwin 1943   352pp
Steel Industry
221   *

Burritt, Elihu
An Account of the Brades Steel Works: being an extract from 'Walks in the Black Country and its Green Borderland'
Oldbury: the firm nd
Hunt, William & Sons   Brades Steel Works
311   316   321   SANDWPL

Burrough, James
The Beefeater Story

1966
Burrough, James
424   GHL

Burroughs Wellcome
The Wellcome Centenary

repr Times 25 Aug 1953   48pp illus
Burroughs Wellcome
257   §

Burrows
A Store Record 1824-1949: Burrows

Plaistow: Curwen Press nd   pamphlet
Burrows
                                            §

Burrows, V E
Tramways in Metropolitan Essex

Upminster: author 1967-76   2 vols illus
Tramways in Metropolitan Essex
721   ENFLDPL

Burt, Boulton & Haywood
A Century of Progress 1848-1948

the firm 1948   66pp illus
Burt, Boulton & Haywood
251   613   §

Burt, Roger
John Taylor: Mining Entrepreneur and Engineer 1779-1863

Buxton: Moorland Publishing 1977   91pp illus index sources
Taylor, John
111   210   *

Burt, Roger
The Lead Industry in England and Wales 1700-1880

London PhD 1971
Lead Industry
224

Burt, Roger
The London Mining Exchange 1850-1900

Business History   vol XIV no 2 1972
London Mining Exchange
831

Burton, Thomas
Royton Industrial Co-operative Society Ltd: History of the Society's Formation and Progress 1857-1907
Manchester: C W S 1907   26pp illus
Royton Industrial Co-op Soc
656   OLDHMPL

Busby, J H
London Trust Company Limited 1889-1964

1964

Bush, W J & Co
> *Centenary Album: A Pictorial Record of Bush World-wide Development 1851-1951*
> Hackney: the firm 1951   70pp illus
> Bush, W J & Co
> 251   256   HACKPL

Bushell, T A
> *'Royal Mail': A Centenary History of the Royal Mail Line 1839-1939*
> Transport & Travel Publ1939   xvi 270pp illus
> Royal Mail Shipping Group
> 740   * §

Bussey, Gordon
> *The Story of Pye Wireless*
>
> the firm 1979
> Pye   Philips Group
> 345

Butler Machine Tool Co
> *Butler: 100 Years 1869-1968*
>
> Halifax: the firm 1968   44pp illus
> Butler Machine Tool Co
> 322   HLFXPL

Butler, Rodney
> *The History of Kirkstall Forge Through Seven Centuries 1200-1954: The Story of England's Oldest Ironworks*
> York: William Sessions 1954   vii 265pp illus index
> Kirkstall Forge
> 221   312   §

Butler, Thomas Howard
> *The History of Wm Butler & Co (Bristol) Ltd 1843 to 1943*
>
> Bristol: the firm 1954   92pp illus
> Butler, Wm & Co (Bristol)
> 251   257   *

Butlin, Billy with Dacre, P
> *The Butlin Story: A Showman to the End*
>
> Robson 1982   287pp
> Butlins
> 667   * §

Butt, John
> *James Young, Scottish Industrialist and Philanthropist*
>
> Glasgow PhD 1964
> Young, James

Butt, John
> *Life Assurance in War and Depression: The Standard Life Assurance Company and its Environment 1914-1939*
> see Westall, Oliver M (ed) 1984
> Standard Life Assurance
> 820

Butt, John (ed)

Robert Owen, Prince of Cotton Spinners: A Symposium

Newton Abbot: David & Charles 1971 265pp illus
Owen, Robert   New Lanark
432   *

Butterley

Butterley through Nine Reigns

typescript 1953   20pp illus
Butterley Co
111   221   241   DERBYPL

Buxton, N K & Aldcroft, D H (eds)

British Industry between the Wars: Instability and Industrial Development 1919-1939
Scolar Press 1979   308pp index sources

                                                                          *

Buxton, Neil K

Coalmining

see Buxton, N K & Aldcroft, D H (eds)
Coal Industry
111

Buxton, Neil K

The Scottish Shipbuilding Industry between the Wars: A Comparative Study
Business History   vol X no 2 1968
Shipbuilding in Scotland
361

Byatt, Ian Charles Rayner

The British Electrical Industry 1875-1914: The Economic Returns to a New Technology
Oxford: Clarendon 1979   xii 228pp index sources
Crompton & Co
161   342   837   *

Byres, T J

Entrepreneurship in the Scottish Heavy Industries 1870-1900

see Payne, Peter L (ed) 1967
Heavy Industries in Scotland
300

Cable, Boyd

A Hundred Year History of the P & O: Peninsular and Oriental Steam Navigation Company 1837-1937
Nicholson & Watson 1937   x 289pp illus index
P & O
740   *

Cadbury

Cadburys of Bournville: The Building of a Modern Business

Bournville: the firm 1966   23pp illus
Cadbury Bros
421   *

Cadbury
Industrial Challenge: The Experience of Cadburys of Bournville in the Post-War Years
Sir Isaac Pitman & Sons 1964   91pp illus
Cadbury Bros
421   * §

Cadbury
Industrial Record 1919-1939: A Review of the Inter-War Years

Bournville: the firm nd   84pp illus
Cadbury Bros
421   * §

Cadell, Patrick
The Iron Mills at Cramond

Edinburgh: Bratton 1973   84pp illus sources
Cramond Iron Mills
221   311   MLOTHPL

Cain, P J
The British Railway Rates Problem 1894-1913

Business History   vol XX no 1 1978
Railway Rates
710

Cairns, Robert
Carpet Manufacture at Elderslie: A Brief History of A F Stoddard and Company Ltd
Strathclyde BA 1975   48pp sources
Stoddard, A F & Co
438   RNFRWPL

Caldwell and Whitley
Notes on the Firm of Caldwell and Whitley

typescript 1950
Caldwell and Whitley
256   WARRPL

Caldwell, Jon
History of Brighouse and its Co-operative Society

Brighouse: Brighouse News 1899   280pp illus
Brighouse Co-operative Soc
656   HLFXPL

Caledon Shipbuilding Co
An Illustrated Brochure...

Dundee: William Kidd & Son   110pp illus
Caledon Shipbuilding Co
361   DNDEEPL

Calico Printers' Association
Fifty Years of Calico Printing: A Jubilee History of the C P A

Manchester: the firm 1949   64pp
Calico Printers' Association
432   TAMESPL

Callender's
     The Story of Callender's 1882-1932

          the firm 1932   106pp illus index
          Callender's Cable & Construction B I C C
          341   502   BLPES
Callister, Ian
     Chester Grosvenor: A History

          the firm 1983
          Chester Grosvenor Hotel Co
          665
Calvert, Albert Frederick
     *A History of the Salt Union: A Record of 25 Years of Disunion
     and Depreciation Compiled from Official Reports*
          Effingham Wilson 1913   xxxviii 286pp
          Salt Union
          233   *
Calvert, Albert Frederick
     Salt and the Salt Industry

          Pitman 1919   vii 151pp
          Salt Union
          233   *
Calvert, Albert Frederick
     Salt in Cheshire

          E & F N Spon 1915   xxiii 1206pp
          Salt Union
          233   *
Cambridge Instrument Co
     50 Years of Scientific Instrument Manufacture

          Engineering   vol 159 1945
          Cambridge Instrument Co
          371
Cambridge Instrument Co
     75 Years of Successful Endeavour 1881-1956

          the firm 1956   28pp illus
          Cambridge Instrument Co
          371   *
Cameron, A & Farndon, R
     Scenes from Sea and City: Lloyd's List 1734-1984

          Colchester: Lloyd's of London Press   288pp illus
          Lloyd's of London
          837
Cameron, John
     Calico Printing in Campsie

          Kirkintilloch: D Macleod 1892   xiv 248pp
          Lindsay, Smith & Co   Henderson, Semple & Co
          437   *

Cameron, Rondo
Banking and Industrialisation in Britain in the Nineteenth Century
see Slaven, A & Aldcroft, D H (eds)
Banking in Britain
814   815

Camidge, William
York Savings Bank: Its History, Formation and Growth

York: the firm 1886   119pp
York Savings Bank
814

Cammell

Charles Cammell & Co Ltd

the firm 1900
Cammell, Charles & Co
221

Cammell Laird
Builders of Great Ships

Birkenhead: the firm 1959   79pp illus
Cammell Laird & Co
361   §

Campbell, Kenneth L G
Campbell, Smith & Company 1873-1973: A Century of Decorative Craftsmanship
the firm 1973   77pp
Campbell, Smith & Co
316   *

Campbell, L
Scottish Retail Co-operative Societies 1870-1914

Strathclyde PhD 1983
Co-operative Retailing, Scotland
656

Campbell, Roy Hutcheson
A Critique of the Christian Businessman and his Paternalism

see Jeremy, D J (ed) 1987

Campbell, Roy Hutcheson
Carron Company

Edinburgh: Oliver & Boyd 1961   xii 346pp illus index sources
Carron Company
221   311   *

Campbell, Roy Hutcheson
Costs and Contracts; Lessons from Clyde Shipbuilding between the Wars
see Slaven, A & Aldcroft, D H (eds)
Shipbuilding in Scotland
361

Campbell, **Roy Hutcheson**
Early Malleable Iron Production in Scotland

Business History vol IV no 1 1961
Malleable Iron in Scotland
311

Campbell, **Roy Hutcheson**
Men of Politics and Business: A History of the Quaker Pease Dynasty of North East England 1750-1939
Allen & Unwin 1981
Pease, J & J W
111 231 362 430 814

Campbell, **Roy Hutcheson**
The Financing of the Carron Company

Business History vol I no 1 1958
Carron Company
221

Campbell, **Roy Hutcheson**
The North British Locomotive Company between the Wars

Business History vol XX no 2 1978
North British Locomotive Co Neilson, Reid
362

Campbell, **Roy Hutcheson**
The Rise and Fall of Scottish Industry 1907-1939

Edinburgh: John Donald 1980
Industry in Scotland

Campbell, **William**
History of the Incorporation of Cordiners in Glasgow

Glasgow: Anderson 1883 xi 310pp
Cordiners in Glasgow
451 *

Campbell, **William Alec**
The Old Tyneside Chemical Trade

Newcastle: N U P 1964
Chemical Industry on Tyneside
250 *

Camrose, **Lord (Berry, William Ewert)**
British Newspapers and their Controllers

Cassell 1947 x 178pp illus
Amalgamated Press
475 *

Cantrell **& Cochrane**
The Story of Cantrell & Cochrane

Belfast: the firm nd
Cantrell & Cochrane
428

Cantrell, J A
James Nasmyth and the Bridgewater Foundry: Partners and Partnerships
Business History   vol XXIII no 3 1981
Nasmyth, James   Bridgewater Foundry
311   312   320

Cape Asbestos Co
The Story of the Cape Asbestos Company Limited 1893-1953

the firm 1953   85pp illus
Cape Asbestos Co
243   244   §

Carey, Arthur Merwyn
English, Irish and Scottish Firearms Makers

W & R Chambers 1955   xv 121pp illus
Westley Richards
329   *

Carlson, Robert Eugene
The Liverpool & Manchester Railway Project   1821-1831

Newton Abbot: David & Charles 1969 292pp illus index sources
Liverpool & Manchester Railway
710   *

Carmichael, James & Co
History of the House of Carmichael

Dundee: the firm 1924   32pp illus
Carmichael, James & Co
311   323   DNDEEPL

Carnegie, J F
Brownlee 125: The History of Brownlee & Co. Ltd. 1949-1974: A Sequel to 'One Hundred Years in Timber'
Glasgow: the firm nd   80pp illus
Brownlee & Co
613   §

Carr, James C & Taplin, Walter
History of the British Steel Industry

Oxford: Basil Blackwell 1962   xii 632pp illus
Steel Industry
221   *

Carr-Saunders, Alexander Morris et al
Consumers Co-operation in Great Britain: An Examination of the British Co-operative Movement
Allen & Unwin 1938   556pp
Co-operative Movement
656   *

Carter, Alan
The History of St Quintin, Chartered Surveyors 1831-1981

the firm nd   62pp illus
St Quintin
834   837   §

Carter, C J M
The Stephenson Clarke Fleet Story 1730-1958

repr Sea Breezes 1958   52pp
Stephenson Clarke
740   GHL

Carter, George Arthur
The Whitecross Company Ltd 1864-1964: One Hundred Years of Service in the Wire Industry
the firm 1964   48pp
Whitecross Co
223 224   *

Carter, Harry
A History of the Oxford University Press: Vol 1 -to the year 1780
Oxford: Clarendon 1975   xxxi 640pp illus index sources
Oxford University Press
475   *

Carter, Harry
Wolvercote Mill: A Study in Papermaking at Oxford

Oxford: Clarendon 1974   ix 81pp illus index sources
Clarendon Press
471   *

Carter, John W & Pollard, Henry G
The Firm of Charles Ottley, Landon & Co.

Hart Davis 1948   95pp
Ottley, Charles & Landon
             * §

Cartwright, Alan Patrick
Gold Paved the Way: The Story of the Gold Fields Group of Companies
Macmillan 1967   x 326pp illus index
Consolidated Gold Fields
210 839   §

Cartwright, Walter H
The House of K & J: A Booklet Issued to Celebrate the 75th Anniversary of our Foundation
West Bromwich: the firm 1953 70pp illus
Kenrick & Jefferson
475   SANDWPL

Carty
Carty & Son Ltd: Makers of Vats and Wooden Tanks since 1766

the firm 1966   8pp
Carty & Son
464   SWKPL

Carvel, John Lees
Fifty Years of Machine Mining Progress 1899-1949

Motherwell: the firm 1949 112pp illus
Anderson, Boyes & Co
325   §

Carvel, John Lees
  One Hundred Years in Coal: The History of the Alloa Coal Company
  Alloa: the firm 1944   viii 199pp illus index
  Alloa Coal Co
  111   *

Carvel, John Lees
  One Hundred Years in Timber: The History of the City Saw Mills 1849-1949
  Glasgow: the firm nd   168pp illus
  Brownlee & Co
  613   * §

Carvel, John Lees
  Stephen of Linthouse: A Record of Two Hundred Years of Shipbuilding 1750-1950
  Linthouse, Glasgow: the firm 1950   211pp illus index
  Stephen, Alexander & Sons
  361   * §

Carvel, John Lees
  The Alloa Glass Work: An Account of its Development since 1750
  Alloa: the firm 1953   viii 102pp illus index
  Alloa Glass Work Co   United Glass
  247   *

Carvel, John Lees
  The Coltness Iron Company: A Study in Private Enterprise

  Constable 1948   viii 199pp illus index
  Coltness Iron Co
  221   * §

Carvel, John Lees
  The New Cumnock Coalfield: A Record of its Development and Activities
  New Cumnock: the firm 1946   viii 123pp
  New Cumnock Coalfield
  111   *

Cassell, Michael
  Inside Nationwide: One Hundred Years of Cooperation

  the firm 1984   151pp illus sources
  Nationwide Building Society   Co-operative Permanent Bldg Soc
  815   *

Cassis, Youssef
  Les Banquiers de la City à l'Époque Edouardienne 1890-1914

  Genève: Librairie Droz 1984   449pp index sources
  London Bankers
  814   815   BLPES

Cassis, Youssef
  Management and Strategy in the English Joint Stock Banks 1890-1914
  Business History   vol XXVII no 3 1985
  Joint Stock Banks
  814

110

Casson, Mark (ed)
    The Growth of International Business

        Allen & Unwin 1983   xii 276pp illus index sources
        International Business
        839   *

Castner-Kellner
    Fifty Years of Progress : The Story of the Castner-Kellner Alkali Company 1895-1945
        Birmingham: the firm 1947   65pp illus
        Castner-Kellner Alkali Co   I C I
        251   *

Catchpole, William L & Elverston, E
    BIA Fifty 1917-1967: Fifty Years of the British Insurance Association
        Stockport: P H Press 1967   85pp illus index
        British Insurance Association
        820   * §

Cater Ryder & Co
    Cater Ryder: Discount Bankers 1816-1966

        Newman Neame 1966   17pp
        Cater Ryder & Co
        814   *

Catterall, R E
    Electrical Engineering

        see Buxton, N K & Aldcroft, D H (eds)
        British Electrical Mfrs
        340

Cauldwell, E
    Cauldwell of Rowsley: Flour Millers

        Rowsley: the firm 1974   12pp illus
        Cauldwell, E (Rowsley)
        416   DERBYPL

Cave, Austin & Co
    Sixty Years of Trading: A History of Cave, Austin and Co Ltd., Cave's Cafes 1896-1956
        Lewisham: the firm 1957   26pp illus
        Cave, Austin and Co
        617   661   *

Cave, G P & Martin, Janet
    Leicester Trustee Savings Bank 1817-1967: A History of the First 150 Years
        Leicester: the firm 1967   30pp illus
        Leicester Trustee Savings Bank
        814   LEICSPL

Central Mining
    Fiftieth Anniversary

        the firm   32pp illus
        Central Mining & Investment Corp
        815   BLPES

Chalmers, Thomas
100 Years of Guttapercha

the firm nd   53pp illus
Dick, R & J
481   BLPES

Chalmin, Philippe
Tate & Lyle: Géant du Sucre

Paris: Economica 1983   704pp index sources
Tate & Lyle
420   *

Chaloner, William Henry
National Boiler 1864-1964: A Century of Progress in Industrial Safety
the firm 1964   68pp illus
National Boiler
820   §

Chaloner, William Henry
People and Industries

Frank Cass 1963   151pp illus index sources

                                                            *

Chaloner, William Henry
The Social and Economic Development of Crewe 1780-1923

Manchester: M U P 1973   xx 326pp illus index
London & North Western Railway
362   710   *

Chaloner, William Henry
Vulcan: The History of One Hundred Years of Engineering and Insurance 1859-1959
Stockport: the firm 1959   viii 65pp illus
Vulcan Boiler & General Insurance
820   * §

Champness, A
A Century of Progress

1937   62pp
General Life Assurance
820   GHL

Chance Brothers
100 Years of British Glass Making 1824-1924

the firm 1924   23pp illus
Chance Brothers
247   SANDWPL

Chance Brothers
Mirror for Chance

Smethwick: the firm 1951   72pp illus
Chance Brothers
247   *

Chance, J W
United Glass 1932-1957: Jubilee in Glass

    the firm 1958   29pp illus
    United Glass
    247   §

Chance, James Frederick
A History of the Firm of Chance Brothers & Co, Glass and Alkali Manufacturers
    Spottiswoode & Ballantyne 1919   iv 302pp
    Chance Brothers   Pilkington Brothers
    247   251   *

Chance, James Frederick
The Lighthouse Work of Sir James Chance

    Smith, Elder & Co 1902   x 162pp
    Chance Brothers
    247   *

Chandler, Alfred D
Managerial Hierarchies

    Cambridge, Mass: 1982

Chandler, Alfred D
Strategy and Structure: Chapters in the History of the American Industrial Enterprise
    Cambridge, Mass: MIT Press 1962   xiv 463pp index sources

Chandler, Alfred D
The Visible Hand: The Managerial Revolution in American Business
    Cambridge, Mass: Harvard U P 1977   xvi 608pp index sources

Chandler, Dean & Lacey, A Douglas
The Rise of the Gas Industry in Britain

    British Gas Council 1949   xii 156pp illus index sources
    Gas Industry
    162   *

Chandler, George
Four Centuries of Banking: The Bankers, Customers and Staff Associated with the Constituent Banks of Martins Bank Ltd.
    Batsford 1964-68   2 vols illus index sources
    Martins Bank   Barclays Bank
    814   * §

Channon, Geoffrey
A Nineteenth Century Investment Decision: The Midland Railway's London Extension
    Economic History Review   2nd ser vol XXV no 3 1972
    Midland Railway
    710

Channon, Geoffrey
The Great Western Railway under the British Railways Act of 1921
Business History Review   vol LV no 2 1981
Great Western Railway
710

Chantler, Philip
The British Gas Industry: An Economic Study

Manchester: M U P 1938   xi 141pp index sources
Gas Industry
162   *

Chapman, Dennis
The New Shipwright Building Company of Dundee 1826-31

Economic History Review   vol 10 no 2 1940
New Shipwright Building Co
361

Chapman, Elaine
Ellsons the Bakers

typescript nd   27pp illus
Ellsons the Bakers
419   LEICSPL

Chapman, Stanley David
Hogg Robinson: The Rise of a Lloyd's Broker

see Westall, Oliver M (ed) 1984
Hogg Robinson
820

Chapman, Stanley David
Jesse Boot of Boots The Chemists: A Study in Business History

Hodder & Stoughton 1974   221pp illus index sources
Boots The Chemists
257   643   * §

Chapman, Stanley David
N M Rothschild 1777-1836

the firm 1977   25pp illus sources
Rothschild
814   *

Chapman, Stanley David
Stanton and Staveley: A Business History

Cambridge: Woodhead-Faulkner 1981 240pp illus index sources
Stanton & Staveley
221   DERBYPL

Chapman, Stanley David
The Life of William Felkin of Nottingham 1795-1874

Nottingham MA 1960
Felkin, William of Nottingham
436   439

Chapman, Stanley David
The Peels in the Early English Cotton Industry

Business History   vol XI no 2 1969
Peels
432

Chapman, Stanley David
The Rise of Merchant Banking

Allen & Unwin 1984   xi 224pp illus index sources
Baring Brothers   Rothschild
814   *

Chapman-Huston, W W Desmond M
Sir James Reckitt: A Memoir

Faber & Gwyer 1927   xvii 349pp illus
Reckitt & Sons
259   418   *

Chapman-Huston, W W Desmond M & Cripps, Ernest C
Through a City Archway: The Story of Allen & Hanburys 1715-1954
John Murray 1954   xv 326pp illus index sources
Allen & Hanbury   Glaxo
257   413   643   * §

Charles, A A S
The Steel Pen Trade 1930-1980: A Record of the Principal Manufacturers, Manufacturing Processes, Selling Practices
Highley, Shropshire: the firm 1983   48pp illus
Leonhardt, D & Co   Highley Pens
495   SOLHLPL

Chater, Michael
Family Business: A History of Grosvenor Chater 1690-1977

the firm 1977   64pp illus
Grosvenor Chater
471   619   StBRD

Chatterton, D A
State Control of Public Utilities in the Nineteenth Century: The London Gas Industry
Business History   vol XIV no 2 1972
Gas Industry in London
162

Chaytor, Mark Hamilton Freer
The Wilsons of Sharrow: The Snuffmakers of Sheffield

Sheffield: J W Northend 1962   xiii 191pp illus
Wilsons of Sharrow
429   *

Checkland, Sydney George
Cultural Factors and British Business Men 1815-1914

see Fuji Conference 2, 1975
Cultural Factors and Business

Checkland, Sydney George
Scottish Banking: A History 1695-1973

    Glasgow: Collins 1975   xxvi 785pp illus index sources
    Banking in Scotland
    814   *

Checkland, Sydney George
The Mines of Tharsis: Roman, French & British Enterprise in Spain
    Allen & Unwin 1967   288pp illus index sources
    Tharsis/Tennant   Tennant, Charles & Co
    210   230   839   *

Cheney & Sons
Cheney's of Banbury 1767-1967

    Banbury: the firm 1967   36pp illus
    Cheney & Sons
    475   *

Cheney, Christopher R, John & Walter G
John Cheney and his Descendants: Printers in Banbury since 1767
    Banbury: the firm 1936   81pp illus sources
    Cheney & Sons
    475   *

Chevalier, W S (ed)
London's Water Supply 1903-1953: A Review of the Work of the Metropolitan Water Board
    the firm 1953   xv 368pp illus index
    Metropolitan Water Board
    170   §

Childe, W H
A Brief History of Batley Co-operative Society 1867-1917

    Manchester: Co-op Printing Soc 1919 148pp illus
    Batley Co-operative Soc
    656   HDSFDPL

Childers, James Saxon
Robert McAlpine: A Biography

    the firm 1925   189pp
    McAlpine, Sir Robert & Sons
    500   *

Chilton, P & Poppleston, M
History of Brewers in North East England

    typescript: nd
    Brewing Industry in NE England
    427   NWCSLPL

Chiswick Products
Chiswick Products Ltd., Polish Manufacturers

    the firm 1947   24pp illus
    Chiswick Products
    259   MRC

Christie, Guy
Crieff Hydro

Edinburgh: Oliver & Boyd 1967   184pp illus
Strathearn Hydropathic Estab Crieff Hydro
665   667   *

Christie, Guy
Storeys of Lancaster 1848-1964

Collins 1964   256pp illus index sources
Storey Brothers & Co   Williamson, James & Son
438   483   §

Christy
175 Years of the House of Christy

the firm 1949
Christy & Co
453   SWKPL

Christy, W M
100 Years of the Royal Turkish Towel 1851-1951

Manchester: the firm 1951   27pp illus
Christy, W M & Sons
432   TAMESPL

Chubb & Son's Lock & Safe Co
Men with Pride: The House of Chubb 1818-1948

1948   17pp
Chubb Lock & Safe Co
316   GHL

Chubb Fire Security
Ten Years of Chubb Fire: A Background from 1881

the firm 1981   48pp illus
Chubb Fire Security
316   328   343   §

Chubb, George H & Churcher, Walter G
The House of Chubb 1818-1918

Herbert Jenkins 1919   x 111pp illus
Chubb Lock & Safe Co
316   §

Chudley, John A
Letraset: A Lesson in Growth

Business Books 1974   xi 155pp index
Letraset
495   *

Church, R A & Miller, M
The Big Three: Competition, Management and Marketing in the British Motor Industry 1922-1939
see Supple, Barry (ed) 1977
Motor Industry
351   614   651

Church, Roy Anthony
An Aspect of Family Enterprise in the Industrial Revolution

    Business History   vol IV no 2 1962
    Gotch & Sons
    451   814

Church, Roy Anthony
Family and Failure: Archibald Kenrick & Sons Ltd 1900-1950

    see Supple, Barry (ed) 1977
    Kenrick, Archibald & Sons
    316

Church, Roy Anthony
Herbert Austin: The British Motor Car Industry to 1941

    Europa 1979   lii 233pp illus index sources
    Austin Motor Co
    350   * §

Church, Roy Anthony
Kenricks in Hardware: A Family Business 1791-1966

    Newton Abbot: David & Charles 1969 340pp illus index sources
    Kenrick, Archibald & Sons
    316   * §

Church, Roy Anthony
Labour Supply and Innovation 1800-1860: The Boot and Shoe Industry
    Business History   vol XII no 1 1970
    Boot and Shoe Industry
    451

Church, Roy Anthony
Markets and Marketing in the British Motor Industry before 1914 with some French Comparisons
    Journal of Transport History   3rd ser vol III no 1 1982
    Motor Industry
    351

Church, Roy Anthony
Messrs Gotch & Sons and the Rise of the Kettering Footwear Industry
    Business History   vol VIII no 2 1966
    Gotch & Sons
    451

Church, Roy Anthony
The British Leather Industry and Foreign Competition 1870-1914
    Economic History Review   2nd ser vol XXIV no 4 1971
    Leather Industry
    440

Church, Roy Anthony
The History of the British Coal Industry; vol 3: Victorian Pre-Eminence
    Oxford: O U P 1986   800pp illus index sources
    Coal Industry
    111

Church, Roy Anthony
The Marketing of Automobiles in Britain and the United States before 1939
see Fuji Conference 7, 1980
Motor Industry
351   614   651
Churchill, Charles
The Churchill-Redman Story

typescript; Churchill-TI nd
Churchill, Charles & Co   Churchill-Redman
322
Churchill, Charles
The Story of the Churchill Machine Tool Co. Ltd: A History of Precision Grinding. Golden Jubilee 1906-1956
Manchester: the firm 1956   54pp illus
Churchill, Charles & Co
322   *
Churchill-T I
Churchill-T I

Blaydon on Tyne: the firm ca1965
Churchill, Charles & Co   Churchill-Redman
322
Ciba Geigy
Fifty Years at Duxford

Duxford: the firm 1984   pamphlet
Ciba Geigy Plastics
256   364   462   RAeS
City Engraving
City is Sixty: City Engraving of Hull 1896-1956

York: William Sessions 1956
City Engraving
475
City of London Real Property Co
City of London Real Property Company Limited Centenary 1864-1964
the firm 1964   40pp illus
City of London Real Property Co
850   * §
City of Perth Co-operative Society
City of Perth Co-operative Society Limited 1871-1931: Diamond Jubilee Souvenir
Perth: the firm 1931   56pp illus
City of Perth Co-operative Soc
656   ·   PERTHPL
Clapham, John Harold
The Bank of England: A History

Cambridge: C U P 1944   2 vols illus
Bank of England
814   *

Clapp, Brian William
John Owens: Manchester Merchant

    Manchester: M U P 1965   viii 193pp index sources
    Owens, John
    430   839   * §

Clark, Alec W
Through a Glass Clearly

    Golden Eagle 1980   159pp illus
    Beatson, Clark & Co
    247   * §

Clark, Alexander
A Short History of the Shipmasters' Society or the Seamen's Box of Aberdeen
Aberdeen: William Smith 1911
Shipmasters' Society
740   NESLS

Clark, Edwin Kitson
Kitsons of Leeds 1837-1937: A Firm and its Folk by One of Them
Locomotive Publishing Co 1938   186pp illus
Kitsons of Leeds
320   362   *

Clark, G
Peeps into the Past: Bicentenary of the Old Amicable Society and Centenary of the Norwich Union Life Office 1705-1908
Jarrold 1908   81pp illus
Norwich Union
820   NRFLKPL

Clark, Ronald Harry
100- Not Out: To Commemorate the Centenary of Savages Ltd 1850-1950, Engineers, King's Lynn
King's Lynn: the firm 1950   35pp
Savages
321

Clark, Ronald Harry
Chronicles of a Country Works: A History of Messrs Charles Burrell & Sons Ltd of Thetford, Traction Engine Builders
Percival Marshall 1952   xv 305pp illus index sources
Burrell, Charles & Sons
328   *

Clark, Ronald Harry
Savages Ltd., Engineers, St. Nicholas Ironworks, King's Lynn: A Short History 1850-1964
Norwich: the firm 1964   39pp illus
Savages
321

Clark, Victoria Elizabeth
The Port of Aberdeen: A History of its Trade and Shipping from the 12th Century to the Present Day
Aberdeen: D Wyllie & Son 1921   xiii 178pp illus index
Port of Aberdeen
763   *

Clark, Wallace
    Linen on the Green: An Irish Mill Village 1730-1982

    Belfast: B U P 1982   xi 183pp illus index sources
    Clark, William & Sons
    434   *

Clarke, Joseph Francis
    Power on Land and Sea: A History of R & W Hawthorn Leslie & Co Ltd
    Tyne & Wear: the firm 1979   125pp illus
    Hawthorn Leslie   Clark-Hawthorn
    328   361   BLPES

Clarke, L J & Burbidge, H L
    An Account of the Development of the Business of H Burbidge, Woodturner, Founded in Coventry 1867
    1984   57pp illus
    Burbidge, H
    463   COVNPL

Clarke, P
    Decline and Rise of a Village Store: Roys of Wroxham

    1972   12pp
    Roys of Wroxham
    656   NRFLKPL

Clarke, Philip
    The First House in the City: Child & Co 1673-1973

    the firm 1973   67pp illus sources
    Child & Co
    814   BCROB

Clarke, Philip
    Ties are Their Business: An Excursion thro' 150 Years of Competitive Enterprise....
    Belfast: the firm 1970   51pp illus
    Atkinson, Richard & Co
    432   NEELBPL

Clarke, Sam
    Sam: An East End Cabinet Maker: The Pocket Book of Sam Clarke 1907-1979
    ILEA Geffrye Museum 1983   39pp
    Clarke, Sam
    467   *

Clarkson, H & Co
    The Clarkson Chronicle 1852-1952

    the firm 1953   115pp illus index
    Clarkson, H & Co
    839   GHL

Clay Cross Co
    125 Years of Service to Industry and Public Undertakings 1837-1962
    the firm 1963   18pp illus
    Clay Cross Co
    221   231   241   311   DERBYPL

Clay Cross Co
> *A Hundred Years of Enterprise: Centenary of the Clay Cross Company 1837-1937*
> Derby: the firm 1937   52pp illus
> Clay Cross Co
> 111   210   221   231   DERBYPL

Clay Cross Co
> *Over a Hundred Years of Enterprise 1837-1959*
>
> the firm 1960   28pp illus
> Clay Cross Co
> 221   231   241   311   DERBYPL

Clay, Ewart Waide
> *200 Years of Harris Cleaning 1780-1980*
>
> the firm nd   95pp illus
> Harris, Joseph   Johnson Group Cleaners
> 981   §

Clay, Ewart Waide
> *Waide's 100 Years 1878-1978: A Short History...of Thomas Waide & Sons Ltd, Printers and Carton Manufacturers*
> Leeds: the firm 1978   60pp illus
> Waide, Thomas & Sons
> 472   475   §

Clayton, A K
> *The Elsecar and Milton Ironworks to 1848*
>
> Cusworth Hall Museum   77pp index sources
> Elsecar and Milton Ironworks
> 221   SHEFFPL

Clear, Gwen
> *The Story of W H Smith & Son 1792-1948*
>
> the firm 1949   viii 221pp illus
> Smith, W H & Son
> 619   653   *

Cleary, Esmond John
> *The Building Society Movement*
>
> Elek 1965   320pp index sources
> Building Societies
> 815   *

Cleaver, George and Pamela
> *The Union Discount: A Centenary Album*
>
> the firm 1985   128pp illus index sources
> Union Discount Co
> 814   §

Clegg, Cyril
> *Friend in Deed: The History of a Life Assurance Office from 1858 to 1958...the Refuge Assurance Company Ltd*
> Manchester: the firm 1958   xxxviii 160pp illus index
> Refuge Assurance Co
> 820   * §

Clowes, William Beaufoy
Family Business 1803-1953

the firm 1953　　　　　　　　ix 81pp illus
Clowes, William
475　　　　　　　　　　　　　　　　　　　　　　* §

Cluttons
Cluttons 1765-1965

the firm 1965　　　　　　　　19pp illus
Cluttons
834　　　　　　　　　　　　　　　　　　　　　　§

Cluttons
Cluttons: Some Historical Notes Put Together in 1948

the firm 1950　　　　　　　　49pp illus
Cluttons
834　　　　　　　　　　　　　　　　　　　　GLROHL

Clyne, H R
After Fifty Years 1862-1912: A Story of Industrial Enterprise

Denton: the firm 1912　　　　18pp illus
Moores, J & Sons
453　　　　　　　　　　　　　　　　　　　TAMESPL

Co-operative Wholesale Society
A Consumers' Democracy: An Account of the Origins and Growth of the Co-operative Wholesale Society Ltd
the firm 1951　　　　　　　160pp illus
Co-operative Wholesale Society
619　　　　656　　　　　　　　　　　　　　　§

Coad, Roy
Laing: The Biography of Sir John W Laing CBE 1879-1978

Hodder & Stoughton 1979　　238pp illus index sources
Laing, John
500　　　　　　　　　　　　　　　　　　　BLPES

Coal Merchants, Society of
Historical Notes on the London Coal Exchange

1950　　　　　　　　　　　50pp
London Coal Exchange
612　　　　630　　　　　　　　　　　　　　GHL

Coalbrookdale Company
250th Anniversary of the Successful Use of Coke in Ironmaking: four papers presented at Birmingham
typescripts 1959　　　　　73pp sources
Coalbrookdale Co
221　　　　311　　　　　　　　　　　　DUDLYPL

Coates, J B M
A History of Coates Brothers & Company Ltd, 1877-1977

Westerham Press 1977　　　102pp illus index
Coates Bros
255　　　　　　　　　　　　　　　　　　　§

Coats, Robert Hay
In Memoriam: Robert Hall Best

Birmingham: Kynoch 1925   6pp
Best & Lloyd
316   *

Cochrane, Alfred
The Early History of Elswick

Newcastle: Mawson Swan 1909   90pp illus
Armstrong, Whitworth & Co
329   *

Cochrane, James Aikman
Dr. Johnson's Printer: The Life of William Strahan

Routledge & Kegan Paul 1964   xiii 225pp illus index sources
Strahan, William
475   *

Cockburn, Robert & John
A Centenary Retrospect: R & J Cockburn 1805: Cockburn & Campbell Ltd 1831-1931
Edinburgh: the firm 1931   28pp illus
Cockburn & Campbell
426   *

Cockerell, Hugh Anthony Lewis
Sixty Years of the Chartered Insurance Institute 1897-1957

the firm 1957   92pp illus
Chartered Insurance Institute
820   * §

Cocks Biddulph & Co
Cocks Biddulph & Co 1759-1920

Cocks Biddulph & Co   Martins Bank
814   §

Cocks, Edward J & Walters, Bernhardt
A History of the Zinc Smelting Industry in Britain

Harrap 1968   ix 224pp illus index sources
Zinc Smelting
224   * §

Coe, W E
The Engineering Industry of the North of Ireland

Newton Abbot: David & Charles 1967 224pp illus sources
Engineering Ind; N Ireland
320   *

Cohen, George
One Hundred Years 1834-1934

the firm 1934   244pp
Cohen, George & Sons   600 Group
221   621   GHL

Cohen, George
    The 125 Year Book of 600: 1834-1959

    the firm 1959   172pp illus
    Cohen, George & Sons   600 Group
    325   500   621   HMFULPL

Cohen, John Michael
    The Life of Ludwig Mond

    Methuen 1956   xiv 295pp illus index
    I C I   Brunner, Mond
    250   *

Cole, John F & Camerer Cuss, Theodore P
    A Watchmaking Centenary: Usher & Cole 1861-1961

    the firm 1961   20pp illus
    Usher & Cole
    374   *

Coleman, Benfield & Loxley
    Coleman, Benfield & Loxley: Building and Civil Engineering Contractors, Oxford
    Oxford: the firm ca1979   20pp illus
    Coleman, Benfield & Loxley
    501   502   OXFDPL

Coleman, Donald Cuthbert
    Courtaulds and the Beginning of Rayon

    see Supple, Barry (ed) 1977
    Courtaulds
    260   432

Coleman, Donald Cuthbert
    Courtaulds: An Economic and Social History

    Oxford: Clarendon 1969-80   3 vols illus index sources
    Courtaulds
    260   432   * §

Coleman, Donald Cuthbert
    The British Paper Industry 1495-1860: A Study in Industrial Growth
    Oxford: Clarendon 1958   xvi 367pp illus
    Paper Industry
    471   *

Coleridge, Ernest Hartley
    The Life of Thomas Coutts, Banker 1735-1822

    John Lane 1920   2 vols illus index
    Coutts & Co
    814   * §

Collidge, W H
    Judkins, 1460-1966: A Short History of Judkins of Heyford, Northants and Judkins Quarries at Nuneaton
    Nuneaton: the firm 1966   36pp sources
    Judkins
    231   COVNPL

Collier, L J

Development and Location of the Clay-Brickmaking Industry in the South-East Midlands of England since 1800
London PhD 1966
Clay-Brickmaking
241

Collins, M

The Bank of England at Liverpool 1827-1844

Business History   vol XIV no 2 1972
Bank of England
814

Collins, Michael

The Business of Banking: English Bank Balance Sheets 1840-1880
Business History   vol XXVI no 1 1984
Banking Industry
814   815

Collinson, Francis

The Life and Times of William Grant

Dufftown: the firm 1979   102pp illus
Glenfiddich Distillery   Grant, William & Sons
424   §

Collis, Maurice

Wayfoong: The Hongkong and Shanghai Banking Corporation: A Study of East Asia's Transformation during the last 100 Years
Faber 1965   xii 269pp illus
Hongkong & Shanghai Bank
814   839   *

Colman, H C

J J Colman

Norwich: the firm 1905   464pp illus
Colman, J & J   Reckitt & Colman
259   418   §

Colman, J & J

Souvenir of the Centenary 1805-1905

Norwich: the firm 1905   25pp illus
Colman, J & J
257   258   426   839   NRFLKPL

Colnaghi, Paul & Dominic

Colnaghi's 1760-1960

the firm 1960   18pp illus
Colnaghi, P & D & Co
977   *

Colne Valley Water

The Colne Valley Water Company 1873-1973

Watford: the firm 1973   77pp illus
Colne Valley Water Co
170   HERTSPL

Colvin, C J L
>   The Baptist Insurance Company Limited: A Short History of
>   Seventy-Five Years 1905-1980
>   the firm 1980   24pp
>   Baptist Insurance Co   Central Insurance Co
>   820   §

Commercial Bank of Scotland
>   Our Bank: The Story of the Commercial Bank of Scotland Ltd
>   1810-1946
>   Nelson 1946   94pp illus
>   Commercial Bank of Scotland
>   814   EDNBRPL

Commercial Bank of Wales
>   The Commercial Bank of Wales: A Banking Enterprise
>
>   the firm nd
>   Commercial Bank of Wales   Hodge Group
>   814

Commercial Union Assurance Co: Exeter Branch
>   The Origin and Development of the West of England Fire and
>   Life Insurance Co of Exeter 1807-1894
>   Exeter: the firm 1952   43pp illus
>   Commercial Union Group   West of England Fire & Life
>   820   §

Conder, William S
>   The Story of the London Life Association Limited
>
>   the firm 1979   304pp illus index
>   London Life Association
>   820   §

Conn, Michael
>   Hillman's Airways and Saloon Coaches Ltd 1928-35
>
>   typescript nd   illus index sources
>   Hillman's Airways
>   721   750   ROMFDPL

Consett Iron
>   Leaves from Consett Iron Company Letter Books 1887-1893
>
>   Newcastle: the firm 1962   192pp
>   Consett Iron Co
>   221   UBRIS

Cook, Arthur Norton
>   British Enterprise in Nigeria
>
>   Frank Cass 1964   ix 330pp sources
>   Royal Nigeria Co
>   839   *

Cook, Clifford J
>   A Barge on the Blocks: A Short History of Walter Cook and Son,
>   Boatbuilders, Maldon, Essex 1894-1970
>   Maldon: the firm ca1980   64pp illus
>   Cook, Walter & Son
>   361   ESSEXPL

Cook, F W

The Centenary of the House of Cook 1819-1919: Souvenir and various pamphlets
Dudley: the firm 1919   illus
Cook, F W
656   DUDLYPL

Cook, Norman

Higsons Brewery 1780-1980

the firm nd   50pp illus
Higsons Brewery
427   662   §

Cook, Son & Co (St.Pauls)

Cooks of St Pauls: 150 Years 1807-1957

the firm 1957   19pp
Cook, Son & Co (St.Pauls)
450   616   647   GHL

Cook, William

Co-operation in Coalsnaughton: Golden Jubilee: An Historical Sketch of the Coalsnaughton Society 1872-1922
Tillicoultry: Bett 1922   18pp
Coalsnaughton Co-op Soc   Forth Valley Co-op
656   CLKMNPL

Cooke, A J

Baxter's of Dundee

Dundee: D U P 1980   80pp illus sources
Baxter Brothers   Low & Bonar
435   455   DNDEEPL

Coope, B

The People's Carriage 1874-1974: The History of the Bristol Omnibus Co Ltd
Bristol: the firm 1974   xi 92pp illus
Bristol Omnibus Co
721   §

Cooper Brothers

A History of Cooper Brothers & Co 1854 to 1954

Batsford 1954   ix 116pp illus index
Cooper Brothers & Co   London & County Bank
814   §

Copeland, W T & Sons

W T Copeland & Sons

Stoke-on-Trent: 1950   76pp illus
Copeland, W T & Sons   Spode
248   §

Copeman, John & Sons

Copeman's of Norwich 1789-1946

Norwich: Jarrold 1946   47pp illus
Copeman, John & Sons
617   * §

Corah, N
Corah's of Leicester

the firm 1950   120pp illus
Corah, N & Sons
436   MRC

Corina, Maurice
Fine Silks and Oak Counters: Debenhams 1778-1978

Hutchinson Benham 1978   200pp illus index
Debenham
656   * §

Corina, Maurice
Pile It High, Sell It Cheap: The Authorised Biography of Sir John Cohen, Founder of Tesco
Weidenfeld & Nicolson 1978   x 204pp illus index
Tesco
641   656   * §

Corina, Maurice
Trust in Tobacco: The Anglo-American Struggle for Power

Michael Joseph 1975   320pp illus
Carreras
429   *

Cork Savings Bank
The Cork Savings Bank 1817-1917: A Brief Historical Memoir

Cork: Guy 1918   18pp illus
Cork Savings Bank
814   CORKPL

Corley, Thomas Anthony Buchanan
A History of the Burmah Oil Company 1886-1924

Heinemann 1983   xvi 331pp illus index sources
Burmah Oil
130   140   612   652   * §

Corley, Thomas Anthony Buchanan
Domestic Electrical Appliances

Jonathan Cape 1966   160pp illus
Electrical Appliances
346   *

Corley, Thomas Anthony Buchanan
From National to Multinational Enterprise: The Beecham Business 1848-1945
U Reading Disc Paper   no 76, 1983
Beecham
257   258

Corley, Thomas Anthony Buchanan
How Quakers Coped with Business Success: Quaker Industrialists 1860-1914
see Jeremy, D J (ed) 1987
Quaker Industrialists

Corley, Thomas Anthony Buchanan
Quaker Enterprise in Biscuits: Huntley & Palmers of Reading 1822-1972
Hutchinson 1972   xvi 320pp illus index sources
Huntley & Palmers
419   *

Corley, Thomas Anthony Buchanan
Simonds' Brewery at Reading 1760-1960

Berks Arch Journal   vol 68 1975-76
Simonds, H & G
427

Corley, Thomas Anthony Buchanan
Some Notes on the History of Huntley, Boorne and Stevens, Tin Box Manufacturers of Reading from 1832 to 1918
typescript 1972   17pp
Huntley, Boorne and Stevens
316   BERKSPL

Corley, Thomas Anthony Buchanan
Strategic Factors in the Growth of a Multinational Enterprise: The Burmah Oil Company 1886-1928
see Casson, Mark (ed) 1983
Burmah Oil
130   140

Cormack, Alexander Allan
Our Ancient and Honourable Craft 1750-1933: Paper Making in Scotland and at Culter, Aberdeen in particular
Paper Market 1933   39pp illus sources
Paper Industry in Scotland
471   ABRDNPL

Cormack, Alexander Allan
The Chalmers Family and Aberdeen Newspapers: Links between Aberdeen and Gothenburg
Aberdeen: the firm 1958   39pp illus
Aberdeen Journals
475   *

Cormack, W S
An Economic History of Shipbuilding and Marine Engineering with special reference to the West of Scotland
Glasgow PhD 1931
Shipbuilding in W Scotland
361

Cornford, Leslie Cope
A Century of Sea Trading 1824-1924: The General Steam Navigation Company Limited
A & C Black 1924   x 182pp illus index
General Steam Navigation Co
740   BLPES

Cornford, Leslie Cope
The Sea Carriers 1825-1925: The Aberdeen Line

the firm 1925   iii 79pp illus
Aberdeen Line   Thompson, George & Co
740   *

Corran, T H
James Deady, Henry Meux and the Griffin Brewery: Fraud in an Early Nineteenth Century Business
Business History   vol XXIII no 3 1981
Meux, Reid & Co   Griffin Brewery
427

Corrins, R D
William Baird & Company, Coal and Iron Masters 1830-1914

Strathclyde PhD 1974
Baird, William & Co
111   221

Corti, Egon Caesar (tr Brian & Beatrix Lunn)
The Rise and Reign of the House of Rothschild 1770-1871

Gollancz 1928   2 vols illus index sources
Rothschild
814   * §

Cory, William & Son
One Hundred Years: A Brief History of the Cory Fleet

1960   20pp
Cory, William & Son
612   740   *

Cossor, A C
1859-1959

the firm 1959
Cossor, A C & Son(Surgical)
345   372

Cossor, A C
Half a Century of Progress 1896-1947: History of a Noted Firm in Radio and Electronics Industry
the firm 1947   33pp illus
Cossor, A C
345   ISLTNPL

Coster, Ian
The Sharpest Edge in the World: The Story of the Rise of a Great Industry
the firm 1948   78pp illus
Gillette Industries
316   *

Cottrell, E
The Giant with Feet of Clay: The British Steel Industry 1945-1981
Centre for Policy Studies 1981   vi 222pp illus
Steel Industry
221

Cottrell, P L
British Overseas Investment in the Nineteenth Century

Macmillan 1975   79pp index sources
Overseas Investment
814   839   *

Cottrell, P L
Industrial Finance 1830-1914: The Finance and Organisation of English Manufacturing Industry
Methuen 1980   xii 298pp index sources
Finance... of Engl Mfr Ind
                                                          *

Cottrell, P L
London Financiers and Austria 1863-1875: The Anglo-Austrian Bank
Business History   vol XI no 2 1969
Anglo-Austrian Bank
814

Cottrell, P L
The Steamship on the Mersey 1815-80: Investment and Ownership
see Cottrell & Aldcroft (eds) 1981
Mersey Steamship Co
740

Cottrell, P L & Aldcroft, D H (eds)
Shipping, Trade and Commerce

Leicester: L U P 1981   200pp index sources
Shipping
740   *

Cottrell, W F
The Jubilee Record of the Pendleton Co-operative Industrial Society Limited 1860-1910
Manchester: C W S 1910   269pp illus
Pendleton Co-op Ind Soc
656   SALFDPL

County Chemical Co
County Chemical Co Ltd (Chemico) 1895-1945: Fifty Years of Progress
the firm 1945   16pp
County Chemical Co   Chemico
256   SOLHLPL

Couper, W J
The Millers of Haddington, Dunbar & Dunfermline: A Record of Scottish Bookselling
T Fisher Unwin 1914   319pp illus index
Millers
653   *

Course, Alfred George
Painted Ports: The Story of the Ships of Devitt & Moore

Hollis & Carter 1961   230pp illus
Devitt & Moore
740   *

Course, Alfred George
The Wheel's Kick and the Wind's Song

1968   xiv 264pp illus
Stewart, John & Co
740   *

132

Courtaulds
Courtaulds: The Anatomy of a Multinational

Gen Federation of Trade Unions 1975 112pp
Courtaulds
260   432   UBRIS

Coventry Building Society
Coventry Permanent Economic Building Society: An Economic Record of Fifty Years 1884-1934
1934   14pp illus
Coventry Building Society
815   COVNPL

Coventry Evening Telegraph
Inside Story

Coventry Newspapers 1972   36pp illus
Coventry Evening Telegraph
475   COVNPL

Coventry Perseverance Co-op Soc
Coventry Perseverance Co-operative Society

Coventry: the firm 1917   xiv 422pp illus
Coventry Perseverance Co-op
656   *

Coventry Provident Building Society
A Century of Progress 1872-1972

1972   27pp illus
Coventry Provident Bldg Soc
815   COVNPL

Cow & Gate
Cow & Gate Limited: The Story of How It Began and What It Has Become after 50 Years
the firm 1959   30pp illus
Cow & Gate
413   *

Cowen, Frank
History of Chesters Brewery Company

Swinton: Neil Richardson 1982   45pp illus
Chesters Brewery Co   Whitbread & Co
427   662   *

Cox, F Hayter
The Oldest Accident Office in the World: Being the Story of the Railway Passengers Assurance Co 1849-1949
the firm 1960   67pp illus
Railway Passengers Assurance
820   * §

Cox, Harold & Chandler, John E
The House of Longman 1724-1924

Longmans Green 1925   94pp illus
Longman
475   * §

Crabtree, John A & Co
Lincoln Works Jubilee

the firm 1948　　　　　　　　　15pp illus
Crabtree, J A
342　　　　　　　　　　　　　　　　　　　　　WALSLPL

Craig, Charles
Glenpatrick House, Elderslie: The Story of an Unsuccessful Distillery
Johnstone: Ambrosia Books 1982　　iv 39pp illus sources
Glenpatrick Distillers
424　　　　　　　　　　　　　　　　　　　　　* §

Craig, J
Lennox Co-operative Society Ltd 1894-1913

Dumbarton: Bennet & Thomson 1913　41pp illus
Lennox Co-operative Soc
656　　　　　　　　　　　　　　　　　　　　　DMBTNPL

Craig, John Herbert McCutcheon
The Mint: A History of the London Mint from AD287 to 1948

Cambridge: C U P 1953　　　　　　xviii 450pp illus index
Royal Mint
491　　　　　　　　　　　　　　　　　　　　　*

Craig, Robert & Sons
A Century of Papermaking 1820-1920

Edinburgh: R & R Clark 1920　　　　144pp illus
Craig, Robert & Sons
471　　　　　　　　　　　　　　　　　　　　　AIRDRPL

Craig, Robin
William Gray & Company: A West Hartlepool Shipping Enterprise 1864-1913
see Cottrell & Aldcroft (eds) 1981
Gray, William & Co
740

Cramb, George E
A History of the Biscuit Makers of Edinburgh

Edinburgh: author 1983　　　　　　12pp
Biscuit Makers of Edinburgh
419　　　　　　　　　　　　　　　　　　　　　EDNBRPL

Cramp, B G
British Midland Airways

Airline Publications 1979　　　　　　208pp illus
British Midland Airways
750　　　　　　　　　　　　　　　　　　　　　*

Crankshaw, W P & Blackburn, Alfred
A Century and a Half of Cotton Spinning 1797-1947: The History of Knowles Ltd of Bolton
Bolton: the firm 1947　　　　　　　39pp illus
Knowles of Bolton
432　　　　　　　　　　　　　　　　　　　　　BOLTNPL

Crapster, Basil L
The London Sunday Advertiser and its Immediate Successors

Business History   vol V no 2 1963
Sunday Advertiser
475

Craven, Wilfred Archer
The First Hundred Years: The Early History of Bradley & Craven Limited, Wakefield, England
Wakefield: the firm 1963   140pp illus
Bradley & Craven
311   351   *

Crawford, Andrew & Co
The 'Vales' of Glasgow: Andrew Crawford & Co Ltd 1895-1955

Glasgow: the firm 1955   77pp illus
Crawford, Andrew & Co
740   UBRIS

Creed
The Breath of Invention: The Story of Frederick C Creed

Brighton: the firm 1976
I T T Creed   Creed & Co
344

Crick, Wilfred F & Wadsworth, John E
A Hundred Years of Joint Stock Banking

Hodder & Stoughton 1936   464pp illus index sources
Midland Bank
814   * §

Crighton, John
Contributions to the Maritime History of Great Britain

1948   95pp
London Graving Dock Co
763   GHL

Crighton, John
The Famous Orchard Dockyard Past and Present

the firm ca1950   36pp illus
London Graving Dock Co   Orchard Dockyard
361   763   §

Cripps, Ernest Charles
Plough Court: The Story of a Notable Pharmacy 1715-1927

the firm 1927   xviii 227pp illus
Allen & Hanbury   Glaxo
257   * §

Critchell, James T & Raymond, Joseph
A History of the Frozen Meat Trade

Constable 1912   xviii 442pp illus
Borthwick, Thomas & Sons
412   617   *

Crittall Manufacturing Co
Crittall Windows: A Brief History and Description of Current Activities
the firm ca1955   16pp
Crittall Manufacturing Co
314   GHL

Croall, Robert
Fifty Years of Family Baking: Scott-Lyon Ltd 1910-1960

Edinburgh: the firm 1960   36pp illus
Scott-Lyon
419   EDNBRPL

Crompton Parkinson & Co
Foundations of the Electrical Industry

the firm ca1929
Crompton Parkinson & Co
340

Crompton, G W
'Efficient and Economical Working'? The Performance of the Railway Companies 1923-1933
Business History   vol XXVII no 2 1985
Railway Companies
710

Crompton, Yorke
Seventy Years and More: The Story of Barnsley Brewery

Newman Neame 1960
Barnsley Brewery Co
427   662

Cronjé, Suzanne; Ling, Margaret & Cronjé, Gillian
Lonrho: Portrait of a Multinational

Julian Friedmann 1976   316pp index sources
Lonrho
839   *

Crosland-Taylor, W James C
Crosville: The Sowing and the Harvest

Liverpool: Littlebury Bros 1948   143pp illus
Crosville Motor Services   Tilling, Thomas
721   CLWYDPL

Crosland-Taylor, W James C
State Owned without Tears: The Story of Crosville 1948-1953

Liverpool: Littlebury Bros 1954   154pp illus index
Crosville Motor Services
721   UBRIS

Cross, C
William Plant: Wood Block and Woodcraft Manufacturers, 67A Great Ancoats St, Manchester
Stockport Museums Service 1977   22pp illus
Plant, William
465   TAMESPL

Crossley Motors
A Short History of Crossley Motors Ltd

Stockport: the firm ca1952
Crossley Motors
351   SKPTPL

Crossley, Julian & Blandford, J
The D C O Story: A History of Banking in Many Countries 1925-1971
the firm 1975   xxx 339pp illus index
Barclays Bank (DC&O)
814   839   *

Crossley, Richard Shaw
Accrington Captains of Industry

Accrington: Wardleworth 1930   xiv 233pp illus
Howard & Bullough   Accrington Industrialists
323   *

Crow, Duncan
A Man of Push and Go: The Life of George Macaulay Booth

Rupert Hart-Davis 1965   192pp illus
Booth, Alfred
611   770   815   *

Croydon Advertiser
Croydon Advertiser 1869-1969

Croydon: the firm 1969   50pp illus
Croydon Advertiser
475   BROMPL

Croydon Gas Co
A Hundred Years of Public Service 1847-1947

Croydon: the firm 1947   36pp illus
Croydon Gas Co
162   *

Crozier, Mary
An Old Silk Family 1745-1945: The Brocklehursts of Brocklehurst-Whiston Amalgamated Ltd.
Aberdeen: A U P 1947   43pp illus
Brocklehurst-Whiston
432   * §

Cruikshank, James
Alex. Pirie and Sons Ltd, Paper Manufacturers, Stoneywood and Waterton Works, Aberdeen 1770-1945
typescript ca1945
Pirie, Alex & Sons
471   ABRDNPL

Crump, William Bunting
The Leeds Woollen Industry 1780-1820

Leeds: Thoresby Society 1931   xi 343pp illus
Leeds Woollen Industry
431   *

Crusha & Son
Sixty Years of Progress

Tottenham: the firm 1921   23pp illus
Tottenham Weekly Herald
475   ENFLDPL

Crutchley, George W
John Mackintosh: A Biography

Hodder & Stoughton 1921   231pp illus index
Mackintosh, John
421   * §

Cullingford & Co
History of Cullingford & Co Ltd

Colchester: the firm 1985   16pp illus
Cullingford & Co
475   ESSEXPL

Culpan, H V
The House of Gestetner: 70th Anniversary Brochure

the firm 1951
Gestetner
330

Culter Paper Mills
History of Culter Paper Mills: Two Hundred Years of Progress
1751-1951
Aberdeen: the firm 1951   63pp illus
Culter Paper Mills
471   *

Cumberland Newspapers Group
Cumberland Newspapers Group Ltd

the firm 1972
Cumberland Newspapers Group
475

Cumbers, Frank
The Book Room: The Story of the Methodist Publishing House
and Epworth Press
Epworth 1956   xii 153pp illus index sources
Methodist Publishing   Epworth Press
475   * §

Cummings, John
Railway Motor Buses and Bus Services in the British Isles
1902-1933
Oxford: Oxford Publishing 1983   318pp illus index sources
Railway Motor Buses
721   *

Curls
Curls of Norwich

Norwich: the firm 1956   36pp illus
Curls
656   NRFLKPL

Curran, Edward
The Edward Curran Companies: A Review of Half a Century 1903-1953
Cardiff: the firm 1953   88pp illus
Curran, Edward, Engineering
311   313   316   324   §

Currie, James Russell Leslie
The Northern Counties Railway

N Abbot: David & Charles 1973-74   2 vols illus index
Northern Counties Railway
710   *

Currier-Briggs, Noel
Contemporary Observations on Security from the Chubb Collecteana 1818-1968
the firm   56pp illus
Chubb Lock & Safe Co
316   BLPES

Currys
The House of Currys 1884-1964

the firm nd
Currys
363   654   648

Curwen, Henry
A History of Booksellers: The Old and the New

Chatto & Windus 1873   483pp illus
Book Trade
653   *

Cussins & Light
The CandL Golden Book: Cussins & Light Ltd.

York: the firm 1971   204pp illus
Cussins & Light   CandL
345   *

Cuthbert, Alan D
Clyde Shipping Company Limited: A History

Glasgow: the firm 1956   125pp illus
Clyde Shipping Co
740   UBRIS

D P Battery Co
The D P Battery Co: A Century of Power 1827-1927

the firm ca1927   19pp illus
D P Battery Co
343   DERBYPL

Dagley, Donald Burdett
Mark Thornhill Wade: Silk Dyer, Soho

Research Publishing 1961   157pp illus
Wade, Mark Thornhill
437   *

Daimler
> *Daimler of Coventry*

> Coventry: the firm 1966   24pp illus
> Daimler Motor Co
> 351   MRC

Daish, Alfred Newman
> *Printers' Pride: The House of Yelf at Newport, Isle of Wight*
> *1816-1966*
> Newport, IoW: the firm 1967   92pp illus index sources
> Yelf Brothers
> 475   *

Dale, Rodney
> *From Ram Yard to Milton Hilton: A History of Cambridge*
> *Consultants*
> Cambridge: the firm 1981   36pp illus
> Cambridge Consultants
> 324   837   940   *

Dale, Rodney
> *The Sinclair Story*

> Duckworth 1985   viii 184pp illus
> Sinclair Research
> 330   940   * §

Dale, Tim
> *Harrods: The Store and the Legend*

> Pan 1981   ix 149pp illus
> Harrods
> 656   * §

Dalton, Barton & Co
> *D B Co Ltd 1825-1929*

> 1929   16pp illus
> Dalton, Barton & Co
> 432   COVNPL

Dane, Eric Surrey
> *Peter Stubs and the Lancashire Hand Tool Industry*

> Altrincham: John Sherratt 1973   xi 291pp illus index sources
> Stubs, Peter
> 316   *

Daniels, Jeff
> *British Leyland: The truth about the Cars*

> Osprey 1980   192pp illus index
> British Leyland
> 351   *

Darbyshire, L C
> *The Story of Vauxhall 1857-1946*

> Luton: the firm 1946   56pp illus
> Vauxhall Motors
> 328   351   UBRIS

Darley, Lionel Seabrook
  Bookbinding Then and Now: A Survey of the First 178 Years of James Burn & Company
  Faber 1959   126pp illus index
  Burn, James & Co
  475   *
Darwin, Bernard Richard Meirion
  Charrington Gardner Locket and Company Limited 1731-1931: Two Hundred Years in the Coal Trade
  the firm 1931   48pp illus
  Charrington, Gardner, Locket & Co
  612   654   *
Darwin, Bernard Richard Meirion
  Robinsons of Bristol 1844-1944

  Bristol: the firm 1945   xiii 72pp illus
  Robinson, E S & A
  471   472   *
Daunton, Martin James
  Aristocrat and Traders: The Bute Docks 1839-1914

  Journal of Transport History   new ser vol III no 2 1975
  Bute Docks
  612   763   770
Daunton, Martin James
  Coal Metropolis: Cardiff 1870-1914

  Leicester: L U P 1977   xi 260pp illus index sources
  Coal Metropolis: Cardiff
  111   612   630   763   *
Daunton, Martin James
  Dowlais Iron Company in the Iron Industry 1800-1850

  Welsh Historical Review   vol 6 no 1 1972
  Dowlais Iron Co
  221   311
Daunton, Martin James
  Royal Mail: The Post Office since 1840

  Athlone 1985   xviii 388pp illus index sources
  Post Office
  790   *
Davenport, John
  The History of R & J Hill, Established 1775, Purveyors to the House of Lords, Contractors to the Admiralty
  the firm 1942   47pp illus
  Hill, R & J   Carreras
  429   HACKPL
Davenport-Hines, R P T & Liebenau, J (eds)
  Business in the Age of Reason

  Frank Cass 1986

  248   320   814   839

141

Davenport-Hines, R P T & Van Helten, J-J
Edgar Vincent and the Eastern Investment Company in London, Constantinople and Johannesburg
Business History   vol XXVIII no 1 1986
Eastern Investment Company   Imperial Ottoman Bank
810   839

Davenport-Hines, Richard P T
British Marketing of Armaments 1885-1939

see Davenport-Hines, R P T (ed)
Armaments
329

Davenport-Hines, Richard P T
Dudley Docker: The Life and Times of a Trade Warrior

Cambridge: C U P 1984   295pp illus index sources
Vickers   B S A
320   329   340   351   814   BLPES

Davenport-Hines, Richard P T
Glaxo as a Multinational before 1963

see Jones, Geoffrey (ed) 1986
Glaxo
257

Davenport-Hines, Richard P T
The British Armaments Industry under Disarmament 1918-1936
Cambridge PhD 1979
Vickers   Armstrong, Whitworth & Co
329

Davenport-Hines, Richard P T
The British Engineers' Association and Markets in China 1900-30
see Davenport-Hines, R P T (ed)
British Engineers' Assoc
320

Davenport-Hines, Richard P T
Vickers as a Multinational before 1945

see Jones, Geoffrey (ed) 1986
Vickers
320

Davenport-Hines, Richard P T
Vickers' Balkan Conscience: Aspects of Anglo-Romanian Armaments 1918-1939
Business History   vol XXV no 3 1983
Vickers
329

Davenport-Hines, Richard P T (ed)
Markets and Bagmen: Studies in Marketing and British Industrial Performance 1830-1939
Aldershot: Gower 1986

257   316   329   353   421

142

Davenport-Hines, Richard P T (ed)
Speculators and Patriots: Essays in Business Biography

Frank Cass 1986   viii 139pp illus index sources

340   412   814   815   831

David Lloyd, Pigott & Co
David Pugh and David Lloyd: One Hundred and Fifty Years 1760-1910
the firm nd
David Lloyd, Pigott & Co
423   839   UBRIS

David Lloyd, Pigott & Co
Two Centuries: The Story of David Lloyd, Pigott & Co 1760-1960
the firm 1960   36pp
David Lloyd, Pigott & Co
423   839   GHL

Davidson, John F
From Collier to Battleships: Palmers of Jarrow 1852-1933

Durham: 1946
Palmers of Jarrow
361

Davies, Alun C
A Welsh Waterway in the Industrial Revolution: The Aberdare Canal 1793-1900
Journal of Transport History   new ser vol IV no 3 1978
Aberdare Canal
726

Davies, Bernard
Eastern Counties Leather Company Ltd: One Hundred Years

Sawston: Crampton & Sons nd   100pp illus
Eastern Counties Leather Co
441   §

Davies, David Wyn
Owen Owen: Victorian Draper

Aberystwyth: Gwasg Cambria 1984   156pp illus index sources
Owen Owen
647   656   * §

Davies, Edward Andrew
An Account of the Formation and Early Years of the Westminster Fire Office
the firm 1952   90pp illus sources
Westminster Fire Office
820   * §

Davies, Glyn
Building Societies and their Branches: A Regional Economic Survey
Franey 1981   xiv 429pp illus index
Building Societies
815   *

Davies, Harvey & Murrell
The Story of Davies, Harvey & Murrell 1919-1949

1949   14pp
Davies, Harvey & Murrell
471   GHL

Davies, J Hathren
History of Dowlais

translated manuscript 1891   35pp
Dowlais Iron Co
221   311   MRTHRPL

Davies, John
Cardiff and the Marquesses of Bute

Cardiff: Wales U P 1981   x 335pp index sources
South Wales Coalowners
111   221   740   763

Davies, Kenneth Gordon
The Royal African Company

Longmans 1957   ix 390pp index sources
Royal African Company
839   * §

Davies, L N A
The History of the Barry Dock and Railways Company in relation to the Development of the South Wales Coalfield
Wales MA 1938
Barry Dock and Railways Co
710   763

Davies, Peter N & Bourn, A M
Lord Kylsant and the Royal Mail

Business History   vol XIV no 2 1972
Royal Mail Shipping Group
740

Davies, Peter Neville
British Shipping and World Trade: Rise and Decline 1820-1939

see Fuji Conference 11, 1984
Shipping and World Trade
740

Davies, Peter Neville
Business Success and the Role of Chance: The Extraordinary Philipps Brothers
Business History   vol XXIII no 2 1981
Royal Mail Shipping Group   Investment Trusts
740   815

Davies, Peter Neville
Group Enterprise, Strengths and Hazards: Business History and the Teaching of Business Management
see Marriner, Sheila (ed) 1978
Elder Dempster   Royal Mail Shipping Group
740

Davies, Peter Neville
Henry Tyrer: A Liverpool Shipping Agent and his Enterprise

Croom Helm 1979   159pp illus
Tyrer, Henry & Co
770

Davies, Peter Neville
Sir Alfred Jones: Shipping Entrepreneur par Excellence

Europa 1978   lxii 162pp index sources
Elder Dempster
740   770   *

Davies, Peter Neville
The African Steam Ship Company

see Harris, J R (ed) 1969
African Steam Ship Co   Royal Mail Shipping Group
740

Davies, Peter Neville
The Trade Makers: Elder Dempster in West Africa 1862-1972

Allen & Unwin 1973   526pp illus index sources
Elder Dempster   Ocean Steam Ship Co
740   770   839   *

Davies, Peter Neville (ed)
Trading in West Africa 1840-1920

Croom Helm 1976   209pp index sources
Trading in West Africa
740   770   839   *

Davies, Randall Robert Henry
The Railway Centenary: A Retrospect

the firm 1925   49pp illus
London & North Eastern Railway Stockton & Darlington Railway
710   *

Davies, Stuart
*Kells of Gloucester and Ross: Agricultural and Implement
Makers*
Bristol & Gloucester Arch Soc   vol 99 1981
Kells
321

Davies, W J
W J Davies & Sons, Ltd 1693-1958: Emery Manufacturers

1958   5p illus
Davies, W J & Sons
246   SWKPL

Davis, Arthur Charles
A Hundred Years of Portland Cement 1824-1924

Concrete Publ 1924   xxii 281pp illus
Portland Cement
242   *

145

Davis, Clarence B
Financing Imperialism: British and American Bankers as Vectors of Imperial Expansion in China 1908-1920
Business History Review   vol LVI no 2 1982
Hongkong & Shanghai Bank   British & Chinese Corp
814

Davis, F C
Historical Survey of Peek, Frean & Co Ltd 1857-1957

typescript 1957
Peek, Frean & Co
419   URDNG

Davis, Martyn
One Hundred Years: Coventry Building Society 1884-1984

Coventry: the firm 1984   24pp illus
Coventry Building Society
815   COVNPL

Davis, Patrick
Number One: A History of the Firm of Gregory, Rowcliffe & Co 1784-1984
the firm 1984   88pp illus
Gregory, Rowcliffe & Co
835   §

Davis, Ralph
Twenty One and a Half, Bishop Lane: A History of J H Fenner & Co. Ltd 1861-1961
Newman Neame 1961   110pp illus
Fenner, J H
442   * §

Davis, Richard Whitlock
The English Rothschilds

Collins 1983   272pp illus index sources
Rothschild
814   *

Davis, Theo
John Fowler and the Business He Founded

the firm 1951
Fowlers of Leeds
321

Davis, Walter Tamsett
The History of the Royal Arsenal Co-operative Society Ltd 1868-1918
Woolwich: the firm 1922   xvi 277pp illus
Royal Arsenal Co-operative Soc
656   *

Dawe, Donovan A
Skilbecks, Drysalters 1650-1950

the firm 1950   xi 116pp illus index sources
Skilbeck Brothers
612   * §

Day, Joan
>   *Bristol Brass: A History of the Industry*
>
>   Newton Abbot: David & Charles 1973 240pp illus index sources
>   Bristol Brass
>   224   * §

Dayer, Roberta A
>   *Strange Bedfellows: J P Morgan & Co, Whitehall and the Wilson Administration during World War I*
>   Business History   vol XVIII no 2 1976
>   Morgan, J P & Co
>   814

De Barr, A E & Sharman, S M
>   *M T I R A 1960-1981: The Machine Tool Industry Research Association*
>   Macclesfield: the firm 1982   119pp illus
>   M T I R A
>   322   940   MACCPL

de Havilland
>   *De Havilland's Fifty Years*
>
>   the firm 1960   27pp illus
>   de Havilland
>   364   RAeS

De Zoete & Gorton
>   *De Zoete & Gorton: A History 1863-1963*
>
>   Harley 1963   80pp
>   De Zoete & Gorton
>   831

Deakins
>   *Deakins Ltd: 100 Years of Bleaching and Dyeing 1850-1950*
>
>   the firm 1950   24pp illus
>   Deakins
>   437   BOLTNPL

Dean, Joseph Normanton
>   *A Brief History of Deans*
>
>   Stockport: the firm
>   Dean & Co (Stockport)
>   441   472   SKPTPL

Deghy, Guy
>   *Paradise in the Strand: The Story of Romano's*
>
>   Richards 1958   256pp illus index sources
>   Romano's
>   661   *

Dempsey, Mike (ed)
>   *Bubbles: Early Advertising Art from A & F Pears*
>
>   Fontana 1978   72pp illus
>   Pears, A & F
>   258   838   *

Dempsey, Mike (ed)
Pipe Dreams: Early Advertising for the Imperial Tobacco Company
Pavilion 1982   96pp illus
Imperial Tobacco
    429   838   *

Dempster, John
Certain Aspects of some 19th Century Scottish Religious Book Publishers: Blackie & Son and Thomas Nelson and Sons
Strathclyde: M A thesis 1983
Blackie & Son   Nelson, Thomas and Sons
    475

Dempster, Robert & Sons
100 years: the Record of a Century of Progress 1855-1955

Elland: the firm 1955   42pp illus
Dempster, Robert & Sons
    320   HLFXPL

Dence, Alexander Henry
The Hovis Jubilee: A Brief Record of the Company's History 1898-1948
the firm 1948   40pp illus
Hovis Co
    416   419   *

Dennett, Laurie
The Charterhouse Group 1925-1979: A History

Gentry 1979   175pp illus index sources
Charterhouse
    814   * §

Denny, William & Bros
Denny Dumbarton 1844-1932

Dumbarton: the firm 1932   114pp illus
Denny, William & Bros
    361   DMBTNPL

Denny, William & Bros
Denny Dumbarton 1844-1950

Edinburgh: McLagan & Cumming 1950 35pp
Denny, William & Bros
    361   *

Denny, William & Bros
Denny's Dumbarton Souvenir 1908

Dumbarton: the firm 1908   155pp illus
Denny, William & Bros
    361   DMBTNPL

Denny, William & Bros
Souvenir of One Thousand Vessels

Dumbarton: the firm 1913   155pp illus
Denny, William & Bros
    361   DMBTNPL

Denny, William & Bros
William Denny & Brothers, Dumbarton 1844-1944

Dumbarton: the firm 1944
Denny, William & Bros
361

Dent & Hellyer
Under Eight Reigns, George I to George V 1730-1930:
Bicentenary
the firm 1930   136pp illus
Dent & Hellyer
503   613   UBRIS

Dent, Joseph Malaby
The House of Dent 1888-1938

J M Dent 1938   xvii 334pp illus index
Dent, J M
475   * §

Derbyshire, F W
History of Thomas Broadbent and Sons Ltd 1864-1950

Huddersfield: typescript ca1950   38pp
Broadbent, Thomas and Sons
320   HDSFDPL

Derry and Sons
Derry's: A Century in Print 1867-1967

Nottingham: the firm 1967   84pp illus
Derry & Sons
475   * §

Devine, Thomas Martin
Kirkman Finlay: A Study of Entrepreneurship and Politics

Strathclyde PhD 1971
Kirkman Finlay
429

Dewar
The House of Dewar 1846-1946

Perth: the firm 1946   68pp illus
Dewar, John & Sons
424   *

Dewey, J & S
Men of Iron: J & S Dewey

Wallingford Arch & Hist Soc   1983
Dewey, J & S   Wilder, J
311

Diack, William
Rise and Progress of the Granite Industry in Aberdeen

Quarry Managers' Journal 1949   iii 123pp illus
Granite Industry in Aberdeen
231   *

Diaper, Stefanie J
Kleinwort Benson: The History of a Merchant Bank

Nottingham PhD 1984
Kleinwort Benson
814

Dick, W F L
A Hundred Years of Alkali in Cheshire

the firm 1973   126pp illus
I C I   Brunner, Mond
251   UBRIS

Dickinson & Co
The Firm of John Dickinson and Company Limited

Chiswick Press 1896   63pp illus
Dickinson, John & Co
475   *

Dickinson, Sue V
*The First Sixty Years: A History of the Imperial Tobacco
Company in the United States of America 1902-1962*
Bristol: the firm 1965   134pp illus sources
Imperial Tobacco
429   AVONPL

Dickson, Peter George Muir
*The Sun Insurance Office 1710-1960: The History of
Two-and-a Half Centuries of British Insurance*
Oxford U P 1960   xiv 324pp illus index sources
Sun Insurance
820   * §

Didham, R C
The Hardwick Colliery Company Ltd

1970   13pp
Hardwick Colliery Co
111   DERBYPL

Dillon, Malcolm
*Some Account of the Works of Palmers Shipbuilding & Iron Co
Ltd*
Newcastle-upon-Tyne: Franklin 1900 55pp illus
Palmers of Jarrow
361   *

Dilnot, George
The Romance of the Amalgamated Press

the firm 1925   101pp illus
Amalgamated Press   Fleetway House
475   *

Dingley, Cyril S
The Story of B I P 1894-1962

Oldbury: the firm 1962   64pp illus
British Industrial Plastics   Turner & Newall
251   483   * §

Dinsdale, Walter Arnoid
History of Accident Insurance in Great Britain

Stone & Cox 1954   xii 362pp
Accident Insurance
820   *

Disher, Maurice W & Bruce, Michael W S
The Personality of the Alhambra and the History of Odeon

Birmingham: the firm 1937   31pp
Odeon Theatre Co   Alhambra Theatre
971   974   *

Divine, David
These Splendid Ships: The Story of the Peninsular and Oriental Line
Frederick Muller 1960   255pp illus index
P & O
740   * §

Dixey, C W & Son
C W Dixey & Son: A History 1777-1977

the firm nd   47pp illus
Dixey, C W & Son
371   §

Dixon, Donald F
Petrol Distribution in the United Kingdom 1900-1950

Business History   vol VI no 1 1963
Petrol Distribution
612

Dobbs, Brian
The Last Shall Be First: The Colourful Story of John Lobb the St James's Street Bootmaker
Elm Tree Books 1972   xi 147pp illus index
Lobb, John
451   *

Dobie, George A
The Role of David Colville and Sons in the Iron and Steel Industry in Motherwell 1870-1890
Glasgow: Notre Dame diss 1979   55pp sources
Colvilles
221   MTHWLPL

Dobson & Barlow
Dobson & Barlow Ltd, Textile Machinists: 134 Years in Progress 1790-1924
Bolton: the firm 1924   119pp illus
Dobson & Barlow
323   BOLTNPL

Dobson & Barlow
Samuel Crompton, Inventor of the Spinning Mule...History of Messrs Dobson & Barlow Ltd
Bolton: the firm 1927   147pp illus
Dobson & Barlow
432   *

Dobson, Charles George
*A Century and a Quarter: The Story of the Growth of our
Business from 1824 to the Present Day*
Croydon: the firm 1951   x 228pp illus index
Hall & Co.
613   648   654   * §

Dobson, E Philip & Ives, John B
*A Century of Achievement: The History of James Ives & Co.
1848-1948: Woollen Manufacturers, Yeadon, Yorkshire*
York: William Sessions 1948   103pp illus
Ives, James
431   *

Dobson, Eric B
Hartonclean 1884-1984: The Story of the First 100 Years

the firm 1984   64pp illus
Johnson Group Cleaners   Hartonclean
981   §

Dobson, P Alan
John Player & Sons: A Short History and Appreciation

typescript 1975
Player, John & Sons   Imperial Tobacco
429

Dobson, Robert Montagu Hume
*Final Night: A Record of the Last Days of the Morning Post as a
Separate Journal*
Uxbridge: King & Hutchings 1938   58pp
Morning Post
475   *

Docherty, C
Steel and Steelworkers: The Sons of Vulcan

Heinemann 1983   x 247pp illus sources
Vulcan Foundry
221   *

Dodwell
The House of Dodwell: A Century of Achievement 1858-1958

the firm 1958   viii 160pp illus
Dodwell & Co   Inchcape
740   839   * §

Don, G Stuart
David Bentley, Ltd. 150 Years of Bowl Making

1934   illus
Bentley, David
320   SALFDPL

Donaldson, Frances Annesley
The Marconi Scandal

Hart-Davis 1962   304pp illus
Marconi
344   *

Donaldson, Gordon
Northwards by Sea

Edinburgh: Paul Harris 1978   162pp illus sources
P & O Ferries   North of Scotland Shipping Co
740   *

Donaldson, Mrs Kathleen
The Cox Family, the Linen Trade and the Growth of Lochee (ca1800-1922)
Dundee BLitt 1972
Cox Family, the Linen Trade
434

Doncaster, Daniel
D D 1778-1978

Sheffield: the firm 1978   30pp illus
Doncaster, Daniel & Sons
221   322   IMECHE

Doncaster, Daniel
Daniel Doncaster & Sons Ltd: The Story of Four Generations 1778-1938
Sheffield: the firm 1938   30pp
Doncaster, Daniel & Sons
221   322   SHEFFPL

Donkin, Bryan
A Brief Account of Bryan Donkin F R S and of the Company He Founded 150 Years Ago 1803-1953
Chesterfield: the firm 1953   69pp illus
Donkin, Bryan & Co
221   SHEFFPL

Donkin, Harry Julyan
The History of Bryan Donkin and Company: Some Notes on the History of an Engineering Firm 1803-1903
the firm 1925   19pp
Donkin, Bryan & Co
221   *

Donnachie, Ian
A History of the Brewing Industry in Scotland

Edinburgh: John Donald 1979   xi 287pp illus index sources
Brewing Industry in Scotland
427   *

Donne, Michael
Leader of the Skies: Rolls-Royce: The First 75 Years

Frederick Muller 1981   160pp illus index sources
Rolls-Royce
351   364   *

Donnelly, Desmond
David Brown's: The Story of a Family Business 1860-1960

Collins 1960   128pp illus index
David Brown
321   322   351   §

Donohue, Joseph Walter (ed)
The Theatrical Manager in England and America: Player of a Dangerous Game
Princeton: P U P 1970 xii 216pp illus
Theatrical Managers
974 *

Dorlay, John S
The Roneo Story

Croydon: the firm 1978 223pp illus index
Roneo Vickers Neostyle Manufacturing Co
330 §

Dormer, Ernest W
Reading and High Wycombe Building Society Centenary 1852-1952
Reading: the firm 1952 10pp illus sources
Reading & High Wycombe Bldg Soc
815 BERKSPL

Dougan, David
The Great Gunmaker

Newcastle: Frank Graham 1971
Armstrong, Whitworth & Co
329

Dougan, David
The History of North East Shipbuilding

Allen & Unwin 1968 258pp illus
Shipbuilding in NE England
361

Douglas, John Monteath
The Truth about the London, Brighton and South Coast Railway: Its Accounts, its Working and its Assailants
Effingham Wilson 1882 16pp
London Brighton & South Coast Rly
710 *

Doulton & Co
The Royal Doulton Potteries: A Brief Account of their History

1959 55pp
Doulton & Co
248 *

Doulton & Co
The Royal Doulton Potteries: A Brief Summary of their Rise and Expansion during Six Reigns
the firm 1924 80pp
Doulton & Co
248 *

Dow, George
Great Central

Locomotive Publishing Co 1959-65 3 vols illus index
Great Central Railway
710 *

154

Dowell, William Chipchase
The Webley Story: A History of Webley Pistols and Revolvers and the Development of the Pistol Cartridge
Leeds: Skyrac 1962   337pp illus index
Webley & Scott
329   SANDWPL

Doxford, William
William Doxford & Company

1921
Doxford, William & Co
328   361

Drage, Charles
Taikoo

Constable 1970   320pp illus index sources
Butterfield & Swire
740   770   839   §

Dray & Drayton
A Century of Service 1856-1956: The Story of G W Dray & Son Ltd. and the Drayton Paper Works Ltd.
the firm 1956   64pp illus
Dray, G W & Son
471   472   GHL

Drew, Bernard
The Fire Office: Being the History of the Essex & Suffolk Equitable Insurance Society Limited 1802-1952
Colchester: the firm 1952   ix 166pp illus index
Essex & Suffolk Equitable Ins
820   * §

Drew, Bernard
The London Assurance: A Chronicle

the firm 1927   xi 155pp illus
London Assurance
820   * §

Drew, Bernard
The London Assurance: A Second Chronicle

the firm 1949   xv 334pp illus sources
London Assurance
820   * §

Dreweatt, Watson and Barton
Dreweatt, Watson and Barton 1759-1959

Newbury: the firm 1959   34pp illus
Dreweatt, Watson and Barton
834   §

Dromey, Jack & Taylor, Graham
Grunwick: The Workers' Story

Lawrence & Wishart 1978   207pp illus index
Grunwick
493   *

Drower, Jill
Good Clean Fun: The Story of Britain's First Holiday Camp

Arcadia Books 1982   63pp illus
Cunningham's Holiday Camp
667   *

Du Cros, Arthur Philip
Wheels of Fortune: A Salute to Pioneers

Chapman & Hall 1938   xiii 316pp illus index
Dunlop Rubber Co
481   453   *

du Garde Peach, Lawrence
The Company of Cutlers in Hallamshire in the County of York 1906-1956
Sheffield: Pawson & Brailsford 1960
Cutlers' Company
316   491   DBB

Duckham, Baron Frederick
Railway Steamship Enterprise: The Lancashire and Yorkshire Railway's East Coast Fleet 1904-14
Business History   vol X no 1 1968
Lancashire & Yorkshire Railway
710   740

Duguid, Charles
The Story of the Stock Exchange

Grant Richards 1901   x 463pp illus
Stock Exchange
831   *

Dumbarton Corporation Gas Undertaking
Dumbarton Corporation Gas Undertaking: A Century of Service 1832-1932
Dumbarton: the firm 1932   32pp illus
Dumbarton Corporation Gas
162   DMBTNPL

Dumbell, Stanley
The Centenary Book of the Liverpool Stock Exchange 1836-1936
Liverpool: the firm 1936   68pp illus
Liverpool Stock Exchange
831   §

Dumbleton, Michael
Brickmaking: A Local Industry

Bracknell & Dist Hist Soc 1978   23pp illus sources
Brickmaking
241   BERKSPL

Dummelow, John
1899-1949: A History of the Metropolitan-Vickers Electrical Co Ltd
Manchester: the firm 1949   250pp illus index
Metropolitan-Vickers
340   * §

Dummett, G A
From Little Acorns: A History of the A P V Company Ltd

Hutchinson Benham 1981   xiv 247pp illus index
A P V
316   320   *
Dunbar, Charles S
The Rise of Road Transport 1919-1939

Ian Allan 1981   144pp illus index sources
Road Transport
720   *
Duncan Brothers & Co
The Duncan Group: Being a Short History of Duncan Brothers, Calcutta and Walter Duncan & Goodricke, London 1859-1959
the firm 1959   184pp illus index
Duncan Brothers & Co   Duncan, Walter & Goodricke
423   435   839   *
Duncan, Flockhart & Co
The History of Duncan, Flockhart & Co: Commemorating the Centenaries of Ether and Chloroform
Edinburgh: the firm 1946   52pp illus
Duncan, Flockhart & Co
257   643   * §
Dundee Eastern Co-operative Society
Dundee Eastern Co-operative Society Diamond Jubilee Souvenir 1873-1933
Dundee: the firm 1933   29pp
Dundee Eastern Co-operative Soc   Dundee C W S
656   DNDEEPL
Dundee Savings Bank
Dundee Savings Bank: Its Origins, Progress and Present Position 1900
Dundee: the firm 1901   85pp illus
Dundee Savings Bank   Trustee Savings Bank
814   DNDEEPL
Dundee, Perth & London Shipping
Dundee, Perth & London Shipping Co: The History of a Hundred Years
Dundee: the firm 1927   31pp illus
Dundee, Perth & London Shipping
740   770   DNDEEPL
Dunhill, Mary
Our Family Business

Bodley Head 1979   146pp illus
Dunhill, Alfred
429   654   GLROHL
Dunlop, T
The British Fisheries Society 1786-1893

Edinburgh: John Donald 1978
British Fisheries Soc
30

Dunn, John Maxwell
The Wrexham, Mold and Connah's Quay Railway

Lingfield: Oakwood 1957   32pp illus sources
Wrexham Mold Connah's Quay Rly
710   *

Dunnett, Alastair MacTavish
The Donaldson Line: A Century of Shipping 1854-1954

Glasgow: Jackson, Son & Co 1960   x 125pp illus
Donaldson Line
740   *

Dunnett, Peter J S
The Decline of the British Motor Industry: The Effects of Government Policy 1945-1979
Croom Helm 1980   201pp illus index sources
Motor Industry
351   *

Dupont-Lhotelain, Hubert
The Story of the Mossley Wool Combing and Spinning Company Ltd 1932-1982
Mossley: the firm ca1982   71pp illus
Mossley Wool Combing & Spinning
431   §

Durham, John Francis Langton
Telegraphs in Victorian London

Cambridge: Golden Head Press 1959   30pp
Universal Private Telegraph Co
790   *

Durtnell, R & Sons
From an Acorn to an Oak Tree: A Study in Continuity

Brasted: the firm 1976   vii 64pp illus
Durtnell, R & Sons
501   *

Dussek Bitumen
50 Years of Dussek Bitumen Procducts

the firm 1956   16pp
Dussek Bitumen
140   WARRPL

Dutton's Blackburn Brewery
Dutton's Blackburn Brewery: 150 Years of the House of Dutton 1799-1949
the firm 1949   68pp illus
Dutton's Blackburn Brewery
427   662   UBRIS

Dutton, H I
The Patent System and Inventive Activity during the Industrial Revolution 1750-1852
Manchester: M U P 1984   232pp index sources
Patent System
320   *

158

Dutton, H I & Jones, S R H
>*Invention and Innovation in the British Pin Industry 1790-1850*
>
>Business History Review   vol LVII no 2 1983
>Pin Industry
>316

Dutton, P A
>*The Employment Effects of Mergers: A Case Study of GEC, AEI and English Electric*
>Warwick PhD 1980
>GEC   English Electric
>340   364

Dwyer, Frederick Joseph
>*The Atlas Ironworks: The History of Thomas Holt Ltd. 1855-1959: Textile Machinists*
>the firm nd   viii 102pp illus index
>Holt, Thomas   Leesona-Holt
>323   *

Dyson, Anthony
>*Pictures to Print: The Nineteenth Century Engraving Trade*
>
>Farrand 1984   xxx 234pp illus index sources
>Dixon Ross
>475   *

E M B Co
>*E M B Jubilee 1908-1958*
>
>West Bromwich: the firm 1958   24pp illus
>E M B Co
>322   362   SANDWPL

Eadie Brothers
>*Eadie Brothers 1871-1971*
>
>Newman Neame 1971   71pp illus
>Eadie Brothers
>323   §

Eagle Star Insurance Co
>*Box 1299*
>
>the firm nd   37pp illus
>Eagle Star Insurance Co
>820   §

Eaglestone, Arthur A & Lockett, Terence A
>*The Rockingham Pottery*
>
>Newton Abbot: David & Charles 1973 159pp illus index
>Rockingham
>248   *

Earl, R A J
>*The Development of the Telephone in Oxford 1877-1977*
>
>Oxford: the firm 1983   ix 158pp illus
>British Telecom
>790   *

Earle, James Basil Foster
>*A Century of Road Materials: The History of the Roadstone Division of Tarmac Ltd.*
>Oxford: Basil Blackwell 1971   xviii 182pp illus index sources
>Tarmac
>231   245   502   * §

Earle, James Basil Foster
>*Black Top: A History of the British Flexible Roads Industry*
>
>Oxford: Basil Blackwell 1974   269pp illus index sources
>Flexible Roads Industry
>231   245   502   *

Earnshaw, Thomas
>*A Short History of South Crosland and Netherton Co-operative Society Ltd*
>Netherton: the firm 1929   40pp
>Crosland & Netherton Co-op
>656   HDSFDPL

East Kent Road Car Co
>*East Kent: A Brief History of the Company's Development*
>
>Canterbury: the firm 1966   15pp illus
>East Kent Road Car Co
>721   MRC

East Lancashire Paper Mill Co
>*East Lancashire Paper Mill Company Ltd 1860-1960: One Hundred Years of Progress*
>Radcliffe: the firm 1960   61pp illus
>East Lancashire Paper Mill Co
>471   * §

Eastbourne Waterworks
>*A Century of Service 1859-1959*
>
>Eastbourne: the firm 1959   10pp illus
>Eastbourne Waterworks
>170   §

Eastern Associated Telegraph Co
>*Fifty Years of 'Via Eastern'...Jubilee of the Eastern Associated Telegraph Co 1922*
>the firm 1922   203pp illus
>Eastern Associated Telegraph Co
>790   *

Easton, Harry Tucker
>*The History of a Banking House: Smith, Payne and Smiths*
>
>Blades, East & Blades 1903   xvi 127pp
>Smith, Payne & Smith
>814   *

Eastwood, J B
>*The Eastwood Story*
>
>1976   36pp
>Eastwood, J B
>10   412   MRC

Economist
> *The Economist 1843-1943: A Centenary Volume*

Oxford U P 1943   178pp index
Economist
475   * §

Edgar, S H
> *History of J & J Colman Ltd*

typescript ca1970
Colman, J & J
257   258   426   NRFLKPL

Edgar, S H
> *Notes on the History of Colman Foods*

typescript nd   306pp
Colman, J & J
257   258   426   NRFLKPL

Edgerton, D E H
> *Innovation in the Photographic Industry*

see Liebenau, Jonathan (ed) 1987
Ilford
259

Edgerton, D E H
> *Technical Innovation, Industrial Capacity & Efficiency: Public Ownership & the British Military Aircraft Industry 1935-48*

Business History   vol XXVI no 3 1984
Military Aircraft Industry
364

Edison-Swan
> *The Pageant of the Lamp*

the firm 1949   72pp illus
Edison-Swan Electric Co
347   ENFLDPL

Edleston, William
> *Woollens: An Historic Survey 1848-1948*

Sowerby Bridge: the firm 1948   24pp illus
Edleston, William
431   HLFXPL

Edmonds, Alexander
> *History of the Metropolitan District Railway Company to June 1908*

the firm 1973   vii 243pp
London Transport
710   *

Edwardes, Michael
> *Back from the Brink: An Apocalyptic Experience*

Collins 1983   301pp illus index
British Leyland
351   * §

Edwards, Chris & Liz
Concorde: Ten Years and a Billion Pounds Later

Pluto Press 1972   48pp sources
British Aircraft Corporation
364   AVONPL

Edwards, E
Personal Recollections of Birmingham and Birmingham Men

Birmingham: Midland 1877   168pp illus
Birmingham Banks   Muntz, George Frederick
221   224   495   814   §

Edwards, Harold Raymond
Competition and Monopoly in the British Soap Industry

Oxford: Clarendon 1962   x 270pp index sources
Unilever   Hedley, Thomas
258   * §

Edwards, Ifor
The British Iron Company

Trans Denbigh Hist Soc   vol 31 1982
British Iron Company
221   SANDWPL

Edwards, Norman
One Hundred Years of British Engine

the firm 1978   72pp illus
British Engine Insurance Co
820   * §

Edwards, Ronald S & Townsend, Harry
Business Enterprise: Its Growth and Organisation

Macmillan 1958   xvii 607pp

                                         *

Edwards, Ronald S & Townsend, Harry
Business Growth

Macmillan 1966   xxiv 410pp

                                         *

Eglin, Roger & Ritchie, Barry
Fly Me, I'm Freddie!

Weidenfeld & Nicolson 1980   238pp sources
Laker Airways
750   *

Elkington, George
The National Building Society 1849-1934

Cambridge: W Heffer 1935   79pp illus
National Building Society
815   * §

Ellerman Lines
The Development of British Shipping

1924   63pp
Ellerman Lines
740   GHL

Elliotts of Reading
Elliotts of Reading

Reading: the firm 1952   16pp
Elliotts of Reading
460   BERKSPL

Ellis & Everard
The History of Ellis & Everard Ltd and Joseph Ellis & Sons Ltd

the firm 1924   64pp
Ellis & Everard   Ellis, Joseph & Sons
654   LEICSPL

Ellis, Aytoun
Bold Adventure: A History of the National Provincial Bank

1953   26pp illus
National Provincial Bank
814   * §

Ellis, Aytoun
Heirs of Adventure: The Story of Brown, Shipley & Co.,
Merchant Bankers 1810-1960
the firm 1960   vi 165pp illus index
Brown, Shipley & Co.
814   * §

Ellis, Aytoun
Three Hundred Years on London River: The Hay's Wharf Story
1651-1951
Bodley Head 1952   133pp illus index
Hay's Wharf
763   * §

Ellis, Aytoun
Vitesse: The Story of 'Continental Express' 1849-1949

the firm 1949   46pp illus
Continental Express   Hay's Wharf
770   * §

Ellis, Aytoun
Yorkshire Magnet: The Story of John Smith's Tadcaster Brewery

Tadcaster: the firm 1953   illus
Smith, John; Tadcaster Brewery
427   662   *

Ellis, Colin D B
The Centenary Book of Ellis & Everard Ltd 1848-1948

Leicester: the firm 1948   64pp illus
Ellis & Everard
612   613   654   LEICSPL

Ellis, Cuthbert Hamilton
  London Midland and Scottish: A Railway in Retrospect

  Ian Allan 1970   224pp illus
  London Midland & Scottish Rly
  710   *

Ellis, Cuthbert Hamilton
  The Midland Railway   *and many other titles of individual*
  railway companies
  Ian Allan 1953   viii 192pp illus
  Midland Railway
  710   *

Ellis, H G
  Broughs Limited: The Story of a Business

  the firm 1952   157pp illus
  Broughs
  617   641   UBRIS

Ellis, Joseph & Sons
  The Centenary History of Joseph Ellis & Sons Ltd 1839-1939

  Leicester: 1939   59pp illus
  Ellis, Joseph & Sons   Ellis & Everard
  654   LEICSPL

Ellis, Shirley
  A Mill on the Soar

  the firm 1978   147pp illus sources
  Donisthorpe
  430   LEICSPL

Elsas, Madeleine (ed)
  Iron in the Making: Dowlais Iron Co. Letters 1782-1860

  Glamorgan County Records 1960   247pp illus index
  Dowlais Iron Co   Guest Keen Iron & Steel Co
  221   * §

Elson, C H & Sons
  From Such Small Beginnings: Being a Brief History of the House
  of C H Elson & Sons, Proprietors of the London Laundry
  the firm ca1933   18pp illus
  London Laundry, Coventry   Elson, C H & Sons
  981   COVNPL

Elvin, Laurence
  Bishop and Son, Organ Builders: The Story of J C Bishop and his
  Successors
  Lincoln: author 1984   356pp illus index
  Bishop, J C
  492   GLROHL

Ely, Vernon N
  Fifty Years - Hard: An Autobiography. Elys of Wimbledon: The
  Family and the Store
  Linen & Woollen Drapers...Homes1976 185pp illus
  Elys (Wimbledon)
  656   MERTNPL

Emery, N
   Pease & Partners and the Deerness Valley

   Durham MA 1984
   Pease & Partners
   111   231   362   430   814
Enfield Manufacturing Co.
   Moscow Mill and its People

   Oswaldtwistle: the firm nd   40pp illus
   Enfield Manufacturing Co
   430   BLPES
Enfield, A L
   90 Years Young: A Brief History of Arden & Cobden Hotels Ltd

   the firm 1977
   Arden & Cobden Hotels
   665
Enock, Arthur Guy
   This Milk Business: A Study from 1895 to 1943

   H K Lewis & Co 1943   lii 243pp illus
   United Dairies   Express Dairy
   413   617   641   *
Ensor & Co
   Ensor & Co Ltd

   typescript nd   75pp illus
   Ensor & Co
   248   §
Erdman, Edward L
   People and Property

   Batsford 1982   x 214pp illus index
   Erdman, Edward L
   834   *
Erickson, Charlotte
   British Industrialists: Steel and Hosiery 1850-1950

   Cambridge: C U P 1959   xxi 276pp index sources
   Steel Industry   Hosiery Industry
   221   436   *
Escombe, W M L
   The History of Escombe, McGrath & Company Limited

   the firm 1969   vii 131pp illus
   Escombe, McGrath & Co
   740   770   * §
Evans Medical
   The Story of Evans Medical 1809-1959

   Liverpool: the firm 1959   68pp illus
   Evans Medical Supplies
   257   * §

Evans, David Ewart
Lister's: The First Hundred Years

    Gloucester: Alan Sutton 1979   256pp illus index sources
    Lister, R A & Co
    328   *

Evans, George
The Old Snuff House of Fribourg and Treyer 1720-1920

    author 1921   50pp illus
    Fribourg & Treyer
    429   *

Evans, Harold
Vickers: Against the Odds 1956-1977

    Hodder & Stoughton 1978   287pp illus index sources
    Vickers
    221   329   361   364   * §

Evans, Joan
The Endless Web: John Dickinson & Co Ltd 1804-1954

    Jonathan Cape 1955   xvi 274pp illus index
    Dickinson, John & Co
    472   * §

Evans, Joan
Time and Chance: The Story of Arthur Evans and his Forbears

    Longmans 1943   xi 410pp illus
    Dickinson, John & Co
    472   *

Evans, Lewis
The Firm of John Dickinson & Company Limited

    1896
    Dickinson, John & Co
    472   *

Evans, Mike
In the Beginning: The Manchester Origins of Rolls-Royce

    Derby: Rolls-Royce Heritage 1984   169pp illus
    Rolls-Royce
    328   352   364   §

Evans, Richard
The Romance of Coal: Haydock Collieries, St. Helens, Lancs.

    Albion Publishing 1928   31pp illus
    Evans, Richard & Co
    111   StHLNS

Everard, Stirling
The History of the Gas Light and Coke Company 1812-1949

    Benn 1949   428pp illus index
    Gas Light & Coke Co
    162   *

Evered & Co
Evered 1809-1959: An Interim Report

Smethwick: the firm 1959   24pp illus
Evered & Co
311   §
Everett, Edgcumbe & Co
The Making of a Name

1954
Everett, Edgcumbe & Co
371
Eversheds & Vignoles
Eversheds: Their Place in British Industry 1885-1932

the firm 1932   47pp
Eversheds & Vignoles
320   340   617   *
Eves, Alec
Frederick Parker and its Subsidiaries

Leicester Graphic 1978   24pp illus
Parker, Frederick
311   325   LEICSPL
Ewer, George
*60 Years of Coaching 1919-1979: The George Ewer Group: A
History of the Company and Coach Fleet*
Ewer Group Enthusiasts Club 1979   44pp illus
Ewer, George
721   MRC
Exell, Arthur
The Morris Garages' Story

typescript 1979   22pp
Morris Garages
351   OXFDPL
Express Dairy
Express Story 1864-1964

the firm 1964   55pp illus
Express Dairy
413   617   641   *
Express Lift Company
The Express Lift Company Ltd 1770-1982

Northampton: the firm 1982   16pp illus
Express Lift Company
325   NHPTNPL
Eyles, Desmond
*Royal Doulton 1815-1965: The Rise and Expansion of the Royal
Doulton Potteries*
Hutchinson 1965   viii 208pp illus index
Royal Doulton
248   *

Eyles, W E
Electricity in Bath 1890-1974

Bath City Council/SWEB 1974   64pp
South Western Electricity
161   ELECC

Fabes, Gilbert H
The Romance of a Bookshop 1904-1938

the firm 1938   64pp
Foyle, W & G
653   *

Fache, E C
Lancaster & Locke: A Pedigree

the firm ca1933
Lancaster & Locke
210   224

Fagg, Alan
Westrays: A Record of J B Westray & Co Ltd

the firm 1957   117pp illus
Westrays
740   770   UBRIS

Fairfax-Blakeborough, John Freeman
A Short History of Redcar Race Course
and many other individual racecourse titles
Reid-Hamilton 1950   32pp
Redcar Race Course
979   *

Fairfield Shipbuilding
Fairfield 1860-1960

Glasgow: the firm nd   100pp illus
Fairfield Shipbuilding
361   IMECHE

Fairfield Shipbuilding
The Fairfield Shipbuilding and Engineering Works: History of
the Company...and Description of the Works
1909
Fairfield Shipbuilding
361

Fairrie, Geoffrey
The Sugar Refining Families of Great Britain

the firm 1951   xii 41pp illus
Tate & Lyle   Martineau
420   *

Falkland Islands Co
The Falkland Islands Company Ltd 1851-1951

1951   34pp
Falkland Islands Co
616   839   GHL

Falkus, Malcolm
The Development of Municipal Trading in the Nineteenth Century
Business History   vol XIX no 2 1977
Municipal Trading
162

Fallon, Ivan & Strodes, James
DeLorean: The Rise and Fall of a Dream Maker

Hamish Hamilton 1983   417pp illus
DeLorean
351   *

Fallows and Birkett
Notes on the Firm

typescript 1950
Fallows and Birkett
256   WARRPL

Falmouth Hotel Co
The Falmouth Hotel Company 1882-1982

the firm 1982
Falmouth Hotel Co
665

Farnie, Douglas Anthony
Platt Brothers & Co of Oldham, Machine Makers to Lancashire and the World: ...Cotton Spinning Spindles 1880-1914
Business History   vol XXIII no 1 1981
Platt Brothers & Co
323

Farnie, Douglas Anthony
The English Cotton Industry and the World Market 1815-1896

Oxford: Clarendon 1979   xiii 399pp index sources
Cotton Industry
432   *

Farnie, Douglas Anthony
The Manchester Ship Canal and the Rise of the Port of Manchester
Manchester: M U P 1980   xii 208pp illus index sourcespp
Manchester Ship Canal   Manchester, Port of
763   * §

Farnie, Douglas Anthony
The Structure of the British Cotton Industry 1846-1914

see Fuji Conference 8, 1981
Cotton Industry
432

Farnol, J
Portrait of a Gentleman in Colours: The Romance of Mr Lewis Berger
Sampson Low ca1935   85pp
Berger, Lewis & Sons
255   *

Farr, F & Co
Farrs Centenary: The Golden Square Story

the firm 1963   34pp illus
Farr, F & Co
645   *

Farr, Grahame
The Bristol City Line of Bristol, England

American Neptune   vol XIV no 2 1954
Bristol City Line
740   AVONPL

Farrant, J P
The History of Scont Motors Ltd of Salisbury 1902-1921

Salisbury: Group for Ind Arch   24pp illus
Scont Motors
721   MRC

Farrow, Howard
Howard Farrow Limited: A Story of Fifty Years 1908-1958

Harley 1958   72pp illus
Farrow, Howard
500   *

Faulkner, Alan H
Claytons of Oldbury

Kettering: Robert Wilson 1978   48pp illus
Clayton, Thomas
726   DUDLYPL

Faulkner, Alan H
F M C: A Short History of Fellows, Morton and Clayton Ltd

Kettering: Robert Wilson 1975   48pp illus
Fellows, Morton and Clayton
726   DUDLYPL

Faulkner, Ewart
The Birmingham Temperance Society 1830-1969

the firm 1969
Birmingham Temperance Soc
850

Fayle, Charles Ernest
Lloyd's List & Shipping Gazette 1734-1934

the firm 1934   pamphlet
Lloyd's List & Shipping Gazette
837   §

Fearon, P
Aircraft Manufacturing

see Buxton, N K & Aldcroft, D H (eds)
Aircraft Mfr
364

Fearon, Peter
The British Airframe Industry and the State 1918-35

Economic History Review   2nd ser vol XXVII no 2 1974
Airframe Industry
364

Fearon, Peter
The Formative Years of the British Aircraft Industry 1913-1924
Business History Review   vol 43 1969
Aircraft Industry
364

Fearon, Peter
The Vicissitudes of a British Aircraft Company: Handley Page Ltd between the Wars
Business History   vol XX no 1 1978
Handley Page
364

Feeny, Alfred
South Staffordshire Water Works Co: Inauguration of New Works Constructed under the Company's Act of 1875
Birmingham: Billing Bros 1880   41pp
South Staffs Water Works Co
170   SANDWPL

Felce, Ernest
Norwich Union Fire Insurance Society: An Historical Sketch 1797-1897
Norwich: the firm 1897   47pp
Norwich Union
820   *

Fenn, George Manville
Memoir of Benjamin Franklin Stevens

the firm 1903   310pp illus index
Stevens & Brown
653   * §

Fenter, Frances Margaret
Copec Adventure: The Story of Birmingham Copec House Improvement Society
Birmingham: the firm 1960   vii 74pp illus
Birmingham Copec Soc
850   *

Fereday, R P
The Career of Richard Smith (1783-1868), Manager of Lord Dudley's Mines and Ironworks
Keele MA 1966
Lord Dudley's Mines and Ironworks
111   221

Ferguson
Centenary: Ferguson Brothers, Carlisle 1824-1924

Carlisle: Charles Thurnam 1924   68pp illus index
Ferguson Brothers
430   BLPES

Ferguson, James D
The Story of Aberdeen Airport 1934-1984

Glasgow: the firm 1984   79pp illus
Aberdeen Airport
764   ABRDNPL

Ferneyhough, Frank
Liverpool and Manchester Railway 1830-1980

Hale 1980   xii 193pp illus index sources
Liverpool & Manchester Railway
710   §

Ferodo
The Ferodo Story: Sixty Years of Safety 1897-1957

Chapel-en-le-Frith: the firm 1957   64pp illus
Ferodo   Turner & Newall
244   353   §

Ferranti
Centenary of Sebastian Ziani de Ferranti DSc FRS, Founder of Ferranti Ltd 1882
Hollinwood: the firm 1964   35pp illus
Ferranti
340   *

Ferranti
Ferranti in Scotland

Edinburgh: the firm 1974   illus
Ferranti
344   364   DNDEEPL

Ferranti
The Good News Is....

Cheadle: the firm 1982   24pp
Ferranti
344   364   DNDEEPL

Ferranti
Yesterday and Today: A Brief Story of the Ferranti Organisation
Hollinwood: the firm 1957   37pp illus
Ferranti
340   *

Ferranti, Gertrude Ziani de & Ince, Richard
The Life and Letters of Sebastian Ziani de Ferranti

Williams & Norgate 1934   240pp illus
Ferranti
340   *

Ferrier, R W
The History of the British Petroleum Company: vol 1   The Developing Years 1901-1932
Cambridge: C U P 1982   xxx 801pp illus index sources
B P
130   140   251   612   652   * §

Ferris, Paul
> *The House of Northcliffe: The Harmsworths of Fleet St.*
>
> Weidenfeld & Nicolson 1971   340pp illus index sources
> Associated Newspapers
> 475   *

Ferris, T
> *The Ulster Railway 1835-48*
>
> Belfast MA 1980
> Ulster Railway
> 710

Field, H
> *The Story of the Old Works...of John Harper & Co at Willenhall,*
> *Staffordshire   1790-1949*
> Willenhall: the firm 1949   42pp illus
> Harper, John & Co
> 316   320   * §

Field, Henry Martyn
> *The Story of the Atlantic Telegraph*
>
> Gay & Bird 1893   415pp
> Atlantic Telegraph Co
> 790   *

Field, Molly & Dick
> *The History of Clapham Brothers Ltd., Keighley 1837-1962*
>
> Marsworth, Tring: Field 1983   220pp illus sources
> Clapham Brothers
> 311   320   BLPES

Fieldhouse, David Kenneth
> *Unilever Overseas: The Anatomy of a Multinational 1895-1965*
>
> Croom Helm 1978   620pp index sources
> Unilever
> 258   411   414   * §

Fielding, T J
> *History of Bakelite Limited*
>
> the firm 1948   80pp illus
> Bakelite
> 251   §

Finch, R
> *The Flying Wheel: I & R Morley*
>
> 1924   89pp
> Morley, I & R
> 437   GHL

Finch, Robert
> *A World-Wide Business*
>
> Bournville: the firm nd   64pp illus
> Cadbury Bros
> 421   SANDWPL

Finch, Robert J & Roberts, Alfred
> *The History of the National Mutual Life Assurance Society 1830-1930*
> the firm 1930   93pp illus
> National Mutual Life Assurance
> 820   *

Findlay, J A
> *The Baltic Exchange: Being a Short History of the Baltic Mercantile and Shipping Exchange...1744-1927*
> the firm 1927   55pp illus
> Baltic Exchange
> 832   *

Fine Cotton Spinners
> *Behind the Distaff: An Account of the Activities of the Fine Cotton Spinners' and Doublers' Association*
> Manchester: the firm ca1946   109pp illus
> Fine Cotton Spinners & Doublers
> 432   UBRIS

Fine Cotton Spinners
> *Jubilee 'Distaff' 1898-1948*
>
> Manchester: the firm 1948   73pp illus
> Fine Cotton Spinners & Doublers   Houldsworth
> 432   SKPTPL

Fine Cotton Spinners
> *The Fine Cotton Spinners' and Doublers' Association*
>
> Manchester: the firm 1909
> Fine Cotton Spinners & Doublers
> 432

Finlay, James & Co
> *James Finlay and Company Limited: Manufacturers and East India Merchants 1750-1950*
> Glasgow: Jackson Son & Co 1951   xix 276pp illus index sources
> Finlay, James & Co
> 423   432   435   839   §

Finn, Ralph Leslie
> *Tottenham Hotspur F C: The Official History*
>
> Robert Hale 1972   221pp illus
> Tottenham Hotspur F C
> 979   *

Finsbury & City Savings Bank
> *Finsbury & City of London Savings Bank: One Hundred and Twenty Five Years of Progress 1816-1941*
> 1941   30pp illus
> Finsbury & City...Savings Bank
> 814   ISLTNPL

Firth Brown
> *100 Years in Steel: Firth Brown Centenary 1837-1937*
>
> Sheffield: the firm 1937   76pp
> Firth, Thos & Sons   Brown, John
> 221   329   361   * §

Firth-Derihon
Historical Summary and Essential Facts

typescript nd   4pp
Firth-Derihon Stampings   Firth Brown
311   322   DERBYPL

Fitton, Robert S & Wadsworth Alfred P
The Strutts and the Arkwrights 1758-1830: A Study of the Early Factory System
Manchester: M U P 1958   xii 361pp illus index sources
Strutt, W G & J   English Sewing Cotton Co
430   *

Flanagan, James A
Co-operation in Sauchie 1865-1915: A Retrospect on...the Jubilee of the Newtonshaw Co-operative Society Ltd
New Sauchie: the firm 1915   72pp illus
Newtonshaw Co-op Soc   Forth Valley Co-op
656   CLKMNPL

Flanagan, James A
Wholesale Co-operation in Scotland: The Fruits of Fifty Years' Efforts 1868-1918: The Scottish Co-operative Wholesale Soc
Glasgow: the firm 1920   xiv 478pp illus index
Scottish Co-op Wholesale Soc
619   656   *

Flanders, A D; Pomeranz & Woodward
Experiment in Industrial Democracy: A Study of the John Lewis Partnership
Faber 1968   261pp index sources
John Lewis Partnership
656   * §

Flanders, Allan David
The Fawley Productivity Agreements

Faber
Esso Petroleum Co
140   §

Flavel, Sidney & Co
How We Build: part 1 - 160 Years' Progress, The New Flavel Gas Cooker; part 2 - The English Fireplace
Leamington: the firm 1937   74pp illus
Flavel, Sidney & Co   Glynwed
311   316   *

Fletch, A M
An Account of the Introduction of the Northrop Loom into the Mills of Ashton Bros & Co at Hyde, Cheshire in 1902
Hyde: the firm 1902   25pp illus
Ashton Bros & Co   Courtaulds
432   TAMESPL

Fletcher & Stewart
F S: A Brief History

the firm ca1976   4pp illus
Fletcher & Stewart
324   DERBYPL

175

Fletcher, R S
>
> *The History of the Leeds General Cemetery Company*
> *1833-1965*
> Leeds MPhil 1975
> Leeds General Cemetery Co
> 989

Fletcher, Samuel Billyeald
> *The Fletcher House of Lace and its Wider Family Associations*
>
> Derby: the firm 1957   xvi 307pp illus
> Fletcher, William & Sons
> 439   *

Flinn, M W with Stoker, D
> *The History of the British Coal Industry vol 2: The Industrial*
> *Revolution 1700-1830*
> Oxford: Clarendon 1983   xxi 512pp illus index sources
> Coal Industry
> 111   * §

Flinn, Michael Walter
> *Men of Iron: The Crowleys in the Early Iron Industry*
>
> Edinburgh: E U P 1962   xii 270pp illus index sources
> Crowleys of Stourbridge
> 221   * §

Flinn, Michael Walter
> *The Law Book of the Crowley Ironworks*
>
> Surtees Society 1957   xxxviii 193pp
> Crowleys of Stourbridge
> 221   311   *

Flinn, Michael Walter
> *The Lloyds in the Early English Iron Industry*
>
> Business History   vol II no 1 1959
> Lloyds
> 221

Floud, Roderick C
> *The British Machine Tool Industry 1850-1914*
>
> Cambridge: C U P 1976   xiv 217pp illus index sources
> Machine Tool Industry
> 322   *

Floud, Roderick C
> *The Metal-working Machine Tool Industry in England*
> *1850-1914: Greenwood and Batley Ltd*
> Oxford DPhil 1970
> Greenwood & Batley
> 322

Foley, John
> *The Food Makers: A History of General Foods Ltd*
>
> Banbury: the firm 1972   65pp
> Bird, Alfred & Sons   General Foods
> 410   423   *

Forbes, William
>*Memoirs of a Banking House*
>
>Edinburgh: the firm 1860   ix 96pp illus
>Union Bank of Scotland   Coutts & Co
>814   *

Ford & Weston
>*The Story of Ford & Weston*
>
>Derby & Cheltenham: the firm 1966 88pp illus
>Ford & Weston
>501   *

Ford, John
>*Ackermann 1783-1983: The Business of Art*
>
>Ackermann 1983   256pp illus index sources
>Ackermann Publications
>475   §

Fordath
>*The First Fifty Years...*
>
>West Bromwich: the firm 1970   20pp illus
>Fordath
>251   327   SANDWPL

Foreman-Peck, James S
>*Diversification and the Growth of the Firm: The Rover Company to 1914*
>Business History   vol XXV no 2 1983
>Rover Co   Starley, J K & Co
>351   363

Foreman-Peck, James S
>*Economies of Scale and the Development of the British Motor Industry before 1930*
>London PhD 1978
>Motor Industry
>351

Foreman-Peck, James S
>*Exit, Voice and Loyalty as Responses to Decline: The Rover Company in the Inter-War Years*
>Business History   vol XXIII no 2 1981
>Rover Co
>351   363

Forres, Lord
>*Balfour, Williamson & Company and Allied Firms: Memoirs of a Merchant House*
>the firm 1929   vii 100pp
>Balfour, Williamson
>740   770   839   *

Fort, George Seymour
>*Alfred Beit: A Study of the Man and his Work*
>
>Ivor Nicholson & Watson 1932   221pp illus
>British South Africa Co   De Beers
>630   815   839   *

Foster & Braithwaite
Foster & Braithwaite 1825-1931

the firm 1931   11pp illus
Foster & Braithwaite
831   §

Foster & Braithwaite
One Hundred Years at 27 Austin Friars 1865-1965

ca1965   8pp
Foster & Braithwaite
831   GHL

Foster, Richard
*F Cape & Co of St. Ebbe's Street, Oxford: From Draper's Shop to
Department Store*
Oxford City Museum 1973   29pp illus
Cape, F & Co
645   656   OXFDPL

Fosters
The Story of Fosters: The Hitchin Building Firm

Ed. J Burrow 1965   57pp illus
Fosters
501   HERTSPL

Fowler, Alan & Lesley
A History of the Nelson Weavers Association

Nelson: 1984
Nelson Weavers Association
432

Fowler, E
100 Years in the Shoe Trade 1862-1962

Norwich: the firm 1962   20pp illus
Buckingham, J & Sons
451   NRFLKPL

Fox Brothers & Co
Fox Brothers & Co Ltd: 175 Years, 1772-1947

Wellington: the firm 1947   18pp illus
Fox Brothers & Co
431   814   SOMPL

Fox, Hubert
*Quaker Homespun: The Life of Thomas Fox of Wellington, Serge
Maker and Banker 1747-1821*
Allen & Unwin 1958   136pp illus
Fox Brothers & Co
431   814   *

Fox, Humphrey & J
A Century and a Half of Progress 1814-1964

Willenhall: the firm 1964   24pp illus
Fox, Humphrey & J
316   WALSLPL

Fox, Joseph Hoyland
The Woollen Manufacture at Wellington, Somerset

Humphreys 1914   viii 121pp illus
Fox Brothers & Co
431   *

Fox, W E
Imperial Chemical Industries Ltd: One of the Biggest Trusts in Britain with World Ramifications
Martin Lawrence 1934   31pp
I C I
250   *

Fox, W E
Taximen and Taxi Owners: A Study of Organisation, Ownership and Working Conditions in the London Taxi Trade
Labour Research Dept 1935   23pp
Taxi Trade in London
722   *

France, Wm, Fenwick & Co
Wm France, Fenwick & Co Ltd: Its History and its Predecessors

the firm 1933   27pp
France, Wm, Fenwick & Co
740   *

Francis, Anne
A Guinea a Box: A Biography

Hale 1968   191pp illus index
Beecham
257   258   *

Francis, Anthony John
The Cement Industry 1796-1914: A History

Newton Abbot: David & Charles 1978 319pp illus index sources
Cement Industry
242   * §

Francis, Eric Vernon
London and Lancashire History: The History of the London and Lancashire Insurance Company Ltd
Newman Neame 1962   171pp illus index
London & Lancashire Insurance
820   *

Francis, F
F Francis Centenary Year 1869-1969: 100 Years Old and Moving Forward
SE London Mercury 1 May 1969   32pp illus
Francis, F

SWKPL

Francis, J R
A History of Cannock Chase Colliery Company

Staffs Ind Arch Soc 1979   73pp illus
Cannock Chase Colliery Co
111

Francis, J Roger
A History of the Cannock Chase Colliery Company

Staffs Ind Arch Soc 1980   73pp illus sources
Cannock Chase Colliery Co
111   SANDWPL

Francis, John
History of the Bank of England: Its Times and Traditions

Willoughby & Co 1847   2 vols index
Bank of England
814   *

Francis, Pat
Taddy & Co: Snuff & Tobacco Manufacturers

Brighton: John L Noyce 1983   20pp
Taddy & Co
429   MERTNPL

Franklin, S E
Samuel Montagu & Co: A Brief Account of the Development of the Firm
unpublished memoir 1967: the firm
Samuel Montagu & Co
814

Fraser, Colin
Harry Ferguson, Inventor and Pioneer

John Murray 1972   vii 294pp illus
Ferguson, Harry   Massey-Harris-Ferguson
321   *

Fraser, John Foster
Pullars of Perth: Dyers and Cleaners 1824-1924: The Romance of Cleaning and Dyeing
Perth: the firm 1924   46pp illus
Pullars of Perth
981   PERTHPL

Fraser-Stephen, Elspet
Two Centuries in the London Coal Trade: The Story of Charringtons
the firm 1952   viii 157pp illus index
Charrington, Gardner, Locket & Co
612   654   * §

Freeman, J D F; Jowitt, R E & Murphy, R J
King Alfred Motor Services: The Story of a Winchester Family Business
Southampton: Kingfisher 1984   208pp illus sources
King Alfred Motor Services
721

Friederichs, Hulda
The Life of Sir George Newnes, Bart.

Hodder & Stoughton 1911   xi 304pp
Newnes, George
475   *

Friends' Provident & Century Insurance Office
Friends' Provident & Century Insurance Offices 1832-1957

1957   35pp
Friends' Provident & Century Ins
820   GHL
Friends' Provident & Century Insurance Office
The Beginnings of Insurance and the Origins of the Friends'
Provident & Century Insurance Office
1955   24pp
Friends' Provident & Century Ins
820   GHL
Frost, George H
Munitions of War: A Record of the B S A and Daimler Companies
during the World War 1914-1918
Birmingham: the firm 1921   222pp illus
B S A   Daimler Co
329   350   *
Frostick, Michael
Bentley: Cricklewood to Crewe

Osprey 1980   302pp illus index sources
Bentley   Rolls-Royce
351   *
Fry, J S & Sons
Fry's of Bristol Established 1728

Bristol: the firm nd   30pp illus
Fry, J S & Sons
421   §
Fry, J S & Sons
Fry's Works Magazine - Bicentenary Number 1728-1928

the firm 1928   86pp illus
Fry, J S & Sons   British Cocoa & Chocolate Co
421   *
Fry, J S & Sons
History of J S Fry and Sons

typescript; archives of the firm
Fry, J S & Sons
421
Fry, Richard
Bankers in West Africa: The Story of the Bank of British West
Africa Limited
Hutchinson Benham 1976   xviii 270pp illus index sources
Standard Chartered Bank   Bank of British West Africa
820   839   * §
Fudge, Muriel K
An Enquiry into the History of the Leather Glove Trade

Bristol MA 1930
Leather Glove Trade
453

Fuji Conference
Fuji International Conference on Business History: annual
report volumes
Tokyo: T U P 1974-

BLPES

Fulford, Roger Thomas Baldwin
Five Decades of B E T: The Story of the British Electric
Traction Company Limited
the firm 1946   84pp illus
British Electric Traction
161   162   721   981   *

Fulford, Roger Thomas Baldwin
Glyn's 1753-1953: Six Generations in Lombard Street

Macmillan 1953   xi 267pp illus index
Glyn Mills & Co
814   * §

Fulford, Roger Thomas Baldwin
The Sixth Decade: 1946-1956

the firm 1956   xxi 86pp illus
British Electric Traction   Rediffusion
161   162   721   974   981   * §

Fullard, Harold J
Story of the House of Philip

typescript: the firm 1985
Philip, George & Son
475

Fuller Electrical & Manufacturing Co
A History of Asea Electric Ltd and Fuller Electrical &
Manufacturing Co during 50 Years
the firm 1949   110pp
Fuller Electrical   A S E A
340   GHL

Fuller Electrical & Manufacturing Co
Sixty Years of Progress: A Pictorial History

1958   40pp illus
Fuller Electrical   A S E A
340   GHL

Fuller, Robert P
The Chairman's Memories of the Early Days of the Avon India
Rubber Co Ltd
the firm 1947   16pp illus
Avon Rubber Co
481   UBRIS

Fuller, Roland
The Bassett-Lowke Story

New Cavendish 1984   352pp illus index sources
Bassett-Lowke
371   494   *

182

Funnell, K J
> *Snodland Paper Mill: C Townsend Hook and Company from 1854*

the firm ca1985   104pp illus
C Townsend Hook
471   * §

Gale, Walter Keith Vernon
> *A History of Bromford 1780-1980*

Publicitywise 1983   66pp illus
Bromford Iron & Steel Co
311   SANDWPL

Gale, Walter Keith Vernon
> *A History of the Pensnett Railway*

Cambridge: Goose & Son 1975   111pp illus index sources
Pensnett Railway
710   *

Gale, Walter Keith Vernon
> *Boulton, Watt and the Soho Undertakings*

Birmingham Museum 1952   40pp illus
Boulton & Watt
328   *

Gale, Walter Keith Vernon
> *Soho Foundry*

Birmingham: the firm 1948   49pp illus
Avery, W & T   Boulton & Watt
328   *

Gale, Walter Keith Vernon
> *The Coneygre Story*

Tipton: the firm 1954   30pp illus sources
Coneygre Foundry
311   *

Gale, Walter Keith Vernon & Nicholls, C R
> *The Lilleshall Co Ltd: A History 1764-1964*

Ashbourne: the firm 1979   134pp illus index
Lilleshall Co
111   221   241   320   *

Gallaher
> *Gallaher Ltd and Subsidiary Companies 1857-1956*

the firm 1956
Gallaher
429

Galloway, John
> *Galloways of Balerno*

Newman Neame 1968   51pp illus
Galloway, John & Co
471   §

Galloway, R L (ed B F Duckham)
A History of Coal Mining in Great Britain (1882)

Newton Abbot: David & Charles 1969 xi 273pp index sources
Coal Industry
111   *

Gammons, Walter
Forty Years in Transport

1931   163pp
Gammons, Walter
723   GHL

Garbutt, John L
Manbré & Garton Ltd 1855-1955: A Hundred Years of Progress

the firm 1955   32pp illus
Manbré & Garton   Tate & Lyle
420   * §

Gardiner, Alfred George
The Life of George Cadbury

Cassell 1923   ix 324pp illus index
Cadbury Bros
421   *

Gardiner, Leslie
Bartholomew 150 Years

Edinburgh: the firm 1976   111pp illus
Bartholomew, John & Son
475   §

Gardiner, Leslie
The Making of John Menzies: 150th Anniversary 1833-1983

the firm 1983   96pp illus
Menzies, John & Co
475   653   * §

Gardner, Charles
British Aircraft Corporation: A History

Batsford 1981   320pp illus index sources
British Aircraft Corporation
364   * §

Gardner, Joseph & Sons
History of Joseph Gardner & Sons Limited, Liverpool and London 1748-1947
Liverpool: the firm 1948   34pp illus
Gardner, Joseph & Sons
613   UBRIS

Garlands
Garlands of Norwich 1862-1962: 100 Years of Fashion

Norwich: the firm 1962   10pp illus
Garlands
656   NRFLKPL

184

Garlick, Peter C
*The Sheffield Cutlery and Allied Trades and their Markets in
the 18th and 19th Centuries*
Sheffield MA 1951
Sheffield Cutlery
316

Garner, James & Sons
Garner, James & Sons: Tanners & Leather Manufacturers

1953   14pp
Garner, James & Sons
441   GHL

Garnett, G & Sons
Garnett, G & Sons: West Yorkshire

York: William Sessions 1962
Garnett, G & Sons

Garnett, Ronald G
*A Century of Co-operative Insurance: The Co-operative
Insurance Society 1867-1967: A Business History*
Allen & Unwin 1968   324pp illus index sources
Co-operative Insurance Society
820   §

Garnett, Walter Onslow
Wainstalls Mills: The History of I & I Calvert Ltd. 1821-1951

Halifax: the firm 1951   52pp illus
Calvert, I & I
431   *

Garrett
*Garrett 200: A Bicentenary History of Garretts of Leiston
1778-1978*
Transport Bookman 1978
Garretts of Leiston
325   DBB

Garrod, P
The Bradford Worsted Industry 1900-39

Leeds MPhil 1982
Bradford Worsted
431

Gas Light & Coke
*Gas Light & Coke Company: An Account of the Progress of the
Company from its Incorporation 1812-1912*
the firm 1912   91pp illus
Gas Light & Coke Co
162   *

Gas Light & Coke Co
The Gas Light & Coke Company: A Record of Progress

the firm 1930-31   2 parts illus
Gas Light & Coke Co
162   *

Gauldie, Enid
> *The Scottish Country Miller 1700-1900: A History of*
> *Water-Powered Meal Milling in Scotland*
> Glasgow: Bell & Bain 1981   ix 254pp index sources
> Scottish Country Miller
> 416   *

Gavin, William
> *Ninety Years of Family Farming: The Story of Lord Rayleigh's*
> *and Strutt & Parker Farms*
> Hutchinson 1967   246pp illus
> Strutt & Parker Farms   Rayleigh, Lord; Farms
> 10   *

Gay, Philip W & Smith, Robert L
> *The British Pottery Industry*
>
> Butterworth 1974   293pp illus sources
> Pottery Industry
> 248   *

Geddes, R Stanley
> *Burlington Blue-Grey: A History of the Slate Quarries,*
> *Kirkby-in-Furness*
> Kirkby-in-Furness: author 1975   318pp illus index sources
> Burlington Slate Quarries
> 231   UBRIS

Gee, Walker & Slater
> *Gee, Walker & Slater Ltd: Building and Civil Engineering*
> *Contractors 1864-1950*
> the firm 1950   illus
> Gee, Walker & Slater
> 500

Gemmell, Peter
> *A Short History of the Old Green Markets and of the Waverley*
> *Market*
> 1906   64pp illus
> Waverley Market, Edinburgh
> 617   641   EDNBRPL

General Accident, Fire & Life
> *Romance of a Business: Forty Years' Work 1885-1924*
>
> Perth: the firm 1924   42pp illus
> General Accident, Fire & Life
> 820   PERTHPL

General Accident, Fire & Life
> *The Building of a Business: Quarter Century Memento*
> *1885-1911*
> Perth: the firm 1911   41pp illus
> General Accident, Fire & Life
> 820   PERTHPL

General Life Assurance
> *A Century of Progress*
>
> · the firm 1937   62pp
> General Life Assurance
> 820

George's of Bristol
: *George's of Bristol 1847-1972: 125 Years of Bookselling*

    Illustrated Bristol News Sept 1972 16pp illus
    George's, William & Sons
    653   AVONPL

George, F L
: *The Spencers of Coventry: The Story of M H Spencer Ltd 1823-1973*
    1973   36pp illus
    Spencer, M H
    323   COVNPL

Georges & Co
: *Georges Bristol Brewery: The Art of Brewing 1788-1951*

    Bristol: the firm 1951   32pp
    Bristol Brewery Georges & Co
    427   §

Gere, Charlotte
: *Morris & Company 1861-1939*   *(in catalogue of exhibition 1979)*
    Fine Art Society 1979   56pp illus
    Morris & Co
    438   467   648   MERTNPL

Gerrard, J & Sons
: *J G & S Ltd*

    Swinton: 1953   23pp
    Gerrard, J & Sons
    501   MRC

Gerretson, Frederik Carel
: *History of the Royal Dutch*

    Leiden: E J Brill 1953-57   4 vols illus index
    Royal Dutch/Shell
    130   140   251   612   652   * §

Gestetner
: *Gestetner 1834-1934*

    the firm 1934   20pp illus
    Gestetner
    330   §

Gestetner
: *Gestetner*

    1953   20pp
    Gestetner
    330   GHL

Gettmann, Royal Alfred
: *A Victorian Publisher: A Study of the Bentley Papers*

    Cambridge: C U P 1960   xi 272pp illus index sources
    Bentley
    475   *

Gibb, David Eric Watson
Lloyd's of London: A Study in Individualism

    Macmillan 1957   ix 387pp illus index
    Lloyd's of London
    820   *

Gibb, Mildred A & Beckwith, Frank
The Yorkshire Post: Two Centuries

    Leeds: the firm 1954   xi 112pp illus index
    Yorkshire Post
    475   * §

Gibbons, Stanley
The Stanley Gibbons Centenary

    the firm 1956   40pp illus
    Stanley Gibbons
    648   §

Gibbs, Antony
Merchants and Bankers: Antony Gibbs & Sons and its Associated Houses' Business during 150 Years 1808-1958
    the firm 1958   136pp illus
    Gibbs, Antony
    814   * §

Gibbs, John Arthur
The History of Antony and Dorothea Gibbs...The Early Years of the House of Antony Gibbs and Sons
    the firm 1922   xvi 509pp illus
    Gibbs, Antony and Dorothea
    814   839   *

Gibbs, John Morel
Morels of Cardiff: The History of a Family Shipping Firm

    Amgueddfa Genedlaethol Cymru 1982 183pp illus index sources
    Morel   Dowlais Iron Co
    361   740   763   770   * §

Gibbs, T A
Metropolitan Electric Tramways: A Short History

    Tramway & Light Railway Soc 1962   24pp illus
    Metropolitan Electric Tramways
    721   ENFLDPL

Gibson, John Frederic
Brocklebanks 1770-1950

    Liverpool: Henry Young 1953   2 vols illus index sources
    Brocklebank Line
    740   §

Gibson-Jarvie, Robert
The London Metal Exchange: A Commodity Market

    Cambridge: Woodhead-Faulkner 1976 viii 191pp illus
    London Metal Exchange
    630   831   * §

Gieve, David W
Gieves & Hawkes 1785-1985: The Story of a Tradition

the firm 1985   123pp illus
Gieves & Hawkes
453   §

Gill & Co
The Story of Gill & Co Ltd, Oxford Ironmongers

Oxford: the firm 1930   12pp illus
Gill & Co
648   OXFDPL

Gipson, R
A History of Hunts of Earls Colne, Essex 1825-1921

BA Reading 1979   73pp
Hunts
321

Girtin, T H
In Love and Unity: A Book about Brushmaking

Hutchinson 1961   112pp illus
Hamilton & Co
465   *

Glascock, J L's Successors
Noblest of all Arts

Bishop's Stortford: 1977   20pp
Glascock, J L's Successors
501   MRC

Glasgow Stock Exchange
Records of the Glasgow Stock Exchange Association 1844-1926

Glasgow: Jackson, Wylie & Co 1927   128pp illus
Glasgow Stock Exchange
831   UBRIS

Glen Line
Glen Line

1949   22pp
Glen Line
740   GHL

Glenlivet
*Glenlivet Being the Annals of the Glenlivet Distillery Founded
by George Smith in 1824*
the firm 1959   40pp illus
Glenlivet
424   BCROB

Glenlivet
Glenlivet Distillery 1824-1924

the firm 1924   32pp illus
Glenlivet
424   §

Glossop, W & J
W & J Glossop Ltd, Halifax (Road Construction) 1906-1966

York: William Sessions 1966
Glossop, W & J
502

Gloucester Railway Carriage & Wagon Co
A History of the Gloucester Railway Carriage & Wagon Co.

Weidenfeld & Nicolson 1960   64pp illus
Gloucester Railway Carriage
362   BLPES

Glover, Frederick J
Dewsbury Mills: A History of Messrs Wormalds and Walker Ltd, Blanket Manufacturers of Dewsbury
Leeds PhD 1959
Wormalds & Walker
431

Glover, Frederick J
The Rise of the Heavy Woollen Trade of the West Riding of Yorkshire in the Nineteenth Century
Business History   vol IV no 1 1961
Yorks Heavy Woollen Trade
431

Goad, Rigg & Co
The History of Goad, Rigg & Co

1952   15pp
Goad, Rigg & Co
456   *

Goblin B V C
The Goblin Story: A Short History of the Companies in the Goblin B V C Ltd Group of Companies
1969   24pp
Goblin B V C
343   GHL

Godwin, George Stanley
Hansons of Eastcheap: The Story of the House of Samuel Hanson & Son Ltd.
the firm 1947   99pp illus
Hanson, Samuel
641   839   * §

Gold, Alec H
Four-in-Hand: A History of W & A Gilbey Ltd 1857-1957

the firm 1957   83pp illus
Gilbey, W & A
424   642   §

Golding, Cecil F & Page, Douglas K
Lloyd's

New York: McGraw-Hill 1952   vii 220pp
Lloyd's of London
820   *

Goodale, Ernest William
Weaving and the Warners 1870-1970

Leigh-on-Sea: F Lewis 1971   58pp illus
Warner & Sons
430   *

Goodall, Francis
*Marketing Consumer Products before 1914: Rowntrees and
Elect Cocoa*
see Davenport-Hines, R P T (ed)
Rowntree
421

Goodall, Michael Harold
*The Wight Aircraft: The History of the Aviation Department of
J Samuel White and Co Ltd 1913-1919*
Gentry 1973   194pp illus index sources
White, J Samuel & Co
364   *

Goodden, Susanna
At the Sign of the Four-poster: A History of Heal's

the firm 1984   127pp illus
Heal's   Habitat
467   615   656   * §

Goodey, Charles
The First Hundred Years: The Story of Richards Shipbuilders

Ipswich: Boydell Press 1976   111pp illus index
Richards Shipbuilders
361   *

Goodhart, Charles Albert Eric
The Business of Banking 1891-1914

Weidenfeld & Nicolson 1972   ix 628pp sources
Joint Stock Banking
814   *

Goodman, Jean
The Mond Legacy: A Family Saga

Weidenfeld & Nicolson 1982   xv 272pp illus index sources
I C I   Brunner, Mond
250   *

Goodwin, Michael
Artist and Colourman: Reeves & Sons 200th Anniversary

Enfield: Michael Goodwin 1966   51pp illus sources
Reeves & Sons
255   BCROB

Gordon, B
*One Hundred Years of Electricity Supply 1881-1981: Growth
and Development over the Last Century*
                                     83pp illus
Southern Electricity
161

Gordon, Charles
    The Two Tycoons: A Personal Memoir of Charles Clore and Jack
    Cotton
    Hamish Hamilton 1984   242pp illus index
    City Centre Properties   City and Central
    850   * §

Gordon, Donald Ian
    The East Anglian Railway Company: A Study in Railway and
    Financial History
    Nottingham PhD 1964
    East Anglian Railway Co
    710

Gordon, Donald Ian
    The Eastern Counties: A Regional History of the Railways of
    Great Britain
    Newton Abbot: David & Charles 1968 252pp illus sources
    Railways in the E Counties
    710   *

Gordon, George
    Prying with the Pynours 1498-1978: An Intimate Look at the
    Aberdeen Shore Porters' Society and their Times
    Aberdeen: Taylor & Henderson 1978 319pp illus
    Aberdeen Shore Porters' Soc
    763   NESLS

Gordon, George
    The Shore Porters' Society of Aberdeen 1498-1969

    Aberdeen: Alex P Reid & Son 1970   127pp illus
    Aberdeen Shore Porters' Soc
    763   *

Gordon, Thomas Crouther
    History of Alva Co-operative Bazaar Ltd 1845-1947

    Alva: the firm 1948   112p illus
    Alva Co-operative Bazaar   Forth Valley Co-op
    656   CLKMNPL

Gosnell, John & Co
    Through the Fragrant Years: A History of the House of Gosnell
    1677-1947
    the firm 1947   24pp illus
    Gosnell, John & Co
    258   *

Gosse, Edmund William
    Sir Henry Doulton: The Man of Business as a Man of Imagination

    Hutchinson 1970   xiv 218pp illus index
    Doulton & Co
    248   * §

Gott, Ron
    Henry Bolckow: Founder of Teesside

    Middlesbrough: author 1968
    Bolckow, Vaughan & Co
    221

Gould, Maurice P
Frank Hornby: The Boy Who Made $1,000,000 with a Toy

New York: the firm 1915
Meccano   Hornby
494

Gould, Roger
David Allens 1857-1957

John Murray 1957   xii 57pp illus
Allen, David
838   *

Gourvish, T R & Wilson, R G
Profitability in the Brewing Industry 1885-1914

Business History   vol XXVII no 2 1985
Brewing Industry   Allsops
427

Gourvish, Terence Richard
Captain Mark Huish: A Pioneer in the Development of Railway Management
Business History   vol XII no 1 1970
London & North Western Railway
710

Gourvish, Terence Richard
Mark Huish and the London & North Western Railway: A Study of Management
Leicester: L U P 1972   319pp illus index sources
London & North Western Railway
710   *

Gourvish, Terence Richard
Mechanical Engineering

see Buxton, N K & Aldcroft, D H (eds)

320

Gourvish, Terence Richard
Railways and the British Economy 1830-1914

Macmillan 1980   70pp index sources
Railways
710   *

Gourvish, Terence Richard
The Performance of British Railway Management after 1860: The Railways of Watkin and Forbes
Business History   vol XX no 2 1978
South Eastern Rly   London Chatham & Dover Rly
710   721

Gowans, L M
The Caffyn Story: The Story of Caffyns from 1865

the firm 1957   28pp illus
Caffyn
614   651   671   §

Gowing, Margaret
Independence and Deterrence: Britain and Atomic Energy 1945-1952
Macmillan 1974   2 vols index sources
Atomic Energy
150   161   *

Grace, D R & Phillips, D C
Ransomes of Ipswich: A History of the Firm and Guide to its Records
Reading: Inst Agricultural Hist 1975 64pp illus sources
Ransomes, Sims & Jefferies
321   §

Grace, Darbyshire & Todd
A Short Account of Grace, Darbyshire & Todd: Chartered Accountants of Bristol 1818-1957
the firm 1957
Grace, Darbyshire & Todd
836

Graham, O
The Jute Industry of Dundee 1830-1855

Manchester MA 1928
Jute Industry
435

Graham, Richard
A British Industry in Brazil: Rio Flour Mills 1886-1920

Business History   vol VIII no 1 1966
Rio Flour Mills
416   839

Graham, Richard
Britain and the Onset of Modernisation in Brazil

Cambridge: C U P 1968   xv 384pp illus sources
Modernisation in Brazil
839   *

Grant, Allan John
Steel and Ships: The History of John Brown's

Michael Joseph 1950   97pp illus
Brown, John   Firth Brown
221   329   361   * §

Grant, Hilda Kay
Samuel Cunard: Pioneer of the Atlantic Steamship

Abelard-Schuman 1967   192pp illus index
Cunard
740   *

Grant, William S
Reminiscences

Bradford-on-Avon: 1949   24pp illus
Aberdeen Granite Mfrs' Assoc
231   NESLS

Granville-Smith, J
>   *Jones, Yarrell & Co: Bi-centenary 1960*

>   the firm 1960   15pp illus
>   Jones, Yarrell & Co
>   472   GHL

Gray, Imrie E
>   *A Business Epic 1885-1935: General Accident, Fire & Life*
>   *Assurance Corporation Limited*
>   Perth: the firm 1935   72pp illus
>   General Accident, Fire & Life
>   820   PERTHPL

Gray, Malcolm
>   *Organisation and Growth in the East-Coast Herring Fishing*
>   *1800-1885*
>   see Payne, Peter L (ed) 1967
>   Herring Fishing
>   30

Gray, Paul; Keeley, Malcolm & Seale, John
>   *Midland Red: A History of the Company and its Vehicles from*
>   *1940-1970*
>   Glossop: Transport Publ Co 1978-79 2 vols illus
>   Birmingham & Midland Motor Bus   Midland Red
>   721   *

Gray, Robert Archibald Speir
>   *Rolls on the Rocks: The Rise, Decline and Fall of the Most*
>   *Famous Name in the History of Industry*
>   Panther/Granada 1971   95pp illus
>   Rolls-Royce
>   328   350   364   *

Gray, William Forbes
>   *A Brief Chronicle of the Scottish Union & National Insurance*
>   *Company 1824-1924*
>   Edinburgh: the firm 1924   192pp illus
>   Scottish Union & National Ins
>   820   * §

Great Universal Stores
>   *Great Universal Stores 1932-1957: Twenty Five Years of*
>   *Progress*
>   the firm 1957   56pp illus
>   Great Universal Stores
>   656   §

Greaves & Thomas
>   *The Golden Jubilee of Greaves & Thomas 1905-1955*

>   the firm 1955   28pp illus
>   Greaves & Thomas   Put-U-Up
>   467   *

Green, Daniel
>   *C P C (United Kingdom): A History*

>   Publications for Companies 1980   32pp illus
>   Corn Products Co   Brown & Polson
>   418   423   §

Green, E & Son
Waste Not: The Story of Green's Economiser

Harley 1956   166pp illus
Green, E & Son, Wakefield
320   UBRIS

Green, Edwin
Debtors to their Profession: A History of the Institute of
Bankers 1879-1979
Methuen 1979   245pp illus index sources
Institute of Bankers
814   * §

Green, Edwin
The Making of a Modern Banking Group: A History of the Midland
Bank since 1900
the firm 1979
Midland Bank
814

Green, Edwin
Very Private Enterprise: Ownership and Finance in British
Shipping 1825-1940
see Fuji Conference 11, 1984
Royal Mail Shipping Group
740

Green, Edwin & Moss, Michael
A Business of National Importance: The Royal Mail Shipping
Group 1902-1937
Methuen 1982   xii 291pp illus index sources
Royal Mail Shipping Group
740   * §

Green, Henry & Wigram, Robert
Chronicles of Blackwall Yard: part 1

Whitehead Morris & Lowe 1881
Blackwall Yard
361   *

Green, M H
The World-wide Organisation: The Origin and Activities of Cory
Brothers
'Syren and Shipping' 1946   16pp
Cory Bros & Co
612   740   GHL

Green, Tom
Yates Duxbury & Sons, Papermakers of Bury 1863-1963

Newman Neame 1963   56pp illus
Yates Duxbury & Sons
471   *

Greenall, Gilbert & John
Distillers and Wine Merchants since 1761

the firm 1979   12pp
Greenall, Gilbert & John
424   WARRPL

Greenberg, M
British Trade and the Opening of China 1800-1842

Cambridge: C U P 1951   xii 238pp
Jardine, Matheson
839   *

Greene, Dorothy
The Glass Works, Rotherham 1751-1951

Rotherham: the firm 1952   51pp illus
Beatson, Clark & Co
247   §

Greenhill, Robert G
Britain and the Cocoa Trade in Latin America before 1914

Cambridge: ca1971   34pp
Cocoa Trade
421   839   *

Greenhill, Robert G
British Export Houses, the Brazilian Coffee Houses and the Question of Control 1850-1914
Cambridge: ca1972   58pp
Coffee Trade
423   617   839   .   *

Greenhill, Robert G
British Shipping Links with South America with special reference to the Royal Mail Steam Packet Company
Exeter PhD 1971
Royal Mail Shipping Group
740

Greenhill, Robert G
The State under Pressure: The West Indian Mail Contract 1905

Business History   vol XI no 2 1969
Royal Mail Shipping Group   Elder Dempster
740   790

Greening, Edward Owen
A Democratic Co-partnership Successfully Established by the Wigston Hosiers Ltd
Leicester: Co-op Printing Soc 1921   125pp illus
Wigston Hosiers
436   LEICSPL

Greening, Edward Owen
A Pioneer Co-partnership: History of the Leicester Co-op Boot & Shoe Manufacturing Society ('Equity' Brand)
Co-partnership Assn 1923   xviii 192pp illus
Leicester Co-op Boot 'Equity'
451   LEICSPL

Greensmith, J
A History of the Fullers Earth Industry in Surrey up to 1900

Reigate: Greenwood 1983   12pp sources
Fullers Earth Union
231   *

Greenstock, Harry
 Go On and Prosper: Reminiscences of the Early Days of the Plastics Industry
 the firm 1981　　　　　　　　36pp illus
 British Xylonite Co　　　BXL Plastics
 251　　　　483　　　　　　　　　　　　　　　　§
Greenwood, George A
 Taylor of Batley: A Story of 102 Years

 Max Parrish 1957　　　　　　188pp index
 Taylor of Batley
 431　　　　　　　　　　　　　　　　　　　　*
Greenwood, J
 Jubilee of the Luddenden Industrial Co-operative Society Limited 1860-1910
 Manchester: C W S 1910　　　106pp illus
 Luddenden Industrial Co-op Soc
 656　　　　　　　　　　　　　　　　　　HLFXPL
Greg, R

 R Greg & Co Ltd

 Stockport: the firm ca1939
 Greg, R & Co
 432　　　·　　　　　　　　　　　　　　SKPTPL
Gregory, Robert & Co
 Gregory's of Liverpool: Three Score Years and Ten 1875-1945

 the firm 1945　　　　　　38pp illus
 Gregory, Robert & Co
 770　　　　　　　　　　　　　　　　　　　§
Gregory, Theodore Emanuel Gugenheim
 The Westminster Bank through a Century

 Oxford: O U P 1936　　　　2 vols illus index sources
 Westminster Bank
 814　　　　　　　　　　　　　　　　　* §
Greig, John
 The Mint: A History of the London Mint from AD 287 to 1948

 Cambridge: C U P 1953　　　450pp
 Royal Mint
 491
Gresham House Estate Company
 Gresham House Estate Company Ltd 1857-1957: Centenary Review by the Chairman
 the firm 1957
 Gresham House Estate Co
 850
Gresham Life Assurance Society
 Gresham Life Assurance Society: A Centenary Souvenir 1848-1948
 the firm 1948　　　　　　40pp illus
 Gresham Life Assurance Soc
 820　　　　　　　　　　　　　　　　　　　§

Grey, Henry **M**
> *Lloyd's Yesterday and Today*

> Syren & Shipping 1922   115pp illus
> Lloyd's of London
> 820   *

Greysmith, **Brenda**
> *The History of Staffordshire Agricultural Society*

> the firm nd   72pp illus sources
> Staffs Agricultural Soc
> 10   841   963   BCROB

Gridley **Miskin**
> *Gridley Miskin & Co Ltd 1865-1965*

> the firm 1965   16pp illus
> Gridley Miskin
> 613   KINGSPL

Grierson, **Edward**
> *A Little Farm Well Tilled*

> Keighley: the firm ca1960   84pp illus
> Dean, Smith & Grace
> 322   UBRIS

Griffin, **Alan R**
> *Mining in the East Midlands 1550-1947*

> Frank Cass 1971   xvi 338pp illus sources
> Mining in E Midlands
> 111

Griffin, **Gary Stephen**
> *H Brown (Fulham) Ltd: The Rise of a Small Retail*
> *Confectioner-Tobacconist to a Wholesale Business 1932-1978*
> typescript 1980   50pp illus sources
> Brown (Fulham), H
> 642   617   HMFULPL

Griffin, **W C**
> *The Northampton Boot and Shoe Industry...from 1800 to1914*

> Wales (Cardiff) MA 1968
> Boot and Shoe Industry
> 451

Griffiths, **A J**
> *The Industrial Estate at Bridgend*

> typescript nd   41pp sources
> Bridgend Industrial Estate
> 850   MGLAMPL

Griffiths, **Percival**
> *A History of the Inchcape Group*

> the firm 1977   211pp illus index
> Inchcape   P & O
> 740   770   839   §

Griffiths, **Percival**
A History of the Joint Steamer Companies

the firm 1979 156pp illus
Inchcape P & O
740 770 839 BLPES

Griffiths, **Thomas**
Richard Thomas & Baldwins Ltd: The History and Growth of the Company to 1948
lecture notes nd 24pp
Richard Thomas & Baldwins
221 MGLAMPL

Grimbly **Hughes**
The Story of Grimbly Hughes, Oxford Grocers

Oxford: ca1925 illus
Grimbly Hughes
641 OXFDPL

Grindlay's
Grindlay's 1828-1928

the firm 1928 15pp
Grindlay's Bank
814 §

Grindon, **Leopold Hartley**
Manchester Banks and Bankers: Historical, Biographical and Anecdotal
Manchester 1877 vi 332pp
Manchester Banks
814 * §

Grinling, **Charles Herbert**
British Railways as Business Enterprises

see Ashley, William James (ed)
Railways
710 *

Grinling, **Charles Herbert**
The History of the Great Northern Railway 1845-1922

Allen & Unwin 1966 xviii 490pp illus index
Great Northern Railway
710 *

Grinyer, **P H & Spender, J-C**
Turnaround: Managerial Recipes for Strategic Success: The Fall and Rise of Newton Chambers Group
Assoc Business Press 1979 xii 211pp illus
Newton Chambers Ransomes & Rapier
251 311 320 325 328 *

Groves, **J W P & Keith G**
The History of a Brewery 1835-1949: The...Partnership and Limited Company of the House of Groves and Whitnall
the firm 1949 32pp illus
Groves & Whitnall
427 662 * §

Guardian Assurance Co
Record of the Guardian Assurance Company Ltd 1821-1921

the firm 1921   153pp illus
Guardian Assurance Co
820   * §

Guest Keen Baldwins
Guest Keen Baldwins Iron & Steel Co Ltd

E T W Dennis 1937   68pp illus
Guest Keen Baldwins
221   MGLAMPL

Guest, Keen & Nettlefolds
Guest, Keen & Nettlefolds: An Outline History of this Group of Companies
Birmingham: the firm ca1925
GKN
313

Guinness
St. James's Gate Brewery: History and Guide

the firm 1935   110pp illus
Guinness
427   §

Gulvin, Clifford
The Scottish Hosiery and Knitwear Industry 1680-1980

Edinburgh: John Donald 1984   ix 163pp index sources
Pringle, Robert & Son   Lyle & Scott
436   *

Gulvin, Clifford
The Tweedmakers: A History of the Scottish Fancy Woollen Industry 1600-1914
Newton Abbot: David & Charles 1973 240pp illus index sources
Fancy Woollen Ind in Scotland
431   NESLS

Gulvin, Clifford (ed)
Journal of Henry Brown, Woollen Manufacturer, Galashiels 1828-1829
Scottish Ind Hist Soc 1978
Henry Brown, Woollen Mfr
431   BORDRPL

Gunston, Bill
By Jupiter! The Life of Sir Roy Fedden

Royal Aeronautical Soc 1978   ix 157pp illus index
Bristol Aeroplane Co
364   750   *

Gurr, Duncan & Hunt, J
The Cotton Mills of Oldham

Oldham Leisure Services 1985   60pp illus sources
Oldham Cotton Mills
432   §

Guttery, David Reginald
From Broad Glass to Cut Crystal: A History of the Stourbridge Glass Industry
Leonard Hill 1956   xiii 161pp illus index sources
Stourbridge Glass
247   *
Guy Motors
Forty Years of Achievement

the firm 1954   pamphlet
Guy Motors
351   §
Haber, Ludwig Fritz
From Alkali to Petrochemicals: Economic Development and Technological Diffusion: British Chemical Industry 1914-64
see Fuji Conference 6, 1979
Chemical Industry
250
Haber, Ludwig Fritz
The Chemical Industry 1900-1930: International Growth and Technical Change
Oxford: Clarendon 1971   xi 452pp sources
Chemical Industry
250   *
Haber, Ludwig Fritz
The Chemical Industry during the Nineteenth Century: The Economic Aspect of Applied Chemistry in Europe & N America
Oxford: Clarendon 1958   x 292pp sources
Chemical Industry
250   *
Hackett, Dennis
The History of the Future: The Bemrose Corporation 1826-1976

Scolar 1976   144pp illus index
Bemrose & Sons
475   §
Hacking, Barbara
Municipalisation of Bolton Gas Company 1818-1872

thesis 1968   51pp sources
Bolton Gas Co
162   BOLTNPL
Hackman, Rowan M B H
The Fleet Past and Present of Hunting & Son Ltd

Newcastle: the firm 1961   44pp illus
Hunting Group
740   750   *
Haden, George Nelson & Sons
Haden 150 Years

Newman Neame 1966   56pp illus
Haden, G N & Sons
503   *

202

Haden, Harry Jack
The Story of Mark & Moody Limited 1840-1957

Stourbridge: the firm 1958   35pp illus
Mark & Moody
653   *

Hadfields
A Short Description of Hadfields Ltd: Its History, Plant and Manufactures
Sheffield: the firm 1938
Hadfields
221   311

Hadfields
Hadfield's Steel Foundry Company Limited

Sheffield: the firm 1905
Hadfields
221   311

Hadley, Peter
The History of Bovril Advertising

the firm 1972   112pp illus
Bovril
412   838   *

Haggar, Reginald George
The Masons of Lane Delph and the Origin of Masons Patent Ironstone China
the firm 1952   xvii 104pp illus
Ashworth, G L & Bros.   Masons
248   *

Hague, D & Wilkinson, G
The I R C: An Experiment in Industrial Intervention

Allen & Unwin 1983
Industrial Reorganisation Corp
340   364

Haigh, A
History of the Meltham Industrial Co-operative Trading Society Ltd; Jubilee 1861-1911
Manchester: Co-op Printing 1911   88pp
Meltham Industrial Co-op
656   HDSFDPL

Haimes, Thomas & Co
Castle Mills: The 150th Anniversary of the Founding of the Firm of Thomas Haimes & Co Ltd
Melbourne, Derbyshire: the firm 1962 32pp illus
Haimes, Thomas & Co
436   453   *

Halford Cycle Co
50 Years of Progress 1907-1957

Edgbaston: the firm 1957   24pp illus
Halford Cycle Co
363   654   GHL

Halfpenny, E
Pickfords - Expansion and Crisis in the Early Nineteenth Century
Business History   vol I no 1; vol II no 1 1958/59
Pickfords
723

Halifax Building Society
80 Years of Home Building-the Halifax Plan: The Romantic History of the Halifax Building Society...during 84 Years
Halifax: the firm 1937   x 123pp illus
Halifax Building Society
815   *

Halifax Building Society
The Faith of 'Fifty-Three': A Brief History of the Halifax Permanent Benefit Building Society 1853-1921
Halifax: the firm 1921   95pp illus
Halifax Building Society
815   HLFXPL

Halifax Building Society
The History of the Halifax Permanent Benefit Building Society: A Jubilee Memorial of this Society
Reed & Co 1903   200pp illus
Halifax Building Society
815   HLFXPL

Halifax Flour Society
Jubilee Celebration

Manchester: Co-op Printing Soc 1897 110pp illus index
Halifax Flour Society
416   HLFXPL

Hall Harding
One Hundred Years of Family Enterprise, 1853-1953

the firm 1953   24pp
Hall Harding
330   653   GHL

Hall's Barton Ropery Co
The Story of the Hall-Mark

the firm 1975   26pp illus
Hall's Barton Ropery Co
223   439   UBRIS

Hall, F G
History of the Bank of Ireland

Dublin: Hodges Figgis 1949   viii 429pp index sources
Bank of Ireland
814   §

Hall, Fred
The History of the Co-operative Printing Society 1869-1919

Manchester: the firm 1919   352pp
Co-operative Printing Society
475   *

Hall, Philip J
> *A Handful of History: The Story of Qualter Hall & Co Ltd*
> *1860-1960*
> the firm nd 47pp
> Qualter Hall & Co
> 837 SHEFFPL

Hall, Richard
> *The Making of Molins: The Growth and Transformation of a*
> *Family Business 1874-1977*
> the firm 1978 102pp
> Molins Ltd
> 324 BLPES

Hallam, Douglas J
> *The First Two Hundred Years: A Short History of Rabone*
> *Chesterman Ltd*
> Birmingham: the firm 1984 136pp illus
> Rabone Chesterman
> 316 322 * §

Hallam, Winfield B
> *Blow Five: A History of the Alexandra Towing Company Ltd*
>
> Liverpool: Journal of Commerce 1976 107pp illus
> Alexandra Towing Co
> 763 §

Halstead, R
> *History of Walsall Locks and Cart Gear Ltd 1873-1923: Fifty*
> *Years of Co-partnership Endeavour*
> the firm ca1924 47pp illus
> Walsall Locks & Cart Gear
> 316 WALSLPL

Halstead, R
> *The Story of a Village Industrial Democracy: ...The Glenfield*
> *'Progress' Co-operative Boot and Shoe Manufacturing Society*
> Leicester: Co-op Printing Soc 1914 59pp illus
> Glenfield 'Progress' Co-op
> 451 LEICSPL

Hambro's Bank
> *Hambro's Bank, London Ltd 1839-1939*
>
> the firm 1939 43pp illus
> Hambro's Bank
> 814 §

Hammond and Hussey
> *The Hammond and Hussey Story 1769-1969*
>
> the firm 1969 20pp illus
> Hammond & Hussey
> 648 CROYPL

Hampson, Cyril G
> *150th Anniversary of Robert Fletcher & Son Ltd*
>
> Radcliffe: the firm 1973 69pp illus sources
> Fletcher, Robert & Son Cromptons
> 471 *

Hamshere, N & Sutton, J
Happy Family: The Story of Yellow Bus Services, Stoughton

authors 1978   76pp illus
Yellow Bus Services of Stoughton
721   *

Hancock, H E
Semper Fidelis: The Saga of the 'Navvies' 1924-1948: The Services of the General Steam Navigation Company
the firm 1949   xv 140pp illus index
General Steam Navigation Co
740   *

Hancock, Laurie W J
The Perkins Story

Peterborough: the firm 1969
Perkins Engine Co
351

Hancocks, H
History of Tinplate Manufacture in Llanelly

Wales (Swansea) MA 1965
Tinplate Manufacture in Llanelly
221

Hand-in-Hand Fire & Life
Hand-in-Hand Fire and Life Assurance Society Bi-Centenary Notice 12th November 1896
the firm 1896   27pp illus
Hand-in-Hand Fire and Life Ass
820   *

Hand-in-Hand Fire & Life
The Origin and History of the Hand-in-Hand Fire and Life Assurance Society
1891   32pp
Hand-in-Hand Fire and Life Ass
820   GHL

Handover, Phyllis Margaret
A History of the London Gazette 1665-1965

HMSO 1965   vii 95pp illus sources
London Gazette
475   *

Hannah, Leslie
Electricity Before Nationalisation: A Study of the Development of the Electricity Supply Industry in Britain to 1948
Macmillan 1979   xiii 467pp index sources
Electricity Supply
161   * §

Hannah, Leslie
Engineers, Managers and Politicians: The First Fifteen Years of Nationalised Electricity Supply in Britain
Macmillan 1982   xiii 336pp index sources
Electricity Supply
161   * §

Hannah, Leslie
Government and Business in Britain: The Evolution of the
Modern Relationship
see Fuji Conference 5, 1978
Government & Business

Hannah, Leslie
Managerial Innovation and the Rise of the Large-Scale Company
in Interwar Britain
Economic History Review   2nd ser vol XXVII no 2 1974

Hannah, Leslie
The Rise of the Corporate Economy: The British Experience

Methuen 1976   xii 243pp index sources
Corporate Economy
                                                                    *

Hannah, Leslie (ed)
Management Strategy and Business Development: An Historical
and Comparative Study
Macmillan 1976   xi 267pp index
Management Strategy
                                                                    *

Hanson, James & Sons
James Hanson: A Rolling Stone: Sixty Years' Retrospect
1886-1946
Liverpool: the firm   550pp illus
Hanson, J & Sons, Modern Dairies
617   641   UBRIS

Hanson, Simon G
Argentine Meat and the British Market

Oxford U P 1938   vii 294pp
Argentine Meat
412   740   770   *

Harbutts of Bath
The Plasticine People: Harbutts of Bath 1897-1972

York: William Sessions 1972
Harbutts of Bath
495

Harcourt, Freda
The P & O Company: Flagships of Imperialism

see Palmer, S R & Williams, G (eds)
P & O
740

Hardie, David William Ferguson
A History of the Chemical Industry in Widnes

the firm 1950   xi 250pp illus index sources
I C I   United Alkali Co
250   * §

207

Hardie, David William Ferguson
A History of the Modern British Chemical Industry

Oxford: Pergamon 1966   xi 380pp illus index sources
Chemical Industry
250   *

Harding, John Shepherd
*History of the Tamworth Industrial Co-operative Society Ltd
1886-1907*
Manchester: C W S 1910   222pp illus
Tamworth Industrial Co-op
656   UBRIS

Hardinge, G N
The Development and Growth of Courage's Brewery 1787-1932

the firm 1932   54pp illus
Courage & Co
427   * §

Hardinge, G N
*To Celebrate the 150th Anniversary of Courage's Brewery
1787-1937*
the firm 1937   52pp illus
Courage & Co
427   SWKPL

Hardwick Colliery Co
Williamthorpe Colliery

the firm 1946   16pp
Hardwick Colliery Co
111   DERBYPL

Hare, A E C
The Anthracite Trade of the Swansea District

Swansea: University College 1940
Anthracite Trade
111

Hargraves, Ian
*They Always Come Back: The...Owen Owen Organisation's
Contribution to the Shopping Public during the Last 100 Years*
Liverpool: the firm 1968   50pp illus
Owen Owen
656   §

Hargreaves, Henry and Sons
History of Hargreaves: A Century of Growth 1872-1972

Hargreaves, Henry & Sons
503   328   BURYPL

Hargreaves, R
*William Heaton & Sons Ltd, Lostock Junction Mills: A
Miscellany*
typescript 1974   15pp illus
Heaton, William & Sons
432   BOLTNPL

Harker, Ronald W
    The Engines Were Rolls-Royce: An Informal History of that
    Famous Company
    Collier Macmillan 1979   xxi 202pp illus index
    Rolls-Royce
    351   364   *

Harley, Basil
    A History of the Serck Group

    Solihull: the firm 1982   85pp illus
    Serck Group
    328   SOLHLPL

Harmer, F W & Co
    Story of a Norwich Industry

    Norwich: the firm 1949   25pp illus
    Harmer, F W & Co
    453   NRFLKPL

Harris and Pearson
    Harris and Pearson Ltd, Stourbridge 1852-1952: One Hundred
    Years of Firebrick Making
    Stourbridge: the firm ca1952   7pp
    Harris & Pearson
    248   DUDLYPL

Harris, C W J
    100 Years of Bookbinding in Bath

    Bath: Cedric Chivers 1978   29pp illus
    Cedric Chivers
    475   SOMPL

Harris, John Raymond
    The Copper King: A Biography of Thomas Williams of Llanidan

    Liverpool: L U P 1964   xiii 194pp index sources
    Parys & Mona Mines
    210   *

Harris, John Raymond (ed)
    Liverpool and Merseyside: Essays in the Economic and Social
    History of the Port and its Hinterland
    Frank Cass 1969   xiv 287pp index sources

    432   740   *

Harris, Leonard
    London General Shipowners' Society, 1811-1961

    the firm 1961   48pp illus
    London General Shipowners' Soc
    740   963   *

Harrison & Sons
    Harrison: A Family Imprint 1750-1950

    the firm 1950   36pp illus
    Harrison & Sons
    475   *

Harrison, **A E**
F Hopper & Co: The Problems of Capital Supply in the Cycle Manufacturing Industry 1891-1914
Business History   vol XXIV no 1 1982
Hopper, F & Co
363

Harrison, **A E**
Joint Stock Company Flotation in the Cycle, Motor-Vehicle and Related Industries 1882-1914
Business History   vol XXIII no 2 1981
Cycle & Motor Industries
350   363

Harrison, **Cecil R & H G**
The House of Harrison, Printers to the King

the firm 1914   118pp illus
Harrison & Sons
475   *

Harrison, **George & Co**
Harrisons of Edinburgh, Clothmakers 1863-1963

Edinburgh: the firm 1963   19pp illus
Harrison, George & Co
431   EDNBRPL

Harrison, **Godfrey Percival**
Borthwicks: A Century in the Meat Trade 1863-1963

the firm 1963   212pp illus
Borthwick, Thomas & Sons
412   617   * §

Harrison, **Godfrey Percival**
Bristol Cream

Batsford 1955   162pp illus index sources
Harvey, John & Sons
426   617   * §

Harrison, **Godfrey Percival**
V Y B: A Century of Metal Broking 1859-1959

the firm 1959   103pp illus index
Vivian, Younger & Bond
630   831   *

Harrisons **& Crosfield**
One Hundred Years as East India Merchants 1844-1943

the firm   69pp illus
Harrisons & Crosfield
740   839   §

Harrods
In Memoriam: Sir Richard Burbidge Bart (1917)

the firm 1917
Harrods
656

Harrop, J
Rayon

see Buxton, N K & Aldcroft, D H (eds)
Courtaulds
260   430

Hart & Levy
The Story of Hart & Levy and John Manners 1859-1959

Harley 1959   38pp illus
Hart & Levy   Manners, John
453   645   UBRIS

Harte, Negley B
A History of George Brettle & Co Ltd 1801-1964

typescript the firm 1975
Courtaulds   Brettle, George
436   DERBYPL

Harte, Negley B
A History of Samuel Heap & Son Ltd 1823-1964

typescript nd   69pp sources
Heap, Samuel & Son   Courtaulds
437   §

Hartley, Peter
Matchless: Once the Largest British Motorcycle Manufacturers

Osprey 1980   208pp illus index
Matchless
363   *

Hartley, Peter
The Story of Royal Enfield Motor Cycles

Cambridge: Patrick Stephens 1981   128pp illus index
Royal Enfield
363   329   *

Hartley, Peter
The Story of Rudge Motorcycles

Wellingborough: Stephens 1985   128pp illus index
Rudge-Whitworth
363   *

Hartwell, R M
The Yorkshire Woollen and Worsted Industries 1800-1850

Oxford DPhil 1955
Yorkshire Woollen and Worsted
431

Harvey & Beard
Harvey & Son and Beard & Co of Lewes, Founded 1790

Martlet 1977   48pp
Harvey & Beard
427   ESUSXPL

Harvey, Charles E
*Business History and the Problem of Entrepreneurship: The
Case of the Rio Tinto Company 1873-1939*
Business History   vol XXI no 1 1979
Rio Tinto
839
Harvey, Charles E
*The Rio Tinto Company: An Economic History of a Leading
International Mining Concern 1873-1954*
Penzance: Alison Hodge 1981   xiv 390pp index sources
Rio Tinto
210   224   839   * §
Harvey, Charles Malcolm Barclay
A History of the Great North of Scotland Railway

Locomotive Publishing 1949   231pp illus index
Great North of Scotland Railway
710   *
Harvey-Bailey, Alec H
Rolls-Royce: Hives, the Quiet Tiger

Paulerspury: Royce Mem Found 1985   101pp illus
Rolls-Royce
328   351   364   §
Harvey-Bailey, Alec H
Rolls-Royce: The Formative Years 1906-1939

Derby:Rolls-Royce Heritage 1982   95pp illus
Rolls-Royce
328   351   364   * §
Haselgrove, D & Murray, J (eds)
*John Dwight's Fulham Pottery 1672-1978: A Collection of
Documentary Sources*
Journal of Ceramic Hist   no 11 1979
Fulham Pottery
248   HMFULPL
Haskins & Sells
Haskins & Sells: Our First Seventy Five Years

Garland 1984   192pp
Haskins & Sells
836
Haslam, James
*Accrington and Church Industrial Co-operative Society
Limited: History of Fifty Years' Progress 1860-1910*
Manchester: Co-op Newspaper 1910   208pp illus
Accrington Industrial Co-op Soc
656   *
Haslam, James
*History of Fifty Years Progress: Eccles Provident Industrial
Co-operative Society Jubilee 1857-1907*
Manchester: the firm 1907   235pp illus
Eccles Provident Ind Co-op
656   SALFDPL

212

Haslam, James
Woolfold Co-operative Society Ltd, Bury: History of Fifty Years' Progress: Jubilee 1865-1915
the firm nd   illus
Woolfold Co-op Soc, Bury
656   BURYPL

Haslam, Malcolm
The Martin Brothers, Potters

Richard Dennis 1978   174pp illus index sources
Martinware   Martin Brothers, Potters
248   EALNGPL

Haslam, William Heywood & Morris, F E
John Haslam & Co Ltd 1816-1920

Bolton: the firm 1971   13pp illus
Haslam, John & Co
432   BOLTNPL

Hawick Co-operative Store Co
History of the Hawick Co-operative Store Company Limited 1839-1888
Hawick: the firm 1889   111pp
Hawick Co-operative Store Co
656

Hawkins, Alexander
Alexander Hawkins & Sons Ltd: Centenary 1844-1944

the firm 1944   12pp illus
Hawkins, Alexander
648   SWKPL

Hawkins, Kevin H
A History of Bass Charrington

Oxford: the firm 1978   ix 228pp illus sources
Bass Charrington   Charrington & Co
427   662   §

Hawkins, Kevin H
The Conduct and Development of the Brewing Industry in England and Wales 1880-1938
Bradford PhD 1983
Brewing Industry
427

Hawkins, Kevin H & Pass, C L
The Brewing Industry: A Study in Industrial Organisation and Public Policy
Heinemann 1979   ix 169pp illus index
Brewing Industry
427   *

Hay's Wharf
Some Facts about Hay's Wharf

1966   51pp
Hay's Wharf
763   GHL

Hay's Wharf Cartage Co
> *Transport Saga 1646-1947*

> the firm 1947   63pp illus
> Hay's Wharf   Pickfords
> 723   §

Hay, William
> *William Hay Limited*

> Hull: the firm ca1948   78pp illus
> Hay, William
> 257   UBRIS

Haybittle, J
> *Gillett & Johnston Ltd.: Bellfounders of Croydon: A History 1844-1950*
> Sheffield BA 1985   54pp
> Gillett & Johnston
> 311   CROYPL

Hayes, P A
> *The Houldsworth Cotton Mill and its Community 1866-1976*

> typescript 1976
> Fine Cotton Spinners & Doublers   Houldsworth
> 432   SKPTPL

Hayman, Leslie C R
> *An Account of W Williams & Son (Bread Street) Limited 1819-1975*
> the firm nd   28pp illus
> Williams, W & Son (Bread Street)
> 616   645   656   GLROHL

Hayward, R A
> *Fairbairns of Manchester: The History of an Engineering Works in the Nineteenth Century*
> Manchester (UMIST) MSc 1971
> Fairbairns of Manchester
> 320

Haywards
> *Years of Reflection 1783-1953: The Story of Haywards of the Borough*
> Harley 1953   106pp illus
> Haywards of the Borough
> 221   247   314   613   615   *

Hazell, Stanley
> *A Record of the First Hundred Years of the National Provident Institution for Mutual Life Assurance 1835-1935*
> the firm 1935   96pp illus sources
> National Provident Institution
> 820   * §

Hazell, Watson & Viney
> *Hazells in Aylesbury 1867-1967: A Scrapbook to Commemorate the First 100 Years*
> the firm 1968   188pp illus
> Hazell, Watson & Viney
> 475   §

Hazzlewood, T
    Pittards 1826-1976: A Commemorative History

    Yeovil: the firm 1976   80pp illus
    Pittard, C W & Co
    441   SOMPL

Head, Victor
    A Triumph of Hope: The Story of the National Farmers' Union Mutual Insurance Society Limited
    Stratford-upon-Avon: the firm 1985 125pp illus index
    Farmers' Mutual Insurance Soc
    820   §

Heal, David Walter
    The Steel Industry in Post-War Britain

    Newton Abbot: David & Charles 1974 224pp illus
    Steel Industry
    221   *

Heaton, Paul Michael
    Reardon Smith Line: The History of a South Wales Shipping Venture
    Risca, Newport: Starling Press 1984 133pp illus sources
    Reardon Smith Line
    740   *

Heaton, Paul Michael
    The Abbey Line: History of a Cardiff Shipping Venture

    Risca, Newport: Starling Press 1983 151pp illus
    Abbey Line
    740   * §

Heaton, Paul Michael
    The Usk Ships: History of a Newport Shipping Venture

    Risca, Newport: Starling Press 1982 88pp illus
    Usk Ships
    740   *

Hebden Bridge Fustian
    Hebden Bridge Fustian Manufacturing Co-op Soc: Report of the Coming-of-Age Celebrations, Sept 23rd & 26th 1891
    Hebden Bridge: Co-op News 1891   93pp illus
    Hebden Bridge Fustian Mfr Co-op
    432   HLFXPL

Hebden Bridge Ind Co-op Soc
    A Century's Progress 1848-1948

                           24pp illus
    Hebden Bridge Industrial Co-op
    656   HLFXPL

Hebden, C Donald
    The Trustee Savings Bank of Yorkshire and Lincoln: The Story of its Formation and of its Six Constituents
    Hull: the firm 1981   382pp illus
    Trustee Savings Bank of Yorks
    814   *

Hedges, J A
Crisis and Rationalisation in the English Cotton Industry 1928-34
Bristol PhD 1983
Cotton Industry
432

Hellyer, Bertram
Under Eight Reigns: George I - George V

the firm ca1930   136pp illus
Dent & Hellyer
503   613   BLPES

Helps, Arthur
Life and Labours of Mr Brassey 1805-1870

Bath: Adams & Dart nd
Building Railways
502   710

Hempstead, C A (ed)
Cleveland Iron and Steel: Background and Nineteenth Century History
Redcar: the firm 1979   x 275pp illus
British Iron & Steel Corporation
221   *

Henckel du Buisson & Co
Henckel du Buisson & Co Ltd 1697-1947

the firm 1948   43pp
Henckel du Buisson & Co
617   §

Henderson, A J
Progress of the Prince Line

the firm 1949
Prince Line
740

Henderson, A J
Under the Furness Flag

C Birchall & Son 1951   24pp
Furness, Withy & Co
740   GHL

Henderson, Hogg & Co
Henderson, Hogg & Co: 100

Paisley: James Paton 1970   40pp illus
Henderson, Hogg & Co
612   617   RNFRWPL

Henderson, Thomas
The Savings Bank of Glasgow: One Hundred Years of Thrift

Glasgow: the firm 1936   xii 91pp illus
Savings Bank of Glasgow
814   *

Hendry, John
Prolonged Negotiations: The British Fast Computer Project and the Early History of the British Computer Industry
Business History   vol XXVI no 3 1984
Ferranti   Elliott Brothers
330
Hennessey, Roger Anthony Sean
The Electric Revolution

Newcastle upon Tyne: Oriel 1972   x 190pp illus
Electrical Industry
340   *
Hennessy, Elizabeth
Stockbrokers for 150 Years: A History of Sheppards and Chase 1827-1977
the firm 1978   68pp illus sources
Sheppards & Chase
831   §
Henriques, Robert David Quixano
Marcus Samuel, First Viscount Bearsted and Founder of the Shell Transport and Trading Company 1853-1927
Barrie & Rockliff 1960   xi 676pp illus index sources
Shell   Royal Dutch/Shell
130   140   612   652   *
Henriques, Robert David Quixano
Sir Robert Waley Cohen 1877-1952: A Biography

Secker & Warburg 1966   424pp illus

814   815   *
Henry, James Archibald
The First Hundred Years of the Standard Bank

Oxford U P 1963   ix 371pp illus index sources
Standard Bank
814   839   * §
Herbert, Alfred
Alfred Herbert Ltd: A Coventry Firm 1888-1983

Coventry City Council 1983   19pp illus sources
Herbert, Alfred
322   COVNPL
Herbert, Charles
A Merchant Adventurer: Being the Biography of Leonard Hugh Bentall, Kingston upon Thames
Waterlow 1936   163pp illus index
Bentalls of Kingston
656   *
Hercock, Robert J & Jones, George A
Silver by the Ton: The History of Ilford Ltd. 1879-1979

McGraw-Hill 1979   170pp illus index sources
Ilford
259   * §

Herring, Daw & Manners
Herring, Daw and Manners:- Surveyors, Valuers and Estate Agents
the firm 1973   pamphlet
Herring, Daw & Manners
834   837   §

Herrmann, Frank
Sotheby's: Portrait of an Auction House

Chatto & Windus 1980   xxvi 468pp illus index sources
Sotheby Parke Bernet
654   839   * §

Herson, John D
Industrial Restructuring and a Small Firm: The Case of Adamsez Ltd
Progress in Planning   vol 20 no 1 1983
Adamsez
248   BLPES

Hertner, P & Jones, G
Multinationals: Theory and History

Aldershot: Gower 1986   200pp index sources

Hesketh, Everard
J & E Hall Ltd 1785 to 1935

Glasgow: G U P 1935   viii 58pp illus
Hall, J & E
320   325   351   * §

Hetherington, G
Portrait of a Company: Thermal Syndicate Limited 1906-1981

Wallsend: the firm 1981   253pp
Thermal Syndicate
248   SciMus

Hetherington, G
Portrait of a Company: Thermal Syndicate Ltd 1906-1981

the firm 1981   xv 253pp illus
Thermal Syndicate
248

Hewins, Ralph
Mr. Five Per Cent: The Biography of Calouste Gulbenkian

Hutchinson 1957   xix 254pp illus
Iraq Petroleum Co   Royal Dutch/Shell
130   140   251   *

Hewit, J & Sons
J Hewit & Sons Ltd, Tanners and Leather Dressers 1806-1956

Edinburgh: the firm nd   20pp illus
Hewit, J & Sons
441   EDNBRPL

Hewlett, C J & Son
A Century of Progress

the firm 1932   35pp illus
Hewlett, C J & Son
257   §

Heydemann, N & Co
Centenary of N Heydemann & Co Ltd, Bradford 1852-1952

the firm nd   29pp illus
Heydemann, N & Co
431   630   UBRIS

Heyes, Philip
The Protector Lamp and Lighting Company Limited 1873-1973:
The First Hundred Years
Eccles, Manchester: the firm 1973   54pp illus
Protector Lighting Company
343   347   §

Heywood, Arthur Sons & Co
Arthur Heywood Sons & Co 1773-1883

Heywood, Arthur Sons & Co   Martins Bank
814   §

Hibbs, John
The History of British Bus Services

Newton Abbot: David & Charles 1968 280pp illus
Bus Services
721   *

Hick, Hargreaves & Co
100 Years of Engineering Progress: 1833-1933 at the Soho
Ironworks, Bolton
Bolton: the firm 1933   20pp illus
Hick, Hargreaves & Co   Soho Ironworks, Bolton
310   320   328   BOLTNPL

Hicks, Agnes Hedvig
The Story of the Forestal

the firm 1956   viii 102pp illus
Forestal Land Timber & Railways
441   815   839   850   * §

Hidy, Ralph Willard
The House of Baring in American Trade and Finance: English
Merchant Bankers at Work 1763-1861
Cambridge, Mass: Harvard U P 1949   xxiv 631pp illus index
Baring Brothers
814   *

Higgins, J P
A History of W M Christy and Sons 1833-1913

Christy, W M & Sons   Courtaulds
432

219

Higgs & Hill
50th Anniversary of Higgs & Hill Ltd. 1898-1948

the firm 1948   39pp illus
Higgs & Hill
500   MRC

Higgs & Hill
Higgs & Hill 1874-1974

New Malden: Crown Journal   no 178 1974
Higgs & Hill
500   MRC

Higham, Robin David Stewart
*Britain's Imperial Air Routes 1918 to 1939: The Story of
Britain's Overseas Airlines*
G T Foulis 1960   407pp illus sources
Imperial Airways
750   *

Higham, Robin David Stewart
*The British Rigid Airship 1908-1931: A Study in Weapons
Policy*
G T Foulis 1961   xxii 426pp illus
Royal Airship Works   Vickers
364   *

Highet, Campbell
The Glasgow and South Western Railway

Lingfield: Oakwood Press 1965   92pp illus index sources
Glasgow & South Western Railway
710   *

Highland Railway Company
*The Highland Railway Company and its Constituents and
Successors 1855-1955*
Stephenson Locomotive Soc 1955   121pp illus
Highland Railway Company
710   ABRDNPL

Hiley, Edgar Nathaniel
Brass Saga

Benn 1957   166pp illus index
National Brass Foundry Assoc
316   * §

Hill, Brian
Whitbread's Brewery

the firm 1951   92pp illus index sources
Whitbread & Co
427   662   BLPES

Hill, Edwin Darley (ed)
*The Northern Banking Company Limited: A Century of Banking in
Ireland by the First Joint-Stock Bank Established 1824-1924*
Belfast: M'Caw,Stephenson 1925   xv 301pp
Northern Banking Co
814   *

Hill, G W
Electricity Supply in the South of England after 1930

Strathclyde MLitt 1983
Electricity Supply
161

Hill, Howard
Secret Ingredient: The Story of Fletchers' Seven Bakeries

Wakefield: E P Publishing 1978   94pp illus index
Fletchers
419   CROYPL

Hill, John Charles Gathorne
Shipshape and Bristol Fashion

Liverpool: Journal of Commerce 1952 viii 110pp illus
Bristol City Line   Hill, Charles & Sons
740   UBRIS

Hill, Mervyn Frederick
Magadi: The Story of the Magadi Soda Company

Birmingham: Kynoch 1964   x 199pp illus
Magadi Soda Co   Brunner, Mond
251   *

Hill, N K
*The History of the Imperial Continental Gas Association
1824-1900: A Study in British Economic Enterprise in...Europe*
London PhD 1951
Imperial Continental Gas
162   839

Hillier, Bevis
Asprey of Bond Street 1781-1981

Quartet 1981   144pp illus index
Asprey & Co
654   *

Hillier, Richard
Clay That Burns: A History of the Fletton Brick Industry

the firm 1981   100pp illus index sources
London Brick Co
241   * §

Hills, Richard L
Beyer Peacock: Locomotive Builders to the World

Glossop: Transport Publishing 1982   302pp illus index sources
Beyer Peacock
362   IMECHE

Hilton, J A
A History of the Medway Navigation Company

author nd   37pp
Medway Navigation Co
740

Hilton, John Peter
   Britain's First Municipal Savings Bank, ie that in Birmingham:
   The Romance of a Great Achievement
   Leicester: Blackfriars Press 1927   xvii 251pp
   Birmingham Municipal Savings
   814   *

Hinckley U D Council Gas Department
   A Short History of the Hinckley Gas Supply

   Hinckley: the firm 1945   28pp illus
   Hinckley Gas
   162   LEICSPL

Hinde, F & Sons
   Story of Norwich Silks: The Manufacture of Silks by Fras. Hinde
   & Sons Ltd from 1810 to the Present Time
   Norwich: the firm 1948   63pp illus
   Hinde, F & Sons
   432   NRFLKPL

Hindle, Wilfrid Hope
   The 'Morning Post' 1772-1937: Portrait of a Newspaper

   Routledge 1937   xi 260pp
   Morning Post
   475   *

Hindley, Charles
   The History of the Catnach Press at Berwick-upon-Tweed,
   Alnwick, Newcastle-upon-Tyne and Seven Dials, London
   Charles Hindley 1886   308pp illus index
   Catnach Press
   475   *

Hirst
   Smoke Rings 1815-1965: The Story of the House of Hirst

   the firm nd   pamphlet
   Hirst   Great Northern Tobacco Co
   429   642   §

Hirst, Geo C
   History of C J Hirst and Sons Ltd; Fancy Woollen Manufacturers

   Huddersfield: Wheatley Dyson 1942   60pp illus sources
   Hirst, C J & Sons
   431   HDSFDPL

Hirst, Hugo
   Two Autobiographical Fragments

   Business History   vol XXVIII no 1 1986
   G E C
   340

Hoare, Henry Peregrine Rennie
   Hoare's Bank: A Record 1672-1955: The Story of a Private Bank

   Collins 1955   116pp illus
   Hoare's Bank
   814   §

Hobbs, Hart & Co
A Century of Making Security Equipment 1851-1951

1951   24pp
Hobbs, Hart & Co
316   GHL

Hobson
Hobson: A Personal Story of Fifty Years

Wolverhampton: the firm 1953   49pp Illus
Hobson, H M
764   RAeS

Hobson, H; Knightley, P & Russell, L
The Pearl of Days: An Intimate Memoir of 'The Sunday Times'
1822-1972
Hamish Hamilton 1972   506pp illus index
Sunday Times
475   StBRDS

Hobson, Oscar Rudolf
A Hundred Years of the Halifax: The History of the Halifax
Building Society 1853-1953
Batsford 1953   x 190pp illus index sources
Halifax Building Society
815   * §

Hobson, Oscar Rudolf
The Post Office Savings Bank 1861-1961

H M S O 1961   23pp illus
Post Office Savings Bank
814   ABRDNPL

Hodder, T K
Sutton's at Reading

Journal Royal Horticultural Soc   vol LXXXI no 5 1956
Sutton's Seeds
10   BERKSPL

Hodge Group
A Short History of Gwent and the Hodge Group

the firm 1963
Hodge Group
814   820

Hodges, Sheila
Gollancz: The Story of a Publishing House 1928-1978

Gollancz 1978   256pp illus index sources
Gollancz, Victor
475   * §

Hodgson, Geoffrey
Lloyd's of London: A Reputation at Risk

Allen Lane 1984   378pp index
Lloyd's of London
820   §

Hodgson, H
Fifty Years of Co-operation in Great Horton and District: Jubilee History of Great Horton Co-operative 1859-1909
Manchester: Co-operative Soc 1909   191pp
Great Horton Co-operative Soc
656

Hodson, George & F W
History and Description of the Loughborough Waterworks

the firm 1906   63pp
Loughborough Waterworks
170   LEICSPL

Hoe, Susanna
The Man Who Gave his Company Away: A Biography of Ernest Bader; Founder, Scott Bader Commonwealth
Heinemann 1978   xiii 242pp illus index sources
Scott Bader & Co
251   255   *

Hogg, James (ed)
Fortunes Made in Business

Griffith, Farren 1891   406pp illus
Fortunes Made in Business

Hogg, Oliver Frederick Gillilan
The Royal Arsenal: Its Background, Origins and Subsequent History
Oxford U P 1963   2 vols illus
Royal Arsenal
329   *

Holden & Brooke
Holden & Brooke Ltd 1883-1983: The First Hundred Years

the firm 1983
Holden & Brooke
328

Holden, L T
The Rise of the Motor Industry at Luton 1914-45

Open University MPhil 1984
Vauxhall Motors   General Motors
351

Holden, M
William Holden of Belper 1850-1934: The Years Between

author 1983   31pp illus
Holden, William of Belper
467

Holland, Hannen & Cubitts
This is Cubitts

the firm 1975   85pp
Holland, Hannen & Cubitts
500   MRC

Hollerith Group
The Tabulator, Golden Jubilee Issue July 1958

the firm 1958   55pp illus
Hollerith Group
330   §

Hollett, Dave
From Cumberland to Cape Horn: Thomas and John Brocklebank of Whitehaven and Liverpool: The World's Oldest Shipping Co
Fairplay 1984   204pp index sources
Brocklebank Line
740   *

Holliday, Bob
The Story of B S A Motor Cycles

Cambridge: Patrick Stephens 1978   128pp illus index
B S A
363   *

Hollowood, Albert Bernard
Cornish Engineers: A History of Holman Brothers Ltd of Camborne
Camborne: the firm 1951   95pp illus
Holman Bros
328   §

Hollowood, Albert Bernard
The story of J & G Meakin

the firm nd   64pp illus
Meakin, J & G
248   BLPES

Hollowood, Albert Bernard
The Story of Morro Velho

the firm 1955   88pp illus
St John d'el Rey Mining Co
210   839   * §

Holmes, Graeme M
Fifty Years of British Benzol: A History of British Benzol and Coal Distillation Ltd
Cardiff: the firm 1979
British Benzol & Coal Distillation
120   140   162

Holmes, W C
100 Years of Service 1850-1950

Manchester: Cross Courtenay 1950   64pp illus
Holmes, W C & Co
320   HDSFDPL

Holmes, W C
W C Holmes & Co Ltd 1850-1950

Huddersfield: typescript ca1950   6pp
Holmes, W C & Co
320   HDSFDPL

Holt, Cecil R (ed)
The Diary of John Holt with the Voyage of the 'Maria'

Liverpool: the firm 1948   xxvii 279pp illus
Holt, John & Co
740   839   §

Holt, John
Merchant Adventure: John Holt & Co (Liverpool) Ltd

Liverpool: the firm 1947   80pp illus
Holt, John & Co
740   839   §

Holt, John Alphonse
The Early Years of an African Trader: John Holt Who Sailed for West Africa on 23rd June 1862
Newman Neame nd   28pp
Holt, John & Co
740   839   *

Holyoake, George Jacob
The History of Co-operation in England   *also author of many histories of individual co-operative societies*
T Fisher Unwin 1908   xxi 691pp illus
Co-operation in England
610   656   *

Holyoake, George Jacob
The History of the Rochdale Pioneers 1844-1892

Swan Sonnenschein 1907   191pp
Rochdale Pioneers
656   UBRIS

Holyoake, George Jacob
The Jubilee History of the Leeds Industrial Co-operative Society from 1847-1897 Traced Year by Year
Leeds: the firm 1897   xii 260pp illus
Leeds Industrial Co-operative Soc
656   *

Home, Gordon
The Great Western Railway

A & C Black 1913   iv 92pp illus
Great Western Railway
710   ABRDNPL

Honeycombe, Gordon
Selfridges: Seventy Five Years: The Story of a Store 1909-1984
the firm 1984   240pp illus index sources
Selfridges
656   * §

Hook, Elizabeth
A Guide to the Papers of John Swire and Sons Ltd

London U Sch Oriental...Studies 1977 176pp sources
Butterfield & Swire   Swire, John & Sons
740   770   839   *

Hoole, Kenneth
North Road Locomotive Works, Darlington 1863-1966

Roundhouse Books 1967   xiv 102pp illus
Darlington Locomotive Works
362   *

Hooper, W & Co
A Record of the History and Peculiarities of the Business of W Hooper & Co
nd
Hooper, W & Co
643   GHL

Hoover
Opening of the Factory of Hoover Limited at Pentrebach, Merthyr Tidfil, October 12th 1948
the firm 1948   89pp
Hoover
342   346   MRTHRPL

Hope, Henry & Sons
A Short History of Henry Hope & Sons Ltd, Halford Works, Smethwick, Birmingham 1818-1958
Smethwick: the firm 1958   33pp illus
Hope, Henry & Sons
314   *

Hope, Iain
The Campbells of Kilmun: Shipowners 1853-1980

Johnstone: Aggregate Publ 1981   86pp illus
Campbell, P & A
740   *

Hopkin & Williams
Hopkin & Williams Ltd: A Century of Progress 1850-1950

Chadwell Heath: the firm 1950   36pp illus
Hopkin & Williams
256   WMNSTPL

Hopkins, Charles Henry Gordon
Pallion 1874-1954: Church and People in a Shipyard Parish

Sunderland: Wearside Printing 1954 143pp illus
Short Brothers
361   *

Hopkins, Leon
The Hundredth Year

Macdonald & Evans 1980
Cooper Brothers & Co
836

Hopkinson
The Hopkinson Story

the firm 1981   16pp illus
Hopkinsons
328   HDSFDPL

Hopwood, Bert
Whatever Happened to the British Motorcycle Industry

Yeovil: Haynes 1981   315pp illus index
Motorcycle Industry
363   *

Hornby & Clarke
The Ideal District with the Ideal Service (Farm & Dairy)

Ed J Burrow 1930   32pp illus
Hornby & Clarke
10   413   RCHMDPL

Horne, H Oliver
A History of Savings Banks

the firm 1947   xii 407pp
Trustee Savings Bank
814

Horne, H Oliver
Ellon Savings Bank 1839-1939

Aberdeen Journals 1939   19pp illus
Ellon Savings Bank
814

Horne, H Oliver
Insch and Upper Garioch Savings Bank 1838-1938
and many other titles
Aberdeen Journals 1938   25pp illus
Insch, Upper Garioch Savings Bank
814

Hornsby, R M
History of the Consett Iron Company

Consett the firm 1958
Consett Iron Co
221

Horrockses, Crewdson & Co
Cotton: The Magic Transformation

Manchester: the firm 1936   39pp illus
Horrockses, Crewdson & Co
432   BOLTNPL

Horrockses, Crewdson & Co
History, Origin and Development of the Firm of Horrockses,
Crewdson & Co Ltd 1791-1912
Preston: the firm 1913
Horrockses, Crewdson & Co
432

Horrockses, Crewdson & Co
The Story of Horrockses: Founded 1791

Preston: the firm 1950   68pp illus
Horrockses, Crewdson & Co
430   BLPES

Horsfall, John H C
The Iron Masters of Penns 1720-1970

    Kineton: Roundwood 1971   xii 331pp illus index sources
    Webster & Horsfall
    221   223   *

Horsley, Smith & Co
Horsley, Smith & Co 1871-1971

    Norwich: the firm ca1971   10pp
    Horsley, Smith & Co   Jewson & Sons
    613   NRFLKPL

Houghton, J C & Co
Fruitful Years 1852-1952: The Centenary of J C Houghton & Co

    Liverpool: the firm nd   26pp illus
    Houghton, J C & Co
    617   630   §

House, Jack
A Century of Box-Making: A History of Andrew Ritchie and Son Limited from 1850 to 1950
    Glasgow: the firm 1950   77pp illus
    Ritchie, Andrew & Son
    464   472   483   *

House, Jack
A Family Affair: The Story of David Carlaw & Sons Ltd of Glasgow
    Edinburgh: the firm 1960   70pp illus
    Carlaw, David & Sons
    327   614   *

House, Jack
Lochrin's Hundred Years: The Story of William Bain & Co Ltd of Coatbridge
    Edinburgh: the firm ca1959   92pp illus
    Bain, William & Co   Lochrin's
    221   223   320   *

House, Jack
Pride of Perth: The Story of Arthur Bell & Sons Ltd.: Scotch Whisky Distillers
    Hutchinson Benham 1984   135pp illus
    Bell, Arthur & Son
    424   * §

House, Jack
Robert Paterson, Builder 1827-1977

                              96pp illus
    Paterson, Robert
    501   AIRDRPL

House, Jack
The Plumber in Glasgow: The History of the Firm of Hugh Twaddle & Son Ltd, Glasgow from 1848 to 1948
    Glasgow: the firm 1949   63pp illus
    Twaddle, Hugh & Son
    503   *

Houseman, Lorna
The House that Thomas Built: The Story of De La Rue

Chatto & Windus 1968   xv 207pp illus index sources
de la Rue, Thomas
475   * §

Houston, Henry James
The Real Horatio Bottomley

Hurst & Blackett 1923   287pp illus
John Bull
475   831   *

Howard & Sons
Howards 1797-1947

Ilford: the firm 1947   25pp illus
Howard & Sons
257   643   UBRIS

Howard Rotovator Co
1938-1967

West Horndon: nd   8pp illus
Howard Rotovator Co
321   MRC

Howard, John & Son
The Britannia Ironworks, Bedford

The Engineer   vol 30, 1870
Howard, John & Son
321

Howard, Michael Spencer
Jonathan Cape, Publisher: Herbert Jonathan Cape, G Wren Howard
Cape 1971   351pp illus index sources
Jonathan Cape
475   * §

Howard, Peter Dunsmore
Beaverbrook: A Study of Max the Unknown

Hutchinson 1964   164pp
Express Newspapers   Beaverbrook Press
475   *

Howard, R B
Amicable and Fraternal Society: Summary of its History to 1890
1903   48pp
Amicable and Fraternal Soc
820   GHL

Howarth, William
Barclay and Company Limited: Being a History of the Old Banking Firm...and...Various Institutions...Amalgamated
Lombard Press 1901   72pp
Barclays Bank
814   *

Howarth, William
The Three Crowns and the Lucky Guinea: Being an Account of the Famous Banking House of Messrs Coutts & Co
Lombard Press 1900   33pp
Coutts & Co
814   GHL

Howden, Alexander
Alexander Howden: 150 Years of Shipping and Insurance

1972   16pp
Howden, Alexander
832   GHL

Howden, James & Co
A Hundred Years of Howden Engineering: A Brief History 1854-1954
Glasgow: the firm nd   56pp illus
Howden, James & Co
328   UBRIS

Howe, Anthony
The Cotton Masters 1830-1860

Oxford: Clarendon 1984   359pp sources
Cotton Industry
432   *

Howe, Anthony C
Churchmen and Cotton Masters in Victorian England

see Jeremy, David J (ed) 1987
Cotton Masters
432

Howe, Ellic
Bushills: The Story of a Coventry Firm of Printers and Boxmakers 1856-1956
Coventry: the firm 1956   66pp illus
Bushills
472   475   *

Howe, L
The North Staffordshire Coalfield

Keele MA 1982
North Staffs Coalfield
111

Howitt, Harold Gibson
The History of the Institute of Chartered Accountants in England and Wales 1870-1965
Heinemann 1966   xiv 269pp illus index sources
Chartered Accountants
836   963   * §

Howse, R M & Harley, F H
History of the Mining Engineering Company 1909-1959

Worcester: the firm 1959   123pp illus
Mining Engineering Co
325   §

Hubback, David
> *No Ordinary Press Baron: A Life of Walter Layton*

    Weidenfeld & Nicolson 1985   271pp illus index sources
    Economist   Associated Newspapers
    475   BLPES

Hudson, Bramwell
> *History of Co-operation in Cainscross and District: Jubilee of the Cainscross & Ebley Co-operative Society 1863-1913*
> the firm 1913   166pp illus
> Cainscross & Ebley Co-op
> 656   UBRIS

Hudson, Graham S
> *The Aberford Railway and the History of the Garforth Collieries*
> Newton Abbot: David & Charles 1971 184pp illus index sources
> Aberford Railway   Garforth Collieries
> 111   710   §

Hudson, Kenneth
> *The Bath and West: A Bicentenary History 1976*

    Moonraker 1976   251pp illus index sources
    Bath & West Agricultural Soc
    10   841   963   BCROB

Hudson, Kenneth
> *The Bowler Collection*

    Bath Industrial Trust 1978   8pp illus
    Bowler, J B
    224   SOMPL

Hudson, Kenneth
> *The History of English China Clays: Fifty Years of Pioneering & Growth*
> Newton Abbot: David & Charles 1968 189pp illus index
> English China Clays
> 231   245   *

Hudson, Kenneth
> *Towards Precision Shoemaking: C & J Clark and the Development of the British Shoe Industry*
> Newton Abbot: David & Charles 1968 109pp illus index
> Clark, C & J
> 451   *

Hudson, Pat
> *The Role of Banks in the Finance of the West Yorkshire Wool Textile Industry ca1780-1850*
> Business History Review   vol LV no 3 1981
> WestRiding Wool Textile Ind
> 431

Hughes, F A
> *F A Hughes Centenary Year*

    Epsom: the firm 1969
    Hughes, F A   Distillers Co
    250

Hughes, Fielden
Into the Future: The Continuing Story of the Temperance Permanent Builing Society
the firm ca1971   99pp illus
Temperance Permanent Bldg Soc
815   §
Hughes, John
Liverpool Banks and Bankers 1760-1837

Liverpool: Henry Young 1906   xvi 243pp illus index
Liverpool Banks
814
Hughes, William J & Thomas, Joseph L
The Sentinel: A History of Alley & MacLellan and the Sentinel Waggon Works vol 1- 1875-1930
Newton Abbot: David & Charles 1973 320pp illus index
Alley & MacLellan
362   *
Hugill, Antony
Sugar and All That: A History of Tate & Lyle

Gentry 1978   320pp illus index sources
Tate & Lyle
420   * §
Hulanicki, Barbara
From A to Biba

Hutchinson 1983   168pp illus
Biba
645   *
Hulme, A G
Squirrel Horn Ltd

typescript 1967
Squirrel Horn
421   SKPTPL
Hume, John R & Moss, Michael S
A Bed of Nails: The History of P MacCallum & Sons Ltd of Greenock 1781-1981: A Study in Survival
Greenock: Lang & Fulton 1981   xii 148pp illus index sources
MacCallum, P & Sons
361   * §
Hume, John R & Moss, Michael S
Beardmore: The History of a Scottish Industrial Giant

Heinemann 1979   xx 364pp illus index sources
Beardmore, William & Co
311   320   351   361   *
Humpherson, L H
The First Hundred Years of the Marine and General Mutual Life Assurance Society
the firm 1952   46pp illus
Marine & General Mutual Life
820   §

Humphreys, B K
>*Trooping and the Development of the British Independent Airlines*
>Journal of Transport History   new ser vol V no 1 1979
>Independent Airlines
>750

Hunt Edmunds & Co
>*Hunt Edmunds & Co Ltd 1896-1946: With an Account of the Earlier Forms of the Business*
>Banbury: the firm 1946   47pp illus
>Hunt Edmunds & Co
>427   §

Hunt, Leslie B
>*George Matthey and the Building of the Platinum Industry*
>
>Platinum Metals Review 1979
>Johnson, Matthey
>224

Hunt, R
>*The Rise and Progress of Steam Cultivation at Watling Works, Stony Stratford, Bucks*
>Birmingham: the firm 1863   19pp
>Martin & Son
>321   ICIVILE

Hunt, Roope & Co
>*The Story and Origin of Hunt, Roope & Co 1395-1951*
>
>the firm 1951   32pp illus
>Hunt, Roope & Co
>426   GHL

Hunt, Wallis
>*Heirs of Great Adventure: The History of Balfour, Williamson & Company Ltd 1851-1951*
>the firm 1957-60   2 vols illus index
>Balfour, Williamson
>740   770   839   * §

Hunting & Son
>*Centenary Review*
>
>Hunting Fleet Magazine   no 80, 1974
>Hunting Group
>740   750

Hunting, Percy
>*The Group and I: An Account of the Hunting Group*
>
>the firm 1968   xi 136pp illus
>Hunting Group
>740   750   * §

Huntley & Palmers
>*The History of Huntley and Palmers Ltd*
>
>Reading: the firm 1927   24pp illus
>Huntley & Palmers
>419   BERKSPL

Huntley & Palmers
The Progress of Biscuit Town in the Nineteenth Century

the firm ca1900   59pp illus
Huntley & Palmers
419   MRC

Huntley & Palmers
The Seventh Wonder of the Commercial World

the firm ca1910   12pp illus
Huntley & Palmers
419   MRC

Huntsman, Benjamin
A Brief History of the Firm of B Huntsman Ltd. 1742-1930

Sheffield 1930
Huntsman, B
221   SHEFFPL

Hurd, Edgar
Eighty-Six Years Plus: The Story of the London Graving Dock Co Ltd 1890-1976
the firm 1976   xiv 83pp
London Graving Dock Co
763   §

Hurd, Michael
Vincent Novello - and Company

Granada 1981   ix 163pp illus index sources
Novello & Co
475   * §

Hurn, Elizabeth
Wheatsheaf Works, Opened 1891: The Largest Boot Factory in Europe
typescript 1982   27pp illus sources
Wheatsheaf Works
451   LEICSPL

Hurren, George
Phoenix Renascent: A History of the Phoenix Assurance Co Ltd 1782-1968
the firm 1973   xviii 173pp illus index
Phoenix Assurance
820   §

Hurst, J G
Edmund Potter and Dinting Vale

Manchester: the firm 1948   xiii 89pp illus sources
Potter, Edmund & Co
437   *

Hurst, Margery
No Glass Slipper

Arlington Books 1967   176pp illus
Brook Street Bureau
839   *

Hutchisons of Kirkcaldy
>Hutchisons of Kirkcaldy: A History of the Family and the Firm

    typescript 1948   sources
    Hutchisons of Kirkcaldy
    416   KCLDYPL

Huws, Richard E
>*A History of the House of Spurrell, Carmarthen, 1840-1969*

    Wales(Aberystwyth) FLA1981   352pp sources
    Spurrell, W & Son
    475   DYFEDPL

Hyde, Francis Edwin
>*Blue Funnel: A History of Alfred Holt and Company of Liverpool from 1865 to 1914*

    Liverpool: L U P 1956   xvii 201pp illus index sources
    Holt, Alfred & Co   Ocean Steam Ship Co
    740   * §

Hyde, Francis Edwin
>*Cunard and the North Atlantic 1840-1973: A History of Shipping and Financial Management*

    Macmillan 1975   xx 382pp illus index sources
    Cunard
    740   *

Hyde, Francis Edwin
>*Liverpool and the Mersey: An Economic History of a Port 1700-1970*

    Newton Abbot: David & Charles 1971 xvi 269pp illus index sources
    Mersey Docks & Harbour Board
    763   *

Hyde, Francis Edwin
>*Shipping Enterprise and Management 1830-1939: Harrisons of Liverpool*

    Liverpool: L U P 1967   xx 208pp illus index sources
    Harrisons of Liverpool
    740   *

Hyde, Harford Montgomery
>*Mr. and Mrs. Beeton*

    Harrap 1951   189pp illus
    Beeton, Samuel O
    475   *

Hyde, W G S (ed)
>*Greater Manchester Transport Review*

    Mossley: the firm 1978   128pp illus sources
    Greater Manchester Transport
    721   BOLTNPL

Hyman, Alan
>*The Rise and Fall of Horatio Bottomley: The Biography of a Swindler*

    Cassell 1972   xv 304pp illus index sources
    John Bull
    475   831   §

Hytner, B A & Irvine, I A N
Roadships Ltd: Report of an Investigation ...under the
Companies Act 1948
HMSO 1976
Roadships   Hilton Transport Services
723
Imperial & Queen Laundries
Imperial & Queen Laundries, Uttoxeter 1902-1962

York: William Sessions 1962
Imperial & Queen Laundries
981
Imperial Chemical Industries
Imperial Chemical Industries and its Founding Companies:
vol.1- Nobel's Explosives Co. & Nobel Industries 1871-1926
the firm 1938   xii 240pp illus
I C I
250   *
Imperial Continental Gas
Imperial Continental Gas Association 1824-1974

the firm 1974   xi 51pp illus
Imperial Continental Gas
162   839   * §
Inchcape Group
The Inchcape Group including Inchcape & Co Ltd and Subsidiary
and Associated Companies
the firm 1963   86pp illus
Inchcape
740   770   §
Incorporated Stone & Marble Co
A Retrospect of Eighty Years

1961   12pp
Incorporated Stone & Marble Co
245   501   GHL
Incorporation of Bakers of Glasgow
The Incorporation of Bakers of Glasgow   and other titles of
Glasgow Incorporations
Glasgow 1931   212pp
Bakers of Glasgow
419   *
Ind Coope
Collection of material on Romford Brewery

manuscripts, pamphlets etc
Ind Coope Romford Brewery
427   ROMFDPL
Ingram, J G & Son
A Century of Progress and Development of Ingram, J G & Son,
The London India Rubber Works, Hackney Wick
the firm 1947
Ingram, J G & Son
481   HACKPL

Insurance Institute of London
The History and Development of Protecting and Indemnity Clubs

the firm 1957   55pp
Insurance Institute of London
820   §
International Conference of Applied Chemistry
The Rise and Progress of the British Explosives Industry

1909   418pp
Explosives Industry
256   §
International Harvester
The First 100 Years of McCormick International in Great Britain
the firm 1951   16pp
International Harvester Co of GB
321
International Paints
International Paints 1881-1956: Seventy Five Years of Paint-Making
the firm 1958   72pp illus
International Paints
255   UBRIS
Ionian Bank
Ionian Bank Limited: A History

the firm 1953   41pp illus
Ionian Bank
814   §
Irvine, A S
A History of the Alkali Division (formerly Brunner, Mond & Co Ltd)
Birmingham: Kynoch1958   46pp
I C I   Brunner, Mond
250
Irving, R J
An Economic History of the North Eastern Railway Company 1870-1914
Birmingham PhD 1972
North Eastern Railway
710
Irving, R J
British Railway Investment and Innovation 1900-1914: The North Eastern and London & North Western Railway Companies
Business History   vol XIII no 1 1971
North Eastern Railway   London & North Western Railway
710
Irving, R J
New Industries for Old? Some Investment Decisions of Sir W G Armstrong, Whitworth & Co Ltd 1900-1914
Business History   vol XVII no 2 1975
Armstrong, Whitworth & Co
221   310   320   361

238

Irving, R J
  The North Eastern Railway Co, 1870-1914: An Economic
  History
  Leicester: L U P 1976   320pp illus index sources
  North Eastern Railway
  710   *

Isaac, Peter Charles Gerald
  William Davison of Alnwick, Pharmacist and Printer
  1781-1858
  Oxford: Clarendon 1968   vii 38pp illus sources
  Davison, William of Alnwick
  475   643   *

Jackson, Alan A C & Croome, Desmond F
  Rails Through the Clay: A History of London's Tube Railways

  Allen & Unwin 1962   406pp illus
  London Transport
  710   *

Jackson, Gordon
  The British Whaling Trade

  A & C Black 1978   xvi 310pp index sources
  Whaling Trade
  30   *

Jackson, Lionel George
  The Story of Streets: Streets Advertising

  typescript nd
  Street, G & Co
  838

Jackson, R & Co
  Jacksons of Piccadilly

  1973
  Jackson, R & Co
  423   641   GHL

Jackson, Robert
  The Nuffield Story

  Frederick Muller 1964   254pp illus
  Morris Motors
  351   *

Jacobs, Bertram
  Axminster Carpets (Hand-Made) 1755-1957

  Leigh-on-Sea: F Lewis 1970   79pp illus
  Axminster Carpets
  438   *

Jacobson, Michael
  The Cliffe Brewery 1723-1973

  the firm 1973   60pp illus
  Tollemache & Cobbold
  427   UBRIS

Jacobson, Michael
> *Two Hundred Years of Beer: The Story of Boddingtons'*
> *Strangeways Brewery 1778-1978*
> the firm 1978   95pp illus
> Boddingtons' Brewery
> 427   §

Jaffrey, Thomas
> *The Aberdeen Savings Bank: Its History, Development and*
> *Present Position*
> Aberdeen: 1896   64pp illus
> Aberdeen Savings Bank
> 814   NESLS

Jagger, C
> *Paul Philip Barraud in the Family Business 1750-1929*

> 1968
> Barraud
> 374   GHL

Jaguar Cars
> *Case History: The Story of Jaguar Cars Ltd and its Subsidiary*
> *Companies*
> Coventry: the firm 1964   57pp illus
> Jaguar Cars
> 351   COVNPL

Janes, Hurford
> *A Wonderful Heritage: The Hadley Story*

> Henry Melland 1977   104pp illus
> Hadley, Joseph (Holdings)
> 820   §

Janes, Hurford
> *Albion Brewery 1808-1958: The Story of Mann, Crossman &*
> *Paulin Ltd*
> Harley 1958   115pp illus
> Mann, Crossman & Paulin
> 427   662   *

Janes, Hurford
> *De Zoete & Gorton: A History*

> 1963   80pp
> De Zoete & Gorton
> 831   GHL

Janes, Hurford
> *Full Ahead: The Story of Brown, Jenkison & Co Limited*
> *1860-1969*
> Harley 1960   71pp illus
> Brown, Jenkison & Co
> 770   839   UBRIS

Janes, Hurford
> *Hall & Woodhouse 1777-1977: Independent Family Brewers*

> Henry Melland 1977   80pp illus
> Hall & Woodhouse
> 427   662   *

Janes, Hurford
Sons of the Forge: The Story of B & S Massey Ltd. 1861-1961

Harley 1961   105pp illus
Massey, B & S
312   *

Janes, Hurford
Stone's 1740-1965: The Story of the Finsbury Distillery

Harley 1965   55pp illus
Stone's Finsbury Distillery
424   ISLTNPL

Janes, Hurford
The Master Millers: The Story of the House of Rank Issued by Joseph Rank Ltd...Their 80th Anniversary
Harley nd   98pp illus
Rank, Joseph
416   BLPES

Janes, Hurford
The Red Barrel: A History of Watney Mann

John Murray 1963   226pp illus index sources
Watney Mann
427   662   *

Janes, Hurford
Two Centuries: The Story of David Lloyd Pigott and Company of London: Tea and Coffee Merchants 1760-1960
Harley 1960   36pp illus
David Lloyd, Pigott & Co
423   839   *

Janes, Hurford & Sayers, H J
The Story of Czarnikow

Harley 1963   176pp illus index
Czarnikow
420   839   * §

Jaques, John
Jaques: 150th Anniversary

the firm 1945   20pp illus
Jaques, John & Son
494   CROYPL

Jardine, Matheson
Jardine, Matheson & Company: An Outline of the History of a China House for a Hundred Years 1832-1932
the firm 1934   87pp
Jardine, Matheson
839

Jardine, Matheson
Jardine, Matheson and Company: An Historical Sketch

Hongkong: the firm 1969   64pp illus
Jardine, Matheson
210   630   839   §

Jardine, Matheson
Jardines and E W O Interests

the firm 1947 52pp illus
Jardine, Matheson
839 §

Jardine, Matheson & Co (Japan)
Jardines' Centenary in Japan 1859-1959

Tokyo: the firm 1959 47pp illus
Jardine, Matheson
839 UBRIS

Jarrold
The House of Jarrolds 1823-1923: A Brief History of One Hundred Years
Norwich: the firm 1924 55pp illus
Jarrold & Sons
475 NRFLKPL

Jarrold, John & Sons
Jarrold 1770-1970

Jarrold 1970 illus
Jarrold & Sons
475 *

Jeans, James Stephen
Jubilee Memorial of the Stockton & Darlington Railway and a Record of its Results: first edition, Longmans Green 1875
Newcastle upon Tyne: Graham !974 315pp illus
Stockton & Darlington Railway
710 *

Jeans, James Stephen
Pioneers of the Cleveland Iron Trade

Middlesbrough: H G Reid 1875
Cleveland Iron Trade
210 221 *

Jefferson, Herbert
Viscount Pirrie of Belfast

Belfast: Wm Mullen 1948 xii 336pp illus
Harland & Wolff Royal Mail Shipping Group
361 740

Jeffery, A E
The History of Scruttons

1971 173pp
Scruttons
740 GHL

Jefferys, James Bavington
Business Organisation in Great Britain 1856-1914

London PhD 1970
Business Organisation

Jefferys, James Bavington
Retail Trading in Britain 1850-1950

Cambridge: C U P 1954   xvii 497pp illus
Retail Trading
640   650   *

Jeffrey, David Cockburn
Down by the Riverside: The History of the Alloa Riverfront and the Jeffrey Shipyard
Alloa: Clackmannan Library 1984   10pp illus
Jeffrey, Robert   Vickers
361   CLKMNPL

Jenkin, Alfred
Tootals in Bolton

typescript nd   10pp
Tootal, Broadhurst, Lee
432   BOLTNPL

Jenkin, Alfred Kenneth Hamilton
Wendron Tin

Helston: the firm 1978   65pp illus index sources
Wendron Forge
210   224   *

Jenkin, Roger
The Wig-making Clarksons: In Search of their Life and Times

Ilfracombe: Arthur H Stockwell 1982 208pp illus index sources
Clarkson, W
453   974   *

Jenkins, Alan
Built on Teamwork

Heinemann 1980   xvi 245pp illus index sources
Taylor Woodrow
500   * §

Jenkins, Alan
Drinka Pinta: The Story of Milk and the Industry that Serves It

Heinemann 1970   xii 242pp illus index sources
Milk Marketing Board
413   617   641   * §

Jenkins, Alan
On Site 1921-1971

Heinemann 1971   xiv 226pp illus index sources
Taylor Woodrow
500   * §

Jenkins, Alan
The Stock Exchange Story

Heinemann 1973   x 212pp illus index sources
Stock Exchange
831   *

243

Jenkins, David
Jenkins Brothers of Cardiff: A Ceredigion Family's Shipping Ventures
Cardiff: Nat Museum of Wales 1985   112pp illus sources
Jenkins Brothers
740   §

Jenkins, David
The History of B P B Industries

the firm 1973   xvii 147pp illus index
British Plaster Board Industries
243   §

Jenkins, David Trevor
The West Riding Wool Textile Industry 1770-1835: A Study of Fixed Capital Formation
Edington: Pasold Research Fund nd   xvi 336pp illus index sources
West Riding Wool Textile Ind
431   *

Jenkins, David Trevor & Ponting, Kenneth G
The British Wool Textile Industry 1770-1914

Heinemann 1982   xii 388pp index sources
Wool Textile Industry
431   * §

Jenkins, John Geraint
Evan Thomas Radcliffe: A Cardiff Shipowning Company

Cardiff: Nat Museum of Wales 1982   92pp illus sources
Radcliffe, Evan Thomas & Co
740   * §

Jenkins, John Geraint
The Welsh Woollen Industry

Cardiff: Nat. Museum of Wales 1969   xviii 410pp illus sources
Welsh Woollen Industry
431   *

Jennings, Elizabeth
Sir Isaac Holden 1807-97: The First Comber in Europe

Bradford PhD 1982
Holden, Isaac
323   431

Jennings, Eric
Mansfields: Transport and Distribution in South-East Asia

Singapore: Meridian ca1974   48pp illus
Ocean Transport & Trading   Mansfields
740   770   839   §

Jennings, Fred H & Sons
1913-1983: Seventy Years

Netherton: the firm 1983   16pp illus
Jennings, Fred H & Sons
343   SANDWPL

244

Jennings, Paul Francis
Dunlopera: The Works and Workings of the Dunlop Rubber Company
the firm 1961   157pp illus
Dunlop Rubber Co
453   481   * §
Jenson & Nicholson
The Story of an English Firm: Jenson & Nicholson Ltd Founded 1821
the firm 1948   36pp illus
Jenson & Nicholson
255   *
Jephcott, Harry
The First Fifty Years: The Early Life of Joseph Edward Nathan and...his Merchandise Business that Became the Glaxo Group
the firm 1969   118pp illus
Glaxo
257   413   * §
Jephcott, William Ellery
The House of Izons: The History of a Pioneer Firm of Ironfounders
Murray-Watson 1948   45pp illus
Izons & Co
311   SANDWPL
Jeremy, David J
Anatomy of the British Business Elite 1860-1980

Business History   vol XXVI no 1 1984

Jeremy, David J
Chapel in the Career of a Late-Victorian Businessman: The Case of John Mackintosh
see Jeremy, David J (ed) 1987
Mackintosh, John
421
Jeremy, David J
Religious Affiliations of the Business Leaders in the 'Dictionary of Business Biography'
see Jeremy, David J (ed) 1987

Jeremy, David J
The Big Issues in Business and Religion

see Jeremy, David J (ed) 1987

Jeremy, David J
Transatlantic Industrial Revolution: The Diffusion of Textile Technologies between Britain and America 1790-1830s
Oxford: Basil Blackwell 1981   xvii 384pp illus index sources
Textile Technology
323   430   *

Jeremy, David J (ed)
Business and Religion: Cases and Issues in Victorian and Edwardian Britain
Aldershot: Gower 1987
Business and Religion

Jessop, William
Visit to a Steelworks

Sheffield 1913   59pp
Jessop, William
221   SHEFFPL

Jessup, Edward
Ernest Oppenheimer: A Study in Power

Rex Collings 1979   357pp illus index sources
Anglo American Corporation
210   815   839   *

Jevons, Herbert Stanley
The British Coal Trade

Kegan Paul, Trench, Trübner 1915   xii 876pp illus sources
Coal Trade
111   612   630   763   *

Jewell, J
Engineering for Life: The Story of Martin Baker

Higher Denham: the firm 1979   108pp illus
Martin Baker Aircraft Co
364   RAeS

Jewish Chronicle
The Jewish Chronicle 1841-1941: A Century of Newspaper History
the firm 1949   xv 187pp illus
Jewish Chronicle
475   * §

Jewson & Sons
The House of Jewson 1836-1956

Norwich: the firm 1956   17pp illus
Jewson & Sons
613   NRFLKPL

Joby, Richard S
The Development of Railways in N E Norfolk 1872-1914

Leicester MPhil 1982
Railways in N E Norfolk
710

Joby, Richard S
The Railway Builders

Newton Abbot: David & Charles 1983 200pp illus index sources
Great Western Railway   London & North Western Railway
502   *

John Bull Rubber Co
>*The Story of John Bull 1906-1956: A History of the John Bull Rubber Company Limited*
>Leicester: the firm nd   37pp illus
>John Bull Rubber Co
>481   UBRIS

John, Arthur Henry
>*A Liverpool Merchant House: Being the History of Alfred Booth and Company 1863-1958*
>Allen & Unwin 1959   197pp illus index sources
>Booth, Alfred
>440   740   *

John, Arthur Henry (ed)
>*The Walker Family, Ironfounders and Lead Manufacturers 1741-1893*
>Council Pres Bus Archives 1951   76pp illus index
>Walkers, Parker & Co   Walker, Samuel & Co
>221   251   311   SHEFFPL

Johnsen & Jorgensen
>*Johnsen & Jorgensen 1884-1984*
>
>the firm 1984   81pp illus
>Johnsen & Jorgensen
>247   *

Johnson, C J
>*The Origin and Development of the Alcester Waterworks Co 1875-1947*
>Bath MSc 1980
>Alcester Waterworks Co
>170

Johnson, D G
>*History of Geo Bassett & Co Ltd.*
>
>typescript 1967   32pp illus
>Bassett, Geo & Co
>421   SHEFFPL

Johnson, F G L
>*The James Russell Story*
>
>Margate: Eyre & Spottiswoode 1962   17pp illus
>Russell, James & Co
>221   222   SANDWPL

Johnson, H R
>*William Strutt's Cotton Mills 1793-1812*
>
>Trans Newcomen Soc   vol 30 1957
>Strutt, William, Cotton Mills
>432   DERBYPL

Johnson, J H & Randell, W L
>*Colonel R E B Crompton and the Evolution of the Electrical Industry*
>Longmans 1945   27pp
>Crompton & Co
>342   837   *

Johnson, Leslie
Johnson Brothers, Dyers & Cleaners: 150 Years

Newman Neame 1967   36pp illus
Johnson Group Cleaners
981   *

Johnson, Robert L
A Shetland Country Merchant: Being an Account of the Life and Times of James Williamson of Mid Yell 1800-1872
Lerwick: Shetland Publ Co 1979   110pp illus
Williamson, James
656   STLDPL

Johnson, W
The Development of the Kent Coalfield 1896-1946

Kent PhD 1972
Kent Coalfield
111

Johnston, C H
'Black Diamonds' by Sea

Repr. from 'Sea Breezes' 1948   16pp
Cory, William & Son
740   612   GHL

Johnston, W & A K
One Hundred Years of Map Making: The Story of W & A K Johnston
Edinburgh: the firm ca1925   20pp illus
Johnston, W & A K
475   EDNBRPL

Jolly, William Percy
Lord Leverhulme: A Biography

Constable 1976   viii 246pp illus index sources
Lever Brothers   Unilever
257   258   411   414   *

Jones, A E
The Romance of a Century 1826-1926: Account of Bemrose & Sons, Printers, Derby
Derby: the firm 1926   27pp illus
Bemrose & Sons
475   DERBYPL

Jones, Albert Everett
An E J Keepsake

Decimus 1982
Everett
838   HISTAD

Jones, B Alcwyn
The Story of Halfords 1907-82

Redditch: the firm 1982   72pp illus
Halford Cycle Co   Burmah Oil
654   *

Jones, Barry M
The Story of Panther Motorcycles

Cambridge: Patrick Stephens 1983   136pp illus index
Phelon & Moor
363   *

Jones, Charles A
Competition and Structural Change in the Buenos Aires Fire
Insurance Market: The Local Board of Agents 1875-1921
see Westall, Oliver M (ed) 1984
Buenos Aires Fire Ins Market
820   839

Jones, Clement Wakefield
Pioneer Shipowners

Liverpool: Birchall & Sons 1935-38   2 vols illus index
Shipping
740   *

Jones, Clement Wakefield
Sea Trading and Sea Training: Being a Short History of the Firm
of Devitt & Moore
Arnold 1936   192pp illus
Devitt & Moore
740   *

Jones, Colin
A Record of 150 Years of Merchant Banking

the firm 1958   26pp illus
Gibbs, Antony
814   §

Jones, F
The Cotton Spinning Industry in the Oldham District from
1896-1914
Manchester MA 1959
Cotton Spinning in Oldham
432

Jones, G P
The Dorothea Slate Quarry ca1828-1970

Wales(Bangor) MA 1981
Dorothea Slate Quarry
231

Jones, Geoffrey
Admirals and Oilmen: The Relationship between the Royal Navy
and the Oil Companies 1900-1924
see Palmer, S R & Williams, G (eds)
Burmah Oil   Anglo-Persian Oil Co
130   140

Jones, Geoffrey
Banking and Empire in Iran: Banking and Oil: The History of the
British Bank of the Middle East
Cambridge: C U P 1986   2 vols illus index sources
Imperial Bank of Persia   British Bank of the Middle East
814   839

Jones, Geoffrey
Courtaulds in Continental Europe 1920-1945

see Jones, Geoffrey (ed) 1986
Courtaulds
260   432

Jones, Geoffrey
Lombard Street on the Riviera: The British Clearing Banks and Europe 1900-1960
Business History   Vol XXIV no 2 1982
Clearing Banks
814   839

Jones, Geoffrey
Multinational Chocolate: Cadbury Overseas 1918-1939

Business History   vol XXVI no 1 1984
Cadbury Bros
421

Jones, Geoffrey
The 'Old Aunts': Government, Politicians and the Oil Buiness

see Turner, John (ed) 1984
Anglo-Persian Oil Co   Royal Dutch/Shell
130   140

Jones, Geoffrey
The Chocolate Multinationals: Cadbury, Fry and Rowntree 1918-1939
see Jones, Geoffrey (ed) 1986
Cadbury Bros   Fry, J S & Sons
421

Jones, Geoffrey
The Expansion of British Multinational Manufacturing 1890-1939
see Fuji Conference 9, 1982
Multinational Manufacturing

Jones, Geoffrey
The Gramophone Company: An Anglo-American Multinational 1898-1931
Business History Review   vol 59 no 1 1985
Gramophone Company   Victor Company
345

Jones, Geoffrey
The Growth and Performance of British Multinational Firms before 1939: The Case of Dunlop
Economic History Review   2nd ser vol XXXVII no 1 1984
Dunlop Rubber Co
481

Jones, Geoffrey
The Multinational Expansion of Dunlop 1890-1939

see Jones, Geoffrey (ed) 1986
Dunlop Rubber Co
480

Jones, Geoffrey
The Oil Companies and the British Government 1900-1925

Cambridge PhD 1977
Oil Companies
130   140
Jones, Geoffrey
The Performance of British Multinational Enterprise 1890-1945
see Hertner & Jones (eds)

Jones, Geoffrey
The State and the Emergence of the British Oil Industry

Macmillan 1981   xi 264pp index sources
B P   Burmah Oil
130   140   * §
Jones, Geoffrey (ed)
British Multinationals: Origins, Management and Performance

Aldershot: Gower 1986

221   247   320   421   480
Jones, H Edgar
Accountancy and the British Economy 1840-1980: The Evolution of Ernst & Whinney
Batsford 1981   288pp illus index sources
Ernst & Whinney
836   * §
Jones, H Edgar
Guest Keen & Nettlefolds: Innovation and Enterprise vol 1; 1759-1918
Macmillan 1987
G K N
221   311   313   320
Jones, H Edgar
Guest, Keen & Nettlefolds: Their Entry, Dominance and Development of the U K Market in Automotive Transmissions
see Davenport-Hines, R P T (ed) 1986
G K N
320   353
Jones, H Edgar
Steel and Engineering Overseas: Guest, Keen & Nettlefolds' Multinational Growth 1918-1965
see Jones, Geoffrey (ed) 1986
G K N
320
Jones, H Kay
Butterworths: History of a Publishing House

Butterworths 1980   x 285pp illus index sources
Butterworth & Co
475   * §

Jones, H Quentin
Centenary 1823-1923: William Walker & Sons Limited, Rose
Hill Tannery, Bolton
Bolton: the firm 1923   12pp illus
Walker, William & Sons
441   442   BOLTNPL

Jones, H Quentin
William Walker & Sons Ltd: Tanners, Curriers and Belting
Manufacturers, Bolton, England
Bolton: the firm 1924   32pp illus
Walker, William & Sons
441   442   BOLTNPL

Jones, Linda Lloyd
Fifty Penguin Years

Harmondsworth: Penguin 1985   142pp illus
Penguin Books
475   §

Jones, P d'A & Simons, E N
Story of the Saw: Spear & Jackson Limited 1760-1960

Newman Neame 1961   80pp illus index sources
Spear & Jackson
316   322   §

Jones, Robert & Marriott, Oliver
Anatomy of a Merger: A History of G E C, A E I & English
Electric
Jonathan Cape 1970   346pp index sources
G E C   A E I
340   364   *

Jones, Roderick
A Life in Reuters

Hodder & Stoughton 1951   496pp index
Reuters
839   * §

Jones, S G
The Leisure Industry in the Inter-War Years

Manchester PhD 1983
Leisure Industry
665   969   979

Jones, S R H
Hall, English & Co 1813-41: A Study of Entrepreneurial
Response in the Gloucester Pin Industry
Business History   vol XVIII no 1 1976
Hall, English & Co
316

Jones, S R H
John English & Co, Feckenham: A Study of Enterprise in the
West Midlands Needle Industry in the 18th & 19th Centuries
London PhD 1981   418pp illus sources
English, John & Co, Feckenham
316   HWORCPL

Jones, Samuel
150 Years on Paper

the firm 1960   39pp illus
Jones, Samuel & Co   Wiggins Teape
472
Jones, Samuel
Samuel Jones & Co Quarterly Magazine

the firm   vols 1-16 illus 1913-37
Jones, Samuel & Co   Wiggins Teape
472
*
Jones, Stephanie
A Maritime History of the Port of Whitby 1700-1914

London PhD 1982
Port of Whitby
763
Jones, Stephanie
Two Centuries of Overseas Trading: The Origins and Growth of the Inchcape Group
Macmillan 1986   xxii 328pp illus index sources
Inchcape
740   770   839
Jones, Stuart
The Cotton Industry and Joint Stock Banking in Manchester 1825-1850
Business History   vol XX no 2 1978
Cotton & Banking in Manchester
432   814
Jones, T (ed Middlemas, K)
Whitehall Diary 1916-1930

Oxford U P 1969-71   3 vols illus index sources
Politics & Business

*
Jones, Thomas
A Diary with Letters 1931-1950

Oxford U P 1954   582pp
Politics & Business

*
Jones, Tom
Henry Tate 1819-1899: A Biographical Sketch

the firm 1960   32pp illus index sources
Tate & Lyle
420
*
Jopp, Keith
Corah of Leicester 1815-1965

the firm 1965   60pp illus
Corah, N
436
* §

Jopp, Keith
The Hewetson Story 1898-1958

Macclesfield: the firm nd   32pp illus
Hewetson, A W
432   436   455   UBRIS

Jordan & Sons
Jordans 1863-1963: The Story of Jordan & Sons Ltd

the firm 1963   38pp
Jordan & Sons
475   *

Jordan, Alexander
The Balance of Power: The Golden Jubilee of Landis & Gyr

the firm 1963   44pp illus
Landis & Gyr
340   371   BRENTPL

Joscelyne, Clement
Clement Joscelyne 1879-1979

Bishops Stortford: the firm nd   16pp illus
Joscelyne, Clement
647   648

Joslin, David Maelgwyn
A Century of Banking in Latin America: Centenary in 1962 of the Bank of London and South America 1862-1962
Oxford U P 1963   xi 307pp illus index sources
Bank of London & South America   Gibbs, Antony
814   839   *

Jowett Cars
50 Years of Progress 1901-1951

Bradford: the firm 1951   24pp illus
Jowett Cars
351

Jowitt
150 Years in the Wool Trade: Unique Record of a Bradford Firm

Wool Record, Textile World   vol 30, 1926
Jowitt, Robert & Sons
431

Jowitt, George
George Jowitt & Sons Limited: A History

Sheffield: the firm 1966   27pp illus
Jowitt, George & Sons
221   246   §

Jukes, G (ed)
The Story of Belling 1912-1962

Enfield: the firm 1962   95pp illus
Belling & Co
346   *

254

Kaufman, M
        The First Century of Plastics: Celluloid and its Sequel

        Plastics Institute 1963   130pp illus index
        Xylonite Group
        251   483   §
Keefe, H J
        A Century in Print: The Story of Hazell's 1839-1939

        the firm 1939   224pp illus
        Hazell, Watson & Viney
        475   BCRL
Keeling, B S & Wright, A E G
        The Development of the Modern British Steel Industry

        Longman 1964   210pp illus index sources
        Steel Industry
        221   §
Keevil, Ambrose
        The Story of Fitch Lovell 1784-1970

        Phillimore 1972   xvi 304pp illus
        Fitch Lovell
        617   §
Keighley Fleece Mills Co
        The Keighley Fleece Mills Co Ltd...1865-1965

        the firm 1965
        Keighley Fleece Mills Co
        431
Keir, David E & Morgan, Bryan (eds)
        Golden Milestone: 50 Years of the A A

        the firm 1955   240pp illus index
        Automobile Association
        969   * §
Keir, David Edwin
        The Younger Centuries: The Story of William Younger & Co. Ltd.
        1749 to 1949
        Edinburgh: the firm 1951   vi 110pp illus
        Younger, William
        427   662   *
Keir, David Edwin
        The Bowring Story

        Bodley Head 1962   448pp illus index sources
        Bowring, C T & Co
        30   740   832   * §
Keir, David Edwin
        The House of Collins: The Story of a Scottish Family of
        Publishers from 1789 to the Present Day
        the firm 1952   303pp illus index sources
        Collins
        475   * §

255

Keith, Alexander
Aberdeen University Press: An Account of the Press from its Foundation in 1840 until its...new Premises in 1963
Aberdeen: A U P 1963   71pp illus index
Aberdeen University Press
475   *

Keith, Alexander
The North of Scotland Bank Ltd 1836-1936

Aberdeen Journals 1936   viii 188pp illus index
North of Scotland Bank
814   *

Keith, Kenneth
The Achievement of Excellence: The Story of Rolls-Royce

New York: Newcomen Society 1977   31pp illus
Rolls-Royce
351   364   RAeS

Kelly, Alison
The Story of Wedgwood

Faber 1975   152pp illus index sources
Wedgwood, Josiah & Sons
248   BLPES

Kemp's Mercantile Offices
Kemp's Mercantile Offices 1849-1949: The Story of a Century

the firm ca1949   30pp illus
Kemp's Mercantile Offices
653   963   GHL

Kemp, Peter Kemp
The Bentall Story: Commemorating 150 Years' Service to Agriculture   1805-1955
Maldon, Essex: the firm 1955   42pp illus
Bentall, E H & Co
321   *

Kendall
The House of Kendall

Newman Neame 1970   32pp illus
Kendall
453   §

Kennedy, W P & Michie, R
The London and New York Stock Exchanges 1850-1914

Journal of Economic History   1986
Stock Exchange
831

Kennett, Pat
The Foden Story: From Farm Machinery to Diesel Trucks and other vehicle titles
Cambridge: Patrick Stephens 1978   183pp illus index
Foden
351   * §

Kenning Motors Group
Kenning Motors Group 100th Anniversary 1878-1978

the firm 1978   28pp illus
Kenning Motors Group
614   651

Kenrick & Jefferson
Britain's Business Equippers 1878-1928: A Brief Review of...
Kenrick & Jefferson Ltd...
the firm 1928   64pp illus
Kenrick & Jefferson
475

Kenrick & Jefferson
The House of K & J

1953   63pp
Kenrick & Jefferson
472

Kenrick & Jefferson
Their Work Shall Endure: Frederick Thomas Jefferson J P and
John Arthur Kenrick J P
West Bromwich: the firm nd   10pp illus
Kenrick & Jefferson
475

Kensey, M F
Grouts of Enfield Ltd: The History and Archaeology of the Firm

Enfield Archaeological Soc 1975   45pp illus
Grouts of Enfield
648

Kent Insurance Co
Kent Insurance Company 1802-1952

Maidstone: the firm 1952   47pp illus
Kent Insurance Co
820
§

Kent, George
George Kent Limited 1838-1938: A Volume of Reminiscences
and Pictures
the firm 1938   100pp illus
Kent, George
371

Kent, Marian
Oil and Empire: British Policy and Mesopotamian Oil
1900-1920
Macmillan 1976   xiii 273pp illus index sources
Royal Dutch/Shell   Anglo Persian Oil Co
130   140
*

Kenyon, George Hughes
Glass Industry of the Weald

Leicester: L U P 1967   xxii 231pp illus
Glass Industry of the Weald
247
*

Kenyon, James & Son
Kenyons of Bury: Being the Story of James Kenyon & Son Ltd

Manchester 1950   illus
Kenyon, James & Son
431   BURYPL

Kenyon, James & Son
The House of Kenyon 1714-1930

Bury: the firm ca1930   illus
Kenyon, James & Son
431   BURYPL

Kenyon, John
Bi-centenary Celebration 1710-1910: A Short Account of the History of the Firm, Presented to Workpeople
Sheffield: Pawson & Brailsford 1910
Kenyon, John & Co
221

Kenyon, William
William Kenyon & Sons: A Century's Work 1866-1966

Dukinfield: the firm ca1982 82pp illus
Kenyon, William & Sons
320   439   §

Kestner
The Kestner Golden Jubilee Book: Fifty Years of Chemical Engineering Endeavour
the firm 1958   104pp illus index
Kestner Evaporator & Engineering
320   §

Keswick, Maggie (ed)
The Thistle and the Jade: A Celebration of 150 Years of Jardine, Matheson & Co.
Octopus 1982   272pp illus index sources
Jardine, Matheson
740   770   839   §

Ketelbey, Caroline Doris Mabel
The History of R Tullis & Company and Tullis Russell & Co Ltd 1809-1959
Markinch,Fife: the firm 1967 xiii 283pp illus sources
Tullis Russell
471   *

Kettle, Russell
Deloitte & Co. 1845-1958

the firm 1958   xi 171pp illus index
Deloitte, Plender, Griffiths
836   *

Kidd, William
Whitehall Palace Buildings: Celebration of Semi-Jubilee in Young's Room 3rd April 1896
Dundee: William Kidd 1896 55pp
Kidd, William
475   DNDEEPL

Kieve, Jeffrey L
    Electric Telegraph: A Social and Economic History

    Newton Abbot: David & Charles 1973 310pp illus index sources
    Electric Telegraph Co   Telegraph Construction & Maint
    502
                                                                    §
Kieve, Jeffrey L
    The Telegraph Industry 1837-90

    London MPhil 1970
    Telegraph Industry
    790
Killick, J
    *Risk, Speculation and Profit in the Mercantile Sector of the
    19th Century Cotton Trade: Alexander Brown and Sons 1820-80*
    Business History   vol XVI no 1 1974
    Brown, Alexander & Sons
    432
Kilpatrick, J
    *Deloitte Plender Griffiths & Co: Some Notes on the early days
    of the Firm*
    Wyman 1942   32pp
    Deloitte Plender Griffiths
    836
                                                                    §
Kimber, H E
    *Wilfred Nicholson 1821 to 1921: A Brief Record of His Life and
    Work*
    1960   91pp
    Nicholson, Wilfred
    255
                                                                    GHL
Kincaid, J G
    Kincaids 1868-1968

    1968
    Kincaids
    361
King and Hutchings
    King and Hutchings

    Uxbridge: the firm 1970   20pp illus
    King & Hutchings
    475
                                                                    HILLPL
King, Arthur & Stuart, Albert F
    The House of Warne: One Hundred Years of Publishing

    Frederick Warne 1965   x 107pp illus
    Warne, Frederick
    475
                                                                    *
King, David I
    *The House that William Greensmith Built: An Outline History of
    William Greensmith & Son, Harrogate 1832-1985.....*
    Scarborough: the firm 1985   43pp illus
    Greensmith & Thackwray   Greensmith, Wm & Son
    645
                                                                    CHELTPL

                                                                    259

King, Frank A
The Story of the Cannon Brewery 1751-1951

    1951   34pp illus
    Cannon Brewery
    427   ISLTNPL

King, Frank Henry Haviland
Eastern Banking: Essays in the History of the Hongkong and Shanghai Banking Corporation
    Athlone 1983   xvi 791pp illus index sources
    Hongkong & Shanghai Bank
    814   839   * §

King, Henry Charles
The House of Dollond: Two Hundred Years of Optical Service 1750-1950
    1950   35pp
    Dollond & Aitchison
    373   654   GHL

Kingsford, Garlant & J B Marks
Kingsfords: A Brief History

    the firm 1957
    Kingsfords
    836   GHL

Kingsford, Peter Wilfrid
F W Lanchester: A Life of an Engineer

    Arnold 1960   246pp illus index sources
    Lanchester Motor Co
    351   * §

Kingsford, Peter Wilfrid
The Lanchester Engine Company Ltd 1899-1904

    Business History   vol III no 2 1961
    Lanchester Engine Co
    351

Kingsford, Reginald John Lethbridge
The Publishers' Association 1896-1946, with an Epilogue

    Cambridge U P 1970   x 228pp
    Publishers' Association
    475   963   *

Kinloch, James & Butt, John
History of the Scottish Co-operative Wholesale Society

    Manchester: the firm 1981   416pp illus index sources
    Scottish Co-op Wholesale Soc   Co-operative Wholesale Society
    619   656   *

Kinross, John
Fifty Years in the City: Financing Small Business

    John Murray 1982   xiv 238pp illus index
    I C F C   Gresham Trust
    814

Kirby, Maurice W
>   *Men of Business and Politics: The Rise and Fall of the Quaker*
>   *Pease Dynasty of North-East England 1700-1943*
>   Allen & Unwin 1984
>   Pease, J & J W   North Eastern Railway
>   111   231   362   430   814   *

Kirby, Maurice W
>   *The British Coalmining Industry 1870-1946: A Political and*
>   *Economic History*
>   Macmillan 1977   viii 278pp index sources
>   Coal Industry
>   111   *

Kirby, Maurice W
>   *The Failure of a Quaker Business Dynasty: The Peases of*
>   *Darlington   1830-1902*
>   see Jeremy, David J (ed) 1987
>   Pease, J & J W
>   111   231   362   430   814

Kirk, R M
>   *The Growth of the British Textile Machine Industry 1850-1939*
>
>   Salford PhD 1983
>   Textile Machine Industry
>   323

Kirk, R M & Simmons, C
>   *Engineering and the First World War: A Case Study of the*
>   *Lancashire Cotton Spinning Industry*
>   Salford University 1983   39pp
>   Platt Brothers   Dobson & Barlow
>   323

Klapper, Charles Frederick
>   *The Golden Age of Buses*
>
>   Routledge & Kegan Paul 1978   xii 248pp illus index
>   Buses
>   721   *

Klapper, Charles Frederick
>   *The Golden Age of Tramways*
>
>   Routledge & Kegan Paul 1961   xiii 327pp illus
>   Tramways
>   721

Klockner-Moeller
>   *Always One Step Ahead*
>
>   Aylesbury: the firm 1971   24pp illus
>   Klockner-Moeller (England)
>   342   BCRL

Knapman, Geoffrey J
>   *Caring for the Caring: Medical Sickness Annuity & Life*
>   *Assurance Society Limited 1884-1984*
>   Henry Melland 1984   240pp illus index
>   Medical Sickness Annuity & Life
>   820   §

Knight, Arthur W
Private Enterprise and Public Intervention: The Courtaulds Experience
Allen & Unwin 1974   223pp index
Courtaulds
430   CLWYDPL

Knight, Geoffrey
Concorde: The Inside Story

Weidenfeld & Nicolson 1976   ix 174pp illus index
British Aircraft Corporation
364   *

Knightley, Phillip
The Vestey Affair

Macdonald Futura 1981   159pp illus
Union Cold Storage   Vestey
412   641   740   770   *

Knights, G & Farrington, A
History of the Radcliffe and Pilkington District Co-operative Industrial Society Ltd 1860-1910
Manchester: ca1911
Radcliffe & Pilkington Co-op
656   BURYPL

Knott, J R
A Study of Brindley and Foster, Organbuilders of Sheffield 1854-1939
1973
Brindley & Foster
492   SHEFFPL

Knowles & Foster
The History of Knowles & Foster 1828-1948

the firm 1948   92pp illus
Knowles & Foster
814   839   GHL

Knox, Andrew Marshall
Coming Clean: A Postscript after Retirement from Unilever

Heinemann 1976   xii 252pp illus index
Unilever
258   * §

Knox, Collie
Steel at Brierley Hill: The Story of Round Oak Steel Works 1857-1957
Newman Neame 1957   73pp illus
Round Oak Steel Works
221   §

Knox, Diana M
The Development of the London Brewing Industry 1830-1914 with special reference to Whitbread and Company
Oxford BLitt 1956
Whitbread & Co
427

262

Knox, James
> **The Triumph of Thrift: The Story of the Savings Bank of Airdrie Instituted 1835**
> Airdrie: Baird & Hamilton 1927   xvi 366pp illus index
> Airdrie Savings Bank
> 814   *

Knox, Oliver
> **Croft: A Journey of Confidence**
>
> Collins 1978   40pp illus
> Croft & Co
> 617   *

Kohn, Roger
> **Palm Line: The Coming-of-Age 1949-1970**
>
> the firm 1970   80pp illus
> Palm Line   United Africa Company
> 740   770   §

Kornitzer, Margaret (ed)
> **Berisfords the Ribbon People: The Story of 100 Years 1858-1958**
> York: William Sessions 1958   81pp illus
> Berisford Group
> 439   *

Koss, Stephen Edward
> **Fleet Street Radical: A G Gardiner and the 'Daily News'**
>
> Allen Lane 1973   x 339pp index sources
> Daily News
> 475

Koss, Stephen Edward
> **Sir John Brunner: Radical Plutocrat, 1842-1919**
>
> Cambridge U P 1970   xii 314pp illus sources
> Brunner, Mond   I C I
> 250   *

Koss, Stephen Edward
> **The Rise and Fall of the Political Press in Britain**
>
> Hamish Hamilton 1981-4   2 vols illus index
> Political Press
> 475   *

Kraft
> **Kraft 1924-1974: Golden Jubilee**
>
> the firm 1974   24pp illus
> Kraft
> 413   HILLPL

Kynaston, D T A
> **The London Stock Exchange 1870-1914: An Institutional History**
> London PhD 1983
> Stock Exchange
> 831

Kynoch
>
> *Under Five Flags: The Story of Kynoch Works, Witton*
> *Birmingham 1862-1962*
> Birmingham: the firm 1962   100pp illus
> Kynoch   I C I
> 329   *

Labour Research Dept
> *Coal Combines in Yorkshire*
>
> Labour Research Dept 1935   29pp
> Coal Combines in Yorkshire
> 111   *

Labour Research Dept
> *Ten Years of Railway Finance*
>
> Labour Research Dept 1932   23pp
> Railway Finance
> 710   *

Labour Research Dept
> *The Food Combines*
>
> Labour Research Dept 1931   26pp
> Food Combines
> 410   420   *

Labour Research Dept
> *Who's Who in Anthracite? A Study of the Ownership,*
> *Organisation & Profits of the Welsh Anthracite Coal Industry*
> Labour Research Dept 1935   23pp
> Welsh Anthracite Coal
> 111   *

Lackey, Clifford
> *Quality Pays...The Story of Joshua Tetley & Son*
>
> Ascot: Springwood Books 1985   160pp illus index
> Tetley, Joshua & Son
> 427   662   §

Lacre
> *The Lacre Story*
>
> St.Albans: the firm ca1974   16pp illus
> Lacre
> 352   MRC

Laing, John & Son
> *Teamwork: The Story of John Laing & Son Ltd*
>
> the firm 1950   108pp illus
> Laing, John
> 500   GHL

Laird, Dorothy
> *Paddy Henderson: A History of the Scottish Shipping Firm P*
> *Henderson & Co...1834-1961*
> Glasgow: George Outram 1961   230pp illus
> Henderson, P & Co
> 740   KCLDYPL

Lamb, P G
Electricity in Bristol 1863-1948

Bristol: Hist Assoc 1981
Bristol Electricity
161

Lambert Howard
Lambert Howard Group History

manuscript nd
Lambert Howard
451

Lambert, Richard Stanton
The Railway King 1800-1871: A Study of George Hudson and the
Business Morals of his Time
Allen & Unwin 1934   340pp illus sources
Midland Railway
710   815   *

Lambert, Richard Stanton
The Universal Provider: A Study of William Whiteley and the
Rise of the London Department Store
Harrap 1938   276pp illus index sources
Whiteley, William
656   * §

Lambert, Zeta E & Wyatt, Robert J
Lord Austin the Man

Sidgwick & Jackson 1968   187pp illus
Austin Motor Co
351   *

Lambeth Building Society
Lambeth Building Society 1852-1952

the firm 1952   30pp illus
Lambeth Building Soc
815   §

Lancashire & Yorkshire Bank
The Story of the Lancashire & Yorkshire Bank Ltd 1872-1922

Manchester: Sherratt & Hughes 1922 100pp illus
Lancashire & Yorkshire Bank
814   SALFDPL

Lancashire Cotton Corporation
The Mills and Organisation of the Lancashire Cotton
Corporation 1929-1950
the firm 1950   57pp illus
Lancashire Cotton Corporation
432   §

Lancashire Watch Company
The Lancashire Watch Company, Prescot, Lancashire: Its Rise
and Progress
Prescot: the firm 1893
Lancashire Watch Company
374

Lancaster J Y & Wattleworth, D R
The Iron & Steel Industry of West Cumberland: An Historical Survey
Workington & Barrow: the firm 1977 xii 198pp illus index sources
British Steel Corporation
210   221   *

Lanchbery, Edward
A V Roe: A Biography of Sir Alliott Verdon-Roe

Bodley Head 1956   140pp illus
Avro   Saunders-Roe
364   *

Lane, Michael R
The Story of the Steam Plough Works: Fowlers of Leeds

Northgate 1980   410pp illus index
Fowlers of Leeds
321   *

Lang, T B
An Historical Summary of the Post Office in Scotland: Compiled from Authentic Records & Documents; 1856
Edinburgh: Castlelaw reprint 1984   16pp sources
Post Office in Scotland
790   MTHWLPL

Langley, S J
The History and Development of the Iron and Steel Welded Tube Trade...and the Town of Wednesbury, Staffordshire
Birmingham MCom 1948
Welded Tube Trade
221

Langworth, Richard & Robson, Graham
Triumph Cars: The Complete 75 Year History

1975   312pp illus index
Triumph Cars
351   *

Laporte Chemicals
An Account of the Development and Activities of the House of Laporte 1888-1947
Luton: the firm 1947   92pp illus
Laporte Chemicals
250   *

Lascelles, Thomas Spooner
The City and South London Railway

Lingfield: Oakwood Press 1955   36pp illus
City & South London Railway
710   *

Last, Donald
A Centenary Review 1868-1968

the firm 1968
Foreign & Colonial Investment Co
815

Latham, Edward Bryan
History of Timber Trade Federation of the United Kingdom: The
First Seventy Years
Ernest Benn 1965   176pp illus index
Timber Trade Federation
613   * §

Latham, Edward Bryan
Timber: Its Development and Distribution...includes 1757-1957
The Story of James Latham
Harrap 1957   305pp illus
Latham, James
613   *

Latham, Joseph
Take-Over: The Facts and the Myths of the G E C / A E I Battle

Iliffe Books 1969   128pp index
G E C   A E I
340   *

Laughton, George A
A Century of Achievement: The Story of Laughton & Sons Ltd.
1860-1960
York: William Sessions 1960   xv 170pp illus
Laughton & Sons   Jarrett, Rainsford & Laughton
316   483   491   §

Launchbury, G T
John Allen & Son (Oxford) Ltd 1868-1952

Oxford: the firm 1952-54
Allen, John & Son (Oxford)
321   OXFDPL

Laurence, Alastair
Alex. Laurence & Sons, Leicester

typescript 1982   23pp illus
Laurence, Alex & Sons
436   LEICSPL

Laver, James
Hatchards of Piccadilly 1797-1947: One Hundred and Fifty
Years of Bookselling
the firm 1947   47pp illus
Hatchards
653   * §

Laver, James
The House of Haig

Markinch: the firm 1958   viii 74pp illus
Haig, John & Co
424   *

Laver, James
The Liberty Story

the firm 1959   40pp illus
Liberty & Co
494   654   §

Law, Rupert S
> *The End of a Chapter: The Story of Whiffen & Sons Limited, Fine Chemical Manufacturers*
> pamphlet ca1973
> Whiffen & Sons   Fisons
> 257

Lawford, G L & Nicholson, L R
> *The Telcon Story 1850-1950*
>
> the firm 1950   176pp illus
> Telegraph Construction & Maint   Telcon
> 502   * §

Lawlor, Harold C
> *Rise of the Linen Merchants: The Ewarts of Belfast*
>
> Fibres & Fabrics Journal   vol 10 1943
> Ewarts of Belfast
> 434

Lawson, William E
> *A History of Clydebank Co-operative Society Ltd*
>
> Glasgow: S C W S ca1948   106pp illus index
> Clydebank Co-operative Soc
> 656   UBRIS

Layton, Walter Thomas
> *The Early Years of the South Metropolitan Gas Company 1833-1871*
> Spottiswoode Ballantyne 1920   45pp illus index
> South Metropolitan Gas Co
> 162   IGASE

Lazell, Henry George
> *From Pills to Penicillin: The Beecham Story: A Personal Account*
> Heinemann 1975   208pp illus index
> Beecham
> 257   *

Lazonick, William
> *Industrial Organisation and Technological Change: The Decline of the British Cotton Industry*
> Business History Review   vol LVII no 2 1983
> Cotton Industry
> 432

Le Fevour, Edward
> *Western Enterprise in Late Ch'ing China: A Selective Survey of Jardine, Matheson & Co's Operations 1842-1895*
> Cambridge, Mass: Harvard U P 1968   215pp
> Jardine, Matheson
> 839

Leach, Cyril
> *Decision and Destiny: The Story of 100 Years of Co-operation in Warrington and District 1860-1960*
> C W S 1961   80pp
> Warrington Co-op
> 656   WARRPL

Leach, Hubert C
>*Hubert C Leach 1933-1983: Golden Jubilee Anniversary Brochure*
>the firm nd   19pp illus
>Leach, Hubert C
>501   HERTSPL

Leach, Robert
>*Let the Ink Flow: The History of the First Fifty Years of Fishburn Ink*
>Watford: the firm 1980   100pp illus
>Fishburn Printing Ink Co   Interchemical Corporation
>255   * §

Leader, Robert Eadon
>*A Century of Thrift: An Historical Sketch of the Sheffield Savings Bank 1819-1919*
>Sheffield: the firm 1920   vii 87pp illus index
>Sheffield Savings Bank
>814   *

Leader, Robert Eadon
>*History of Elkington & Co*
>
>typescript ca1913   53pp
>Elkington & Co
>316   491   *

Leader, Robert Eadon
>*History of the Company of Cutlers in Hallamshire*
>
>Sheffield: Pawson & Brailsford 1905 2 vols
>Cutlers' Company
>316   491   *

Leader, Robert Eadon
>*The Sheffield Banking Company Limited: An Historical Sketch 1831-1916*
>Sheffield: the firm 1916   vii 137pp illus index
>Sheffield Banking Co
>814   * §

Leapman, Michael
>*Barefaced Cheek: The Apotheosis of Rupert Murdoch*
>
>Hodder & Stoughton 1983   269pp illus index sources
>News International   Thomson Organisation
>475   *

Ledbetter, R M
>*Sheffield's Industrial History from about 1700, with special Reference to the Abbeydale Works*
>thesis 1971   320pp index sources
>Tyzack, William & Sons
>221   316   ROTHMPL

Lee, Alan J
>*The Origins of the Popular Press in England 1855-1914*
>
>Croom Helm 1976   310pp illus index sources
>Popular Press
>475   *

Lee, Arthur
Lee of Sheffield: A Family Enterprise

Sheffield: the firm 1962   47pp
Lee, Arthur & Sons
221   SHEFFPL

Lee, C J
The First Hundred Years: A Short Survey of the Work of the
Salisbury Railway and Market House Company
Salisbury: author 1956   20pp
Salisbury Railway & Market House
656   710   WILTSPL

Lee, Charles Edward
The Metropolitan District Railway
and many other titles
Lingfield: Oakwood Press 1956   51pp illus
London Transport
710   *

Lee, Clive Howard
A Cotton Enterprise 1795-1840: A History of M'Connel &
Kennedy- Fine Cotton Spinners
Manchester: M U P 1972   viii 188pp index sources
M'Connel & Kennedy
432   * §

Lee, Clive Howard
Marketing Organisation and Policy in the Cotton Trade:
M'Connel & Kennedy of Manchester 1795-1835
Business History   vol X no 2 1968
M'Connel & Kennedy
432

Lee, Clive Howard
Some Aspects of the Coastal Shipping Trade: The Aberdeen
Steam Navigation Company 1835-80
Journal of Transport History   new ser vol III no 2 1975
Aberdeen Steam Navigation Co
740

Lee, G A
The Tramways of Kingston-upon-Hull 1871-1945

Sheffield PhD 1968
Hull Tramways
721

Lee, Joseph
The Construction Costs of Irish Railways 1830-1853

Business History   vol XI no 2 1967
Irish Railways
502   710

Lee, Norman & Stubbs, Peter C
The History of Dorman Smith 1878-1972

Newman Neame 1972   176pp illus index sources
Dorman Smith
342   *

270

Lee, T A
*Company Financial Statements: An Essay in Business History
1830-1950*
see Marriner, Sheila (ed) 1978
Company Financial Statements   Distillers Co
424
Leech, Bosdin Thomas
History of the Manchester Ship Canal

Manchester: Sherratt & Hughes 1907 2 vols
Manchester Ship Canal
763   *
Leeds, Herbert
Romance of a Business House

the firm   32pp illus
Caley, A J & Son
421   BLPES
Leeman, Francis William
*Co-operation in Nottingham: A History of One Hundred Years of
Nottingham Co-operative Society Ltd*
Nottingham: the firm 1963   176pp illus index
Nottingham Co-operative Soc
656   *
Lees, J B & S
The Story of One Hundred Years 1852-1952

West Bromwich: the firm 1952   36pp illus
Lees, J B & S
223   SANDWPL
Lehane, Brendan
C & J Clark 1825-1975

Street: the firm 1975   52pp illus
Clark, C & J
451   * §
Leicester Co-operative Printing Society Ltd
*Twenty One Years of Co-partnership Printing: Being a Souvenir
of the Coming-of-Age of the Society*
Leicester: the firm 1913   48pp illus
Leicester Co-op Printing Soc
475   LEICSPL
Leicester Water Department
Leicester Water Department: 1847-1947: An Historical Review

Leicester: the firm 1974   84pp illus
Leicester Water
170   *
Leigh-Bennett, Ernest Pendarves
*Men behind the Meters: An Account of Certain Activities of the
Gas Light & Coke Company*
Curwen 1934   24pp
Gas Light & Coke Co
162   *

Leigh-Bennett, Ernest Pendarves
    On This Evidence: A Study in 1936 of the Legal and General
    Assurance Society since its Formation in 1836
    Baynard Press 1936   121pp illus sources
    Legal & General Assurance Soc
    820   * §

Leigh-Bennett, Ernest Pendarves
    Weighing the World: Two Hundred Years of an English House of
    Business...1730-1930
    Birmingham: the firm 1930   90pp illus
    Avery, W & T
    328   *

Leighton-Boyce, John Alfred Stuart
    Smiths the Bankers 1658-1958

    the firm 1958   337pp illus index sources
    Smiths the Bankers   National Provincial Bank
    814   * §

Leleux, Sydney Arthur
    Brotherhoods, Engineers

    Dawlish: David & Charles 1965   85pp illus sources
    Brotherhoods
    320   *

Lenman, Bruce
    Pitfour Brickworks, Glencarse, Perth

    Industrial Archaeology   vol 6 1969
    Small, Robert & Co
    231   241   DNDEEPL

Lenman, Bruce & Donaldson, Kathleen
    Partners' Incomes, Investment and Diversification in the
    Scottish Linen Area 1850-1921
    Business History   vol XIII no 1 1971
    Jute Industries of Dundee
    435

Lerner, Harry
    Currys: The First 100 Years

    Cambridge: Woodhead-Faulkner 1984 112pp illus
    Currys   Dixons
    363   648   654   §

Leslie, Ian M
    The First Two Hundred Years: Rosser and Russell Bi-centenary

    the firm 1974   36pp illus
    Rosser & Russell
    328   503   HMFULPL

Lesser Columbus (pseud. Laurence Cowen)
    Greater Bristol

    Pelham Press 1893   300pp illus

    421   429   450   471   AVONPL

Lethaby, W & Co
Leda: Fifty Years of Numbering Machines

the firm 1963   53pp illus
Lethaby, W & Co
330   *

Leubuscher, Charlotte
The West African Shipping Trade 1909-1959

Leyden: A W Sythoff 1962   109pp
West African Shipping
740   770   839   *

Leverhulme
Viscount Leverhulme by his Son

Allen & Unwin 1927   325pp illus index
Lever Brothers   Unilever
257   258   411   414   §

Levin, Hillel
John DeLorean: The Maverick Mogul

Orbis 1983   268pp
DeLorean
351   *

Lewchuck, Wayne A
*The Economics of Technical Change: A Case Study of the
British Motor Vehicle Industry 1896-1932*
Cambridge PhD 1982
Motor Vehicle Industry
350   363

Lewchuk, Wayne A
*The Return to Capital in the British Motor Vehicle Industry
1896-1939*
Business History   vol XXVII no 1 1985
Motor Vehicle Industry
350

Lewinsohn, Richard
The Man behind the Scenes: The Career of Sir Basil Zaharoff

Gollancz 1929   214pp illus
Vickers
320   361   *

Lewis, C M
*British Railways in Argentina 1857-1914: A Case Study of
Foreign Investment*
Athlone 1983   259pp
Baring Brothers
814   839   *

Lewis, Edward Roberts
No C. I. C.

Universal Royalties 1956   95pp
Decca Gramophone Co
344   345   * §

273

Lewis, G
> *Cherry Blossom Boot Polish 1851-1951: One Hundred Shining Years*
> the firm 1951   8pp illus
> Cherry Blossom Boot Polish
> 259   §

Lewis, Harry
> *From an Acorn the Tree: A History of the Wandsworth Gas Company 1834-1949*
> the firm 1949   44pp illus
> Wandsworth & District Gas Co
> 162   *

Lewis, Henry King
> *Lewis's: 1844-1944: A Brief Account of a Century's Work*
>
> the firm 1945   89pp illus
> Lewis, H K & Co
> 475   * §

Lewis, John Spedan
> *Partnership for All*
>
> Kerr-Cross Publishing 1948   xviii 532pp
> John Lewis Partnership
> 656   *

Lewis, M J
> *G T Clark and the Dowlais Iron Company 1852-97: An Entrepreneurial Case Study*
> Wales(Aberystwyth) MSc(Econ) 1983
> Dowlais Iron Co
> 221

Lewis, R Stanley
> *Eighty Years of Enterprise 1869-1949: Ransomes & Rapier Ltd of the Waterside Works, Ipswich*
> Ipswich: W S Cowell 1949   112pp illus
> Ransomes & Rapier
> 320   * §

Lewis, Reginald
> *Lord Glenesk and the 'Morning Post'*
>
> Alston Rivers 1910   443pp index
> Morning Post
> 475   StBRD

Lewis, Victor
> *The Iron Dale*
>
> Stanton, Notts: the firm 1959   47pp illus
> Stanton Ironworks
> 221   * §

Liebenau, Jonathan M
> *A History of the British Pharmaceutical Industry*
>
> Manchester, M U P forthcoming
> Pharmaceutical Industry
> 257

Liebenau, Jonathan M
Industrial R & D in Pharmaceutical Firms in the Early Twentieth Century
Business History   vol XXVI no 3 1984
Burroughs Wellcome   Allen & Hanbury
257

Liebenau, Jonathan M
Marketing High Technology: Educating Physicians to Use Innovative Medicines
see Davenport-Hines, R P T (ed)
Innovative Medicines
257

Liebenau, Jonathan M (ed)
The Challenge of New Technology: Innovation in British Business
Aldershot: Gower 1987

Lind, Peter & Co
Lind, Peter & Co 40th Anniversary: Concrete Achievements

the firm 1955   57pp illus
Lind, Peter & Co
502   §

Lindgren, Håkan
Corporate Growth: The Swedish Match Industry in its Global Setting
Stockholm: Liber Förlag 1979   447pp illus index sources
Bryant & May   Swedish Match
256

Lindsay Parkinson
This Way Forward: A Résume and a Record of Building and Construction during 75 Eventful Years
the firm nd
Lindsay Parkinson
500

Lindsay, Jean
A History of the North Wales Slate Industry

Newton Abbot: David & Charles 1974 376pp illus sources
Slate Industry
231   *

Linen Thread Co
The Faithful Fibre: The Story of the Development of the Linen Thread Company Ltd
Glasgow: the firm 1956   68pp illus
Linen Thread Co
434   UBRIS

Lines, C J
The Development and Location of the Specialist Agricultural Engineering Industry with special reference to East Anglia
London MSc 1961
Agricultural Engineering Industry
321

Lines, Walter
Looking Backwards and Forwards, Being a Short History

the firm 1958   76pp illus
Lines Bros   Triang
494   MERTNPL

Lipman, Michael Isaac
Memoirs of a Socialist Business Man

Lipman Trust 1980   iii 407pp
Lipman   EKCO
345   630

Lipton
Golden Jubilee of Lipton Ltd., 1948

the firm 1948   30pp illus
Lipton   Allied Suppliers
423   617   641   §

Lischka, J R
Ludwig Mond and the British Alkali Industry: A Study in the Interrelations of Science, Engineering, Industry & Government
Duke PhD 1970
Brunner, Mond   Alkali Industry
251

Little, Bryan
Capper Pass 150: The First Hundred and Fifty Years

Newman Neame 1963   33pp sources
Capper Pass
224   320   * §

Little, Bryan
David Jones 1862-1962: A Hundred Years of Wholesale Grocery

Newman Neame 1962   47pp illus
Jones, David & Co, Liverpool
617   * §

Littler, Eric Raymond
A Striking Industry in Bishops Stortford

the firm 1971   68pp illus
United Match Industries
256   HERTSPL

Littler, Eric Raymond
A Striking Industry in Heywood

typescript 1975   22pp illus
Hargreaves & Clegg
256   *

Littler, Eric Raymond
A Striking Industry in Irlam

Wigan: author 1979   20pp illus
Hulme Patent Advertising Match
256   838   *

Littler, Eric Raymond
A Striking Industry in Letchworth

typescript 1973   47pp illus
Anglia Match Co
256   HERTSPL

Littler, Eric Raymond
A Striking Industry in Welwyn Garden City

typescript 1969   23pp
Welwyn Match Co
256   MRC

Liu, Kwang-Ching
Anglo-American Steamship Rivalry in China 1862-1874

Cambridge, Mass: Harvard U P 1962   xvi 218pp
Steamship Rivalry in China
740   770   839   *

Liveing, Edward George Downing
A Century of Insurance: The Commercial Union Group of Insurance Companies 1861-1961
Witherby 1961   xvi 320pp illus index sources
Commercial Union Group
820   * §

Liveing, Edward George Downing
Adventure in Publishing: The House of Ward Lock 1854-1954

Ward Lock 1954   108pp illus index
Ward Lock
475   * §

Liveing, Edward George Downing
Pioneers of Petrol: A Centenary History of Carless, Capel and Leonard 1859-1959
Witherby 1959   xxiii 94pp illus index
Carless, Capel & Leonard
140   612   * §

Liveing, Edward George Downing
The House of Harrild 1801-1948

the firm 1949   ix 70pp illus
Harrild & Sons
327   *

Liverpool Corn Trade
Liverpool Corn Trade Association 1853-1953

Liverpool: 1953   64pp illus
Liverpool Corn Trade Assoc
963   611   *

Livingstone, E & S
Footprints on the Sands of Time 1863-1963: The Story of the House of Livingstone, Medical, Scientific & Dental Publishers
Edinburgh: Livingstone 1963   71pp illus
Livingstone, E & S
475   EDNBRPL

Lloyd's List and Shipping Gazette
Lloyd's List and Shipping Gazette 1734-1934

the firm 1934   47pp illus
Lloyd's List & Shipping Gazette
837   §

Lloyd's Packing Warehouses
The Story of the Bale

Manchester: the firm 1926   27pp illus
Lloyd's Packing Warehouses
770   TAMESPL

Lloyd's Register of Shipping
Annals of Lloyd's Register: Centenary Edition 1934

the firm 1934   274pp index
Lloyd's Register of Shipping
837   *

Lloyd, Attree & Smith
Lloyd, Attree & Smith: One Hundred Years

the firm 1957   37pp
Lloyd, Attree & Smith
453   HACKPL

Lloyd, Geoffrey I H
The Cutlery Trades: An Historical Essay in the Economics of Small Scale Production
Longmans Green 1913 repr 1968
Cutlery Trades
316   491   SHEFFPL

Lloyd, Humphrey
The Quaker Lloyds in the Industrial Revolution

Hutchinson 1975   xiv 322pp illus index sources
Lloyds Bank   Old Park Colliery Co
111   221   814   * §

Lloyd, Ian
Rolls-Royce: The Growth of a Firm; The Merlin at War; The Years of Endeavour
Macmillan 1978   3 vols illus index sources
Rolls-Royce
328   351   364   *

Lloyd, John
The Early History of the Old South Wales Iron Works 1760-1840
Bedford Press 1906   viii 218pp illus
South Wales Iron Works
221   311   *

Lloyd, Keith J
The Highgate Brewery, Walsall

Tipton: Black Country Soc 1982   20pp illus
Highgate Brewery   Mitchells & Butlers
427   WALSLPL

Lloyd, Samuel
> *The Lloyds of Birmingham: With Some Account of the Founding of Lloyds Bank*
>
> Birmingham: Cornish Bros 1907   xvi 246pp
> Lloyds Bank
> 814   *

Lloyd-Jones, R & Lewis, M J
> *Industrial Structure and Firm Growth: The Sheffield Iron and Steel Industry 1880-1901*
>
> Business History   vol XXV no 3 1983
> Sheffield Iron & Steel
> 221

Loasby, B J
> *The Swindon Project: A Report on the Relocation of W H Smith & Son Ltd's Lambeth Warehouse*
>
> Pitman Publishing 1973   76pp index
> Smith, W H & Son
> 619   653   UBRIS

Lockwood, Arthur
> *Co-operation in the Thames Valley*
>
> Reading: the firm 1949   134pp illus
> Reading Co-operative Soc
> 656   BERKSPL

Logan, John C
> *An Economic History of the Scottish Electricity Supply Industry 1878-ca1930*
>
> Strathclyde PhD 1983
> Electricity Supply in Scotland
> 161

Logan, John C
> *The Dumbarton Glass Work Company ca1777-ca1850*
>
> Strathclyde MLitt 1970   222pp sources
> Dumbarton Glass Work Co
> 247   DMBTNPL

Logan, John C
> *The Dumbarton Glass Works Company: A Study in Entrepreneurship*
>
> Business History   vol XIII no 2 1971
> Dumbarton Glass Works Co
> 247

London & South Western Bank
> *A Short History of the London & South Western Bank Limited: Jubilee Year 1862-1912*
>
> Blades East & Blades 1913   32pp
> London & South Western Bank
> 814

London and Lancashire Insurance Co
> *After Fifty Years*
>
> 1912   61pp
> London & Lancashire Insurance
> 820   GHL

Long, Anne & Russell
A Shipping Venture: Turnbull Scott & Co 1872-1972

Hutchinson Benham 1974 xix 326pp illus index sources
Turnbull Scott & Co
740 §

Long, Joan
A First Class Job: The Story of Frank Murphy, Radio Pioneer, Furniture Designer and Industrial Idealist
Sheringham, Norfolk: author 1985 208pp illus index
Murphy Radio
345 *

Longhurst, Henry Carpenter
Adventure in Oil: The Story of British Petroleum

Sidgwick & Jackson 1959 286pp illus
B P
130 140 251 612 652 * §

Longhurst, Henry Carpenter
The Borneo Story: The History of the First 100 Years of Trading in the Far East by the Borneo Company Ltd
Newman Neame 1956 120pp illus
Borneo Co
839 * §

Longley
A Royal Occasion

the firm 1958
Longley, James & Co
501

Longley
Longleys of Crawley 1863-1963

the firm 1963 47pp illus
Longley, James & Co
501 *

Longworth, J E
Oldham Master Cotton Spinners Association Ltd: Centenary Year 1866-1966
the firm 1966 43pp illus
Oldham Master Cotton Spinners
432 OLDHMPL

Loring, Henry
From the Beginning

Jarrold ca1905 114pp illus
Robertson Electric Lamps G E C
347 *

Louis, Harry & Currie, Bob
The Story of Triumph Motor Cycles

Cambridge: Patrick Stephens 1978 128pp illus index
Triumph Motor Cycles
363 *

Lovell, Y J
>*Bi-centenary Lovell 1786-1986: Two Centuries Strong and Building*
>the firm 1986   36pp illus
>Lovell, Y J
>500   §

Low, David
>*'With All Faults'*
>
>Tehran: Amate Press 1973   118pp illus
>David Low
>653   StBRD

Low, James F
>*James F Low & Co, Monifieth: An Account of its Progress*
>
>the firm nd   12pp
>Low, James F
>323   DNDEEPL

Lowe & Oliver
>*Lowe & Oliver Ltd 1923-1966*
>
>Oxford Mail 1966   12pp illus
>Lowe & Oliver
>503   OXFDPL

Lowe, C J
>*The Building Society Movement: A Half-Century Record ...The Bristol, West of England & S. Wales Permanent Building Soc*
>Bristol: W Crofton Hemmings 1901   158pp illus index
>Bristol & West Building Soc
>815   BLPES

Lowe, Dorothy P
>*The Furniture Industry of High Wycombe since 1870*
>
>London MPhil 1983
>High Wycombe Furniture Industry
>467

Lowe, Thomas & Sons
>*1825-1975 Thomas Lowe & Sons Ltd*
>
>Burton upon Trent: nd   19pp
>Lowe, Thomas & Sons
>501   MRC

Lucas Aerospace
>*Turning Industrial Decline into Expansion- A Trade Union Initiatiave*
>Lucas Trade Union Committee 1979   400pp typescript sources
>Lucas Aerospace
>340   343   BLPES

Luke and Spencer
>*Luke and Spencer Ltd 1877-1977 Centenary Year: 100 Years of Grinding Wheel Manufacture*
>the firm 1977
>Luke & Spencer   Unicorn Industries U K
>246

Lukens, John
>*The Sanger Story: Being George Sanger Coleman's Story of His Life with His Grandfather 'Lord' George Sanger*
>Hodder & Stoughton 1956
>Sanger, 'Lord' George
>974   979   *

Lumbys
>*Our First Hundred Years 1858-1958*
>
>Halifax: the firm 1958   39pp illus
>Lumbys
>320   HLFXPL

Lumsden, Harry & Aitken, P Henderson
>*History of the Hammermen of Glasgow: A Study Typical of Scottish Craft Life and Organisation*
>Paisley: 1912   xxv 446pp illus
>Hammermen of Glasgow
>312   *

Lusty, Robert
>*Bound To Be Read*
>
>Jonathan Cape nd   314pp ind
>Jonathan Cape   Hutchinson
>475   StBRD

Lyddon, Denis W & Marshall, Peter A
>*Paper in Bolton: A Papermaker's Tale*
>
>Altrincham: John Sherratt 1975   208pp illus index sources
>Trinity Paper Mills   Cromptons, Creams
>471   *

Lye and Sons
>*Lye and Sons 1857-1957*
>
>Luton: the firm 1957   24pp illus
>Lye & Sons
>439   §

Lyle of Westbourne, Lord
>*Mr. Cube's Fight Against Nationalisation*
>
>Hollis & Carter 1954   306pp illus
>Tate & Lyle
>420   UBRIS

Lyle, Oliver
>*The Plaistow Story*
>
>the firm 1960
>Tate & Lyle
>420

Lynch, Henry Foulks & Co
>*Seventy Years of Progress in Accountancy Education*
>
>. the firm 1955   63pp illus
>Lynch, H Foulks & Co
>836   *

Lynch, Patrick & Vaizey, John
Guinness's Brewery in the Irish Economy 1759-1876

Cambridge: C U P 1960   viii 278pp illus index sources
Guinness
427   *

Lynes, Alice
A History of Coventry Textiles

Coventry Textile Society 1952
Coventry Textiles
430

Lynn, Richard (ed)
The Entrepreneurs: Eight Case Studies

Allen & Unwin 1974   175pp

10   345   371   665   723   *

Lyons, J
Lyons of London: The Rise of a Great Business

typescript   30pp
Lyons, J & Co
419   423   661   GLROHL

Lysaght
The Lysaght Century 1857-1957

Bristol: the firm 1957   64pp illus
Lysaght, John
220   UBRIS

Lythe, Samuel George Edgar
Gourlays of Dundee: The Rise and Fall of a Scottish Shipbuilding Firm
Dundee: Abertay Hist Soc 1964   20pp
Gourlays Brothers & Co
361   *

Lythe, Samuel George Edgar
Shipbuilding at Dundee down to 1914

Scot Journal Political Econ 1962
Shipbuilding at Dundee
361

Maber, John M
North Star to Southern Cross

Prescot: T Stephenson & Sons 1967 xv 335pp illus
Orient Line
740   *

Macartney, Sylvia & West, John
A History of the Lewisham Silk Mills

Lewisham Local History Soc 1979   26pp illus
Lewisham Silk Mills
432   BLPES

Macaulay, P Tarbet
Jubilee History of the Queensbury Industrial Society Ltd from 1855-1905
Manchester: Co-op Printing 1905   115pp illus
Queensbury Industrial Soc
656   HLFXPL

Macaulay, R H
History of the Bombay Burmah Trading Corporation Ltd

the firm 1934   161pp
Bombay Burmah Trading Corp
839   §

MacDermot, B H D
Panmure Gordon & Co 1876-1976: A Century of Stockbroking

the firm 1976   v 71pp illus
Panmure Gordon & Co
831   §

MacDermot, Edward T (Clinker, C R & Nott, O S eds)
History of the Great Western Railway (revised edition)

Ian Allan 1964-67   3 vols illus index
Great Western Railway
710   *

MacDonald, Donald
Percival Norton Johnson: The Biography of a Pioneer Metallurgist
the firm 1951   224pp illus
Johnson, Matthey
224   *

MacDonald, Donald
The Johnsons of Maiden Lane

Martins 1964   180pp illus index sources
Johnson, Matthey
224   *

MacDonald, Donald & Hunt, Leslie B
A History of Platinum and its Allied Metals

the firm 1983   460pp
Johnson, Matthey
224   *

Macdonald, Gilbert
In Pursuit of Excellence: One Hundred Years of Wellcome 1880-1980
the firm 1983   120pp illus
Wellcome Foundation   Burroughs Wellcome
257   §

Macfarlane, Lang & Co
Macfarlane, Lang & Co Ltd, Glasgow and London 1817-1925: A Brief History
the firm 1925   32pp illus
Macfarlane, Lang & Co
419   HMFULPL

MacGregor, David Roy
   The China Bird: The History of Captain Killick and 100 Years of Steam and Sail
   Chatto & Windus 1961   366pp illus index sources
   Ben Line Steamers   Killick Martin & Co
   740   770   *

Machin, Donald J & Smyth, R Leslie
   The Changing Structure of the British Pottery Industry 1935-1968
   Newcastle, Staffs: Keele U P 1969   127pp illus
   Pottery Industry
   248   *

Mack, Peter Hughes
   The Golden Weed: A History of Tobacco and of the House of Andrew Chalmers 1865-1965
   Newman Neame 1965   xvi 64pp illus index sources
   Chalmers, Andrew & Co
   617   * §

Mack, R J
   Andrew Chalmers & Company Established 1865: The Story of the Company down to 1950
   the firm 1950   32pp illus
   Chalmers, Andrew & Co
   429   UBRIS

Mackenzie, Edward Montague Compton
   Brockhouse: A Study in Industrial Evolution

   West Bromwich: the firm 1945   54pp illus index
   Brockhouse, J & Co
   223   311   312   320   353   SANDWPL

Mackenzie, Edward Montague Compton
   Realms of Silver: One Hundred Years of Banking in the East

   Routledge 1954   xiv 333pp illus index
   Chartered Bank
   814   * §

Mackenzie, Edward Montague Compton
   The House of Coalport 1750-1950

   Collins 1951   128pp illus
   Coalport China Co
   248   *

Mackenzie, Edward Montague Compton
   The Sankey Story

   typescript ca1958
   Sankey, Joseph & Sons   G K N Sankey
   310   353

Mackie
   Centenary Souvenir of the House of Mackie 1825-1925

   Edinburgh: the firm 1925   24pp illus
   Mackie, House of
   419   EDNBRPL

Mackie, A D
>*A Centenary History of Waddie & Co. Limited, Edinburgh & London*
>the firm 1960 78pp illus
>Waddie & Co
>475 EDNBRPL

Mackie, W
>*Century of Craftsmanship: Alexander Hall and Son (Builders) Ltd 1880-1980*
>Aberdeen: Mearns & Gill 1980 100pp illus
>Hall, Alexander & Son
>501 ABRDNPL

Mackie, W Euan
>*The Mallinson Story 1877-1977*
>
>the firm 1977 109pp illus
>Mallinson, William & Denny Mott
>613 *

Mackintosh, Eric D
>*Norwich Adventure: An Account of Events at Chapel Field Works 1932-1942*
>the firm 1947 96pp illus
>Caley, A J & Son Mackintosh, John
>421

Mackintosh, Harold Vincent
>*By Faith and Work: The Autobiography of the First Viscount Mackintosh of Halifax*
>Hutchinson 1966 296pp illus index
>Mackintosh, John
>421 * §

Mackintosh, John & Sons
>*The Mackintosh Story*
>
>Norwich: the firm 1967
>Mackintosh, John
>421 NRFLKPL

MacLaren, Moray David Shaw
>*Sanderson & Murray: Fellmongers and Wool Merchants 1844-1954*
>Galashiels: the firm 1955 83pp illus
>Sanderson & Murray
>441 BORDRPL

Maclean, John S
>*The Newcastle and Carlisle Railway 1825-1862 Compiled from Official Reports, Documents and Records*
>Newcastle upon Tyne: Robinson 1948 vi 121pp illus index
>Newcastle & Carlisle Railway
>710 *

Maclehose, James
>*The Glasgow University Press 1638-1931*
>
>Glasgow: G U P 1931 xx 285pp illus index sources
>Glasgow University Press
>475 *

Macleod, William H & Houldsworth, Henry H
The Beginnings of the Houldsworths of Coltness

Glasgow: Jackson Son & Co 1937   xi 164pp illus
Coltness Iron Co   Fine Cotton Spinners & Doublers
221   *

Macmillan, David S
The Transfer of Company Control from Scotland to London in the 19th Century: The Case of the Scottish Australian Company
Business History   vol XII no 2 1970
Scottish Australian Company
814   839

Macnab, A & J
A & J Macnab Ltd: A Company History

Edinburgh: the firm 1960   62pp illus
Macnab, A & J
431   981   EDNBRPL

Macpherson, Hugh (ed)
John Spedan Lewis 1885-1963 Remembered by some of his Contemporaries in the Centenary Year of his Birth
the firm 1985   222pp illus index
John Lewis Partnership
656   §

MacRae, R J
The Life and Times of the 'Old Lady of Hertford Street' 1835-1935
Coventry: the firm 1935   24pp illus
Coventry Savings Bank
814   *

Maggs, C W & Co (Melksham)
150th Anniversary: Being a Record of One Hundred and Fifty Years of Progress
Melksham: the firm 1953   15pp illus
Maggs, C W & Co (Melksham)
                                                               WILTSPL

Magnusson, Mamie
A Length of Days: The Scottish Mutual Assurance Society 1883-1983
Henry Melland 1983   154pp illus
Scottish Mutual Assurance Soc   Scot Temperance Assurance Soc
820   * §

Maguire, Edward
The Sirocco Story: The Birth and Growth of an Industry

Belfast: the firm nd   36pp illus
Davidson & Co   Sirocco
328   SEELBPL

Mahony, Martin & Bros
Two Hundred Years: The Story of a Family and an Industry 1750-1950
Blarney: the firm 1950   24pp illus
Mahony, Martin & Bros   Cork Woollen Mills
431   CORKPL

Mainland, J F & Howard, E H
   Indemnity Mutual Marine Assurance Co: A Centenary Retrospect
   1824-1924
   the firm 1924   65pp illus index
   Indemnity Mutual Marine
   820   * §

Mais, Stuart Peter Brodie
   A History of N. Greening & Sons Ltd., Warrington, England: From
   1799 to 1949
   the firm 1949   60pp illus
   Greening, N & Sons
   223   224   *

Malcolm, Charles Alexander
   The Bank of Scotland 1695-1945

   Edinburgh: the firm 1948   viii 322pp illus index
   Bank of Scotland
   814   * §

Malcolm, Charles Alexander
   The History of the British Linen Bank

   Edinburgh: the firm 1950   xii 253pp illus index sources
   British Linen Bank
   814   * §

Malcolm, D O
   The British South Africa Company 1889-1939

   1939   73pp
   British South Africa Co
   839   GHL

Malin, John C
   The West Riding Recovered Wool Industry ca1813-1939

   York DPhil 1979
   Recovered Wool Industry
   431

Mallett, Alan S
   Idyll of the Kings: The History of the King Line 1889-1979

   Kendal: World Ship Soc 1980   64pp illus
   King Line   British & Commonwealth
   470   §

Manchester Gas Dept
   One Hundred and Forty Three Years of Gas in Manchester

   Manchester: the firm 1949   67pp illus
   Manchester Gas Dept
   162   *

Manchester Tramway Dept
   Souvenir Brochure on the Abandonment of the Last Tram
   Service
   Manchester: Manchester Corp 1949 31pp
   Manchester Tramway Dept
   721   NRMYORK

Manchester, Port of
    Manchester Ship Canal Company Past and Present

    Manchester: the firm 1978
    Manchester Ship Canal
    763
Mander
    The History of Mander Brothers

    Wolverhampton: the firm 1955   255pp illus
    Mander Brothers
    255   SANDWPL
Manfield & Sons
    In the Service of a Famous Firm: 50th Anniversary Brochure

    Northampton: the firm 1936   20pp illus
    Manfield & Sons
    451   NHPTNPL
Manfield & Sons
    The Story of a British Industry: Manfield & Sons

    Northampton: Joseph Rogers 1908
    Manfield & Sons
    451
Manifoldia
    Fifty Years of Achievement 1903-1953

    West Bromwich: the firm 1953   86pp illus
    Manifoldia
    475   SANDWPL
Mann Judd Gordon & Co
    Of a Going Concern: Mann Judd Gordon & Company, Chartered
    Accountants, Glasgow circa 1817 to 1967
    the firm 1967   58pp illus
    Mann Judd Gordon & Co
    836   §
Mann, Amos
    Democracy in Industry: 21 Years of the Leicester Anchor Boot
    & Shoe Productive Society Ltd.
    Leicester: Co-op Printing Soc 1914   73pp illus
    Anchor Boot Society
    451   LEICSPL
Mann, Cecil
    The Alden Heating Story: A History of Fred. G Alden (Heating)
    Ltd, Oxford
    Alden Press 1981   66pp illus
    Alden, Fred. G
    503   *
Manning, Peter
    The Origins and Early History of Barclays Bank in Pall Mall

    the firm 1985   28pp illus
    Barclays Bank   Ransom Bouverie & Co
    814   §

Mansbridge, Albert
Brick upon Brick: 50 Years of the Co-operative Permanent Building Society 1884-1934
Dent 1934 xxii 236pp illus index
Co-operative Permanent Bldg Soc
815 * §

Mappin Fraser, J N
History of Mappin & Webb Ltd

typescript 1957
Mappin & Webb
316 491

Marconi's Wireless Telegraph Co
Jubilee Year: The Marconi Company

Chelmsford: the firm 1947 57pp illus
Marconi
790 *

Mardon, Heber
Landmarks in the History of a Bristol Firm 1824-1904

Bristol: the firm 1918 66pp illus
Mardon, Son & Hall
472 475 *

Marillier, H C
Christies: 1766 to 1925

Constable 1926 xii 311pp illus
Christies
839 *

Marine Insurance Co
The Marine Insurance Company Ltd 1836-1936

the firm 1936 81pp illus
Marine Insurance Co
820 §

Marley
Marley Diamond Jubilee 1924-1984: 60 Years of Achievement

Sevenoaks: the firm 1984 56pp illus
Marley
241 483 BROMPL

Marment, Arthur Verriour
Marments, Cardiff 1879-1979: In Fashion Now as in 1879

Cardiff: the firm 1979 20pp illus
Marments
645 SGLAMPL

Marriage, E
Annals of One Hundred Years of Flour Milling

Colchester: the firm 1940 illus
Marriage, E & Son
416 ESSEXPL

Marriner, **Sheila**
Rathbones of Liverpool 1845-1873

Liverpool: L U P 1961   xi 246pp illus index sources
Rathbones
740   *
Marriner, **Sheila**
*Sir Alfred Mond's Octopus: A Nationalised House Building
Business*
Business History   vol XXI no 1 1979
Office of Works
501
Marriner, **Sheila & Hyde, Francis E**
*The Senior John Samuel Swire 1825-98: Management in Far
Eastern Shipping Trades*
Liverpool: L U P 1967   xv 224pp illus index sources
Butterfield & Swire   Holt, Alfred & Co
740   770   839   * §
Marriner, **Sheila (ed)**
*Business and Businessmen: Studies in Business, Economic and
Accounting History*
Liverpool: L U P 1978   xiv 300pp index sources

424   710   740   820   *
Marsden, **Frederick**
*Textiles for Manufacture, Frederick Marsden Ltd:
Commemorating the Sixtith Jubilee 1890-1950*
1950   42pp illus
Marsden, Frederick
430   COVNPL
Marsden, **J S & Brock, D B S**
Eagley Mills 1800-1965

typescript nd   101pp
Coats, T & P   Eagley Mills
432   BOLTNPL
Marsh, **J**
*One Hundred Years: The Story of White, Wolfe Barry & Partners
1856-1956*
1956   30pp
White, Wolfe Barry & Partners
837   GHL
Marshall, **A C & Newbould, Herbert**
The History of Firth's 1842-1918

Sheffield: the firm 1924   112pp illus
Firth, Thos & Sons
221   *
Marshall, **Chapman Frederick Dendy**
A History of the Southern Railway

the firm 1936   xi 708pp illus index sources
Southern Railway
710   *

Marshall, John
The Lancashire and Yorkshire Railway

N Abbot: David & Charles 1969-72   2 vols illus index sources
Lancashire & Yorkshire Railway
710   *

Marshall, John Duncan
Furness and the Industrial Revolution: An Economic History of
Furness 1711-1900 and the Town of Barrow 1757-1897
Barrow Central Library 1958   xxii 438pp illus sources
Furness and Barrow
210   221   329   361   *

Martin Baker Aircraft
The Story of an Enterprise 1929-1955

Higher Denham: the firm 1955   80pp illus
Martin Baker Aircraft Co
764   RAeS

Martin, Albert A
Cazenove & Co 1785-1955

the firm 1955   16pp illus
Cazenove & Co
831   *

Martin, Bill
Harry Ferguson Ltd

Holywood: Ulster Folk Museum 1984   30pp illus
Ferguson, Harry
321   353   NEELBPL

Martin, C W
Under Eight Monarchs: C W Martin & Sons Limited 1823-1953

the firm 1953   69pp illus
Martin, C W & Sons
456   616   * §

Martin, Frederick W
The History of Lloyd's and of Marine Insurance in Great Britain

1876   416pp
Lloyd's of London
820   *

Martin, John
The Garnkirk and Glasgow Railway

Bishopbriggs: Strathkelvin 1983   64pp illus sources
Garnkirk & Glasgow Railway
710   SKLVNPL

Martin, John Biddulph
The 'Grasshopper' in Lombard Street

Leadenhall Press 1892   xx 328pp illus index
Martins Bank
814   * §

Martin, P W
History of the Heart of England Building Society

    Warwick: the firm 1981   200pp illus index
    Heart of England Building Soc
    815   §

Martins Bank
Martins Bank Ltd: A Short Account of over a Century and a Quarter of Progress and Development
    Liverpool: the firm 1962   illus
    Martins Bank
    814   *

Martins, Susanna Wade
A Great Estate at Work: The Holkham Estate and its Inhabitants in the Nineteenth Century
    Cambridge: C U P 1980   xiv 289pp illus index sources
    Holkham Estate
    10   *

Masefield, Peter Gordon
To Ride the Storm: The Story of the Airship R 101

    William Kimber 1982   560pp illus index
    Royal Airship Works
    364   *

Mason, Alfred Edward Woodley
Sir George Alexander and the St James's Theatre

    Macmillan 1935   x 247pp illus
    St James's Theatre
    974   *

Mason, Alfred Edward Woodley
The Royal Exchange: A Note on the...Bicentenary of the Royal Exchange Assurance
    the firm 1920   103pp
    Royal Exchange Assurance
    820   *

Mason, Eric
The Lancashire & Yorkshire Railway in the Twntieth Century

    Ian Allan 1975   236pp illus index
    Lancashire & Yorkshire Railway
    710   *

Mason, John D
A Manufacturing and Bleaching Enterprise during the Industrial Revolution: The Sykeses of Edgeley
    Business History   vol XXIII no 1 1981
    Sykeses of Edgeley
    432   437

Mason, Joseph & Co
Joseph Mason Paints: Into Two Centuries

    Derby: the firm 1966   12pp illus
    Mason, Joseph & Co
    255   DERBYPL

Mason, N M
*Unprofitable Railway Companies in England and Wales
1845-1923 with special reference to the S Midlands*
London PhD 1982
Railway Companies, Unprofitable
710

Mathew, William M
The House of Gibbs and the Peruvian Guano Monopoly

Royal Historical Society 1981   xii 281pp index sources
Gibbs, Antony
814   *

Mathias, Peter
*Capital and Entrepreneurship as Factor Markets in British
Industry   1750-1914*
see Fuji Conference 3, 1976
Capital & Entrepreneurship

Mathias, Peter
*Manufacturers and Retailing in the Food Trades: The Struggle
over Margarine*
see Supple, Barry (ed) 1977
Margarine
411   641

Mathias, Peter
*Retailing Revolution: A History of Multiple Retailing in the
Food Trades: Allied Suppliers Group*
Longman 1967   xix 425pp illus index sources
Allied Suppliers   Lipton
617   641   * §

Mathias, Peter
The Brewing Industry in England 1700-1830

Cambridge: C U P 1959   xxviii 596pp illus index sources
Brewing Industry
427   * §

Mathieson, George
The Sugar Convention from a Confectioner's Standpoint

Cassell 1889   31pp
Clarke, Nicholls and Coombs   Clarnico
421   *

Matthews, Philip W & Tuke, Anthony W
History of Barclays Bank Limited

Blades, East & Blades 1926   xiv 441pp illus index sources
Barclays Bank
814   *

Matthews, Wrightson Group
*Irons in the Fire: A Record of the Matthews, Wrightson Group
of Companies 1901-1951*
the firm 1952   83pp illus
Matthews, Wrightson Group
820   §

294

Maude, Evelyn John (ed)
> *The Story of the Royal United Kingdom Beneficent Association 1863-1963*
> the firm 1963   v 86pp
> Royal U K Beneficent Assoc
> 820   *

Maude, Wilfred
> *Merchants and Bankers: A Brief Record of Antony Gibbs & Sons Ltd 1808-1958*
> the firm 1958   136pp illus
> Gibbs, Antony
> 814   *

Maudslay
> *Memories of Maudslay, Son & Field*
>
> the firm nd   24pp illus
> Maudslay, Son & Field
> 320   328   IMECHE

Maxwell, Herbert Eustace
> *Annals of the Scottish Widows' Fund Life Assurance Society during One Hundred Years 1815-1914*
> Edinburgh: the firm 1914   vii 132pp illus
> Scottish Widows' Fund Life
> 820   *

Maxwell, Herbert Eustace
> *Half a Century of successful Trade: Being a Sketch of the Rise and Development of the Business of W A Gilbey 1857-1907*
> the firm 1907   85pp illus index
> Gilbey, W & A
> 424   642   *

Maxwell, Herbert Eustace
> *Life and Times of the Right Honourable W H Smith MP*
>
> Edinburgh: Blackwood & Sons 1893   2 vols illus
> Smith, W H & Son
> 619   653   *

Maxwell, William
> *First Fifty Years of St Cuthbert's Co-operative Association Ltd 1859-1909*
> Edinburgh: the firm 1909   275pp illus
> St Cuthbert's Co-op Assoc
> 656   UBRIS

May (Hop Merchants)
> *Welcome You to May's Acre*
>
> ca1961   14pp illus
> May (Hop Merchants)
> 617   SWKPL

May, Garry
> *The Challenge of B E A: The Story of a Great Airline's First 25 Years*
> Wolfe 1971   175pp illus
> British European Airways
> 750   *

May, Henry B
Seventy Years in Horticulture

Cable Printing 1928 92pp illus
May Horticulture
10 ENFLDPL

May, R
R May & Son Ltd, Timber Merchants est. 1853, Acorn Wharf 1855-1955: The Story of R May & Son Ltd
illus
May, R & Son
613 SWKPL

Mayer, H C
The History of Griffin & George Ltd

Alperton,Wembley: typescript 1980
Griffin & George
371

Mayes, Leonard John
The History of Chair Making in High Wycombe

Routledge & Kegan Paul 1960 xiv 174pp illus
High Wycombe Chair Making
467 *

McAlpine, Sir Robert
Sir Robert McAlpine & Sons Ltd 1869-1969: Souvenir Brochures and Brief History
the firm 1969 174pp illus
McAlpine, Sir Robert & Sons
500 HMLTNPL

McBurnie, John M
The Story of the Lancashire and Yorkshire Bank Limited 1872-1922
Manchester: Sherratt & Hughes 1922 108pp illus
Lancashire & Yorkshire Bank
814 HLFXPL

McChesney, John S
Adam Wilson & Sons: The History of a Firm of Timber Merchants
Ayr: the firm 1980 40pp illus
Wilson, Adam & Sons
613 §

McCloskey, Donald N
Economic Maturity and Entrepreneurial Decline: British Iron and Steel 1870-1913
Methuen 1971 xv 439pp
Steel Industry
221 *

McConnell, Brian
At the Sign of the Crane: 350 Years of Burrup, Mathieson and Company Limited 1628-1978
the firm 1978 xii 44pp illus
Burrup, Mathieson
475 §

296

McCreary, Alf
Spirit of the Age: The Story of 'Old Bushmills'

Belfast: the firm 1983   232pp illus
Bushmills Distillery
424   * §

McCulloch, John Herries & Stirling, Kenneth James
The Edinburgh Savings Bank: A Review of its Century of Service 1836-1936
Edinburgh: the firm 1936   xiv 120pp illus
Edinburgh Savings Bank
814   *

McEwan, Ann M C
Shotts Iron Company 1800-1850

Strathclyde MLitt 1972   272pp sources
Shotts Iron Co
221

McEwans of Perth
Window on St John Street: A Short History of McEwans of Perth 1868-1968
Perth: the firm 1968   36pp illus
McEwans of Perth
656   PERTHPL

McFarlane, Larry A
British Investment and the Land: Nebraska 1877-1946

Business History Review   vol LVII no 2 1983
Land Investment and Nebraska
839   850

McGarvie, Michael
Bowlingreen Mill: A Centenary History

Street: the firm 1979   154pp illus index sources
Avalon Leatherboard Co
441   442   * §

McGarvie, Michael
Castle Cary: Industrial & Social History with special reference to Boyd's Hair Factory
Street: the firm 1980   48pp illus sources
Boyd, John & Co.   Avalon Industries
439   * §

McGill, Jack
Crisis on the Clyde: The Story of Upper Clyde Shipbuilders

Davis-Poynter 1973   144pp
U C S (Upper Clyde Shipbuilders) Fairfield Shipbuilding
361   *

McGrandle, Leith
Two Centuries of Lewis & Peat (now the Guinness Peat Group)

the firm 1975   64pp
Lewis & Peat   Guinness Peat
815   §

McKay, J A
Kirkcaldy and District Savings Bank: Short History

1939 23pp illus
Kirkcaldy & District Savings Bank
814 KCLDYPL

McKechnie, John D
The McKechnie Story

Newman Neame 1965 28pp illus
McKechnie Brothers
224 * §

McKitterick, David
Four Hundred Years of University Printing and Publishing 1584-1984
Cambridge: C U P 1984 vii 183pp illus index sources
Cambridge University Press
475 * §

McLachlan, Sandy
The National Freight Buy-Out

Macmillan 1983 xiv 208pp illus index
National Freight Consortium
723 *

McLean, D
Nicholl's Ironmaking in the Forest of Dean

1981 82pp illus
Nicholl's
210 §

McLean, Ruari
Joseph Cundell: A Victorian Publisher

Pinner: Private Libraries Assoc 1976 96pp illus index sources
Cundell, Joseph
475 StBRD

McLellan, R S
Anchor Line, 1856-1956

Glasgow: the firm 1956 184pp illus
Anchor Line Handysides & Co
740 *

McMaster, Charles
Alloa Ale: A History of the Brewing Industry in Alloa: Sponsored to Commemorate 175 Years of Brewing in Alloa
Edinburgh: the firm 1985 70pp illus sources
Alloa Brewery Co
427 §

McMillan, Stewart
Port Line Story: A Short History of the Company

the firm 1964 75pp
Port Line
740

McNeill, Valerie
Mustads: The Story of the Horseshoe Nail

typescript 1981   70pp illus sources
Mustad Manufacturing Co
313   AVONPL

McRobb, John
The and Now 1854-1912: The Aberdeen Lime Company Ltd

Aberdeen: the firm 1912   32pp illus
Aberdeen Lime Co
242   ABRDNPL

McRoberts, J
The Houston Story

Sea Breezes   vol 44 Mar-May 1970
Houston
740

Meat Trade (various authors)
The Meat Trade

Gresham 1934   3 vols illus
Borthwick, Thomas & Sons
412   617   *

Mee, F
*Market Harborough Building Society: The First 100 Years: A
Record of Progress 1870-1970*
Market Harborough: the firm ca1970 48pp illus
Market Harborough Building Soc
815   LEICSPL

Mee, L Graham
*The Earls Fitzwilliam and the Management of the Collieries
and other Enterprises on the Wentworth Estate 1795-1857*
Nottingham PhD 1972
Wentworth Estate
111

Meggitt & Jones
Fifty Years 1884-1934: History of the Firm

Cardiff: the firm 1934   79pp illus
Meggitt & Jones
613   SGLAMPL

Melling, Joseph
*Industrial Strife and Business Welfare Philosophy: The Case of
the South Metropolitan Gas Company from the 1880s to the War*
Business History   vol XXI no 2 1979
South Metropolitan Gas Co
162

Mellor, A J L
Aspects of the Development of Dover Harbour since 1918

Kent MPhil 1981
Dover Harbour
763

299

Melrose, Andrew & Co
Centenary of the Famous Tea House of Andrew Melrose & Co 1812-1912
Edinburgh: the firm 1912   24pp illus
Melrose, Andrew
423   641   839   EDNBRPL

Meneight, W A
A History of the United Molasses Co Ltd

the firm 1977   212pp illus index
United Molasses Co
420   UBRIS

Mennell, G H
The Romance of a Great Industry,1725-1921

Darlington Echo 1922   11pp illus
Rowntree
421   BLPES

Mensforth, Eric
Family Engineers

Ward Lock 1981   168pp illus index sources
Metropolitan-Vickers   Brown, John
111   221   320   322   361   IMECHE

Menzies, John
The House of Menzies: 123 Years of Bookselling

Edinburgh: the firm 1958   76pp illus
Menzies, John & Co
619   642   653   * §

Menzies, John
The Menzies Group

Edinburgh: the firm 1965   63pp
Menzies, John & Co
619   642   653   ABRDNPL

Mercer, Tony
Mercer Chronometers: Radical Tom Mercer and the House He Founded
Ashford: Brant Wright 1978   xxiv 251pp illus index sources
Mercer Chronometers
374   *

Merriam, John
Pioneering in Plastics

Ipswich: East Anglian Magazine 1976 118pp illus
British Xylonite Co3
251   483   BLPES

Merriday, Frank (pseud)
Matthew Pomfret Limited, Soda Water Manufacturers, Albion Street, Elton, Bury: The Rise and Development of the Firm
Bury: T Crompton 1885
Pomfret, Matthew
428   BURYPL

Merrill, John
    A Hundred Years of History: Lockwood & Carlisle Ltd
    1876-1976
    Sheffield: the firm 1976
    Lockwood & Carlisle
        320   SHEFFPL
Merry, Ian D
    The Westcotts and their Times

    National Maritime Museum 1977   x 149pp illus index sources
    Westcotts
        361   740   UBRIS
Merryweather & Sons
    A Record of Two Centuries: Being a Short History of the House
    of Merryweather & Sons 1690-1901
    Merritt & Hatcher 1901   85pp
    Merryweather & Sons
        351   *
Mersey Docks
    Business in Great Waters: An Account of the Activities of the
    Mersey Docks & Harbour Board 1858-1958
    Newman Neame 1958   40pp illus
    Mersey Docks & Harbour Board
        763   §
Merthyr Tidfil County Borough
    Fifty Years of Merthyr Buses 1924-1974

    Merthyr Tidfil: 1975   47pp
    Merthyr Buses
        721   MRTHRPL
Mervyn, J F A
    Looking Back 250 Years at Lye Forge: A Short History of a
    Pioneer Firm of Iron and Steel Forgers 1699-1949
    Murray-Watson 1949   44pp illus
    Lye Forge
        312   UBRIS
Metal Box
    Metal Box, Palmers Green 1929-1979

    Southgate: the firm 1979   22pp illus
    Metal Box
        316   ENFLDPL
Metropolitan-Vickers
    1899-1949: Fifty Years in Brief

    Manchester: the firm 1949   44pp illus
    Metropolitan-Vickers   Westinghouse
        340   TAMESPL
Meux, Valerie Susie
    History of Meux's Brewery

    1891   40pp
    Meux's Brewery
        427   *

Michie, Ranald C
Crisis and Opportunity: The Formation and Operation of the British Assets Trust 1897-1914
Business History   vol XXV no 2 1983
British Assets Trust
815

Middlemas, Robert K & Barnes, A John L
Baldwin. A Biography

Weidenfeld & Nicolson 1969   1149pp illus
Baldwins
221

Middlemas, Robert Keith
The Master Builders: Thomas Brassey, John Aird, Lord Cowdray, John Norton-Griffiths
Hutchinson 1963   328pp illus index sources
Building
500   *

Middleton, D H
Airspeed: The Company and Its Aeroplanes

Lavenham: Terence Dalton 1982   206pp illus
Airspeed
364   *

Middleton, Judy
The Royal Escape with a History of the Old Ship Hotel, Brighton

the firm 1982
Old Ship Hotel, Brighton
665

Midland Iron Co
Midland Iron Co Ltd Centenary 1844-1944

the firm 1944   28pp illus
Midland Iron Co
221   ROTHMPL

Midland Motor Cylinder Co
Midcyl Golden Jubilee 1915-1965

the firm 1965   .   27pp illus
Midland Motor Cylinder Co
221   353   SANDWPL

Midland Tar Distillers
M T D Magazine: Oldbury Works Centenary 1865-1965

M T D Magazine   no 48 & 49
Demuth, Lewis and Co   Midland Tar Distillers
251   *

Midlands Counties Dairy
Souvenir of the 25th Birthday of the Midlands Counties Dairy Ltd
Birmingham: the firm 1934
Midlands Counties Dairy
617   641

302

Miles Aircraft
Milestones

Reading: the firm 1946
Miles Aircraft
364   *

Millar, Alexander Hastie
The 'Dundee Advertiser': A Centenary Memoir 1801-1901

Dundee, John Leng 1901   123pp illus
Leng, John & Co   Thomson, D C & Co
475   *

Millar, John
William Heap and his Company 1866

Liverpool: the firm 1976   246pp illus index sources
Heap & Partners
320   *

Miller, Harry
Halls of Dartford 1785-1985: Founded in the Industrial
Revolution, Pioneer of Refrigeration: 200 Years of Progress
Hutchinson Benham 1985   232pp illus index sources
Hall, J & E   Hall-Thermotank
320   325   351   §

Miller, Harry
Service to the Services: The Story of Naafi

Newman Neame 1971   156pp illus index
NAAFI
663   664   §

Miller, Harry
Tools that Built a Business: The Story of A A Jones & Shipman
Ltd
Hutchinson Benham 1972   128pp illus
Jones, A A & Shipman
322   LEICSPL

Miller, M & Church, R A
Motor Manufacturing

see Buxton, N K & Aldcroft, D H (eds)
Motor Industry
350

Miller, Michael B
The Bon Marché: Bourgeois Culture and the Department Store
1869-1920
Allen & Unwin 1981   xii 266pp illus index sources
Bon Marché
656   * §

Miller, Rory
Small Business in the Peruvian Oil Industry: Lobitos Oilfields
Limited before 1934
Business History Review   vol LVI no 3 1982
Lobitos Oilfields
130   140

Miller, Thomas Ronald
The Monkland Tradition

Nelson 1958   xiv 154pp illus sources
Motherwell Bridge & Engineering   Monkland
320   502   *

Miller, V
L Steel & Co: The Development of a Family Firm

typescript nd   33pp illus sources
Steel, L & Co   Coles, Henry J
311   325   503   613   §

Milliken, H T
Saga of a Family: The Story Behind the House of Woolley

the firm 1967   49pp illus
Woolley, James & Sons   British Drug Houses
257   TAMESPL

Mills, Cyril Bertram
Bertram Mills Circus: Its Story

Hutchinson 1967   271pp illus
Bertram Mills Circus
979   *

Mills, Godfrey Hope Saxon
There Is a Tide...The Life and Work of Sir William Crawford

Heinemann 1954   viii 197pp illus
Crawford, W S
838   *

Mills, Mary
Profit Sharing in the South Metropolitan Gas Company 1889-1920

CNAA MPhil 1983
South Metropolitan Gas Co
162

Mills, William Haslam
Sir Charles W Macara, Bart.: A Study of Modern Lancashire

Manchester: Sherratt & Hughes 1917 333pp
Master Cotton Spinners' Assoc
432   *

Mills, William Haslam
The Manchester Guardian: A Century of History

Chatto & Windus 1921   146pp illus
Manchester Guardian   Guardian
475   *

Miln, John
The Dundee Savings Bank

Dundee: the firm 1901   85pp
Dundee Savings Bank   Trustee Savings Bank
814   DNDEEPL

Milne, Alan Hay
Sir Alfred Lewis Jones KCMG: A Story of Energy and Success

Liverpool: Henry Young & Sons 1914   vii 113pp illus
Elder Dempster
740   770   DBB

Milne, T E
A British Ship-owning Company in the Late 19th and Early 20th Centuries...Voyage Accounts of William Thompson & Co
Glasgow BLitt 1966
Thompson, William & Co
740

Milne, T E
British Shipping in the Nineteenth Century: A Study of the Ben Line Papers
see Payne, Peter L (ed)
Ben Line
740

Milward
The Milward Story: Centenary Publication 1857-1957

Reading: the firm 1957   26pp illus
Milward's of Reading
451   BERKSPL

Minchinton, Walter Edward
The British Tinplate Industry: A History

Oxford: Clarendon 1957   xiv 286pp
Tinplate Industry
221   *

Mingay, G E
Fifteen Years On: The B E T Goup 1956-1971

the firm 1973   xi 117pp illus
British Electric Traction   Rediffusion
463   721   723   842   981   §

Minkes, A L & Tucker, D G
J A Crabtree: A Pioneer of Business Management

Business History   vol XXI no 2 1979
Crabtree, J A
342

Minney, Rubeigh James
Viscount Southwood

Odhams 1954   384pp illus index sources
John Bull   People
475   * §

Minnitt, Jack
The Sun Life Story 1810-1985

the firm 1985   111pp illus sources
Sun Life
820   §

Mirrlees, Bickerton & Day
50 Years of Diesel Progress

Hazel Grove: the firm 1957
Mirrlees, Bickerton & Day
328   SKPTPL

Mirrlees, Bickerton & Day
A British Engineering Shop During the War

Hazel Grove: the firm 1918
Mirrlees, Bickerton & Day
328   SKPTPL

Mitchell's Auction Company
Centenary of Mitchell's Auction Company Limited

the firm 1973
Mitchell's Auction Co
834

Mitchell, Albert & Grayling, Christopher
The History of Oldham Brewery

Manchester: the firm 1985   50pp illus
Boddingtons' Brewery
427   §

Mitchell, Brian Rodman
Economic Development of the British Coal Industry 1800-1914

Cambridge: C U P 1984   xv 381pp index sources
Coal Industry
111   * §

Mitchell, William H & Sawyer, L A
*The Cape Run: The Story of Union-Castle Service to South
Africa and of the Ships Employed*
Lavenham: Dalton 1984   ix 214pp illus index
Union-Castle
740   *

Mitchells & Butlers
Fifty Years of Brewing 1879-1929

Smethwick: the firm 1929   120pp illus
Mitchells & Butlers
427   *

Mitchells & Butlers
The Mitchells & Butlers Story

the firm 1981   18pp illus
Mitchells & Butlers
427   SANDWPL

Mobbs and Lewis
75 Years of Progress 1885-1960

Kettering: the firm 1960   22pp illus
Mobbs & Lewis
465   NHPTNPL

Monckton, H A
Whitbread's Breweries: A Chronological Survey of the Evolution of One of the Oldest Groups of Breweries in Britain
the firm 1984
Whitbread & Co
427

Mond
The Story of Mond Nickel

the firm 1951   63pp
Mond Nickel Co
224   210   SANDWPL

Mondey, David
Planemakers 2: Westland

Janes 1982   162pp illus
Westland Aircraft
364   RAeS

Monks, Hall & Co
Monks, Hall & Co Centenary 1874-1974

the firm 1974   17pp
Monks, Hall & Co
500   WARRPL

Monstead, Otto
Progress or the Romance of a British Industry

the firm 1914   31pp illus
Monstead, Otto   Maypole Dairy Co
411   413   617   641   EALNGPL

Montagu of Beaulieu, E J B D S
Jaguar: A Biography

Cassell 1961   xx 273pp illus
Jaguar Cars
351   *

Montagu of Beaulieu, E J B D S
Rolls of Rolls-Royce: A Biography of the Hon C S Rolls

Cassell 1966   xiii 250pp illus
Rolls-Royce
351   *

Montagu of Beaulieu, E J B D S
The Early Days of Rolls-Royce and the Montagu Family

Derby: Rolls-Royce Heritage 1983   51pp illus
Rolls-Royce
328   351   364   §

Montagu of Beaulieu, Lord J W D S
Argyll Motor Works: Inaugural Brochure

Alexandria: the firm 1906   23pp illus
Argyll Motors
351   DMBTNPL

Moore, A S
A History of the Belfast Engineering Firm of Jas. Mackie &
Sons Ltd...to Celebrate its Centenary
typescript in Belfast City Library   1946
Mackie, Jas & Sons
323

Moore, Charles W
Timing a Century: History of the Waltham Watch Company

Cambridge, Mass: Harvard U P 1945
Waltham Watch Company
374

Moran, James Charles
Clays of Bungay

Bungay,Suffolk: the firm 1978   160pp illus sources
Clays of Bungay
475   StBRD

Moran, James Charles
Cox & Wyman Ltd. 1777-1977: A Company History

Norwich: the firm 1977   45pp illus
Cox & Wyman
475   619   656   BCROB

Moran, James Charles
Henry George, Printer, Bookseller, Stationer and Bookbinder,
Westerham 1830-ca1846
Westerham: Westerham Press 1972   72pp illus
George, Henry
475   653   BROMPL

Moran, James Charles
Stephen Austin's of Hertford: Two Hundred Years of Print: A
Bicentenary History
Hertford: the firm 1968   72pp illus index
Austin, Stephen
475   * §

More, C
Armaments and Profits: The Case of Fairfield

Business History   vol XXIV no1 1982
Fairfield Shipbuilding
329   361

Morgan Grenfell & Co
George Peabody & Co; J S Morgan & Co; Morgan Grenfell & Co
1838-1958
the firm 1958   xiii 30pp illus
Morgan, J S & Co   Peabody, George & Co
814   * §

Morgan, Aubrey Neil
David Morgan 1833-1919: The Life and Times of a Master
Draper in South Wales
Risca: Starling Press 1977   181pp illus sources
Morgan, David
645   *

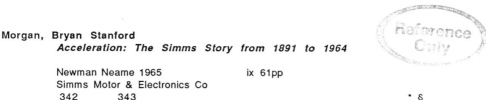

Morgan, Bryan Stanford
Acceleration: The Simms Story from 1891 to 1964

Newman Neame 1965   ix 61pp
Simms Motor & Electronics Co
342   343   * §
Morgan, Bryan Stanford
*Apothecary's Venture: The Scientific Quest of the
International Nicholas Organisation*
the firm 1959   60pp illus
Aspro-Nicholas   Nicholas International
257   * §
Morgan, Bryan Stanford
*Express Journey 1864-1964: A Centenary of the Express Dairy
Company Ltd*
Newman Neame 1964   xv 139pp illus
Express Dairy
413   617   641   * §
Morgan, Bryan Stanford
The Rolls-Royce Story

Collins 1971   46pp illus
Rolls-Royce
328   351   364   DERBYPL
Morgan, Bryan Stanford
*Total To Date: The Evolution of the Adding Machine: The Story
of Burroughs*
the firm 1953   70pp illus
Burroughs Adding Machine Co
330   * §
Morgan, Charles
The House of Macmillan 1843-1943

Macmillan 1944   xii 248pp index
Macmillan
475   * §
Morgan, David
The First Hundred Years

the firm 1979
Morgan, David
645
Morgan, Edward Victor & Thomas, William A
The Stock Exchange, Its History and Functions

Elek 1969   293pp illus index sources
Stock Exchange
831   * §
Morgan, H Llewellyn
*The History of James Lock & Co, Hatters: 6 St James's Street,
London*
the firm 1948   16pp illus
Lock, James & Co
453   *

Morgan, J S
The Colonel Stephens Railways

Newton Abbot: David & Charles 1970
Colonel Stephens Railways
710

Morgan, Robert M
Callender's 1882-1945

Prescot: the firm 1982   ix 256pp illus index
B I C C   Callender's Cable & Const
341   502   * §

Morgan, Susan L
The Aberdeenshire Canal: A Study in Transport History

Aberdeen thesis 1973   50pp illus sources
Aberdeenshire Canal
761   NESLS

Morison, Stanley
John Bell 1745-1831: Bookseller, Printer, Typefounder, Journalist etc.
First Edition Club 1930   166pp illus index sources
Bell, John
327   475   653   *

Morley, C
Yates, Haywood & Co Ltd: 150 Years of Stove Grate Manufacture

typescript 1977   36pp illus sources
Yates, Haywood & Co
311   ROTHMPL

Morpurgo, Jack Eric
Allen Lane: King Penguin

Hutchinson 1979   406pp illus index sources
Allen Lane   Penguin Books
475   *

Morrah, Dermot MacGregor
A History of Industrial Life Assurance

Allen & Unwin 1955   243pp index
Life Assurance
820   * §

Morris Motors
Making Cars: A History of Car Making in Cowley...by the People who make the Cars (Television History Workshop)
Routledge & Kegan Paul 1985   131pp illus index
Morris Motors   British Leyland
351   ABRDNPL

Morris, Charles F
Origins, Orient and 'Oriana'

Brighton: Teredo 1980   xx 491pp illus index
Orient Line   P & O
740

Morris, Gregory
*A History of One Hundred Years of Accountancy Practice
1852-1952*
Manchester: the firm 1953
Morris, Gregory & Co
836

Morris, James A
A Romance of Industrial Engineering

Kilmarnock: the firm 1939   148pp illus
Glenfield & Kennedy
320   * §

Morris, John H & Williams, Lawrence J
The South Wales Coal Industry 1841-1875

Cardiff: Wales U P 1958   xii 289pp
South Wales Coal
111   *

Morton, Frederic
The Rothschilds: A Family Portrait

Secker & Warburg 1962   264pp illus index sources
Rothschild
814   *

Morton, G R & LeGuillou
Alfred Hickman Ltd 1866-1932

West Midlands Studies   no 3 1969
Hickman, Alfred
111   221

Morton, G R & Smith, W A
The Bradley Ironworks of John Wilkinson

J Iron & Steel Inst July 1966   18pp illus sources
Bradley Ironworks
221   DUDLYPL

Morton, James
1906-1956: Fifty Years of Sundour

Carlisle: the firm 1956   40pp
Sundour   Morton Sundour
431   432   §

Morton, Jocelyn
Three Generations in a Family Textile Firm

Routledge & Kegan Paul 1971   xxi 481pp illus index
Morton, Alexander & Co   Morton Sundour
432   437   439   *

Morton, John
*Thomas Bolton & Sons Ltd. 1783-1983: The Bicentenary History
of a Major Copper and Brass Manufacturer*
Ashbourne: Moorland 1983   154pp illus index sources
Bolton, Thomas & Sons   B I C C
224   *

Mosers

>*Mosers of the Borough: A Brief Record of the History of the Firm from 1787-1937*
>the firm 1938   32pp illus
>Mosers of the Borough   Nettlefold & Sons
>648   §

Moss, D J

>*The Private Banks of Birmingham 1800-1827*
>
>Business History   vol XXIV no 1 1982
>Attwoods & Spooner
>814

Moss, M S & Hume, J R

>*The Making of Scotch Whisky: A History of the Scotch Whisky Distilling Ind (Bruichladdich Distillery, Islay 1881-1981)*
>Edinburgh: James & James 1981   303pp illus index sources
>Bruichladdich Distillery Co   Distillers Co
>424   §

Moss, M S & Hume, J R

>*Workshop of the British Empire: Engineering and Shipbuilding in the West of Scotland*
>Heinemann 1977   xv 192pp illus index sources
>Eng & Shipbuilding in Scotland
>220   320   360   §

Moss, Michael S & Hume John R

>*A History of Harland and Wolff 1853-1985*
>
>Blackstaff 1986
>Harland & Wolff
>361

Mottram, R H & Coote, Colin

>*Through Five Generations: The History of the Butterley Company*
>Faber 1950   181pp illus index
>Butterley Co
>111   221   * §

Mountfield, Stuart

>*Western Gateway: A History of the Mersey Docks and Harbour Board*
>Liverpool: L U P 1965   xi 228pp illus
>Mersey Docks & Harbour Board
>763   *

Mountford, Colin E

>*The History of John Bowes and Partners up to 1914*
>
>Durham MA 1967
>Bowes, John and Partners
>111

Mowat, Charles Loch

>*The Golden Valley Railway: Railway Enterprise in the Welsh Border in Late Victorian Times*
>Cardiff: U Wales P 1964   x 121pp illus index sources
>Golden Valley Railway   Great Western Railway
>710   *

Mowlem, John & Co
>*150 Years of Construction: Mowlem*
>*also other pamphlets and brochures*
>Brentford: 1977   12pp
>Mowlem, John & Co
>500   MRC

Moxon, Stanley
>*A Fox Centenary: Umbrella Frames, 1848-1948*
>
>Stocksbridge: the firm 1948 55pp illus
>Fox, Samuel & Co
>453   *

Mui, Hoh-Cheung & Lorna H
>*Andrew Melrose: Tea Dealer and Grocer of Edinburgh*
>*1812-1833*
>Business History   vol XI no 1 1967
>Melrose, Andrew
>423   641   839

Mui, Hoh-Cheung & Lorna H
>*William Melrose in China 1845-1855: The Letters of a Scottish*
>*Tea Merchant*
>Edinburgh: Scottish Hist Soc 1973 lxxvii 301pp index sources
>Melrose, William
>423   839   §

Muir, Augustus
>*75 Years, A Record of Progress: Smith's Stamping Works*
>*(Coventry) Ltd: Smith-Clayton Forge Ltd, Lincoln*
>Coventry: the firm 1958 104pp illus
>Smith's Stamping Works Smith-Clayton Forge
>312   §

Muir, Augustus
>*Andersons of Islington: The History of C F Anderson & Son*
>*Limited 1863-1963*
>Newman Neame 1963   xii 52pp illus
>Anderson, C F & Son
>501   613   * §

Muir, Augustus
>*Blyth, Greene, Jourdain & Company Limited 1810-1960*
>
>Newman Neame 1961   55pp illus
>Blyth, Greene, Jourdain & Co
>839   *

Muir, Augustus
>*Churchill and Sim 1813-1963: A Short History*
>
>Newman Neame 1963   84pp index
>Churchill and Sim
>613   * §

Muir, Augustus
>*In Blackburne Valley: The History of Bowers Mills*
>
>Cambridge: Heffer 1969 90pp illus
>Taylor, J S   Bowers Mills
>430   *

Muir, Augustus
Nairns of Kirkcaldy: A Short History of the Company 1847-1956
Cambridge: Heffer 1956   vii 158pp illus
Nairn, Michael & Co
438   483   *

Muir, Augustus
The Fife Coal Company: A Short History

Leven, Fife: the firm 1952   vii 133pp illus index
Fife Coal Co
111   * §

Muir, Augustus
The History of Baker Perkins

Cambridge: Heffer 1968   x 214pp illus index
Baker Perkins
324   327   * §

Muir, Augustus
The Kenyon Tradition: The History of James Kenyon & Son Ltd 1664-1964
Cambridge: Heffer 1964   112pp illus index sources
Kenyon, James
431   * §

Muir, Augustus
The Story of Shotts: A Short History of the Shotts Iron Company Limited
Edinburgh: the firm 1952   vi 80pp illus index
Shotts Iron Co
221   §

Muir, Augustus & Davies, M
A Victorian Shipowner: A Portrait of Sir Charles Cayzer, Baronet of Gartmore
the firm 1978   320pp index
Cayzer Irvine & Co
740   *

Muir, Percy Horace
Minding My Own Business: An Autobiography

Chatto & Windus 1956   224pp illus index
Muir, Percy
653   *

Mumby, Frank A & Stallybrass, Frances H S
From Swan Sonnenschein to George Allen & Unwin Ltd

Allen & Unwin 1955   100pp index sources
Allen & Unwin
475   *

Mumby, Frank Arthur
The House of Routledge 1834-1934: With a History of Kegan Paul, Trench, Trübner and associated Firms
George Routledge 1934   xiii 232pp illus index
Routledge
475   *

Munn, Charles W
Scottish Provincial Banking Companies: An Assessment

Business History   vol XXIII no 1 1981
Provincial Banking in Scotland
814

Munn, Charles W
The Development of Joint Stock Banking in Scotland 1810-1865
see Slaven, A & Aldcroft, D H (eds)
Joint Stock Banking in Scotland
814

Munn, Charles W
The Development of Joint-Stock Banking in the British Isles in the Nineteenth Century: A Comparative Approach
Economic History Conference 1986
Joint Stock Banking
814

Munn, Charles W
The Scottish Provincial Banking Companies 1747-1864

Edinburgh: John Donald 1981 306pp index sources
Aberdeen Banking Co   Dundee Banking Co
814   *

Munro, Neil
The History of the Royal Bank of Scotland 1727-1927

Edinburgh: the firm 1928   xvii 417pp illus
Royal Bank of Scotland
814   * §

Munro, R W
R W Munro Centenary 1864-1964: A Century of Instrument Making and Precision Engineering
the firm 1964   57pp
Munro, R W
370   §

Munting, R
Ransomes in Russia: An English Agricultural Engineering Company's Trade with Russia to 1917
Economic History Review   2nd Ser vol XXXI no 2 1978
Ransomes, Sims & Jefferies
321

Murphy, R J
J D W Coaches: The first Sixty Years. The J D W Transport Company Ltd 1920-1980
Ipswich: the firm 1980   39pp illus
J D W Transport Co
721   MRC

Murray, Andrew
Fifty Years of Slamannan Co-operative Society Limited 1861-1911
the firm 1911   145pp illus
Slamannan Co-operative Soc
656   MTHWLPL

Murray, David
The York Building Company: A Chapter in Scotch History (first published 1883)
Edinburgh: Bratton 1973   131pp index
York Building Co
500   MLOTHPL

Murray, George McIntosh
The Press and the Public: The Story of the British Press Council
Carbondale: S Illinois U P 1972   xi 243pp
Press Council
475   *

Murray, Marischal
Union Castle Chronicle 1853-1953

Longmans Green 1953   xvii 392pp illus index
Union-Castle
740   * §

Murray, R (vols 1 & 2) & McWhirter, J (vol 3)
History of Barrhead Co-operative Society

Barrhead: the firm 1911-1962   3 vols illus
Barrhead Co-operative Society
656   RNFRWPL

Murray, William
Coalsnaughton Co-operative Society Ltd: The Continuation of a Historical Sketch of the Society 1922-1947
Tillicoultry: Tribune 1947   15pp
Coalsnaughton Co-op Soc   Forth Valley Co-op
656   CLKMNPL

Musgrave Spinning Co
The Musgrave Spinning Co Ltd, Atlas Mills, Bolton

Bolton: the firm ca1930   12pp illus
Musgrave Spinning Co
432   BOLTNPL

Muskett, A E
A A McGuckian: A Memorial Volume

Belfast: McGuckian Memorial 1956   191pp illus
McGuckian
10   NEELBPL

Musson, Albert Edward
An Early Engineering Firm: Peel, Williams & Co of Manchester

Business History   vol III no 1 1960
Peel, Williams & Co
320

Musson, Albert Edward
Enterprise in Soap and Chemicals: Joseph Crosfield & Sons Ltd. 1815-1965
Manchester: M U P 1965   xi 384pp illus index sources
Crosfield, Joseph   Unilever
251   258   * §

Musson, Albert Edward
Joseph Whitworth and the Growth of Mass Production Engineering
Business History   vol XVII no 2 1975
Whitworth, Joseph
310   320
Musson, Albert Edward
The Typographical Association: Origins and History up to 1949

Oxford U P 1954   viii 550pp index sources
Typographical Association
475   963   * §
Mutton, Norman
The Foster Family 1786 1899: A Study of a Midland Industrial Dynasty
London PhD 1974
Stourbridge Ironworks
221
Myer, Ewart
Myer's First Century 1876-1976: The Story of Myer's Comfortable Beds
the firm 1976   52pp illus
Myer, Horatio & Co
467   §
Mytholmroyd Industrial Society
Jubilee Celebration 1861-1911: A Short History of the Society

Mytholmroyd: the firm 1911   16pp illus
Mytholmroyd Industrial Soc
656   HLFXPL
Mytton-Davies, Cynric
Their First Two Centuries: The History of Fullwood and Bland of Ellesmere
the firm 1977   70pp illus
Fullwood & Bland
321   BCROB
Nathan, Archie John
Costumes by Nathan

Newnes 1960   207pp illus index
Nathan
974   979   *
National Bank of Scotland
National Bank of Scotland Ltd: Centenary 1825-1925 and a Short History of the Bank
the firm 1925/47   2 vols illus
National Bank of Scotland   Royal Bank of Scotland
820   EDNBRPL
National Cash Register Co
Booklet 1947 and various pamphlets

the firm 1974   43pp illus
National Cash Register Co
330   *

National Coal Board, Scottish Division
Short History of the Scottish Coal Mining Industry

the firm 1958   116pp illus index sources
National Coal Board, Scottish Div
111   MTHWLPL

Naylor, Gillian
A History of Gordon Russell Limited

the firm 1976
Gordon Russell
467

Naylor, R A
The Naylors of Warrington: Timber Importers and Saw Millers:
A Century in Timber
Newton-le-Willows: the firm 1972 49pp
Naylor, R A
613   WARRPL

Naylor, Stanley (ed)
An International Oilman: Autobiography of Sir Henri Deterding

Ivor Nicholson & Watson 1934 126pp
Royal Dutch/Shell   Asiatic Petroleum
130 140 251 612 652   *

Neal, F

Liverpool Shipping in the Early Nineteenth Century

see Harris, J R (ed) 1969
Liverpool Shipping
740

Neal, William K & Back, David H
Forsyth & Co, Patent Gunmakers

Bell 1969   xix 280pp illus
Forsyth & Co
329

Neal, William K & Back, David H
The Mantons, Gunmakers

Herbert Jenkins 1967   xv 300pp illus
Manton, J & J
329

Neale, J

Burwell and District Motor Service

author nd   41pp illus
Burwell & Dist Motor Service
721   MRC

Neale, W G
At the Port of Bristol 1848-1914

Bristol: the firm 1968-70 2 vols illus
Port of Bristol
763   *

318

Negretti & Zambra
Negretti & Zambra Centenary 1850-1950

the firm 1950   24pp illus
Negretti & Zambra
371   BCRL

Neill, W
The Cassel Cyanide Co Ltd: A Short History

typescript 1927   13pp sources
Cassel Cyanide Co   I C I
251   UBRIS

Nelson, James
Nelsons of Nelson: The Story of James Nelson Ltd 1881-1951

Harley 1951   53pp illus
Nelson, James
432   UBRIS

Nelstrop, Wm
William Nelstrop & Co Ltd Stockport: 150 Years 1820-1970

Stockport: the firm nd
Nelstrop, Wm & Co
416   SKPTPL

Nestlé
A Nestlés Condensery

Hayes: the firm nd   20pp illus
Nestlé
413   HILLPL

Netherwood and Dalton
Netherwood and Dalton, History: vols 1-3, 1868-1951

microfilm nd
Netherwood & Dalton
475   HDSFDPL

Neufeld, Edward Peter
A Global Corporation: A History of the International Development of Massey-Ferguson Limited
Toronto: T U P 1969   ix 427pp illus index
Massey-Ferguson   Perkins Engine Co
321   328   351   * §

Nevett, Terry R
Advertising in Britain: A History

Heinemann 1982   xiii 231pp illus index sources
Advertising
838   * §

Nevile, Sydney Oswald
Seventy Rolling Years

Faber 1958   288pp illus index
Whitbread & Co
427   * §

Neville, T & E
    Building a Name

    Luton: 1975   30pp
    Neville, T & E
    501   MRC
Newman, Bernard
    One Hundred Years of Good Company: Published on the Occasion
    of the Ruston Centenary 1857-1957
    the firm 1957   vii 272pp illus index
    Ruston & Hornsby
    328   *
Newman, Karin
    The Selling of British Telecom

    Holt, Rinehart & Winston 1986   176pp
    British Telecom
    790
Newman, Tom Seth
    History of the Hearts of Oak Benefit Society 1842-1942

    the firm 1942   205pp illus
    Hearts of Oak Benefit Soc
    820   BLPES
Newman, William & Sons
    The Story of William Newman & Sons Ltd, Established 1750

    the firm 1950   40pp illus
    Newman, William & Sons
    311   320   UBRIS
Newth, Jack D
    Adam & Charles Black 1807-1957: Some Chapters in the
    History of a Publishing House
    Black 1957   115pp illus index
    Black, Adam & Charles
    475   * §
Newton, David
    Men of Mark: Makers of East Midland Allied Press

    Peterborough: the firm 1977   238pp illus index
    East Midland Allied Press
    475   CAMBSPL
Newton, Ernest Edward
    A Short Account of Twinings in the Strand

    the firm 1922   20pp illus
    Twining, R & Co
    423   617   641   *
Nicholls & Clarke
    Nicholls & Clarke, Shoreditch, London: 100th Anniversary

    1975   8pp
    Nicholls & Clarke
    613   GHL

Nicholls, **Robert**
Ten Generations of a Potting Family

Hanley: Wood Mitchell 1931   xxvi 135pp illus index
Adams, William
248   *
Nichols, **Philip Peter Ross**
A Centenary Memoir 1864-1964 of Carlisle & Gregson
(Jimmy's) Ltd, Tutorial College
the firm 1964   17pp
Carlisle & Gregson (Jimmy's)
933   *
Nicholson, **Hubert C**
The Pegler-Hattersley Group: An Historical Review 1871-1971

Sheffield: the firm 1974   73pp illus index
Pegler-Hattersley Group   Northern Rubber
311   328   481   §
Nicolson, **James Robert**
Hay & Company: Merchants in Shetland

Lerwick: the firm 1982   228pp illus index
Hay & Co (Lerwick)
610   640   650   *
Nicolson, **James Robert**
Lerwick Harbour 1877-1977

Lerwick: Harbour Trust 1977   viii 212pp illus index
Lerwick Harbour
763   *
Nicolson, **John**
Arthur Anderson: A Founder of the P & O Company

Lerwick: T & J Manson 1932   110pp illus
P & O
740   *
Nixon, St **John Cousins**
A Record of Fifty Years of the Daimler Company: Daimler
1896-1946
Foulis 1946   232pp illus index
Daimler Motor Co   B S A
351   * §
Nixon, St **John Cousins**
The Simms Story from 1891

the firm 1955   64pp illus
Simms Motor & Electronics Co
343   353   432   * §
Nixon, St **John Cousins**
The Story of the S M M T 1902-1952

the firm 1952   131pp illus index
S M M T   Motor Manufacturers & Traders
350   963

321

Nixon, St John Cousins
Wolseley: A Saga of the Motor Industry

    G T Foulis 1949   157pp illus
    Wolseley Tool & Motor Car Co   Morris Motors
    351   *

Noad, L M
A Short History of Noad and Son, Chartered Surveyors

    Chippenham: the firm 1980   18pp illus
    Noad & Son
    834   WILTSPL

Noakes, Aubrey
Principality Building Society 1860-1960: A Commemorative History
    Cardiff: H F & G Witherby 1960   viii 55pp illus
    Principality Building Soc
    815   * §

Noakes, Aubrey
The County Fire Office 1807-1957: A Commemorative History

    H F & G Witherby 1957   xv 189pp illus sources
    County Fire Office
    820   * §

Noal, James
100 Years of Service to Safety 1868-1968

    Hyde: the firm 1968   42pp illus
    Noal, James & Sons
    453   TAMESPL

Noall, Cyril
Geevor

    Penzance: the firm 1983   167pp
    Geevor Tin Mines
    210   SciMus

Nock, Oswald Stevens
The Caledonian Railway

    Ian Allan 1964   190pp illus index
    Caledonian Railway
    710   *

Nock, Oswald Stevens
The Lancashire & Yorkshire Railway: A Concise History

    Ian Allan 1969   159pp illus index
    Lancashire & Yorkshire Railway
    710   *

Nock, Oswald Stevens
*The South Eastern and Chatham Railway
and many other similar titles*
    1961
    South Eastern & Chatham Rly
    710   *

Nockolds, Harold
Lucas: The First Hundred Years: The Successors

N Abbot: David & Charles 1976/78   2 vols illus index sources
Lucas Industries
343   * §

Nockolds, Harold
Rescue from Disaster: The History of the R F D Group

Newton Abbot: David & Charles 1980 224pp illus index sources
R F D Group   G Q Parachute Co
364   481   * §

Nockolds, Harold
The Magic of a Name

Foulis nd   xiii 283pp illus index
Rolls-Royce
328   351   364   * §

Noël, A & Sons
The Centenary of a Family Business 1860-1960

1960   27pp
Noël, A & Sons
423   617   UBRIS

Nokes, B C G
John English of Feckenham, Needle Manufacturer

Business History   vol XI no 1 1969
English, John & Co, Feckenham
316

Normington, Thomas
The Lancashire & Yorkshire Railway

Manchester: John Heywood 1898   375pp illus index
Lancashire & Yorkshire Railway
710   *

Norrington, A L P
Blackwell's 1879-1979: The History of a Family Firm

Oxford: Basil Blackwell 1983   xiii 191pp illus index
Blackwell
475   653   * §

North British & Mercantile Insurance Co
North British and Mercantile Insurance Company: Centenary 1809-1909
the firm 1909   75pp illus
North British & Mercantile Ins
820   §

North British Distillery Co
The North British Distillery Company Limited 1885-1960

Edinburgh: the firm 1960   43pp illus
North British Distillery Co
424   EDNBRPL

North British Locomotive
A History of the North British Locomotive Co. Ltd. 1903-1953:
Sharp Stewart & Co., Neilson Reid & Co., Dubs & Co.
Glasgow: the firm nd   115pp illus
North British Locomotive   Sharp Stewart & Co
362   DMBTNPL

North British Rubber Co
North British Rubber and Gorgie-Dairy Living Memory Project:
Stretch a Mile
Edinburgh: the firm 1985   2 vols illus
North British Rubber Co
481   EDNBRPL

North East London Polytechnic/Greater London Council
Dockland: An illustrated Historical Survey of Life and Work in
East London
Dagenham: N E L P 1986   400pp illus index sources
Dockland
763

North Metropolitan Electrical Power Distribution Co
The Enfield Electricity Works

Enfield: the firm 1907   10pp illus
Enfield Electricity Works
161   ENFLDPL

North of Scotland Bank
Contract of a Co-Partnership of the North of Scotland Banking
Co 1836
Aberdeen: 1836   53pp
North of Scotland Bank
814   NESLS

North, Rex
The Butlin Story

Jarrolds 1962   150pp illus index
Butlins
667   *

Norton Abrasives
Norton Abrasives Ltd: 50th Anniversary

the firm nd   32pp illus
Norton Abrasives
246   HERTSPL

Norton Villiers Triumph
Meriden: Historical Summary 1972-1974

Meriden: the firm 1974   37pp
Norton Villiers Triumph   Meriden
363   SANDWPL

Nortons Tividale
Nortons Tividale

Tipton: the firm 1957   64pp illus
Nortons Tividale
325   §

Nottingham Water Works
A Short History of the Water Works

Nottingham: City Water Dept 1930
Nottingham Water Works
170
Novello
A Century and a Half in Soho: A Short History of the Firm of Novello, Publishers and Printers of Music 1811-1961
Novello 1961   ix 84pp illus
Novello & Co
475   * §
Nowell-Smith, Simon
The House of Cassell 1848-1958

Cassell 1958   x 299pp illus index sources
Cassell & Co
475   §
Nuffield
At Cowley: A Chronicle of Morris Activities

Cowley: the firm ca1930   20pp illus
Morris Motors
361   OXFDPL
Nuffield
The Nuffield Organisation

Oxford: the firm ca1947   40pp illus
Morris Motors
361   OXFDPL
Nulty, Geoffrey
Guardian Country 1853-1978: Being the Story of the First 125 Years of Cheshire County Newspapers Ltd
the firm 1978   143pp
Cheshire County Newspapers
475   WARRPL
O'Connor, Denis
Barrow Bridge, Bolton; Dean Mills Estate: A Victorian Model Achievement
Bolton: author 1972   38pp illus sources
Gardner & Bazley   Lord, John & Robert of Halliwell
432   BOLTNPL
O'Connor, Denis
Samuel Chatwood, Bankers' Engineer: An Account of the Chatwood Safe Co Ltd
typescript 1979   41pp illus sources
Chatwood Safe Co
316   BOLTNPL
O'Connor, G W
The First Hundred Years: The Royal Mail Steam Packet Co Ltd

Southampton: the firm 1961   107pp illus
Royal Mail Shipping Group   Red Funnel Steamers
740   * §

O'Connor, Thomas Power
The House of Spicer 1796-1922: To Celebrate the Reunion of the Two Great Spicer Paper Houses
the firm 1922   15pp
Spicer Bros
471   *

O'Dell, Andrew Charles
The Railways of Scotland: Papers of Andrew C O'Dell edited by R E H Mellor
Aberdeen: A U P 1984   53pp illus source
Railways of Scotland
710   *

O'Donoghue, K & Heaton, Paul M
Kaye, Son & Co Ltd

Kendal: World Ship Society 1983   48pp
Kaye, Son & Co   Royal Mail Shipping Group
740

O'Gráda, Cormac
The Beginnings of the Irish Creamery System 1880-1914 (Irish Agricultural Organisation Society)
Economic History Review   2nd Ser vol XXX no 2 1977
Irish Agric Organisation Soc
413

O'Hagan, Henry Osborne
Leaves from my Life

John Lane, Bodley Head 1929   2 vols index

814   815   831   *

O'Mahoney, B M E
Newhaven-Dieppe 1825-1980: The History of an Anglo-French Joint Venture
author 1979   x 160pp illus
Newhaven-Dieppe
740

O'Sullivan, Timothy
Julian Hodge: A Biography

Routledge & Kegan Paul 1981   xi 210pp illus index
Hodge Group   Commercial Bank of Wales
814   820   *

Oakey, John
Centenary of John Oakey & Sons Ltd. 1833-1933

the firm 1933   43pp
Oakey, John
246   GHL

Odhams, William James Bond
The Business and I

Martin Secker 1935   xii 193pp illus
Odhams Press
475

Oetzmann & Co
        The House of Oetzmann 1848-1948

        1948   15pp
        Oetzmann & Co
        648   GHL
Ogborn, Maurice Edward
        Equitable Assurances: The Story of Life Assurance in the
        Experience of the Equitable Life Assurance Society
        Allen & Unwin 1962   271pp illus index
        Equitable Life Assurance
        820   * §
Ogden, Eric
        Northern Counties of Wigan

        Glossop: Transport Publishing 1976   116pp illus index
        Northern Counties of Wigan
        352   WIGANPL
Ogden, J H
        Failsworth Industrial Society Jubilee History 1859-1909

        Manchester: Co-op Printing Soc 1909 240 pp illus
        Failsworth Industrial Soc
        656   OLDHMPL
Ogilvy, David Mackenzie
        Confessions of an Advertising Man

        Mayflower 1966   208pp
        Ogilvy Benson & Mather
        838   *
Oldaker, John
        A Century of Progress: The Story of a Family Business
        1859-1959
        the firm 1959   vii 40pp illus
        Previté & Co
        245   *
Oldham
        Story of an Enterprise 1865-1948

        Denton: the firm 1948   52pp illus
        Oldham & Son
        343   TAMESPL
Oldham
        Vintage: Centenary issue of the Grid House Magazine

        Denton: the firm 1965   52pp illus
        Oldham & Son
        343   *
Oldham Equitable & Industrial Co-op
        Co-operation in Oldham 1850-1950: Centenary of the Equitable
        and Industrial Co-operative Societies
        the firm 1950   64pp illus
        Oldham Equitable & Ind Co-op
        656   OLDHMPL

                                                                    327

Oldham, Wilton Joseph
The Hyphen In Rolls-Royce: A Biography of Claude Johnson

Foulis 1967 xxii 194pp illus
Rolls-Royce
328 351 364 *

Oldham, Wilton Joseph
The Ismay Line: The White Star Line and the Ismay Family Story
Liverpool: Journal of Commerce 1961 xviii 283pp illus
White Star Line Oceanic Steam Navigation Co
740 *

Oliphant, Mrs & Porter, Mrs
Annals of a Publishing House: William Blackwood and his Sons: Their Magazine and Friends
Edinburgh: Blackwood 1897/98 3 vols illus index
Blackwood, William & Sons
475 EDNBRPL

Oliver, George (Footwear) Ltd
Oliver's 1860-1950

Leicester: Edgar Backus 1950 27pp illus
Oliver, George (Footwear) Ltd
451 646 *

Oliver, John L
The Development and Structure of the Furniture Industry

Oxford: Pergamon 1966 xviii 187pp illus
Furniture Industry
467 *

Ollerenshaw, P G
The Belfast Banks 1820-ca1900: Aspects of Banking in 19th Century Ireland
Sheffield PhD 1982
Belfast Banks
814

Openshaw, C
C Openshaw & Sons, Todmorden 1805-1955

York: William Sessions 1955
Openshaw, C & Sons
430

Orbell, M John
Baring Brothers & Co Limited: A History to 1939

the firm 1985 93pp illus index sources
Baring Brothers
814 BLPES

Orbell, M John with Green, Ed & Moss, M
From Cape to Cape: The History of Lyle Shipping Company

Edinburgh: Paul Harris 1978 xiii 239pp illus index sources
Lyle Shipping Co
740 * §

Orchard, Vincent Robert
Tattersalls: Two Hundred Years of Sporting History

Hutchinson 1953   312pp illus index
Tattersalls
839   *

Orchardson, I K
Sir William Mackinnon, Shipowner 1823-93

London PhD 1970
Mackinnon, William
740

Orr's Zinc White
Orr's Zinc White: The First Fifty Years at the Vine Works,
Widnes
the firm 1948   61pp illus
Orr's Zinc White   Imperial Smelting Corporation
224   251   UBRIS

Osborn, Frederick Marmaduke
The Story of the Mushets

Nelson 1952   xii 195pp illus index sources
Whitecliff Iron Works   Osborn, Samuel & Co
221   * §

Overend, Gurney & Co
Report of the Committee of the Defence Association

the firm 1867   68pp
Overend, Gurney & Co
814   §

Overy, Richard James
William Morris, Viscount Nuffield

Europa 1976   xlvi 151pp illus index sources
Morris Motors
351   *

Owen Mumford
Owen Mumford   Ltd: 25th Anniversary 1952-1977

Woodstock: the firm 1977   12pp illus
Mumford, Owen
372   OXFDPL

Owen Organisation
An Industrial Commonwealth: The Owen Organisation of Great
Britain
the firm 1951   104pp
Owen Organisation   Electro-Hydraulics
328   839   WARRPL

Owen Organisation
The Owen Organisation

the firm 1954   43pp
Owen Organisation
328   839   WARRPL

Owen, C C

Thornwill & Warham: Samuel Briggs & Co Ltd

typescript nd   23pp sources
Thornwill & Warham   Briggs, Samuel & Co
311   320   §

Owen, Colin

The Leicestershire and South Derbyshire Coalfield 1200-1900

Ashbourne: Moorland Publishing 1984 321pp illus index sources
Leicester & S Derby Coalfield
111   LEICSPL

Owen, David

The Manchester Ship Canal

Manchester: M U P 1983   ix 133pp illus index sources
Manchester Ship Canal
763   §

Owen, David John

A Short History of the Port of Belfast

Belfast: Mayne, Boyd & Son 1917   ix 96pp illus
Port of Belfast
763   *

Owen, John Alastair

The History of the Dowlais Iron Works 1759-1970

Newport, Gwent: Starling 1977   161pp illus index sources
Dowlais Iron Co   G K N
221   311   *

Owen, K

Concorde: New Shape in the Sky

Janes 1982   292pp sources
British Aircraft Corporation
364   *

Owen, Louise

Northcliffe; The Facts

author 1931   334pp
Associated Newspapers
475   *

Owen, Roderic

Lepard & Smiths Limited 1757-1957

the firm 1957   16pp illus
Lepard & Smiths
471   *

Oxford and District Gas Company

Oxford and District Gas Company 1818-1948

the firm 1948   24pp illus
Oxford & District Gas Co
162   OXFDPL

P E P (Political and Economic Planning)
Report on the British Press

    P E P 1938   333pp
    Newspaper Industry
    475   *

P E P (Political and Economic Planning)
Report on the Supply of Electricity in Great Britain

    P E P 1936   171pp
    Electricity Supply
    161   *

P E P (Political and Economic Planning)
The British Film Industry

    P E P 1952   307pp
    Film Industry
    971   *

P E P (Political and Economic Planning)
The Market for Household Appliances

    P E P 1945   xxxviii 398pp

    316   346   *

Pafford, Elizabeth R & John, H P
Employer and Employed: Ford, Ayrton & Co Ltd, Silk Spinners with Worker Participation 1870-1970
Edington: Pasold Research 1974   77pp index sources
Ford, Ayrton
    432   BLPES

Pagan, William & Young, Robert
Fifty Years of Service: A Historical Sketch of Broxburn Co-operative Society from 1879 till 1929
Glasgow: Scottish C W S 1929   60pp illus
Broxburn Co-operative Soc
    656   WLOTHPL

Page, Donald T
An Early History of Seccombe Marshall and Campion Limited 1919-1947
typescript 1968
Seccombe Marshall & Campion
    814

Page, Ken
Greene King Biggleswade Brewery 1764-1984

    the firm 1984   51pp illus sources
    Greene King
    427   §

Paget-Tomlinson, Edward William
Bibby Line: 175 years of Achievement

    Liverpool: the firm 1982   69pp illus
    Bibby Line
    740   LPOOLPL

Paget-Tomlinson, Edward William
The History of the Bibby Line

Liverpool: 1969   78pp illus
Bibby Line
740   §

Painting, M H
The Development of the Gas Industry in the Bristol Region
1810-1950
Bath PhD 1979
Bristol Gas
162

Palfreyman, David
John Jeyes: The Making of a Household Name

Thetford: the firm 1977   127pp illus index sources
Jeyes Group
257   §

Palmer, S R & Williams, G (eds)
Charted and Uncharted Waters: Conference on the Study of
Maritime History 1981
National Maritime Museum 1982   iii 262pp illus
Maritime History
361   740   *

Palmer, Sarah Rosalind
'The Most Indefatigable Activity': The General Steam
Navigation Company 1824-1850
Journal of Transport History   3rd ser vol III no 2 1982
General Steam Navigation Co
740

Palmer, Sarah Rosalind
The Character and Organisation of the Shipping Industry of the
Port of London 1815-1849
London PhD 1979
Port of London
740   763   770

Palmer, Sarah Rosalind
The Indemnity in the London Marine Insurance Market 1824-50

see Westall, Oliver M (ed) 1984
Indemnity Marine Insurance
820

Pantin, W & C
W & C Pantin Ltd: A Brief History of the Firm

Woodford: the firm 1932   15pp illus
Pantin, W & C
466   §

Pardoe, F E
John Baskerville of Birmingham: Letter Founder and Printer

Frederick Muller 1975   181pp illus index sources
Baskerville, John
475   327   StBRD

Parker, J Francis
A History of British Rolling Mills Ltd

the firm 1979   36pp illus
British Rolling Mills
311   DUDLYPL

Parker, Thomas H
The House of Parker: Bicentenary 1750 to 1950: Looking Back 200 Years
the firm 1950   33pp illus
Parker Gallery
654   977   * §

Parker, W M
The House of Oliver & Boyd: A Record from 1778 to 1948

typescript nd   103pp sources
Oliver & Boyd
475   EDNBRPL

Parkes, Josiah & Sons
Union: Josiah Parkes & Sons Ltd, Manufacturers of Locks for over a Century 1840-1958
typescripts ca1960   100pp illus
Parkes, Josiah & Sons   Union
316   319   §

Parkinson, J R
Shipbuilding

see Buxton, N K & Aldcroft, D H (eds)
Shipbuilding Industry
361

Parry, T V
The Incorporated Church Building Society 1818-1851

Oxford MLitt 1984
Incorporated Church Building Soc
815

Parsons, John F
J E Beale Ltd and the Growth of Bournemouth: The Story of a Business Enterprise in a Growing Resort 1881-1914
Bournemouth Loc Studies 1980-82   2 vols illus
Beales
656

Parsons, Richard M
The White Ships: The Banana Trade at the Port of Bristol

City of Bristol Museum 1982   90pp illus index sources
Imperial Direct West India Mail   Elders & Fyffes
740   763   *

Parsons, Richard M
Turner Edwards: 150 Years of History in the Wine Trade 1834-1984
Bristol: the firm 1984   20pp illus
Turner Edwards   P & O Wine Services
617   AVONPL

Parsons, Thomas & Sons
150 Years of Paint and Varnish Manufacturing

the firm 1952   63pp illus
Parsons, Thomas & Sons
255   *

Partington, S
Jubilee of the Middleton & Tonge Industrial Society Ltd

Manchester: C W S 1900   190pp illus
Middleton & Tonge Industrial Soc
656   UBRIS

Pascall, James
Pascall: One Hundred Years 1866-1966

Mitcham: the firm 1966   28pp illus
Pascall, James
421   MERTNPL

Pascoe, W H
C C C: The History of the Cornish Copper Company

Redruth: Cornish Publications 1982   202pp illus index sources
Cornish Copper Co
210   *

Pasold, Eric W
Ladybird Ladybird: A Story of Private Enterprise

Manchester: M U P 1977   xvi 668pp illus index
Pasold   Coats, Paton & Baldwin
436   838   * §

Paton, Alexander Forrester
The Romance of Paton's Yarn 1813-1920

Alloa: the firm repr 1984   17pp
Paton, John   Coats, Paton & Baldwin
431   CLKMNPL

Patrick Motors Group
Patrick Motors Group 1930-1980: Fifty Years of Dedicated Service
Birmingham: the firm 1980   40pp illus
Patrick Motors Group
651   671   SOLHLPL

Pattison, G W
The London and Indian Dock Companies 1864-1909

London PhD 1971
London & Indian Dock Co
763

Pattullo Higgs & Co
60 Years with Pattullo Higgs

the firm 1964   27pp illus
Pattullo Higgs & Co
251   611   BROMPL

Paul, Philip
    City Voyage: The Story of Erlebach & Company Limited
    1867-1967
    Morden: Harley 1967   84pp illus
    Erlebach & Co
    770   UBRIS

Paulden, Sydney M & Hawkins, Bill
    Whatever Happened at Fairfields?

    Gower 1969   x 214pp
    Fairfield Shipbuilding   Upper Clyde Shipbuilders
    361   *

Payne, George
    The First Fifty Years

    the firm 1946   36pp
    Payne, George & Co
    421   SWKPL

Payne, Peter Lester
    Colvilles and the Scottish Steel Industry

    Oxford: Clarendon 1979   xxi 458pp index sources
    Colvilles
    220   * §

Payne, Peter Lester
    Family Business in Britain: An Historical and Analytical Study

    see Fuji Conference 10, 1983
    Family Business

Payne, Peter Lester
    Railways and Rubber in the Nineteenth Century: A Study of the
    Spencer Papers 1853-1891
    Liverpool: L U P 1961   246pp
    Spencer, George & Co   Spencer Moulton
    481   710   BLPES

Payne, Peter Lester
    Rationality and Personality: A Study of Mergers in the Scottish
    Iron and Steel Industry 1916-1936
    Business History   vol XIX no 2 1977
    Steel Industry in Scotland
    221

Payne, Peter Lester
    The Govan Collieries 1804-1805

    Business History   vol III no 2 1961
    Govan Collieries
    111

Payne, Peter Lester
    The House of Spencer 1853-1891: A Study in Business History

    Nottingham PhD 1954
    Spencer, George & Co   Spencer Moulton
    481   710

Payne, Peter Lester
The Savings Bank of Glasgow 1836-1914

see Payne, Peter L (ed) 1967
Savings Bank of Glasgow
814

Payne, Peter Lester (ed)
Studies in Scottish Business History

Frank Cass 1967   xviii 436pp

30   111   300   740   814   *

Payne, Sara
The Gurteens of Haverhill: Two Hundred Years of Suffolk Textiles
Cambridge: Woodhead-Faulkner 1984 96pp illus index sources
Gurteens of Haverhill
431   §

Peaples, F W
History of the Great & Little Bolton Co-operative Society Limited Showing Fifty Years' Progress 1859-1909
Manchester: the firm 1910   670pp illus index
Bolton Co-operative Society
656   *

Pearce Bros Builders
1867-1967: Pearce Bros Builders: The First Hundred Years

Bromley: nd   20pp
Pearce Bros Builders
501   MRC

Pearce, D & Hodges, D I
Wellworthy: The First Fifty Years

the firm ca1969   191pp illus
Wellworthy
350   §

Pearson and Co
Stoneware from Chesterfield: An Account of the History and Activities of Pearson and Co (Chesterfield) Ltd
the firm nd   6pp
Pearson and Co
248   DERBYPL

Pearson, James Denning
The Development and Organisation of Rolls-Royce Ltd.

Derby: the firm 1964   29pp
Rolls-Royce
351   364   RAeS

Peddie, R
The United Steel Companies Ltd. 1918-1968: A History

the firm 1969   70pp illus
United Steel
221   222   SHEFFPL

336

Peden, George
Arms, Government and Businessmen 1935-1945

see Turner, John (ed)
Vickers-Armstrong   Royal Ordnance Factories
329
Peden, J A
The History of Kirkless Ironworks

typescript ca1965   65pp sources
Wigan Coal & Iron Co
111   311   WIGANPL
Pedler, Frederick Johnson
The Lion and the Unicorn in Africa: A History of the Origins of the United Africa Company 1787-1931
Heinemann 1974   xv 343pp illus index sources
United Africa Company   Unilever
411   839   *
Pedrick, Gale
The Story of Horrockses

Preston: the firm 1950   71pp illus
Horrockses, Crewdson & Co
432   UBRIS
Peebles, Bruce & Co
The Story of Bruce Peebles 1866-1954

Edinburgh: the firm 1955   51pp illus
Peebles, Bruce & Co
343   EDNBRPL
Peek, Frean
Peek, Frean & Co: A Hundred Years of Biscuit Making 1857-1957
the firm 1957   49pp illus
Peek, Frean & Co
419   SWKPL
Peel, David
A Pride of Potters: The Adams Family of Burslem and their Work
Arthur Barker 1957   40pp illus
Adams, William
248   *
Peel, Derek Wilmot Douglas
A Garden in the Sky: The Story of Barkers of Kensington 1870-1957
W H Allen 1960   175pp illus
Barkers of Kensington
656   *
Peirson, J Gordon
Great Ship Builders: The Rise of Harland & Wolff

Arthur H Stockwell 1935   24pp illus
Harland & Wolff
361   *

Pena, R O & Duhalde, E L
Baring Brothers y la Historia Politica Argentina

Buenos Aires: Sudestada 1968   213pp
Baring Brothers
814   839   §

Penguin Books
Penguins' Progress 1935-1960

Harmondsworth: Penguin 1960   86pp illus
Penguin Books
475   HILLPL

Penmaenmawr and Welsh Granite Co
Moving Mountains

Penmaenmawr 1958   74pp illus
Penmaenmawr and Welsh Granite
231   *

Penrose, Harald
British Aviation: The Pioneer Years 1903-1914

Cassell 1980   viii 309pp illus index
British Airways
750   *

Penrose, Harald
British Aviation: The Adventuring Years 1920-1929

Putnam 1973   727pp illus index
British Airways
750   *

Penrose, Harald
British Aviation: Widening Horizons 1930-1934

HMSO 1979   viii 340pp illus index
British Airways
750   *

Penrose, Harald
British Aviation: Ominous Skies 1935-1939

HMSO 1980   viii 318pp illus index
British Airways
750   *

Penrose, Harald
Wings Across the World: An Illustrated History of British
Airways
Cassell 1980   304pp illus index
British Airways
750   §

Penzer, Norman Mosley
Paul Storr: The Last of the Goldsmiths

Batsford 1954   292pp illus
Storr, Paul
491   *

338

Perkin Dyeworks
100 Years of Synthetic Dyestuffs

Pergamon 1958   136pp illus index
Perkin Dyeworks
251   EALNGPL

Perkins, Edwin Judson
Financing Anglo-American Trade: The House of Brown
1800-1880
Cambridge, Mass: Harvard U P 1975   323pp index sources
Brown, Shipley & Co
814   *

Perkins, Edwin Judson
Managing a Dollar Sterling Exchange Account: Brown, Shipley &
Co in the 1850s
Business History   vol XVI no 1 1974
Brown, Shipley & Co
814

Perkins, Herbert H
The Rise of Bentalls: Over 80 Years' Progress 1867-1951

Kingston upon Thames: the firm 1951 47pp illus
Bentalls of Kingston
656   CROYPL

Perks, R B
Real Profit Sharing: William Thomson & Sons of Huddersfield
1886-1925
Business History   vol XXIV no 2 1982
Thomson, William & Sons
431

Perren, Richard
John Fleming & Company Limited 1877-1977

Aberdeen: the firm 1977   96pp illus index sources
Fleming, John & Co
613   * §

Perren, Richard
The Meat Trade in Britain 1840-1914

Routledge & Kegan Paul 1978   x 258pp illus index
Meat Trade
412   617   *

Perrotts
A History of 250 Years of Clothworking

1962   46pp
Perrotts
645   GHL

Perry, Charles R
The British Post Office 1836-1914: A Study in Nationalisation
and Administrative Expansion
Harvard PhD 1976
Post Office
790

Perry, G
Movies from the Mansion: A History of Pinewood Studio

Elm Tree 1983   182pp illus
Pinewood Studio
971   §
Peterborough Provincial Benefit Building Society
Peterborough Provincial Benefit Building Society: The First
Hundred Years 1860-1960
the firm nd   21pp illus
Peterborough Provincial Bldg Soc
815   CAMBSPL
Peterhead Savings Bank
Rules and Regulations of the Peterhead Savings Bank

Peterhead: P Buchan 1825
Peterhead Savings Bank
814   NESLS
Petter, Percival Waddams
The Story of Petters Limited:- Told for my Children

typescript/Dr Norah Sims nd
Petters   Westland Aircraft
328   364
Pettigrew, Andrew M
The Awakening Giant: Continuity and Change in Imperial
Chemical Industries
Oxford: Basil Blackwell 1985   542pp index sources
I C I
250   *
Philip, George
The Story of the House of Philip during the last 100 Years: A
Geographical Record   1834-1934
George Philip & Son 1934   108pp illus
Philip, George & Son
475   * §
Philips, J & N
Philips, J & N & Co: 1747-1947 Bicentenary

Tean, Staffs: the firm 1947   10pp illus
Philips, J & N
439   MRC
Phillips, Alastair
Glasgow's Herald 1783-1983

Glasgow: Richard Drew 1982   192pp illus index
Glasgow Herald
475   StBRD
Phillips, Barty
Conran and the Habitat Story

Weidenfeld & Nicolson 1984   ix 150pp illus index
Habitat   Conran Associates
647   648   * §

340

Phillips, David C
*The Wantage Engineering Co. Ltd. and its Predecessors
1826-1910*
J Road Locomotive Soc   vol 33 1980
Wantage Engineering Co
321

Phillips, Elizabeth
A History of the Pioneers of the Welsh Coalfield

Cardiff: Western Mail 1925   viii 261pp
Welsh Coalfield
111   MRTHRPL

Phillips, J
A History of the United Wire Works, Established 1825

Edinburgh: Granton 1947   63pp illus
United Wire Works
223   §

Phillips, J A & Co
*Sixty Years of Cycle Craftsmanship: Marking the Diamond
Jubilee of the Phillips Organisation*
the firm 1952   48pp illus
Phillips, J A & Co
363   SANDWPL

Phillips, R J
History of Ramsbury Building Society

Ramsbury: the firm 1982   116pp illus sources
Ramsbury Building Soc
815   §

Phipps-Faire
150th Anniversary Brochure 1822-1972

Northampton: the firm 1972   12pp illus
Phipps-Faire
451   NHPTNPL

Phoenix Assurance Co
Phoenix Family Story

the firm 1953   156pp
Phoenix Assurance
820   GHL

Phoenix Assurance Co
The Phoenix Assurance Company Ltd. 1782-1915

the firm 1915   104pp illus
Phoenix Assurance
820   *

Pick, J B
*The Pick Knitwear Story 1856-1956: An Account of J Pick &
Sons Ltd, Leicester, Manufacturers for 100 Years*
Leicester: the firm 1956   45pp illus
Pick, J & Sons
436   LEICSPL

341

Pigott, Stanley
Hollins: A Study of Industry 1784-1949

Nottingham: the firm 1949 151pp illus index sources
Hollins, William
432 436 * §
Pigott, Stanley
O B M: A Celebration: 125 Years in Advertising

the firm 1975 84pp sources
Ogilvy Benson & Mather
838 *
Pilkington
Now Thus- Now Thus 1826-1926

St Helens: the firm 1926 93pp illus
Pilkington Brothers
247 *
Piller, Norman
Instead of the Butler's Apron

Luton: Cortney 1974 vii 433pp illus
Bloore & Piller
613 648 *
Pitman
The House of Pitman

the firm (photocopy) nd 63pp illus
Pitman, Isaac & Sons
475 BLPES
Pittard
Pittards 1826-1976: A Commemorative History

Yeovil: the firm nd 88pp illus
Pittard, C W & Co
441 BLPES
Plaisted, H
Prudential Past and Present: Story of the Rise and Progress of the Prudential Assurance Company
C & E Layton 1917 viii 262pp
Prudential Assurance
820 *
Plant, Marjorie
The English Book Trade

Allen & Unwin 1974 518pp illus index sources
Book Trade
475
Plant, William
Brief History of the Firm

Manchester: the firm nd
Plant, William & Sons
453 SKPTPL

Playne, Arthur Twisden & Long, Arthur Leslie
200th Anniversary: A History of Playne of Longfords Mills

Gloucester: the firm 1959   64pp illus
Playne, William & Co
431   UBRIS

Plowright Brothers
The Plowright Story

the firm 1960   12pp
Plowright Brothers
320   DERBYPL

Plumb, J H
*A History of the Leicester Co-operative Boot and Shoe
Manufacturing Society Limited*
Leicester: the firm 1936   94pp illus
Leicester Co-op Boot & Shoe
451   LEICSPL

Plummer, Alfred
The London Weavers' Company 1600-1970

Routledge & Kegan Paul 1972   xviii 476pp illus index sources
Weavers' Company
431   *

Plummer, Alfred
*The Witney Blanket Industry: The Records of the Witney
Blanket Weavers*
George Routledge 1934   ix 284pp index sources
Witney Blanket Industry
431   * §

Plummer, Alfred & Early, Richard E
*The Blanket Makers 1669-1969: A History of Charles Early &
Marriott (Witney) Ltd.*
Routledge & Kegan Paul 1969   xii 205pp illus index sources
Early, Charles   Witney Blanket Industry
431   *

Pochin, R Eric
Over my Shoulder and Beyond

Leicester: the firm 1954   87pp illus
Goodwin Barsby & Co
325   LEICSPL

Pochin, R Eric with Olive, E A
Over my Shoulder and Beyond

Leicester: the firm 1971   109pp illus
Aveling-Barford Group
325   LEICSPL

Pocock Bros
Shoe and Leather News: Pocock 1815-1962

1962   55pp
Pocock Bros
451   GHL

Pocock, Douglas Charles David
A Comparative Study of Three Steel Towns: Corby, Scunthorpe and Middlesbrough
Dundee PhD 1969
Steel Towns
221

Pointer, **Michael**
Ruston & Hornsby, Grantham, 1918-1963

Grantham: Bygone Grantham 1977   36pp
Ruston & Hornsby
321

Pointon, **Arnold Cecil**
The Bombay Burmah Trading Corporation Limited 1863-1967

Southampton: Millbrook 1964   143pp illus index sources
Bombay Burmah Trading Corp
839   §

Pointon, **Arnold Cecil**
Wallace Brothers

the firm 1974   vi 120pp illus index sources
Wallace Brothers & Co (Holdings)
839   * §

Pole, **William**
The Life of Sir William Siemens

John Murray 1888   xii 412pp illus
Siemens Brothers & Co
221   *

Pole, **William (ed)**
The Life of Sir William Fairbairn Bart, partly written by himself (first published 1877)
Newton Abbot: David & Charles 1970 507pp index sources
Fairbairns of Manchester
320   328   361   362   502   §

Political **and Economic Planning**
Report on the British Coal Industry

P E P 1936   214pp
Coal Industry
111   *

Political **and Economic Planning**
Report on the British Cotton Industry

P E P 1934   147pp
Cotton Industry
432   *

Political **and Economic Planning**
Report on the Gas Industry in Great Britain

P E P 1939   213pp
Gas Industry
162   *

Political and Economic Planning
The British Fuel and Power Industries

P E P 1947   xi 406pp
Fuel & Power Industries
111   161   162   *

Pollard, Sidney
Notes on a Typefoundry: The Rise of Stephenson Blake & Co Ltd

Sheffield: the firm nd   19pp
Stephenson Blake & Co
224   SHEFFPL

Pollard, Sidney
Shirley Aldred & Co Ltd 1796-1958

Worksop: the firm 1959   41pp illus
Shirley Aldred & Co
251   §

Pollard, Sidney
Stephenson Blake & Co Ltd, Sheffield: Typefounders (No Title on Volume)
ca1960: only one copy printed   277pp
Stephenson Blake & Co
327   StBRD

Pollard, Sidney
Three Centuries of Sheffield Steel: The Story of a Family Business
Sheffield: the firm 1954   82pp illus
Marsh Brothers & Co
221   * §

Pollard, Sidney & Marshall, J D
The Furness Railway and the Growth of Barrow

Journal of Transport History   vol I no 2 1953
Furness Railway
710

Pollard, Sidney & Robertson, Paul
The British Shipbuilding Industry 1870-1914

Cambridge, Mass: Harvard U P 1979   xiii 312pp illus index sources
Cammell, Charles & Co
361   *

Pollard, Sidney & Turner, R
Profit Sharing and Autocracy: The Case of J T and J Taylor of Batley, Woollen Manufacturers 1892-1966
Business History   vol XVIII no 1 1976
Taylor, J T & J
431

Polley, Bernard
The Candor Story: Sixty Years of Service to the Colchester Motorist 1922-1982
Colchester: the firm 1984   38pp illus
Candor Motors
652   671   §

Pollins, H
Railway Contractors and the Finance of Railway Development in Britain
Journal of Transport History   vol 3 no 1 1957

500   710
Pollock, Walter
The Pollocks as Engineers

Tunbridge Wells: the firm 1939   228pp
Pollock, Walter
361   *

Poole Pottery
Poole Pottery: The First Hundred Years

Bournemouth: the firm 1973   48pp illus
Poole Pottery
248   INVRNPL

Popham, Hugh
Esso in Britain: 100 Years of History

the firm 1978
Esso Petroleum Co
130   140   612   652

Popham, Hugh
The History of Job's Dairy

Feltham: the firm 1977   29pp illus
Job, H A
617   641   *

Portal, Francis Spencer
Portals: The Church, the State and the People, Leading to 250 Years of Papermaking
the firm 1962   xii 99pp illus sources
Portals
471   * §

Porteous, Crichton
Pill Boxes and Bandages: A Documentary Biography of the First Two Generations of Robinsons of Chesterfield 1839-1916
Chesterfield: the firm 1960   188pp illus index
Robinson & Sons
257   * §

Porter, Andrew
Donald Currie and Southern Africa 1870 to 1912: Strategies for Survival
see Palmer, S R & Williams, G (eds)
Union-Castle
740

Porter, Dilwyn
A Trusted Guide of the Investing Public: Harry Marks and the 'Financial News' 1884-1916
Business History   vol XXVIII no 1 1986
Financial News
475   831

Porter, J H
Cotton and Wool Textiles

see Buxton, N K & Aldcroft, D H (eds)
Textile Industry
431   432

Porter, J H
The Development of a Provincial Department Store 1870-1939

Business History   vol XIII no 1 1971
Broadbents of Southport
656

Potter, Stephen
The Magic Number: The Story of "57"

Max Reinhardt 1959   182 pp illus index
Heinz, H J & Co
410   * §

Potter, Walter C
The House of Mallinson 1877-1947

Southern Editorial Syndicate 1947   175pp illus
Mallinson, William & Denny Mott
613   UBRIS

Potters of Darwen
Potters of Darwen 1839-1939: A Century of Wallpaper Printing

the firm 1940   120pp illus
Potters of Darwen   Wall Paper Manufacturers
472   §

Potts, Bob
The Firm that Used Round Base Codd-Hybrids, Matthew Pomfret Ltd , Bury, Lancashire

Pomfret, Matthew
428   BURYPL

Potts, J D
Platt of Rotherham: Mason-Architects 1700-1810

Sheffield: author 1959   20pp illus
Platt of Rotherham
501   837   *

Pound, Reginald
Selfridge: A Biography

Heinemann 1960   268pp illus
Selfridges
656   *

Pound, Reginald
The Fenwick Story

Newcastle: the firm 1972
Fenwicks
656

Pound, Reginald & Harmsworth, A Geoffrey
 Northcliffe

    Cassell 1959   xvi 933pp illus index sources
    Associated Newspapers
    475   *

Powell Duffryn
 The Powell Duffryn Steam Coal Company Limited 1864-1914

    the firm 1914   95pp illus
    Powell Duffryn Steam Coal Co
    111   *

Powell, Christopher G
 An Economic History of the British Building Industry 1815-1979
    Methuen 1982
    Building
    500

Power-Gas
 The Stockton Scene

    Stockton: the firm nd   42pp
    Power-Gas   Ashmore, Benson, Pease & Co
    320

Premier
 Premier Omnibus Co: Premier Line Ltd

    Blackpool: Dryhurst 1962   23pp illus
    Premier Omnibus Co
    721   MRC

Prescott's Bank
 Prescott's Bank 1766-1966

    1966
    Prescott's Bank   National Provincial Bank
    814   GHL

Pressed Steel
 Pressed Steel Co Ltd.

    Oxford: the firm ca1960   69pp illus
    Pressed Steel
    312   351   OXFDPL

Pressed Steel
 The Pressed Steel Co Ltd: 24 Years of Progress 1926-1950

    Oxford: the firm 1950   28pp illus
    Pressed Steel
    312   351   OXFDPL

Pressed Steel
 The Prestcold Story

    Oxford: the firm 1953   40pp illus
    Pressed Steel   Prestcold
    312   346   OXFDPL

Pressed Steel
The Story of Pressed Steel

Oxford: the firm ca1930
Pressed Steel
312   351   OXFDPL

Preston, J M
A Short History: A History of Short Bros. Aircraft Activities in Kent 1908-1964
Rochester: North Kent Books 1979   42pp illus
Short Brothers
364   BROMPL

Prestwich, Wm.
Diamond Jubilee 1889-1949

the firm 1950   32pp illus
Prestwich, Wm & Sons
243   245   DERBYPL

Prevost, Augustus
History of Morris, Prevost & Co

the firm 1904   16pp
Morris, Prevost & Co
616   647   *

Price's (Bromborough)
The History of Price's of Bromborough 1854-1954

Bromborough: the firm 1954   43pp
Price's (Bromborough)
251

Price's Patent Candle Co
A Brief History of Price's Patent Candle Company

Waterlow 1891   15pp
Price's Patent Candle Co
259   *

Price's Patent Candle Co
Price's Patent Candle Co: Jubilee Memoir 1847-1897

the firm 1897   38pp illus
Price's Patent Candle Co
259   WANDSPL

Price's Patent Candle Co
Still the Candle Burns: Price's Patent Candle Co Centenary 1847-1947
the firm 1947   43pp illus
Price's Patent Candle Co
259   * §

Price, Barrie
The Lea-Francis Story

Batsford 1978   144pp illus index
Lea-Francis
351   §

Price, F G Hilton
    The Marygold by Temple Bar: Being a History of...the Banking
    House of Messrs Child & Co
    Quaritch 1902   202pp illus index
    Child & Co
    814   §

Price, Forbes
    And at Lloyd's: The Story of Price, Forbes and Company Limited

    Harley 1954   viii 71pp illus
    Price, Forbes & Co
    820   §

Price, J R
    A History of Mountain and Gibson

    Hartley Nemo 1980   illus
    Mountain & Gibson
    362   BURYPL

Price, Seymour J
    From Queen to Queen: The Centenary Story of the Temperance
    Permanent Building Society 1854-1954
    Franey 1954   xiii 134pp illus index
    Temperance Permanent Bldg Soc
    815   * §

Price, Seymour James
    Building Societies: Their Origin and History

    Franey 1958   xiii 598pp illus index sources
    Building Societies Association
    815   * §

Price, Thomas L
    One Hundred Years of Progress: Blackstone & Co Ltd of
    Stamford, Lincs from...1837 to the Present Day
    Dursley: F Bailey & Son ca1937   43pp illus
    Blackstone & Co   Lister-Blackstone
    321   328   UBRIS

Price, Waterhouse & Co
    Price, Waterhouse & Co: History of the Firm: The First Fifty
    Years 1850-1900
    typescript nd   15pp illus
    Price, Waterhouse & Co
    836   §

Price-Hughes, H A
    B T H Reminiscences: 60 Years of Progress; British Thomson
    Houston Co
    the firm 1946   176pp illus
    British Thomson Houston Co
    340   * §

Priestley, John H
    The History of the Ripponden Co-operative Society Limited
    1832-1932
    Halifax: F King 1932   185pp illus
    Ripponden Co-operative Soc
    656   HLFXPL

Prince, Peter
John Bell and the 'Universal Advertiser'

Business History   vol XI no 2 1969
Bell, John
475

Pringle, Robert and Sons
The House of Pringle 1835-1935

the firm nd   23pp illus
Pringle, Robert & Sons
374   491   654   ISLTNPL

Proudfoot, William Bryce
The Origin of Stencil Duplicating

Hutchinson 1972   128pp illus index
Gestetne
330   495   * §

Prudential Assurance
History of the Prudential Assurance Company

1880   81pp
Prudential Assurance
820   GHL

Prudential Assurance
History of the Prudential Assurance Company

the firm 1880   82pp
Prudential Assurance
820   §

Public Wharfingers
The London Association of Public Wharfingers 1854-1954

1954   24pp
Public Wharfingers
763   GHL

Puddefoot, Bowers & Simonett
Ivory: An Unbroken Tradition of 250 Years 1685-1935

the firm 1935   6pp
Puddefoot, Bowers & Simonett
495   *

Pudney, John Sleigh
A Draught of Contentment: The Story of the Courage Group

New English Library 1971   152pp illus
Courage & Co
427   §

Pudney, John Sleigh
Bristol Fashion: Some Account of the Earlier Days of Bristol Aviation
Putnam 1960   102pp illus
Bristol Aeroplane Co
364   *

Pudney, John Sleigh
The Seven Skies: A Study of B O A C and its Forerunners since 1919
the firm 1959   320pp illus
British Overseas Airways Corp   Imperial Airways
750   *

Pudney, John Sleigh
The Thomas Cook Story

Michael Joseph 1953   264pp index
Cook, Thomas
770   *

Pugh, Charles H
Charles H Pugh: One Hundred Years Old

the firm 1965   34pp illus
Pugh, Charles H   Atco
313   328   §

Purvis, W F
Nine Generations of Fur Trading: P R Poland & Son

1951   16pp
Poland, P R & Son
456   GHL

Quail, G
Garnkirk Fire-Clay

Bishopbriggs: Strathkelvin 1985   48pp illus
Garnkirk Fire-Clay Co
231   248   SKLVNPL

Qualter Hall & Co
A Handful of History: The Story of Qualter Hall & Co Ltd 1860-1960
Barnsley: the firm 1960   47pp illus
Qualter Hall & Co
325   UBRIS

Quin-Harkin, A J
Imperial Airways 1924-40

Journal of Transport History   vol 1 1954
Imperial Airways
750

Quinn, Esther
The Ravenscraig Decision

Strathclyde PhD 1981   331pp sources
British Steel
221   MTHWLPL

Radford, J B
A Century of Progress: Centenary Brochure of the Derby Carriage and Wagon Works
the firm 1976   56pp illus sources
British Rail Engineering
362   DERBYPL

Radmore, D F
The Origins of Julia Hanson and Sons Ltd

typescript 1981   6pp illus sources
Hanson, Julia & Sons
427   DUDLYPL

Rae, John B
Harry Ferguson and Henry Ford

Belfast: Ulster Hist Foundation 1980 x 32pp illus
Ferguson, Harry   Ford Motor
321   *

Rae, William Fraser
The Business of Travel: A Fifty Years' Record of Progress

the firm 1891   318pp
Cook, Thomas
770   *

Raistrick, Arthur
Coalbrookdale 1709-1959

Wellington: the firm 1959   29pp illus
Coalbrookdale Co   Allied Ironfounders
221   311   *

Raistrick, Arthur
Dynasty of Ironfounders: The Darbys and Coalbrookdale

Longmans Green 1953   xvi 308pp illus index sources
Coalbrookdale Co   Allied Ironfounders
221   311   * §

Raistrick, Arthur
Two Centuries of Industrial Welfare: The London (Quaker) Lead Co 1692-1905
Buxton: Moorland 1977   168pp illus index sources
London (Quaker) Lead Co
720   * §

Rait, Robert S
The History of the Union Bank of Scotland

Glasgow: John Smith 1930   xviii 392pp illus index sources
Union Bank of Scotland
814   * §

Raithby Lawrence & Co
1776-1876 Raithby Lawrence & Co 1876-1976: De Montfort Press
Leicester: the firm 1976   90pp illus
Raithby Lawrence & Co
475   *

Raleigh
Raleigh Industries: A Story of Great Achievement

the firm 1957
Raleigh Industries
363   *

Ralfe, Pilcher G
Sixty Years of Banking 1865-1925: A Short History of the Isle of Man Banking Company Limited
Douglas: L G Meyer 1925   59pp illus
Isle of Man Banking Co
820   *

Ralli Trading Group
History and Activities of the Ralli Trading Group: Commodity Merchants for 160 Years
the firm 1979   80pp illus
Ralli Trading Group   Bowater
630   839   * §

Rambotham, J W
J W Rambotham Reach their Half-Century

Edmonton: the firm 1957   8pp illus
Rambotham & Co
646   ENFLDPL

Randall, Robert W
British Company and Mexican Community: The English at Real del Monte 1824-1849
Business History Review   vol 59 no 4 1985
Real del Monte Co   Silver Mining
210   839

Rank, Joseph
The Master Millers: The Story of the House of Rank...Issued on their Eightieth Anniversary
Harley 1955   98pp illus
Rank, Joseph
416   UBRIS

Rankin, John
A History of our Firm; Pollok, Gilmour & Co and its Offshoots and Connections 1804-1920
Liverpool: Henry Young 1921   ix 330pp index
Pollok, Gilmour & Co
613   770   *

Ransomes
Wherever the Sun Shines: 175 years of Progress by Ransomes

Ipswich: the firm nd   36pp illus
Ransomes, Sims & Jefferies
321   328   §

Ransomes, Sims and Jefferies
Ransomes' 'Royal' Records: A Century and a Half in the Service of Agriculture
Ipswich: the firm ca1939   96pp illus
Ransomes, Sims a& Jefferies
321   UBRIS

Ravage, Marcus Eli
Five Men of Frankfort: The Story of the Rothschilds 1789-1900

Harrap 1929   331pp
Rothschild
814   *

Raw, Charles
>*Slater Walker: An Investigation of a Financial Phenomenon*

Deutsch 1977   368pp index
Slater Walker
815   *

Raw, Charles; Hodgson, Godfrey & Page, Bruce
>*Do You Sincerely Want to Be Rich? Bernard Cornfeld and I O S; An International Swindle*

Deutsch 1971   464pp illus
Investors Overseas Services
831   *

Raybould, Trevor J
>*The Economic Emergence of the Black Country: A Study of the Dudley Estate*

Newton Abbot: David & Charles 1973 272pp
Dudley Estate   Round Oak Steel Works
111   210   221   *

Rea, Vincent (comp)
>*Palmer's Yard and the Town of Jarrow*

Jarrow 1975
Palmers of Jarrow
361

Read, Ian F
>*Premier Albanian Coaches: A History of Independent Bus and Coach Operation from 1923*

the firm 1985   64pp illus
Premier Coaches   Albanian Coaches
721   HERTSPL

Read, Joan
>*Ellis, Wood, Bickersteth & Hazel 1883-1983*

the firm 1983   55pp illus
Ellis, Wood, Bickersteth & Hazel
835   * §

Reader, Ernest R
>*The History of the B & I Line including the City of Cork Steam Packet Co*

the firm 1952   64pp illus
B & I Line
740   CORKPL

Reader, William Joseph
>*A House in the City: A Study of the City and of the Stock Exchange...The Records of Foster & Braithwaite 1825-1975*

Batsford 1979   x 198pp illus index sources
Foster & Braithwaite
831   * §

Reader, William Joseph
>*Architect of Air Power: The Life of the First Viscount Weir of Eastwood 1877-1959*

Collins 1968   351pp illus index sources
Weir, G & J
320   *

Reader, William Joseph
Birds Eye: The Early Years

Walton on Thames: the firm 1963   48pp illus sources
Birds Eye Foods Ltd.
411   414   415   617   * §

Reader, William Joseph
Bowater: A History

Cambridge: C U P 1981   xv 426pp illus index sources
Bowater
20   471   472   * §

Reader, William Joseph
Fifty Years of Unilever 1930-1980

Heinemann 1980   xi 148pp illus index sources
Unilever
258   411   414   * §

Reader, William Joseph
Hard Roads and Highways: S P D Limited 1918-1968: A Study in Distribution
Batsford 1969   152pp illus index sources
S P D   Unilever
723   * §

Reader, William Joseph
Imperial Chemical Industries: A History

Oxford U P 1970-75   2 vols illus index sources
I C I
250   * §

Reader, William Joseph
Metal Box: A History

Heinemann 1976   xii 256pp illus index sources
Metal Box
316   * §

Reader, William Joseph
The Chemical Industry

see Buxton, N K & Aldcroft, D H (eds)
Chemical Industry
250

Reader, William Joseph
The Macadam Family and the Turnpike Roads 1798-1861

Heinemann 1980   xii 241pp illus index sources
Macadam
245   502   *

Reader, William Joseph
The United Kingdom Soapmakers' Association and the English Soap Trade
Business History   vol I no 2 1959
Soap Trade
258

Reader, William Joseph
The Weir Group: A Centenary History

Weidenfeld & Nicolson 1971 238pp illus index sources
Weir, G & J
320 *

Reader, William Joseph
To Have and To Hold: An Account of Frederick Baudet's Life in Business
the firm 1983 xviii 277pp illus index
Hunting Gate Group
850 *

Reader, William Joseph
Unilever: A Short History

the firm 1960 60pp sources
Unilever
258 411 414 UBRIS

Readhead
Readheads of South Shields

South Shields: the firm 1965 illus
Readhead, John & Sons
361 *

Rebbeck, D
The History of Iron Shipbuilding on the Queen's Island up to July 1874
Queen's University, Belfast PhD 1950
Harland & Wolff
361

Reckitt, Basil Norman
The History of Reckitt & Sons Ltd.

Norwich: Brown 1951 xvi 113pp illus
Reckitt & Colman
259 418 *

Recknell, George Hugh
King Street, Cheapside and the National Mutual Life Assurance

the firm 1936 53pp illus
National Mutual Life Assurance
820 * §

Redden, Richard
A History of the Britannia Building Society 1856-1985

Franey 1985 168pp illus index
Britannia Building Society
815 MACCPL

Redfern
Redfern's Rubber Works: Our Jubilee 1900-1950

Hyde: the firm 1950 32pp illus
Redfern's Rubber Works
481 TAMESPL

Redfern, Percy
The New History of the CWS

Dent 1938 xiv 624pp illus index
Co-operative Wholesale Society
619 656 *

Redfern, Percy
The Story of the CWS: The Jubilee History of the Co-operative Wholesale Society Limited 1863-1913
Manchester: the firm 1913 viii 439pp illus index
Co-operative Wholesale Society
619 656 *

Redford, Arthur (ed)
Manchester Merchants and Foreign Trade 1794-1858

Manchester: M U P 1934 2 vols
Manchester Merchants
740 839 *

Redman, M
The Evening and the Morning

Solihull: Toon & Heath 1957 103pp illus
Armstrong Siddeley Motors
351 MRC

Redmayne, Ronald
Ideals in Industry; Being the Story of Montague Burton Ltd. 1900-1950
Leeds: the firm 1951 481pp illus
Montague Burton
453 645 UBRIS

Reed, Austin
Fine and Fifty

the firm 1950 36pp
Austin Reed
453 645 GHL

Reed, B
Crewe Locomotive Works and Its Men

Newton Abbot: David & Charles 1982 240pp illus
London & North Western Railway Crewe Works
362 710

Reed, M C
A History of James Capel & Co.

the firm 1975 xiii 129pp illus index sources
Capel, James
814 §

Reed, Richard
National Westminster Bank: A Short History

the firm 1983 56pp illus
Westminster Bank National Provincial Bank
814 §

Reeder, D A
A Victorian Building Firm in Fulham 1878-1884

typescript nd 6pp
Gibbs & Flew
501 HMFULPL
Rees, Morgan Goronwy
St. Michael: A History of Marks and Spencer

Weidenfeld & Nicolson 1966 261pp illus index sources
Marks & Spencer
645 656 * §
Regan, Simon
Rupert Murdoch: A Business Biography

Angus & Robertson 1976 viii 246pp illus index
News International
475 *
Reid, A
Continuous Venture: The Story of a Steel Works

Shotton: the firm 1948 47pp illus
Summers, John & Sons
221 TAMESPL
Reid, James Macarthur
James Lithgow, Master of Work

Hutchinson 1964 254pp
Lithgow Scott Lithgow
361 *
Reid, James Macarthur
The First Hundred Years

the firm 1958 67pp illus
Bayne and Duckett
616 646 *
Reid, James Macarthur
The History of the Clydesdale Bank 1838-1938

Glasgow: Blackie 1938 ix 299pp illus index
Clydesdale Bank
814 *
Reid, Margaret Isabel
The Secondary Banking Crisis 1973-75: The Inside Story of Britain's Biggest Banking Upheaval
Macmillan 1982 ix 219pp index sources
Secondary Banking Crisis London & County Securities
814 815 * §
Reliance Bank
The Reliance Bank Ltd.

the firm 1951 28pp illus
Reliance Bank Salvation Army Bank
814 §

359

Renault UK

Renault UK Ltd 1902-1982: An Historic Account of the Activities of Renault UK

the firm 1982   20pp illus

Renault UK

614   §

Rendell

A Good Job Well Done: Rendell, a West Country Builder

Stocker & Hocknell 1984   iii 175pp illus

Rendell

501

Rennison, R W

Water to Tyneside: A History of the Newcastle & Gateshead Water Company

Newcastle upon Tyne: the firm 1969 xx 361pp illus index sources

Newcastle & Gateshead Water Co

170   §

Repath, Elizabeth

Print is our Business: A History of Alabaster Passmore & Sons Ltd

Maidstone: the firm 1983   50pp illus

Alabaster Passmore

475   §

Reynolds & Co

The Firm of Reynolds: 110 Years of Service

Ed J Burrow ca1933   16pp illus

Reynolds & Co

648   RCHMDPL

Reynolds, Bryan

Don't Trudge It: Rudge It

Yeovil: Haynes 1977   174pp illus index

Rudge-Whitworth

363   *

Reynolds, Jack

The Great Paternalist: Titus Salt and the Growth of Nineteenth-Century Bradford

Maurice Temple Smith 1983   382pp

Salt, Titus

431   BLPES

Rhondda, Margaret, Viscountess

D A Thomas, Viscount Rhondda

Longmans 1921   ix 335pp illus

Cambrian Collieries

111   *

Richards Tiles

Richards Tiles Ltd 1837-1953

Staffordshire: the firm 1953   36pp

Richards Tiles

248

Richards, Archibald B
Touche Ross & Co 1899-1981: The Origins and Growth of the United Kingdom Firm
the firm 1981   xiv 145pp illus
Touche Ross & Co
836   *

Richards, E S
The Finances of the Liverpool and Manchester Railway Again

Economic History Review   2nd ser vol XXV no 2 1972
Liverpool & Manchester Railway
710

Richards, G E
History of the Firm: The First Fifty Years 1850-1900

typescript the firm 1950   13pp
Price, Waterhouse & Co
836   §

Richards, John
A History of the Simpkiss Breweries

Manchester: Neil Richardson 1984   27pp illus
Simpkiss Breweries
427   DUDLYPL

Richardson, D J
The History of the Catering Industry with special reference to the History of J Lyons & Co Ltd to 1939
Kent PhD 1970
Lyons, J & Co
419   423   661   664

Richardson, H W & Bass, J M
The Profitability of the Consett Iron Company before 1914

Business History   vol VII no 2 1965
Consett Iron Co
221   311

Richardson, Harry W & Aldcroft, Derek H
Building in the British Economy between the Wars

Allen & Unwin 1968   355pp illus index sources
Building
500   *

Richardson, J E
Chronicle of Fitzroy Works and of Frederick Braby and Co Ltd

the firm 1925   338pp
Braby Group
223   313   316   §

Richardson, J N
Bessbrook

the firm 1945
Bessbrook Spinning Co
434

Richardson, K
>*Ragosine Centenary*

the firm 1978   pamphlet
Ragosine
140   §

Richardson, Kenneth
>*The British Motor Industry 1896-1939*

Macmillan 1977   xiii 258pp illus index sources
Motor Industry
350   *

Richardson, Kenneth
>*Twentieth-Century Coventry*

Macmillan 1972   xi 380pp illus
Motor Industry
350   *

Richardson, Neil
>*A History of Joseph Holt*

Swinton: the author 1984   28pp illus
Holt, Joseph
427   *

Richardson, Neil
>*A History of Wilsons Brewery 1834-1984 to Commemorate 150 Years of Brewing at Newton Heath*
Manchester: author 1983   30pp illus
Wilsons Brewery
427   * §

Richardson, P
>*Nobels and the Australian Mining Industry 1907-1925*

Business History   vol XXVI no 2 1984
Nobel's Explosive Co
256

Richardson, Ralph
>*Coutts & Co., Bankers, Edinburgh and London*

Elliot Stock 1900   xii 166pp illus index
Coutts & Co
814   *

Richardson, William
>*The CWS in War and Peace 1938-1976: The CWS in the Second World War and Post-War Years*
Manchester: the firm 1977   xiii 399pp
Co-operative Wholesale Society
619   656   *

Richardson, William
>*The History of the Parish of Wallsend: General, Ecclesiastical, Industrial and Biographical*
Northumberland Press 1923   538pp illus
Wallsend Parish
740   *

362

Riden, Philip J
> *The Butterley Company 1790-1830: A Derbyshire Ironworks in the Industrial Revolution*
> author 1973   63pp sources
> Butterley Co
> 111   221   DERBYPL

Rigby, Thomas
> *The Origins and the History of Co-operation in Bury...Jubilee of the Bury District Co-operative Society Ltd 1855-1905*
> Bury: 1905
> Bury District Co-operative Soc
> 656   BURYPL

Rimmer, William Gordon
> *Joseph Watson: Soap Manufacturer 1873-1922*
>
> Leeds Journal   vol 32; 1961
> Watson, Joseph & Sons   Lever Brothers
> 258   411

Rimmer, William Gordon
> *Leeds Leather Industry in the Nineteenth Century*
>
> Publ Thoresby Society   Miscellany 13
> Leeds Leather Industry
> 440

Rimmer, William Gordon
> *Marshalls of Leeds: Flax Spinners 1788-1886*
>
> Cambridge: C U P 1960   xiii 342pp illus index sources
> Marshalls
> 434   * §

Rippon, Guy S O
> *The Flintshire Oil and Cannel Co Ltd 1864-1872*
>
> London MA 1977
> Flintshire Oil & Cannel Co
> 120   130

Ritchie, Arthur Edwin
> *The Kent Coalfield: Its Evolution and Development*
>
> Iron & Coal Trades Review 1919   x 309pp illus
> Kent Coal Concessions
> 111   612   *

Rivington, Septimus
> *The Publishing House of Rivington: History of the Family Business since 1711*
> Rivington 1894   81pp illus
> Rivington, Percival & Co
> 475   *

Robbins, Richard Michael
> *The North London Railway*
>
> Godalming: Oakwood 1937   31pp illus sources
> North London Railway
> 721   *

Robbins, Richard Michael
The Railway Age

Routledge & Kegan Paul 1962   x 227pp illus index sources
Railways
710   *

Robens, Alfred
Ten Year Stint

Cassell 1972   342pp index
National Coal Board
111   §

Roberts, C P & Co
The House that Roberts Built 1868-1968

Potters Bar: the firm nd   41pp
Roberts, C P & Co
501   MRC

Roberts, Cecil
Achievement: A Record of Fifty Years' Progress of Boots Pure Drug Company Ltd 1888-1938
the firm nd   70pp illus
Boots The Chemists
257   643   §

Roberts, Cecil R J
The First Fifty Years of 'Millbay'

Plymouth: Underhill 1948   61pp illus
Millbay Laundry, Cleaning
981   *

Roberts, Colin William
A Legacy from Victorian Enterprise: The Briton Ferry Ironworks and the Daughter Companies
Gloucester: Alan Sutton 1983   x 277pp illus index sources
Briton Ferry Ironworks   Dowlais Iron Co
221   *

Roberts, David E
The Grimsby Gas Undertaking 1836-1949

Leicester: East Midlands Gas 1983   38pp illus sources
Grimsby Gas
162   §

Roberts, David E
The Leicester Gas Undertaking 1821-1921

Leicester: East Midlands Gas 1978   50pp illus sources
Leicester Gas
162   §

Roberts, David E
The Lincoln Gas Undertaking 1828-1949

Leicester: East Midlands Gas 1981   46pp illus sources
Lincoln Gas Light & Coke Co
162   * §

Roberts, David E
The Nottingham Gas Undertaking 1921-1949

Leicester: East Midlands Gas 1980   54pp illus sources
Nottingham Gas-Light and Coke Co
162   §

Roberts, David E
The Nottingham Gas-Light and Coke Company 1818-1874

Loughborough MA 1976
Nottingham Gas-Light and Coke Co
162

Roberts, David E
The Sheffield Gas Undertaking 1818-1949

Leicester: East Midlands Gas 1979   46pp illus sources
Sheffield Gas Undertaking
162   §

Roberts, David E & Frisby, J H
The Northampton Gas Undertaking 1823-1949

Leicester: East Midlands Gas 1980   38pp illus sources
Northampton Gas
162   §

Roberts, J
The John Roberts Press: The Oldest Firm in Clerkenwell Green 1898-1974
1974   12pp illus
Roberts, J
475   ISLTNPL

Roberts, Peter
The Old Vic Story: A Nation's Theatre 1818-1976

W H Allen 1976   x 203pp illus index sources
Old Vic
974   *

Roberts, R O
The Operations of the Brecon Old Bank of Wilkins & Co 1778-1890
Business History   vol I no 2 1959
Wilkins & Co   Brecon Old Bank
814

Roberts, S C
The Evolution of Cambridge Publishing

Cambridge: C U P 1956   ix 67pp illus
Cambridge University Press
475   * §

Roberts, T J
The Richard Evans Company and The Development of Haydock 1830-1980
Exeter MA 1984
Richard Evans Co   Haydock

Robertson, A J
Lord Beaverbrook and the Supply of Aircraft 1940-1941

see Slaven, A & Aldcroft, D H (eds)
Aircraft Industry
364

Robertson, Alex J
Robert Owen and the Campbell Debt 1810-1822

Business History   vol XI no 1 1969
New Lanark
432   814

Robertson, Alex J
The Decline of the Scottish Cotton Industry

Business History   vol XII no 2 1970
Cotton Industry in Scotland
432

Robertson, P L
*Shipping and Shipbuilding: The Case of William Denny and
Brothers*
Business History   vol XVI no 1 1974
Denny, William & Bros
361

Robinson, Harry Perry
The Employers' Liability Assurance Corporation 1880-1930

the firm 1930   viii 177pp
Employers' Liability Assurance
820   *

Robinson, Howard
*Britain's Post Office: A History of Development from the
Beginnings to the Present Day*
Oxford U P 1953   xiv 299pp illus index sources
Post Office
790   *

Robinson, Philip Moffat
The Robinson Family of Bolsover and Chesterfield

Chesterfield: the firm 1961   320pp illus
Robinson & Sons
257   *

Robinson, Philip Moffat
*The Smiths of Chesterfield: A History of the Griffin Foundry,
Brampton 1775-1833*
Chesterfield: the firm 1957   104pp illus index
Robinson & Sons   Griffin Foundry
221   311   * §

Robinson, Ralph Mosley
Coutts: The History of a Banking house

John Murray 1929   xii 189pp illus index sources
Coutts & Co
814   * §

Robinson, Sydney
Seeboard: The First Twenty-Five Years

Hove: the firm 1974   115pp illus index
Seeboard
161   * §

Robinsons of Chesterfield
Achievement: The Story of Robinsons of Chesterfield

Chesterfield: the firm 1963   50pp illus
Robinson & Sons
257   DERBYPL

Robinsons of Chesterfield
Robinsons of Chesterfield Centenary 1839-1939

Chesterfield: the firm nd   48pp illus
Robinson & Sons
257   UBRIS

Robson, Graham
The Rover Story

Cambridge: Patrick Stephens 1984   201pp illus index
Rover Co   Starley, J K & Co
351   * §

Robson, M
R & D in Response to the First World War: The Pharmaceutical Industry
see Liebenau, Jonathan (ed) 1987
Pharmaceutical Industry
257

Robson, Robert
The Cotton Industry in Britain

Macmillan 1957   xx 364pp
Cotton Industry
432   *

Robson, Robert
The Man-Made Fibres Industry

Macmillan 1958   vii 135pp
Man-Made Fibres Industry
260   430   *

Roche, J C
The History, Development and Organisation of the Birmingham Jewellery & Allied Trdes
Birmingham MComm 1927   113pp
Dennison Watch Case Co   Birmingham Jewellery Trade
374   491   BLPES

Rock Life Assurance Co
Centenary 1806-1906: Rock Life Assurance Company

the firm 1906   140pp illus
Rock Life Assurance Co
820   *

Rock Life Assurance Co
>*Life Assurance in the 19th Century as Illustrated by the Rock*
>*Life Assurance Co*
>the firm 1901   viii 105pp
>Rock Life Assurance Co
>820   *

Rodgers, Joseph & Son
>*Under Five Sovereigns*
>
>Sheffield: the firm 1920   38pp illus
>Rodgers, Joseph & Son
>316   §

Rodgers, Terence
>*Sir Alan Smith, the Industrial Group and the Politics of*
>*Unemployment 1919-1924*
>Business History   vol XXVIII no 1 1986
>Industrial Group   Politics of Unemployment

Rogers, T B
>*A Century of Progress 1831-1931: Cadbury, Bournville*
>
>Bournville: the firm 1931   89pp illus
>Cadbury Bros
>421   *

Roll, Eric
>*An Early Experiment in Industrial Organisation: Being a History*
>*of the Firm of Boulton & Watt 1775-1805*
>Frank Cass 1968   xvi 320pp index sources
>Boulton & Watt
>328   * §

Rolt, Lionel Thomas Caswall
>*A Hunslet Hundred: One Hundred Years of Locomotive Building*
>*by the Hunslet Engine Co*
>Newton Abbot: David & Charles 1964 177pp illus index sources
>Hunslet Engine Co   Avonside Engine Co
>362   * §

Rolt, Lionel Thomas Caswall
>*Charles Churchill 1865-1965*
>
>Birmingham: the firm 1965
>Churchill, Charles & Co   Churchill-Redman
>322

Rolt, Lionel Thomas Caswall
>*George and Robert Stephenson: The Railway Revolution*
>
>Longman 1960   xviii 356pp illus index sources
>Railways
>502   710   *

Rolt, Lionel Thomas Caswall
>*Holloways of Millbank: The First Seventy-Five Years*
>
>Newman Neame 1958   56pp illus
>Holloway Brothers
>500   * §

Rolt, Lionel Thomas Caswall
Isambard Kingdom Brunel

Longman 1957   447pp illus index sources
Great Western Railway
502   710   *

Rolt, Lionel Thomas Caswall
Mariners' Market: Burnyeat Limited, Growth Over a Century

Newman Neame 1961   62pp illus
Burnyeat
610   *

Rolt, Lionel Thomas Caswall
The Dowty Story: parts I & II

the firm 1962-73   2 vols illus
Dowty Group
325   328   364   CHELTPL

Rolt, Lionel Thomas Caswall
Thomas Telford

Longman 1958   224pp illus index sources
Telford, Thomas
502   *

Rolt, Lionel Thomas Caswall
Waterloo Iron Works: A History of Taskers of Andover 1809-1968
Newton Abbot: David & Charles 1969 240pp illus index
Taskers of Andover
321   352   *

Romain, W J
A Good Job Well Done: The Story of Rendell, a West Country Builder
Amersham: Stocker Hocknell 1983   178pp illus index
Rendell
501   §

Roper, D H & Harrison, John
The First Hundred Years 1868-1968: The Story of the National Deposit Friendly Society
the firm 1968   vii 47pp illus
National Deposit Friendly Soc
820   *

Rose, A
Personalities and Progress 1858-1969: The Story of Strong & Co of Romsey Ltd
Romsey: the firm 1970   40pp illus
Strong & Co of Romsey
427

Rose, Downs & Thompson
At the Tail of Two Centuries: A Brief History...the Foundation and Development of the Old Foundry, Hull
Hull: the firm 1949   24pp illus
Rose, Downs & Thompson
328   *

Rose, Mary B
> *Diversification of Investment by the Greg Family 1800-1914*

    Business History   vol XXI no 1 1979
    Greg, Samuel & Co
    432

Rose, Mary B
> *Gregs of Styal*

    Styal: Quarry Bank Mill Trust 1978   40pp illus sources
    Greg, Samuel & Co
    432   *

Rose, Mary B
> *The Role of the Family in Providing Capital and Managerial Talent in Samuel Greg and Company 1784-1840*

    Business History   vol XIX no 1 1977
    Greg, Samuel & Co
    432

Ross, Catherine
> *The Development of the Glass Industry on the Rivers Tyne and Wear 1700-1900*

    Newcastle upon Tyne PhD 1982
    Glass Industry
    247

Rossington, T
> *The Story of Treeton Colliery: One Hundred Years of Coalmining 1875-1975*

    Rotherham: Borough Library 1976
    Treeton Colliery
    111

Rotax
> *The Story of a Company*

    the firm 1969   64pp illus
    Rotax
    364   RAeS

Roth, H Ling
> *The Genesis of Banking in Halifax with Sidelights on Country Banking*

    Halifax: F King 1914   51pp illus
    Halifax Banks
    814   §

Rotherham Advertiser
> *The 'Rotherham Advertiser' 1858-1928: A Seventy Years' Record*

    Rotherham: the firm 1928   20pp illus
    Garnett, Henry & Co
    475   ROTHMPL

Roughdale Brickworks
> *History of Roughdale Brickworks*

    the firm typescript ca1980   52pp sources
    Roughdale Brickworks   Ibstock Brick Roughdales
    241   StHLNS

Routley, John
    A Saga of British Industry: The story of The British Plaster Board Group
    the firm 1959   xvi 172pp illus index
    British Plaster Board Industries
    243   * §

Rowat, David
    Jubilee Book of Paisley Provident Co-operative Society Ltd 1860-1910
    Paisley: the firm 1910   202pp illus
    Paisley Provident Co-op Soc
    656   *

Rowe, David John
    Lead Manufacturing in Britain: A History

    Croom Helm 1983   xiv 427pp illus index sources
    Associated Lead   Walkers, Fishwick & Co
    210   224   * §

Rowland, John & Basil, 2nd Lord Cadman
    Ambassador for Oil: The Life of John, First Baron Cadman

    Herbert Jenkins 1960   191pp illus
    British Petroleum
    130   140   251   612   652   *

Rowland, John Herbert Shelley
    Progress in Power: The Contribution of Charles Merz & his Associates to 60 Years of Electrical Development 1899-1959
    Newman Neame 1960   130pp illus
    Merz & McLellan
    342   837   * §

Rowland, L & C
    L & C Rowland, Chemists of Wrexham 1810-1960

    York: William Sessions 1960
    Rowland, L & C
    643

Rowlands, John
    Copper Mountain

    Llangefni: Anglesey Antiq Soc 1966   203pp illus index sources
    Parys & Mona Mines
    210   *

Rowlinson, P J
    Regulation of the Gas Industry in the Early 19th Century 1800-1860
    Oxford DPhil 1984
    Gas Industry Regulation
    162

Rowntree & Sons
    A Century and a Half of Progress

    Scarborough: the firm 1930   20pp illus
    Rowntree & Sons
    641   §

Rowntree, Arthur (ed)
The Birmingham Battery and Metal Company: One Hundred Years
1836-1936
the firm 1936   109pp illus
Birmingham Battery & Metal Co
343   612   *

Royal Bank of Scotland
The Royal Bank of Scotland 1727-1977

Edinburgh: the firm 1977   55pp illus
Dundee Banking Co   Royal Bank of Scotland
814   * §

Royal Bank of Scotland
Warrants for the Royal Charters & Acts of Parliament

Edinburgh: the firm 1908   292pp index
Royal Bank of Scotland
814   EDNBRPL

Royal Dutch Petroleum Co
The Royal Dutch Petroleum Company 1890-1950: Diamond
Jubilee Book
The Hague: the firm 1950   204pp illus
Royal Dutch Petroleum Co   Shell
130   140   612   652   §

Royal Mail Steam Packet Co
A Link of Empire or 70 Years of British Shipping: The 70th Year
of Incorporation of the Royal Mail Steam Packet Co
the firm 1909   94pp illus
Royal Mail Shipping Group
740   *

Royden, Ernest B
Thomas Royden & Sons: Shipbuilders, Liverpool 1818-1893

Liverpool: the firm 1953   56pp illus
Royden, Thomas & Sons
361   UBRIS

Royston, George P
A History of the Park Gate Iron and Steel Company Ltd
1823-1923
the firm 1923   95pp illus
Park Gate Iron & Steel Co
221   ROTHMPL

Royton Spinning Company
Royton Spinning Company Ltd Eightieth Anniversary 1871-1951

the firm 1951   22pp illus
Royton Spinning Co
432   OLDHMPL

Rubery Owen
Owen Organisation: The Vital Link in World Industry

the firm ca1950   67pp illus
Rubery Owen Holdings   Owen Organisation
320   WALSLPL

Rudden, Bernard
The New River: A Legal History

Oxford: Clarendon 1985 xiii 335pp illus index sources
New River Company Metropolitan Water Board
170 *

Rumsby, W N
This is your Firm

typescript the firm ca1972
Carmichael, James
500

Russell, McDonough
Sheep into Shoes: The Development of Morlands Warm-Lined Footwear
Glastonbury: the firm 1962 64pp illus
Clark, Son & Morland Morlands
441 451 §

Russell, Samuel & Co
A Century of Progress 1838-1938

8pp illus
Russell, Samuel & Co
311 WALSLPL

Russell, Samuel & Sons
The Russell Story 1864-1964

Leicester: the firm nd 32pp illus
Russell, Samuel & Sons
311 UBRIS

Rutherford, Wilfrid
The Man Who Built the 'Mauritania': The Life Story of Sir George B Hunter
Hillside 1934 170pp illus
Swan Hunter Wigham Richardson
320 361 *

Rutter, Owen
At the Three Sugar Loaves and Crown: Davison, Newman & Co: A Brief History of the Firm
the firm 1938 39pp illus
Davison, Newman & Co West Indian Produce Association
617 839 §

Ryan, Roger J
A History of the Norwich Union Fire and Life Insurance Societies from 1797 to 1914
East Anglia PhD 1984
Norwich Union
820

Ryan, Roger J
The Early Expansion of the Norwich Union Life Insurance Society 1808-1837
Business History vol XXVII no 2 1985
Norwich Union
820

Ryan, Roger J
The Norwich Union and the British Fire Insurance Market in the early Nineteenth Century
see Westall, Oliver M (ed) 1984
Norwich Union
820

Ryder, Thomas & Son
Machines to Make Machines: Thomas Ryder & Son Ltd, Turner Bridge Works, Bolton, Lancashire 1865-1965
Bolton: the firm 1965   34pp illus
Ryder, Thomas & Son
322   BOLTNPL

Ryerson, Barry
The Giants of Small Heath: The History of B S A

Yeovil: Haynes 1980   190pp illus index sources
B S A
329   363   *

Rylands of Warrington
Rylands of Warrington 1805-1955: The Story of Rylands Brothers Limited
Harley 1956   141pp illus
Rylands Brothers
223   224   UBRIS

Ryott, David
John Barran's of Leeds 1851-1951

Leeds: the firm 1951   60pp illus
Barran, John
453   UBRIS

Sakamoto, T
Technology and Business in the British Electrical Industry 1880-1914
see Fuji Conference 6, 1979
Electrical Industry
161   340

Sampson Low
Fortunes Made in Business

Sampson Low 1884   3 vols
Fortunes Made in Business
                                                                          *

Sanctuary, A C
The Development of the Bridport Rope, Twine and Net Industry

1969
Bridport Rope, Twine & Net Ind
439   BLPES

Sandberg, Lars G
Lancashire in Decline: A Study in Entrepreneurship, Technology and International Trade
Columbus, Ohio: O U P 1974   xii 276pp sources
Lancashire Cotton Industry
432   BLPES

374

Sanderson Kayser
> *400 Years of Iron and Steel*

    Sheffield: the firm 1972   24pp illus
    Sanderson Kayser
    221

Sanderson, Arthur & Sons
> *A Century of Sanderson 1860-1960*

    the firm 1960   39pp illus
    Sanderson, Arthur & Sons   Wall Paper Manufacturers
    432   472   *

Sanger, George
> *Seventy Years a Showman: My Life and Adventures in Camp and Caravan the World over*

    C A Pearson 1908   128pp
    Sanger, 'Lord' George
    974   979   *

Sarson, Henry
> *Family Tradition: The Biography of a Business 1641-1941*

    typescript ca1960   89pp sources
    Sarsons   British Vinegars
    423   §

Saul, S B
> *The Machine Tool Industry in Britain to 1914*

    Business History   vol X no 1 1968
    Machine Tool Industry
    322

Saul, S B
> *The Mechanical Engineering Industries in Britain 1860-1914*

    see Supple, Barry (ed) 1977
    Mechanical Engineering
    320

Saul, S B
> *The Motor Industry in Britain to 1914*

    Business History   vol V no 1 1962
    Motor Industry
    351

Saunders, Alan
> *Development and Organisation of the British Sugar Corporation Limited*

    the firm 1957   38pp illus
    British Sugar Corporation
    420   CAMBSPL

Saunders, Philip Thomas
> *Stuckey's Bank*

    Taunton: Barnicott & Pearce 1928   viii 116pp illus
    Stuckey's Banking Co
    814   * §

Savings Bank of the County and City of Perth
  A Brief Sketch of the...Savings Bank of the County and City of
  Perth: Centenary 1815-1915
  Perth: the firm nd   108pp
  Perth Savings Bank
  814
Savory, A C S
  The Savorys of Savory and Moore

  Lymington: the author 1982   80pp index
  Savory and Moore
  257   643   CHELTPL
Saxton, Chas A W
  The Origin and Progress of the Worcester Co-operative Society
  Ltd 1881-1931
  Worcester: the firm nd   178pp illus
  Worcester Co-operative Society
  656   UBRIS
Sayers, Richard Sidney
  Gilletts in the London Money Market 1867-1967

  Oxford: Clarendon 1968   x 204pp illus index sources
  Gillett Brothers Discount Co
  814   831   * §
Sayers, Richard Sidney
  Lloyds Bank in the History of English Banking

  Oxford: Clarendon 1957   xii 381pp illus index sources
  Lloyds Bank
  814   * §
Sayers, Richard Sidney
  The Bank of England 1891-1944

  Cambridge: C U P 1976   3 vols index sources
  Bank of England
  814   * §
Schooling, William
  Alliance Assurance 1824-1924

  the firm 1924   119pp illus index
  Alliance Assurance
  820   * §
Schooling, William
  The Standard Life Assurance Company 1825-1925

  Edinburgh: Blackwood 1925   122pp illus index
  Standard Life Assurance
  820   §
Schück, J H E & Sohlman, R (tr Lunn)
  The Life of Alfred Nobel

  Heinemann 1929   ix 353pp illus
  . Nobel's Explosive Co   I C I
  251   256   *

376

Scopes, Frederick
The Development of Corby Works

Corby: the firm 1968   xiv 283pp illus index sources
Stewarts & Lloyds
221   222   * §

Scotsman
The Glorious Privilege: The History of 'The Scotsman'

Nelson 1967   196pp illus index
Scotsman
475   StBRD

Scott Bader and Co
Scott Bader: Forty Years of Chemical Pioneering

Wollaston: the firm 1961   28pp illus
Scott Bader and Co
251   NHPTNPL

Scott, Alexander T
Balfour, Beatty: Fifty Years 1909-1959

the firm 1959
Balfour, Beatty & Co
502

Scott, George & Son
One Hundred Years of Chemical Engineering

1934   32pp
Scott, George & Son
324   GHL

Scott, George Edwin
Reporter Anonymous: The Story of the Press Association

Hutchinson 1968   307pp illus index
Press Association
839   * §

Scott, James Maurice
Extel 100: The Centenary History of the Exchange Telegraph Company
Benn 1972   xi 239pp illus index
Exchange Telegraph Co
790   * §

Scott, John
Legibus: A History of Clifford-Turner 1900-1980

King, Thorne & Stace 1980   211pp illus index sources
Clifford-Turner
835   * §

Scott, John Dick
Siemens Brothers 1858-1958: An Essay in the History of Industry
Weidenfeld & Nicolson 1958   279pp illus index sources
Siemens Brothers & Co
342   344   * §

Scott, John Dick
        Vickers: A History

        Weidenfeld & Nicolson 1962   xxiii 416pp illus index sources
        Vickers
        329   361   364   *
Scott, John William Robertson
        The Story of the Pall Mall Gazette

        Oxford U P 1950   xi 470pp illus index sources
        Pall Mall Gazette
        475   *
Scott, Samuel H & Scott, F C
        Personal Account: Some Recollections of Fifty Years of the
        Provincial Insurance Company
        Kendal: the firm 1953   46pp
        Provincial Insurance Co
        820   * §
Scott, William Maddin
        A Hundred Years A-Milling: Commemorating an Ulster Mill
        Centenary
        Dundalk: the firm 1956   xviii 266pp illus
        Scott, W & C, Excelsior Mills
        416   *
Scottish Amicable
        The Scottish Amicable Jubilees 1892-1942 & 1892-1952

        Edinburgh: the firm 1942/52   2 vols illus
        Scottish Amicable Bldg Soc
        815   EDNBRPL
Scottish Co-operative Wholesale Society
        Scottish Co-operative Wholesale Society Ltd 1868 till 1929:
        Historical and Descriptive Handbook
        the firm ca1930
        Scottish Co-op Wholesale Soc
        619   656   MTHWLPL
Scottish Equitable Life Office
        Prospectus or the Formative Years of the Scottish Equitable
        Life Office
        Edinburgh: the firm 1963   23pp illus
        Scottish Equitable Life Office
        820   EDNBRPL
Scottish Widows' Fund
        Life Assurance...the Origin, Constitution and early History of
        the Scottish Widows' Fund and Life Assurance Society
        Edinburgh: the firm 1901   160pp illus
        Scottish Widows' Fund
        820   EDNBRPL
Scotts
        Two Centuries of Shipbuilding by the Scotts at Greenock

        Manchester: W Hopwood 1950   280pp illus index
        Scotts of Greenock
        361   BCROB

378

Scotts

Two Hundred and Fifty Years of Shipbuilding by the Scotts at Greenock
Greenock: the firm 1961   xx 279pp illus index
Scotts of Greenock
361   §

Scourfield, Elfyn
John Williams & Son, Phoenix Iron Works, Rhuddlan

J Flintshire Hist Soc   vol 28 1977-78
Williams, John & Son
321

Scourfield, Elfyn
Powell Brothers and Whitaker, Agricultural Implement Makers

Trans Denbigh Hist Soc   vol 25 1976
Powell Brothers and Whitaker
321

Scrope Hugh E
Golden Wings: The Story of Fifty Years of Aviation by the Vickers Group of Companies 1908-1958
the firm 1960   90pp
Vickers
364   RAeS

Seacombe, Andrew
The Edbro Story

typescript 1974   34pp
Edbro   Bromilow & Edwards
                                                                       BOLTNPL

Seager Evans & Co
Mr Seager & Mr Evans: The Story of a Great Partnership, Seager Evans & Co
the firm 1963   48pp illus
Seager Evans & Co
424   *

Seal, Helen
The Gas Industry in Bristol 1815-53

Bristol BA 1975   10pp sources
Bristol Gas
162   AVONPL

Sears, J & Co
The Story of 'True-Form'

Northampton: the firm 1925   16pp illus
Sears, J & Co   True-Form Boot Co
451   NHPTNPL

Seaton, R
Malcolm Graham: Sixty Years in the News

the firm 1983
Express & Star (Wolverhampton)
475

Sebire, Charles B
  Berisfords: The Ribbon People: The Story of a Family Business

    York: William Sessions 1966   125pp illus
    Berisford Group
    439   MACCPL

Sebire, J F
  A Reputation in Ribbons

    Congleton: the firm 1985   107pp sources
    Berisford Group
    439   MACCPL

Seed, Thomas Alexander
  Pioneers for a Century 1852-1952: A History of   Samuel Osborn & Co Ltd, Clyde Steel Works, Sheffield
    Sheffield: the firm 1952   82pp illus
    Osborn, Samuel & Co
    221   * §

Segrave, Edmond
  Ten Years of Penguins

    Harmondsworth: Penguin 1945
    Penguin Books
    475

Segreto, Luciano
  More Trouble than Profit: Vickers' Investment in Italy 1905-1939
    Business History   vol XXVII no 3 1985
    Vickers
    329   361   364

Selfridge
  The House of Selfridge 1909-1959

    the firm 1959   37pp
    Selfridges
    656   WMNSTPL

Selfridge, Harry Gordon
  The Romance of Commerce

    John Lane 1918   xviii 422pp illus
    Selfridges
    656   *

Semmens, Peter William Brett
  History of the Great Western Railway

    Allen & Unwin 1985   3 vols illus index
    Great Western Railway
    710   *

Serocold, Walter P
  The Story of Watneys

    the firm 1949   130pp illus
    Watney, Combe, Reid & Co
    427   BCROB

Sessions of York
Sessions of York and their Printing Forbears

York: William Sessions 1985   x 69pp illus index
Sessions, William
475

Sessions, William K & E Margaret
The Tukes of York

York: William Sessions 1971   x 117pp illus index sources
Tuke & Co
421   641

Seth-Smith, Michael
The Long Haul: A Social History of the British Commercial Vehicle Industry
Hutchinson 1975   189pp illus index sources
Commercial Vehicle Industry
351   723   * §

Seth-Smith, Michael
Two Hundred Years of Richard Johnson & Nephew

Manchester: the firm 1973   xiv 292pp illus index sources
Johnson, Richard & Nephew
223   313   *

Settle, Alison
A Family of Shops

the firm 1951   37pp illus
Marshall & Snelgrove
656   LEICSPL

Sewell, Gordon
Echoes of a Century: The Centenary History of Southern Newspapers Limited 1864-1964
Southampton: the firm 1964   xii 159pp illus index sources
Southern Newspapers
475   * §

Sewell, V
Standard Chartered Bank: A Story Brought up to Date

the firm 1983   99pp
Standard Chartered Bank   Chartered Bank
814   839   §

Sharp, Cecil Martin
An Outline of de Havilland History

Faber 1960
de Havilland
364

Sharp, Cecil Martin
D H: A History of De Havilland

Shrewsbury: Airlife 1982   487pp illus index
de Havilland   Hawker Siddeley
364   *

Sharp, T J
>   *The Kent Fruit Industry in the later 19th Century*

>   Kent PhD 1983
>   Kent Fruit Industry
>   10
Sharpe, Len
>   *The Lintas Story: Impressions and Recollections*

>   the firm 1964   112pp illus
>   Lintas
>   838   HISTAD
Shaw, Christine
>   *The Large Manufacturing Employers of 1907*

>   Business History   vol XXV no 1 1983
>   Manufacturing Employers of 1907

Shaw, H
>   *Magnets and Memories: A Celebration of the 200 Years of H*
>   *Shaw (Magnets) 1783-1983*
>   Sheffield: the firm 1983   48pp illus index
>   Shaw, H (Magnets)
>   221   313   §
Shaw, Herbert
>   *The story of Nalder and Collyer's Croydon Brewery and its*
>   *Licensed Houses in Bromley*
>   typescript 1977   9pp
>   Nalder and Collyer
>   427   BROMPL
Shaw, M
>   *Story of the Mann Egerton Group of Companies*

>   Norwich: Norfolk Fair 1972   6pp illus
>   Mann Egerton
>   614   651   671   NRFLKPL
Shaw, Simeon
>   *History of the Staffordshire Potteries (1829 edition)*

>   Newton Abbot: David & Charles 1970 244pp
>   Pottery Industry
>   248   *
Shearer, W Russell
>   *Century of Service 1872-1972: Methodist Insurance Company*
>   *Limited*
>   the firm 1972   32pp
>   Methodist Insurance Co
>   820   §
Shears, William Sydney
>   *William Nash of St. Paul's Cray, Papermakers*

>   Batchworth: the firm 1950   ix 177pp illus index
>   Nash, William
>   471   *

382

Sheffield Smelting Company
Sheffield Smelting Company Limited 1760-1960

Sheffield: the firm 1960   28pp illus
Sheffield Smelting Co
224   *

Sheffield Trustee Savings Bank
150 Years of Thrift; Sheffield Trustee Savings Bank 1819-1969
the firm 1969   16pp
Sheffield Trustee Savings Bank
814   SHEFFPL

Sheldon, Peter
A History of Swindon and District Mineral Water Manufacturers

Swindon: Thamesdown Council 1980 36pp illus sources
Swindon Mineral Water
428   WILTSPL

Shell Transport & Trading
1897-1947: To Mark the Jubilee of the Shell Transport & Trading Company
1947   20pp
Shell Transport & Trading Co   Royal Dutch/Shell
130   140   612   652   GHL

Shepherd & Woodward
Shepherd & Woodward Centenary 1877-1977

Oxford Mail 24 Nov 1977   8pp illus
Shepherd & Woodward
645   OXFDPL

Shepherd, A F
Links with the Past: A Brief Chronicle of the Public Service of a Notable Institution
the firm 1917   xi 297pp illus
Eagle & British Dominions Ins Co
820   * §

Sheppard, Francis Henry Wollaston
Brakspear's Brewery, Henley on Thames 1779-1979

Henley on Thames: the firm 1979   viii 103pp illus
Brakspear, W H & Sons
427   *

Shepshed Lace Manufacturing Co
Fifty Years of Lace

Loughborough: the firm 1956   26pp illus
Shepshed Lace Manufacturing Co
439   LEICSPL

Sherriff, Francis Henry
From Then Till Now: Being a Short History of the Provident Mutual Life Assurance Association 1840-1940
1940   122pp illus
Provident Mutual Life Assurance
820   §

Sherwen, Theo
The Bomford Story: A Century of Service to Agriculture

Evesham: the firm 1978   104pp illus
Bomford & Evershed
321   * §

Shields, E H
Fifty Years at Bardsley Vale: A Record of Pharmaceutical
Progress
Bardsley: the firm 1946   46pp illus
Kerfoot, Thomas & Co
257   * §

Shiloh
The Shiloh Story 1874-1974

Royton: the firm 1974   52pp illus
Shiloh Spinners
432   BLPES

Shinkfield, H J
Ironmongers & Builders' Merchants, 20-22 Lordship Lane S E
22; Founded 1894
ca1960   11pp illus
Shinkfield, H J
648   613   SWKPL

Shirley Aldred
Shirley Aldred & Co Ltd 1796-1958

the firm 1958   41pp illus
Shirley Aldred & Co   Warwick, T O & Co
251   ROTHMPL

Short Brothers
Mowbray Quay to Pallion Yard 1850-1950

Sunderland: the firm 1950
Short Brothers
361

Shuttleworth, William Sewell
The Shuttleworth Story 1830-1953

Harley 1954   51pp illus
Shuttleworth, W S & Co
                                                                       *

Sibley, Brian
The Book of Guinness Advertising

Guinness Books 1985   224pp illus index
Guinness
427   §

Sieff, Israel Moses
Memoirs

Weidenfeld & Nicolson 1970   214pp illus index
Marks & Spencer
645   656   *

Siepmann, Harry Arthur (ed)
    The First Hundred Years of the Standard Bank

    Oxford U P 1963   ix 371pp illus
    Standard Bank
    820   839   *

Sigsworth, Eric Milton
    A History of Messrs John Forster and Son Ltd 1819-1891

    Leeds PhD 1954
    Forster, John & Sons
    431

Sigsworth, Eric Milton
    Black Dyke Mills: A History

    Liverpool: L U P 1958   xvii 385pp illus index sources
    Black Dyke Mills   Forster, John & Sons
    431   * §

Silcock, R & Sons
    The Silcock Story

    the firm nd   51pp illus
    Silcock, R & Sons
    416   422   UBRIS

Simmonds, Reginald Claud
    An Account of the Institute of Actuaries 1848-1948

    the firm 1948   xi 317pp illus
    Institute of Actuaries
    832   *

Simmons, Douglas A
    Schweppes: The First 200 Years

    Springwood 1983   160pp illus index sources
    Schweppes   Cadbury-Schweppes
    428   * §

Simmons, Jack
    The Railway in England and Wales 1830-1914: The System and its Working
    Leicester: L U P 1978   295pp illus index sources
    Railway
    710   *

Simmons, Jack
    Thomas Cook of Leicester

    Trans Leics Arch Hist Soc   vol 49 1973-74
    Cook, Thomas
    770

Simmons, Jack (ed)
    The Birth of the Great Western Railway: Extracts from the Diary and Correspondence of George Henry Gibbs
    Bath: Adams & Dart 1971   96pp illus index sources
    Great Western Railway
    362   500   710   *

Simmons, W H
A Short History of the Royal Gunpowder Factory at Waltham Abbey
H M S O 1963   98pp illus
Royal Gunpowder Factory
329   ENFLDPL

Simon, Anthony
The Simon Engineering Group

Stockport: the firm 1953   liv 119pp illus
Simon Engineering Group
320   §

Simon, Herbert
Song and Words: A History of the Curwen Press

Allen & Unwin 1973   vii 261pp illus index sources
Curwen Press
475   *

Simonds, H & G
The House of Simonds through Nine Reigns

Reading: the firm nd   8pp illus
Simonds, H & G
427   BERKSPL

Simons, Eric N & Sessions, E M
Jenkins of Rotherham 1856-1981: 125 Years of Industrial History
York: William Sessions 1981   120pp illus index
Jenkins, Robert & Co
320   *

Simons, Eric Norman
Lockwood and Carlisle Ltd. of Sheffield: A Chapter of Marine History
Sheffield: the firm 1962   62pp illus
Lockwood & Carlisle
328   351   * §

Simons, Eric Norman
The Story of a Great Steel Firm

Sheffield: E A magazine 1953-58
Allen, Edgar
221

Simpson, James Dyer
1936: Our Centenary Year

the firm nd   160pp illus index
Liverpool & London & Globe Ins
820   *

Simpson, Michael
Urban Transport and the Development of Glasgow's West End 1830-1914
Journal of Transport History   new ser vol I no 3 1972
Glasgow Tramways   Glasgow City & District Railway
710   721

Simpson, Stephen
History of the Firm of Stephen Simpson 1829-1929

Preston: the firm 1929   74pp illus index
Simpson, Stephen
491   §

Sinclair, Robert George
The Faithful Fibre: The Story of the Linen Thread Co Ltd

Glasgow: the firm 1956   68pp illus
Linen Thread Co
434   *

Singleton, Frank
Tillotsons 1850-1950: Centenary of a Family Business

Bolton: Tillotson 1950   x 94pp illus index sources
Tillotson & Son
475   * §

Sirocco
Sirocco: Behind the Trade Mark

Belfast: the firm nd   16pp illus
Davidson & Co   Sirocco
328   SEELBPL

Skelmanthorpe Industrial and Co-operative Provident Society
Centenary Souvenir 1834-1934

Manchester: Co-op Printing Soc 1934 80pp illus
Skelmanthorpe Industrial Co-op
656   HDSFDPL

Skelton, C J
Announcing One Hundred Years of Progress 1855-1955

Sheffield: the firm 1955
Skelton, C J & Co
221

Skinner, Basil Chisholm
The Cramond Iron Works

Edinburgh: Dept Adult Education 1965 49pp illus sources
Cramond Iron Mills
221   311   EDNBRPL

Skinner, Basil Chisholm
The Lime Industry in the Lothians

Edinburgh: Dept Adult Education 1969 64pp illus index sources
Lime Industry in the Lothians
242   MLOTHPL

Slade, E H
A History of the Londonderry Shirt Industry from 1800

Belfast MA 1937
Londonderry Shirt Industry
453

Slater, A W
A London Firm of Still-Makers

Business History   vol VIII no 1 1966
Dore, John & Co
324

Slater, A W
Howards, Chemical Manufacturers 1797-1837: A Study in Business History
London MSc 1956
Howards
251

Slater, Ernest
One Hundred Years 1837-1937: The History of Henley's

the firm 1937   77pp
Henley's Telegraph Works   G E C
341   344   *

Slater, J Norman
A Brewer's Tale: The Story of Greenall Whitley & Co Ltd through Two Centuries
Warrington: the firm 1980   230pp illus index
Greenall Whitley
427   662   §

Slaven, A & Aldcroft, D H (eds)
Business, Banking and Urban History

Edinburgh: John Donald 1982   235pp sources

111   361   364   814   * §

Slaven, Anthony
A Shipyard in Depression: John Browns of Clydebank

Business History   vol XIX no 2 1977
Brown, John
361

Slaven, Anthony
British Shipbuilders: Market Trends and Order Book Patterns between the Wars
Journal of Transport History   3rd ser vol III no 2 1982
Shipbuilding
361

Slaven, Anthony
Earnings and Productivity in the Scottish Coal-Mining Industry during the Nineteenth Century: The Dixon Enterprises
see Payne, Peter L (ed)
Dixon, William & Sons   Govan Collieries
111

Slaven, Anthony
Management and Shipbuilding 1890-1938: Structure and Strategy in the Shipbuilding Firms on the Clyde
see Slaven, A & Aldcroft, D H (eds)
Shipbuilding in Scotland
361

388

Slaven, Anthony
Self-Liquidation: The National Shipbuilders Security Ltd and
British Shipbuilding in the 1930s
see Palmer, S R & Williams, G (eds)
National Shipbuilders Security
361

Slinn, Judith
A History of Freshfields

the firm 1984   208pp illus index sources
Freshfields
836   * §

Slinn, Judith
A History of May & Baker 1834-1984

Cambridge: Hobsons 1984   196pp illus index sources
May & Baker
257   * §

Sloan, Alfred Pritchard
My Years with General Motors

Sidgwick & Jackson 1965   xxix 472pp illus
General Motors   Vauxhall Motors
350   *

Slough Estates
Slough Estates Ltd 1920-1970

the firm nd   36pp illus
Slough Estates
850   §

Smallpeice, Basil
Of Comets and Queens: An Autobiography

Shrewsbury: Airlife 1981   274pp illus index
Cunard   British Overseas Airways Corp
740   750   *

Smedley, John
The World of John Smedley: Lea Mills

typescript nd
Smedley, John
436   DERBYPL

Smeeton, Arthur E
The Story of Evans Medical 1809-1959

the firm 1959   illus
Evans Medical Supplies
257   *

Smith and Nephew
Smith and Nephew 1856-1956: A Record of Service to Surgery
and Medicine
the firm 1956   52pp illus
Smith & Nephew
257   §

Smith Brothers
Romance of 'The Globe', 1884-1934: A Record of Enterprise and Success
Dundee: William Kidd 1934   12pp illus
Smith Brothers
645   647   DNDEEPL
Smith, Alan
The Lancashire Watch Company, Prescot, Lancashire, England, 1889-1910
New Hampshire: Ken Roberts 1973
Lancashire Watch Company
374
Smith, Arthur C
Arthur C Smith, Typewriter Accessories 1931-1981

York: William Sessions 1981
Smith, Arthur C
495   614
Smith, Arthur William
Wray (Optical Works) Ltd 1850-1971: A Short History

typescript 1971   21pp
Wray (Optical Works)
373   BROMPL
Smith, Barbara M D
The Galtons of Birmingham: Quaker Gun Merchants and Bankers 1702-1831
Business History   vol XI no 2 1967
Galtons of Birmingham
329   814
Smith, Barbara M D
The History of the British Motorcycle Industry 1945-75

Centre Urban Reg Studies no 3, 1980 v 57pp illus sources
Enfield Cycle Co   B S A
363   *
Smith, Bell
Under Four Flags: The Story of Smith, Bell & Company in the Philippines
the firm ca1971   68pp illus
Smith, Bell
839   §
Smith, David L
The Dalmellington Iron Company: Its Engines and Men

Newton Abbot: David & Charles 1967 256pp illus index
Dalmellington Iron Co   Coltness Iron Co
111   221   328   UBRIS
Smith, Frederick H
Proud Heritage: A History of Thomas Smith & Sons (Rodley) Ltd, Established 1820
the firm ca1947   56pp illus
Smith, Thomas & Sons
                                                             UBRIS

390

Smith, George & Sons
A Short History of the Firm

the firm 1935   22pp illus
Smith, George & Sons
456   GHL

Smith, H Charles
Co-operation in Enfield and its Environs

Enfield: the firm 1932   95pp illus
Enfield Highway Co-op Soc   Co-operative Wholesale Society
656   ENFLDPL

Smith, J W & Holden, T S
Where Ships Are Born: Sunderland 1346-1946

Sunderland: Thomas Reed 1946   97pp illus
Shipbuilding in NE England
361   * §

Smith, James & Co
James Smith & Co (Derby) Ltd 1830-1966

the firm 1967   16pp illus
Smith, James & Co
453   DERBYPL

Smith, L D
The Carpet Weavers of Kidderminster 1800-1850

Birmingham PhD 1982
Kidderminster Carpet Industry
438

Smith, Mackenzie & Co
The History of Smith, Mackenzie & Company Ltd

the firm ca1936   62pp
Smith, Mackenzie & Co

                                      §

Smith, Malcolm
Planning and Building the British Bomber Force 1934-1939

Business History Review   vol LIV no 1 1980
Avro   Vickers
364

Smith, R
Sea Coal for London: The History of Coal Factors in the London Market
1961   388pp
London Coal Exchange
612   630   GHL

Smith, R
The Lancashire Cotton Industry 1873-96

Birmingham PhD 1954
Lancashire Cotton Industry
432

Smith, R Grenville & Barrie, Alexander
Aspro: How a Family Business Grew Up

the firm 1976	x 182pp illus index
Aspro-Nicholas	Nicholas International
257	* §

Smith, Rhonda
Longleys of Crawley: A Pictorial History of James Longley & Co

the firm 1983	95pp illus
Longley, James & Co	
501	§

Smith, Roland
An Oldham Limited Liability Company 1875-1896

Business History	vol IV no 1 1961
Moorfield Spinning Co	
432	

Smith, W H & Son
The Story of W H Smith & Son

the firm 1955	242pp illus
Smith, W H & Son	
619 653	UBRIS

Smout, T C
Leadmining in Scotland 1650-1850

see Payne, Peter L (ed)
Leadmining in Scotland
210

Smyth, Hazel Pauline
The B & I Line: A History of the British and Irish Steam Packet Company

Dublin: Gill & MacMillan 1984	246pp illus index
B & I Line	
740	*

Smyth, Hazel Pauline
Two Hundred Years a'Growing: The Story of Mackey's Seeds Limited

Dublin Hist Records	vol XXXV no 3
Mackey's Seeds	
611	

Snow, Frederick
Sir Frederick Snow and Partners, Consulting Engineers 1943-1968

the firm 1968	128pp illus
Snow, Frederick	
837	*

Snowden, James Keighley
The Master Spinner: A Life of Sir Swire Smith

Allen & Unwin 1921	352pp
Smith, Swire	
432	*

Solloway, William J
Motor Cars in Needle Land: Enfield Autocar Co, Hunt End, Redditch 1906-1908

typescript 1960   108pp illus index
Enfield Autocar Co
351   HWORCPL

Solloway, William J
The Townsend Story

typescript 1966   40pp illus sources
Townsend, George & Co, Redditch
316   363   HWORCPL

Somervell, John
After 90 Years: The Evolution of K Shoes

the firm ca1932   52pp illus
K Shoes   Somervell Brothers
451   UBRIS

Somner, Graeme
Ben Line: Fleet List and Short History

Kendal: World Ship Soc 1980   120pp illus index
Thomson, Wm & Co   Ben Line Steamers
361   740   *

Somner, Graeme
From 70 North to 70 South: A History of the Christian Salvesen Fleet

Edinburgh: the firm 1984   142pp illus index
Salvesen of Leith
30   740   EDNBRPL

South Metropolitan Gas
A Century of Gas in South London

the firm 1924   23pp illus
South Metropolitan Gas Co
162   IGASE

South Staffordshire Waterworks Co
A Century of Service 1853-1953

the firm 1953   32pp illus
South Staffs Waterworks Co
170   SANDWPL

Southard
An Outline of the Foundation and Development of Southards since 1814
the firm nd   93pp illus
Southard & Co
617   §

Southdown
The Southdown Story 1915-1965: A History of Southdown Motor Services Limited
the firm 1965   102pp illus
Southdown Motor Services
721   §

Spalding, C W
    Tubes of Steel, Being the History of Howell & Co. Ltd.
    Sheffield Tube Works 1865-1971
    typescript nd   77pp illus
    Howell & Co   Tube Investments
    222   §
Sparks, W L
    Story of Shoemaking in Norwich

    Norwich: Inst Boot Ind 1948   119pp illus index
    Norvic Shoe Co   Buckingham, J & Sons
    451
Spater, E
    Eagle Star Insurance Co: Box 1299

    the firm nd   37pp illus
    Eagle Star Insurance Co
    820   §
Spear & Jackson
    Spear & Jackson: Continual Progress since 1774

    Sheffield: the firm nd
    Spear & Jackson
    221   316
Spenceley, G F R
    The English Pillow Lace Industry 1840-1880: A Rural Industry
    in Competition with Machinery
    Business History   vol XIX no 1 1977
    Pillow Lace Industry
    439
Spenceley, G F R
    The English Pillow Lace Industry: A Study of Rural Industry in
    Competition during the 19th Century
    Hull PhD 1975
    Pillow Lace Industry
    439
Spencer Moulton
    1848-1948: A Hundred Years of Rubber Manufacture

    the firm 1948
    Spencer Moulton
    481
Spencer-Clark
    Spencer-Clark Bi-centenary: 200 Years of Metal Craftsmanship

    Sheffield: the firm 1978
    Spencer-Clark
    221
Spender, John Alfred
    Weetman Pearson, First Viscount Cowdray 1856-1927

    Cassell 1930   316pp illus index
    Pearson, S & Son
    130   500   815   *

Spicer
>*Albert Spicer 1847-1934: A Man of his Times*

Simpkin Marshall 1938
Spicer Bros
471

Spiller, Brian
>*The Chameleon's Eye: James Buchanan & Co Ltd 1884-1984*

the firm 1984   148pp illus sources
Buchanan , James & Co
424   BLPES

Spink, Reginald
>*The Story of the Danish Bacon Co 1902-1977*

Welwyn Garden City: the firm 1977   96pp illus index sources
Danish Bacon Co
412   617   *

Spring, A E
>*The Bicentenary of the House of Kings*

the firm ca1946
King & Co
648

Spurrell, William & Son
>*The House of Spurrell*

Carmarthen: the firm 1940   32pp illus
Spurrell, W & Son
475   DYFEDPL

St Cuthbert's Co-operative Association
>*One Hundred Years of Co-operation: The History of St Cuthbert's Co-operative Association 1859-1959*

Manchester: Co-op Press 1959   71pp illus index
St Cuthbert's Co-op Assoc
656   UBRIS

Staddon, Tommy G
>*History of Cambrian Airways, the Welsh Airline from 1935-1976*

Hounslow: Airline 1979   111pp illus
Cambrian Airways
750   *

Stammers, Michael K
>*The Passage Makers: The History of the Black Ball Line of Australian Packets 1852-1871*

Brighton: Teredo Books 1978   xx 508pp illus index sources
Black Ball Line
740   *

Standard Chartered Bank
>*A Story Brought up to Date*

the firm 1983   99pp illus
Standard Chartered Bank   Chartered Bank
814   * §

Standard **Engineering Co**
The First Fifty Years 1894-1944

the firm nd   80pp illus
Standard Engineering Co
327   LEICSPL

Standard **Telephones & Cables**
The Story of S T C 1883-1958

the firm 1958   108pp illus
S T C
341   §

Stander, **C S**
A History of the Pharmaceutical Industry with particular
reference to Allen and Hanbury 1775-1843
London MSc 1956
Allen & Hanbury
257

Stanford, **Edward**
The House of Edward Stanford 1852-1952

1952   15pp
Stanford, Edward   Philip, George & Son
475   653   GHL

Stansfield, **Hazel**
Samuel Fox and Company Ltd. 1842-1967

Stocksbridge: the firm 1967   31pp illus
Fox, Samuel & Co   United Steel
221   *

Stanton **Ironworks Co**
The Stanton Ironworks Co Ltd near Nottingham, England

the firm 1960   25pp illus
Stanton Ironworks
221   222   DERBYPL

Stanton, **George**
The Story of an Industrial Democracy 1896-1917: The...
Kettering 'Union' Boot and Shoe Productive Society Ltd
Leicester: Co-op Printing Soc 1918   52pp illus
Kettering 'Union' Boot and Shoe
451   LEICSPL

Stapleton, **Henry Edward Champneys(ed)**
A Skilful Master Builder: The Continuing Story of a Yorkshire
Family Business, Craftsmen for Seven Generations
Osbaldwick: the firm 1975   viii 72pp illus sources
Anelay, William
501   * §

Star
The Story of the 'Star' 1888-1930

the firm 1930   111pp illus
Star
475

396

Star Aluminium Co
The First Twenty Five Years 1933/4-1958/9

Wolverhampton: the firm 1960
Star Aluminium Co
224   *

Staveley Industries
Centenarians of Vigour

the firm 1964   16pp illus
Staveley Industries
111   221   222   DERBYPL

Stead & Simpson
Stead & Simpson: A History 1834-1984

Leicester: the firm 1984   36pp illus
Stead & Simpson
451   646   LEICSPL

Steel, Wilfred L
The History of the London & North Western Railway

Railway & Travel Monthly 1914   xii 502pp illus index
London & North Western Railway
710   *

Stephen, Alexander and Sons
A Shipbuilding History 1750-1932: A Record of the Business
Founded about 1750 by Alexander Stephen at Burghead
Ed J Burrow 1932   212pp illus
Stephen, Alexander & Sons   Dundee Shipbuilders' Co
361   * §

Stephen, J Thomson
Social Redemption or the Fifty Years' Story of the Leicester
Co-operative Society Ltd 1860-1910
Leicester: Co-op Printing Soc 1911   160pp illus
Leicester Co-operative Soc
656   LEICSPL

Stephen, Walter M
The Binnend Oilworks and the Binn Village

Kirkcaldy: Fife Education 1969   48pp illus sources
Binnend Oilworks
130   140   KCLDYPL

Stephenson, Clifford
Great Grandfather Had a Wheelbarrow

Huddersfield: Regent Printers 1978   28pp illus
Shaw, Benjamin & Sons
428   HDSFDPL

Stephensons of Oxford
Stephensons of Oxford 1876-1976, Centenary

the firm 1976   49pp illus
Stephensons of Oxford
613   OXFDPL

397

Stern, W M
The First London Dock Boom and the Growth of West India Docks
Economica   Feb 1952
West India Docks
763   GHL

Steuart, Mary D
The Scottish Provident Institution 1837-1937

Edinburgh: the firm 1937   56pp illus
Scottish Provident Institution
820   *

Stevens, Edward Frank
One Hundred Years of Houlders 1849-1950

the firm 1950   101pp illus index
Houlder Brothers
740   * §

Stevenson, L W
The Lee Howl Story 1880-1980

Tipton: the firm 1980   80pp illus
Lee Howl & Co
328   SANDWPL

Steward, S F
Twenty-five Years of South Western Electricity

Bristol: S W E B 1973   44pp
South Western Electricity
161   ELECC

Stewart, James
History of the Tillicoultry Co-operative Store Coy Ltd 1839-1889
Scottish C W S 1889   55pp
Tillicoultry Co-op Society   Forth Valley Co-op
656   CLKMNPL

Stewarts and Lloyds
Stewarts and Lloyds 1903-1953

the firm ca1954   160pp illus
Stewarts & Lloyds
221   320   MTHWLPL

Stirling, T B
History of the Vale of Leven Co-operative Society Ltd 1862-1912
Alexandria: the firm 1915   204pp illus
Vale of Leven Co-op Soc
656   DMBTNPL

Stivers, William
International Politics and Iraqi Oil 1918-1928: A Study in Anglo-American Diplomacy
Business History Review   vol LV no 4 1981
Anglo-Persian Oil Co   Turkish Petroleum Co
130   140

Stockdale, Edmund
The Bank of England in 1934

the firm 1967   316pp
Bank of England
814   ABRDNPL

Stockport Co-operative Society
Stockport Co-operative Society: Centenary 1860-1960

Stockport: the firm 1960
Stockport Co-operative Society
656   SKPTPL

Stocks, Leslie A
The History of John Maden & Son Ltd. 1837-1977

the firm nd   54pp
Maden, John
430   BLPES

Stoddard, A F & Co
The Carpet Makers: One Hundred Years of Designing and Manufacturing Carpets of Quality
Paisley: the firm 1962   72pp illus
Stoddard, A F & Co
438   *

Stoddard, Jeanne
Manbré: A Hundred Years of Sugar Refining in Hammersmith 1874-1974
Fulham Hist Soc 1974   54pp illus index
Manbré & Garton   Tate & Lyle
420   *

Stoff, Michael B
The Anglo-American Oil Agreement and the Wartime Search for Foreign Oil Policy
Business History Review   vol LV no 1 1981
Anglo-Iranian Oil Co   Iraq Petroleum Co
130   140

Stoker, R B
Sixty Years on the Western Ocean

the firm 1958
Manchester Liners
740

Stone, Sheila
Barrow Bridge, Bolton, Lancashire: An Attempt to Create a Model Industrial Community in the Nineteenth Century
Southampton: dissertation 1974   61pp illus sources
Gardner & Bazley   Lord, John & Robert of Halliwell
432   BOLTNPL

Stopps, Leslie B
Burgess & Son (Abingdon) Ltd 1827-1980: A Short History

Abingdon: the firm 1980   63pp illus
Burgess & Son (Abingdon)
475   §

399

Storey, Graham
Reuters' Century 1851-1951

Max Parrish 1951   xii 276pp illus index sources
Reuters
839   * §

Storrs, Ronald Henry Amherst
Dunlop in War and Peace

Hutchinson 1946   xii 147pp illus
Dunlop Rubber Co
453   481   * §

Stote, Amos
1910-1935: Twenty-Five Eventful Years

West Bromwich: the firm 1935   47pp
Kenrick & Jefferson
475   SANDWPL

Strain, Wm & Sons
*Our Jubilee Souvenir: William Strain & Sons, Belfast
1859-1909*
Belfast: the firm 1909   47pp illus
Strain, Wm & Sons
472   SEELBPL

Straker Bros
Bishopsgate Press 1800-1925

1925
Straker Bros
475   GHL

Straker Bros
The House of Straker

1950   38pp
Straker Bros
472   GHL

Straus, Ralph
Lloyd's of London: An Historical Sketch

Hutchinson 1937   292pp illus index
Lloyd's of London
820   *

Stray, J F
Inside an International: Forty Years with 'Cable and Wireless'

Regency 1982   332pp illus index
Cable & Wireless
790   *

Street, Eric & Glenn, R
*The History of the National Mutual Life Assurance Society
1830-1980*
the firm 1980   v 122pp illus
National Mutual Life Assurance
820   * §

Street, George Slythe
The London Assurance 1720-1920

the firm 1920   51pp illus
London Assurance
820   * §

Strong, Leonard Alfred George
*A Brewer's Progress 1757-1957: A Survey of Charrington's
Brewery on Its Bicentenary*
the firm 1957   88pp illus
Charrington & Co
427   UBRIS

Strong, Leonard Alfred George
*A Brewer's Progress 1757-1957: A Survey of Charrington's
Brewery on the Occasion of its Bicentenary*
the firm 1957   viii 88pp illus
Charrington & Co
427   *

Strong, Leonard Alfred George
The Annals of One Hundred Years of Flour Milling

the firm 1940
Marriage, E & Son
416

Stuarts & Jacks
*Stuarts & Jacks Ltd, Musselburgh, Scotland: Fishing Net and
Twine Manufacturers, Cotton Spinners and Doublers*
Musselburgh: the firm ca1924   40pp illus
Stuarts & Jacks
439   432   ELOTHPL

Sturgess, R W (ed)
The Great Age of Industry in the North East
                                                            \
Durham: Durham Loc Hist Soc 1981   64pp
NE England Industries
220   300   *

Sturney, Alfred Charles
The Story of Mond Nickel

the firm 1951   63pp
Mond Nickel Co   International Nickel
224   *

Submarine Cables
The Story of the Submarine Cable

the firm 1960   28pp
Submarine Cables
341   *

Subutec
*A Brief History of SUBUTEC Oxford Exhaust Systems
1919-1979*
Oxford: the firm 1979   12pp
Subutec   Osberton Radiators
353   OXFDPL

401

Sudarshan, Ratna M
The Development of the Telephone Service in Britain 1912-39

Cambridge MSc 1983
Telephone Service
790

Suddards, Roger Whitley
Titus of Salts

Bradford: Watmough 1976   64pp illus sources
Salt, Titus
431   *

Sugden, Alan V & Entwisle, Eric A
Potters of Darwen 1839-1939: A Century of Wallpaper Printing by Machinery
Manchester: the firm 1939   120pp illus sources
Potters of Darwen
472   *

Sugiyama, Shinya
Thomas B Glover: A British Merchant in Japan 1861-1870

Business History   vol XXV no 2 1984
Glover & Co   Jardine, Matheson
839

Sully, J & A W
Towards the Centenary 1865-1951: Notes on the Origin and History of an Accountancy Practice
the firm 1951   40pp illus
Sully, J & A W & Co
836   *

Summers, John & Sons
History of the Company

Shotton: the firm ca1955   20pp illus
Summers, John & Sons
221   CLWYDPL

Sun Mill Co, Oldham
The Story of a Great Enterprise 1858-1958

Oldham: the firm 1958   33pp illus
Sun Mill Co, Oldham
432   OLDHMPL

Supple, Barry Emanuel
Corporate Growth and Structural Change in a Service Industry: Insurance 1870-1914
see Supple, Barry (ed)
Insurance
820

Supple, Barry Emanuel
The Royal Exchange Assurance: A History of British Insurance 1720-1970
Cambridge: C U P 1970   584pp illus index sources
Royal Exchange Assurance
820   *

Supple, Barry Emanuel (ed)
Essays in British Business History

Oxford: Clarendon 1977 viii 267pp sources

Sutcliffe, Peter
The Oxford University Press: An Informal History

Oxford: Clarendon 1978 xxviii 303pp illus index sources
Oxford University Press
475 * §
Sutcliffe, R J & Edward D
Richard Sutcliffe: The Pioneer of Underground Belt Conveying

the firm 1955 143pp illus
Sutcliffe, Richard
325 §
Suter, A F & Co
Fifty Worthwhile Years

the firm 1956 25pp illus
Suter, A F & Co
256 259 UBRIS
Sutton, George Barry
A History of Shoemaking in Street, Somerset: C & J Clark,
1833-1903
York: William Sessions 1979 viii 208pp illus index sources
Clark, C & J
451 *
Sutton, George Barry
The Marketing of Ready Made Footwear in the Nineteenth
Century: A Study of the Firm of C & J Clark
Business History vol VI no 2 1964
Clark, C & J
451
Swale, S E
Forerunners of the North Western Electricity Board

Manchester: NORWEB 1963 107pp
North Western Electricity
161 ELECC
Swan Hunter & Wigham Richardson
Launching Ways: Swan, Hunter Jubilee

Wallsend-on-Tyne: the firm 1953 40pp illus
Swan Hunter Wigham Richardson
320 361 * §
Swan Hunter & Wigham Richardson
Swan Hunter & Wigham Richardson, Engineers and Shipbuilders

Wallsend-on-Tyne: the firm 1906 40pp illus
Swan Hunter Wigham Richardson
320 361 *

Swan, Malcolm S
*Jubilee History of the Greenock Central Co-operative Society
1870-1930*
Glasgow: Scottish C W S 1930   viii 132pp illus
Greenock Central Co-op Soc
656   *
Sweet & Maxwell
*Then and Now 1799-1974: Commemorating 175 Years of Law
Bookselling & Publishing*
Sweet & Maxwell 1974   xii 219pp illus
Sweet & Maxwell
475   653   *
Swindin, Norman
Engineering without Wheels: A Personal History

Weidenfeld & Nicolson 1962   255pp illus index
Nordac
251   324   837   *
Swinglehurst, Edmund
*The Romantic Journey: The Story of Thomas Cook and Victorian
Travel*
Pica Editions 1974   208pp illus index sources
Cook, Thomas & Son
770   * §
Swire, John & Sons
The Swire Group

the firm ca1975   60pp illus
Swire, John & Sons   Butterfield & Swire
740   770   839   §
Sykes, Alan John
Concerning the Bleaching Industry

Manchester: the firm 1925   ix 120pp illus
Bleachers' Association
437   *
Sykes, Philip
Albert E Reed and the Creation of a Paper Business 1860-1960

the firm 1981   viii 493pp illus
Reed International
471   *
Syme & Duncan
The History of Syme & Duncan Ltd 1870 to 1970

Beckenham: nd   12pp
Syme & Duncan
501   MRC
Symington, R & W H & Co
*In Our Own Fashion 1856-1956: The story of R & W H Symington
& Co Ltd, Market Harborough*
Harley 1956   104pp illus
Symington, R & W H & Co
436   453   LEICSPL

404

Symons, Julian
Horatio Bottomley

Cresset 1955   287pp illus
John Bull   Bottomley, Horatio
475   831   *

Tamaki, Norio
The Life Cycle of the Union Bank of Scotland 1830-1954

Aberdeen: A U P 1983   xx 242pp index sources
Union Bank of Scotland
814   §

Tangye, Richard
One and All: An Autobiography of Richard Tangye of the
Cornwall Works
S W Partridge 1889   190pp illus
Tangyes
328   *

Tangyes
1856-1950: A Brief History of Cornwall Works

the firm 1950   16pp illus
Tangyes
328   SANDWPL

Tangyes
A Hundred Years of Engineering Craftsmanship 1857-1957

Smethwick: the firm 1957   109pp illus
Tangyes
328   §

Tann, Jennifer
Gloucestershire Woollen Mills

Newton Abbot: David & Charles 1967 254pp illus
Woollen Mills
431   *

Tann, Jennifer (ed)
The Selected Papers of Boulton & Watt; vol 1- The Engine
Partnership   1775-1825
Diploma 1981   xv 425pp illus index sources
Boulton & Watt
320   *

Tanner, Geo. & Wicks, P O
Geo. Tanner & P O Wicks Ltd

Braintree: 1968   12pp
Tanner, Geo. & Wicks, P O
501   MRC

Tanqueray, Gordon & Co
The House of Gordon: The Story of Gordon's London Dry Gin

                                 31pp illus
Tanqueray, Gordon & Co   Gordon's
424   ISLTNPL

Taphouse, Charles & Son
The Story of a Music Shop 1857-1957

Oxford: the firm 1957   15pp illus
Taphouse, Charles & Son
648   OXFDPL

Tapper, Oliver
Roots in the Sky: A History of British Aerospace Aircraft

IPC 1980   96pp illus

364   *

Tarn, A W & Byles, C E
A Record of the Guardian Assurance Company Limited 1821-1921
the firm 1921   153pp illus index
Guardian Assurance Co
820   * §

Tate & Lyle
Tate & Lyle: A Record of the Activities of the Tate & Lyle Group
the firm 1965   88pp illus
Tate & Lyle
420   §

Tatham, Bromage & Co
Tatham's Log 1858-1958: The Centenary of Tatham, Bromage & Company Ltd
the firm 1958   100pp illus
Tatham, Bromage & Co
740   §

Taylor, Alan John Percivale
Beaverbrook

Hamish Hamilton 1972   xvii 712pp illus sources
Express Newspapers   Beaverbrook Press
475   DBB

Taylor, Audrey Mary
Gilletts: Bankers at Banbury and Oxford: A Study in Local Economic History
Oxford: Clarendon 1964   xiv 247pp illus index sources
Gillett Brothers Discount Co
814   831   * §

Taylor, E & Wilson, J S
At the Sign of the Orrery

ca1967
Cooke, Troughton & Simms
370   GHL

Taylor, Frank
Johnstone and Co-operation: Jubilee Souvenir 1866-1916

Johnstone: the firm 1916   144pp illus
Johnstone Co-operative Society
656   RNFRWPL

Taylor, H A & D
Two Hundred Years of Malting

Sawbridgeworth: the firm nd   19pp illus
Taylor, H A & D
427   HERTSPL

Taylor, J
The Beginning of Derwent Works

1911
Derwent Works
                                       BLPES

Taylor, J T
The Jubilee History of the Oldham Industrial Co-operative Society Ltd 1850-1900
Manchester: C W S 1900   180pp illus
Oldham Industrial Co-op
656   SALFDPL

Taylor, James
Ellermans: A Wealth of Shipping

Wilton House Gentry 1976   320pp illus index
Ellerman Lines
740   * §

Taylor, John
John Taylors Ltd: Centenary Souvenir 1856-1956

Bolton: Tillotsons 1956   32pp illus
Taylor, John
431   HDSFDPL

Taylor, John W R & Allward, Maurice F
Westland 50

Shepperton: Ian Allan 1965   216pp illus
Westland Aircraft
364   *

Taylor, Leslie B
A Brief History of the Westley Richards Firm 1812-1913

the firm 1913   94pp illus
Westley Richards
329   *

Taylor, Michael John Haddrick
Shorts the Planemakers

Janes 1984   160pp illus index
Short Brothers   Harland & Wolff
364   *

Taylor, Theodore Cooke
One Hundred Years: Records, Recollections and Reflections

Leeds: Whitehead & Miller 1946   69pp illus
Taylor of Batley
431   HDSFDPL

Taylor-Hobson

Taly Ho - In Pursuit of Precision: The Taylor-Hobson Story 1886-1956

Leicester: the firm 1956   32pp illus sources
Taylor, Taylor & Hobson   Rank Precision Industries
371   373   UBRIS

Teesdale, E

Queen's Gunstonemaker

Seaford: Lindel 1984   125pp
Gunstonemaker
231   256   ESUSXPL

Teetgen & Co

One Hundred Years of Trading

1934
Teetgen & Co
423   839   GHL

Tennant

Enterprise: An Account of the Activities of the Tennant Group of Companies First Established in 1797
Adprint ca1945   168pp illus
Tennant, Charles & Co
251   770   839   BLPES

Tennant

One Hundred and Forty Years of the Tennant Companies: 1797-1937
the firm 1937   65pp illus
Tennant, Charles & Co
251   §

Tennant, E W D

A Short Account of the Tennant Companies 1797-1922

the firm 1922   53pp illus
Tennant, Charles & Co
251   770   DMBTNPL

Terry's

Terry's of York 1767-1967

the firm 1967   24pp illus
Terry, Joseph
421   BCROB

Terry, C

A Pioneer Bank in a Pioneer Land

Cape Town: Flesch & Partners 1979
Standard Chartered Bank
839   BAC

Tetley, Joshua & Son

Joshua Tetley & Son: A Hundredth Birthday 1823-1923

Leeds: the firm 1937   28pp illus
Tetley, Joshua & Son
427   * §

Teversham, Traviss Frederick
The Story of a Country Printing House

Cambridge: 1962   57pp illus
Crampton & Sons
475   §

Tewson, W F
The British Cotton Growing Association: Golden Jubilee
1904-1954
the firm 1954   xiv 83pp illus
British Cotton Growing Assoc
432   §

Thames & Mersey Marine Insurance Co
Thames & Mersey Marine Insurance Company Limited
1860-1960
Liverpool: the firm 1960   79pp illus
Thames & Mersey Marine Ins Co
820   * §

Thames Conservancy
The Thames Conservancy 1857-1957

the firm nd   100pp illus index
Thames Conservancy
761   UBRIS

Thane, Pat
Financiers and the British State: The Case of Sir Ernest Cassel

Business History   vol XXVIII no 1 1986
Cassell, Ernest
810   831

Thetford Moulded Products
100 Years Thetford Moulded Products Limited 1879-1979

the firm 1979
Thetford Moulded Products
483

Thomas, David A
The Canning Story 1785-1985

Springwood 1985   xi 195pp illus index sources
Canning
140   256   311   344

Thomas, David G & Sowan, Brenda J
W A Crips & Sons: Bermondsey's Last Chainsmiths

Greater London Ind Arch Soc 1977   26pp illus
Crips, W A & Sons
313   SWKPL

Thomas, Earl B
Guest, Keen & Nettlefolds Group of Companies

Steel Review   vol 17 Jan 1960
G K N
313

Thomas, Edward Wynne
The House of Yardley 1770-1953

Sylvan Press 1953   106pp illus index
Yardley
258   *

Thomas, Frederick Moy
I & R Morley: A Record of a Hundred Years

the firm 1900   x 103pp illus
Morley, I & R   Brettle, George
436   *

Thomas, Joan
A History of the Leeds Clothing Industry

Hull: Yorks Bull Econ Res 1955
Leeds Clothing
453

Thomas, John
The North British Railway

N Abbot: David & Charles 1969-75   2 vols illus index sources
North British Railway
710   *

Thomas, John
The Springburn Story: The History of the Scottish Railway Metropolis
Dawlish: David & Charles 1964   260pp illus index
Springburn
362   710   *

Thomas, Ronald Henry George
London's First Railway: The London and Greenwich

Batsford 1972   270pp illus
London & Greenwich Railway
710   *

Thomas, Ronald Henry George
The Liverpool & Manchester Railway

Batsford 1980   264pp illus index sources
Liverpool & Manchester Railway
710   *

Thomas, William Miles Webster
Out On a Wing

Michael Joseph 1964
Morris Motors   British Overseas Airways Corp
351   750   *

Thompson, C R
From Ship to Shore: The Biography of William Schermuly and the History of the Company
the firm 1946   xii 79pp illus
Schermuly Pistol Rocket Co
256   *

Thompson, Francis G
Harris Tweed: The Story of a Hebridean Industry

Newton Abbot: David & Charles 1969 191pp illus index
Harris Tweed
431   *

Thompson, J Hannay & Ritchie, Geo G
Dundee Harbour Trust: A Brief History of the Harbour of Dundee together with Notes on its Trade
Ed J Burrow 1952   64pp illus
Dundee Harbour Trust
740   770   *

Thoms, David
Workshop of War: The West Midlands 1939-1945

Croom Helm 1987
West Midlands Industries
320   350

Thoms, David & Donnelly, Tom
The Motor Car Industry in Coventry since the 1890s

Croom Helm 1985   243pp index sources
Motor Industry in Coventry
351   *

Thomson, Alistair G
The Paper Industry in Scotland 1590-1861

Edinburgh: Scottish Academic 1974   229pp illus index sources
Paper Industry in Scotland
471   *

Thomson, D C
The Thomson-Leng Story in Pictures

Dundee: Thomson-Leng 1954   44pp illus
Thomson, D C & Co   Leng, John & Co
475   DNDEEPL

Thomson, J G & Co
J G Thomson & Co: Two Hundred and Fifty Years 1709-1959

Edinburgh: the firm 1959   36pp illus sources
Thomson, J G & Co
617   642   EDNBRPL

Thornton
Thorntons 1911-1981: The Story of a Family Firm

Sheffield: the firm 1981   16pp illus
Thornton
421   SHEFFPL

Thornton, Robert
A Story of Woollen Rag Sales 1860-1960

Harley 1960   32pp illus
Thornton, Robert & Sons
431   622   * §

Thorpe, T W
The Shepherd's Crook

C Nicholls 1950 32pp illus
Thorpe, T W
431 HDSFDPL

Threlfall, Richard Evelyn
The Story of 100 Years of Phosphorus Making 1851-1951

Oldbury: the firm 1951 400pp illus index sources
Albright & Wilson
251 *

Tilbury Contracting & Dredging Co
*Tilbury Contracting & Dredging Co: An Account of some
Achievements and Present Activities*
1955 36pp
Tilbury Contracting & Dredging Co
502 763 GHL

Till, Roger
Wills of Bristol 1786-1901

the firm nd 74pp illus index
Wills, W D & H O
429 UBRIS

Tilling, John
Kings of the Highway

1957 126pp illus
Tilling, Thomas
723 *

Tillmanns, Martin
*Bridge Hall Mills: Three Centuries of Paper & Cellulose Film
Manufacture*
Tisbury, Wilts: Compton 1978 xi 219pp illus index sources
Bridge Hall Mills Transparent Paper
471 483 * §

Timaeus, C E
*A Century and a Half of Wire Weaving: The Story of C H Johnson
and Sons Ltd*
the firm 1952 56pp illus
Johnson, C H and Sons
223 UBRIS

Timings, F L
The Birmingham Steel Pen Trade after 1826

Birmingham MComm 1926
Birmingham Steel Pen Trade
495

Timmins, John Geoffrey
*The Commercial Development of the Sheffield Crucible Steel
Industry*
Sheffield MA 1976
Sheffield Crucible Steel
221

412

Timmins, John Geoffrey (ed)
     Workers in Metal Since 1784: A History of W & G Sissons Ltd. -
     Bicentenary 1784-1984
     Sheffield: the firm 1984   20pp illus
     Sissons, W & G
     316

Timpson, D J
     William Timpson Limited: A Century of Service 1865-1965

     Kettering: the firm 1965   68pp illus
     Timpson, William
     451   646   * §

Tinsley Wire
     The First Twenty-Five Years: Being a Short History of Tinsley
     Wire Industries Ltd 1933-1958
     the firm nd   40pp
     Tinsley Wire Industries
     223   SHEFFPL

Tinsley, H
     Tinsley's History 1904-1964

     South Norwood: the firm 1964   32pp illus
     Tinsley, H & Co
     344   CROYPL

Tippett, Leonard Henry Caleb
     A Portrait of the Lancashire Textile Industry

     Oxford U P 1969   x 170pp illus
     Lancashire Textile Industry
     432   *

Titheridge, Alan
     Hythe Pier and Ferry: A History

     Southampton: Itchen 1981   112pp illus
     Hythe Pier & Southampton Ferry
     740   763

Todd, Murray
     A Short History of Todd Bros (St. Helens and Widnes) Ltd

     St. Helens: the firm 1947   27pp
     Todd Bros
     221   StHLNS

Tolliday, Steven
     Tariffs and Steel 1916-1934: The Politics of Industrial
     Decline
     see Turner, John (ed)
     Steel Tariffs
     221

Tomkinson
     Tomkinson's Centenary 1869-1969

     Carpet Review   64pp illus
     Tomkinsons Carpets
     438   HWORCPL

Tomlinson, W W
The North Eastern Railway: Its Rise and Development

Newcastle-upon-Tyne: A Reid 1914　　xvi 820pp illus index sources
North Eastern Railway
710　　　　　　　　　　　　　　　　　　　　　　　　　　NRMYORK

Toms, Stanley J
A Record of the History of Derry & Toms

typescript 1963　　　　　　　　　　8pp illus
Derry & Toms
656　　　　　　　　　　　　　　　　　　　　　　　　　　KENSPL

Toomey, R R
A Study of the Firm in the Copper and Related Industries with special reference to Vivian & Sons 1809-1924
Wales (Swansea) PhD 1980
Vivian & Sons
224

Topham, A J
The Credit Structure of the West Riding Wool Textile Industry in the 19th Century
Leeds MA 1955
West Riding Wool Textile Industry
431　　　　　814

Torrens, Hugh S
Men of Iron: The History of the McArthur Group

Bristol: the firm 1984　　　　　　76pp illus sources
McArthur Group
210　　　　221　　　　311　　　　612　　　　615　　　　　　§

Torrens, Hugh S
The Evolution of a Family Firm: Stothert and Pitt of Bath

Bath: the firm 1978　　　　　　v 86pp illus index sources
Stothert & Pitt
311　　　　325　　　　　　　　　　　　　　　　　　　* §

Tottenham & District Gas
Tottenham & District Gas 1847-1947

the firm 1947　　　　　　　　57pp illus
Tottenham & District Gas
162　　　　　　　　　　　　　　　　　　　　　　　　　　§

Tottington Industrial Co-operative Society
Tottington Industrial Co-operative Society Jubilee 1861-1911

Bury: the firm 1911
Tottington Industrial Co-op Soc
656　　　　　　　　　　　　　　　　　　　　　　　　BURYPL

Toulson, Norman
The Squirrel and the Clock: National Provident Institution 1835-1985
Henry Melland 1985　　　　　　140pp illus index
National Provident Institution
820　　　　　　　　　　　　　　　　　　　　　　　　　§

414

Towles Ltd
>*50 Years of Paramount Progress*
>
>Loughborough: the firm 1956   20pp illus
>Towles
>436   LEICSPL

Tozer Kemsley and Millbourn
>*Tozer Kemsley and Millbourn Limited 1899-1949: Fifty Years of Service*
>the firm 1949   66pp illus
>Tozer Kemsley and Millbourn
>815   §

Tramayne, Arthur
>*One Hundred Years After: Being a Little History of a Great Achievement*
>Birmingham: the firm 1912
>Dennison Watch Case Co
>374

Travers, Frank
>*Chronicles of Cannon Street: A Few Records of an Old Firm*
>
>the firm 1957   64pp illus index
>Travers, Joseph & Sons
>420   617   839   * §

Travers, Joseph & Sons
>*Past and Present in an Old Firm*
>
>the firm 1907   55pp illus
>Travers, Joseph & Sons
>420   617   839   *

Treasure, John A P
>*The History of British Advertising Agencies 1875-1939*
>
>Edinburgh: Scottish Academic P 1977 20pp
>Advertising Agencies
>838   *

Trebilcock, Ronald Clive
>*Phoenix Assurance and the Development of British Insurance vol 1 1782-1870*
>Cambridge: C U P 1985   xx 792pp illus index sources
>Phoenix Assurance
>820   * §

Trebilcock, Ronald Clive
>*The Vickers Brothers: Armaments and Enterprise, 1854-1914*
>
>Europa 1977   xl 181pp illus index sources
>Vickers
>320   361   * §

Treble, J H
>*The Pattern of Investment of the Standard Life Assurance Company 1875-1914*
>Business History   vol XXII no 2 1980
>Standard Life Assurance
>820

Treble, J H
The Record of the Standard Life Assurance Company in the Life
Insurance Market of the United Kingdom 1850-1864
see Westall, Oliver M (ed) 1984
Standard Life Assurance
820

Tredrey, F D
The House of Blackwood 1804-1954: The History of a
Publishing Firm
Edinburgh: Blackwood 1954   ix 282pp illus index sources
Blackwood, William & Sons
475   * §

Tregoning, David & Cockerell, Hugh
Friends for Life: Friends' Provident Life Office 1832-1982

Henry Melland 1982   196pp illus index
Friends' Provident Life   Century Insurance Co
820   * §

Tregonning, Kennedy Gordon Philip
Home Port Singapore: A History of the Straits Steamship
Company Limited 1890-1965
Singapore: Oxford U P 1967   xii 321pp illus index sources
Straits Steamship Co
740   839   * §

Tremlett, George
The First Century: The Exciting Story of the Working Men's Club
& Institute Union
the firm 1962   145pp illus
Working Men's Club & Inst Union
663   *

Trethowan, D M
The Rise and Decline of Porthleven Harbour 1810-1960

Exeter MA 1972
Porthleven Harbour
763

Trewin, John C & King, Evelyn M
Printer to The House: The Story of Hansard

Methuen 1952   xv 272pp illus index sources
Hansard
475   *

Trinder, Barrie Stuart
The Darbys of Coalbrookdale

Chichester: Phillimore 1974   79pp illus index
Coalbrookdale Co
221   311   DUDLYPL

Tripp, Basil Howard
Grand Alliance: A Chapter of Industrial History

Chantry 1951   56pp illus
Allied Ironfounders
311   *

Tripp, Basil Howard
Renold Chains: A History of the Company and the Rise of the Precision Chain Industry 1879-1955
Allen & Unwin 1956   191pp illus index
Renold Chains
326   * §
Tripp, Basil Howard
Renold Limited 1956-1967

Allen & Unwin 1969   188pp illus index
Renold Chains
326   §
Trollope & Colls
City Builders for 200 Years 1778-1978: The History of Trollope & Colls
Precision 1978
Trollope & Colls
500
Trotter, R (ed)
I C I and its Founding Companies: Vol 1; The History of Nobel's Explosives Company and Nobel Industries Limited 1871-1926
the firm 1938
I C I
250
Trowell, Frank
Nineteenth-Century Speculative Housing in Leeds: With Special Reference to the Suburb of Headingley 1838-1914
York DPhil 1982
Walmsley Brothers
501
Trumans
Trumans the Brewers 1666-1966: The Story of Truman Hanbury Buxton & Co Ltd, London & Burton
Newman Neame 1966   63pp illus
Truman Hanbury Buxton
427   662   * §
Trumper, George F
George F Trumper, Curzon St, London: Court Hairdressers for 200 Years
York: William Sessions 1980
Trumper, George F
982
Trussed Concrete Steel Co
Truscon: The First Fifty Years: A Short History of the Truscon Co 1907-1957
1957   38pp
Truscon
243   GHL
Tse, K K
Marks & Spencer: Anatomy of Britain's Most Efficiently Managed Company
Oxford: Pergamon 1985   viii 239pp illus index sources
Marks & Spencer
645   656   * §

Tuck, Raphael
The Romance of the House of Raphael Tuck & Sons Ltd.

the firm 1966   pamphlet
Tuck, Raphael
475   §

Tucker, D G
The Slate Islands of Scotland: The History of the Scottish Slate Industry
Business History   vol XIX no 1 1977
Slate Industry in Scotland
231

Tucker, K A
Business History: Selected Readings

Frank Cass 1977   xvi 442pp illus index sources

                                                                       *

Tucker, M T
Vincent & Son Ltd, Cabinet Makers; Brick Lane, London

Greater London Ind Arch Soc 1977   8pp illus
Vincent & Son
467

Tuke Mennell & Co
Tea: An Historical Sketch

1926   63pp
Tuke & Co   Mennell, R C & Co
423   839   GHL

Tuke, Anthony W & Gillman, Richard J H
Barclays Bank Limited 1926-1969: Some Recollections

the firm 1972   vii 167pp illus
Barclays Bank
814   *

Turnbull & Stockdale
Turnbull & Stockdale Jubilee 1881-1931

Manchester: the firm 1931   illus
Turnbull & Stockdale
                                                         BURYPL

Turnbull, Geoffrey (ed)
A History of the Calico Printing Industry of Great Britain

Altrincham: J Sherratt & Son 1951   xv 501pp illus
Calico Printers' Association
432   *

Turnbull, Gerard L
Traffic and Transport: An Economic History of Pickfords

Allen & Unwin 1979   xii 196pp index sources
Pickfords   Hay's Wharf Cartage Co
723   * §

Turner & Newall
Turner & Newall Limited: The First Fifty Years 1920-1970

the firm 1970   87pp illus
Turner & Newall
243   244   * §

Turner, D H
The Wigan Coal and Iron Company,1865-1885

typescript ca1969   48pp sources
Wigan Coal & Iron Co
111   311   WIGANPL

Turner, Graham
Business in Britain

Eyre & Spottiswoode 1969   451pp index

                                                              *

Turner, Graham
The Car Makers

Eyre & Spottiswoode 1963   262pp
Motor Industry
351   *

Turner, Graham
The Leyland Papers

Eyre & Spottiswoode 1971   216pp illus index
British Leyland
351   *

Turner, J Howard
The London Brighton and South Coast Railway

Batsford 1977-79   3 vols illus index sources
London Brighton & South Coast Rly
710   NRMYORK

Turner, John (ed)
Businessmen and Politics: Studies of Business Activity in British Politics 1900-1945
Heinemann 1984   vii 200pp index
Politics & Business
                                                              *

Turner, John (ed)
Businessmen and Politics: Studies of Business Activity in British Politics 1900-1945
Aldershot: Gower 1984   208pp index
Business Activity in Politics
140   221   328   814   *

Turner, Joshua
Joshua Turner, Gentlemen's Hatter

ca1930   23pp
Turner, Joshua
453   GHL

Turner, William
William Adams: An Old English Potter

    Chapman & Hall 1904   xxii 252pp illus
    Adams, William
    248   *

Turrell, Robert
Sir Frederic Philipson Stow: The Unknown Diamond Magnate

    Business History   vol XXVIII no 1 1986

Tute, Warren Stanley
The Grey Top Hat: The Story of Moss Bros of Covent Garden

    Cassell 1961   153pp illus index
    Moss Bros
    453   645   846   §

Tweedale, Geoffrey
English versus American Hardware: British Marketing Techniques and Business Performance in the U S A
see Davenport-Hines, R P T (ed)
Steel Tools & Hardware
316   322

Tweedale, Geoffrey
Giants of Sheffield: The Men Who Made Sheffield the Steel Capital of the World
Sheffield: Sheffield City Lib 1986
Sheffield Steel
221

Tweedale, Geoffrey
Science, Innovation and the 'Rule of Thumb': A Case Study of Metallurgy and the British Steel Industry 1850-1930
see Liebenau, Jonathan (ed)
Steel Industry
221   310   320

Tweedale, Geoffrey
Sheffield Steel and America: A Century of Commercial and Technological Interdependence 1830-1930
Cambridge: C U P
Sheffield Steel
221

Tweedale, Geoffrey
Sheffield Steel and America: Aspects of the Atlantic Migration of Special Steelmaking Technology 1850-1930
Business History   vol XXV no 3 1983
Sheffield Speciality Steels
221

Tweedale, Geoffrey
The Sheffield Steel Industry and its Allied Trade and the American Market 1850-1930
London PhD 1984
Sheffield Steel
221

Tweedale, Geoffrey
Transatlantic Speciality Steels: Sheffield High-Grade Steel Firms and the U S A 1860-1940
see Jones, Geoffrey (ed)
Sheffield Speciality Steels
221

Twelvetrees, Richard W R & Squire, Pepys
Why Dennis - And How

Guildford: the firm 1945   106pp illus
Dennis Brothers
351   UBRIS

Twining
The Twinings in Three Centuries: The Annals of a Great London Tea House 1710-1910
the firm nd   42pp illus
Twining, R & Co
423   617   641   *

Twining, Stephen H
The House of Twining 1706-1956: Being a Short History of the Firm of R. Twining & Co. Ltd: Tea and Coffee Merchants
the firm 1956   xi 115pp illus index
Twining, R & Co
423   617   641   * §

Twining, Stephen H
Two Hundred and Twenty Five Years in the Strand 1706-1931: A History of the Firm
the firm 1931   40pp illus
Twining, R & Co
423   617   641   * §

Twiston Davies, William
Fifty Years of Progress: An Account of the African Organisation of the Imperial Tobacco Company 1907-1957
Bristol: the firm nd   92pp illus
Imperial Tobacco
429   617   * §

Twitchett, John & Bailey, Betty
Royal Crown Derby

Barrie & Jenkins 1980   224pp illus index sources
Royal Crown Derby
248   *

Tylors of London
Tylors during Nine Reigns 1787-1957

the firm 1957   15pp
Tylors of London
325   §

Tyson, Geoffrey
100 Years of Banking in Asia and Africa: A History of National & Grindlays Bank Limited 1863-1963
the firm 1963   xii 246pp illus index
National & Grindlays Bank
814   839   BLPES

Tyson, R E
Scottish Investment in American Railways: The Case of the
City of Glasgow Bank 1856-1881
see Payne, Peter L (ed) 1967
City of Glasgow Bank
814
Tyson, R E
The Sun Mill Company Limited: A Study in Democratic
Investment 1858-1959
Manchester MA 1962
Sun Mill Co
432
Tyzack, Wm
Centenary Souvenir 1812-1912

Sheffield: the firm 1912
Tyzack, William & Sons
221   316   322   SHEFFPL
Ulster Bank
Decades of the Ulster Bank 1836-1964

Belfast: the firm 1965   274pp illus index
Ulster Bank
814   BLPES
Unigate
The Cow and Gate Story

the firm 1959
Cow & Gate   Unigate
413   617
Unilever
Unilever's World: C I S Anti-Report

C I S ca1980   103pp illus sources
Unilever
258   UBRIS
Union Bank of Scotland
Brief Historical Sketch of the Union Bank of Scotland

Edinburgh: Maclehose 1910   37pp illus
Union Bank of Scotland
814   EDNBRPL
Union Marine and General Insurance Co
Centennial Story: The Union Marine and General Insurance Co
Ltd 1863-1963
Liverpool: the firm 1963   99pp illus
Union Marine & General Ins Co
820   * §
United Alkali Co
The Struggle for Supremacy: Chapters in the History of the
Leblanc Alkali Industry in Great Britain
Liverpool: the firm 1907   77pp illus
United Alkali Co
251   UBRIS

422

United Clubs Brewery Co
Golden Jubilee of the South Wales and Monmouthshire United Clubs Brewery Co Ltd, 1969
the firm 1969   25pp illus
United Clubs Brewery Co
427   MGLAMPL

United Wire Works
The History of the United Wire Works

Edinburgh: Pillans & Wilson 1948   63pp illus
United Wire Works
223   EDNBRPL

Unwin, George; Hulme, Arthur & Taylor, George
Samuel Oldknow and the Arkwrights: The Industrial Revolution at Stockport and Marple
Manchester: M U P 1924   xvi 260pp index sources
Oldknow and the Arkwrights
430   *

Unwin, Philip
The Printing Unwins: A Short History of Unwin Brothers, The Gresham Press 1826-1976
Allen & Unwin 1976   159pp illus index sources
Unwin Brothers, Gresham Press
475   *

Unwin, Philip
The Publishing Unwins

Heinemann 1972   x 182pp illus index sources
Allen & Unwin
475   *

Unwin, Stanley
The Truth about a Publisher: An Autobiographical Record

Allen & Unwin 1960   455pp illus index
Allen & Unwin
475   *

Unwin, Stanley
The Truth about Publishing

Allen & Unwin 1976   256pp index sources
Allen & Unwin
475   *

Urquhart, Robert
History of the Scottish Milk Marketing Board

the firm 1979   90pp illus
Scottish Milk Marketing Board
617   RNFRWPL

Vaizey, John Ernest
The Brewing Industry 1886-1951: An Economic Study

Isaac Pitman & Sons 1960   xxiv 173pp
Brewing Industry
427   *

Vaizey, John Ernest
The History of British Steel

Weidenfeld & Nicolson 1974   xvii205pp illus index sources
British Steel
221   * §

Vale, Henry Edmund Theodoric
The Harveys of Hayle: Engine Builders, Shipwrights &
Merchants of Cornwall
Truro: Bradford Barton 1966   356pp illus index sources
Harvey & Co
328   361   * §

Vale, Vivian
The Government and the Cunard Contract of 1903

Journal of Transport History   new ser vol V no 1 1979
Cunard
740   790

Vallance, Aylmer
Very Private Enterprise: An Anatomy of Fraud and High Finance

Thames & Hudson 1955   v 205pp
Fraud and High Finance
800

Vamplew, Wray
Salvesen of Leith

Edinburgh: Scot Academic 1975   xii 311pp illus index sources
Salvesen of Leith
30   740   *

Van Moppes
Diamonds in the Service of Industry: The Story of the Van
Moppes Group
Basingstoke: the firm nd   40pp illus
Van Moppes, L M & Sons
246   322   §

Varley, Donald Emerson
A History of the Midland Counties Lace Manufacturers'
Association 1915-1958
Long Eaton: Lace Productions 1959   212pp illus index sources
Midland Counties Lace Mfrs' Assoc
439   *

Varley, Donald Emerson
John Heathcote 1783-1861: Founder of the Machine-made Lace
Industry
Newton Abbot: David & Charles 1969 40pp illus
Heathcote, John
439   *

Vaughan, Anthony
The Vaughans, East End Cabinet Makers: Three Hundred Years of
a London Family
ILEA 1984   95pp illus sources
Vaughan Family
467   §

Vaughan-Thomas, Wynford
Dalgety: The Romance of a Business

Henry Melland 1984   96pp illus
Dalgety   Spillers
416   422   427   641   839   §

Vauxhall
A History of Vauxhall

Luton: the firm 1980   68pp illus
Vauxhall Motors
351   §

Veeder-Root
Notes on the History of the Company in Dundee

the firm nd
Veeder-Root
340   344   DNDEEPL

Venesta
Our First Fifty Years

the firm 1948   11pp illus
Venesta
224   462   MRC

Vere-Hodge, Edmund Reginald
Imperial British East Africa Company

Macmillan 1960   vii 95pp
Imperial British East Africa Co
839   *

Vernon, Anne
A Quaker Business Man: The Life of Joseph Rowntree 1836-1925

Allen & Unwin 1958   207pp illus index sources
Rowntree
421   *

Vertigan, Sean A
J & J Cash Limited: A Business History 1846-1928

Nottingham B A 1982
Cash, J & J
439

Vickers and Sons
Vickers and Sons Ltd: 125 years

Leeds: the firm 1954   162pp illus
Vickers and Sons
320   §

Vickers, Benjn R & Sons
This Family Business, Vickers

Leeds: the firm 1954   60pp illus
Vickers, Benjn R & Sons
411   UBRIS

Victor

Victor: The First Fifty Years 1929-1979

Wallsend: the firm 1979
Victor Products
325

Villiers Engineering Co

Villiers Engineering Co Ltd: 1898-1958 Sixty Progressive Years

Wolverhampton: the firm 1958   21pp
Villiers Engineering Co
328   363   §

Vincent, James Edmund

John Nixon, Pioneer of the Steam Coal Trade in South Wales: A Memoir

J Murray 1900   viii 245pp
S Wales Steam Coal Trade
111   612   *

Vincents

Vincents: The first Hundred Years 1867-1967

Reading: the firm 1967   26pp illus
Vincents
651   BERKSPL

Volk, Conrad

Magnus Volk of Brighton

Chichester: Phillimore 1971   240pp illus index sources
Volk's Electric Railway
342   721   §

Vulcan Foundry

Built by Stephenson: The Early History of the Vulcan Foundry Ltd and Stephenson & Hawthorne Ltd

1958   241pp
Vulcan Foundry   Stephenson & Hawthorne
362   WARRPL

Vulcan Foundry

The Vulcan Locomotive Works 1830-1930

Locomotive Publishing Co 1930   122pp illus
Vulcan Foundry
362   *

Vulcan Foundry

Vulcan's Heritage: A Brief History of the Vulcan Site

the firm 1975
Vulcan Foundry   General Electric Co
311   328   362

Wade, Malcolm

Malcolm Wade, Ink Makers 1800-1955

York: William Sessions 1955
Wade, Malcolm
255

Wade, Malcolm & Co
Seventy Five Years of Achievement 1880-1955

1955   15pp
Wade, Malcolm & Co
255   GHL

Wainwright, David
Broadwood By Appointment: A History

Quiller 1982   360pp illus index sources
Broadwood, John & Sons
492   * §

Wainwright, David
Brooke Bond: A Hundred Years

Newman Neame nd   60pp illus
Brooke Bond Liebig
423   617   * §

Wainwright, David
Cranes and Craftsmen: The Story of Herbert Morris Limited

Hutchinson Benham 1974   88pp illus
Morris, Herbert
325   LEICSPL

Wainwright, David
Henderson: A History of the Life of Alexander Henderson, First Lord Faringdon and of Henderson Administration
Quiller 1985   112pp illus index sources
Henderson Administration
815   §

Wainwright, David
Richard Ellis 1773-1973

Hutchinson Benham 1973   71pp illus
Ellis, Richard
834   BCROB

Wainwright, David
The Piano Makers

Hutchinson 1975   192pp illus index sources
Piano Makers
492   *

Wake, Joan
Mott, Hay & Anderson

Newman Neame 1965
Mott, Hay & Anderson
837   §

Wakefield, C C & Co
The First Fifty Years of Castrol:1909-1959

1959   48pp
Wakefield, C C & Co   Castrol
140   GHL

Wakefield, C C & Co
The Romance of Wakefields 1899-1949

    1949   72pp
    Wakefield, C C & Co   Castrol
    140   GHL
Waldron, Robin
G M S: A Short History 1925-76

    the firm 1977   32pp illus
    G M S Syndicate
                                                      *

Walker Bros (London)
Walker Bros (London) Ltd: A Brief History of the Business

    1948   35pp
    Walker Bros (London)
    740   GHL
Walker, Denis
G H Williamson & Sons, Providence Works, Worcester

    Worcester: the firm 1976   91pp illus
    Metal Box   Williamson, G H
    316   HWORCPL
Walker, Densmore
Some Account of Walker Bros (Wigan) Ltd

    typescript 1973   25pp
    Walker Bros (Wigan)
    325   WIGANPL
Walker, H C
Reminiscences of 70 Years in the Lift Industry

    1934   100pp
    Otis Elevator   Waygood-Otis
    325   GHL
Walker, Peter & Son
Walker's Warrington Ales: A History and Description of the Firm

    the firm 1897   80pp
    Walker, Peter & Son
    427   617   662   WARRPL
Walker, Selwyn Joseph Sykes
History of Joseph Sykes Brothers

    Huddersfield: typescript 1976   46pp
    Sykes, Joseph Bros
    431   HDSFDPL
Wall Paper Manufacturers
Wall Paper Manufacturers Ltd: The Pattern of a Great Organisation 1899-1949

    Manchester: the firm 1949   296pp illus
    Wall Paper Manufacturers
    255   472   *

428

Wall, T
>   *Wall's Way*
>
>   the firm ca1960   illus
>   Wall, T & Co
>   412   421   TAMESPL

Wallace, William
>   *Prescription for Partnership: A Study of Industrial Relations*
>
>   Pitman 1959   xvi 228pp
>   Rowntree & Co
>   421   *

Waller, Robert J
>   *The Dukeries Transformed: The Social and Political*
>   *Development of a Twentieth-Century Coalfield*
>   Oxford: Clarendon 1983   319pp index sources
>   National Coal Board
>   111   *

Wallis, G E & Sons
>   *A Century of Building 1860-1960:   also Wallis News 25-26,*
>   *1975-76 (includes history of S. Wales branch)*
>   Maidstone: nd   17pp
>   Wallis, G E & Sons
>   501   MRC

Wallis, Philip
>   *At the Sign of the Ship: Notes on the House of Longman*
>   *1724-1974*
>   Longmans Green 1974   viii 79pp illus index sources
>   Longman
>   475   §

Wallis, Thomas & Co
>   *A Hundred Years in Holborn*
>
>   the firm ca1926   24pp illus
>   Wallis, Thomas & Co
>   645   656   CAMDNPL

Walmsley (Bury) Group
>   *the House of Walmsley*
>
>   Bury: the firm 1961   30pp illus
>   Walmsley (Bury) Group
>   471   BOLTNPL

Walpamur Co
>   *The Walpamur Co Ltd , London and Darwen 1906-1956*
>
>   the firm 1956   34pp illus
>   Walpamur Co   Wall Paper Manufacturers
>   472   255   ABRDNPL

Walsall Lithographic Co
>   *Golden Jubilee of Seal Production*
>
>   Walsall: the firm 1964   23pp illus
>   Walsall Lithographic Co
>   495   475   WALSLPL

Walshaw, George R & Behrendt, Carl A J
The History of Appleby-Frodingham

the firm 1950   x 172pp illus
Appleby-Frodingham Steel Co   United Steel
221   *

Walters, Chas
Jubilee of Co-operation in Oldham 1900: A Combined History of the Equitable and Industrial Societies Limited
Manchester: C W S 1900   180pp illus
Oldham Equitable & Indust Co-op
656   OLDHMPL

Walters, R H
The Economic and Business History of the S Wales Steam Coal Industry 1840-1914
Oxford DPhil 1975
S Wales Steam Coal Industry
111

Wandsworth & District Gas Co
A Century of Progress 1834-1934

the firm 1934   44pp illus
Wandsworth & District Gas Co
162   *

Warburton, Ray
Electricity Generation in Bolton

typescript 1984   12pp sources
Bolton Electricty Dept
161   BOLTNPL

Warburtons
100 Years of Baking 1876-1976

the firm 1976   32pp illus
Warburtons Bakery
419   BOLTNPL

Ward, Donovan M
The Other Battle: Being a History of the Birmingham Small Arms Co Ltd
Birmingham: the firm 1946   180pp illus
B S A
329   351   363   * §

Ward, George
Fort Grunwick

Maurice Temple Smith 1977   123pp
Grunwick
493   *

Ward, T W
60 Years of Service 1878-1938

the firm 1938   illus
Ward, Thomas W
501   502   DERBYPL

Ward, T W
> *Outline of Progress: T W W, 1878-1953: Commemorating 75 Years of Service to Industry*
> Sheffield: the firm 1953   212pp illus
> Ward, Thomas W
> 313   362   501   502   621   * §

Ward, W Jesse
> *Jesse Ward, Native of Ipswich and Townsman of Croydon who Founded 'The Croydon Advertiser', Feb 13th, 1869*
> Croydon: the firm 1951   78pp illus
> Croydon Advertiser
> 475   *

Ward-Jackson, Cyril Henry
> *A History of Courtaulds: An Account of the Origin and Rise of Courtaulds Ltd and the American Viscose Corporation*
> Curwen Press 1941   ix 177pp illus
> Courtaulds   Viscose Corporation
> 430   *

Ward-Jackson, Cyril Henry
> *Stephens of Fowey: A Portrait of a Cornish Merchant Fleet 1867-1939*
> National Maritme Museum 1980   115pp illus index sources
> Stephens of Fowey
> 740   UBRIS

Ward-Jackson, Cyril Henry
> *The 'Cellophane' Story: Origins of a British Industrial Group*
> Bridgwater: the firm 1977   144pp illus index sources
> British Cellophane
> 483   251   BLPES

Warde, Edmund (ed)
> *The House of Dodwell: A Century of Achievement 1858-1958*
> the firm 1958   159pp
> Dodwell & Co
> 839   *

Wardle, Arthur C
> *Benjamin Bowring and his Descendants: A Record of Mercantile Achievement*
> Hodder & Stoughton 1938   229pp illus
> Bowring, C T & Co
> 832   *

Wardle, Arthur C
> *Steam Conquers the Pacific: A Record of Maritime Achievement 1840-1940*
> Hodder & Stoughton 1940   208pp illus
> Pacific Steam Navigation Co
> 740   *

Waring & Gillow
> *Gillow's: A Record of a Furnishing Firm during Two Centuries*
> the firm 1901   84pp
> Waring & Gillow
> 648   GHL

Warn, C R

>The Development of Motor Bus Services in Northumberland
>1904-1975
>Newcastle MA 1977
>Bus Services in Northumberland
>721

Warren, Henry

>The Story of the Bank of England: A History of English Banking
>and a Sketch of the Money Market
>Jordan & Sons 1903   251pp
>Bank of England
>814   §

Warren, James G H

>A Century of Locomotive Building by Robert Stephenson & Co
>1823-1923
>Newton Abbot: David & Charles 1970 vii 461pp illus
>Stephenson, Robert & Co
>362   *

Warren, K

>Iron and Steel

>see Buxton, N K & Aldcroft, D H (eds)
>Steel Industry
>221

Warren, Kenneth

>Chemical Foundations: The Alkali Industry in Britain to 1926

>Oxford: Clarendon 1980   viii 208pp illus index sources
>Brunner, Mond   United Alkali Co
>250

Warren, Kenneth

>The British Iron and Steel Sheet Industry since 1840

>Bell 1970   xvi 313pp illus
>Iron & Steel
>221   *

Warren, Kenneth

>The Sheffield Rail Trade 1861-1930

>Trans Inst Brit Geographers   vol 34 1964
>Sheffield Rail Trade
>221

Warren, P G

>One Hundred Years of Stockbroking 1851-1951

>the firm 1951   31pp
>Heseltine, Powell & Co
>831   UBRIS

Warrillow, Ernest James Dalzell

>History of Etruria, Staffordshire, England 1760-1951

>Stoke-on-Trent: Etruscan 1953   408pp
>Wedgwood, Josiah & Sons
>248

432

Waterhouse, Rachel Elizabeth
A Hundred Years of Engineering Craftsmanship: A Short History of Tangyes Ltd Smethwick 1857-1957
Smethwick: the firm 1957   109pp illus
Tangyes
328   * §

Waters, Sydney David
Shaw Savill Line: One Hundred Years of Trading

Christchurch, N Z: Whitcombe 1961   158pp illus index
Shaw Savill & Albion Co
740   UBRIS

Waterston, George & Sons
Two Hundred and Twenty Five Years: A History of George Waterston & Sons Limited 1752-1977
Edinburgh: the firm 1952   69pp illus
Waterston, George & Sons
653   §

Watford Observer
West Herts & Watford Observer Centenary 1863-1963

the firm 1963   pamphlet
Watford Observer
475   §

Watkins & Stafford
Watkins & Stafford Golden Jubilee 1902-1952

Peterborough: the firm nd   12pp illus
Watkins & Stafford
467   647   CAMBSPL

Watkins, Chris; Harvey, W & Senft, R
Shelley Potteries: The History & Production of a Staffordshire Family of Potters
Barrie & Jenkins 1980   176pp illus index sources
Shelley Potteries
248   * §

Watson, Arthur J
The First Fifty Years: Being the Story of Municipal Mutual Insurance Limited 1903-1953
the firm 1953
Municipal Mutual Insurance
820

Watson, Bernard
A Unique Society: A History of the Salvation Army Assurance Society
the firm 1968   135pp illus
Salvation Army Assurance Soc
820   *

Watson, J A
A Hundred Years of Sugar Refining: The Story of Love Lane Refinery 1872-1972
Liverpool: the firm 1973   155pp illus
Tate & Lyle
420   §

Watson, John Arthur Fergus
Savills: A Family and a Firm 1652-1977

Hutchinson Benham 1977   173pp illus index
Savills
834   *

Watson, Rowland
The House of Howard: The Story of an English Firm

the firm 1952   39pp illus
Howard, W W Brothers & Co
613   UBRIS

Watts, John I
The First 50 Years of Brunner, Mond & Co

Derby: the firm 1923   106pp illus
Brunner, Mond   I C I
250   UBRIS

Waugh, Alexander Raban
Merchants of Wine: Being a Centenary Account of the Fortunes of the House of Gilbey
Cassell 1957   135pp illus index
Gilbey, W & A
424   642   * §

Waugh, Alexander Raban
The Lipton Story: A Centennial Biography

Cassell 1951   277pp illus
Lipton
423   617   641   * §

Waugh, Arthur
A Hundred Years of Publishing: Being the Story of Chapman & Hall Ltd 1830-1930
Chapman & Hall 1930   xvii 326pp illus index sources
Chapman & Hall
475   *

Wear, Russell & Lees, Eric
Stephen Lewin and the Poole Foundry

Industrial Railway Soc 1978   101pp illus index sources
Lewin
362   *

Weatherill, Lorna Mary
One Hundred Years of Papermaking: An Illustrated History of the Guard Bridge Paper Co 1873-1973
the firm 1974   122pp illus index sources
Guard Bridge Paper Co
471   StBRD

Webb, C W
An Historical Record of N Corah & Sons Ltd, St Margaret's Works, Leicester
the firm ca1947   120pp illus
Corah, N
436   LEICSPL

Webb, H J
>The Story of Joseph Webb and Sons of Bury, Lancashire
1846-1970
1975   illus
Webb, Joseph & Sons
311   BURYPL

Webster, Eric
>The Record of a Continuous Progress: The 19th Century
Development of John Crossley & Sons...
from 'Industrial Archaeology'   15pp
Crossley, John & Sons
438   HLFXPL

Weeden, Cyril
>The Finances of an Early Nineteenth Century Glasshouse

Glass Technology   vol 26 no 3 1985
Phoenix Glassworks, Bristol
247   AVONPL

Weetch, Kenneth Thomas
>The Dowlais Iron Works and its Industrial Community
1760-1850
London MSc(Econ) 1963   242pp
Dowlais Iron Co
221   311

Weir, G & J
>A Fifty Years' Retrospect 1886-1936

the firm nd   24pp illus
Weir, G & J
320   UBRIS

Weir, Ronald B
>A History of the Scottish American Investment Company
Limited 1873-1973
Edinburgh: the firm 1973   36pp illus
Scot American Investment Co
815   839   850   EDNBRPL

Weir, Ronald B
>The Development of the Distilling Industry in Scotland in the
19th & Early 20th Centuries
Edinburgh PhD 1974
Distilling Industry in Scotland
424

Wellcome Foundation
>The Wellcome Centenary

'Times' Supplement 25 Aug 1953   47pp
Wellcome Foundation   Burroughs Wellcome
257   GHL

Wells, Frederick Arthur
>Hollins and Viyella: A Study in Business History

Newton Abbot: David & Charles 1968 264pp illus index sources
Hollins, William   Viyella
430   453   616   * §

Wells, Frederick Arthur

The British Hosiery and Knitwear Industry: Its History and Organisation

Newton Abbot: David & Charles 1972 256pp illus index sources

Hosiery and Knitwear

436   * §

West Calder Co-op

West Calder and its Co-operative Society: Issued as a Memento of the Society's Coming of Age 13th June 1896

Glasgow: Scottish C W S 1896   142pp illus

West Calder Co-op

656   WLOTHPL

West Country Brewery Holdings

200 Years of Brewing in the West Country

Cheltenham: the firm 1960   48pp illus

West Country Brewery Holdings

427   HWORCPL

West's Cornice Pole Co

West's Cornice Pole Co Ltd 1889-1949

Salford: the firm 1949   8pp illus

West's Cornice Pole Co

463   §

West, Allen

The Allen West Story 1910-1960: Fifty Years of Electrical Control Gear Development

Brighton: the firm 1960   60pp illus

Allen West

342   §

West, Richard

River of Tears: The Rise of the Rio Tinto-Zinc Mining Corporation

Earth Island 1972   201pp sources

Rio Tinto

210   224   839   *

Westall, Oliver M (ed)

The Historian and the Business of Insurance

Manchester: M U P 1984   ix 196pp illus index sources

Norwich Union   Standard Life Assurance

820   *

Western Motor Works (Chislehurst)

The Horseless Carriage

Chislehurst: the firm 1955   30pp illus

Western Motor Works

614   651   671   BROMPL

Weston-Webb, W F M

The Autobiography of a British Yarn Merchant

Cayme Press 1929   247pp illus

Holland & Webb   Hollins, William

616   630   *

Wheldon, Frederick W
A Norvic Century and the Men who Made It 1846-1946

Norwich: Jarrold 1946   160pp illus
Norvic Shoe Co
451   *

Whessoe
The History of Whessoe

the firm nd   26pp illus
Whessoe
320   BCROB

Whitaker, John
The Best: A History of H H Martyn and Co

Cheltenham: author 1985   349pp illus index
Martyn, H H & Co   Gloster Aircraft Co
221   245   311   364   465   CHELTPL

Whitbourn, Frank
Mr. Lock of St James's Street: His Continuing Life and Changing Times
Heinemann 1971   xiii 192pp illus index sources
Lock of St James's Street
453   * §

Whitbread
The Story of Whitbreads

the firm 1964   54pp illus
Whitbread & Co
427   662   ENFLDPL

White, Frank James
The Hargreaves Story: Including a Full History of the 'Cotswold Cider Company'
Bodley Head 1953   192pp
Cotswold Cider Company
426   800   * §

White, Horace
"Fossetts": A Record of Two Centuries of Engineering

Bromborough: the firm 1958   96pp illus sources
Fawcett Preston & Co
320   *

White, Horace
Battleship Wharf

Blyth: the firm 1961   vi 68pp illus
Hughes Bolckow
361   * §

White, J S
Whites of Cowes, Shipbuilders

Cowes, I o W: the firm ca1950   104pp illus
White, J Samuel & Co
361   §

White, John
The John White Story

    Higham Ferrers: the firm 1969   28pp illus
    White, John
    451   NHPTNPL
White, O'Loughlin Molly
Belfast: The Story of Shorts' Big Lifter

    Leicester: Midlands Counties 1984   124pp illus
    Short Brothers
    364   *
White, Valerie
Wimpey: The First Hundred Years 1880-1980

    the firm 1980   48pp illus
    Wimpey
    500   §
Whitechapel Bellfoundry
The History of the Whitechapel Bellfoundry

    Trans London & Middx Arch Soc   no 5 1923
    Whitechapel Bellfoundry
    311   GHL
Whitehead Aircraft
The New Dominion: The Book of Whitehead Aircraft, Richmond

    Richmond: the firm 1917   24pp illus
    Whitehead Aircraft
    364   *
Whitehead, David C & Edwards, Lawrence
Packhouse: The Story of E K P

    the firm 1970   39pp illus
    East Kent Packers
    10   BCROB
Whitehead, David Charles
Gardners of Patricroft 1868-1968

    Newman Neame 1968   40pp illus
    Gardners
    328   * §
Whitehead, Robert Arthur
A Century of Service: An Illustrated History of Eddison Plant Ltd
    Belton, Lincs.: the firm 1968   40pp illus
    Eddison Plant
    842   *
Whitehead, Robert Arthur
Garrett 200: A Bicentenary History of Garretts of Leiston 1778-1978
    Brentford: Transport Bookman 1978 248pp
    Garrett, Richard
    321   *

Whitehead, Robert Arthur
Garretts of Leiston: 1778-1964

Percival Marshall 1964   319pp illus index sources
Garrett, Richard
321   * §

Whitehead, Robert Arthur
Wallis and Steevens: A History

Farnham: Road Locomotive Soc 1983   82pp illus sources
Wallis & Steevens
321   325

Whitehurst, Henry and Sons
Progress 1792-1960

Bolton: the firm 1960   8pp illus
Whitehurst, Henry & Sons
432   BOLTNPL

Whiteley, John & Sons
Centenary Commemoration 17th July 1891

Halifax: the firm 1891   32pp
Whiteley, John & Sons
431   HLFXPL

Whitelock, G C H
250 Years in Coal: The History of Barber, Walker and Company Limited 1680-1946
Derby: the firm 1955
Barber, Walker & Co
111

Whiting, R C
The View from Cowley: The Impact of Industrialisation upon Oxford 1918-1939
Oxford: Clarendon 1983   ix 214pp illus index sources
Morris Motors   Pressed Steel
350   *

Whittaker, F Garth
Edward Marsden: The Story of a Company

the firm 1978   66pp illus
Marsden, Edward   Holden, Arthur & Sons
471   StBRD

Whitting, Harriet Anna
Alfred Booth 1834-1914: Some Memories, Letters and other Family Records
Liverpool: Henry Young 1917   214pp illus
Booth, Alfred
611   770   *

Whymper, W N
The Royal Exchange Assurance: An Historical Sketch

the firm 1895   36pp
Royal Exchange Assurance
820   *

Whyte, A J A
    Swallow to S S to Jaguar

    1976
    Jaguar Cars   Swallow
    351   363   BLPES
Whyte, Adam Gowans
    Forty Years of Electrical Progress: The Story of G E C

    Benn 1930   166pp illus
    G E C
    340   *
Whyte, Andrew
    Jaguar: The History of a Great British Car

    Wellingborough: P Stephens 1985   252pp illus index
    Jaguar Cars   S S Cars
    351   * §
Whyte, Lewis
    One Increasing Purpose: The Annals of an Investor

    Hutchinson Benham nd   141pp index
    Buckmaster & Moore
    831   §
Wigfull Mill
    The Wigfull Mill 1750-1948

                            48pp
    Wigfull Mill
    416   SHEFFPL
Wiggin, Henry
    History of Henry Wiggin & Co Ltd 1835-1935: Centenary
    Publication
    the firm 1935
    Wiggin, Henry
    250   DBB
Wiggins Teape and Co
    Wiggins Teape and Co(1919) Ltd: Glory Paper Mills, Wooburn
    Green, High Wycombe, Bucks.
    High Wycombe: the firm 1956   illus
    Wiggins Teape Group
    471   BCRL
Wiggins Teape Group
    The Dartford Paper Mills

    the firm nd   40pp illus
    Wiggins Teape Group
    471   *
Wigham, Eric Leonard
    The Power to Manage: A History of the Engineering Employers'
    Federation
    Macmillan 1973   x 326pp
    Engineering Employers' Federation
    963   *

Wilkins, **Charles**
The History of the Iron, Steel, Tinplate and other Trades of Wales
Mrthyr Tidfil: J Williams 1903   vi 448pp illus
Iron & Steel in Wales
220   *

Wilkins, **Charles**
The South Wales Coal Trade and its Allied Industries

Cardiff: Owen 1888   xii 405pp
South Wales Coal Trade
111   612   *

Wilkins, **Mira**
The History of European Multinationals: A New Look

J European Econ Hist   1986

Wilkins, **Mira**
The Making of Multinational Enterprise: American Business Abroad from 1914 to 1970
Cambridge, Mass: Harvard U P 1976   xvi 590pp index sources
Multinational Enterprise   Ford Motor
351   *

Willcock, **H D(ed) for Mass Observation**
Brown's and Chester: Portrait of a Shop 1780-1946

Lindsay Drummond   vii 255pp illus
Brown's of Chester
645   647   * §

Willcox, **W H**
Willcox's Centenary 1878-1978: People, Places and Events over 100 Years
1978   36pp illus
Willcox, W H
614   SWKPL

Willesden **Dux**
The Romance of Willesden Dux Oriental, likewise Anti-Gas

the firm 1941   177pp illus
Willesden Paper & Canvas Works   Dux Chemical Solutions
256   455   471   §

Willett, **William**
Willetts of Sloane Square: A Brief History

reprint ca1960
Willetts of Sloane Square
501   KENSPL

Williams **& Womersley**
Williams & Womersley of Wakefield

Wakefield: the firm 1952   32pp illus
Williams & Womersley
311   UBRIS

Williams **Deacon's Bank**
Williams Deacon's 1771-1970

Manchester: the firm 1971 180pp illus index
Williams Deacon's Bank Williams & Glyn's Bank
814 §

Williams, **Alfred Harry**
No Name on the Door: A Memoir of Gordon Selfridge

W H Allen 1956 255pp illus index
Selfridges
656 *

Williams, **C J**
The Llandudno Copper Mines

Nelson: Northern Mine Research 1979 54pp
Llandudno Old, New & Ty Gwyn
210 GWYNPL

Williams, **D M**
Liverpool Merchants and the Cotton Trade 1820-1850

see Harris, J R (ed)
Liverpool Merchants & Cotton
432 611 740

Williams, **David James**
Capitalist Combination in the Coal Industry

Labour Publishing 1924 176pp
Coal Industry
111 *

Williams, **David M**
Merchanting in the First Half of the Nineteenth Century: The Liverpool Timber Trade
Business History vol VIII no 2 1966
Liverpool Timber Trade
613 630 839

Williams, **Edmund**
The Story of Sunlight 1884-1984

the firm 1984 34pp illus
Unilever Lever Brothers
258 838 §

Williams, **Harry**
Historical Notes Showing the Trends of Development of the Park Gate Works from 1823 to 1945
typescript 1982 54pp illus
Park Gate Iron & Steel Co
221 ROTHMPL

Williams, **Iolo Aneurin**
The Firm of Cadbury 1831-1931

Constable 1931 ix 295pp illus index
Cadbury Bros British Cocoa & Chocolate Co
421 *

442

Williams, **L J**
The Monmouthshire and South Wales Coalowners' Association
1873-1914
Wales MA 1957
South Wales Coalowners' Assoc
111
Williams, **M E**
Many a Lifetime: A History of Aristoc Ltd, Langley Mill

1954
Aristoc
436
Williams, **Mari E W**
Choices in Oil Refining: The Case of B P 1900-1960

Business History   vol XXVI no 3 1984
B P   Anglo Persian Oil Co
130   140
Williams, **Mari E W**
Innovation in Scientific Instruments: A Key Science-based
Sector
see Liebenau, Jonathan (ed)

370   371
Williams, **N**
Centenary History of the City of London Building Society
1862-1962
1962
City of London Building Soc
815   GHL
Williams, **Samuel & Sons**
A Company's Story in its Setting: Samuel Williams & Sons Ltd
1855-1955
the firm 1955   88pp illus
Williams, Samuel & Sons   Dagenham Dock
320   740   763   * §
Williams, **Trevor I**
A History of the British Gas Industry

Oxford U P 1981   304pp illus index sources
Gas Industry
162   * §
Williams, **William Emrys**
Allen Lane: A Personal Portrait

Bodley Head 1973   96pp index
Allen Lane   Penguin Books
475   *
Williams, **William Emrys**
The Penguin Story MCMXXXV-MCMLVI

Harmondsworth: Penguin 1956   124pp illus
Penguin Books
475   *

Williams-Thomas, R S
The Crystal Years: A Tribute to the Skills and Artistry of Stevens and Williams, Royal Brierley Crystal
Brierley Hill: the firm 1983   80pp illus index
Stevens & Williams
247   *

Williamson, Geoffrey
Wheels within Wheels: The Story of the Starleys of Coventry

Bles 1966   160pp illus index sources
Starley, J A & Co
363   UBRIS

Williamson, J W
A British Railway behind the Scenes: A Study in the Science of Industry
Benn 1933   ix 213pp illus
London Midland & Scottish Rly
710   *

Williamson, James & Son
Williamsons of Lancaster: A Centenary Memoir

Lancaster: the firm 1944
Williamson, James & Son   Storey Brothers & Co
483   *

Willis, W G
Skinningrove Iron Company Ltd: A History

the firm ca1968   46pp illus
Skinningrove Iron Co
221   UBRIS

Willis, W G
South Durham Steel & Iron Co. Ltd

the firm 1969   ix 54pp illus
South Durham Steel
221   §

Willis-Fear, M J W
The History of the Pottery Firm of W H Goss of Stoke-on-Trent

the firm 1965   pamphlet
Goss, W H
248   §

Willmer, Edgar Wrayford
Family Business: The Story of Willmer Brothers & Haram Ltd

Birkenhead: the firm 1961   86pp illus
Willmer Brothers & Haram
475   * §

Willmott, Frank G
Bricks and Brickies

Rainham: Meresborough Books 1977   x 78pp illus
Eastwoods
241   726   *

Willmott, John Edward
A Short History of the Firm of Thomas Walker and Son Limited,
Birmingham, Nautical Instrument Makers
Birmingham: the firm 1951   27pp illus
Walker, Thomas & Son
371   *

Willoughby's
Willoughby's: A Century of Good Service 1850-1950

the firm nd
Willoughby's
642   661   SKPTPL

Willoughby, Joan
A Short History of Willoughby & Sons, est. 1845

Bournemouth: typescript 1984   48pp
Willoughby & Sons
834   CROYPL

Wills, John
Wilkinson & Riddell Limited 1851-1951

Birmingham: the firm 1951   64pp illus sources
Wilkinson & Riddell
645   * §

Willson, B F
James Cocks and Family: 'Reading Sauce'

typescript 1981   36pp illus sources
Cocks, James & Sons
423   BERKSPL

Wilson
Wilson's Cooperage Co: The Story of Wilson's Cooperage

1965   illus
Wilson's Cooperage Co
464   SWKPL

Wilson Brothers Bobbin Co
Wilson Brothers Bobbin Co: One Hundred Years 1823-1923

Liverpool: the firm ca1924   77pp illus
Wilson Brothers Bobbin Co
323   465   UBRIS

Wilson, A S
The Consett Iron Company Limited: A Case Study in Victorian
Business History
Durham MPhil 1973
Consett Iron Co
221

Wilson, Ambrose
The Ambron Story: Biography of a Business

the firm 1961   37pp illus
Wilson, Ambrose   Ambron
453   656   §

Wilson, Andrew
The Concorde Fiasco

Harmondsworth: Penguin 1973   157pp
British Aircraft Corporation
364   *

Wilson, Arnold T & Levy, Hermann J
Industrial Assurance: An Historical and Critical Study

Oxford: O U P 1937   xxxiii 519pp
Industrial Assurance
820   *

Wilson, Charles
First with the News: The History of W H Smith 1792-1972

Jonathan Cape 1985   416pp illus index sources
Smith, W H & Son
619   653   *

Wilson, Charles
Management and Policy in Large-Scale Enterprise: Lever Brothers and Unilever 1918-38
Oxford: Clarendon 1977
Lever Brothers   Unilever
257   258   411   414

Wilson, Charles
The History of Unilever: A Study in Economic Growth and Social Change
Cassell 1954   2 vols index sources
Unilever   Lever Brothers
257   258   411   414   * §

Wilson, Charles
Unilever 1945-1965: Challenge & Response in the Post-War Industrial Revolution
Cassell 1968   xii 290pp index sources
Unilever   Lever Brothers
257   258   411   414   * §

Wilson, Charles & Reader, William
Men and Machines: A History of D Napier & Son Engineers Ltd. 1808-1958
Weidenfeld & Nicolson   !87pp illus index sources
Napier D & Son
364   320   * §

Wilson, Charles Henry
A Man and his Times: A Memoir of Sir Ellis Hunter

Newman Neame 1962   53pp
Dorman Long
221   *

Wilson, Elena
The Story of the Blue Back Chart 1670-1937

the firm 1937   40pp illus
Imray, Laurie, Norie & Wilson
475   837   * §

446

Wilson, Geoffrey
London United Tramways: A History 1874-1933

Allen & Unwin 1971   240pp illus index sources
London United Tramways
721

Wilson, George F
The Old Days of Price's Patent Candle Co Ltd

James Gilbert 1876   207pp sources
Price's Patent Candle Co
259   WANDSPL

Wilson, Ian
John Kelly: An History

Belfast: the firm   44pp illus
Kelly, John
612   654   740   NEELBPL

Wilson, Ian
Neills of Bangor

author 1982   82pp
Neills of Bangor
612   654   740   NEELBPL

Wilson, J F
*The Ferrantis and the Growth of the Electrical Industry
1882-1914*
Manchester PhD 1980
Ferranti
340

Wilson, John
*A Strategy of Expansion and Combination: Dick, Kerr & Co
1897-1914*
Business History   vol XXVII no 1 1985
Dick, Kerr & Co
340

Wilson, Joseph
*House of Wilson of Denton: Makers of Distinguished Hats since
1872*
the firm 1947
Wilson, Joseph & Sons
453   TAMESPL

Wilson, Martyn & Spink, Karen
*Coles 100 Years: The Growth Story of Europe's Leading Crane
Manufacturer 1879-1979*
Uxbridge: the firm 1978   63pp illus
Acrow   Coles Cranes
325   §

Wilson, Paul N
*Gilkes's 1853 to 1975: 122 Years of Water Turbine and Pump
Manufacture*
Trans Newcomen Soc   vol 47 1974-76
Gilkes's
328   342   353   §

Wilson, Richard G
    Greene King: A Business and Family History

        Bodley Head 1983   xiii 338pp illus index sources
        Greene King
        427   662   * §

Wilson, Ronald E
    Two Hundred Precious Metal Years: A History of the Sheffield
    Smelting Company Limited 1760-1960
        Ernest Benn 1960   xxii 316pp illus index sources
        Sheffield Smelting Co
        224   *

Wilson, Ross
    The House of Sanderson

        Edinburgh: the firm 1963   108pp illus
        Sanderson, William
        424   EDNBRPL

Wilson, Sons & Co
    Wilson, Sons & Co Ltd 1837-1950: An Historical and
    Descriptive Account of the Organisation
        1950   44pp
        Wilson, Sons & Co
        839   GHL

Windsor, David Burns
    The Quaker Enterprise: Friends in Business

        Frederick Muller 1980   176pp illus index
        Coalbrookdale Co   Lloyds Bank
        221   257   419   421   814   *

Winkler, John Kennedy
    Tobacco Tycoon: The Story of James Buchanan Duke

        New York: Random House 1942   337pp
        British American Tobacco
        429   *

Winsbury, Rex
    Thomson McLintock & Co.: The First Hundred Years

        the firm 1977   xi 164pp illus
        Thomson McLintock
        836   §

Winton, J R
    Lloyds Bank 1918-1969

        Oxford: O U P 1982   viii 203pp illus index sources
        Lloyds Bank
        814   * §

Wisdom, T H & Riddihough, N E
    50 Years of Progress: The History of the Automotive Products
    Organisation over the past 50 Years
        Leamington Spa: the firm 1970   48pp illus
        Automotive Products
        353   MRC

Wise and Co

Centenary of Wise and Company in the Philippines 1826-1926

the firm nd 123pp
Wise & Co
839 UBRIS

Wise, S

Painton 1935-1956

Northampton: the firm 1956 40pp illus
Painton & Co
344 NHPTNPL

Withers, Hartley

National Provincial Bank 1833 to 1933

the firm 1933 xvii 90pp illus
National Provincial Bank
814 * §

Withers, Hartley

Pioneers of British Life Assurance

Staples Press 1951 112pp index
United Kingdom Provident Ins London Assurance
820 §

Wood, Alan

Mr. Rank: A Study of J Arthur Rank and British Films

Hodder & Stoughton 1952 228pp
Rank Organisation
971 *

Wood, Alan

The True History of Lord Beaverbrook

Heinemann 1965 xiii 359pp illus
Express Newspapers Beaverbrook Press
475 *

Wood, F A S & Cressey, S

Croda - The Fastest Growing Name: A History of the First Fifty Years of a Chemical Company 1925-1975
the firm nd
Croda
256 UBRIS

Woodall, Doris

A Short History of the House of Kent: G B Kent & Sons Ltd, Brush Manufacturers Established 1777
the firm 1959 50pp illus
Kent, G B & Sons
466 * §

Woodall-Duckham

Woodall-Duckham 1903-1978

the firm 1978
Woodall-Duckham
320

Woodhouse, G B
Hull, Blyth & Company Limited: A Short History

the firm 1979   60pp sources
Hull, Blyth & Co   Union-Castle
740   §

Woodruff, William
The Rise of the British Rubber Industry during the Nineteenth Century
Liverpool: L U P 1958   xvii 246pp illus
Moulton & Co
451   481   *

Woods, Oliver & Bishop, James
The Story of The Times: Bicentenary Edition 1785-1985

Michael Joseph 1985   392pp illus index
Times Newspapers
475   * §

Woodward, Herbert William
Art, Feat and Mystery: The Story of Thomas Webb & Sons, Glassmakers
Stourbridge: Mark and Moody 1978   61pp illus index sources
Webb, Thomas & Sons
247   *

Woodward, Herbert William
The Story of Edinburgh Crystal

Penicuik: the firm 1984   v 92pp illus index
Dema Glass   Edinburgh Crystal
247   *

Woolley, James
Woolleys of Manchester: A Record of 150 Years in Pharmacy

Manchester: the firm 1946   32pp illus
Woolley, James & Sons   British Drug Houses
257   *

Woolworth
Woolworth in Britain

the firm 1959
Woolworth, F W
656

Woolworth
Woolworth's First 75 Years: The Story of Everybody's Store

the firm 1954   62pp
Woolworth, F W
656   *

Workington Iron and Steel Co
Workington Iron and Steel Co: Branch of the United Steel Companies Ltd
Workington: the firm nd
Workington Iron & Steel Co   United Steel
221   UBRIS

Workman, Clark
>*Shipbuilding at Belfast 1880-1933*

>Belfast: the firm 1935
>Workman, Clark
>361

Worsley, Frank A & Griffith, Glyn
>*The Romance of Lloyd's from Coffee-House to Palace*

>Hutchinson 1932   292pp illus index
>Lloyd's of London
>820   * §

Worthington-Simpson
>*Worthington-Simpson Ltd: A History of Worthington-Simpson Ltd and the Simpson Family*
>ca1970   35pp
>Worthington-Simpson
>328   GHL

Wrangham, Cuthbert Edward
>*The History of Shorts Is the History of Aviation*

>Belfast: the firm 1968
>Short Brothers
>361   364   RAeS

Wright & Sons
>*The Story of a Family Business: Ponders End Mill*

>Enfield: the firm 1963   15pp illus
>Wright & Sons
>416   ENFLDPL

Wright, Charles & Fayle, C Ernest
>*A History of Lloyd's: From the Founding of Lloyd's Coffee House to the Present Day*
>Macmillan 1928   xxi 475pp illus index
>Lloyd's of London
>820   *

Wright, Louise
>*The Road from Aston Cross: An Industrial History 1875-1975*

>Leamington Spa: the firm 1975   79pp illus
>Smedley-HP Foods   Midland Vinegar Co
>414   423   §

Wright, P E
>*75 Years of History: Published by Ernest Wright & Son Ltd on the Occasion of their 75th Anniversary 1977*
>Sheffield: S Yorkshire Printers 1977
>Wright, Ernest & Son
>221

Wrights of Richmond
>*Wrights of Richmond 1877-1937: Sixty Years of Progress*

>Ed J Burrow 1937   40pp illus
>Wrights of Richmond
>656   RCHMDPL

Wrottesley, John
The Great Northern Railway

Batsford 1979-81 3 vols illus index sources
Great Northern Railway British Rail
710 *

Xenos, Stefanos
*Depredations or Overend, Gurney & Co and the Greek & Oriental
Steam Navigation Company*
the author 1869 viii 377pp
Overend, Gurney & Co Greek & Oriental Steam Navigation Co
740 814 839 §

Xylonite Group
Fifty Years 1877-1927

the firm 1927
British Xylonite Co Xylonite Group
251 483 HACKPL

Yale Security Products
Yale News: Centenary Issue 1868-1968

the firm nd 19pp illus
Yale Security Products Scovill
316 WALSLPL

Yarrow
Yarrow and Company Limited 1865-1977

Glasgow: the firm 1977 158pp illus index
Yarrow
361 *

Yarrow, Lady Eleanor C & Barnes, E C
Alfred Yarrow: His Life and Work

E Arnold 1923 xv 328pp illus
Yarrow
361 *

Yates Brothers Wine Lodges
*Yates Brothers Wine Lodges Ltd 1884-1984: A Century's
Reputation for Honesty, Excellence and Purity*
Manchester: the firm 1984 71pp illus sources
Yates Brothers Wine Lodges
662 §

Yeo, Alfred William
*Atlas Reminiscent: An Account of the Development of the Atlas
Assurance Company 1808-1908*
J M Dent 1908 83pp illus
Atlas Assurance Co
820 * §

Ynysybwl Co-operative Society
*The Gleaming Vision: Being the History of the Ynysybwl
Co-operative Society Ltd 1889-1954*
Pontypridd: the firm 1954 156pp illus
Ynysybwl Co-operative Soc
656 UBRIS

452

Yonekawa, Shin-ichi
The Strategy and Structure of Cotton and Steel Enterprises in Britain 1900-1939
see Fuji Conference 1, 1974
Cotton and Steel Enterprises
221   432

Yorkshire Insurance Co
The Centenary of the Yorkshire Insurance Company Limited 1824-1924
York: the firm nd   51pp illus
Yorkshire Insurance Co
820   UBRIS

Young, Desmond
Member for Mexico: A Biography of Weetman Pearson, First Viscount Cowdray
Cassell 1966   279pp illus
Pearson, S & Son
130   500   *

Young, Edward Preston
Forty Years of Motoring 1919-1959: The Story of National Benzole
Stanley Paul 1959   190pp illus
National Benzole Co
120   162   612   652   *

Young, Fred H
A Century of Carpet Making 1839-1939

Glasgow: the firm 1943   80pp
Templeton, James & Co
438   UBRIS

Young, James
Co-operation In Uddingston 1861-1911

Uddingston: the firm 1911   121pp illus
Uddingston Co-operative Soc
656   MTHWLPL

Young, Peter
Power of Speech: A History of Standard Telephones and Cables 1883-1983
Allen & Unwin 1983   x 220pp illus index sources
S T C
344   341   * §

Young, Stephen & Hood, Neil
Chrysler UK: A Corporation in Transition

New York: Praeger 1977   xix 342pp index sources
Chrysler   Rootes
350   *

Younger, George
A Short History of George Younger & Son Ltd 1762-1925

Alloa: the firm 1925   35pp illus
Younger, George
427   CLKMNPL

Youngs, Crawshay & Youngs
Coronation Souvenir Brochure

the firm 1936   100pp illus
Youngs, Crawshay & Youngs
427   NRFLKPL

4   Company index

600 Group	Cohen, George
600 Group	Cohen, George
A E C	A E C
A E I	Dutton, P A
A E I	Jones, Robert & Marriott, Oliver
A E I	Latham, Joseph
A P V	Dummett, G A
A S E A	Fuller Electrical & Manufacturing Co
A S E A	Fuller Electrical & Manufacturing Co
Abbey Line	Heaton, Paul Michael
Abbey National	Bellman, Charles Harold
Abbey Road Soc	Bellman, Charles Harold
Aberdare Cables	Aberdare Cables
Aberdare Canal	Davies, Alun C
Aberdeen Airport	Ferguson, James D
Aberdeen Banking Co	Munn, Charles W
Aberdeen Granite Mfrs' Assoc	Grant, William S
Aberdeen Journals	Cormack, Alexander Allan
Aberdeen Lime Co	McRobb, John
Aberdeen Line	Cornford, Leslie Cope
Aberdeen Savings Bank	Aberdeen Savings Bank
Aberdeen Savings Bank	Jaffrey, Thomas
Aberdeen Shore Porters' Soc	Gordon, George
Aberdeen Shore Porters' Soc	Gordon, George
Aberdeen Steam Navigation Co	Lee, Clive Howard
Aberdeen University Press	Keith, Alexander
Aberdeenshire Canal	Morgan, Susan L
Aberford Railway	Hudson, Graham S
Accident Insurance	Dinsdale, Walter Arnold

Accles & Pollock	Accles & Pollock
Accles & Pollock	Accles & Pollock
Accrington Industrial Co-op Soc	Haslam, James
Accrington Industrialists	Crossley, Richard Shaw
Ackermann Publications	Ford, John
Acrow	Acrow
Acrow	Acrow
Acrow	Wilson, Martyn & Spink, Karen
Adams, William	Adams, Percy Walter Lewis
Adams, William	Nicholls, Robert
Adams, William	Peel, David
Adams, William	Turner, William
Adamsez	Adamsez
Adamsez	Benwell Community Project
Adamsez	Herson, John D
Addis	Beaver, Patrick
Advertising	Nevett, Terry R
Advertising Agencies	Treasure, John A P
Aerialite	Aerialite
African Steam Ship Co	Davies, Peter Neville
Agnew's	Agnew, Geoffrey
Agricultural Engineering Industry	Lines, C J
Aircraft Industry	Fearon, Peter
Aircraft Industry	Robertson, A J
Aircraft Mfr	Fearon, P
Airdrie Savings Bank	Blake, George
Airdrie Savings Bank	Knox, James
Airframe Industry	Fearon, Peter
Airspeed	Middleton, D H
Aiton & Co (Derby)	Aiton & Co
Alabaster Passmore	Repath, Elizabeth
Albanian Coaches	Read, Ian F
Albright & Wilson	Albright & Wilson
Albright & Wilson	Threlfall, Richard Evelyn
Alcester Waterworks Co	Johnson, C J
Alden, Fred. G	Mann, Cecil
Alexander, W & Sons	Brown, Stewart J
Alexanders	Alexanders
Alexandra Towing Co	Hallam, Winfield B
Alhambra Theatre	Disher, Maurice W & Bruce, Michael W S
Alkali Industry	Lischka, J R
Allen & Hanbury	Chapman-Huston, W W Desmond M & Cripps,
Allen & Hanbury	Cripps, Ernest Charles
Allen & Hanbury	Liebenau, Jonathan M
Allen & Hanbury	Stander, C S
Allen & Unwin	Mumby, Frank A & Stallybrass, Frances H S
Allen & Unwin	Unwin, Philip
Allen & Unwin	Unwin, Stanley
Allen & Unwin	Unwin, Stanley
Allen Lane	Morpurgo, Jack Eric
Allen Lane	Williams, William Emrys
Allen Line	Jones, Clement Wakefield
Allen West	West, Allen
Allen, David	Allen, William Edward David
Allen, David	Gould, Roger

Allen, Edgar	Simons, Eric Norman
Allen, John & Son (Oxford)	Launchbury, G T
Allen, Thomas	Allen, Thomas
Alley & MacLellan	Hughes, William J & Thomas, Joseph L
Alliance Assurance	Alliance Assurance
Alliance Assurance	Schooling, William
Alliance Box Co	Alliance Box Co
Allied Breweries	Allied Breweries
Allied Ironfounders	Raistrick, Arthur
Allied Ironfounders	Raistrick, Arthur
Allied Ironfounders	Tripp, Basil Howard
Allied Suppliers	Lipton
Allied Suppliers	Mathias, Peter
Alloa Brewery Co	McMaster, Charles
Alloa Co-operative Society	Alloa Co-operative Society
Alloa Coal Co	Carvel, John Lees
Alloa Glass Work Co	Carvel, John Lees
Allsops	Gourvish, T R & Wilson, R G
Alsford, J	Beaver, Patrick
Aluminium Corporation	Aluminium Corporation
Aluminium Corporation	Aluminium Corporation
Alva Co-operative Bazaar	Gordon, Thomas Crouther
Amalgamated Cotton Mills Trust	Amalgamated Cotton Mills Trust
Amalgamated Press	Bridges, T C & Tiltman, H H
Amalgamated Press	Burnham, Lord (Lawson, Edward Frederick)
Amalgamated Press	Camrose, Lord (Berry, William Ewert)
Amalgamated Press	Dilnot, George
Ambron	Wilson, Ambrose
Amicable and Fraternal Soc	Howard, R B
Anchor Boot Society	Mann, Amos
Anchor Line	Jones, Clement Wakefield
Anchor Line	McLellan, R S
Anderson, Boyes & Co	Carvel, John Lees
Anderson, C F & Son	Muir, Augustus
Andrews, Isaac & Sons	Andrews, Sydney; Burls, John (ed)
Anelay, William	Stapleton, Henry Edward Champneys(ed)
Anglia Match Co	Littler, Eric Raymond
Anglo American Corporation	Jessup, Edward
Anglo Persian Oil Co	Williams, Mari E W
Anglo-Austrian Bank	Cottrell, P L
Anglo-Iranian Oil Co	Stoff, Michael B
Anglo-Persian Oil Co	Jones, Geoffrey
Anglo-Persian Oil Co	Jones, Geoffrey
Anglo-Persian Oil Co	Kent, Marian
Anglo-Persian Oil Co	Stivers, William
Anglo-South American Bank	Anglo-South American Bank
Angus, George & Co	Angus, George & Co
Anthracite Trade	Hare, A E C
Appleby-Frodingham Steel Co	Walshaw, George R & Behrendt, Carl A J
Archdale, James	Archdale
Arden & Cobden Hotels	Enfield, A L
Argentine Meat	Hanson, Simon G
Argyll Motors	Montagu of Beaulieu, Lord J W D S
Aristoc	Allen, Philip
Aristoc	Williams, M E

Armaments	Davenport-Hines, Richard P T
Armstrong Siddeley Motors	Redman, M
Armstrong, Whitworth & Co	Cochrane, Alfred
Armstrong, Whitworth & Co	Davenport-Hines, Richard P T
Armstrong, Whitworth & Co	Dougan, David
Armstrong, Whitworth & Co	Irving, R J
Army & Navy Co-operative Soc	Army & Navy Stores
Arnold, E J & Son	Arnold, E J & Son
Arnold, William & Son	Arnold, H
Arrol, Sir William & Co	Arrol, Sir William & Co
Arthur, J F & Co	Barclay, John Francis
Artizans' & General Properties Co	Artizans
Ashmore, Benson, Pease & Co	Power-Gas
Ashton & Mitchell	Brereton, Austin
Ashton Bros & Co	Ashton Bros
Ashton Bros & Co	Fletch, A M
Ashworth	Boyson, Rhodes
Ashworth	Boyson, Rhodes
Ashworth and Parker	Ashworth and Parker
Ashworth, G L & Bros.	Haggar, Reginald George
Asiatic Petroleum	Naylor, Stanley (ed)
Asprey & Co	Hillier, Bevis
Aspro-Nicholas	Morgan, Bryan Stanford
Aspro-Nicholas	Smith, R Grenville & Barrie, Alexander
Assam Company	Antrobus, Hinson Allan
Assoc Owners of City Properties	Associated Owners of City Properties
Associated Equipment Co	A E C
Associated Lead	Rowe, David John
Associated Newspapers	Ferris, Paul
Associated Newspapers	Hubback, David
Associated Newspapers	Owen, Louise
Associated Newspapers	Pound, Reginald & Harmsworth, A Geoffrey
Associated Paper Mills	Allan, Charles M
Associated Portland Cement	Associated Portland Cement
Atco	Pugh, Charles H
Atco	Pugh, Charles H
Atkins of Hinckley	Atkins of Hinckley
Atkinson, Richard & Co	Clarke, Philip
Atlantic Passenger Services	Bonsor, Noel Reginald Pixell
Atlantic Passenger Services	Bonsor, Noel Reginald Pixell
Atlantic Telegraph Co	Bright, Edward B & Charles
Atlantic Telegraph Co	Field, Henry Martyn
Atlas Assurance Co	Yeo, Alfred William
Atlas Forge	Brough, Joseph
Atomic Energy	Gowing, Margaret
Attwoods & Spooner	Moss, D J
Austin Motor Co	Austin Motor Co
Austin Motor Co	Austin Motor Co
Austin Motor Co	Church, Roy Anthony
Austin Motor Co	Lambert, Zeta E & Wyatt, Robert J
Austin Reed	Reed, Austin
Austin, James & Sons(Dewsbury)	Austin, James
Austin, Stephen	Moran, James Charles
Automobile Association	Barty-King, Hugh
Automobile Association	Keir, David E & Morgan, Bryan (eds)

Automotive Products	Wisdom, T H & Riddihough, N E
Avalon Industries	McGarvie, Michael
Avalon Leatherboard Co	McGarvie, Michael
Aveling-Barford Group	Aveling-Barford
Aveling-Barford Group	Barford, Edward
Aveling-Barford Group	Pochin, R Eric with Olive, E A
Avery, W & T	Avery, W & T
Avery, W & T	Broadbent, L H
Avery, W & T	Gale, Walter Keith Vernon
Avery, W & T	Leigh-Bennett, Ernest Pendarves
Avon Rubber Co	Avon Industrial Polymers
Avon Rubber Co	Avon Rubber
Avon Rubber Co	Fuller, Robert P
Avonside Engine Co	Rolt, Lionel Thomas Caswall
Avro	Avro
Avro	Lanchbery, Edward
Avro	Smith, Malcolm
Axminster Carpets	Jacobs, Bertram
B & I Line	Reader, Ernest R
B & I Line	Smyth, Hazel Pauline
B I C C	Banbury, Lawrence G
B I C C	Callender's
B I C C	Morgan, Robert M
B I C C	Morton, John
B I P	British Industrial Plastics
B P	Anderson, John Richard Lane
B P	Beable, William Henry
B P	British Petroleum
B P	Ferrier, R W
B P	Jones, Geoffrey
B P	Longhurst, Henry Carpenter
B P	Williams, Mari E W
B S A	Bird, Anthony C & Hutton-Stott, Francis H
B S A	Birmingham Small Arms Co
B S A	Birmingham Small Arms Co
B S A	Davenport-Hines, Richard P T
B S A	Frost, George H
B S A	Holliday, Bob
B S A	Nixon, St John Cousins
B S A	Ryerson, Barry
B S A	Smith, Barbara M D
B S A	Ward, Donovan M
Bagnall, W G	Baker, Allan C & Civil, Thomas D A
Bahr, Behrend	Behrend, Arthur
Baileys of Matlock	Bailey, E H
Bain, A W & Sons	Bain, Patrick
Bain, William & Co	House, Jack
Bainbridges of Newcastle	Airey, Angela & John
Baird, William & Co	Corrins, R D
Bakelite	Fielding, T J
Baker and Bessemer	Baker, Henry
Baker Perkins	Muir, Augustus
Bakers of Glasgow	Incorporation of Bakers of Glasgow
Baking Industry	Burnett, John
Baldwins	Middlemas, Robert K & Barnes, A John L

459

Balfour, Arthur	Balfour, Arthur
Balfour, Beatty & Co	Balfour, Beatty & Co
Balfour, Beatty & Co	Scott, Alexander T
Balfour, Williamson	Forres, Lord
Balfour, Williamson	Hunt, Wallis
Ballantyne, Hanson	Ballantyne
Balston, W & R Ltd	Balston, Thomas
Baltic Exchange	Barty-King, Hugh
Baltic Exchange	Findlay, J A
Baltic Exchange	Jones, Clement Wakefield
Bambergers	Bamberger, Louis
Bamfords	Bamfords
Bamforth & Co	Alderson, Frederick
Bampton	Bampton, D
Bank Line	Bank Line
Bank of British West Africa	Fry, Richard
Bank of England	Acres, W Marston
Bank of England	Clapham, John Harold
Bank of England	Collins, M
Bank of England	Francis, John
Bank of England	Sayers, Richard Sidney
Bank of England	Stockdale, Edmund
Bank of England	Warren, Henry
Bank of Ireland	Hall, F G
Bank of London & South America	Joslin, David Maelgwyn
Bank of Scotland	Malcolm, Charles Alexander
Banking in Britain	Cameron, Rondo
Banking in Scotland	Checkland, Sydney George
Banking Industry	Collins, Michael
Bannerman, Charles & Sons	Bridges, T C & Tiltman, H H
Banthrone of Newton	Banthrone of Newton
Baptist Insurance Co	Colvin, C J L
Barber, Walker & Co	Whitelock, G C H
Barclay & Fry	Barclay & Fry
Barclay, Curle	Barclay, Curle
Barclay, Perkins & Co	Barclay, Perkins
Barclay, Perkins & Co	Barclay, Perkins
Barclay, Perkins & Co	Barclay, Perkins
Barclay, Perkins & Co	Barclay, Perkins
Barclays Bank	Barclays Bank
Barclays Bank	Bidwell, William Henry
Barclays Bank	Chandler, George
Barclays Bank	Howarth, William
Barclays Bank	Manning, Peter
Barclays Bank	Matthews, Philip W & Tuke, Anthony W
Barclays Bank	Tuke, Anthony W & Gillman, Richard J H
Barclays Bank (DC&O)	Barclays Bank (DC&O)
Barclays Bank (DC&O)	Crossley, Julian & Blandford, J
Barford & Perkins	Barford & Perkins
Baring Brothers	Chapman, Stanley David
Baring Brothers	Hidy, Ralph Willard
Baring Brothers	Lewis, C M
Baring Brothers	Orbell, M John
Baring Brothers	Pena, R O & Duhalde, E L
Barker & Co	Barker & Co

Barkers of Kensington	Peel, Derek Wilmot Douglas
Barnards	Barnards
Barnsley Brewery Co	Barnsley Brewery Co
Barnsley Brewery Co	Crompton, Yorke
Barran, John	Ryott, David
Barraud	Jagger, C
Barrett, W & Co	Barrett, W & Co
Barrhead Co-operative Society	Murray, R (vols 1 & 2) & McWhirter, J (vol
Barrow's Stores	Barrow's Stores
Barrow, Hepburn & Gale	Bardens, Dennis
Barry Dock and Railways Co	Davies, L N A
Barry Railway	Barrie, Derek Stiven Maxwelton
Bartholomew, John & Son	Gardiner, Leslie
Barton, William & Sons	Barton, William & Sons
Bartrum, Harvey & Co	Bartrum, Harvey & Co
Baskerville, John	Pardoe, F E
Bass & Co	Beable, William Henry
Bass Charrington	Hawkins, Kevin H
Bassett, Geo & Co	Johnson, D G
Bassett-Lowke	Fuller, Roland
Batchelors Foods	Batchelors Foods
Batchelors Peas	Batchelors Peas
Bateman, G C	Bateman, G C
Bath & Portland Group	Bezzant, Norman
Bath & West Agricultural Soc	Hudson, Kenneth
Batley Co-operative Soc	Childe, W H
Batsford	Bolitho, Henry Hector
Baume & Co	Baume & Co
Baxter Brothers	Cooke, A J
Baxter, Payne and Lepper	Baxter, Payne and Lepper
Bayne and Duckett	Reid, James Macarthur
Beales	Beale, J Bennett
Beales	Parsons, John F
Beardmore, William & Co	Hume, John R & Moss, Michael S
Beatson, Clark & Co	Clark, Alec W
Beatson, Clark & Co	Greene, Dorothy
Beaven, J & T	Beaven, J & T
Beaven, J & T	Beaven, J & T
Beaverbrook Press	Howard, Peter Dunsmore
Beaverbrook Press	Taylor, Alan John Percivale
Beaverbrook Press	Wood, Alan
Bedford, John & Sons	Bedford, John
Beecham	Corley, Thomas Anthony Buchanan
Beecham	Francis, Anne
Beecham	Lazell, Henry George
Beeton, Samuel O	Hyde, Harford Montgomery
Begg, Cousland	Begg, Cousland
Behrens, Jacob	Behrens
Belfast Banks	Ollerenshaw, P G
Belfast Harbour Commissioners	Belfast Harbour Commissioners
Bell, Arthur & Son	House, Jack
Bell, John	Morison, Stanley
Bell, John	Prince, Peter
Belling & Co	Jukes, G (ed)
Belling & Lee	Belling and Lee

461

Belling & Lee	Belling and Lee
Bemrose & Sons	Bemrose, Henry Howe
Bemrose & Sons	Hackett, Dennis
Bemrose & Sons	Jones, A E
Ben Line	Milne, T E
Ben Line Steamers	Blake, George
Ben Line Steamers	MacGregor, David Roy
Ben Line Steamers	Somner, Graeme
Benefit Footwear	Benefit Footwear
Benfield & Loxley	Benfield & Loxley
Benfield & Loxley	Benfield & Loxley
Benham & Sons	Benham, Stanley J
Benn, Ernest	Abel, Deryck Robert Endsleigh
Bennett, Opie	Bennett, Opie
Bennetts Dairies & Farms	Bennetts Dairies and Farms
Bentall, E H & Co	Kemp, Peter Kemp
Bentalls of Kingston	Bentall, Rowan
Bentalls of Kingston	Herbert, Charles
Bentalls of Kingston	Perkins, Herbert H
Bentley	Frostick, Michael
Bentley	Gettmann, Royal Alfred
Bentley, David	Don, G Stuart
Bentley, Isaac & Co	Bentley, Isaac
Benzie & Miller	Benzie and Miller
Berger, Lewis & Sons	Armitage, F
Berger, Lewis & Sons	Berger, Thomas B
Berger, Lewis & Sons	Farnol, J
Berisford Group	Kornitzer, Margaret (ed)
Berisford Group	Sebire, Charles B
Berisford Group	Sebire, J F
Berry Bros & Rudd	Allen, Herbert Warner
Bertram Mills Circus	Mills, Cyril Bertram
Bertrams	Bertrams
Berwick Salmon Fisheries Co	Berwick Salmon Fisheries Company
Bessbrook Spinning Co	Bessbrook
Bessbrook Spinning Co	Bessbrook
Bessbrook Spinning Co	Richardson, J N
Best & Hobson	Best, Robert Dudley
Best & Lloyd	Coats, Robert Hay
Bevington, Vaizey and Foster	Bevington, Vaizey and Foster
Beyer Peacock	Hills, Richard L
Biba	Hulanicki, Barbara
Bibby Line	Bibby Line
Bibby Line	Bibby Line
Bibby Line	Paget-Tomlinson, Edward William
Bibby Line	Paget-Tomlinson, Edward William
Bibby, J & Sons	Bibby, J & Sons
Bibby, J & Sons	Bibby, John B
Bibby, J & Sons	Bibby, John B & Bibby, Charles L
Bilsland Brothers	Bilsland Brothers
Binnend Oilworks	Stephen, Walter M
Birch, Wm & Sons	Birch, Wm. & Sons
Bird	Bird, Leslie
Bird, Alfred & Sons	Foley, John
Birds Eye Foods Ltd.	Reader, William Joseph

462

Birkin Group	Birkin, Guy
Birmingham & Midland Motor Bus	Gray, Paul; Keeley, Malcolm & Seale, John
Birmingham & the Black Country	Allen, George Cyril
Birmingham Aluminium Casting	Birmingham Aluminium Casting Co
Birmingham Banks	Edwards, E
Birmingham Battery & Metal Co	Rowntree, Arthur (ed)
Birmingham Co-operative Society	Birmingham Co-operative Society
Birmingham Copec Soc	Fenter, Frances Margaret
Birmingham Jewellery Trade	Roche, J C
Birmingham Municipal Savings	Hilton, John Peter
Birmingham Steel Pen Trade	Timings, F L
Birmingham Temperance Soc	Faulkner, Ewart
Biscuit Makers of Edinburgh	Cramb, George E
Bishop, J C	Elvin, Laurence
Black Ball Line	Jones, Clement Wakefield
Black Ball Line	Stammers, Michael K
Black Dyke Mills	Sigsworth, Eric Milton
Black, Adam & Charles	Newth, Jack D
Blackburn & General Aircraft	Blackburn
Blackburn & Sutcliffe	Barlow, Ronald
Blackie & Son	Blackie, Agnes Anna Coventry
Blackie & Son	Dempster, John
Blackstone & Co	Price, Thomas L
Blackwall Yard	Green, Henry & Wigram, Robert
Blackwell	Norrington, A L P
Blackwood, William & Sons	Oliphant, Mrs & Porter, Mrs
Blackwood, William & Sons	Tredrey, F D
Blantyre Co-operative Soc	Blantyre Co-operative Society
Blaxill & Co	Blaxill, Edwin Alec
Bleachers' Association	Sykes, Alan John
Bloore & Piller	Piller, Norman
Blue Circle	Associated Portland Cement
Blue Funnel	Jones, Clement Wakefield
Blundell's Collieries	Atkinson, Glen
Blundell, Spence & Co	Blundell, Spence & Co
Blundells Collieries	Anderson, Donald
Blundells Collieries	Anderson, Donald
Blundells Collieries	Anderson, Donald with Lane, Jane
Blyth, Greene, Jourdain & Co	Muir, Augustus
Boardman, W & Co	Atkinson, Glen
Boatmens' Building Society	Boatmens' Building Society
Boddingtons' Brewery	Jacobson, Michael
Boddingtons' Brewery	Mitchell, Albert & Grayling, Christopher
Bolckow, Vaughan & Co	Bolckow, Vaughan & Co
Bolckow, Vaughan & Co	Gott, Ron
Bolsover Colliery Co	Bolsover Colliery Co
Bolton and Leigh Railway Co	Basnett, Lois
Bolton Co-operative Society	Peaples, F W
Bolton Corporation Transport	Bolton County Borough Transport Departme
Bolton Electricty Dept	Warburton, Ray
Bolton Gas Co	Hacking, Barbara
Bolton, Thomas & Sons	Morton, John
Bombay Burmah Trading Corp	Macaulay, R H
Bombay Burmah Trading Corp	Pointon, Arnold Cecil
Bomford & Evershed	Sherwen, Theo

Bon Marché	Miller, Michael B
Book Trade	Curwen, Henry
Book Trade	Plant, Marjorie
Boot and Shoe Industry	Church, Roy Anthony
Boot and Shoe Industry	Griffin, W C
Booth's Distilleries	Balfour, John Patrick Douglas
Booth, Alfred	Crow, Duncan
Booth, Alfred	John, Arthur Henry
Booth, Alfred	Jones, Clement Wakefield
Booth, Alfred	Whitting, Harriet Anna
Bootham Engineers	Bootham Engineers
Boots The Chemists	Beable, William Henry
Boots The Chemists	Chapman, Stanley David
Boots The Chemists	Roberts, Cecil
Borax Holdings	Borax Holdings
Borneo Co	Longhurst, Henry Carpenter
Borthwick, Thomas & Sons	Critchell, James T & Raymond, Joseph
Borthwick, Thomas & Sons	Harrison, Godfrey Percival
Borthwick, Thomas & Sons	Meat Trade (various authors)
Bottomley, Horatio	Symons, Julian
Boulton & Paul	Boulton & Paul
Boulton & Watt	Gale, Walter Keith Vernon
Boulton & Watt	Gale, Walter Keith Vernon
Boulton & Watt	Roll, Eric
Boulton & Watt	Tann, Jennifer (ed)
Bourlet, James & Sons	Bourlet, James & Sons
Bovril	Armstrong, John
Bovril	Bennett, Richard
Bovril	Hadley, Peter
Bowater	Ralli Trading Group
Bowater	Reader, William Joseph
Bowers Mills	Muir, Augustus
Bowes, John and Partners	Mountford, Colin E
Bowler, J B	Hudson, Kenneth
Bowmans (Warrington)	Bowmans (Warrington)
Bowring, C T & Co	Bowring
Bowring, C T & Co	Keir, David Edwin
Bowring, C T & Co	Wardle, Arthur C
Boyd, Alexander & Co	Bass, Hugh G
Boyd, John & Co.	McGarvie, Michael
Braby Group	Richardson, J E
Bradbury Wilkinson	Bradbury Wilkinson
Brades Steel Works	Burritt, Elihu
Bradford Dyers' Association	Bradford Dyers' Association Ltd
Bradford Property Trust	Brennan, John
Bradford Worsted	Garrod, P
Bradley & Craven	Craven, Wilfred Archer
Bradley Ironworks	Morton, G R & Smith, W A
Bradley, Edwin H	Bradley, Edwin H
Bradshaw & Co	Bradshaw, J B
Brain, S A & Co	Brain, Jennifer
Brakspear, W H & Sons	Sheppard, Francis Henry Wollaston
Brampton Brewery Co	Brampton Brewery
Brearley, Harry	Brearley, Harry
Brecon Old Bank	Roberts, R O

464

British Rail	Bonavia, Michael Robert
British Rail	Wrottesley, John
British Rail Engineering	Radford, J B
British Rolling Mills	Parker, J Francis
British Shipowners' Co	Jones, Clement Wakefield
British South Africa Co	Fort, George Seymour
British South Africa Co	Malcolm, D O
British Steel	British Steel
British Steel	British Steel
British Steel	Quinn, Esther
British Steel	Quinn, Esther
British Steel	Vaizey, John Ernest
British Steel Corporation	Bryer, R A, Brignall, T J & Maunders, A R
British Steel Corporation	Lancaster J Y & Wattleworth, D R
British Sugar Corporation	Saunders, Alan
British Telecom	Earl, R A J
British Telecom	Newman, Karin
British Thomson Houston Co	Price-Hughes, H A
British United Shoe Machinery Co	British United Shoe Machinery Co
British Vinegars	Sarson, Henry
British Xylonite Co	Ashlee, Peter C
British Xylonite Co	British Xylonite Co
British Xylonite Co	Greenstock, Harry
British Xylonite Co	Xylonite Group
British Xylonite Co3	Merriam, John
Briton Brush Co	Briton Brush Co
Briton Ferry Ironworks	Roberts, Colin William
Britton, G B & Sons	Britton, George Bryant & Sons
Broadbent and Turner	Broadbent and Turner
Broadbent, Thomas and Sons	Broadbent, Thomas
Broadbent, Thomas and Sons	Derbyshire, F W
Broadbents of Southport	Porter, J H
Broadwood, John & Sons	Wainwright, David
Brockhouse, J & Co	Brockhouse, J & Co
Brockhouse, J & Co	Mackenzie, Edward Montague Compton
Brocklebank Line	Gibson, John Frederic
Brocklebank Line	Hollett, Dave
Brocklebanks	Jones, Clement Wakefield
Brocklehurst-Whiston	Brocklehurst
Brocklehurst-Whiston	Crozier, Mary
Bromford Iron & Steel Co	Gale, Walter Keith Vernon
Bromilow & Edwards	Seacombe, Andrew
Brook Street Bureau	Hurst, Margery
Brooke Bond Liebig	Wainwright, David
Brotherhoods	Leleux, Sydney Arthur
Broughs	Ellis, H G
Brown & Polson	Green, Daniel
Brown & Tawse Group	Brown & Tawse Group
Brown (Fulham), H	Griffin, Gary Stephen
Brown Bayleys	Brown Bayleys
Brown's of Chester	Willcock, H D(ed) for Mass Observation
Brown, Alexander & Sons	Killick, J
Brown, Jenkison & Co	Janes, Hurford
Brown, John	Brown, John
Brown, John	Firth Brown

Brown, John	Grant, Allan John
Brown, John	Mensforth, Eric
Brown, John	Slaven, Anthony
Brown, Muff & Co	Brown, Muff & Co
Brown, Muff & Co	Brown, Muff & Co
Brown, Shipley & Co	Brown, John Crosby
Brown, Shipley & Co	Perkins, Edwin Judson
Brown, Shipley & Co	Perkins, Edwin Judson
Brown, Shipley & Co.	Ellis, Aytoun
Brownlee & Co	Carnegie, J F
Brownlee & Co	Carvel, John Lees
Broxburn Co-operative Soc	Pagan, William & Young, Robert
Bruichladdich Distillery Co	Moss, M S & Hume, J R
Brunner, Mond	Bolitho, Henry Hector
Brunner, Mond	Cohen, John Michael
Brunner, Mond	Dick, W F L
Brunner, Mond	Goodman, Jean
Brunner, Mond	Hill, Mervyn Frederick
Brunner, Mond	Irvine, A S
Brunner, Mond	Koss, Stephen Edward
Brunner, Mond	Lischka, J R
Brunner, Mond	Warren, Kenneth
Brunner, Mond	Watts, John I
Brunner, Mond & Co	Brunner, Mond
Brunton (Musselburgh)	Adam, Alastair T
Bryant & May	Beable, William Henry
Bryant & May	Beaver, Patrick
Bryant & May	Bryant & May
Bryant & May	Lindgren, Håkan
Brymbo Steel Works	Brymbo
Buchan's Breweries	Buchan, Andrew
Buchanan , James & Co	Spiller, Brian
Buchanan, James & Co	Atherton, F W
Buckingham, J & Sons	Fowler, E
Buckingham, J & Sons	Sparks, W L
Buckmaster & Moore	Whyte, Lewis
Budgett, Samuel	Arthur, William
Buenos Aires Fire Ins Market	Jones, Charles A
Building	Bowley, Marian
Building	Middlemas, Robert Keith
Building	Powell, Christopher G
Building	Richardson, Harry W & Aldcroft, Derek H
Building Railways	Helps, Arthur
Building Societies	Ashworth, Herbert
Building Societies	Boddy, Martin
Building Societies	Cleary, Esmond John
Building Societies	Davies, Glyn
Building Societies Association	Price, Seymour James
Bulmer, H P & Co	Bulmer, Edward F
Burbidge, H	Clarke, L J & Burbidge, H L
Burgess & Son (Abingdon)	Stopps, Leslie B
Burlingham, H	Burlingham, H
Burlington Slate Quarries	Geddes, R Stanley
Burmah Oil	Corley, Thomas Anthony Buchanan
Burmah Oil	Corley, Thomas Anthony Buchanan

468

Burmah Oil	Jones, B Alcwyn
Burmah Oil	Jones, Geoffrey
Burmah Oil	Jones, Geoffrey
Burman & Sons	Burman, Thomas
Burn, James & Co	Darley, Lionel Seabrook
Burnyeat	Rolt, Lionel Thomas Caswall
Burrell, Charles & Sons	Clark, Ronald Harry
Burrough, James	Burrough, James
Burroughs Adding Machine Co	Morgan, Bryan Stanford
Burroughs Wellcome	Burroughs Wellcome
Burroughs Wellcome	Liebenau, Jonathan M
Burroughs Wellcome	Macdonald, Gilbert
Burroughs Wellcome	Wellcome Foundation
Burrows	Burrows
Burrup, Mathieson	McConnell, Brian
Burt, Boulton & Haywood	Burt, Boulton & Haywood
Burwell & Dist Motor Service	Neale, J
Bury District Co-operative Soc	Rigby, Thomas
Bus Services	Hibbs, John
Bus Services in Northumberland	Warn, C R
Buses	Klapper, Charles Frederick
Buses in London	Blacker, Ken
Bush, W J & Co	Bush, W J & Co
Bushills	Howe, Ellic
Bushmills Distillery	McCreary, Alf
Business Activity in Politics	Turner, John (ed)
Business and Religion	Jeremy, David J (ed)
Business Organisation	Jefferys, James Bavington
Bute Docks	Daunton, Martin James
Butler Machine Tool Co	Butler Machine Tool Co
Butler, Wm & Co (Bristol)	Butler, Thomas Howard
Butlins	Butlin, Billy with Dacre, P
Butlins	North, Rex
Butterfield & Swire	Drage, Charles
Butterfield & Swire	Hook, Elizabeth
Butterfield & Swire	Marriner, Sheila & Hyde, Francis E
Butterfield & Swire	Swire, John & Sons
Butterley Co	Butterley
Butterley Co	Mottram, R H & Coote, Colin
Butterley Co	Riden, Philip J
Butterworth & Co	Jones, H Kay
BXL Plastics	Greenstock, Harry
C Townsend Hook	Funnell, K J
Cable & Wireless	Baglehole, K C
Cable & Wireless	Barty-King, Hugh
Cable & Wireless	Stray, J F
Cadbury Bros	Beable, William Henry
Cadbury Bros	Cadbury
Cadbury Bros	Cadbury
Cadbury Bros	Cadbury
Cadbury Bros	Finch, Robert
Cadbury Bros	Gardiner, Alfred George
Cadbury Bros	Jones, Geoffrey
Cadbury Bros	Jones, Geoffrey
Cadbury Bros	Rogers, T B

Cadbury Bros	Williams, Iolo Aneurin
Cadbury-Schweppes	Simmons, Douglas A
Cadell & Davies	Besterman, Theodore (ed)
Caffyn	Gowans, L M
Caffyn	Gowans, L M
Cainscross & Ebley Co-op	Hudson, Bramwell
Caldwell and Whitley	Caldwell and Whitley
Caledon Shipbuilding Co	Caledon Shipbuilding Co
Caledonian Railway	Nock, Oswald Stevens
Caley, A J & Son	Leeds, Herbert
Caley, A J & Son	Mackintosh, Eric D
Calico Printers' Association	Calico Printers' Association
Calico Printers' Association	Turnbull, Geoffrey (ed)
Callender's Cable & Const	Morgan, Robert M
Callender's Cable & Construction	Callender's
Calvert, I & I	Garnett, Walter Onslow
Cambrian Airways	Staddon, Tommy G
Cambrian Collieries	Rhondda, Margaret, Viscountess
Cambridge Consultants	Dale, Rodney
Cambridge Instrument Co	Cambridge Instrument Co
Cambridge Instrument Co	Cambridge Instrument Co
Cambridge University Press	Black, Michael H
Cambridge University Press	McKitterick, David
Cambridge University Press	Roberts, S C
Cammell Laird & Co	Cammell Laird
Cammell, Charles & Co	Cammell
Cammell, Charles & Co	Pollard, Sidney & Robertson, Paul
Campbell, P & A	Hope, Iain
Campbell, Smith & Co	Campbell, Kenneth L G
CandL	Cussins & Light
Candor Motors	Polley, Bernard
Canning	Thomas, David A
Cannock Chase Colliery Co	Francis, J R
Cannock Chase Colliery Co	Francis, J Roger
Cannon Brewery	King, Frank A
Cantrell & Cochrane	Cantrell & Cochrane
Cape Asbestos Co	Cape Asbestos Co
Cape, F & Co	Foster, Richard
Capel, James	Reed, M C
Capital & Entrepreneurship	Mathias, Peter
Capper Pass	Little, Bryan
Carlaw, David & Sons	House, Jack
Carless, Capel & Leonard	Liveing, Edward George Downing
Carlisle & Gregson (Jimmy's)	Nichols, Philip Peter Ross
Carmichael, James	Rumsby, W N
Carmichael, James & Co	Carmichael, James & Co
Carpenters' Company	Alford, Bernard W E & Barker, Theodore C
Carr's Milling Industries	Burgess, Clare et al
Carreras	Corina, Maurice
Carreras	Davenport, John
Carron Company	Campbell, Roy Hutcheson
Carron Company	Campbell, Roy Hutcheson
Carty & Son	Carty
Cash, J & J	Vertigan, Sean A
Cassel Cyanide Co	Neill, W

470

Cassell & Co	Beable, William Henry
Cassell & Co	Nowell-Smith, Simon
Cassell, Ernest	Thane, Pat
Castner-Kellner Alkali Co	Castner-Kellner
Castrol	Wakefield, C C & Co
Castrol	Wakefield, C C & Co
Cater Ryder & Co	Cater Ryder & Co
Catnach Press	Hindley, Charles
Cauldwell, E (Rowsley)	Cauldwell, E
Cave, Austin and Co	Cave, Austin & Co
Cayzer Irvine & Co	Muir, Augustus & Davies, M
Cazenove & Co	Martin, Albert A
Cedric Chivers	Harris, C W J
Cement Industry	Francis, Anthony John
Central Insurance Co	Colvin, C J L
Central Mining & Investment Corp	Central Mining
Century Insurance Co	Tregoning, David & Cockerell, Hugh
Chalmers, Andrew & Co	Mack, Peter Hughes
Chalmers, Andrew & Co	Mack, R J
Chance Brothers	Chance Brothers
Chance Brothers	Chance Brothers
Chance Brothers	Chance, James Frederick
Chance Brothers	Chance, James Frederick
Chapman & Hall	Waugh, Arthur
Charrington & Co	Hawkins, Kevin H
Charrington & Co	Strong, Leonard Alfred George
Charrington & Co	Strong, Leonard Alfred George
Charrington, Gardner, Locket & Co	Darwin, Bernard Richard Meirion
Charrington, Gardner, Locket & Co	Fraser-Stephen, Elspet
Chartered Accountants	Howitt, Harold Gibson
Chartered Bank	Mackenzie, Edward Montague Compton
Chartered Bank	Sewell, V
Chartered Bank	Standard Chartered Bank
Chartered Insurance Institute	Cockerell, Hugh Anthony Lewis
Charterhouse	Dennett, Laurie
Chatwood Safe Co	O'Connor, Denis
Cheltenham & Gloucester Bldg Soc	Ansell, Walter
Chemical Industry	Haber, Ludwig Fritz
Chemical Industry	Haber, Ludwig Fritz
Chemical Industry	Haber, Ludwig Fritz
Chemical Industry	Hardie, David William Ferguson
Chemical Industry	Reader, William Joseph
Chemical Industry on Tyneside	Campbell, William Alec
Chemico	County Chemical Co
Cheney & Sons	Cheney & Sons
Cheney & Sons	Cheney, Christopher R, John & Walter G
Cherry Blossom Boot Polish	Lewis, G
Cheshire County Newspapers	Nulty, Geoffrey
Chester Grosvenor Hotel Co	Callister, Ian
Chesters Brewery Co	Cowen, Frank
Child & Co	Clarke, Philip
Child & Co	Price, F G Hilton
Chiltern Motor Holdings	Bridges, Tom
Chiswick Products	Chiswick Products
Christies	Marillier, H C

Christy & Co	Beable, William Henry
Christy & Co	Christy
Christy, W M & Sons	Christy, W M
Christy, W M & Sons	Higgins, J P
Chrysler	Young, Stephen & Hood, Neil
Chubb Fire Security	Chubb Fire Security
Chubb Lock & Safe Co	Chubb & Son's Lock & Safe Co
Chubb Lock & Safe Co	Chubb, George H & Churcher, Walter G
Chubb Lock & Safe Co	Currier-Briggs, Noel
Churchill and Sim	Muir, Augustus
Churchill, Charles & Co	Churchill, Charles
Churchill, Charles & Co	Churchill, Charles
Churchill, Charles & Co	Churchill-T I
Churchill, Charles & Co	Rolt, Lionel Thomas Caswall
Churchill-Redman	Churchill, Charles
Churchill-Redman	Churchill-T I
Churchill-Redman	Rolt, Lionel Thomas Caswall
Ciba Geigy Plastics	Ciba Geigy
City & South London Railway	Lascelles, Thomas Spooner
City and Central	Gordon, Charles
City Centre Properties	Gordon, Charles
City Engraving	City Engraving
City Motor Co (Oxford)	Bridges, Tom
City of Glasgow Bank	Tyson, R E
City of London Building Soc	Williams, N
City of London Real Property Co	City of London Real Property Co
City of Perth Co-operative Soc	City of Perth Co-operative Society
Civil Air Transport	Birkhead, E
Clapham Brothers	Field, Molly & Dick
Clarendon Press	Carter, Harry
Clares Carlton	Atthill, Robin
Clark	Blair, Matthew
Clark	Blair, Matthew
Clark, C & J	Barber, L H
Clark, C & J	Hudson, Kenneth
Clark, C & J	Lehane, Brendan
Clark, C & J	Sutton, George Barry
Clark, C & J	Sutton, George Barry
Clark, John & Thomas	Beckinsale, Robert Percy
Clark, Son & Morland	Russell, McDonough
Clark, William & Sons	Clark, Wallace
Clark-Hawthorn	Clarke, Joseph Francis
Clarke, Nicholls and Coombs	Mathieson, George
Clarke, Sam	Clarke, Sam
Clarkson, H & Co	Clarkson, H & Co
Clarkson, W	Jenkin, Roger
Clarnico	Mathieson, George
Clay Cross Co	Clay Cross Co
Clay Cross Co	Clay Cross Co
Clay Cross Co	Clay Cross Co
Clay-Brickmaking	Collier, L J
Clays of Bungay	Moran, James Charles
Clayton Aniline Co	Abrahart, Edward Noah
Clayton, Thomas	Faulkner, Alan H
Clearing Banks	Jones, Geoffrey

472

Clerical, Medical & General Life	Besant, Arthur Digby
Cleveland Iron Trade	Jeans, James Stephen
Clifford-Turner	Scott, John
Clint & Co	Jones, Clement Wakefield
Clowes, William	Clowes, William Beaufoy
Cluttons	Cluttons
Cluttons	Cluttons
Clyde Shipping Co	Cuthbert, Alan D
Clydebank Co-operative Soc	Lawson, William E
Clydesdale Bank	Reid, James Macarthur
Co-operation in England	Holyoake, George Jacob
Co-operative Insurance Society	Garnett, Ronald G
Co-operative Movement	Carr-Saunders, Alexander Morris et al
Co-operative Permanent Bldg Soc	Cassell, Michael
Co-operative Permanent Bldg Soc	Mansbridge, Albert
Co-operative Printing Society	Hall, Fred
Co-operative Retailing, Scotland	Campbell, L
Co-operative Wholesale Society	Co-operative Wholesale Society
Co-operative Wholesale Society	Kinloch, James & Butt, John
Co-operative Wholesale Society	Redfern, Percy
Co-operative Wholesale Society	Redfern, Percy
Co-operative Wholesale Society	Richardson, William
Co-operative Wholesale Society	Smith, H Charles
Coal Combines in Yorkshire	Labour Research Dept
Coal Industry	Ashworth, William
Coal Industry	Barker, Theodore C & Harris, John R
Coal Industry	Buxton, Neil K
Coal Industry	Church, Roy Anthony
Coal Industry	Flinn, M W with Stoker, D
Coal Industry	Galloway, R L (ed B F Duckham)
Coal Industry	Kirby, Maurice W
Coal Industry	Mitchell, Brian Rodman
Coal Industry	Political and Economic Planning
Coal Industry	Williams, David James
Coal Metropolis: Cardiff	Daunton, Martin James
Coal Trade	Jevons, Herbert Stanley
Coalbrookdale Co	Coalbrookdale Company
Coalbrookdale Co	Raistrick, Arthur
Coalbrookdale Co	Raistrick, Arthur
Coalbrookdale Co	Trinder, Barrie Stuart
Coalbrookdale Co	Windsor, David Burns
Coalport China Co	Mackenzie, Edward Montague Compton
Coalsnaughton Co-op Soc	Cook, William
Coalsnaughton Co-op Soc	Murray, William
Coates Bros	Coates, J B M
Coats, Paton & Baldwin	Blair, Matthew
Coats, Paton & Baldwin	Blair, Matthew
Coats, Paton & Baldwin	Pasold, Eric W
Coats, Paton & Baldwin	Paton, Alexander Forrester
Coats, T & P	Marsden, J S & Brock, D B S
Cockburn & Campbell	Cockburn, Robert & John
Cockhedge Mill	Armitage, G W
Cocks Biddulph & Co	Cocks Biddulph & Co
Cocks, James & Sons	Willson, B F
Cocoa Trade	Greenhill, Robert G

Coffee Trade	Greenhill, Robert G
Cohen, George & Sons	Cohen, George
Cohen, George & Sons	Cohen, George
Coleman, Benfield & Loxley	Coleman, Benfield & Loxley
Coles Cranes	Wilson, Martyn & Spink, Karen
Coles, Henry J	Miller, V
Collins	Keir, David Edwin
Collins Line	Armstrong, Warren
Colman, J & J	Colman, H C
Colman, J & J	Colman, J & J
Colman, J & J	Edgar, S H
Colman, J & J	Edgar, S H
Colnaghi, P & D & Co	Colnaghi, Paul & Dominic
Colne Valley Water Co	Colne Valley Water
Colonel Stephens Railways	Morgan, J S
Colston	Bloom, John
Coltness Iron Co	Carvel, John Lees
Coltness Iron Co	Macleod, William H & Houldsworth, Henry H
Coltness Iron Co	Smith, David L
Colvilles	Dobie, George A
Colvilles	Payne, Peter Lester
Commercial Bank of Scotland	Anderson, James Lawson
Commercial Bank of Scotland	Commercial Bank of Scotland
Commercial Bank of Wales	Commercial Bank of Wales
Commercial Bank of Wales	O'Sullivan, Timothy
Commercial Union Group	Commercial Union Assurance Co: Exeter Bra
Commercial Union Group	Liveing, Edward George Downing
Commercial Vehicle Industry	Seth-Smith, Michael
Company Financial Statements	Lee, T A
Coneygre Foundry	Gale, Walter Keith Vernon
Conran Associates	Phillips, Barty
Consett Iron Co	Consett Iron
Consett Iron Co	Hornsby, R M
Consett Iron Co	Richardson, H W & Bass, J M
Consett Iron Co	Wilson, A S
Consolidated Gold Fields	Cartwright, Alan Patrick
Constable & Co	Arnold, Ralph Crispian Marshall
Continental Express	Ellis, Aytoun
Cook, F W	Cook, F W
Cook, Son & Co (St.Pauls)	Cook, Son & Co (St.Pauls)
Cook, Thomas	Pudney, John Sleigh
Cook, Thomas	Pudney, John Sleigh
Cook, Thomas	Rae, William Fraser
Cook, Thomas	Simmons, Jack
Cook, Thomas & Son	Swinglehurst, Edmund
Cook, Walter & Son	Cook, Clifford J
Cooke, Troughton & Simms	Taylor, E & Wilson, J S
Cooper Brothers & Co	Cooper Brothers
Cooper Brothers & Co	Hopkins, Leon
Copeland, W T & Sons	Copeland, W T & Sons
Copeman, John & Sons	Copeman, John & Sons
Corah, N	Jopp, Keith
Corah, N	Webb, C W
Corah, N & Sons	Corah, N
Cordiners in Glasgow	Campbell, William

Cork Savings Bank	Cork Savings Bank
Cork Woollen Mills	Mahony, Martin & Bros
Corn Products Co	Green, Daniel
Cornish Copper Co	Pascoe, W H
Corporate Economy	Hannah, Leslie
Cory Bros & Co	Green, M H
Cory, William & Son	Cory, William & Son
Cory, William & Son	Johnston, C H
Cossor, A C	Cossor, A C
Cossor, A C & Son(Surgical)	Cossor, A C
Cosworth Engineering Co	Blunsden, John
Cotswold Cider Company	White, Frank James
Cotton & Banking in Manchester	Jones, Stuart
Cotton and Steel Enterprises	Yonekawa, Shin-ichi
Cotton Industry	Farnie, Douglas Anthony
Cotton Industry	Farnie, Douglas Anthony
Cotton Industry	Hedges, J A
Cotton Industry	Howe, Anthony
Cotton Industry	Lazonick, William
Cotton Industry	Political and Economic Planning
Cotton Industry	Robson, Robert
Cotton Industry in Scotland	Robertson, Alex J
Cotton Masters	Howe, Anthony C
Cotton Spinning in Oldham	Jones, F
County Chemical Co	County Chemical Co
County Fire Office	Noakes, Aubrey
Courage & Co	Barnsley Brewery Co
Courage & Co	Hardinge, G N
Courage & Co	Hardinge, G N
Courage & Co	Pudney, John Sleigh
Courtaulds	Ashton Bros
Courtaulds	Coleman, Donald Cuthbert
Courtaulds	Coleman, Donald Cuthbert
Courtaulds	Courtaulds
Courtaulds	Fletch, A M
Courtaulds	Harrop, J
Courtaulds	Harte, Negley B
Courtaulds	Harte, Negley B
Courtaulds	Higgins, J P
Courtaulds	Jones, Geoffrey
Courtaulds	Knight, Arthur W
Courtaulds	Ward-Jackson, Cyril Henry
Coutts & Co	Coleridge, Ernest Hartley
Coutts & Co	Forbes, William
Coutts & Co	Howarth, William
Coutts & Co	Richardson, Ralph
Coutts & Co	Robinson, Ralph Mosley
Coventry Building Society	Coventry Building Society
Coventry Building Society	Davis, Martyn
Coventry Evening Telegraph	Coventry Evening Telegraph
Coventry Perseverance Co-op	Coventry Perseverance Co-op Soc
Coventry Provident Bldg Soc	Coventry Provident Building Society
Coventry Savings Bank	MacRae, R J
Coventry Textiles	Lynes, Alice
Cow & Gate	Cow & Gate

Cow & Gate	Unigate
Cox & Wyman	Moran, James Charles
Cox Family, the Linen Trade	Donaldson, Mrs Kathleen
Crabtree, J A	Crabtree, John A & Co
Crabtree, J A	Minkes, A L & Tucker, D G
Craig, Robert & Sons	Craig, Robert & Sons
Cramond Iron Mills	Cadell, Patrick
Cramond Iron Mills	Skinner, Basil Chisholm
Crampton & Sons	Teversham, Traviss Frederick
Crawford, Andrew & Co	Crawford, Andrew & Co
Crawford, W S	Mills, Godfrey Hope Saxon
Crawshay	Addis, John Philip
Creed & Co	Creed
Crewe Works	Reed, B
Crieff Hydro	Christie, Guy
Crips, W A & Sons	Thomas, David G & Sowan, Brenda J
Crittall Manufacturing Co	Austin, P E
Crittall Manufacturing Co	Crittall Manufacturing Co
Croda	Wood, F A S & Cressey, S
Croft & Co	Knox, Oliver
Crombie Knowles & Co	Allen, John R (ed)
Crompton & Co	Byatt, Ian Charles Rayner
Crompton & Co	Johnson, J H & Randell, W L
Crompton Parkinson & Co	Crompton Parkinson & Co
Cromptons	Hampson, Cyril G
Cromptons, Creams	Lyddon, Denis W & Marshall, Peter A
Cropper, Benson & Co	Jones, Clement Wakefield
Crosfield, Joseph	Musson, Albert Edward
Crosland & Netherton Co-op	Earnshaw, Thomas
Crossley Motors	Crossley Motors
Crossley, John & Sons	Bretton, R
Crossley, John & Sons	Webster, Eric
Crosville Motor Services	Anderson, Roy Claude
Crosville Motor Services	Crosland-Taylor, W James C
Crosville Motor Services	Crosland-Taylor, W James C
Crowleys of Stourbridge	Flinn, Michael Walter
Crowleys of Stourbridge	Flinn, Michael Walter
Crown Agents	Abbott, Arthur William
Croydon Advertiser	Croydon Advertiser
Croydon Advertiser	Ward, W Jesse
Croydon Gas Co	Croydon Gas Co
Cullingford & Co	Cullingford & Co
Culter Paper Mills	Culter Paper Mills
Cultural Factors and Business	Checkland, Sydney George
Cumberland Newspapers Group	Cumberland Newspapers Group
Cunard	Bastin, J
Cunard	Grant, Hilda Kay
Cunard	Hyde, Francis Edwin
Cunard	Jones, Clement Wakefield
Cunard	Smallpeice, Basil
Cunard	Vale, Vivian
Cundell, Joseph	McLean, Ruari
Cunningham's Holiday Camp	Drower, Jill
Curls	Curls
Curran, Edward, Engineering	Curran, Edward

Currys	Currys
Currys	Lerner, Harry
Curwen Press	Simon, Herbert
Cussins & Light	Cussins & Light
Cutlers' Company	du Garde Peach, Lawrence
Cutlers' Company	Leader, Robert Eadon
Cutlery Trades	Lloyd, Geoffrey I H
Cycle & Motor Industries	Harrison, A E
Czarnikow	Janes, Hurford & Sayers, H J
D P Battery Co	D P Battery Co
Dagenham Dock	Williams, Samuel & Sons
Daily News	Koss, Stephen Edward
Daily Telegraph	Burnham, Lord (Lawson, Edward Frederick)
Daimler Co	Frost, George H
Daimler Motor Co	Daimler
Daimler Motor Co	Nixon, St John Cousins
Dale Electric Group	Barty-King, Hugh
Dalgety	Vaughan-Thomas, Wynford
Dalmellington Iron Co	Smith, David L
Dalton, Barton & Co	Dalton, Barton & Co
Danish Bacon Co	Spink, Reginald
Darlington Locomotive Works	Hoole, Kenneth
David Allen Theatre Co	Allen, William Edward David
David Brown	Donnelly, Desmond
David Lloyd, Pigott & Co	David Lloyd, Pigott & Co
David Lloyd, Pigott & Co	David Lloyd, Pigott & Co
David Lloyd, Pigott & Co	Janes, Hurford
David Low	Low, David
Davidson & Co	Maguire, Edward
Davidson & Co	Sirocco
Davies, Harvey & Murrell	Davies, Harvey & Murrell
Davies, W J & Sons	Davies, W J
Davison, Newman & Co	Rutter, Owen
Davison, William of Alnwick	Isaac, Peter Charles Gerald
De Beers	Fort, George Seymour
de Havilland	Birtles, Philip J
de Havilland	de Havilland
de Havilland	Sharp, Cecil Martin
de Havilland	Sharp, Cecil Martin
de la Rue, Thomas	Houseman, Lorna
de Montfort Press	Brewer, Roy
De Zoete & Gorton	De Zoete & Gorton
De Zoete & Gorton	Janes, Hurford
Deakins	Deakins
Dean & Co (Stockport)	Dean, Joseph Normanton
Dean, Smith & Grace	Grierson, Edward
Debenham	Corina, Maurice
Decca Gramophone Co	Lewis, Edward Roberts
Deloitte Plender Griffiths	Kilpatrick, J
Deloitte, Plender, Griffiths	Kettle, Russell
DeLorean	Fallon, Ivan & Strodes, James
DeLorean	Levin, Hillel
Delta Cables	Aerialite
Dema Glass	Woodward, Herbert William
Dempster, Robert & Sons	Dempster, Robert & Sons

Demuth, Lewis and Co	**Midland Tar Distillers**
Dennis Brothers	**Twelvetrees, Richard W R & Squire, Pepys**
Dennison Watch Case Co	**Roche, J C**
Dennison Watch Case Co	**Tramayne, Arthur**
Denny, William & Bros	**Bruce, Alexander Balmain**
Denny, William & Bros	**Denny, William & Bros**
Denny, William & Bros	**Denny, William & Bros**
Denny, William & Bros	**Denny, William & Bros**
Denny, William & Bros	**Denny, William & Bros**
Denny, William & Bros	**Denny, William & Bros**
Denny, William & Bros	**Robertson, P L**
Dent & Hellyer	**Dent & Hellyer**
Dent & Hellyer	**Hellyer, Bertram**
Dent, J M	**Dent, Joseph Malaby**
Derry & Sons	**Derry and Sons**
Derry & Toms	**Toms, Stanley J**
Derwent Works	**Taylor, J**
Devitt & Moore	**Course, Alfred George**
Devitt & Moore	**Jones, Clement Wakefield**
Dewar, John & Sons	**Anderson, John L**
Dewar, John & Sons	**Dewar**
Dewey, J & S	**Dewey, J & S**
Dick, Kerr & Co	**Wilson, John**
Dick, R & J	**Chalmers, Thomas**
Dickens, Charles	**Brooks, Brian**
Dickinson, John & Co	**Dickinson & Co**
Dickinson, John & Co	**Evans, Joan**
Dickinson, John & Co	**Evans, Joan**
Dickinson, John & Co	**Evans, Lewis**
Distillers Co	**Hughes, F A**
Distillers Co	**Lee, T A**
Distillers Co	**Moss, M S & Hume, J R**
Distilling Industry in Scotland	**Weir, Ronald B**
Dixey, C W & Son	**Dixey, C W & Son**
Dixon Ross	**Dyson, Anthony**
Dixon, William & Sons	**Slaven, Anthony**
Dixons	**Lerner, Harry**
Dobson & Barlow	**Dobson & Barlow**
Dobson & Barlow	**Dobson & Barlow**
Dobson & Barlow	**Kirk, R M & Simmons, C**
Dockland	**North East London Polytechnic/Greater Lonc**
Dodwell & Co	**Dodwell**
Dodwell & Co	**Warde, Edmund (ed)**
Doffcocker Turnpike	**Billington, W D**
Dollond & Aitchison	**Barty-King, Hugh**
Dollond & Aitchison	**King, Henry Charles**
Donaldson Line	**Dunnett, Alastair MacTavish**
Doncaster, Daniel & Sons	**Doncaster, Daniel**
Doncaster, Daniel & Sons	**Doncaster, Daniel**
Donisthorpe	**Ellis, Shirley**
Donkin, Bryan & Co	**Baston, Christopher**
Donkin, Bryan & Co	**Donkin, Bryan**
Donkin, Bryan & Co	**Donkin, Harry Julyan**
Dore, John & Co	**Slater, A W**
Dorman Long	**Boswell, Jonathan S**

Dorman Long	Wilson, Charles Henry
Dorman Smith	Lee, Norman & Stubbs, Peter C
Dorothea Slate Quarry	Jones, G P
Doulton & Co	Doulton & Co
Doulton & Co	Doulton & Co
Doulton & Co	Gosse, Edmund William
Dove Brothers	Braithwaite, David
Dover Harbour	Mellor, A J L
Dowlais Iron Co	Daunton, Martin James
Dowlais Iron Co	Davies, J Hathren
Dowlais Iron Co	Elsas, Madeleine (ed)
Dowlais Iron Co	Gibbs, John Morel
Dowlais Iron Co	Lewis, M J
Dowlais Iron Co	Owen, John Alastair
Dowlais Iron Co	Roberts, Colin William
Dowlais Iron Co	Weetch, Kenneth Thomas
Dowty Group	Rolt, Lionel Thomas Caswall
Doxford, William & Co	Doxford, William
Dray, G W & Son	Dray & Drayton
Dreweatt, Watson and Barton	Dreweatt, Watson and Barton
Drivers Jonas	Barty-King, Hugh
Drummonds	Bolitho, Henry Hector & Peel, Derek
Dubs & Co	Campbell, Roy Hutcheson
Dudley Estate	Raybould, Trevor J
Dumbarton Corporation Gas	Dumbarton Corporation Gas Undertaking
Dumbarton Glass Work Co	Logan, John C
Dumbarton Glass Works Co	Logan, John C
Duncan Brothers & Co	Duncan Brothers & Co
Duncan Dunbar	Jones, Clement Wakefield
Duncan, Flockhart & Co	Duncan, Flockhart & Co
Duncan, Walter & Goodricke	Duncan Brothers & Co
Dundee Banking Co	Boase, Charles William
Dundee Banking Co	Munn, Charles W
Dundee Banking Co	Royal Bank of Scotland
Dundee C W S	Dundee Eastern Co-operative Society
Dundee Eastern Co-operative Soc	Dundee Eastern Co-operative Society
Dundee Harbour Trust	Thompson, J Hannay & Ritchie, Geo G
Dundee Port & Trade	Beckles, N I
Dundee Savings Bank	Dundee Savings Bank
Dundee Savings Bank	Miln, John
Dundee Shipbuilders' Co	Stephen, Alexander and Sons
Dundee, Perth & London Shipping	Dundee, Perth & London Shipping
Dunhill, Alfred	Dunhill, Mary
Dunlop Rubber Co	Beable, William Henry
Dunlop Rubber Co	Du Cros, Arthur Philip
Dunlop Rubber Co	Jennings, Paul Francis
Dunlop Rubber Co	Jones, Geoffrey
Dunlop Rubber Co	Jones, Geoffrey
Dunlop Rubber Co	Storrs, Ronald Henry Amherst
Durtnell, R & Sons	Durtnell, R & Sons
Dussek Bitumen	Dussek Bitumen
Dutton's Blackburn Brewery	Dutton's Blackburn Brewery
Dux Chemical Solutions	Willesden Dux
E M B Co	E M B Co
Eadie Brothers	Eadie Brothers

479

Eagle & British Dominions Ins Co	Shepherd, A F
Eagle Star Insurance Co	Eagle Star Insurance Co
Eagle Star Insurance Co	Spater, E
Eagley Mills	Marsden, J S & Brock, D B S
Earle's Shipbuilding & Engineering	Bellamy, Joyce Margaret
Earle, C & W	Bellamy, Joyce Margaret
Early, Charles	Plummer, Alfred & Early, Richard E
East Anglian Railway Co	Gordon, Donald Ian
East Kent Packers	Whitehead, David C & Edwards, Lawrence
East Kent Road Car Co	East Kent Road Car Co
East Lancashire Paper Mill Co	East Lancashire Paper Mill Co
East Midland Allied Press	Newton, David
Eastbourne Waterworks	Eastbourne Waterworks
Eastern Associated Telegraph Co	Eastern Associated Telegraph Co
Eastern Counties Leather Co	Davies, Bernard
Eastern Investment Company	Davenport-Hines, R P T & Van Helten, J-J
Eastwood, J B	Eastwood, J B
Eastwoods	Willmott, Frank G
Eccles Provident Ind Co-op	Haslam, James
Economist	Economist
Economist	Hubback, David
Edbro	Seacombe, Andrew
Eddison Plant	Whitehead, Robert Arthur
Edinburgh Crystal	Woodward, Herbert William
Edinburgh Savings Bank	McCulloch, John Herries & Stirling, Kenneth
Edison-Swan Electric Co	Edison-Swan
Edleston, William	Edleston, William
EKCO	Lipman, Michael Isaac
Elder Dempster	Davies, Peter Neville
Elder Dempster	Davies, Peter Neville
Elder Dempster	Davies, Peter Neville
Elder Dempster	Greenhill, Robert G
Elder Dempster	Jones, Clement Wakefield
Elder Dempster	Milne, Alan Hay
Elders & Fyffes	Beaver, Patrick
Elders & Fyffes	Parsons, Richard M
Electric Telegraph Co	Kieve, Jeffrey L
Electrical Appliances	Corley, Thomas Anthony Buchanan
Electrical Industry	Hennessey, Roger Anthony Sean
Electrical Industry	Sakamoto, T
Electricity Supply	Ballin, H H
Electricity Supply	Hannah, Leslie
Electricity Supply	Hannah, Leslie
Electricity Supply	Hill, G W
Electricity Supply	P E P (Political and Economic Planning)
Electricity Supply in Scotland	Logan, John C
Electro-Hydraulics	Owen Organisation
Elkington & Co	Leader, Robert Eadon
Ellerman Lines	Ellerman Lines
Ellerman Lines	Jones, Clement Wakefield
Ellerman Lines	Taylor, James
Elliott Brothers	Hendry, John
Elliotts of Reading	Elliotts of Reading
Ellis & Everard	Ellis & Everard
Ellis & Everard	Ellis, Colin D B

Ellis & Everard	Ellis, Joseph & Sons
Ellis, Joseph & Sons	Ellis & Everard
Ellis, Joseph & Sons	Ellis, Joseph & Sons
Ellis, Richard	Wainwright, David
Ellis, Wood, Bickersteth & Hazel	Read, Joan
Ellon Savings Bank	Horne, H Oliver
Ellsons the Bakers	Chapman, Elaine
Elsecar and Milton Ironworks	Clayton, A K
Elson, C H & Sons	Elson, C H & Sons
Elys (Wimbledon)	Ely, Vernon N
Empire Stores	Beaver, Patrick
Employers' Liability Assurance	Robinson, Harry Perry
Enfield Autocar Co	Solloway, William J
Enfield Cycle Co	Smith, Barbara M D
Enfield Electricity Works	North Metropolitan Electrical Power Distrit
Enfield Highway Co-op Soc	Smith, H Charles
Enfield Manufacturing Co	Enfield Manufacturing Co.
Eng & Shipbuilding in Scotland	Moss, M S & Hume, J R
Engineering Employers' Federation	Wigham, Eric Leonard
Engineering Ind; N Ireland	Coe, W E
English China Clays	Hudson, Kenneth
English Electric	Andrews, H H
English Electric	Dutton, P A
English Electric-A E I Traction	Baker, Allan C & Civil, Thomas D A
English Sewing Cotton Co	Blyth, Henry Edward
English Sewing Cotton Co	Fitton, Robert S & Wadsworth Alfred P
English, John & Co, Feckenham	Jones, S R H
English, John & Co, Feckenham	Nokes, B C G
Ensor & Co	Ensor & Co
Epworth Press	Cumbers, Frank
Equitable Life Assurance	Anderson, James Gibson
Equitable Life Assurance	Ogborn, Maurice Edward
Erdman, Edward L	Erdman, Edward L
Erlebach & Co	Paul, Philip
Ernst & Whinney	Jones, H Edgar
Escombe, McGrath & Co	Escombe, W M L
Essex & Suffolk Equitable Ins	Drew, Bernard
Esso Petroleum Co	Flanders, Allan David
Esso Petroleum Co	Popham, Hugh
Ethicon	Bailey, L A
Evans Medical Supplies	Evans Medical
Evans Medical Supplies	Smeeton, Arthur E
Evans, Richard & Co	Evans, Richard
Evered & Co	Evered & Co
Everett	Jones, Albert Everett
Everett, Edgcumbe & Co	Everett, Edgcumbe & Co
Eversheds & Vignoles	Eversheds & Vignoles
Ewarts of Belfast	Lawlor, Harold C
Ewer, George	Ewer, George
Exchange Telegraph Co	Scott, James Maurice
Explosives Industry	International Conference of Applied Chemi
Express & Star (Wolverhampton)	Seaton, R
Express Dairy	Enock, Arthur Guy
Express Dairy	Express Dairy
Express Dairy	Morgan, Bryan Stanford

482

Firth, Thos & Sons	Marshall, A C & Newbould, Herbert
Firth-Derihon Stampings	Firth-Derihon
Fishburn Printing Ink Co	Leach, Robert
Fisons	Law, Rupert S
Fitch Lovell	Keevil, Ambrose
Flavel, Sidney & Co	Flavel, Sidney & Co
Fleetway House	Dilnot, George
Fleming, John & Co	Perren, Richard
Fletcher & Stewart	Bradley, D
Fletcher & Stewart	Fletcher & Stewart
Fletcher, Robert & Son	Hampson, Cyril G
Fletcher, William & Sons	Fletcher, Samuel Billyeald
Fletchers	Hill, Howard
Flexible Roads Industry	Earle, James Basil Foster
Flintshire Oil & Cannel Co	Rippon, Guy S O
Foden	Kennett, Pat
Food Combines	Labour Research Dept
Ford & Weston	Ford & Weston
Ford Motor	Beynon, Huw
Ford Motor	Rae, John B
Ford Motor	Wilkins, Mira
Ford, Ayrton	Pafford, Elizabeth R & John, H P
Fordath	Fordath
Foreign & Colonial Investment Co	Last, Donald
Forestal Land Timber & Railways	Hicks, Agnes Hedvig
Forster, John & Sons	Sigsworth, Eric Milton
Forster, John & Sons	Sigsworth, Eric Milton
Forsyth & Co	Neal, William K & Back, David H
Forth Valley Co-op	Alloa Co-operative Society
Forth Valley Co-op	Cook, William
Forth Valley Co-op	Flanagan, James A
Forth Valley Co-op	Gordon, Thomas Crouther
Forth Valley Co-op	Murray, William
Forth Valley Co-op	Stewart, James
Fortunes Made in Business	Hogg, James (ed)
Fortunes Made in Business	Sampson Low
Foseco Minsep	Atterton, David
Foster & Braithwaite	Foster & Braithwaite
Foster & Braithwaite	Foster & Braithwaite
Foster & Braithwaite	Reader, William Joseph
Fosters	Fosters
Fowlers of Leeds	Davis, Theo
Fowlers of Leeds	Lane, Michael R
Fox Brothers & Co	Fox Brothers & Co
Fox Brothers & Co	Fox, Hubert
Fox Brothers & Co	Fox, Joseph Hoyland
Fox, Humphrey & J	Fox, Humphrey & J
Fox, Samuel & Co	Moxon, Stanley
Fox, Samuel & Co	Stansfield, Hazel
Foyle, W & G	Fabes, Gilbert H
France, Wm, Fenwick & Co	France, Wm, Fenwick & Co
Francis, Day & Hunter	Abbott, John
Francis, F	Francis, F
Fraud and High Finance	Vallance, Aylmer
Freshfields	Slinn, Judith

Fribourg & Treyer	Arlott, John
Fribourg & Treyer	Evans, George
Friedheim, Oscar	Brewer, Roy
Friends' Provident & Century Ins	Friends' Provident & Century Insurance Off
Friends' Provident & Century Ins	Friends' Provident & Century Insurance Off
Friends' Provident Life	Tregoning, David & Cockerell, Hugh
Fry, J S & Sons	Fry, J S & Sons
Fry, J S & Sons	Fry, J S & Sons
Fry, J S & Sons	Fry, J S & Sons
Fry, J S & Sons	Jones, Geoffrey
Fuel & Power Industries	Political and Economic Planning
Fulham Pottery	Haselgrove, D & Murray, J (eds)
Fuller Electrical	Fuller Electrical & Manufacturing Co
Fuller Electrical	Fuller Electrical & Manufacturing Co
Fullers Earth Union	Greensmith, J
Fullwood & Bland	Mytton-Davies, Cynric
Furness and Barrow	Marshall, John Duncan
Furness Interests	Boyce, G H
Furness Railway	Pollard, Sidney & Marshall, J D
Furness, Withy & Co	Henderson, A J
Furness, Withy & Co	Jones, Clement Wakefield
Furniture Industry	Oliver, John L
Fyffes	Beaver, Patrick
G E C	Bridges, T C & Tiltman, H H
G E C	Dutton, P A
G E C	Hirst, Hugo
G E C	Jones, Robert & Marriott, Oliver
G E C	Latham, Joseph
G E C	Loring, Henry
G E C	Slater, Ernest
G E C	Whyte, Adam Gowans
G K N	Addis, John Philip
G K N	Guest, Keen & Nettlefolds
G K N	Jones, H Edgar
G K N	Jones, H Edgar
G K N	Jones, H Edgar
G K N	Owen, John Alastair
G K N	Thomas, Earl B
G K N Sankey	Mackenzie, Edward Montague Compton
G M S Syndicate	Waldron, Robin
G Q Parachute Co	Nockolds, Harold
Gallaher	Gallaher
Galloway, John & Co	Galloway, John
Galtons of Birmingham	Smith, Barbara M D
Gamage, A W	Beable, William Henry
Gamage, A W	Bridges, T C & Tiltman, H H
Gammons, Walter	Gammons, Walter
Gardner & Bazley	O'Connor, Denis
Gardner & Bazley	Stone, Sheila
Gardner, Joseph & Sons	Gardner, Joseph & Sons
Gardners	Whitehead, David Charles
Garforth Collieries	Hudson, Graham S
Garlands	Garlands
Garner, James & Sons	Garner, James & Sons
Garnett, G & Sons	Garnett, G & Sons

484

Gillett Brothers Discount Co	Sayers, Richard Sidney
Gillett Brothers Discount Co	Taylor, Audrey Mary
Gillette Industries	Coster, Ian
Gillott, Joseph	Edwards, E
Glascock, J L's Successors	Glascock, J L's Successors
Glasgow & South Western Railway	Highet, Campbell
Glasgow City & District Railway	Simpson, Michael
Glasgow Herald	Phillips, Alastair
Glasgow Stock Exchange	Glasgow Stock Exchange
Glasgow Tramways	Simpson, Michael
Glasgow University Press	Maclehose, James
Glass Industry	Ross, Catherine
Glass Industry of the Weald	Kenyon, George Hughes
Glasshouses	Buckley, Francis
Glaxo	Beable, William Henry
Glaxo	Chapman-Huston, W W Desmond M & Cripps,
Glaxo	Cripps, Ernest Charles
Glaxo	Davenport-Hines, Richard P T
Glaxo	Jephcott, Harry
Glen Line	Glen Line
Glenfiddich Distillery	Collinson, Francis
Glenfield & Kennedy	Morris, James A
Glenfield 'Progress' Co-op	Halstead, R
Glenlivet	Glenlivet
Glenlivet	Glenlivet
Glenpatrick Distillers	Craig, Charles
Glossop, W & J	Glossop, W & J
Gloster Aircraft Co	Whitaker, John
Gloucester Railway Carriage	Gloucester Railway Carriage & Wagon Co
Glover & Co	Sugiyama, Shinya
Glyn Mills & Co	Browne, Eric Gore
Glyn Mills & Co	Browne, Eric Gore
Glyn Mills & Co	Fulford, Roger Thomas Baldwin
Glynn, John & Son	Jones, Clement Wakefield
Glynwed	Flavel, Sidney & Co
Goad, Rigg & Co	Goad, Rigg & Co
Goblin B V C	Goblin B V C
Golden Valley Railway	Mowat, Charles Loch
Gollancz, Victor	Hodges, Sheila
Goodwin Barsby & Co	Pochin, R Eric
Gordon & Gotch	Bell, Roy Frederick
Gordon Russell	Naylor, Gillian
Gordon's	Tanqueray, Gordon & Co
Gosnell, John & Co	Gosnell, John & Co
Goss, W H	Willis-Fear, M J W
Gotch & Sons	Church, Roy Anthony
Gotch & Sons	Church, Roy Anthony
Gourlays Brothers & Co	Lythe, Samuel George Edgar
Gourock Ropework Co	Blake, George
Govan Collieries	Payne, Peter Lester
Govan Collieries	Slaven, Anthony
Government & Business	Hannah, Leslie
Grace, Darbyshire & Todd	Grace, Darbyshire & Todd
Gramophone Company	Jones, Geoffrey
Granite Industry in Aberdeen	Diack, William

Grant, William & Sons	Collinson, Francis
Grassmoor Colliery Co	Bryan, M A
Gray, William & Co	Craig, Robin
Grayson, Rollo and Clover Docks	Brooks, William Collin
Great Central Railway	Dow, George
Great Eastern Railway	Allen, Cecil John
Great Eastern Railway	Barker, Theodore Cardwell
Great Horton Co-operative Soc	Hodgson, H
Great North of Scotland Railway	Harvey, Charles Malcolm Barclay
Great Northern Railway	Grinling, Charles Herbert
Great Northern Railway	Wrottesley, John
Great Northern Tobacco Co	Hirst
Great Universal Stores	Great Universal Stores
Great Western Railway	Bonavia, Michael Robert
Great Western Railway	Channon, Geoffrey
Great Western Railway	Home, Gordon
Great Western Railway	Joby, Richard S
Great Western Railway	MacDermot, Edward T (Clinker, C R & Nott, (
Great Western Railway	Mowat, Charles Loch
Great Western Railway	Rolt, Lionel Thomas Caswall
Great Western Railway	Semmens, Peter William Brett
Great Western Railway	Simmons, Jack (ed)
Greater Manchester Transport	Hyde, W G S (ed)
Greaves & Thomas	Greaves & Thomas
Greek & Oriental Steam Navigation	Xenos, Stefanos
Green, E & Son, Wakefield	Green, E & Son
Greenall Whitley	Slater, J Norman
Greenall, Gilbert & John	Greenall, Gilbert & John
Greene King	Page, Ken
Greene King	Wilson, Richard G
Greening, N & Sons	Mais, Stuart Peter Brodie
Greenock Central Co-op Soc	Swan, Malcolm S
Greensmith & Thackwray	King, David I
Greensmith, Wm & Son	King, David I
Greenwood & Batley	Floud, Roderick C
Greg, R & Co	Greg, R
Greg, Samuel & Co	Rose, Mary B
Greg, Samuel & Co	Rose, Mary B
Greg, Samuel & Co	Rose, Mary B
Gregory, Robert & Co	Gregory, Robert & Co
Gregory, Rowcliffe & Co	Davis, Patrick
Gresham House Estate Co	Burnand, I B
Gresham House Estate Co	Gresham House Estate Company
Gresham Life Assurance Soc	Gresham Life Assurance Society
Gresham Trust	Kinross, John
Gridley Miskin	Gridley Miskin
Griffin & George	Mayer, H C
Griffin Brewery	Corran, T H
Griffin Foundry	Robinson, Philip Moffat
Grimbly Hughes	Grimbly Hughes
Grimsby Gas	Roberts, David E
Grindlay's Bank	Aldington, Lord (Toby Low)
Grindlay's Bank	Grindlay's
Grosvenor Chater	Chater, Michael
Grouts of Enfield	Kensey, M F

Groves & Whitnall	Groves, J W P & Keith G
Grunwick	Dromey, Jack & Taylor, Graham
Grunwick	Ward, George
Guard Bridge Paper Co	Weatherill, Lorna Mary
Guardian	Ayerst, David George Ogilvy
Guardian	Mills, William Haslam
Guardian Assurance Co	Guardian Assurance Co
Guardian Assurance Co	Tarn, A W & Byles, C E
Guest Keen Baldwins	Guest Keen Baldwins
Guest Keen Iron & Steel Co	Elsas, Madeleine (ed)
Guinness	Brown, John Falcon
Guinness	Guinness
Guinness	Lynch, Patrick & Vaizey, John
Guinness	Sibley, Brian
Guinness Peat	McGrandle, Leith
Gunstonemaker	Teesdale, E
Gurney & Co	Bidwell, William Henry
Gurteens of Haverhill	Payne, Sara
Guthries	Allen, George C & Donnithorne, Audrey G
Guy Motors	Guy Motors
Habitat	Goodden, Susanna
Habitat	Phillips, Barty
Haden, G N & Sons	Haden, George Nelson & Sons
Hadfields	Bridges, T C & Tiltman, H H
Hadfields	Hadfields
Hadfields	Hadfields
Hadley, Joseph (Holdings)	Janes, Hurford
Haig, John & Co	Laver, James
Haimes, Thomas & Co	Haimes, Thomas & Co
Halford Cycle Co	Halford Cycle Co
Halford Cycle Co	Jones, B Alcwyn
Halifax Banks	Roth, H Ling
Halifax Building Society	Bacon, R K
Halifax Building Society	Bridges, T C & Tiltman, H H
Halifax Building Society	Halifax Building Society
Halifax Building Society	Halifax Building Society
Halifax Building Society	Halifax Building Society
Halifax Building Society	Hobson, Oscar Rudolf
Halifax Equitable Benefit Bldg Soc	Alderson, J W & Ogden, A E
Halifax Flour Society	Halifax Flour Society
Halifax Industrial Soc	Blatchford, Montagu J
Hall & Co.	Dobson, Charles George
Hall & Woodhouse	Janes, Hurford
Hall Harding	Hall Harding
Hall's Barton Ropery Co	Hall's Barton Ropery Co
Hall, Alexander & Son	Mackie, W
Hall, English & Co	Jones, S R H
Hall, J & E	Hesketh, Everard
Hall, J & E	Miller, Harry
Hall-Thermotank	Miller, Harry
Hambro's Bank	Bramsen, Bo & Wain, Kathleen
Hambro's Bank	Hambro's Bank
Hamilton & Co	Girtin, T H
Hammermen of Glasgow	Lumsden, Harry & Aitken, P Henderson
Hammond & Hussey	Hammond and Hussey

488

Hand-in-Hand Fire and Life Ass	Hand-in-Hand Fire & Life
Hand-in-Hand Fire and Life Ass	Hand-in-Hand Fire & Life
Handley Page	Barnes, Christopher Henry George Bartlett
Handley Page	Fearon, Peter
Handysides & Co	McLellan, R S
Hansard	Trewin, John C & King, Evelyn M
Hanson, J & Sons, Modern Dairies	Hanson, James & Sons
Hanson, Julia & Sons	Radmore, D F
Hanson, Samuel	Godwin, George Stanley
Harbutts of Bath	Harbutts of Bath
Hardwick Colliery Co	Didham, R C
Hardwick Colliery Co	Hardwick Colliery Co
Hardys & Hansons	Bruce, George
Hargreaves & Clegg	Littler, Eric Raymond
Hargreaves, Henry & Sons	Hargreaves, Henry and Sons
Harland & Wolff	Jefferson, Herbert
Harland & Wolff	Moss, Michael S & Hume John R
Harland & Wolff	Peirson, J Gordon
Harland & Wolff	Rebbeck, D
Harland & Wolff	Taylor, Michael John Haddrick
Harmer, F W & Co	Harmer, F W & Co
Harper, John & Co	Field, H
Harrild & Sons	Liveing, Edward George Downing
Harris & Pearson	Harris and Pearson
Harris Tweed	Thompson, Francis G
Harris, Joseph	Clay, Ewart Waide
Harrison & Sons	Harrison & Sons
Harrison & Sons	Harrison, Cecil R & H G
Harrison, George & Co	Harrison, George & Co
Harrisons & Crosfield	Harrisons & Crosfield
Harrisons of Liverpool	Hyde, Francis Edwin
Harrisons of Liverpool	Jones, Clement Wakefield
Harrods	Dale, Tim
Harrods	Harrods
Hart & Levy	Hart & Levy
Hartleys	Beable, William Henry
Hartonclean	Dobson, Eric B
Harvey & Beard	Harvey & Beard
Harvey & Co	Vale, Henry Edmund Theodoric
Harvey, John & Sons	Harrison, Godfrey Percival
Haskins & Sells	Haskins & Sells
Haslam, John & Co	Haslam, William Heywood & Morris, F E
Hatchards	Laver, James
Hawick Co-operative Store Co	Hawick Co-operative Store Co
Hawker Siddeley	Sharp, Cecil Martin
Hawkins, Alexander	Hawkins, Alexander
Hawthorn Leslie	Browne, B C
Hawthorn Leslie	Clarke, Joseph Francis
Hay & Co (Lerwick)	Nicolson, James Robert
Hay's Wharf	Ellis, Aytoun
Hay's Wharf	Ellis, Aytoun
Hay's Wharf	Hay's Wharf
Hay's Wharf	Hay's Wharf Cartage Co
Hay's Wharf Cartage Co	Turnbull, Gerard L
Hay, J & J	Bowman, A I

Hay, William	Hay, William
Haydock	Roberts, T J
Haywards of the Borough	Haywards
Hazell, Watson & Viney	Hazell, Watson & Viney
Hazell, Watson & Viney	Keefe, H J
Heal's	Goodden, Susanna
Heap & Partners	Millar, John
Heap, Samuel & Son	Harte, Negley B
Heart of England Building Soc	Martin, P W
Hearts of Oak Benefit Soc	Newman, Tom Seth
Heath, C E & Co	Brown, Antony
Heathcoat	Allen, Walter Gore
Heathcote, John	Varley, Donald Emerson
Heaton, William & Sons	Hargreaves, R
Heavy Industries in Scotland	Byres, T J
Hebble Motor Services	Bell, David
Hebden Bridge Fustian Mfr Co-op	Hebden Bridge Fustian
Hebden Bridge Industrial Co-op	Hebden Bridge Ind Co-op Soc
Hedley, Thomas	Edwards, Harold Raymond
Heinz, H J	Alberts, Robert Carman
Heinz, H J & Co	Potter, Stephen
Henckel du Buisson & Co	Henckel du Buisson & Co
Henckel, du Buisson & Co	Breton, Norton
Henderson Administration	Wainwright, David
Henderson, Hogg & Co	Henderson, Hogg & Co
Henderson, P & Co	Laird, Dorothy
Henderson, Semple & Co	Cameron, John
Henley's Telegraph Works	Slater, Ernest
Henry Brown, Woollen Mfr	Gulvin, Clifford (ed)
Herbert, Alfred	Herbert, Alfred
Herring Fishing	Gray, Malcolm
Herring, Daw & Manners	Herring, Daw & Manners
Heseltine, Powell & Co	Warren, P G
Hewetson, A W	Jopp, Keith
Hewit, J & Sons	Hewit, J & Sons
Hewlett, C J & Son	Hewlett, C J & Son
Heydemann, N & Co	Heydemann, N & Co
Heywood, Arthur Sons & Co	Heywood, Arthur Sons & Co
Hick, Hargreaves & Co	Hick, Hargreaves & Co
Hickman, Alfred	Morton, G R & LeGuillou
Higgs & Hill	Higgs & Hill
Higgs & Hill	Higgs & Hill
High Wycombe Chair Making	Mayes, Leonard John
High Wycombe Furniture Industry	Lowe, Dorothy P
Highgate Brewery	Lloyd, Keith J
Highland Railway Company	Highland Railway Company
Highley Pens	Charles, A A S
Higsons Brewery	Cook, Norman
Hill, Charles & Sons	Hill, John Charles Gathorne
Hill, R & J	Davenport, John
Hillman's Airways	Conn, Michael
Hilton Transport Services	Hytner, B A & Irvine, I A N
Hinckley Gas	Hinckley U D Council Gas Department
Hinde, F & Sons	Hinde, F & Sons
Hirst	Hirst

490

Hough, Arthur & Sons	Allman, Geoff
Houghton, J C & Co	Houghton, J C & Co
Houlder Brothers	Stevens, Edward Frank
Houldsworth	Fine Cotton Spinners
Houldsworth	Hayes, P A
Houston	Bowen, Frank Charles
Houston	McRoberts, J
Hovis	Beable, William Henry
Hovis Co	Dence, Alexander Henry
Howard & Bullough	Crossley, Richard Shaw
Howard & Sons	Howard & Sons
Howard Rotovator Co	Howard Rotovator Co
Howard, John & Son	Howard, John & Son
Howard, W W Brothers & Co	Watson, Rowland
Howards	Slater, A W
Howden, Alexander	Howden, Alexander
Howden, James & Co	Howden, James & Co
Howell & Co	Spalding, C W
Huddersfield Industrial Soc	Balmforth, Owen
Hughes Bolckow	White, Horace
Hughes, F A	Hughes, F A
Hull Chemists	Bellamy, Joyce Margaret
Hull Flax & Cotton Mill Co	Bellamy, Joyce Margaret
Hull Stearine & Warehousing Co	Brace, Harold Witty
Hull Tramways	Lee, G A
Hull, Blyth & Co	Woodhouse, G B
Hulme Patent Advertising Match	Littler, Eric Raymond
Humberts	Barber, Derek
Hunslet Engine Co	Rolt, Lionel Thomas Caswall
Hunt Edmunds & Co	Hunt Edmunds & Co
Hunt, Roope & Co	Hunt, Roope & Co
Hunt, William & Sons	Burritt, Elihu
Hunting Gate Group	Reader, William Joseph
Hunting Group	Hackman, Rowan M B H
Hunting Group	Hunting & Son
Hunting Group	Hunting, Percy
Huntley & Palmer	Beable, William Henry
Huntley & Palmers	Corley, Thomas Anthony Buchanan
Huntley & Palmers	Huntley & Palmers
Huntley & Palmers	Huntley & Palmers
Huntley & Palmers	Huntley & Palmers
Huntley, Boorne and Stevens	Corley, Thomas Anthony Buchanan
Hunts	Gipson, R
Huntsman, B	Huntsman, Benjamin
Hutchinson	Lusty, Robert
Hutchisons of Kirkcaldy	Hutchisons of Kirkcaldy
Hythe Pier & Southampton Ferry	Titheridge, Alan
I C F C	Kinross, John
I C I	Bolitho, Henry Hector
I C I	Brunner, Mond
I C I	Castner-Kellner
I C I	Cohen, John Michael
I C I	Dick, W F L
I C I	Fox, W E
I C I	Goodman, Jean

John Bull	Hyman, Alan
John Bull	Minney, Rubeigh James
John Bull	Symons, Julian
John Bull Rubber Co	John Bull Rubber Co
John Lewis Partnership	Flanders, A D; Pomeranz & Woodward
John Lewis Partnership	Lewis, John Spedan
John Lewis Partnership	Macpherson, Hugh (ed)
Johnsen & Jorgensen	Johnsen & Jorgensen
Johnson & Phillips	Brooks, William Collin
Johnson Group Cleaners	Bird, Leslie
Johnson Group Cleaners	Clay, Ewart Waide
Johnson Group Cleaners	Dobson, Eric B
Johnson Group Cleaners	Johnson, Leslie
Johnson, C H and Sons	Timaeus, C E
Johnson, Matthey	Hunt, Leslie B
Johnson, Matthey	MacDonald, Donald
Johnson, Matthey	MacDonald, Donald
Johnson, Matthey	MacDonald, Donald & Hunt, Leslie B
Johnson, Richard & Nephew	Seth-Smith, Michael
Johnston, W & A K	Johnston, W & A K
Johnstone Co-operative Society	Taylor, Frank
Joint Stock Banking	Goodhart, Charles Albert Eric
Joint Stock Banking	Munn, Charles W
Joint Stock Banking in Scotland	Munn, Charles W
Joint Stock Banks	Cassis, Youssef
Jonathan Cape	Howard, Michael Spencer
Jonathan Cape	Lusty, Robert
Jones, A A & Shipman	Miller, Harry
Jones, David & Co, Liverpool	Little, Bryan
Jones, Samuel & Co	Jones, Samuel
Jones, Samuel & Co	Jones, Samuel
Jones, Yarrell & Co	Granville-Smith, J
Jordan & Sons	Jordan & Sons
Jorehaut Tea Co	Antrobus, Hinson Allan
Joscelyne, Clement	Joscelyne, Clement
Jowett Cars	Jowett Cars
Jowitt, George & Sons	Jowitt, George
Jowitt, Robert & Sons	Jowitt
Judkins	Collidge, W H
Jute Industries of Dundee	Lenman, Bruce & Donaldson, Kathleen
Jute Industry	Graham, O
K Shoes	Somervell, John
Kaye, Son & Co	O'Donoghue, K & Heaton, Paul M
Kebroyd Land and Milnes	Barlow, Ronald
Keighley Fleece Mills Co	Keighley Fleece Mills Co
Kells	Davies, Stuart
Kelly, John	Wilson, Ian
Kellys Directories	Beable, William Henry
Kemp's Mercantile Offices	Kemp's Mercantile Offices
Kendall	Kendall
Kenning Motors Group	Kenning Motors Group
Kenrick & Jefferson	Cartwright, Walter H
Kenrick & Jefferson	Kenrick & Jefferson
Kenrick & Jefferson	Kenrick & Jefferson
Kenrick & Jefferson	Kenrick & Jefferson

Kenrick & Jefferson	Stote, Amos
Kenrick, Archibald & Sons	Church, Roy Anthony
Kenrick, Archibald & Sons	Church, Roy Anthony
Kent Coal Concessions	Ritchie, Arthur Edwin
Kent Coalfield	Johnson, W
Kent Fruit Industry	Sharp, T J
Kent Insurance Co	Kent Insurance Co
Kent, G B & Sons	Woodall, Doris
Kent, George	Kent, George
Kenyon, James	Muir, Augustus
Kenyon, James & Son	Kenyon, James & Son
Kenyon, James & Son	Kenyon, James & Son
Kenyon, John & Co	Kenyon, John
Kenyon, William & Sons	Kenyon, William
Kerfoot, Thomas & Co	Shields, E H
Kestner Evaporator & Engineering	Kestner
Kettering 'Union' Boot and Shoe	Stanton, George
Kidd, William	Kidd, William
Kidderminster Carpet Industry	Bartlett, James Neville
Kidderminster Carpet Industry	Smith, L D
Killick Martin & Co	MacGregor, David Roy
Kincaids	Kincaid, J G
King & Co	Spring, A E
King & Hutchings	Bland, Leslie
King & Hutchings	King and Hutchings
King Alfred Motor Services	Freeman, J D F; Jowitt, R E & Murphy, R J
King Line	Mallett, Alan S
Kingsfords	Kingsford, Garlant & J B Marks
Kingston Cotton Mill Co	Bellamy, Joyce Margaret
Kirkcaldy & District Savings Bank	McKay, J A
Kirkman Finlay	Devine, Thomas Martin
Kirkstall Forge	Butler, Rodney
Kitcat, G & J	Adams, John
Kitsons of Leeds	Clark, Edwin Kitson
Kleinwort Benson	Diaper, Stefanie J
Klockner-Moeller (England)	Klockner-Moeller
Knowles & Foster	Knowles & Foster
Knowles of Bolton	Crankshaw, W P & Blackburn, Alfred
Kraft	Kraft
Kynoch	Kynoch
Lacre	Lacre
Laing, John	Coad, Roy
Laing, John	Laing, John & Son
Laker Airways	Banks, Howard
Laker Airways	Eglin, Roger & Ritchie, Barry
Lambert Howard	Lambert Howard
Lambeth Building Soc	Lambeth Building Society
Lancashire & Yorkshire Bank	Lancashire & Yorkshire Bank
Lancashire & Yorkshire Bank	McBurnie, John M
Lancashire & Yorkshire Railway	Bolton Environmental Education Project
Lancashire & Yorkshire Railway	Broadbridge, Seymour Albert
Lancashire & Yorkshire Railway	Bulleid, Henry Anthony Vaughan
Lancashire & Yorkshire Railway	Duckham, Baron Frederick
Lancashire & Yorkshire Railway	Marshall, John
Lancashire & Yorkshire Railway	Mason, Eric

Lancashire & Yorkshire Railway	Nock, Oswald Stevens
Lancashire & Yorkshire Railway	Normington, Thomas
Lancashire Cotton Corporation	Lancashire Cotton Corporation
Lancashire Cotton Industry	Sandberg, Lars G
Lancashire Cotton Industry	Smith, R
Lancashire Textile Industry	Tippett, Leonard Henry Caleb
Lancashire Watch Company	Lancashire Watch Company
Lancashire Watch Company	Smith, Alan
Lancaster & Locke	Fache, E C
Lanchester Engine Co	Kingsford, Peter Wilfrid
Lanchester Motor Co	Bird, Anthony C & Hutton-Stott, Francis H
Lanchester Motor Co	Kingsford, Peter Wilfrid
Land Investment and Nebraska	McFarlane, Larry A
Landis & Gyr	Jordan, Alexander
Laporte Chemicals	Laporte Chemicals
Larkhall Victualling Society	Bulloch, Robert
Latham, James	Latham, Edward Bryan
Laughton & Sons	Laughton, George A
Laurence, Alex & Sons	Laurence, Alastair
Laurence, Scott & Electromotors	Barfield, T J
Laxon, E and Co	Brooks, Brian
Lea-Francis	Price, Barrie
Leach, Hubert C	Leach, Hubert C
Lead Industry	Burt, Roger
Leadmining in Scotland	Smout, T C
Leather Glove Trade	Fudge, Muriel K
Leather Industry	Adam, Helen Pearl
Leather Industry	Church, Roy Anthony
Lee Howl & Co	Stevenson, L W
Lee Steel	Brailsford, Michael
Lee, Arthur & Sons	Lee, Arthur
Leeds Clothing	Thomas, Joan
Leeds General Cemetery Co	Fletcher, R S
Leeds Industrial Co-operative Soc	Holyoake, George Jacob
Leeds Leather Industry	Rimmer, William Gordon
Leeds Woollen Industry	Crump, William Bunting
Lees, J B & S	Lees, J B & S
Leesona-Holt	Dwyer, Frederick Joseph
Legal & General Assurance Soc	Leigh-Bennett, Ernest Pendarves
Leicester & S Derby Coalfield	Owen, Colin
Leicester Co-op Boot & Shoe	Plumb, J H
Leicester Co-op Boot 'Equity'	Greening, Edward Owen
Leicester Co-op Hosiery	Blandford, Thomas & Newell, George
Leicester Co-op Printing Soc	Leicester Co-operative Printing Society Lt
Leicester Co-operative Soc	Stephen, J Thomson
Leicester Gas	Roberts, David E
Leicester Trustee Savings Bank	Cave, G P & Martin, Janet
Leicester Water	Leicester Water Department
Leigh Friendly Co-operative Soc	Boydell, Thomas
Leisure Industry	Jones, S G
Leng, John & Co	Millar, Alexander Hastie
Leng, John & Co	Thomson, D C
Lennox Co-operative Soc	Craig, J
Leonhardt, D & Co	Charles, A A S
Lepard & Smiths	Owen, Roderic

Lerwick Harbour	Nicolson, James Robert
Lester, Thomas	Buck, Anne
Lethaby, W & Co	Lethaby, W & Co
Letraset	Chudley, John A
Letterpress Printing	Alford, Bernard William Ernest
Lever Brothers	Beable, William Henry
Lever Brothers	Jolly, William Percy
Lever Brothers	Leverhulme
Lever Brothers	Rimmer, William Gordon
Lever Brothers	Williams, Edmund
Lever Brothers	Wilson, Charles
Lever Brothers	Wilson, Charles
Lever Brothers	Wilson, Charles
Lewin	Wear, Russell & Lees, Eric
Lewis & Peat	McGrandle, Leith
Lewis's	Briggs, Asa
Lewis, H K & Co	Lewis, Henry King
Lewisham Silk Mills	Macartney, Sylvia & West, John
Liberty & Co	Adburgham, Alison
Liberty & Co	Laver, James
Life Assurance	Morrah, Dermot MacGregor
Lilleshall Co	Gale, Walter Keith Vernon & Nicholls, C R
Lime Industry in the Lothians	Skinner, Basil Chisholm
Lincoln Gas Light & Coke Co	Roberts, David E
Lincoln Industries	Alford, L G C
Lincoln Industries	Armstrong, J W
Lind, Peter & Co	Lind, Peter & Co
Lindsay Parkinson	Lindsay Parkinson
Lindsay, Smith & Co	Cameron, John
Linen Thread Co	Linen Thread Co
Linen Thread Co	Sinclair, Robert George
Lines Bros	Lines, Walter
Lintas	Sharpe, Len
Lipman	Lipman, Michael Isaac
Lipton	Bridges, T C & Tiltman, H H
Lipton	Lipton
Lipton	Mathias, Peter
Lipton	Waugh, Alexander Raban
Lister, R A & Co	Evans, David Ewart
Lister-Blackstone	Price, Thomas L
Lithgow	Reid, James Macarthur
Liverpool & London & Globe Ins	Simpson, James Dyer
Liverpool & Manchester Railway	Carlson, Robert Eugene
Liverpool & Manchester Railway	Ferneyhough, Frank
Liverpool & Manchester Railway	Richards, E S
Liverpool & Manchester Railway	Thomas, Ronald Henry George
Liverpool Banks	Hughes, John
Liverpool Corn Trade Assoc	Liverpool Corn Trade
Liverpool Merchants & Cotton	Williams, D M
Liverpool Shipping	Neal, F
Liverpool Stock Exchange	Dumbell, Stanley
Liverpool Timber Trade	Williams, David M
Livingstone, E & S	Livingstone, E & S
Llandudno & Colwyn Bay Rly	Anderson, Roy Claude
Llandudno, Old, New & Ty Gwyn	Williams, C J

Lloyd's List & Shipping Gazette	Fayle, Charles Ernest
Lloyd's List & Shipping Gazette	Lloyd's List and Shipping Gazette
Lloyd's of London	Brown, Antony
Lloyd's of London	Brown, Antony
Lloyd's of London	Cameron, A & Farndon, R
Lloyd's of London	Gibb, David Eric Watson
Lloyd's of London	Golding, Cecil F & Page, Douglas K
Lloyd's of London	Grey, Henry M
Lloyd's of London	Hodgson, Geoffrey
Lloyd's of London	Martin, Frederick W
Lloyd's of London	Straus, Ralph
Lloyd's of London	Worsley, Frank A & Griffith, Glyn
Lloyd's of London	Wright, Charles & Fayle, C Ernest
Lloyd's Packing Warehouses	Lloyd's Packing Warehouses
Lloyd's Register of Shipping	Blake, George
Lloyd's Register of Shipping	Lloyd's Register of Shipping
Lloyd, Attree & Smith	Lloyd, Attree & Smith
Lloyds	Flinn, Michael Walter
Lloyds Bank	Lloyd, Humphrey
Lloyds Bank	Lloyd, Samuel
Lloyds Bank	Sayers, Richard Sidney
Lloyds Bank	Windsor, David Burns
Lloyds Bank	Winton, J R
Lobb, John	Dobbs, Brian
Lobitos Oilfields	Miller, Rory
Lochrin's	House, Jack
Lock of St James's Street	Whitbourn, Frank
Lock, James & Co	Morgan, H Llewellyn
Lockwood & Carlisle	Merrill, John
Lockwood & Carlisle	Simons, Eric Norman
London & County Bank	Cooper Brothers
London & County Securities	Reid, Margaret Isabel
London & Greenwich Railway	Thomas, Ronald Henry George
London & Indian Dock Co	Pattison, G W
London & Lancashire Insurance	Francis, Eric Vernon
London & Lancashire Insurance	London and Lancashire Insurance Co
London & North Eastern Railway	Allen, Cecil John
London & North Eastern Railway	Bonavia, Michael Robert
London & North Eastern Railway	Bonavia, Michael Robert
London & North Eastern Railway	Davies, Randall Robert Henry
London & North Western Railway	Chaloner, William Henry
London & North Western Railway	Gourvish, Terence Richard
London & North Western Railway	Gourvish, Terence Richard
London & North Western Railway	Irving, R J
London & North Western Railway	Joby, Richard S
London & North Western Railway	Reed, B
London & North Western Railway	Steel, Wilfred L
London & South Western Bank	London & South Western Bank
London (Quaker) Lead Co	Raistrick, Arthur
London Assurance	Drew, Bernard
London Assurance	Drew, Bernard
London Assurance	Street, George Slythe
London Assurance	Withers, Hartley
London Bankers	Cassis, Youssef
London Brick Co	Hillier, Richard

London Brighton & South Coast Rly	Douglas, John Monteath
London Brighton & South Coast Rly	Turner, J Howard
London Chatham & Dover Rly	Gourvish, Terence Richard
London Co-operative Society	Brown, William Henry
London Coal Exchange	Coal Merchants, Society of
London Coal Exchange	Smith, R
London Corn Trade Assn	Barty-King, Hugh
London Gazette	Handover, Phyllis Margaret
London General Shipowners' Soc	Harris, Leonard
London Graving Dock Co	Crighton, John
London Graving Dock Co	Crighton, John
London Graving Dock Co	Hurd, Edgar
London Laundry, Coventry	Elson, C H & Sons
London Life Association	Conder, William S
London Metal Exchange	Gibson-Jarvie, Robert
London Midland & Scottish Rly	Ellis, Cuthbert Hamilton
London Midland & Scottish Rly	Williamson, J W
London Mining Exchange	Burt, Roger
London Transport	Baker, John Clifford Yorke
London Transport	Barker, Theodore C & Robbins, R Michael
London Transport	Barman, Christian
London Transport	Bridges, T C & Tiltman, H H
London Transport	Edmonds, Alexander
London Transport	Jackson, Alan A C & Croome, Desmond F
London Transport	Lee, Charles Edward
London United Tramways	Wilson, Geoffrey
Londonderry Shirt Industry	Slade, E H
Longley, James & Co	Longley
Longley, James & Co	Longley
Longley, James & Co	Smith, Rhonda
Longman	Blagden, Cyprian
Longman	Briggs, Asa
Longman	Cox, Harold & Chandler, John E
Longman	Wallis, Philip
Lonrho	Cronjé, Suzanne; Ling, Margaret & Cronjé,
Lord Dudley's Mines and Ironworks	Fereday, R P
Lord, John & Robert of Halliwell	O'Connor, Denis
Lord, John & Robert of Halliwell	Stone, Sheila
Loughborough Waterworks	Hodson, George & F W
Lovell, Y J	Lovell, Y J
Low & Bonar	Cooke, A J
Low, James F	Low, James F
Lowe & Oliver	Lowe & Oliver
Lowe, Thomas & Sons	Lowe, Thomas & Sons
Lucas Aerospace	Lucas Aerospace
Lucas Industries	Nockolds, Harold
Lucy, W & Co	Andrews, Philip W S & Brunner, Elizabeth
Luddenden Industrial Co-op Soc	Greenwood, J
Luke & Spencer	Luke and Spencer
Lumbys	Lumbys
Luxury Trains	Behrend, George
Lye & Sons	Lye and Sons
Lye Forge	Mervyn, J F A
Lyle & Scott	Gulvin, Clifford
Lyle Shipping Co	Orbell, M John with Green, Ed & Moss, M

Lynch, H Foulks & Co	Lynch, Henry Foulks & Co
Lyons, J & Co	Beable, William Henry
Lyons, J & Co	Bridges, T C & Tiltman, H H
Lyons, J & Co	Lyons, J
Lyons, J & Co	Richardson, D J
Lysaght, John	Lysaght
M T I R A	De Barr, A E & Sharman, S M
M'Connel & Kennedy	Lee, Clive Howard
M'Connel & Kennedy	Lee, Clive Howard
Macadam	Reader, William Joseph
MacCallum, P & Sons	Hume, John R & Moss, Michael S
Macfarlane, Lang & Co	Macfarlane, Lang & Co
Machine Tool Industry	Floud, Roderick C
Machine Tool Industry	Saul, S B
Mackey's Seeds	Smyth, Hazel Pauline
Mackie, House of	Mackie
Mackie, Jas & Sons	Moore, A S
Mackinnon, William	Orchardson, I K
Mackintosh, John	Beable, William Henry
Mackintosh, John	Crutchley, George W
Mackintosh, John	Jeremy, David J
Mackintosh, John	Mackintosh, Eric D
Mackintosh, John	Mackintosh, Harold Vincent
Mackintosh, John	Mackintosh, John & Sons
Macmillan	Morgan, Charles
Macnab, A & J	Macnab, A & J
Maden, John	Stocks, Leslie A
Magadi Soda Co	Hill, Mervyn Frederick
Maggs, C W & Co (Melksham)	Maggs, C W & Co (Melksham)
Mahony, Martin & Bros	Mahony, Martin & Bros
Malleable Iron in Scotland	Campbell, Roy Hutcheson
Mallinson, William & Denny Mott	Mackie, W Euan
Mallinson, William & Denny Mott	Potter, Walter C
Man-Made Fibres Industry	Robson, Robert
Management Strategy	Hannah, Leslie (ed)
Manbré & Garton	Garbutt, John L
Manbré & Garton	Stoddard, Jeanne
Manchester & Milford Haven Rly	Bosley, P B
Manchester & Salford Bank	Allman, A H
Manchester Airport	Brookes, K P
Manchester Banks	Grindon, Leopold Hartley
Manchester Gas Dept	Manchester Gas Dept
Manchester Guardian	Mills, William Haslam
Manchester Liners	Stoker, R B
Manchester Merchants	Redford, Arthur (ed)
Manchester Ship Canal	Farnie, Douglas Anthony
Manchester Ship Canal	Leech, Bosdin Thomas
Manchester Ship Canal	Manchester, Port of
Manchester Ship Canal	Owen, David
Manchester Tramway Dept	Manchester Tramway Dept
Manchester, Port of	Farnie, Douglas Anthony
Manchester, Sheffield & Lincs Rly	Gourvish, T R
Mander Brothers	Mander
Manfield & Sons	Manfield & Sons
Manfield & Sons	Manfield & Sons

Manifoldia	Manifoldia
Mann Egerton	Shaw, M
Mann Judd Gordon & Co	Mann Judd Gordon & Co
Mann, Crossman & Paulin	Janes, Hurford
Manners, John	Hart & Levy
Mansfield Brewery Co	Bristow, Philip
Mansfields	Jennings, Eric
Manton, J & J	Neal, William K & Back, David H
Manufacturing Employers of 1907	Shaw, Christine
Mappin & Webb	Mappin Fraser, J N
Marconi	Baker, W J
Marconi	Donaldson, Frances Annesley
Marconi	Marconi's Wireless Telegraph Co
Mardon, Son & Hall	Mardon, Heber
Margarine	Mathias, Peter
Marine & General Mutual Life	Humpherson, L H
Marine Insurance Co	Marine Insurance Co
Maritime History	Palmer, S R & Williams, G (eds)
Mark & Moody	Haden, Harry Jack
Market Harborough Building Soc	Mee, F
Marks & Spencer	Briggs, Asa
Marks & Spencer	Rees, Morgan Goronwy
Marks & Spencer	Sieff, Israel Moses
Marks & Spencer	Tse, K K
Marley	Marley
Marments	Marment, Arthur Verriour
Marriage, E & Son	Marriage, E
Marriage, E & Son	Strong, Leonard Alfred George
Marsden, Edward	Whittaker, F Garth
Marsden, Frederick	Marsden, Frederick
Marsh Brothers & Co	Pollard, Sidney
Marshall & Snelgrove	Settle, Alison
Marshalls	Rimmer, William Gordon
Martin & Son	Hunt, R
Martin Baker Aircraft Co	Jewell, J
Martin Baker Aircraft Co	Martin Baker Aircraft
Martin Brothers, Potters	Haslam, Malcolm
Martin, C W & Sons	Martin, C W
Martineau	Fairrie, Geoffrey
Martins Bank	Chandler, George
Martins Bank	Cocks Biddulph & Co
Martins Bank	Heywood, Arthur Sons & Co
Martins Bank	Martin, John Biddulph
Martins Bank	Martins Bank
Martins Tobacconists	Beable, William Henry
Martinware	Haslam, Malcolm
Martyn, H H & Co	Whitaker, John
Mason, Joseph & Co	Mason, Joseph & Co
Masons	Haggar, Reginald George
Massey, B & S	Janes, Hurford
Massey-Férguson	Neufeld, Edward Peter
Massey-Harris-Ferguson	Fraser, Colin
Master Cotton Spinners' Assoc	Mills, William Haslam
Matchless	Hartley, Peter
Matthews, Wrightson Group	Matthews, Wrightson Group

Maudslay, Son & Field	Maudslay
May & Baker	Slinn, Judith
May (Hop Merchants)	May (Hop Merchants)
May Horticulture	May, Henry B
May, R & Son	May, R
Maypole Dairy Co	Monstead, Otto
McAlpine, Sir Robert & Sons	Childers, James Saxon
McAlpine, Sir Robert & Sons	McAlpine, Sir Robert
McArthur Group	Torrens, Hugh S
McCorquodale & Co	Ball, John D
McEwans of Perth	McEwans of Perth
McGregor, Peter & Sons	Bowman, A I
McGuckian	Muskett, A E
McKechnie Brothers	McKechnie, John D
Meakin, J & G	Hollowood, Albert Bernard
Meat Trade	Perren, Richard
Meccano	Gould, Maurice P
Mechanical Engineering	Saul, S B
Medical Sickness Annuity & Life	Knapman, Geoffrey J
Medway Navigation Co	Hilton, J A
Meggitt & Jones	Meggitt & Jones
Melrose, Andrew	Melrose, Andrew & Co
Melrose, Andrew	Mui, Hoh-Cheung & Lorna H
Melrose, William	Mui, Hoh-Cheung & Lorna H
Meltham Industrial Co-op	Haigh, A
Mennell, R C & Co	Tuke Mennell & Co
Menzies, John & Co	Gardiner, Leslie
Menzies, John & Co	Menzies, John
Menzies, John & Co	Menzies, John
Mercer Chronometers	Mercer, Tony
Meriden	Bruce-Gardyne, Jock
Meriden	Norton Villiers Triumph
Merryweather & Sons	Merryweather & Sons
Mersey Docks & Harbour Board	Hyde, Francis Edwin
Mersey Docks & Harbour Board	Mersey Docks
Mersey Docks & Harbour Board	Mountfield, Stuart
Mersey Steamship Co	Cottrell, P L
Merthyr Buses	Merthyr Tidfil County Borough
Merz & McLellan	Rowland, John Herbert Shelley
Metal Box	Metal Box
Metal Box	Reader, William Joseph
Metal Box	Walker, Denis
Methodist Insurance Co	Shearer, W Russell
Methodist Publishing	Cumbers, Frank
Metropolitan District Railway	Gourvish, T R
Metropolitan Electric Tramways	Gibbs, T A
Metropolitan Railway	Baker, John Clifford Yorke
Metropolitan Water Board	Chevalier, W S (ed)
Metropolitan Water Board	Rudden, Bernard
Metropolitan-Vickers	Dummelow, John
Metropolitan-Vickers	Mensforth, Eric
Metropolitan-Vickers	Metropolitan-Vickers
Meux's Brewery	Meux, Valerie Susie
Meux, Reid & Co	Corran, T H
Middleton & Tonge Industrial Soc	Partington, S

Midland Bank	Crick, Wilfred F & Wadsworth, John E
Midland Bank	Green, Edwin
Midland Counties Lace Mfrs' Assoc	Varley, Donald Emerson
Midland Iron Co	Midland Iron Co
Midland Motor Cylinder Co	Midland Motor Cylinder Co
Midland Railway	Barnes, Eric George
Midland Railway	Channon, Geoffrey
Midland Railway	Ellis, Cuthbert Hamilton
Midland Railway	Lambert, Richard Stanton
Midland Red	Anderson, Roy Claude
Midland Red	Gray, Paul; Keeley, Malcolm & Seale, John
Midland Tar Distillers	Midland Tar Distillers
Midland Vinegar Co	Wright, Louise
Midlands Counties Dairy	Midlands Counties Dairy
Miles Aircraft	Miles Aircraft
Military Aircraft Industry	Edgerton, D E H
Milk Marketing Board	Jenkins, Alan
Milk Trade of London	Atkins, Peter J
Millbay Laundry, Cleaning	Roberts, Cecil R J
Millers	Couper, W J
Milward's of Reading	Milward
Mining Engineering Co	Howse, R M & Harley, F H
Mining in E Midlands	Griffin, Alan R
Minton	Atterbury, Paul
Mirrlees, Bickerton & Day	Mirrlees, Bickerton & Day
Mirrlees, Bickerton & Day	Mirrlees, Bickerton & Day
Mitchell's Auction Co	Mitchell's Auction Company
Mitchells & Butlers	Lloyd, Keith J
Mitchells & Butlers	Mitchells & Butlers
Mitchells & Butlers	Mitchells & Butlers
Mobbs & Lewis	Mobbs and Lewis
Modernisation in Brazil	Graham, Richard
Moira Colliery Co	Beaumont, Philip
Molins Ltd	Hall, Richard
Mond Nickel Co	Mond
Mond Nickel Co	Sturney, Alfred Charles
Monkland	Miller, Thomas Ronald
Monks, Hall & Co	Monks, Hall & Co
Monstead, Otto	Monstead, Otto
Montague Burton	Redmayne, Ronald
Moores, J & Sons	Clyne, H R
Moorfield Spinning Co	Smith, Roland
Morel	Gibbs, John Morel
Morgan Crucible Co	Bennett, Richard
Morgan, David	Morgan, Aubrey Neil
Morgan, David	Morgan, David
Morgan, J P & Co	Dayer, Roberta A
Morgan, J S & Co	Morgan Grenfell & Co
Morlands	Russell, McDonough
Morley, I & R	Finch, R
Morley, I & R	Thomas, Frederick Moy
Morning Post	Dobson, Robert Montagu Hume
Morning Post	Hindle, Wilfrid Hope
Morning Post	Lewis, Reginald
Morris & Co	Gere, Charlotte

504

Morris Garages	Exell, Arthur
Morris Motors	Andrews, Philip W S & Brunner, Elizabeth
Morris Motors	Bridges, T C & Tiltman, H H
Morris Motors	Jackson, Robert
Morris Motors	Morris Motors
Morris Motors	Nixon, St John Cousins
Morris Motors	Nuffield
Morris Motors	Nuffield
Morris Motors	Overy, Richard James
Morris Motors	Thomas, William Miles Webster
Morris Motors	Whiting, R C
Morris, Gregory & Co	Morris, Gregory
Morris, Herbert	Wainwright, David
Morris, Prevost & Co	Prevost, Augustus
Morton Sundour	Morton, James
Morton Sundour	Morton, Jocelyn
Morton, Alexander & Co	Morton, Jocelyn
Mosers of the Borough	Mosers
Moss Bros	Tute, Warren Stanley
Mossley Wool Combing & Spinning	Dupont-Lhotelain, Hubert
Motherwell Bridge & Engineering	Miller, Thomas Ronald
Motor Industry	Church, R A & Miller, M
Motor Industry	Church, Roy Anthony
Motor Industry	Church, Roy Anthony
Motor Industry	Dunnett, Peter J S
Motor Industry	Foreman-Peck, James S
Motor Industry	Miller, M & Church, R A
Motor Industry	Richardson, Kenneth
Motor Industry	Richardson, Kenneth
Motor Industry	Saul, S B
Motor Industry	Turner, Graham
Motor Industry in Coventry	Thoms, David & Donnelly, Tom
Motor Manufacturers & Traders	Nixon, St John Cousins
Motor Vehicle Industry	Lewchuck, Wayne A
Motor Vehicle Industry	Lewchuk, Wayne A
Motorcycle Industry	Hopwood, Bert
Mott, Hay & Anderson	Wake, Joan
Moulton & Co	Woodruff, William
Mountain & Gibson	Price, J R
Mowlem, John & Co	Baines, Frank
Mowlem, John & Co	Mowlem, John & Co
Mudies	Beable, William Henry
Muir, Percy	Muir, Percy Horace
Multinational Enterprise	Wilkins, Mira
Multinational Manufacturing	Jones, Geoffrey
Mumford, Owen	Owen Mumford
Municipal Mutual Insurance	Watson, Arthur J
Municipal Trading	Falkus, Malcolm
Munro, R W	Munro, R W
Muntz, George Frederick	Edwards, E
Murex	Bird, Ernie A
Murphy Radio	Long, Joan
Musgrave Spinning Co	Musgrave Spinning Co
Mustad Manufacturing Co	McNeill, Valerie
Myer, Horatio & Co	Myer, Ewart

Mytholmroyd Industrial Soc	**Mytholmroyd Industrial Society**
NAAFI	**Miller, Harry**
Nairn, Michael & Co	**Muir, Augustus**
Nalder and Collyer	**Shaw, Herbert**
Napier D & Son	**Wilson, Charles & Reader, William**
Nash, William	**Shears, William Sydney**
Nasmyth, James	**Cantrell, J A**
Nathan	**Nathan, Archie John**
National & Grindlays Bank	**Tyson, Geoffrey**
National Bank of Scotland	**National Bank of Scotland**
National Benzole Co	**Young, Edward Preston**
National Boiler	**Chaloner, William Henry**
National Brass Foundry Assoc	**Hiley, Edgar Nathaniel**
National Building Society	**Elkington, George**
National Cash Register Co	**National Cash Register Co**
National Coal Board	**Robens, Alfred**
National Coal Board	**Waller, Robert J**
National Coal Board, Scottish Div	**National Coal Board, Scottish Division**
National Deposit Friendly Soc	**Roper, D H & Harrison, John**
National Freight Consortium	**McLachlan, Sandy**
National Mutual Life Assurance	**Finch, Robert J & Roberts, Alfred**
National Mutual Life Assurance	**Recknell, George Hugh**
National Mutual Life Assurance	**Street, Eric & Glenn, R**
National Provident Institution	**Hazell, Stanley**
National Provident Institution	**Toulson, Norman**
National Provincial Bank	**Ellis, Aytoun**
National Provincial Bank	**Leighton-Boyce, John Alfred Stuart**
National Provincial Bank	**Prescott's Bank**
National Provincial Bank	**Reed, Richard**
National Provincial Bank	**Withers, Hartley**
National Shipbuilders Security	**Slaven, Anthony**
Nationwide Building Society	**Cassell, Michael**
Naylor, R A	**Naylor, R A**
NE England Industries	**Sturgess, R W (ed)**
Negretti & Zambra	**Negretti & Zambra**
Neills of Bangor	**Wilson, Ian**
Neilson, Reid	**Campbell, Roy Hutcheson**
Nelson Weavers Association	**Fowler, Alan & Lesley**
Nelson, James	**Nelson, James**
Nelson, Thomas and Sons	**Dempster, John**
Nelstrop, Wm & Co	**Bramwell, A G**
Nelstrop, Wm & Co	**Nelstrop, Wm**
Neostyle Manufacturing Co	**Dorlay, John S**
Nestlé	**Nestlé**
Netherwood & Dalton	**Netherwood and Dalton**
Nettlefold & Sons	**Mosers**
Neville, T & E	**Neville, T & E**
New Cumnock Coalfield	**Carvel, John Lees**
New Lanark	**Butt, John (ed)**
New Lanark	**Robertson, Alex J**
New River Company	**Rudden, Bernard**
New Shipwright Building Co	**Chapman, Dennis**
Newcastle & Carlisle Railway	**Maclean, John S**
Newcastle & Gateshead Water Co	**Rennison, R W**
Newhaven-Dieppe	**O'Mahoney, B M E**

Newman, William & Sons	Newman, William & Sons
Newnes, George	Beable, William Henry
Newnes, George	Friederichs, Hulda
News International	Leapman, Michael
News International	Regan, Simon
Newspaper Industry	Andrews, W Linton & Taylor, H A
Newspaper Industry	P E P (Political and Economic Planning)
Newton Chambers	Grinyer, P H & Spender, J-C
Newtonshaw Co-op Soc	Flanagan, James A
Nicholas International	Morgan, Bryan Stanford
Nicholas International	Smith, R Grenville & Barrie, Alexander
Nicholl's	McLean, D
Nicholls & Clarke	Nicholls & Clarke
Nicholson, Wilfred	Kimber, H E
Nightingales to Bolton Turnpike	Billington, W D
Noad & Son	Noad, L M
Noal, James & Sons	Noal, James
Nobel's Explosive Co	Richardson, P
Nobel's Explosive Co	Schück, J H E & Sohlman, R (tr Lunn)
Noël, A & Sons	Noël, A & Sons
Nordac	Swindin, Norman
North British & Mercantile Ins	North British & Mercantile Insurance Co
North British Distillery Co	North British Distillery Co
North British Locomotive	North British Locomotive
North British Locomotive Co	Campbell, Roy Hutcheson
North British Railway	Thomas, John
North British Rubber Co	North British Rubber Co
North Eastern Railway	Bell, Robert
North Eastern Railway	Brooke, D
North Eastern Railway	Brooke, D
North Eastern Railway	Irving, R J
North Eastern Railway	Irving, R J
North Eastern Railway	Irving, R J
North Eastern Railway	Kirby, Maurice W
North Eastern Railway	Tomlinson, W W
North London Railway	Robbins, Richard Michael
North of Scotland Bank	Keith, Alexander
North of Scotland Bank	North of Scotland Bank
North of Scotland Shipping Co	Donaldson, Gordon
North Staffs Coalfield	Howe, L
North Western Electricity	Swale, S E
Northampton Gas	Roberts, David E & Frisby, J H
Northern Banking Co	Hill, Edwin Darley (ed)
Northern Clubs' Fed Brewery	Bennison, Brian R
Northern Counties of Wigan	Ogden, Eric
Northern Counties Railway	Currie, James Russell Leslie
Northern Rubber	Nicholson, Hubert C
Norton Abrasives	Norton Abrasives
Norton Villiers Triumph	Norton Villiers Triumph
Norton, Joseph	Brooke, Alan J
Nortons Tividale	Nortons Tividale
Norvic Shoe Co	Sparks, W L
Norvic Shoe Co	Wheldon, Frederick W
Norwich Union	Bignold, Charles Robert
Norwich Union	Blake, Robert Norman William

507

Norwich Union	Clark, G
Norwich Union	Felce, Ernest
Norwich Union	Ryan, Roger J
Norwich Union	Ryan, Roger J
Norwich Union	Ryan, Roger J
Norwich Union	Westall, Oliver M (ed)
Nottingham Co-operative Soc	Leeman, Francis William
Nottingham Gas-Light and Coke Co	Roberts, David E
Nottingham Gas-Light and Coke Co	Roberts, David E
Nottingham Water Works	Nottingham Water Works
Novello & Co	Hurd, Michael
Novello & Co	Novello
Nurdin & Peacock	Baker, Katherine
Oakey, John	Oakey, John
Ocean Steam Ship Co	Davies, Peter Neville
Ocean Steam Ship Co	Hyde, Francis Edwin
Ocean Transport & Trading	Jennings, Eric
Oceanic Steam Navigation Co	Anderson, Roy
Oceanic Steam Navigation Co	Oldham, Wilton Joseph
Odeon Theatre Co	Disher, Maurice W & Bruce, Michael W S
Odhams Press	Beable, William Henry
Odhams Press	Odhams, William James Bond
Oetzmann & Co	Oetzmann & Co
Office of Works	Marriner, Sheila
Ogilvy Benson & Mather	Ogilvy, David Mackenzie
Ogilvy Benson & Mather	Pigott, Stanley
Oil Companies	Jones, Geoffrey
Old Park Colliery Co	Lloyd, Humphrey
Old Ship Hotel, Brighton	Middleton, Judy
Old Vic	Booth, John
Old Vic	Roberts, Peter
Oldham & Son	Oldham
Oldham & Son	Oldham
Oldham Cotton Mills	Gurr, Duncan & Hunt, J
Oldham Equitable & Ind Co-op	Oldham Equitable & Industrial Co-op
Oldham Equitable & Indust Co-op	Walters, Chas
Oldham Industrial Co-op	Taylor, J T
Oldham Master Cotton Spinners	Longworth, J E
Oldknow and the Arkwrights	Unwin, George; Hulme, Arthur & Taylor, Geo
Oliver & Boyd	Parker, W M
Oliver, George (Footwear) Ltd	Oliver, George (Footwear) Ltd
Openshaw, C & Sons	Openshaw, C
Orchard Dockyard	Crighton, John
Orient Line	Maber, John M
Orient Line	Morris, Charles F
Orr's Zinc White	Orr's Zinc White
Osberton Radiators	British Leyland; Radiators Division
Osberton Radiators	Subutec
Osborn, Samuel & Co	Osborn, Frederick Marmaduke
Osborn, Samuel & Co	Seed, Thomas Alexander
Otis Elevator	Walker, H C
Ottley, Charles & Landon	Carter, John W & Pollard, Henry G
Overend, Gurney & Co	Overend, Gurney & Co
Overend, Gurney & Co	Xenos, Stefanos
Overseas Investment	Cottrell, P L

508

Owen Organisation	Owen Organisation
Owen Organisation	Owen Organisation
Owen Organisation	Rubery Owen
Owen Owen	Davies, David Wyn
Owen Owen	Hargraves, Ian
Owen, Robert	Butt, John (ed)
Owens, John	Clapp, Brian William
Oxford & District Gas Co	Oxford and District Gas Company
Oxford University Press	Carter, Harry
Oxford University Press	Sutcliffe, Peter
P & O	Blake, George
P & O	Bolitho, Henry Hector
P & O	Bridges, T C & Tiltman, H H
P & O	Cable, Boyd
P & O	Divine, David
P & O	Griffiths, Percival
P & O	Griffiths, Percival
P & O	Harcourt, Freda
P & O	Morris, Charles F
P & O	Nicolson, John
P & O Ferries	Donaldson, Gordon
P & O Wine Services	Parsons, Richard M
Pacific Steam Navigation Co	Wardle, Arthur C
Painton & Co	Wise, S
Paisley Provident Co-op Soc	Rowat, David
Pall Mall Gazette	Scott, John William Robertson
Palm Line	Kohn, Roger
Palmers of Jarrow	Davidson, John F
Palmers of Jarrow	Dillon, Malcolm
Palmers of Jarrow	Rea, Vincent (comp)
Panmure Gordon & Co	MacDermot, B H D
Pantin, W & C	Pantin, W & C
Paper Industry	Coleman, Donald Cuthbert
Paper Industry in Scotland	Cormack, Alexander Allan
Paper Industry in Scotland	Thomson, Alistair G
Park Gate Iron & Steel Co	Edwards, E
Park Gate Iron & Steel Co	Royston, George P
Park Gate Iron & Steel Co	Williams, Harry
Parker Gallery	Parker, Thomas H
Parker, Frederick	Eves, Alec
Parkes, Josiah & Sons	Parkes, Josiah & Sons
Parsons, Thomas & Sons	Parsons, Thomas & Sons
Parys & Mona Mines	Harris, John Raymond
Parys & Mona Mines	Rowlands, John
Pascall, James	Pascall, James
Pasold	Pasold, Eric W
Patent System	Dutton, H I
Paterson, Robert	House, Jack
Paton, John	Paton, Alexander Forrester
Patrick Motors Group	Patrick Motors Group
Pattullo Higgs & Co	Pattullo Higgs & Co
Payne, George & Co	Payne, George
Peabody, George & Co	Morgan Grenfell & Co
Pearce Bros Builders	Pearce Bros Builders
Pears, A & F	Beable, William Henry

Post Office Savings Bank	Hobson, Oscar Rudolf
Potter & Clarke	Baker, Peter Shaw
Potter, Edmund & Co	Hurst, J G
Potters of Darwen	Potters of Darwen
Potters of Darwen	Sugden, Alan V & Entwisle, Eric A
Pottery Industry	Gay, Philip W & Smith, Robert L
Pottery Industry	Machin, Donald J & Smyth, R Leslie
Pottery Industry	Shaw, Simeon
Powell Brothers and Whitaker	Scourfield, Elfyn
Powell Duffryn Steam Coal Co	Powell Duffryn
Power-Gas	Power-Gas
Premier Coaches	Read, Ian F
Premier Omnibus Co	Premier
Prescott's Bank	Prescott's Bank
Press Association	Scott, George Edwin
Press Council	Murray, George McIntosh
Pressed Steel	Pressed Steel
Pressed Steel	Pressed Steel
Pressed Steel	Pressed Steel
Pressed Steel	Pressed Steel
Pressed Steel	Whiting, R C
Prestcold	Pressed Steel
Prestwich, J A & Co	Buchanan, D J
Prestwich, Wm & Sons	Prestwich, Wm.
Previté & Co	Oldaker, John
Price's (Bromborough)	Price's (Bromborough)
Price's Patent Candle Co	Beable, William Henry
Price's Patent Candle Co	Price's Patent Candle Co
Price's Patent Candle Co	Price's Patent Candle Co
Price's Patent Candle Co	Price's Patent Candle Co
Price's Patent Candle Co	Wilson, George F
Price, Forbes & Co	Price, Forbes
Price, Waterhouse & Co	Price, Waterhouse & Co
Price, Waterhouse & Co	Richards, G E
Prince Line	Henderson, A J
Principality Building Soc	Noakes, Aubrey
Pringle, Robert & Son	Gulvin, Clifford
Pringle, Robert & Sons	Pringle, Robert and Sons
Protector Lighting Company	Heyes, Philip
Provident Mutual Life Assurance	Sherriff, Francis Henry
Provincial Banking in Scotland	Munn, Charles W
Provincial Insurance Co	Scott, Samuel H & Scott, F C
Prudential Assurance	Barnard, R W
Prudential Assurance	Plaisted, H
Prudential Assurance	Prudential Assurance
Prudential Assurance	Prudential Assurance
Public Wharfingers	Public Wharfingers
Publishers' Association	Kingsford, Reginald John Lethbridge
Puddefoot, Bowers & Simonett	Puddefoot, Bowers & Simonett
Pugh, Charles H	Pugh, Charles H
Pugh, Charles H	Pugh, Charles H
Pullars of Perth	Fraser, John Foster
Pullman	Behrend, George
Purdey, James & Sons	Beaumont, Richard
Put-U-Up	Greaves & Thomas

512

Pye	Bussey, Gordon
Quaker Industrialists	Corley, Thomas Anthony Buchanan
Qualter Hall & Co	Hall, Philip J
Qualter Hall & Co	Qualter Hall & Co
Qualter Hall & Co	Qualter Hall & Co
Queensbury Industrial Soc	Macaulay, P Tarbet
R F D Group	Nockolds, Harold
Rabone Chesterman	Hallam, Douglas J
Radcliffe & Pilkington Co-op	Knights, G & Farrington, A
Radcliffe Paper Mill Co	Arthur, Maurice C B
Radcliffe, Evan Thomas & Co	Jenkins, John Geraint
Ragosine	Richardson, K
Railway	Simmons, Jack
Railway Capital	Broadbridge, Seymour Albert
Railway Companies	Crompton, G W
Railway Companies, Unprofitable	Mason, N M
Railway Finance	Labour Research Dept
Railway Interest	Alderman, Geoffrey
Railway Motor Buses	Cummings, John
Railway Passengers Assurance	Cox, F Hayter
Railway Rates	Cain, P J
Railways	Bonavia, Michael Robert
Railways	Bonavia, Michael Robert
Railways	Gourvish, Terence Richard
Railways	Grinling, Charles Herbert
Railways	Robbins, Richard Michael
Railways	Rolt, Lionel Thomas Caswall
Railways in N E Norfolk	Joby, Richard S
Railways in the E Counties	Gordon, Donald Ian
Railways of Scotland	O'Dell, Andrew Charles
Raithby Lawrence & Co	Raithby Lawrence & Co
Raleigh Industries	Bowden, Gregory Houston
Raleigh Industries	Raleigh
Ralli Trading Group	Ralli Trading Group
Rambotham & Co	Rambotham, J W
Ramsbottom Ind Provident Soc	Ashworth, George
Ramsbury Building Soc	Phillips, R J
Rank Organisation	Wood, Alan
Rank Precision Industries	Taylor-Hobson
Rank, Joseph	Janes, Hurford
Rank, Joseph	Rank, Joseph
Ransom Bouverie & Co	Manning, Peter
Ransomes & Rapier	Grinyer, P H & Spender, J-C
Ransomes & Rapier	Lewis, R Stanley
Ransomes, Sims & Jefferies	Grace, D R & Phillips, D C
Ransomes, Sims & Jefferies	Munting, R
Ransomes, Sims & Jefferies	Ransomes
Ransomes, Sims a& Jefferies	Ransomes, Sims and Jefferies
Rathbones	Marriner, Sheila
Rayleigh, Lord; Farms	Gavin, William
Rayon	Beer, Edwin John
Readhead, John & Sons	Readhead
Reading & High Wycombe Bldg Soc	Dormer, Ernest W
Reading Co-operative Soc	Lockwood, Arthur
Readson	Beaver, Patrick

Real del Monte Co	Randall, Robert W
Reardon Smith Line	Heaton, Paul Michael
Reckitt & Colman	Beable, William Henry
Reckitt & Colman	Colman, H C
Reckitt & Colman	Reckitt, Basil Norman
Reckitt & Sons	Black, Mona S
Reckitt & Sons	Chapman-Huston, W W Desmond M
Recovered Wool Industry	Malin, John C
Red Funnel Steamers	O'Connor, G W
Redcar Race Course	Fairfax-Blakeborough, John Freeman
Redfern's Rubber Works	Redfern
Rediffusion	Fulford, Roger Thomas Baldwin
Rediffusion	Mingay, G E
Reed International	Sykes, Philip
Reed, Thomas	Bean, David
Reeves & Sons	Goodwin, Michael
Refuge Assurance Co	Clegg, Cyril
Reliance Bank	Reliance Bank
Renault UK	Renault UK
Rendell	Rendell
Rendell	Romain, W J
Renold Chains	Tripp, Basil Howard
Renold Chains	Tripp, Basil Howard
Retail Trading	Jefferys, James Bavington
Reuters	Jones, Roderick
Reuters	Storey, Graham
Reynolds & Co	Reynolds & Co
Rhymney Railway	Barrie, Derek Stiven Maxwelton
Richard Evans Co	Roberts, T J
Richard Thomas & Baldwins	Griffiths, Thomas
Richards Shipbuilders	Goodey, Charles
Richards Tiles	Richards Tiles
Ricketts, Henry & Co	Alford, Bernard William Ernest
Ridgway	Briggs, J H Y
Rio Flour Mills	Graham, Richard
Rio Tinto	Avery, David
Rio Tinto	Harvey, Charles E
Rio Tinto	Harvey, Charles E
Rio Tinto	West, Richard
Ripponden Co-operative Soc	Priestley, John H
Ritchie, Andrew & Son	House, Jack
Rivington, Percival & Co	Rivington, Septimus
Road Transport	Dunbar, Charles S
Roadships	Hytner, B A & Irvine, I A N
Roan Antelope	Bradley, Kenneth Granville
Roberts, C P & Co	Roberts, C P & Co
Roberts, J	Roberts, J
Robertson Electric Lamps	Loring, Henry
Robinson & Sons	Porteous, Crichton
Robinson & Sons	Robinson, Philip Moffat
Robinson & Sons	Robinson, Philip Moffat
Robinson & Sons	Robinsons of Chesterfield
Robinson & Sons	Robinsons of Chesterfield
Robinson, E S & A	Darwin, Bernard Richard Meirion
Rochdale Pioneers	Holyoake, George Jacob

514

Rochford's Nurseries	Allan, Mea
Rock Life Assurance Co	Rock Life Assurance Co
Rock Life Assurance Co	Rock Life Assurance Co
Rockingham	Eaglestone, Arthur A & Lockett, Terence A
Rodgers, Joseph & Son	Rodgers, Joseph & Son
Rolland Decorators	Barclay, John B
Rolls Razor	Bloom, John
Rolls-Royce	Bridges, T C & Tiltman, H H
Rolls-Royce	Buist, H Massac
Rolls-Royce	Donne, Michael
Rolls-Royce	Evans, Mike
Rolls-Royce	Frostick, Michael
Rolls-Royce	Gray, Robert Archibald Speir
Rolls-Royce	Harker, Ronald W
Rolls-Royce	Harvey-Bailey, Alec H
Rolls-Royce	Harvey-Bailey, Alec H
Rolls-Royce	Keith, Kenneth
Rolls-Royce	Lloyd, Ian
Rolls-Royce	Montagu of Beaulieu, E J B D S
Rolls-Royce	Montagu of Beaulieu, E J B D S
Rolls-Royce	Morgan, Bryan Stanford
Rolls-Royce	Nockolds, Harold
Rolls-Royce	Oldham, Wilton Joseph
Rolls-Royce	Pearson, James Denning
Romano's	Deghy, Guy
Roneo Vickers	Dorlay, John S
Rootes	Young, Stephen & Hood, Neil
Rose, Downs & Thompson	Rose, Downs & Thompson
Rosser & Russell	Leslie, Ian M
Rotax	Rotax
Rothschild	Ayer, Jules
Rothschild	Chapman, Stanley David
Rothschild	Chapman, Stanley David
Rothschild	Corti, Egon Caesar (tr Brian & Beatrix Lunn
Rothschild	Davis, Richard Whitlock
Rothschild	Morton, Frederic
Rothschild	Ravage, Marcus Eli
Roughdale Brickworks	Roughdale Brickworks
Round Oak Steel Works	Knox, Collie
Round Oak Steel Works	Raybould, Trevor J
Routledge	Mumby, Frank Arthur
Rover Co	Foreman-Peck, James S
Rover Co	Foreman-Peck, James S
Rover Co	Robson, Graham
Rowland, L & C	Rowland, L & C
Rownson, Drew & Clydesdale	Beardmore, J
Rowntree	Goodall, Francis
Rowntree	Mennell, G H
Rowntree	Vernon, Anne
Rowntree & Co	Wallace, William
Rowntree & Sons	Rowntree & Sons
Royal African Company	Davies, Kenneth Gordon
Royal Airship Works	Higham, Robin David Stewart
Royal Airship Works	Masefield, Peter Gordon
Royal Arsenal	Hogg, Oliver Frederick Gillilan

Royal Arsenal Co-operative Soc	Davis, Walter Tamsett
Royal Bank of Scotland	Boase, Charles William
Royal Bank of Scotland	Munro, Neil
Royal Bank of Scotland	National Bank of Scotland
Royal Bank of Scotland	Royal Bank of Scotland
Royal Bank of Scotland	Royal Bank of Scotland
Royal Crown Derby	Twitchett, John & Bailey, Betty
Royal Doulton	Eyles, Desmond
Royal Dutch Petroleum Co	Royal Dutch Petroleum Co
Royal Dutch/Shell	Beaton, Kendall
Royal Dutch/Shell	Gerretson, Frederik Carel
Royal Dutch/Shell	Henriques, Robert David Quixano
Royal Dutch/Shell	Hewins, Ralph
Royal Dutch/Shell	Jones, Geoffrey
Royal Dutch/Shell	Kent, Marian
Royal Dutch/Shell	Naylor, Stanley (ed)
Royal Dutch/Shell	Shell Transport & Trading
Royal Enfield	Hartley, Peter
Royal Exchange Assurance	Mason, Alfred Edward Woodley
Royal Exchange Assurance	Supple, Barry Emanuel
Royal Exchange Assurance	Whymper, W N
Royal Gunpowder Factory	Simmons, W H
Royal London Mutual Ins Soc	Allen, Walter Gore
Royal Mail Shipping Group	Bushell, T A
Royal Mail Shipping Group	Davies, Peter N & Bourn, A M
Royal Mail Shipping Group	Davies, Peter Neville
Royal Mail Shipping Group	Davies, Peter Neville
Royal Mail Shipping Group	Davies, Peter Neville
Royal Mail Shipping Group	Green, Edwin
Royal Mail Shipping Group	Green, Edwin & Moss, Michael
Royal Mail Shipping Group	Greenhill, Robert G
Royal Mail Shipping Group	Greenhill, Robert G
Royal Mail Shipping Group	Jefferson, Herbert
Royal Mail Shipping Group	O'Connor, G W
Royal Mail Shipping Group	O'Donoghue, K & Heaton, Paul M
Royal Mail Shipping Group	Royal Mail Steam Packet Co
Royal Mint	Craig, John Herbert McCutcheon
Royal Mint	Greig, John
Royal Nigeria Co	Cook, Arthur Norton
Royal Ordnance Factories	Peden, George
Royal Small Arms, Enfield	Bowbelski, Margaret
Royal U K Beneficent Assoc	Maude, Evelyn John (ed)
Royden, Thomas & Sons	Royden, Ernest B
Roys of Wroxham	Clarke, P
Royton Industrial Co-op Soc	Burton, Thomas
Royton Spinning Co	Royton Spinning Company
Rubery Owen Holdings	Rubery Owen
Rudge-Whitworth	Hartley, Peter
Rudge-Whitworth	Reynolds, Bryan
Russell, James & Co	Johnson, F G L
Russell, Samuel & Co	Russell, Samuel & Co
Russell, Samuel & Sons	Russell, Samuel & Sons
Ruston & Hornsby	Alford, L G C
Ruston & Hornsby	Newman, Bernard
Ruston & Hornsby	Pointer, Michael

Ryder, Thomas & Son	Ryder, Thomas & Son
Rylands Brothers	Rylands of Warrington
S M M T	Nixon, St John Cousins
S P D	Reader, William Joseph
S S Cars	Whyte, Andrew
S T C	Standard Telephones & Cables
S T C	Young, Peter
S Wales Iron & Steel	Addis, John Philip
S Wales Steam Coal Industry	Walters, R H
S Wales Steam Coal Trade	Vincent, James Edmund
Sage, Frederick & Co	Abel, Deryck Robert Endsleigh
Sainsbury, J	Boswell, James (ed)
Salisbury Railway & Market House	Lee, C J
Salt Union	Calvert, Albert Frederick
Salt Union	Calvert, Albert Frederick
Salt Union	Calvert, Albert Frederick
Salt, Titus	Reynolds, Jack
Salt, Titus	Suddards, Roger Whitley
Salter, Geo & Co	Bache, Mary
Salvation Army Assurance Soc	Watson, Bernard
Salvation Army Bank	Reliance Bank
Salvesen of Leith	Somner, Graeme
Salvesen of Leith	Vamplew, Wray
Samuel Montagu & Co	Franklin, S E
Sanderson & Murray	MacLaren, Moray David Shaw
Sanderson Kayser	Sanderson Kayser
Sanderson, Arthur & Sons	Sanderson, Arthur & Sons
Sanderson, William	Wilson, Ross
Sanger, 'Lord' George	Lukens, John
Sanger, 'Lord' George	Sanger, George
Sankey, Joseph & Sons	Mackenzie, Edward Montague Compton
Sarsons	Sarson, Henry
Saunders-Roe	Lanchbery, Edward
Savages	Braithwaite, David
Savages	Clark, Ronald Harry
Savages	Clark, Ronald Harry
Savills	Watson, John Arthur Fergus
Savings Bank of Glasgow	Henderson, Thomas
Savings Bank of Glasgow	Payne, Peter Lester
Savory and Moore	Savory, A C S
Schermuly Pistol Rocket Co	Thompson, C R
Schweppes	Beable, William Henry
Schweppes	Simmons, Douglas A
Scont Motors	Farrant, J P
Scot American Investment Co	Weir, Ronald B
Scot Temperance Assurance Soc	Magnusson, Mamie
Scotsman	Scotsman
Scott Bader & Co	Hoe, Susanna
Scott Bader and Co	Blum, Fred H
Scott Bader and Co	Scott Bader and Co
Scott Lithgow	Reid, James Macarthur
Scott, George & Son	Scott, George & Son
Scott, W & C, Excelsior Mills	Scott, William Maddin
Scott-Lyon	Croall, Robert
Scottish Amicable Bldg Soc	Scottish Amicable

Scottish Australian Company	Macmillan, David S
Scottish Co-op Wholesale Soc	Flanagan, James A
Scottish Co-op Wholesale Soc	Kinloch, James & Butt, John
Scottish Co-op Wholesale Soc	Scottish Co-operative Wholesale Society
Scottish Country Miller	Gauldie, Enid
Scottish Equitable Life Office	Scottish Equitable Life Office
Scottish Milk Marketing Board	Urquhart, Robert
Scottish Mutual Assurance Soc	Magnusson, Mamie
Scottish Provident Institution	Steuart, Mary D
Scottish Union & National Ins	Gray, William Forbes
Scottish Widows' Fund	Scottish Widows' Fund
Scottish Widows' Fund Life	Maxwell, Herbert Eustace
Scotts of Greenock	Scotts
Scotts of Greenock	Scotts
Scovill	Yale Security Products
Scruttons	Jeffery, A E
Seager Evans & Co	Seager Evans & Co
Sears, J & Co	Sears, J & Co
Seccombe Marshall & Campion	Page, Donald T
Secondary Banking Crisis	Reid, Margaret Isabel
Seeboard	Robinson, Sydney
Selfridges	Bridges, T C & Tiltman, H H
Selfridges	Honeycombe, Gordon
Selfridges	Pound, Reginald
Selfridges	Selfridge
Selfridges	Selfridge, Harry Gordon
Selfridges	Williams, Alfred Harry
Serck Group	Harley, Basil
Sessions, William	Sessions of York
Sharp Stewart & Co	North British Locomotive
Sharp, Stewart & Co	Campbell, Roy Hutcheson
Shaw Savill & Albion Co	Bowen, Frank Charles
Shaw Savill & Albion Co	Bryant, Arthur Wynne Morgan
Shaw Savill & Albion Co	Waters, Sydney David
Shaw, Benjamin & Sons	Stephenson, Clifford
Shaw, H (Magnets)	Shaw, H
Sheerness Economical Society	Brown, William Henry
Sheffield Banking Co	Leader, Robert Eadon
Sheffield Crucible Steel	Timmins, John Geoffrey
Sheffield Cutlery	Garlick, Peter C
Sheffield Gas Undertaking	Roberts, David E
Sheffield Iron & Steel	Lloyd-Jones, R & Lewis, M J
Sheffield Rail Trade	Warren, Kenneth
Sheffield Savings Bank	Leader, Robert Eadon
Sheffield Smelting Co	Sheffield Smelting Company
Sheffield Smelting Co	Wilson, Ronald E
Sheffield Speciality Steels	Tweedale, Geoffrey
Sheffield Speciality Steels	Tweedale, Geoffrey
Sheffield Steel	Tweedale, Geoffrey
Sheffield Steel	Tweedale, Geoffrey
Sheffield Steel	Tweedale, Geoffrey
Sheffield Trustee Savings Bank	Sheffield Trustee Savings Bank
Sheffield's Public Markets	Blackman, Janet
Sheldons	Ashworth, A H
Shell	Beaton, Kendall

Shell	Henriques, Robert David Quixano
Shell	Royal Dutch Petroleum Co
Shell Transport & Trading Co	Shell Transport & Trading
Shelley Potteries	Watkins, Chris; Harvey, W & Senft, R
Shepherd & Woodward	Shepherd & Woodward
Sheppards & Chase	Hennessy, Elizabeth
Shepshed Lace Manufacturing Co	Shepshed Lace Manufacturing Co
Shiloh Spinners	Shiloh
Shinkfield, H J	Shinkfield, H J
Shipbuilders, Thames & Medway	Banbury, P
Shipbuilding	Slaven, Anthony
Shipbuilding at Dundee	Lythe, Samuel George Edgar
Shipbuilding in NE England	Dougan, David
Shipbuilding in NE England	Smith, J W & Holden, T S
Shipbuilding in Scotland	Buxton, Neil K
Shipbuilding in Scotland	Campbell, Roy Hutcheson
Shipbuilding in Scotland	Slaven, Anthony
Shipbuilding in W Scotland	Cormack, W S
Shipbuilding Industry	Parkinson, J R
Shipmasters' Society	Clark, Alexander
Shipping	Cottrell, P L & Aldcroft, D H (eds)
Shipping	Jones, Clement Wakefield
Shipping and World Trade	Davies, Peter Neville
Shirley Aldred & Co	Pollard, Sidney
Shirley Aldred & Co	Shirley Aldred
Shops and Shopping	Adburgham, Alison
Shore Porters' Soc of Aberdeen	Bulloch, John
Short Brothers	Hopkins, Charles Henry Gordon
Short Brothers	Preston, J M
Short Brothers	Short Brothers
Short Brothers	Taylor, Michael John Haddrick
Short Brothers	White, O'Loughlin Molly
Short Brothers	Wrangham, Cuthbert Edward
Shotts Iron Co	McEwan, Ann M C
Shotts Iron Co	Muir, Augustus
Shuttleworth, W S & Co	Shuttleworth, William Sewell
Siemens Brothers & Co	Andrews, H H
Siemens Brothers & Co	Pole, William
Siemens Brothers & Co	Scott, John Dick
Silcock, R & Sons	Silcock, R & Sons
Silver Mining	Randall, Robert W
Simms Motor & Electronics Co	Morgan, Bryan Stanford
Simms Motor & Electronics Co	Nixon, St John Cousins
Simon Engineering Group	Simon, Anthony
Simonds, H & G	Corley, Thomas Anthony Buchanan
Simonds, H & G	Simonds, H & G
Simpkiss Breweries	Richards, John
Simpson, Stephen	Simpson, Stephen
Sinclair Research	Dale, Rodney
Singer Sewing Machines	Brandon, Ruth
Sirocco	Maguire, Edward
Sirocco	Sirocco
Sissons, W & G	Timmins, John Geoffrey (ed)
Skelmanthorpe Industrial Co-op	Skelmanthorpe Industrial and Co-operative
Skelton, C J & Co	Skelton, C J

Skilbeck Brothers	Dawe, Donovan A
Skinningrove Iron Co	Willis, W G
Slamannan Co-operative Soc	Murray, Andrew
Slate Industry	Lindsay, Jean
Slate Industry in Scotland	Tucker, D G
Slater Walker	Raw, Charles
Slough Estates	Slough Estates
Small, Robert & Co	Lenman, Bruce
Smedley, John	Smedley, John
Smedley-HP Foods	Wright, Louise
Smith & Nephew	Bennett, Richard
Smith & Nephew	Bennett, Richard & Leavey, J A
Smith & Nephew	Smith and Nephew
Smith & Wellstood	Borthwick, Alastair
Smith Brothers	Smith Brothers
Smith's Stamping Works	Muir, Augustus
Smith, Arthur C	Smith, Arthur C
Smith, Bell	Smith, Bell
Smith, George & Sons	Smith, George & Sons
Smith, James & Co	Smith, James & Co
Smith, John; Tadcaster Brewery	Ellis, Aytoun
Smith, Mackenzie & Co	Smith, Mackenzie & Co
Smith, Payne & Smith	Easton, Harry Tucker
Smith, Swire	Snowden, James Keighley
Smith, Thomas & Sons	Smith, Frederick H
Smith, W H & Son	Beable, William Henry
Smith, W H & Son	Bridges, T C & Tiltman, H H
Smith, W H & Son	Clear, Gwen
Smith, W H & Son	Loasby, B J
Smith, W H & Son	Maxwell, Herbert Eustace
Smith, W H & Son	Smith, W H & Son
Smith, W H & Son	Wilson, Charles
Smith-Clayton Forge	Muir, Augustus
Smiths the Bankers	Leighton-Boyce, John Alfred Stuart
Snow, Frederick	Snow, Frederick
Soap Trade	Reader, William Joseph
Soho Foundry	Avery, W & T
Soho Ironworks, Bolton	Hick, Hargreaves & Co
Somervell Brothers	Somervell, John
Sotheby Parke Bernet	Herrmann, Frank
South Durham Steel	Willis, W G
South Eastern & Chatham Rly	Nock, Oswald Stevens
South Eastern Rly	Gourvish, Terence Richard
South Metropolitan Gas Co	Layton, Walter Thomas
South Metropolitan Gas Co	Melling, Joseph
South Metropolitan Gas Co	Mills, Mary
South Metropolitan Gas Co	South Metropolitan Gas
South Staffordshire Railway Co	Bartlett, P
South Staffs Water Works Co	Feeny, Alfred
South Staffs Waterworks Co	South Staffordshire Waterworks Co
South Wales Coal	Morris, John H & Williams, Lawrence J
South Wales Coal Trade	Wilkins, Charles
South Wales Coalowners	Davies, John
South Wales Coalowners' Assoc	Williams, L J
South Wales Iron Works	Lloyd, John

South Western Electricity	Eyles, W E
South Western Electricity	Steward, S F
Southard & Co	Southard
Southdown Motor Services	Southdown
Southern Electricity	Gordon, B
Southern Newspapers	Sewell, Gordon
Southern Railway	Marshall, Chapman Frederick Dendy
Sowerby Bridge Industrial Soc	Baxendale, W H
Spear & Jackson	Jones, P d'A & Simons, E N
Spear & Jackson	Spear & Jackson
Spencer Moulton	Payne, Peter Lester
Spencer Moulton	Payne, Peter Lester
Spencer Moulton	Spencer Moulton
Spencer, George & Co	Payne, Peter Lester
Spencer, George & Co	Payne, Peter Lester
Spencer, M H	George, F L
Spencer-Clark	Spencer-Clark
Spicer Bros	O'Connor, Thomas Power
Spicer Bros	Spicer
Spillers	Vaughan-Thomas, Wynford
Spode	Copeland, W T & Sons
Spottiswoode	Austen-Leigh, Richard Leigh
Springburn	Thomas, John
Spurrell, W & Son	Huws, Richard E
Spurrell, W & Son	Spurrell, William & Son
Squirrel Horn	Hulme, A G
St Cuthbert's Co-op Assoc	Maxwell, William
St Cuthbert's Co-op Assoc	St Cuthbert's Co-operative Association
St James's Theatre	Mason, Alfred Edward Woodley
St John d'el Rey Mining Co	Hollowood, Albert Bernard
St Quintin	Carter, Alan
Staffs Agricultural Soc	Greysmith, Brenda
Staley, Radford & Co	Archer, J F
Standard Bank	Henry, James Archibald
Standard Bank	Siepmann, Harry Arthur (ed)
Standard Chartered Bank	Fry, Richard
Standard Chartered Bank	Sewell, V
Standard Chartered Bank	Standard Chartered Bank
Standard Chartered Bank	Terry, C
Standard Engineering Co	Standard Engineering Co
Standard Life Assurance	Butt, John
Standard Life Assurance	Schooling, William
Standard Life Assurance	Treble, J H
Standard Life Assurance	Treble, J H
Standard Life Assurance	Westall, Oliver M (ed)
Stanford, Edward	Stanford, Edward
Stanley Gibbons	Gibbons, Stanley
Stanley, W F & Co	Allen, Cecil John
Stanton & Staveley	Chapman, Stanley David
Stanton Ironworks	Lewis, Victor
Stanton Ironworks	Stanton Ironworks Co
Star	Star
Star Aluminium Co	Star Aluminium Co
Star Paper Mill	Ahvenainen, Jorma
Starley, J A & Co	Williamson, Geoffrey

Starley, J K & Co	Foreman-Peck, James S
Starley, J K & Co	Robson, Graham
Stationers' Company	Blagden, Cyprian
Staveley Industries	Staveley Industries
Stead & Simpson	Stead & Simpson
Steamship Rivalry in China	Liu, Kwang-Ching
Steel Brothers & Co	Braund, Harold Ernest Wilton
Steel Industry	Burn, Duncan Lyall
Steel Industry	Burn, Duncan Lyall
Steel Industry	Burnham, Thomas H & Hoskins, George O
Steel Industry	Carr, James C & Taplin, Walter
Steel Industry	Cottrell, E
Steel Industry	Erickson, Charlotte
Steel Industry	Heal, David Walter
Steel Industry	Keeling, B S & Wright, A E G
Steel Industry	McCloskey, Donald N
Steel Industry	Tweedale, Geoffrey
Steel Industry	Warren, K
Steel Industry in Scotland	Payne, Peter Lester
Steel Tariffs	Tolliday, Steven
Steel Tools & Hardware	Tweedale, Geoffrey
Steel Towns	Pocock, Douglas Charles David
Steel, L & Co	Miller, V
Stephen, Alexander & Sons	Carvel, John Lees
Stephen, Alexander & Sons	Stephen, Alexander and Sons
Stephens of Fowey	Ward-Jackson, Cyril Henry
Stephenson & Hawthorne	Vulcan Foundry
Stephenson Blake & Co	Pollard, Sidney
Stephenson Blake & Co	Pollard, Sidney
Stephenson Clarke	Carter, C J M
Stephenson, Robert & Co	Warren, James G H
Stephensons of Oxford	Stephensons of Oxford
Sterne, L & Co Ltd	Beale, Samuel R
Stevens & Brown	Fenn, George Manville
Stevens & Williams	Williams-Thomas, R S
Stevens' Auction Rooms	Allingham, E C
Stewart, John & Co	Course, Alfred George
Stewarts & Lloyds	Boswell, Jonathan S
Stewarts & Lloyds	Scopes, Frederick
Stewarts & Lloyds	Stewarts and Lloyds
Stock Exchange	Duguid, Charles
Stock Exchange	Jenkins, Alan
Stock Exchange	Kennedy, W P & Michie, R
Stock Exchange	Kynaston, D T A
Stock Exchange	Morgan, Edward Victor & Thomas, William /
Stockport Co-operative Society	Stockport Co-operative Society
Stockton & Darlington Railway	Davies, Randall Robert Henry
Stockton & Darlington Railway	Jeans, James Stephen
Stoddard, A F & Co	Bartlett, James Neville
Stoddard, A F & Co	Cairns, Robert
Stoddard, A F & Co	Stoddard, A F & Co
Stone's Finsbury Distillery	Janes, Hurford
Storey Brothers & Co	Christie, Guy
Storey Brothers & Co	Williamson, James & Son
Storr, Paul	Penzer, Norman Mosley

Stothert & Pitt	Torrens, Hugh S
Stourbridge Glass	Guttery, David Reginald
Stourbridge Ironworks	Mutton, Norman
Strahan, William	Cochrane, James Aikman
Strain, Wm & Sons	Strain, Wm & Sons
Straits Steamship Co	Tregonning, Kennedy Gordon Philip
Straker Bros	Straker Bros
Straker Bros	Straker Bros
Strathearn Hydropathic Estab	Christie, Guy
Street, G & Co	Jackson, Lionel George
Strong & Co of Romsey	Rose, A
Strutt & Parker Farms	Gavin, William
Strutt, W G & J	Fitton, Robert S & Wadsworth Alfred P
Strutt, William, Cotton Mills	Johnson, H R
Stuarts & Jacks	Stuarts & Jacks
Stubs, Peter	Ashton, Thomas Southcliffe
Stubs, Peter	Dane, Eric Surrey
Stuckey's Banking Co	Saunders, Philip Thomas
Submarine Cables	Submarine Cables
Subutec	Subutec
Sully, J & A W & Co	Sully, J & A W
Summers, John & Sons	British Steel
Summers, John & Sons	British Steel
Summers, John & Sons	Reid, A
Summers, John & Sons	Summers, John & Sons
Sun Insurance	Baumer, Edward
Sun Insurance	Dickson, Peter George Muir
Sun Life	Minnitt, Jack
Sun Life Agency in Leeds	Beresford, M W
Sun Mill Co	Boothman, J
Sun Mill Co	Tyson, R E
Sun Mill Co, Oldham	Sun Mill Co, Oldham
Sunday Advertiser	Crapster, Basil L
Sunday Times	Hobson, H; Knightley, P & Russell, L
Sunderland Marine	Beaver, Patrick
Sundour	Morton, James
Sutcliffe, Richard	Sutcliffe, R J & Edward D
Suter, A F & Co	Suter, A F & Co
Sutton's Seeds	Hodder, T K
Swallow	Whyte, A J A
Swan Hunter	Rutherford, Wilfrid
Swan Hunter	Swan Hunter & Wigham Richardson
Swan Hunter	Swan Hunter & Wigham Richardson
Swedish Match	Lindgren, Håkan
Sweet & Maxwell	Sweet & Maxwell
Swift Cycle Co	Beable, William Henry
Swindon Mineral Water	Sheldon, Peter
Swire, John & Sons	Hook, Elizabeth
Swire, John & Sons	Swire, John & Sons
Sykes, Joseph Bros	Walker, Selwyn Joseph Sykes
Sykeses of Edgeley	Mason, John D
Syme & Duncan	Syme & Duncan
Symington, R & W H & Co	Symington, R & W H & Co
Taddy & Co	Francis, Pat
Tamworth Industrial Co-op	Harding, John Shepherd

Tangyes	Tangye, Richard
Tangyes	Tangyes
Tangyes	Tangyes
Tangyes	Waterhouse, Rachel Elizabeth
Tanner, Geo. & Wicks, P O	Tanner, Geo. & Wicks, P O
Tanqueray, Gordon & Co	Tanqueray, Gordon & Co
Taphouse, Charles & Son	Taphouse, Charles & Son
Tarmac	Earle, James Basil Foster
Taskers of Andover	Rolt, Lionel Thomas Caswall
Tate & Lyle	Andrews, Allen
Tate & Lyle	Chalmin, Philippe
Tate & Lyle	Fairrie, Geoffrey
Tate & Lyle	Garbutt, John L
Tate & Lyle	Hugill, Antony
Tate & Lyle	Jones, Tom
Tate & Lyle	Lyle of Westbourne, Lord
Tate & Lyle	Lyle, Oliver
Tate & Lyle	Stoddard, Jeanne
Tate & Lyle	Tate & Lyle
Tate & Lyle	Watson, J A
Tatham, Bromage & Co	Tatham, Bromage & Co
Tattersalls	Orchard, Vincent Robert
Taxi Trade in London	Fox, W E
Taylor of Batley	Greenwood, George A
Taylor of Batley	Taylor, Theodore Cooke
Taylor Woodrow	Jenkins, Alan
Taylor Woodrow	Jenkins, Alan
Taylor, H A & D	Taylor, H A & D
Taylor, J S	Muir, Augustus
Taylor, J T & J	Pollard, Sidney & Turner, R
Taylor, John	Burt, Roger
Taylor, John	Taylor, John
Taylor, Taylor & Hobson	Taylor-Hobson
Teetgen & Co	Teetgen & Co
Telcon	Lawford, G L & Nicholson, L R
Telegraph Construction & Maint	Kieve, Jeffrey L
Telegraph Construction & Maint	Lawford, G L & Nicholson, L R
Telegraph Industry	Kieve, Jeffrey L
Telephone Service	Sudarshan, Ratna M
Telford, Thomas	Rolt, Lionel Thomas Caswall
Temperance Permanent Bldg Soc	Hughes, Fielden
Temperance Permanent Bldg Soc	Price, Seymour J
Temple Press	Armstrong, Arthur C
Templeton, James & Co	Young, Fred H
Tennant, Charles & Co	Checkland, Sydney George
Tennant, Charles & Co	Tennant
Tennant, Charles & Co	Tennant
Tennant, Charles & Co	Tennant, E W D
Terry, Joseph	Terry's
Tesco	Corina, Maurice
Tetley, Joshua & Son	Lackey, Clifford
Tetley, Joshua & Son	Tetley, Joshua & Son
Textile Industry	Porter, J H
Textile Machine Industry	Kirk, R M
Textile Technology	Jeremy, David J

524

Thames & Mersey Marine Ins Co	**Thames & Mersey Marine Insurance Co**
Thames Conservancy	**Thames Conservancy**
Tharsis/Tennant	**Checkland, Sydney George**
Theatrical Managers	**Donohue, Joseph Walter (ed)**
Thermal Syndicate	**Hetherington, G**
Thermal Syndicate	**Hetherington, G**
Thetford Moulded Products	**Thetford Moulded Products**
Thompson, George & Co	**Cornford, Leslie Cope**
Thompson, William & Co	**Milne, T E**
Thomson McLintock	**Winsbury, Rex**
Thomson Organisation	**Braddon, Russell Reading**
Thomson Organisation	**Leapman, Michael**
Thomson, D C & Co	**Millar, Alexander Hastie**
Thomson, D C & Co	**Thomson, D C**
Thomson, J G & Co	**Thomson, J G & Co**
Thomson, William & Sons	**Perks, R B**
Thomson, Wm & Co	**Blake, George**
Thomson, Wm & Co	**Somner, Graeme**
Thornton	**Thornton**
Thornton, Robert & Sons	**Thornton, Robert**
Thornwill & Warham	**Owen, C C**
Thornycroft, John I	**Barnaby, Kenneth Cloves**
Thorpe, T W	**Thorpe, T W**
Tilbury Contracting & Dredging Co	**Tilbury Contracting & Dredging Co**
Tillicoultry Co-op Society	**Stewart, James**
Tilling, Thomas	**Brown, Stewart J**
Tilling, Thomas	**Crosland-Taylor, W James C**
Tilling, Thomas	**Tilling, John**
Tillotson & Son	**Singleton, Frank**
Timber Trade Federation	**Latham, Edward Bryan**
Times Newspapers	**Woods, Oliver & Bishop, James**
Timpson, William	**Timpson, D J**
Tinplate Industry	**Minchinton, Walter Edward**
Tinplate Manufacture in Llanelly	**Hancocks, H**
Tinplate Works	**Brooke, Edward Henry**
Tinplate Works	**Brooke, Edward Henry**
Tinsley Wire Industries	**Tinsley Wire**
Tinsley, H & Co	**Tinsley, H**
Tobacco Industry	**Alford, Bernard William Ernest**
Todd Bros	**Todd, Murray**
Tollemache & Cobbold	**Jacobson, Michael**
Tomkinsons Carpets	**Tomkinson**
Tommy Lees, Tyldesley	**Brierly, E**
Tootal, Broadhurst, Lee	**Jenkin, Alfred**
Tottenham & District Gas	**Tottenham & District Gas**
Tottenham Hotspur F C	**Finn, Ralph Leslie**
Tottenham Weekly Herald	**Crusha & Son**
Tottington Industrial Co-op Soc	**Tottington Industrial Co-operative Society**
Touche Ross & Co	**Richards, Archibald B**
Towles	**Towles Ltd**
Townsend, George & Co, Redditch	**Solloway, William J**
Tozer Kemsley and Millbourn	**Tozer Kemsley and Millbourn**
Trading in West Africa	**Davies, Peter Neville (ed)**
Tramways	**Klapper, Charles Frederick**
Tramways in Metropolitan Essex	**Burrows, V E**

Transparent Paper	Tillmanns, Martin
Travers, Joseph & Sons	Travers, Frank
Travers, Joseph & Sons	Travers, Joseph & Sons
Treeton Colliery	Rossington, T
Trenthams	Bruce, George
Triang	Lines, Walter
Trinity Paper Mills	Lyddon, Denis W & Marshall, Peter A
Triumph Cars	Langworth, Richard & Robson, Graham
Triumph Motor Cycles	Bruce-Gardyne, Jock
Triumph Motor Cycles	Louis, Harry & Currie, Bob
Trollope & Colls	Trollope & Colls
True-Form Boot Co	Sears, J & Co
Truman Hanbury Buxton	Birch, L
Truman Hanbury Buxton	Trumans
Trumper, George F	Trumper, George F
Truscon	Trussed Concrete Steel Co
Trustee Savings Bank	Dundee Savings Bank
Trustee Savings Bank	Horne, H Oliver
Trustee Savings Bank	Miln, John
Trustee Savings Bank of Yorks	Hebden, C Donald
Tube Investments	Bowden, Gregory Houston
Tube Investments	Spalding, C W
Tuck, Raphael	Tuck, Raphael
Tuke & Co	Sessions, William K & E Margaret
Tuke & Co	Tuke Mennell & Co
Tullis Russell	Ketelbey, Caroline Doris Mabel
Turkish Petroleum Co	Stivers, William
Turnbull & Stockdale	Turnbull & Stockdale
Turnbull Scott & Co	Long, Anne & Russell
Turner & Newall	Dingley, Cyril S
Turner & Newall	Ferodo
Turner & Newall	Turner & Newall
Turner Edwards	Parsons, Richard M
Turner, Joshua	Turner, Joshua
Twaddle, Hugh & Son	House, Jack
Twining, R & Co	Newton, Ernest Edward
Twining, R & Co	Twining
Twining, R & Co	Twining, Stephen H
Twining, R & Co	Twining, Stephen H
Tylors of London	Tylors of London
Typographical Association	Musson, Albert Edward
Tyrer, Henry & Co	Davies, Peter Neville
Tyzack, William & Sons	Ledbetter, R M
Tyzack, William & Sons	Tyzack, Wm
U C S (Upper Clyde Shipbuilders)	McGill, Jack
Uddingston Co-operative Soc	Young, James
Ulster Bank	Ulster Bank
Ulster Railway	Ferris, T
Unicorn Industries U K	Luke and Spencer
Unigate	Unigate
Unilever	Edwards, Harold Raymond
Unilever	Fieldhouse, David Kenneth
Unilever	Jolly, William Percy
Unilever	Knox, Andrew Marshall
Unilever	Leverhulme

Unilever	Musson, Albert Edward
Unilever	Pedler, Frederick Johnson
Unilever	Reader, William Joseph
Unilever	Reader, William Joseph
Unilever	Reader, William Joseph
Unilever	Unilever
Unilever	Williams, Edmund
Unilever	Wilson, Charles
Unilever	Wilson, Charles
Unilever	Wilson, Charles
Union	Parkes, Josiah & Sons
Union Bank of Scotland	Forbes, William
Union Bank of Scotland	Rait, Robert S
Union Bank of Scotland	Tamaki, Norio
Union Bank of Scotland	Union Bank of Scotland
Union Cold Storage	Knightley, Phillip
Union Discount Co	Cleaver, George and Pamela
Union Marine & General Ins Co	Union Marine and General Insurance Co
Union Marine Insurance Co	Anderson, B L
Union-Castle	Mitchell, William H & Sawyer, L A
Union-Castle	Murray, Marischal
Union-Castle	Porter, Andrew
Union-Castle	Woodhouse, G B
United Africa Company	Kohn, Roger
United Africa Company	Pedler, Frederick Johnson
United Alkali Co	Hardie, David William Ferguson
United Alkali Co	United Alkali Co
United Alkali Co	Warren, Kenneth
United Biscuits	Adam, James S
United Clubs Brewery Co	United Clubs Brewery Co
United Dairies	Enock, Arthur Guy
United Glass	Carvel, John Lees
United Glass	Chance, J W
United Kingdom Provident Ins	Withers, Hartley
United Match Industries	Littler, Eric Raymond
United Molasses Co	Meneight, W A
United Steel	Andrews, Philip W S & Brunner, Elizabeth
United Steel	Boswell, Jonathan S
United Steel	Boswell, Jonathan S
United Steel	Peddie, R
United Steel	Stansfield, Hazel
United Steel	Walshaw, George R & Behrendt, Carl A J
United Steel	Workington Iron and Steel Co
United Wire Works	Phillips, J
United Wire Works	United Wire Works
Universal Private Telegraph Co	Durham, John Francis Langton
Unwin Brothers, Gresham Press	Unwin, Philip
Upper Clyde Shipbuilders	Paulden, Sydney M & Hawkins, Bill
Usher & Cole	Cole, John F & Camerer Cuss, Theodore P
Usk Ships	Heaton, Paul Michael
Vale of Leven Co-op Soc	Stirling, T B
Van Moppes, L M & Sons	Van Moppes
Vaughan Family	Vaughan, Anthony
Vauxhall Motors	Darbyshire, L C
Vauxhall Motors	Holden, L T

Walkley, F (Clogs), Huddersfield	Brierly, E
Wall Paper Manufacturers	Potters of Darwen
Wall Paper Manufacturers	Sanderson, Arthur & Sons
Wall Paper Manufacturers	Wall Paper Manufacturers
Wall Paper Manufacturers	Walpamur Co
Wall, T & Co	Wall, T
Wallace Brothers & Co (Holdings)	Pointon, Arnold Cecil
Wallis & Steevens	Whitehead, Robert Arthur
Wallis, G E & Sons	Wallis, G E & Sons
Wallis, Thomas & Co	Wallis, Thomas & Co
Wallsend Parish	Richardson, William
Wallsend Slipway and Eng Co	Boyd, W
Walmsley (Bury) Group	Walmsley (Bury) Group
Walmsley Brothers	Trowell, Frank
Walmsley, Thomas & Sons	Brough, Joseph
Walpamur Co	Walpamur Co
Walsall Lithographic Co	Walsall Lithographic Co
Walsall Locks & Cart Gear	Halstead, R
Waltham Watch Company	Moore, Charles W
Wandsworth & District Gas Co	Lewis, Harry
Wandsworth & District Gas Co	Wandsworth & District Gas Co
Wantage Engineering Co	Phillips, David C
Warburtons Bakery	Warburtons
Ward Lock	Liveing, Edward George Downing
Ward White Group	Britton, George Bryant & Sons
Ward, Thomas W	Ward, T W
Ward, Thomas W	Ward, T W
Waring & Gillow	Beable, William Henry
Waring & Gillow	Waring & Gillow
Warne, Frederick	King, Arthur & Stuart, Albert F
Warner & Sons	Goodale, Ernest William
Warrington Co-op	Leach, Cyril
Warwick, T O & Co	Shirley Aldred
Waterston, George & Sons	Waterston, George & Sons
Watford Observer	Watford Observer
Watkins & Stafford	Watkins & Stafford
Watkins, William	Bowen, Frank Charles
Watney Mann	Janes, Hurford
Watney, Combe, Reid & Co	Serocold, Walter P
Watson's of Bullionfield	Allan, Charles M
Watson, Angus & Co 'Skipper'	Beable, William Henry
Watson, Angus & Co 'Skipper'	Bridges, T C & Tiltman, H H
Watson, Joseph & Sons	Rimmer, William Gordon
Waverley Market, Edinburgh	Gemmell, Peter
Waygood-Otis	Walker, H C
Weavers' Company	Plummer, Alfred
Webb, Joseph & Sons	Webb, H J
Webb, Thomas & Sons	Woodward, Herbert William
Webley & Scott	Dowell, William Chipchase
Webster & Horsfall	Horsfall, John H C
Webster, W J	Austin, F Earle
Wedgwood & Bentley	Bentley, Richard
Wedgwood, Josiah & Sons	Beable, William Henry
Wedgwood, Josiah & Sons	Kelly, Alison
Wedgwood, Josiah & Sons	Warrillow, Ernest James Dalzell

Weir, G & J	Reader, William Joseph
Weir, G & J	Reader, William Joseph
Weir, G & J	Weir, G & J
Welded Tube Trade	Langley, S J
Wellcome Foundation	Macdonald, Gilbert
Wellcome Foundation	Wellcome Foundation
Wellworthy	Pearce, D & Hodges, D I
Welsh Anthracite Coal	Labour Research Dept
Welsh Coalfield	Phillips, Elizabeth
Welsh Woollen Industry	Jenkins, John Geraint
Welwyn Match Co	Littler, Eric Raymond
Wendron Forge	Jenkin, Alfred Kenneth Hamilton
Wentworth Estate	Mee, L Graham
West African Shipping	Leubuscher, Charlotte
West Calder Co-op	West Calder Co-op
West Country Brewery Holdings	West Country Brewery Holdings
West India Docks	Stern, W M
West Indian Produce Association	Rutter, Owen
West Midlands Industries	Thoms, David
West of England Fire & Life	Commercial Union Assurance Co: Exeter Bra
West Riding Wool Textile Ind	Jenkins, David Trevor
West Riding Wool Textile Industry	Topham, A J
West's Cornice Pole Co	West's Cornice Pole Co
West, Clayton	Brooke, Alan J
Westcotts	Merry, Ian D
Western Motor Works	Western Motor Works (Chislehurst)
Westinghouse	Metropolitan-Vickers
Westland Aircraft	Mondey, David
Westland Aircraft	Petter, Percival Waddams
Westland Aircraft	Taylor, John W R & Allward, Maurice F
Westley Richards	Carey, Arthur Merwyn
Westley Richards	Taylor, Leslie B
Westminster Bank	Gregory, Theodore Emanuel Gugenheim
Westminster Bank	Reed, Richard
Westminster Fire Office	Davies, Edward Andrew
Westrays	Fagg, Alan
WestRiding Wool Textile Ind	Hudson, Pat
Whaling Trade	Jackson, Gordon
Whatman, J	Balston, Thomas
Wheatsheaf Works	Hurn, Elizabeth
Whessoe	Whessoe
Whiffen & Sons	Law, Rupert S
Whisky Distilleries	Barnard, Alfred
Whitbread & Co	Cowen, Frank
Whitbread & Co	Hill, Brian
Whitbread & Co	Knox, Diana M
Whitbread & Co	Monckton, H A
Whitbread & Co	Nevile, Sydney Oswald
Whitbread & Co	Whitbread
White Star Line	Anderson, Roy
White Star Line	Oldham, Wilton Joseph
White, J Samuel & Co	Goodall, Michael Harold
White, J Samuel & Co	White, J S
White, John	White, John
White, Wolfe Barry & Partners	Marsh, J

Whitechapel Bellfoundry	Whitechapel Bellfoundry
Whitecliff Iron Works	Osborn, Frederick Marmaduke
Whitecross Co	Carter, George Arthur
Whitehead Aircraft	Whitehead Aircraft
Whitehurst, Henry & Sons	Whitehurst, Henry and Sons
Whiteley, John & Sons	Whiteley, John & Sons
Whiteley, William	Beable, William Henry
Whiteley, William	Lambert, Richard Stanton
Whitworth, Joseph	Musson, Albert Edward
Widnell & Trollope	Blake, David (ed)
Wigan Coal & Iron Co	Peden, J A
Wigan Coal & Iron Co	Turner, D H
Wigfull Mill	Wigfull Mill
Wiggin, Henry	Wiggin, Henry
Wiggins Teape	Jones, Samuel
Wiggins Teape	Jones, Samuel
Wiggins Teape Group	Wiggins Teape and Co
Wiggins Teape Group	Wiggins Teape Group
Wigham Richardson	Rutherford, Wilfrid
Wigham Richardson	Swan Hunter & Wigham Richardson
Wigham Richardson	Swan Hunter & Wigham Richardson
Wigston Hosiers	Greening, Edward Owen
Wilder, J	Dewey, J & S
Wilkin & Sons	Benham, Maura
Wilkins & Co	Roberts, R O
Wilkinson & Riddell	Wills, John
Willcox, W H	Willcox, W H
Willesden Paper & Canvas Works	Willesden Dux
Willetts of Sloane Square	Willett, William
Williams & Glyn's Bank	Williams Deacon's Bank
Williams & Womersley	Williams & Womersley
Williams Deacon's Bank	Allman, A H
Williams Deacon's Bank	Williams Deacon's Bank
Williams, John & Son	Scourfield, Elfyn
Williams, Samuel & Sons	Williams, Samuel & Sons
Williams, W & Son (Bread Street)	Hayman, Leslie C R
Williamson, G H	Walker, Denis
Williamson, James	Johnson, Robert L
Williamson, James & Son	Christie, Guy
Williamson, James & Son	Williamson, James & Son
Willmer Brothers & Haram	Willmer, Edgar Wrayford
Willoughby & Sons	Willoughby, Joan
Willoughby's	Willoughby's
Wills, W D & H O	Alford, Bernard William Ernest
Wills, W D & H O	Till, Roger
Wilson Brothers Bobbin Co	Wilson Brothers Bobbin Co
Wilson Cammell	Austin, John & Ford, Malcolm
Wilson's Cooperage Co	Wilson
Wilson, Adam & Sons	McChesney, John S
Wilson, Ambrose	Wilson, Ambrose
Wilson, Joseph & Sons	Wilson, Joseph
Wilson, Sons & Co	Wilson, Sons & Co
Wilsons Brewery	Richardson, Neil
Wilsons of Sharrow	Chaytor, Mark Hamilton Freer
Wimpey	White, Valerie

Wise & Co	Wise and Co
Wishaw Co-operative Soc	Battison, George
Witney Blanket Industry	Plummer, Alfred
Witney Blanket Industry	Plummer, Alfred & Early, Richard E
Wolseley Tool & Motor Car Co	Nixon, St John Cousins
Woodall-Duckham	Bridges, T C & Tiltman, H H
Woodall-Duckham	Woodall-Duckham
Wool Textile Industry	Jenkins, David Trevor & Ponting, Kenneth G
Woolfold Co-op Soc, Bury	Haslam, James
Woollen Mills	Tann, Jennifer
Woolley, James & Sons	Milliken, H T
Woolley, James & Sons	Woolley, James
Woolwich Equitable Building Soc	Brooks, William Collin
Woolwich Equitable Building Soc	Brooks, William Collin
Woolworth, F W	Woolworth
Woolworth, F W	Woolworth
Worcester Co-operative Society	Saxton, Chas A W
Working Men's Club & Inst Union	Tremlett, George
Workington Iron & Steel Co	Workington Iron and Steel Co
Workman, Clark	Workman, Clark
Wormalds & Walker	Glover, Frederick J
Worthington-Simpson	Worthington-Simpson
Wortley Ironworks	Andrews, G R & M
Wostenholm, George & Son	Bexfield, Harold
Wray (Optical Works)	Smith, Arthur William
Wrexham Mold Connah's Quay Rly	Dunn, John Maxwell
Wright & Sons	Wright & Sons
Wright, Ernest & Son	Wright, P E
Wrights of Richmond	Wrights of Richmond
Xylonite Group	Ashlee, Peter C
Xylonite Group	British Xylonite Co
Xylonite Group	Kaufman, M
Xylonite Group	Xylonite Group
Yale Security Products	Yale Security Products
Yardley	Thomas, Edward Wynne
Yarrow	Borthwick, Alastair
Yarrow	Yarrow
Yarrow	Yarrow, Lady Eleanor C & Barnes, E C
Yarrow & Co	Bridges, T C & Tiltman, H H
Yates Brothers Wine Lodges	Yates Brothers Wine Lodges
Yates Duxbury & Sons	Green, Tom
Yates, Haywood & Co	Morley, C
Yelf Brothers	Daish, Alfred Newman
Yellow Bus Services of Stoughton	Hamshere, N & Sutton, J
Ynysybwl Co-operative Soc	Ynysybwl Co-operative Society
York Building Co	Murray, David
York Equitable Industrial Society	Briggs, George
York Savings Bank	Camidge, William
Yorks Heavy Woollen Trade	Glover, Frederick J
Yorkshire Bank	Broomhead, Leslie James
Yorkshire Insurance Co	Yorkshire Insurance Co
Yorkshire Post	Gibb, Mildred A & Beckwith, Frank
Yorkshire Woollen and Worsted	Hartwell, R M
Young, James	Butt, John
Younger, George	Younger, George

Younger, William
Youngs, Crawshay & Youngs
Zinc Smelting

Keir, David Edwin
Youngs, Crawshay & Youngs
Cocks, Edward J & Walters, Bernhardt

5 Industrial classification index

111	Church, Roy Anthony
111	Clay Cross Co
111	Corrins, R D
111	Daunton, Martin James
111	Davies, John
111	Didham, R C
111	Emery, N
111	Evans, Richard
111	Fereday, R P
111	Flinn, M W with Stoker, D
111	Francis, J R
111	Francis, J Roger
111	Gale, Walter Keith Vernon & Nicholls, C R
111	Galloway, R L (ed B F Duckham)
111	Griffin, Alan R
111	Hardwick Colliery Co
111	Hare, A E C
111	Howe, L
111	Hudson, Graham S
111	Jevons, Herbert Stanley
111	Johnson, W
111	Kirby, Maurice W
111	Kirby, Maurice W
111	Kirby, Maurice W
111	Labour Research Dept
111	Labour Research Dept
111	Lloyd, Humphrey
111	Mee, L Graham
111	Mensforth, Eric
111	Mitchell, Brian Rodman
111	Morris, John H & Williams, Lawrence J
111	Morton, G R & LeGuillou
111	Mottram, R H & Coote, Colin
111	Mountford, Colin E
111	Muir, Augustus
111	National Coal Board, Scottish Division
111	Owen, Colin
111	Payne, Peter Lester
111	Payne, Peter Lester (ed)
111	Peden, J A
111	Phillips, Elizabeth
111	Political and Economic Planning
111	Political and Economic Planning
111	Powell Duffryn
111	Raybould, Trevor J
111	Rhondda, Margaret, Viscountess
111	Riden, Philip J

536

111	Ritchie, Arthur Edwin
111	Robens, Alfred
111	Rossington, T
111	Slaven, A & Aldcroft, D H (eds)
111	Slaven, Anthony
111	Smith, David L
111	Staveley Industries
111	Turner, D H
111	Vincent, James Edmund
111	Waller, Robert J
111	Walters, R H
111	Whitelock, G C H
111	Wilkins, Charles
111	Williams, David James
111	Williams, L J
120	Anderson, Donald
120	Anderson, Donald
120	Anderson, Donald with Lane, Jane
120	Holmes, Graeme M
120	Rippon, Guy S O
120	Young, Edward Preston
130	Anderson, John Richard Lane
130	Beaton, Kendall
130	British Petroleum
130	Corley, Thomas Anthony Buchanan
130	Corley, Thomas Anthony Buchanan
130	Ferrier, R W
130	Gerretson, Frederik Carel
130	Henriques, Robert David Quixano
130	Hewins, Ralph
130	Jones, Geoffrey
130	Jones, Geoffrey
130	Jones, Geoffrey
130	Jones, Geoffrey
130	Kent, Marian
130	Longhurst, Henry Carpenter
130	Miller, Rory
130	Naylor, Stanley (ed)
130	Popham, Hugh
130	Rippon, Guy S O
130	Rowland, John & Basil, 2nd Lord Cadman
130	Royal Dutch Petroleum Co
130	Shell Transport & Trading
130	Spender, John Alfred
130	Stephen, Walter M
130	Stivers, William
130	Stoff, Michael B

161	Hill, G W
161	Lamb, P G
161	Logan, John C
161	North Metropolitan Electrical Power Distribution Co
161	P E P (Political and Economic Planning)
161	Political and Economic Planning
161	Robinson, Sydney
161	Sakamoto, T
161	Steward, S F
161	Swale, S E
161	Warburton, Ray
162	Barty-King, Hugh
162	Bourne-Paterson, R A
162	British Gas Light Co
162	Chandler, Dean & Lacey, A Douglas
162	Chantler, Philip
162	Chatterton, D A
162	Croydon Gas Co
162	Dumbarton Corporation Gas Undertaking
162	Everard, Stirling
162	Falkus, Malcolm
162	Fulford, Roger Thomas Baldwin
162	Fulford, Roger Thomas Baldwin
162	Gas Light & Coke
162	Gas Light & Coke Co
162	Hacking, Barbara
162	Hill, N K
162	Hinckley U D Council Gas Department
162	Holmes, Graeme M
162	Imperial Continental Gas
162	Layton, Walter Thomas
162	Leigh-Bennett, Ernest Pendarves
162	Lewis, Harry
162	Manchester Gas Dept
162	Melling, Joseph
162	Mills, Mary
162	Oxford and District Gas Company
162	Painting, M H
162	Political and Economic Planning
162	Political and Economic Planning
162	Roberts, David E
162	Roberts, David E
162	Roberts, David E
162	Roberts, David E
162	Roberts, David E
162	Roberts, David E
162	Roberts, David E & Frisby, J H

210	Williams, C J
220	Allen, George Cyril
220	Boswell, Jonathan S
220	Lysaght
220	Moss, M S & Hume, J R
220	Payne, Peter Lester
220	Sturgess, R W (ed)
220	Wilkins, Charles
221	Addis, John Philip
221	Addis, John Philip
221	Andrews, G R & M
221	Andrews, Philip W S & Brunner, Elizabeth
221	Austin, John & Ford, Malcolm
221	Baker, Henry
221	Balfour, Arthur
221	Baston, Christopher
221	Beale, Samuel R
221	Bedford, John
221	Bolckow, Vaughan & Co
221	Boswell, Jonathan S
221	Boyce, G H
221	Brailsford, Michael
221	Brearley, Harry
221	British Steel
221	British Steel
221	Brooke, Edward Henry
221	Brooke, Edward Henry
221	Brown & Tawse Group
221	Brown Bayleys
221	Brown, John
221	Bryer, R A, Brignall, T J & Maunders, A R
221	Brymbo
221	Burn, Duncan Lyall
221	Burn, Duncan Lyall
221	Burnham, Thomas H & Hoskins, George O
221	Butler, Rodney
221	Butterley
221	Cadell, Patrick
221	Cammell
221	Campbell, Roy Hutcheson
221	Campbell, Roy Hutcheson
221	Carr, James C & Taplin, Walter
221	Carvel, John Lees
221	Chapman, Stanley David
221	Clay Cross Co
221	Clay Cross Co
221	Clay Cross Co

221	Clayton, A K
221	Coalbrookdale Company
221	Cohen, George
221	Consett Iron
221	Corrins, R D
221	Cottrell, E
221	Daunton, Martin James
221	Davies, J Hathren
221	Davies, John
221	Dobie, George A
221	Docherty, C
221	Doncaster, Daniel
221	Doncaster, Daniel
221	Donkin, Bryan
221	Donkin, Harry Julyan
221	Edwards, E
221	Edwards, Ifor
221	Elsas, Madeleine (ed)
221	Erickson, Charlotte
221	Evans, Harold
221	Fereday, R P
221	Firth Brown
221	Flinn, Michael Walter
221	Flinn, Michael Walter
221	Flinn, Michael Walter
221	Gale, Walter Keith Vernon & Nicholls, C R
221	Gott, Ron
221	Grant, Allan John
221	Griffiths, Thomas
221	Guest Keen Baldwins
221	Hadfields
221	Hadfields
221	Hancocks, H
221	Haywards
221	Heal, David Walter
221	Hempstead, C A (ed)
221	Hornsby, R M
221	Horsfall, John H C
221	House, Jack
221	Huntsman, Benjamin
221	Irving, R J
221	Jeans, James Stephen
221	Jessop, William
221	John, Arthur Henry (ed)
221	Johnson, F G L
221	Jones, Geoffrey (ed)
221	Jones, H Edgar

221	Jowitt, George
221	Keeling, B S & Wright, A E G
221	Kenyon, John
221	Knox, Collie
221	Lancaster J Y & Wattleworth, D R
221	Langley, S J
221	Ledbetter, R M
221	Lee, Arthur
221	Lewis, M J
221	Lewis, Victor
221	Lloyd, Humphrey
221	Lloyd, John
221	Lloyd-Jones, R & Lewis, M J
221	Macleod, William H & Houldsworth, Henry H
221	Marshall, A C & Newbould, Herbert
221	Marshall, John Duncan
221	McCloskey, Donald N
221	McEwan, Ann M C
221	Mensforth, Eric
221	Middlemas, Robert K & Barnes, A John L
221	Midland Iron Co
221	Midland Motor Cylinder Co
221	Minchinton, Walter Edward
221	Morton, G R & LeGuillou
221	Morton, G R & Smith, W A
221	Mottram, R H & Coote, Colin
221	Muir, Augustus
221	Mutton, Norman
221	Osborn, Frederick Marmaduke
221	Owen, John Alastair
221	Payne, Peter Lester
221	Peddie, R
221	Pocock, Douglas Charles David
221	Pole, William
221	Pollard, Sidney
221	Quinn, Esther
221	Quinn, Esther
221	Raistrick, Arthur
221	Raistrick, Arthur
221	Raybould, Trevor J
221	Reid, A
221	Richardson, H W & Bass, J M
221	Riden, Philip J
221	Roberts, Colin William
221	Robinson, Philip Moffat
221	Royston, George P
221	Sanderson Kayser

222	Johnson, F G L
222	Peddie, R
222	Scopes, Frederick
222	Spalding, C W
222	Stanton Ironworks Co
222	Staveley Industries
223	Adam, Alastair T
223	Begg, Cousland
223	Brockhouse, J & Co
223	Carter, George Arthur
223	Hall's Barton Ropery Co
223	Horsfall, John H C
223	House, Jack
223	Lees, J B & S
223	Mackenzie, Edward Montague Compton
223	Mais, Stuart Peter Brodie
223	Phillips, J
223	Richardson, J E
223	Rylands of Warrington
223	Seth-Smith, Michael
223	Timaeus, C E
223	Tinsley Wire
223	United Wire Works
224	Accles & Pollock
224	Accles & Pollock
224	Aluminium Corporation
224	Aluminium Corporation
224	British Aluminium
224	Burt, Roger
224	Carter, George Arthur
224	Cocks, Edward J & Walters, Bernhardt
224	Day, Joan
224	Edwards, E
224	Fache, E C
224	Harvey, Charles E
224	Hudson, Kenneth
224	Hunt, Leslie B
224	Jenkin, Alfred Kenneth Hamilton
224	Little, Bryan
224	MacDonald, Donald
224	MacDonald, Donald
224	MacDonald, Donald & Hunt, Leslie B
224	Mais, Stuart Peter Brodie
224	McKechnie, John D
224	Mond
224	Morton, John
224	Orr's Zinc White

224	Pollard, Sidney
224	Rowe, David John
224	Rylands of Warrington
224	Sheffield Smelting Company
224	Star Aluminium Co
224	Sturney, Alfred Charles
224	Toomey, R R
224	Venesta
224	West, Richard
224	Wilson, Ronald E
230	Checkland, Sydney George
231	Bezzant, Norman
231	Campbell, Roy Hutcheson
231	Clay Cross Co
231	Clay Cross Co
231	Clay Cross Co
231	Collidge, W H
231	Diack, William
231	Earle, James Basil Foster
231	Earle, James Basil Foster
231	Emery, N
231	Geddes, R Stanley
231	Grant, William S
231	Greensmith, J
231	Hudson, Kenneth
231	Jones, G P
231	Kirby, Maurice W
231	Kirby, Maurice W
231	Lenman, Bruce
231	Lindsay, Jean
231	Penmaenmawr and Welsh Granite Co
231	Quail, G
231	Quail, G
231	Teesdale, E
231	Tucker, D G
233	Calvert, Albert Frederick
233	Calvert, Albert Frederick
233	Calvert, Albert Frederick
239	Borax Holdings
241	Butterley
241	Clay Cross Co
241	Clay Cross Co
241	Collier, L J
241	Dumbleton, Michael
241	Gale, Walter Keith Vernon & Nicholls, C R
241	Hillier, Richard
241	Lenman, Bruce

241	Marley
241	Roughdale Brickworks
241	Willmott, Frank G
242	Associated Portland Cement
242	Bezzant, Norman
242	Davis, Arthur Charles
242	Francis, Anthony John
242	McRobb, John
242	Skinner, Basil Chisholm
243	Aiton & Co
243	Cape Asbestos Co
243	Jenkins, David
243	Prestwich, Wm.
243	Routley, John
243	Trussed Concrete Steel Co
243	Turner & Newall
244	Cape Asbestos Co
244	Ferodo
244	Turner & Newall
245	Earle, James Basil Foster
245	Earle, James Basil Foster
245	Hudson, Kenneth
245	Incorporated Stone & Marble Co
245	Oldaker, John
245	Prestwich, Wm.
245	Reader, William Joseph
245	Whitaker, John
246	Davies, W J
246	Jowitt, George
246	Luke and Spencer
246	Norton Abrasives
246	Oakey, John
246	Van Moppes
247	Alford, Bernard William Ernest
247	Barker, Theodore C & Harris, John R
247	Barker, Theodore Cardwell
247	Barker, Theodore Cardwell
247	Barker, Theodore Cardwell
247	Buckley, Francis
247	Carvel, John Lees
247	Chance Brothers
247	Chance Brothers
247	Chance, J W
247	Chance, James Frederick
247	Chance, James Frederick
247	Clark, Alec W
247	Greene, Dorothy

248	Richards Tiles
248	Shaw, Simeon
248	Turner, William
248	Twitchett, John & Bailey, Betty
248	Warrillow, Ernest James Dalzell
248	Watkins, Chris; Harvey, W & Senft, R
248	Willis-Fear, M J W
250	Bolitho, Henry Hector
250	Brearley, C B E
250	Campbell, William Alec
250	Cohen, John Michael
250	Fox, W E
250	Goodman, Jean
250	Haber, Ludwig Fritz
250	Haber, Ludwig Fritz
250	Haber, Ludwig Fritz
250	Hardie, David William Ferguson
250	Hardie, David William Ferguson
250	Hughes, F A
250	Imperial Chemical Industries
250	Irvine, A S
250	Koss, Stephen Edward
250	Laporte Chemicals
250	Pettigrew, Andrew M
250	Reader, William Joseph
250	Reader, William Joseph
250	Trotter, R (ed)
250	Warren, Kenneth
250	Watts, John I
250	Wiggin, Henry
251	Abrahart, Edward Noah
251	Albright & Wilson
251	Anderson, John Richard Lane
251	Ashlee, Peter C
251	Avon Industrial Polymers
251	Blum, Fred H
251	Bowmans (Warrington)
251	British Industrial Plastics
251	British Petroleum
251	British Xylonite Co
251	Brunner, Mond
251	Burt, Boulton & Haywood
251	Bush, W J & Co
251	Butler, Thomas Howard
251	Castner-Kellner
251	Chance, James Frederick
251	Dick, W F L

311	Brough, Joseph
311	Burritt, Elihu
311	Cadell, Patrick
311	Campbell, Roy Hutcheson
311	Campbell, Roy Hutcheson
311	Cantrell, J A
311	Carmichael, James & Co
311	Clay Cross Co
311	Clay Cross Co
311	Coalbrookdale Company
311	Craven, Wilfred Archer
311	Curran, Edward
311	Daunton, Martin James
311	Davies, J Hathren
311	Dewey, J & S
311	Evered & Co
311	Eves, Alec
311	Field, Molly & Dick
311	Firth-Derihon
311	Flavel, Sidney & Co
311	Flinn, Michael Walter
311	Gale, Walter Keith Vernon
311	Gale, Walter Keith Vernon
311	Grinyer, P H & Spender, J-C
311	Hadfields
311	Hadfields
311	Haybittle, J
311	Hume, John R & Moss, Michael S
311	Jephcott, William Ellery
311	John, Arthur Henry (ed)
311	Jones, H Edgar
311	Lloyd, John
311	Mackenzie, Edward Montague Compton
311	Miller, V
311	Morley, C
311	Newman, William & Sons
311	Nicholson, Hubert C
311	Owen, C C
311	Owen, John Alastair
311	Parker, J Francis
311	Peden, J A
311	Raistrick, Arthur
311	Raistrick, Arthur
311	Richardson, H W & Bass, J M
311	Robinson, Philip Moffat
311	Russell, Samuel & Co
311	Russell, Samuel & Sons

311	Skinner, Basil Chisholm
311	Thomas, David A
311	Torrens, Hugh S
311	Torrens, Hugh S
311	Trinder, Barrie Stuart
311	Tripp, Basil Howard
311	Turner, D H
311	Vulcan Foundry
311	Webb, H J
311	Weetch, Kenneth Thomas
311	Whitaker, John
311	Whitechapel Bellfoundry
311	Williams & Womersley
312	Brockhouse, J & Co
312	Brough, Joseph
312	Butler, Rodney
312	Cantrell, J A
312	Janes, Hurford
312	Lumsden, Harry & Aitken, P Henderson
312	Mackenzie, Edward Montague Compton
312	Mervyn, J F A
312	Muir, Augustus
312	Pressed Steel
312	Pressed Steel
312	Pressed Steel
312	Pressed Steel
313	Curran, Edward
313	Guest, Keen & Nettlefolds
313	Jones, H Edgar
313	McNeill, Valerie
313	Pugh, Charles H
313	Pugh, Charles H
313	Richardson, J E
313	Seth-Smith, Michael
313	Shaw, H
313	Thomas, David G & Sowan, Brenda J
313	Thomas, Earl B
313	Ward, T W
314	Austin, P E
314	Crittall Manufacturing Co
314	Haywards
314	Hope, Henry & Sons
316	Allman, Geoff
316	Arnold, H
316	Ashton, Thomas Southcliffe
316	Benham, Stanley J
316	Best, Robert Dudley

316	Tweedale, Geoffrey
316	Tyzack, Wm
316	Walker, Denis
316	Yale Security Products
319	Parkes, Josiah & Sons
320	Aiton & Co
320	Alexander, Kenneth J W & Jenkins, Carson L
320	Andrews, Philip W S & Brunner, Elizabeth
320	Arrol, Sir William & Co
320	Ashworth and Parker
320	Baston, Christopher
320	Bellamy, Joyce Margaret
320	Bootham Engineers
320	Borthwick, Alastair
320	Brico
320	Broadbent, Thomas
320	Brockhouse, J & Co
320	Cantrell, J A
320	Clark, Edwin Kitson
320	Coe, W E
320	Davenport-Hines, R P T & Liebenau, J (eds)
320	Davenport-Hines, Richard P T
320	Davenport-Hines, Richard P T
320	Davenport-Hines, Richard P T
320	Dempster, Robert & Sons
320	Derbyshire, F W
320	Don, G Stuart
320	Dummett, G A
320	Dutton, H I
320	Eversheds & Vignoles
320	Field, H
320	Field, Molly & Dick
320	Gale, Walter Keith Vernon & Nicholls, C R
320	Gourvish, Terence Richard
320	Green, E & Son
320	Grinyer, P H & Spender, J-C
320	Hayward, R A
320	Hesketh, Everard
320	Hick, Hargreaves & Co
320	Holmes, W C
320	Holmes, W C
320	House, Jack
320	Hume, John R & Moss, Michael S
320	Irving, R J
320	Jones, Geoffrey (ed)
320	Jones, H Edgar
320	Jones, H Edgar

325	Express Lift Company
325	Garrett
325	Grinyer, P H & Spender, J-C
325	Hesketh, Everard
325	Howse, R M & Harley, F H
325	Miller, Harry
325	Miller, V
325	Nortons Tividale
325	Pochin, R Eric
325	Pochin, R Eric with Olive, E A
325	Qualter Hall & Co
325	Qualter Hall & Co
325	Rolt, Lionel Thomas Caswall
325	Sutcliffe, R J & Edward D
325	Torrens, Hugh S
325	Tylors of London
325	Victor
325	Wainwright, David
325	Walker, Densmore
325	Walker, H C
325	Whitehead, Robert Arthur
325	Wilson, Martyn & Spink, Karen
326	Tripp, Basil Howard
326	Tripp, Basil Howard
327	Bertrams
327	British United Shoe Machinery Co
327	Fordath
327	House, Jack
327	Liveing, Edward George Downing
327	Morison, Stanley
327	Muir, Augustus
327	Pardoe, F E
327	Pollard, Sidney
327	Standard Engineering Co
328	Aiton & Co
328	Angus, George & Co
328	Avery, W & T
328	Bache, Mary
328	Baker, Allan C & Civil, Thomas D A
328	Beale, Samuel R
328	Brandon, Ruth
328	Broadbent, L H
328	Chubb Fire Security
328	Clark, Ronald Harry
328	Clarke, Joseph Francis
328	Darbyshire, L C
328	Doxford, William

328	Turner, John (ed)
328	Vale, Henry Edmund Theodoric
328	Villiers Engineering Co
328	Vulcan Foundry
328	Waterhouse, Rachel Elizabeth
328	Whitehead, David Charles
328	Wilson, Paul N
328	Worthington-Simpson
329	Beaumont, Richard
329	Beynon, Huw & Wainwright, Hilary
329	Birmingham Small Arms Co
329	Birmingham Small Arms Co
329	Bowbelski, Margaret
329	Carey, Arthur Merwyn
329	Cochrane, Alfred
329	Davenport-Hines, Richard P T
329	Davenport-Hines, Richard P T
329	Davenport-Hines, Richard P T
329	Davenport-Hines, Richard P T
329	Davenport-Hines, Richard P T (ed)
329	Dougan, David
329	Dowell, William Chipchase
329	Evans, Harold
329	Firth Brown
329	Frost, George H
329	Grant, Allan John
329	Hartley, Peter
329	Hogg, Oliver Frederick Gillilan
329	Kynoch
329	Marshall, John Duncan
329	More, C
329	Neal, William K & Back, David H
329	Neal, William K & Back, David H
329	Peden, George
329	Ryerson, Barry
329	Scott, John Dick
329	Segreto, Luciano
329	Simmons, W H
329	Smith, Barbara M D
329	Taylor, Leslie B
329	Ward, Donovan M
330	Culpan, H V
330	Dale, Rodney
330	Dorlay, John S
330	Gestetner
330	Gestetner
330	Hall Harding

342	Byatt, Ian Charles Rayner
342	Crabtree, John A & Co
342	Hoover
342	Johnson, J H & Randell, W L
342	Klockner-Moeller
342	Lee, Norman & Stubbs, Peter C
342	Minkes, A L & Tucker, D G
342	Morgan, Bryan Stanford
342	Rowland, John Herbert Shelley
342	Scott, John Dick
342	Volk, Conrad
342	West, Allen
342	Wilson, Paul N
343	Andrews, H H
343	Barfield, T J
343	Chubb Fire Security
343	D P Battery Co
343	Goblin B V C
343	Heyes, Philip
343	Jennings, Fred H & Sons
343	Lucas Aerospace
343	Morgan, Bryan Stanford
343	Nixon, St John Cousins
343	Nockolds, Harold
343	Oldham
343	Oldham
343	Peebles, Bruce & Co
343	Rowntree, Arthur (ed)
344	Creed
344	Donaldson, Frances Annesley
344	Ferranti
344	Ferranti
344	Lewis, Edward Roberts
344	Scott, John Dick
344	Slater, Ernest
344	Thomas, David A
344	Tinsley, H
344	Veeder-Root
344	Wise, S
344	Young, Peter
345	Belling and Lee
345	Belling and Lee
345	Bussey, Gordon
345	Cossor, A C
345	Cossor, A C
345	Cussins & Light
345	Jones, Geoffrey

351	Davenport-Hines, Richard P T
351	Donne, Michael
351	Donnelly, Desmond
351	Dunnett, Peter J S
351	Edwardes, Michael
351	Exell, Arthur
351	Fallon, Ivan & Strodes, James
351	Foreman-Peck, James S
351	Foreman-Peck, James S
351	Foreman-Peck, James S
351	Frostick, Michael
351	Guy Motors
351	Hancock, Laurie W J
351	Harker, Ronald W
351	Harvey-Bailey, Alec H
351	Harvey-Bailey, Alec H
351	Hesketh, Everard
351	Holden, L T
351	Hume, John R & Moss, Michael S
351	Jackson, Robert
351	Jaguar Cars
351	Jowett Cars
351	Keith, Kenneth
351	Kennett, Pat
351	Kingsford, Peter Wilfrid
351	Kingsford, Peter Wilfrid
351	Lambert, Zeta E & Wyatt, Robert J
351	Langworth, Richard & Robson, Graham
351	Levin, Hillel
351	Lloyd, Ian
351	Merryweather & Sons
351	Miller, Harry
351	Montagu of Beaulieu, E J B D S
351	Montagu of Beaulieu, E J B D S
351	Montagu of Beaulieu, E J B D S
351	Montagu of Beaulieu, Lord J W D S
351	Morgan, Bryan Stanford
351	Morris Motors
351	Neufeld, Edward Peter
351	Nixon, St John Cousins
351	Nixon, St John Cousins
351	Nockolds, Harold
351	Oldham, Wilton Joseph
351	Overy, Richard James
351	Pearson, James Denning
351	Pressed Steel
351	Pressed Steel

361	Bowman, A I
361	Boyd, W
361	Brown, John
361	Browne, B C
361	Bruce, Alexander Balmain
361	Buxton, Neil K
361	Caledon Shipbuilding Co
361	Cammell Laird
361	Campbell, Roy Hutcheson
361	Carvel, John Lees
361	Chapman, Dennis
361	Clarke, Joseph Francis
361	Cook, Clifford J
361	Cormack, W S
361	Crighton, John
361	Davidson, John F
361	Denny, William & Bros
361	Denny, William & Bros
361	Denny, William & Bros
361	Denny, William & Bros
361	Denny, William & Bros
361	Dillon, Malcolm
361	Dougan, David
361	Doxford, William
361	Evans, Harold
361	Fairfield Shipbuilding
361	Fairfield Shipbuilding
361	Firth Brown
361	Gibbs, John Morel
361	Goodey, Charles
361	Grant, Allan John
361	Green, Henry & Wigram, Robert
361	Hopkins, Charles Henry Gordon
361	Hume, John R & Moss, Michael S
361	Hume, John R & Moss, Michael S
361	Irving, R J
361	Jefferson, Herbert
361	Jeffrey, David Cockburn
361	Kincaid, J G
361	Lewinsohn, Richard
361	Lythe, Samuel George Edgar
361	Lythe, Samuel George Edgar
361	Marshall, John Duncan
361	McGill, Jack
361	Mensforth, Eric
361	Merry, Ian D
361	More, C

362	E M B Co
362	Emery, N
362	Gloucester Railway Carriage & Wagon Co
362	Hills, Richard L
362	Hoole, Kenneth
362	Hughes, William J & Thomas, Joseph L
362	Kirby, Maurice W
362	Kirby, Maurice W
362	North British Locomotive
362	Pole, William (ed)
362	Price, J R
362	Radford, J B
362	Reed, B
362	Rolt, Lionel Thomas Caswall
362	Simmons, Jack (ed)
362	Thomas, John
362	Vulcan Foundry
362	Vulcan Foundry
362	Vulcan Foundry
362	Ward, T W
362	Warren, James G H
362	Wear, Russell & Lees, Eric
363	Birmingham Small Arms Co
363	Birmingham Small Arms Co
363	Bowden, Gregory Houston
363	Bruce-Gardyne, Jock
363	Buchanan, D J
363	Currys
363	Foreman-Peck, James S
363	Foreman-Peck, James S
363	Halford Cycle Co
363	Harrison, A E
363	Harrison, A E
363	Hartley, Peter
363	Hartley, Peter
363	Hartley, Peter
363	Holliday, Bob
363	Hopwood, Bert
363	Jones, Barry M
363	Lerner, Harry
363	Lewchuck, Wayne A
363	Louis, Harry & Currie, Bob
363	Norton Villiers Triumph
363	Phillips, J A & Co
363	Raleigh
363	Reynolds, Bryan
363	Ryerson, Barry

364	Morgan, Bryan Stanford
364	Nockolds, Harold
364	Nockolds, Harold
364	Oldham, Wilton Joseph
364	Owen, K
364	Pearson, James Denning
364	Petter, Percival Waddams
364	Preston, J M
364	Pudney, John Sleigh
364	Robertson, A J
364	Rolt, Lionel Thomas Caswall
364	Rotax
364	Scott, John Dick
364	Scrope Hugh E
364	Segreto, Luciano
364	Sharp, Cecil Martin
364	Sharp, Cecil Martin
364	Slaven, A & Aldcroft, D H (eds)
364	Smith, Malcolm
364	Tapper, Oliver
364	Taylor, John W R & Allward, Maurice F
364	Taylor, Michael John Haddrick
364	Whitaker, John
364	White, O'Loughlin Molly
364	Whitehead Aircraft
364	Wilson, Andrew
364	Wilson, Charles & Reader, William
364	Wrangham, Cuthbert Edward
370	Allen, Cecil John
370	Atthill, Robin
370	Munro, R W
370	Taylor, E & Wilson, J S
370	Williams, Mari E W
371	Allen, Cecil John
371	Cambridge Instrument Co
371	Cambridge Instrument Co
371	Dixey, C W & Son
371	Everett, Edgcumbe & Co
371	Fuller, Roland
371	Jordan, Alexander
371	Kent, George
371	Lynn, Richard (ed)
371	Mayer, H C
371	Negretti & Zambra
371	Taylor-Hobson
371	Williams, Mari E W
371	Willmott, John Edward

412	Spink, Reginald
412	Wall, T
413	Chapman-Huston, W W Desmond M & Cripps, Ernest C
413	Cow & Gate
413	Enock, Arthur Guy
413	Express Dairy
413	Hornby & Clarke
413	Jenkins, Alan
413	Jephcott, Harry
413	Kraft
413	Monstead, Otto
413	Morgan, Bryan Stanford
413	Nestlé
413	O'Gráda, Cormac
413	Unigate
414	Batchelors Foods
414	Batchelors Peas
414	Benham, Maura
414	Fieldhouse, David Kenneth
414	Jolly, William Percy
414	Leverhulme
414	Reader, William Joseph
414	Reader, William Joseph
414	Reader, William Joseph
414	Wilson, Charles
414	Wilson, Charles
414	Wilson, Charles
414	Wright, Louise
415	Batchelors Foods
415	Reader, William Joseph
416	Andrews, Sydney; Burls, John (ed)
416	Bailey, E H
416	Bradshaw, J B
416	Bramwell, A G
416	Burgess, Clare et al
416	Cauldwell, E
416	Dence, Alexander Henry
416	Gauldie, Enid
416	Graham, Richard
416	Halifax Flour Society
416	Hutchisons of Kirkcaldy
416	Janes, Hurford
416	Marriage, E
416	Nelstrop, Wm
416	Rank, Joseph
416	Scott, William Maddin
416	Silcock, R & Sons

416	Strong, Leonard Alfred George
416	Vaughan-Thomas, Wynford
416	Wigfull Mill
416	Wright & Sons
418	Black, Mona S
418	Chapman-Huston, W W Desmond M
418	Colman, H C
418	Green, Daniel
418	Reckitt, Basil Norman
419	Adam, James S
419	Bilsland Brothers
419	Burnett, John
419	Chapman, Elaine
419	Corley, Thomas Anthony Buchanan
419	Cramb, George E
419	Croall, Robert
419	Davis, F C
419	Dence, Alexander Henry
419	Hill, Howard
419	Huntley & Palmers
419	Huntley & Palmers
419	Huntley & Palmers
419	Incorporation of Bakers of Glasgow
419	Lyons, J
419	Macfarlane, Lang & Co
419	Mackie
419	Peek, Frean
419	Richardson, D J
419	Warburtons
419	Windsor, David Burns
420	Andrews, Allen
420	Bradley, D
420	Chalmin, Philippe
420	Fairrie, Geoffrey
420	Garbutt, John L
420	Hugill, Antony
420	Janes, Hurford & Sayers, H J
420	Jones, Tom
420	Labour Research Dept
420	Lyle of Westbourne, Lord
420	Lyle, Oliver
420	Meneight, W A
420	Saunders, Alan
420	Stoddard, Jeanne
420	Tate & Lyle
420	Travers, Frank
420	Travers, Joseph & Sons

420	Watson, J A
421	Cadbury
421	Cadbury
421	Cadbury
421	Crutchley, George W
421	Davenport-Hines, Richard P T (ed)
421	Finch, Robert
421	Fry, J S & Sons
421	Fry, J S & Sons
421	Fry, J S & Sons
421	Gardiner, Alfred George
421	Goodall, Francis
421	Greenhill, Robert G
421	Hulme, A G
421	Jeremy, David J
421	Johnson, D G
421	Jones, Geoffrey
421	Jones, Geoffrey
421	Jones, Geoffrey (ed)
421	Leeds, Herbert
421	Lesser Columbus (pseud. Laurence Cowen)
421	Mackintosh, Eric D
421	Mackintosh, Harold Vincent
421	Mackintosh, John & Sons
421	Mathieson, George
421	Mennell, G H
421	Pascall, James
421	Payne, George
421	Rogers, T B
421	Sessions, William K & E Margaret
421	Terry's
421	Thornton
421	Vernon, Anne
421	Wall, T
421	Wallace, William
421	Williams, Iolo Aneurin
421	Windsor, David Burns
422	Bibby, J & Sons
422	Bibby, John B
422	Bibby, John B & Bibby, Charles L
422	Silcock, R & Sons
422	Vaughan-Thomas, Wynford
423	Antrobus, Hinson Allan
423	Antrobus, Hinson Allan
423	Armstrong, John
423	Bennett, Richard
423	David Lloyd, Pigott & Co

423	David Lloyd, Pigott & Co
423	Duncan Brothers & Co
423	Finlay, James & Co
423	Foley, John
423	Green, Daniel
423	Greenhill, Robert G
423	Jackson, R & Co
423	Janes, Hurford
423	Lipton
423	Lyons, J
423	Melrose, Andrew & Co
423	Mui, Hoh-Cheung & Lorna H
423	Mui, Hoh-Cheung & Lorna H
423	Newton, Ernest Edward
423	Noël, A & Sons
423	Richardson, D J
423	Sarson, Henry
423	Teetgen & Co
423	Tuke Mennell & Co
423	Twining
423	Twining, Stephen H
423	Twining, Stephen H
423	Wainwright, David
423	Waugh, Alexander Raban
423	Willson, B F
423	Wright, Louise
424	Anderson, John L
424	Atherton, F W
424	Balfour, John Patrick Douglas
424	Banthrone of Newton
424	Barnard, Alfred
424	Burrough, James
424	Collinson, Francis
424	Craig, Charles
424	Dewar
424	Glenlivet
424	Glenlivet
424	Gold, Alec H
424	Greenall, Gilbert & John
424	House, Jack
424	Janes, Hurford
424	Laver, James
424	Lee, T A
424	Marriner, Sheila (ed)
424	Maxwell, Herbert Eustace
424	McCreary, Alf
424	Moss, M S & Hume, J R

427	Hardinge, G N
427	Hardinge, G N
427	Harvey & Beard
427	Hawkins, Kevin H
427	Hawkins, Kevin H
427	Hawkins, Kevin H & Pass, C L
427	Hill, Brian
427	Hunt Edmunds & Co
427	Ind Coope
427	Jacobson, Michael
427	Jacobson, Michael
427	Janes, Hurford
427	Janes, Hurford
427	Janes, Hurford
427	Keir, David Edwin
427	King, Frank A
427	Knox, Diana M
427	Lackey, Clifford
427	Lloyd, Keith J
427	Lynch, Patrick & Vaizey, John
427	Mathias, Peter
427	McMaster, Charles
427	Meux, Valerie Susie
427	Mitchell, Albert & Grayling, Christopher
427	Mitchells & Butlers
427	Mitchells & Butlers
427	Monckton, H A
427	Nevile, Sydney Oswald
427	Page, Ken
427	Pudney, John Sleigh
427	Radmore, D F
427	Richards, John
427	Richardson, Neil
427	Richardson, Neil
427	Rose, A
427	Serocold, Walter P
427	Shaw, Herbert
427	Sheppard, Francis Henry Wollaston
427	Sibley, Brian
427	Simonds, H & G
427	Slater, J Norman
427	Strong, Leonard Alfred George
427	Strong, Leonard Alfred George
427	Taylor, H A & D
427	Tetley, Joshua & Son
427	Trumans
427	United Clubs Brewery Co

427	Vaizey, John Ernest
427	Vaughan-Thomas, Wynford
427	Walker, Peter & Son
427	West Country Brewery Holdings
427	Whitbread
427	Wilson, Richard G
427	Younger, George
427	Youngs, Crawshay & Youngs
428	Cantrell & Cochrane
428	Merriday, Frank (pseud)
428	Potts, Bob
428	Sheldon, Peter
428	Simmons, Douglas A
428	Stephenson, Clifford
429	Alford, Bernard William Ernest
429	Alford, Bernard William Ernest
429	Chaytor, Mark Hamilton Freer
429	Corina, Maurice
429	Davenport, John
429	Dempsey, Mike (ed)
429	Devine, Thomas Martin
429	Dickinson, Sue V
429	Dobson, P Alan
429	Dunhill, Mary
429	Evans, George
429	Francis, Pat
429	Gallaher
429	Hirst
429	Lesser Columbus (pseud. Laurence Cowen)
429	Mack, R J
429	Till, Roger
429	Twiston Davies, William
429	Winkler, John Kennedy
430	Allen, Walter Gore
430	Atthill, Robin
430	Beaver, Patrick
430	Campbell, Roy Hutcheson
430	Clapp, Brian William
430	Ellis, Shirley
430	Emery, N
430	Enfield Manufacturing Co.
430	Ferguson
430	Fitton, Robert S & Wadsworth Alfred P
430	Goodale, Ernest William
430	Harrop, J
430	Horrockses, Crewdson & Co
430	Jeremy, David J

430	Kirby, Maurice W
430	Kirby, Maurice W
430	Knight, Arthur W
430	Lynes, Alice
430	Marsden, Frederick
430	Muir, Augustus
430	Openshaw, C
430	Robson, Robert
430	Stocks, Leslie A
430	Unwin, George; Hulme, Arthur & Taylor, George
430	Ward-Jackson, Cyril Henry
430	Wells, Frederick Arthur
431	Allen, John R (ed)
431	Beckinsale, Robert Percy
431	Blair, Matthew
431	Blair, Matthew
431	Bradford Dyers' Association Ltd
431	Brooke, Alan J
431	Crump, William Bunting
431	Dobson, E Philip & Ives, John B
431	Dupont-Lhotelain, Hubert
431	Edleston, William
431	Fox Brothers & Co
431	Fox, Hubert
431	Fox, Joseph Hoyland
431	Garnett, Walter Onslow
431	Garrod, P
431	Glover, Frederick J
431	Glover, Frederick J
431	Greenwood, George A
431	Gulvin, Clifford
431	Gulvin, Clifford (ed)
431	Harrison, George & Co
431	Hartwell, R M
431	Heydemann, N & Co
431	Hirst, Geo C
431	Hudson, Pat
431	Jenkins, David Trevor
431	Jenkins, David Trevor & Ponting, Kenneth G
431	Jenkins, John Geraint
431	Jennings, Elizabeth
431	Jowitt
431	Keighley Fleece Mills Co
431	Kenyon, James & Son
431	Kenyon, James & Son
431	Macnab, A & J
431	Mahony, Martin & Bros

431	Malin, John C
431	Morton, James
431	Muir, Augustus
431	Paton, Alexander Forrester
431	Payne, Sara
431	Perks, R B
431	Playne, Arthur Twisden & Long, Arthur Leslie
431	Plummer, Alfred
431	Plummer, Alfred
431	Plummer, Alfred & Early, Richard E
431	Pollard, Sidney & Turner, R
431	Porter, J H
431	Reynolds, Jack
431	Sigsworth, Eric Milton
431	Sigsworth, Eric Milton
431	Suddards, Roger Whitley
431	Tann, Jennifer
431	Taylor, John
431	Taylor, Theodore Cooke
431	Thompson, Francis G
431	Thornton, Robert
431	Thorpe, T W
431	Topham, A J
431	Walker, Selwyn Joseph Sykes
431	Whiteley, John & Sons
432	Amalgamated Cotton Mills Trust
432	Angus, George & Co
432	Armitage, G W
432	Ashton Bros
432	Beer, Edwin John
432	Bellamy, Joyce Margaret
432	Blair, Matthew
432	Blair, Matthew
432	Blyth, Henry Edward
432	Boothman, J
432	Boyson, Rhodes
432	Boyson, Rhodes
432	Brocklehurst
432	Brown, Charles
432	Butt, John (ed)
432	Calico Printers' Association
432	Chapman, Stanley David
432	Christy, W M
432	Clarke, Philip
432	Coleman, Donald Cuthbert
432	Coleman, Donald Cuthbert
432	Courtaulds

432	Crankshaw, W P & Blackburn, Alfred
432	Crozier, Mary
432	Dalton, Barton & Co
432	Dobson & Barlow
432	Farnie, Douglas Anthony
432	Farnie, Douglas Anthony
432	Fine Cotton Spinners
432	Fine Cotton Spinners
432	Fine Cotton Spinners
432	Finlay, James & Co
432	Fletch, A M
432	Fowler, Alan & Lesley
432	Greg, R
432	Gurr, Duncan & Hunt, J
432	Hargreaves, R
432	Harris, John Raymond (ed)
432	Haslam, William Heywood & Morris, F E
432	Hayes, P A
432	Hebden Bridge Fustian
432	Hedges, J A
432	Higgins, J P
432	Hinde, F & Sons
432	Horrockses, Crewdson & Co
432	Horrockses, Crewdson & Co
432	Howe, Anthony
432	Howe, Anthony C
432	Jenkin, Alfred
432	Johnson, H R
432	Jones, F
432	Jones, Geoffrey
432	Jones, Stuart
432	Jopp, Keith
432	Killick, J
432	Lancashire Cotton Corporation
432	Lazonick, William
432	Lee, Clive Howard
432	Lee, Clive Howard
432	Longworth, J E
432	Macartney, Sylvia & West, John
432	Marsden, J S & Brock, D B S
432	Mason, John D
432	Mills, William Haslam
432	Morton, James
432	Morton, Jocelyn
432	Musgrave Spinning Co
432	Nelson, James
432	Nixon, St John Cousins

432	O'Connor, Denis
432	Pafford, Elizabeth R & John, H P
432	Pedrick, Gale
432	Pigott, Stanley
432	Political and Economic Planning
432	Porter, J H
432	Robertson, Alex J
432	Robertson, Alex J
432	Robson, Robert
432	Rose, Mary B
432	Rose, Mary B
432	Rose, Mary B
432	Royton Spinning Company
432	Sandberg, Lars G
432	Sanderson, Arthur & Sons
432	Shiloh
432	Smith, R
432	Smith, Roland
432	Snowden, James Keighley
432	Stone, Sheila
432	Stuarts & Jacks
432	Sun Mill Co, Oldham
432	Tewson, W F
432	Tippett, Leonard Henry Caleb
432	Turnbull, Geoffrey (ed)
432	Tyson, R E
432	Whitehurst, Henry and Sons
432	Williams, D M
432	Yonekawa, Shin-ichi
434	Andrews, Sydney; Burls, John (ed)
434	Bellamy, Joyce Margaret
434	Bessbrook
434	Bessbrook
434	Boyle, Emily
434	Clark, Wallace
434	Donaldson, Mrs Kathleen
434	Lawlor, Harold C
434	Linen Thread Co
434	Richardson, J N
434	Rimmer, William Gordon
434	Sinclair, Robert George
435	Cooke, A J
435	Duncan Brothers & Co
435	Finlay, James & Co
435	Graham, O
435	Lenman, Bruce & Donaldson, Kathleen
436	Allen, Philip

436	Atkins of Hinckley
436	Blandford, Thomas & Newell, George
436	Chapman, Stanley David
436	Corah, N
436	Erickson, Charlotte
436	Greening, Edward Owen
436	Gulvin, Clifford
436	Haimes, Thomas & Co
436	Harte, Negley B
436	Jopp, Keith
436	Jopp, Keith
436	Laurence, Alastair
436	Pasold, Eric W
436	Pick, J B
436	Pigott, Stanley
436	Smedley, John
436	Symington, R & W H & Co
436	Thomas, Frederick Moy
436	Towles Ltd
436	Webb, C W
436	Wells, Frederick Arthur
436	Williams, M E
437	Adburgham, Alison
437	Barlow, Ronald
437	Cameron, John
437	Dagley, Donald Burdett
437	Deakins
437	Finch, R
437	Harte, Negley B
437	Hurst, J G
437	Mason, John D
437	Morton, Jocelyn
437	Sykes, Alan John
438	Bartlett, James Neville
438	Bartlett, James Neville
438	Bretton, R
438	Cairns, Robert
438	Christie, Guy
438	Gere, Charlotte
438	Jacobs, Bertram
438	Muir, Augustus
438	Smith, L D
438	Stoddard, A F & Co
438	Tomkinson
438	Webster, Eric
438	Young, Fred H
439	Birkin, Guy

439	Blake, George
439	Buck, Anne
439	Chapman, Stanley David
439	Fletcher, Samuel Billyeald
439	Hall's Barton Ropery Co
439	Kenyon, William
439	Kornitzer, Margaret (ed)
439	Lye and Sons
439	McGarvie, Michael
439	Morton, Jocelyn
439	Philips, J & N
439	Sanctuary, A C
439	Sebire, Charles B
439	Sebire, J F
439	Shepshed Lace Manufacturing Co
439	Spenceley, G F R
439	Spenceley, G F R
439	Stuarts & Jacks
439	Varley, Donald Emerson
439	Varley, Donald Emerson
439	Vertigan, Sean A
440	Adam, Helen Pearl
440	Beaven, J & T
440	Beaven, J & T
440	Church, Roy Anthony
440	John, Arthur Henry
440	Rimmer, William Gordon
441	Bardens, Dennis
441	Davies, Bernard
441	Dean, Joseph Normanton
441	Garner, James & Sons
441	Hazzlewood, T
441	Hewit, J & Sons
441	Hicks, Agnes Hedvig
441	Jones, H Quentin
441	Jones, H Quentin
441	MacLaren, Moray David Shaw
441	McGarvie, Michael
441	Pittard
441	Russell, McDonough
442	Davis, Ralph
442	Jones, H Quentin
442	Jones, H Quentin
442	McGarvie, Michael
450	Cook, Son & Co (St.Pauls)
450	Lesser Columbus (pseud. Laurence Cowen)
451	Barber, L H

451	Barrett, W & Co
451	Benefit Footwear
451	Brierly, E
451	Britton, George Bryant & Sons
451	Campbell, William
451	Church, Roy Anthony
451	Church, Roy Anthony
451	Church, Roy Anthony
451	Dobbs, Brian
451	Fowler, E
451	Greening, Edward Owen
451	Griffin, W C
451	Halstead, R
451	Hudson, Kenneth
451	Hurn, Elizabeth
451	Lambert Howard
451	Lehane, Brendan
451	Manfield & Sons
451	Manfield & Sons
451	Mann, Amos
451	Milward
451	Oliver, George (Footwear) Ltd
451	Phipps-Faire
451	Plumb, J H
451	Pocock Bros
451	Russell, McDonough
451	Sears, J & Co
451	Somervell, John
451	Sparks, W L
451	Stanton, George
451	Stead & Simpson
451	Sutton, George Barry
451	Sutton, George Barry
451	Timpson, D J
451	Wheldon, Frederick W
451	White, John
451	Woodruff, William
453	Beable, William Henry
453	Beaver, Patrick
453	Broadbent and Turner
453	Christy
453	Clyne, H R
453	Du Cros, Arthur Philip
453	Fudge, Muriel K
453	Gieve, David W
453	Haimes, Thomas & Co
453	Harmer, F W & Co

453	Hart & Levy
453	Jenkin, Roger
453	Jennings, Paul Francis
453	Kendall
453	Lloyd, Attree & Smith
453	Morgan, H Llewellyn
453	Moxon, Stanley
453	Noal, James
453	Plant, William
453	Redmayne, Ronald
453	Reed, Austin
453	Ryott, David
453	Slade, E H
453	Smith, James & Co
453	Storrs, Ronald Henry Amherst
453	Symington, R & W H & Co
453	Thomas, Joan
453	Turner, Joshua
453	Tute, Warren Stanley
453	Wells, Frederick Arthur
453	Whitbourn, Frank
453	Wilson, Ambrose
453	Wilson, Joseph
455	Cooke, A J
455	Jopp, Keith
455	Willesden Dux
456	Goad, Rigg & Co
456	Martin, C W
456	Purvis, W F
456	Purvis, W F
456	Smith, George & Sons
460	Elliotts of Reading
461	Boulton & Paul
462	Ciba Geigy
462	Venesta
463	Boulton & Paul
463	Clarke, L J & Burbidge, H L
463	Mingay, G E
463	West's Cornice Pole Co
464	Carty
464	House, Jack
464	Wilson
465	Alford, Bernard W E & Barker, Theodore C
465	Austin, F Earle
465	Blaxill, Edwin Alec
465	Brierly, E
465	Briton Brush Co

471	Lesser Columbus (pseud. Laurence Cowen)
471	Lyddon, Denis W & Marshall, Peter A
471	O'Connor, Thomas Power
471	Owen, Roderic
471	Portal, Francis Spencer
471	Reader, William Joseph
471	Shears, William Sydney
471	Spicer
471	Sykes, Philip
471	Thomson, Alistair G
471	Tillmanns, Martin
471	Walmsley (Bury) Group
471	Weatherill, Lorna Mary
471	Whittaker, F Garth
471	Wiggins Teape and Co
471	Wiggins Teape Group
471	Willesden Dux
472	Barclay & Fry
472	Clay, Ewart Waide
472	Darwin, Bernard Richard Meirion
472	Dean, Joseph Normanton
472	Dray & Drayton
472	Evans, Joan
472	Evans, Joan
472	Evans, Lewis
472	Granville-Smith, J
472	House, Jack
472	Howe, Ellic
472	Jones, Samuel
472	Jones, Samuel
472	Kenrick & Jefferson
472	Mardon, Heber
472	Potters of Darwen
472	Reader, William Joseph
472	Sanderson, Arthur & Sons
472	Strain, Wm & Sons
472	Straker Bros
472	Sugden, Alan V & Entwisle, Eric A
472	Wall Paper Manufacturers
472	Walpamur Co
475	Abbott, John
475	Abel, Deryck Robert Endsleigh
475	Adams, John
475	Alderson, Frederick
475	Alford, Bernard William Ernest
475	Allen, William Edward David
475	Andrews, W Linton & Taylor, H A

475	Derry and Sons
475	Dickinson & Co
475	Dilnot, George
475	Dobson, Robert Montagu Hume
475	Dyson, Anthony
475	Economist
475	Ferris, Paul
475	Ford, John
475	Friederichs, Hulda
475	Fullard, Harold J
475	Gardiner, Leslie
475	Gardiner, Leslie
475	Gettmann, Royal Alfred
475	Gibb, Mildred A & Beckwith, Frank
475	Hackett, Dennis
475	Hall, Fred
475	Handover, Phyllis Margaret
475	Harris, C W J
475	Harrison & Sons
475	Harrison, Cecil R & H G
475	Hazell, Watson & Viney
475	Hindle, Wilfrid Hope
475	Hindley, Charles
475	Hobson, H; Knightley, P & Russell, L
475	Hodges, Sheila
475	Houseman, Lorna
475	Houston, Henry James
475	Howard, Michael Spencer
475	Howard, Peter Dunsmore
475	Howe, Ellic
475	Hubback, David
475	Hurd, Michael
475	Huws, Richard E
475	Hyde, Harford Montgomery
475	Hyman, Alan
475	Isaac, Peter Charles Gerald
475	Jarrold
475	Jarrold, John & Sons
475	Jewish Chronicle
475	Johnston, W & A K
475	Jones, A E
475	Jones, H Kay
475	Jones, Linda Lloyd
475	Jordan & Sons
475	Keefe, H J
475	Keir, David Edwin
175	Keith, Alexander

475	Kenrick & Jefferson
475	Kenrick & Jefferson
475	Kidd, William
475	King and Hutchings
475	King, Arthur & Stuart, Albert F
475	Kingsford, Reginald John Lethbridge
475	Koss, Stephen Edward
475	Koss, Stephen Edward
475	Leapman, Michael
475	Lee, Alan J
475	Leicester Co-operative Printing Society Ltd
475	Lewis, Henry King
475	Lewis, Reginald
475	Liveing, Edward George Downing
475	Livingstone, E & S
475	Lusty, Robert
475	Mackie, A D
475	Maclehose, James
475	Manifoldia
475	Mardon, Heber
475	McConnell, Brian
475	McKitterick, David
475	McLean, Ruari
475	Millar, Alexander Hastie
475	Mills, William Haslam
475	Minney, Rubeigh James
475	Moran, James Charles
475	Moran, James Charles
475	Moran, James Charles
475	Moran, James Charles
475	Morgan, Charles
475	Morison, Stanley
475	Morpurgo, Jack Eric
475	Mumby, Frank A & Stallybrass, Frances H S
475	Mumby, Frank Arthur
475	Murray, George McIntosh
475	Musson, Albert Edward
475	Netherwood and Dalton
475	Newth, Jack D
475	Newton, David
475	Norrington, A L P
475	Novello
475	Nowell-Smith, Simon
475	Nulty, Geoffrey
475	Odhams, William James Bond
475	Oliphant, Mrs & Porter, Mrs
475	Owen, Louise

491	Broadley, Alexander Meyrick
491	Craig, John Herbert McCutcheon
491	du Garde Peach, Lawrence
491	Greig, John
491	Laughton, George A
491	Leader, Robert Eadon
491	Leader, Robert Eadon
491	Lloyd, Geoffrey I H
491	Mappin Fraser, J N
491	Penzer, Norman Mosley
491	Pringle, Robert and Sons
491	Roche, J C
491	Simpson, Stephen
492	Bamberger, Louis
492	Elvin, Laurence
492	Knott, J R
492	Wainwright, David
492	Wainwright, David
493	Dromey, Jack & Taylor, Graham
493	Ward, George
494	Fuller, Roland
494	Gould, Maurice P
494	Jaques, John
494	Laver, James
494	Lines, Walter
495	Charles, A A S
495	Chudley, John A
495	Edwards, E
495	Harbutts of Bath
495	Proudfoot, William Bryce
495	Puddefoot, Bowers & Simonett
495	Smith, Arthur C
495	Timings, F L
495	Walsall Lithographic Co
500	B P B
500	Balfour, Beatty & Co
500	Bowley, Marian
500	Bradley, Edwin H
500	Braithwaite, David
500	Bruce, George
500	Childers, James Saxon
500	Coad, Roy
500	Cohen, George
500	Farrow, Howard
500	Gee, Walker & Slater
500	Higgs & Hill
500	Higgs & Hill

500	Holland, Hannen & Cubitts
500	Jenkins, Alan
500	Jenkins, Alan
500	Laing, John & Son
500	Lindsay Parkinson
500	Lovell, Y J
500	McAlpine, Sir Robert
500	Middlemas, Robert Keith
500	Monks, Hall & Co
500	Mowlem, John & Co
500	Murray, David
500	Pollins, H
500	Powell, Christopher G
500	Richardson, Harry W & Aldcroft, Derek H
500	Rolt, Lionel Thomas Caswall
500	Rumsby, W N
500	Simmons, Jack (ed)
500	Spender, John Alfred
500	Trollope & Colls
500	White, Valerie
500	Young, Desmond
501	Abel, Deryck Robert Endsleigh
501	Baines, Frank
501	Benfield & Loxley
501	Benfield & Loxley
501	Birch, Wm. & Sons
501	Coleman, Benfield & Loxley
501	Durtnell, R & Sons
501	Ford & Weston
501	Fosters
501	Gerrard, J & Sons
501	Glascock, J L's Successors
501	House, Jack
501	Incorporated Stone & Marble Co
501	Leach, Hubert C
501	Longley
501	Longley
501	Lowe, Thomas & Sons
501	Mackie, W
501	Marriner, Sheila
501	Muir, Augustus
501	Neville, T & E
501	Pearce Bros Builders
501	Potts, J D
501	Reeder, D A
501	Rendell
501	Roberts, C P & Co

613	B P B
613	Bamberger, Louis
613	Beaver, Patrick
613	Burt, Boulton & Haywood
613	Carnegie, J F
613	Carvel, John Lees
613	Dent & Hellyer
613	Dobson, Charles George
613	Ellis, Colin D B
613	Gardner, Joseph & Sons
613	Gridley Miskin
613	Haywards
613	Hellyer, Bertram
613	Horsley, Smith & Co
613	Jewson & Sons
613	Latham, Edward Bryan
613	Latham, Edward Bryan
613	Mackie, W Euan
613	May, R
613	McChesney, John S
613	Meggitt & Jones
613	Miller, V
613	Muir, Augustus
613	Muir, Augustus
613	Naylor, R A
613	Nicholls & Clarke
613	Perren, Richard
613	Piller, Norman
613	Potter, Walter C
613	Rankin, John
613	Shinkfield, H J
613	Stephensons of Oxford
613	Watson, Rowland
613	Williams, David M
614	Alexanders
614	Bridges, Tom
614	Church, R A & Miller, M
614	Church, Roy Anthony
614	Gowans, L M
614	Gowans, L M
614	House, Jack
614	Kenning Motors Group
614	Renault UK
614	Shaw, M
614	Smith, Arthur C
614	Western Motor Works (Chislehurst)
614	Willcox, W H

617	Monstead, Otto
617	Morgan, Bryan Stanford
617	Newton, Ernest Edward
617	Noël, A & Sons
617	Parsons, Richard M
617	Perren, Richard
617	Popham, Hugh
617	Reader, William Joseph
617	Rutter, Owen
617	Southard
617	Spink, Reginald
617	Thomson, J G & Co
617	Travers, Frank
617	Travers, Joseph & Sons
617	Twining
617	Twining, Stephen H
617	Twining, Stephen H
617	Twiston Davies, William
617	Unigate
617	Urquhart, Robert
617	Wainwright, David
617	Walker, Peter & Son
617	Waugh, Alexander Raban
618	Baker, Peter Shaw
618	Bennett, Richard
618	Bennett, Richard & Leavey, J A
619	Arthur, William
619	Chater, Michael
619	Clear, Gwen
619	Co-operative Wholesale Society
619	Flanagan, James A
619	Kinloch, James & Butt, John
619	Loasby, B J
619	Maxwell, Herbert Eustace
619	Menzies, John
619	Menzies, John
619	Moran, James Charles
619	Redfern, Percy
619	Redfern, Percy
619	Richardson, William
619	Scottish Co-operative Wholesale Society
619	Smith, W H & Son
619	Wilson, Charles
621	Cohen, George
621	Cohen, George
621	Ward, T W
622	Thornton, Robert

604

641	Twining, Stephen H
641	Vaughan-Thomas, Wynford
641	Waugh, Alexander Raban
642	Allen, Herbert Warner
642	Arlott, John
642	Briggs, Asa
642	Brooks, Brian
642	Gold, Alec H
642	Griffin, Gary Stephen
642	Hirst
642	Maxwell, Herbert Eustace
642	Menzies, John
642	Menzies, John
642	Thomson, J G & Co
642	Waugh, Alexander Raban
642	Willoughby's
643	Baker, Peter Shaw
643	Bellamy, Joyce Margaret
643	Chapman, Stanley David
643	Chapman-Huston, W W Desmond M & Cripps, Ernest C
643	Duncan, Flockhart & Co
643	Hooper, W & Co
643	Howard & Sons
643	Isaac, Peter Charles Gerald
643	Roberts, Cecil
643	Rowland, L & C
643	Savory, A C S
645	Adburgham, Alison
645	Bass, Hugh G
645	Briggs, Asa
645	Farr, F & Co
645	Foster, Richard
645	Hart & Levy
645	Hayman, Leslie C R
645	Hulanicki, Barbara
645	King, David I
645	Marment, Arthur Verriour
645	Morgan, Aubrey Neil
645	Morgan, David
645	Perrotts
645	Redmayne, Ronald
645	Reed, Austin
645	Rees, Morgan Goronwy
645	Shepherd & Woodward
645	Sieff, Israel Moses
645	Smith Brothers
645	Tse, K K

606

651	Gowans, L M
651	Gowans, L M
651	Kenning Motors Group
651	Patrick Motors Group
651	Shaw, M
651	Vincents
651	Western Motor Works (Chislehurst)
652	Anderson, John Richard Lane
652	Beaton, Kendall
652	British Petroleum
652	Corley, Thomas Anthony Buchanan
652	Ferrier, R W
652	Gerretson, Frederik Carel
652	Henriques, Robert David Quixano
652	Longhurst, Henry Carpenter
652	Naylor, Stanley (ed)
652	Polley, Bernard
652	Popham, Hugh
652	Rowland, John & Basil, 2nd Lord Cadman
652	Royal Dutch Petroleum Co
652	Shell Transport & Trading
652	Young, Edward Preston
653	Bell, Roy Frederick
653	Besterman, Theodore (ed)
653	Blagden, Cyprian
653	Bolitho, Henry Hector
653	Clear, Gwen
653	Couper, W J
653	Curwen, Henry
653	Fabes, Gilbert H
653	Fenn, George Manville
653	Gardiner, Leslie
653	George's of Bristol
653	Haden, Harry Jack
653	Hall Harding
653	Kemp's Mercantile Offices
653	Laver, James
653	Loasby, B J
653	Low, David
653	Maxwell, Herbert Eustace
653	Menzies, John
653	Menzies, John
653	Moran, James Charles
653	Morison, Stanley
653	Muir, Percy Horace
653	Norrington, A L P
653	Smith, W H & Son

653	Stanford, Edward
653	Sweet & Maxwell
653	Waterston, George & Sons
653	Wilson, Charles
654	Barty-King, Hugh
654	Bateman, G C
654	Broadley, Alexander Meyrick
654	Currys
654	Dobson, Charles George
654	Ellis & Everard
654	Ellis, Colin D B
654	Ellis, Joseph & Sons
654	Herrmann, Frank
654	Hillier, Bevis
654	Jones, B Alcwyn
654	King, Henry Charles
654	Laver, James
654	Lerner, Harry
654	Parker, Thomas H
654	Pringle, Robert and Sons
654	Wilson, Ian
654	Wilson, Ian
656	Adburgham, Alison
656	Airey, Angela & John
656	Alloa Co-operative Society
656	Army & Navy Stores
656	Arthur, William
656	Ashworth, George
656	Balmforth, Owen
656	Battison, George
656	Baxendale, W H
656	Beale, J Bennett
656	Beaver, Patrick
656	Bentall, Rowan
656	Benzie and Miller
656	Birmingham Co-operative Society
656	Blantyre Co-operative Society
656	Blatchford, Montagu J
656	Boswell, James (ed)
656	Boydell, Thomas
656	Briggs, Asa
656	Briggs, Asa
656	Briggs, George
656	Brown, Muff & Co
656	Brown, Muff & Co
656	Brown, William Henry
656	Brown, William Henry

656	Bulloch, Robert
656	Burton, Thomas
656	Caldwell, Jon
656	Campbell, L
656	Carr-Saunders, Alexander Morris et al
656	Childe, W H
656	City of Perth Co-operative Society
656	Clarke, P
656	Co-operative Wholesale Society
656	Cook, F W
656	Cook, William
656	Corina, Maurice
656	Corina, Maurice
656	Cottrell, W F
656	Coventry Perseverance Co-op Soc
656	Craig, J
656	Curls
656	Dale, Tim
656	Davis, Walter Tamsett
656	Dundee Eastern Co-operative Society
656	Earnshaw, Thomas
656	Ely, Vernon N
656	Flanagan, James A
656	Flanders, A D; Pomeranz & Woodward
656	Garlands
656	Goodden, Susanna
656	Gordon, Thomas Crouther
656	Great Universal Stores
656	Greenwood, J
656	Haigh, A
656	Harding, John Shepherd
656	Hargraves, Ian
656	Harrods
656	Haslam, James
656	Haslam, James
656	Haslam, James
656	Hawick Co-operative Store Co
656	Hayman, Leslie C R
656	Hebden Bridge Ind Co-op Soc
656	Herbert, Charles
656	Hodgson, H
656	Holyoake, George Jacob
656	Holyoake, George Jacob
656	Honeycombe, Gordon
656	Hudson, Bramwell
656	Johnson, Robert L
656	Kinloch, James & Butt, John

656	Knights, G & Farrington, A
656	Lambert, Richard Stanton
656	Lawson, William E
656	Leach, Cyril
656	Lee, C J
656	Leeman, Francis William
656	Lewis, John Spedan
656	Lockwood, Arthur
656	Macaulay, P Tarbet
656	Macpherson, Hugh (ed)
656	Maxwell, William
656	McEwans of Perth
656	Miller, Michael B
656	Moran, James Charles
656	Murray, Andrew
656	Murray, R (vols 1 & 2) & McWhirter, J (vol 3)
656	Murray, William
656	Mytholmroyd Industrial Society
656	Ogden, J H
656	Oldham Equitable & Industrial Co-op
656	Pagan, William & Young, Robert
656	Parsons, John F
656	Partington, S
656	Peaples, F W
656	Peel, Derek Wilmot Douglas
656	Perkins, Herbert H
656	Porter, J H
656	Pound, Reginald
656	Pound, Reginald
656	Priestley, John H
656	Redfern, Percy
656	Redfern, Percy
656	Rees, Morgan Goronwy
656	Richardson, William
656	Rigby, Thomas
656	Rowat, David
656	Saxton, Chas A W
656	Scottish Co-operative Wholesale Society
656	Selfridge
656	Selfridge, Harry Gordon
656	Settle, Alison
656	Sieff, Israel Moses
656	Skelmanthorpe Industrial & Co-op Provident Soc
656	Smith, H Charles
656	St Cuthbert's Co-operative Association
656	Stephen, J Thomson
656	Stewart, James

656	Stirling, T B
656	Stockport Co-operative Society
656	Swan, Malcolm S
656	Taylor, Frank
656	Taylor, J T
656	Toms, Stanley J
656	Tottington Industrial Co-operative Society
656	Tse, K K
656	Wallis, Thomas & Co
656	Walters, Chas
656	West Calder Co-op
656	Williams, Alfred Harry
656	Wilson, Ambrose
656	Woolworth
656	Woolworth
656	Wrights of Richmond
656	Ynysybwl Co-operative Society
656	Young, James
661	Cave, Austin & Co
661	Deghy, Guy
661	Lyons, J
661	Richardson, D J
661	Willoughby's
662	Barclay, Perkins
662	Barclay, Perkins
662	Barclay, Perkins
662	Barclay, Perkins
662	Bristow, Philip
662	Bruce, George
662	Cook, Norman
662	Cowen, Frank
662	Crompton, Yorke
662	Keir, David Edwin
662	Lackey, Clifford
662	Slater, J Norman
662	Trumans
662	Walker, Peter & Son
662	Whitbread
662	Wilson, Richard G
662	Yates Brothers Wine Lodges
663	Miller, Harry
663	Tremlett, George
664	Miller, Harry
664	Richardson, D J
665	Callister, Ian
665	Christie, Guy
665	Enfield, A L

710	Brooke, D
710	Bulleid, Henry Anthony Vaughan
710	Cain, P J
710	Carlson, Robert Eugene
710	Chaloner, William Henry
710	Channon, Geoffrey
710	Channon, Geoffrey
710	Crompton, G W
710	Currie, James Russell Leslie
710	Davies, L N A
710	Davies, Randall Robert Henry
710	Douglas, John Monteath
710	Dow, George
710	Duckham, Baron Frederick
710	Dunn, John Maxwell
710	Edmonds, Alexander
710	Ellis, Cuthbert Hamilton
710	Ellis, Cuthbert Hamilton
710	Ferneyhough, Frank
710	Ferris, T
710	Gale, Walter Keith Vernon
710	Gordon, Donald Ian
710	Gordon, Donald Ian
710	Gourvish, Terence Richard
710	Gourvish, Terence Richard
710	Gourvish, Terence Richard
710	Gourvish, Terence Richard
710	Grinling, Charles Herbert
710	Grinling, Charles Herbert
710	Harvey, Charles Malcolm Barclay
710	Highet, Campbell
710	Highland Railway Company
710	Home, Gordon
710	Irving, R J
710	Irving, R J
710	Irving, R J
710	Jackson, Alan A C & Croome, Desmond F
710	Jeans, James Stephen
710	Joby, Richard S
710	Labour Research Dept
710	Lambert, Richard Stanton
710	Lascelles, Thomas Spooner
710	Lee, C J
710	Lee, Charles Edward
710	Lee, Joseph
710	MacDermot, Edward T (Clinker, C R & Nott, O S eds)
710	Maclean, John S

710	Marriner, Sheila (ed)
710	Marshall, Chapman Frederick Dendy
710	Marshall, John
710	Martin, John
710	Mason, Eric
710	Mason, N M
710	Morgan, J S
710	Mowat, Charles Loch
710	Nock, Oswald Stevens
710	Nock, Oswald Stevens
710	Nock, Oswald Stevens
710	Normington, Thomas
710	O'Dell, Andrew Charles
710	Payne, Peter Lester
710	Payne, Peter Lester
710	Pollard, Sidney & Marshall, J D
710	Pollins, H
710	Reed, B
710	Richards, E S
710	Robbins, Richard Michael
710	Rolt, Lionel Thomas Caswall
710	Rolt, Lionel Thomas Caswall
710	Semmens, Peter William Brett
710	Simmons, Jack
710	Simmons, Jack (ed)
710	Simpson, Michael
710	Steel, Wilfred L
710	Thomas, John
710	Thomas, John
710	Thomas, Ronald Henry George
710	Thomas, Ronald Henry George
710	Tomlinson, W W
710	Turner, J Howard
710	Williamson, J W
710	Wrottesley, John
720	Dunbar, Charles S
720	Raistrick, Arthur
721	Anderson, Roy Claude
721	Anderson, Roy Claude
721	B E T:
721	Baker, John Clifford Yorke
721	Barker, Theodore C & Robbins, R Michael
721	Barman, Christian
721	Bell, David
721	Blacker, Ken
721	Bolton County Borough Transport Department
721	Brown, Stewart J

721	Brown, Stewart J
721	Burrows, V E
721	Conn, Michael
721	Coope, B
721	Crosland-Taylor, W James C
721	Crosland-Taylor, W James C
721	Cummings, John
721	East Kent Road Car Co
721	Ewer, George
721	Farrant, J P
721	Freeman, J D F; Jowitt, R E & Murphy, R J
721	Fulford, Roger Thomas Baldwin
721	Fulford, Roger Thomas Baldwin
721	Gibbs, T A
721	Gray, Paul; Keeley, Malcolm & Seale, John
721	Hamshere, N & Sutton, J
721	Hibbs, John
721	Hyde, W G S (ed)
721	Klapper, Charles Frederick
721	Klapper, Charles Frederick
721	Lee, G A
721	Manchester Tramway Dept
721	Merthyr Tidfil County Borough
721	Mingay, G E
721	Murphy, R J
721	Neale, J
721	Premier
721	Read, Ian F
721	Robbins, Richard Michael
721	Simpson, Michael
721	Southdown
721	Volk, Conrad
721	Warn, C R
721	Wilson, Geoffrey
722	Fox, W E
723	Allen, Thomas
723	Barker, Theodore Cardwell
723	Gammons, Walter
723	Halfpenny, E
723	Hay's Wharf Cartage Co
723	Hytner, B A & Irvine, I A N
723	Lynn, Richard (ed)
723	McLachlan, Sandy
723	Mingay, G E
723	Reader, William Joseph
723	Seth-Smith, Michael
723	Tilling, John

740	Drage, Charles
740	Dundee, Perth & London Shipping
740	Dunnett, Alastair MacTavish
740	Ellerman Lines
740	Escombe, W M L
740	Fagg, Alan
740	Farr, Grahame
740	Forres, Lord
740	France, Wm, Fenwick & Co
740	Gibson, John Frederic
740	Glen Line
740	Grant, Hilda Kay
740	Green, Edwin
740	Green, Edwin & Moss, Michael
740	Greenhill, Robert G
740	Greenhill, Robert G
740	Griffiths, Percival
740	Griffiths, Percival
740	Hackman, Rowan M B H
740	Hancock, H E
740	Harcourt, Freda
740	Harris, Leonard
740	Harrisons & Crosfield
740	Heaton, Paul Michael
740	Heaton, Paul Michael
740	Heaton, Paul Michael
740	Henderson, A J
740	Henderson, A J
740	Hill, John Charles Gathorne
740	Hilton, J A
740	Hollett, Dave
740	Holt, Cecil R (ed)
740	Holt, John
740	Holt, John Alphonse
740	Hook, Elizabeth
740	Hope, Iain
740	Hunt, Wallis
740	Hunting & Son
740	Hunting, Percy
740	Hyde, Francis Edwin
740	Hyde, Francis Edwin
740	Hyde, Francis Edwin
740	Inchcape Group
740	Jeffery, A E
740	Jenkins, David
740	Jenkins, John Geraint
740	Jennings, Eric

740	Johnston, C H
740	Jones, Clement Wakefield
740	Jones, Clement Wakefield
740	Jones, Stephanie
740	Keir, David Edwin
740	Keswick, Maggie (ed)
740	Knightley, Phillip
740	Kohn, Roger
740	Laird, Dorothy
740	Lee, Clive Howard
740	Leubuscher, Charlotte
740	Liu, Kwang-Ching
740	Long, Anne & Russell
740	Maber, John M
740	MacGregor, David Roy
740	Marriner, Sheila
740	Marriner, Sheila & Hyde, Francis E
740	Marriner, Sheila (ed)
740	McLellan, R S
740	McMillan, Stewart
740	McRoberts, J
740	Merry, Ian D
740	Milne, Alan Hay
740	Milne, T E
740	Milne, T E
740	Mitchell, William H & Sawyer, L A
740	Morris, Charles F
740	Muir, Augustus & Davies, M
740	Murray, Marischal
740	Neal, F
740	Nicolson, John
740	O'Connor, G W
740	O'Donoghue, K & Heaton, Paul M
740	O'Mahoney, B M E
740	Oldham, Wilton Joseph
740	Orbell, M John with Green, Ed & Moss, M
740	Orchardson, I K
740	Paget-Tomlinson, Edward William
740	Paget-Tomlinson, Edward William
740	Palmer, S R & Williams, G (eds)
740	Palmer, Sarah Rosalind
740	Palmer, Sarah Rosalind
740	Parsons, Richard M
740	Payne, Peter Lester (ed)
740	Porter, Andrew
740	Reader, Ernest R
740	Redford, Arthur (ed)

740	Richardson, William
740	Royal Mail Steam Packet Co
740	Smallpeice, Basil
740	Smyth, Hazel Pauline
740	Somner, Graeme
740	Somner, Graeme
740	Stammers, Michael K
740	Stevens, Edward Frank
740	Stoker, R B
740	Swire, John & Sons
740	Tatham, Bromage & Co
740	Taylor, James
740	Thompson, J Hannay & Ritchie, Geo G
740	Titheridge, Alan
740	Tregonning, Kennedy Gordon Philip
740	Vale, Vivian
740	Vamplew, Wray
740	Walker Bros (London)
740	Ward-Jackson, Cyril Henry
740	Wardle, Arthur C
740	Waters, Sydney David
740	Williams, D M
740	Williams, Samuel & Sons
740	Wilson, Ian
740	Wilson, Ian
740	Woodhouse, G B
740	Xenos, Stefanos
750	Aldcroft, Derek Howard
750	Banks, Howard
750	Barnes, Christopher Henry George Bartlett
750	Birkhead, E
750	Conn, Michael
750	Cramp, B G
750	Eglin, Roger & Ritchie, Barry
750	Higham, Robin David Stewart
750	Humphreys, B K
750	May, Garry
750	Penrose, Harald
750	Penrose, Harald
750	Penrose, Harald
750	Penrose, Harald
750	Penrose, Harald
750	Pudney, John Sleigh
750	Pudney, John Sleigh
750	Quin-Harkin, A J
750	Quin-Harkin, A J
750	Smallpeice, Basil

764	Ferguson, James D
764	Hobson
764	Martin Baker Aircraft
770	Allen, G C & Donnithorne, A G
770	Allen, George C & Donnithorne, Audrey G
770	Behrend, Arthur
770	Blake, George
770	Bolitho, Henry Hector
770	Brereton, Austin
770	Crow, Duncan
770	Daunton, Martin James
770	Davies, Peter Neville
770	Davies, Peter Neville
770	Davies, Peter Neville
770	Davies, Peter Neville
770	Davies, Peter Neville
770	Davies, Peter Neville (ed)
770	Davies, Peter Neville (ed)
770	Ellis, Aytoun
770	Gibbs, John Morel
770	Gregory, Robert & Co
770	Griffiths, Percival
770	Griffiths, Percival
770	Griffiths, Percival
770	Griffiths, Percival
770	Hanson, Simon G
770	Hook, Elizabeth
770	Hook, Elizabeth
770	Hunt, Wallis
770	Hunt, Wallis
770	Janes, Hurford
770	Keswick, Maggie (ed)
770	Knightley, Phillip
770	Kohn, Roger
770	Leubuscher, Charlotte
770	Liu, Kwang-Ching
770	Lloyd's Packing Warehouses
770	MacGregor, David Roy
770	Marriner, Sheila & Hyde, Francis E
770	Milne, Alan Hay
770	Palmer, Sarah Rosalind
770	Paul, Philip
770	Pudney, John Sleigh
770	Pudney, John Sleigh
770	Rae, William Fraser
770	Rankin, John
770	Simmons, Jack

814	Browne, Eric Gore
814	Browne, Eric Gore
814	Cameron, Rondo
814	Camidge, William
814	Campbell, Roy Hutcheson
814	Cassis, Youssef
814	Cassis, Youssef
814	Cater Ryder & Co
814	Cave, G P & Martin, Janet
814	Chandler, George
814	Chapman, Stanley David
814	Chapman, Stanley David
814	Checkland, Sydney George
814	Church, Roy Anthony
814	Clapham, John Harold
814	Clarke, Philip
814	Cleaver, George and Pamela
814	Cocks Biddulph & Co
814	Coleridge, Ernest Hartley
814	Collins, M
814	Collins, Michael
814	Collis, Maurice
814	Commercial Bank of Scotland
814	Commercial Bank of Wales
814	Cooper Brothers
814	Cork Savings Bank
814	Corti, Egon Caesar (tr Brian & Beatrix Lunn)
814	Cottrell, P L
814	Cottrell, P L
814	Crick, Wilfred F & Wadsworth, John E
814	Crossley, Julian & Blandford, J
814	Davenport-Hines, R P T & Liebenau, J (eds)
814	Davenport-Hines, Richard P T
814	Davenport-Hines, Richard P T (ed)
814	Davis, Clarence B
814	Davis, Richard Whitlock
814	Dayer, Roberta A
814	Dennett, Laurie
814	Diaper, Stefanie J
814	Dundee Savings Bank
814	Easton, Harry Tucker
814	Edwards, E
814	Ellis, Aytoun
814	Ellis, Aytoun
814	Emery, N
814	Finsbury & City Savings Bank
814	Forbes, William

814	Fox Brothers & Co
814	Fox Brothers & Co
814	Fox, Hubert
814	Fox, Hubert
814	Francis, John
814	Franklin, S E
814	Fulford, Roger Thomas Baldwin
814	Gibbs, Antony
814	Gibbs, John Arthur
814	Goodhart, Charles Albert Eric
814	Green, Edwin
814	Green, Edwin
814	Gregory, Theodore Emanuel Gugenheim
814	Grindlay's
814	Grindon, Leopold Hartley
814	Hall, F G
814	Hambro's Bank
814	Hebden, C Donald
814	Henderson, Thomas
814	Henriques, Robert David Quixano
814	Henry, James Archibald
814	Heywood, Arthur Sons & Co
814	Hidy, Ralph Willard
814	Hill, Edwin Darley (ed)
814	Hilton, John Peter
814	Hoare, Henry Peregrine Rennie
814	Hobson, Oscar Rudolf
814	Hodge Group
814	Horne, H Oliver
814	Horne, H Oliver
814	Horne, H Oliver
814	Howarth, William
814	Howarth, William
814	Hughes, John
814	Ionian Bank
814	Jaffrey, Thomas
814	Jones, Colin
814	Jones, Geoffrey
814	Jones, Geoffrey
814	Jones, Stuart
814	Jones, Stuart
814	Joslin, David Maelgwyn
814	Keith, Alexander
814	King, Frank Henry Haviland
814	Kinross, John
814	Kirby, Maurice W
814	Kirby, Maurice W

624

814	Knowles & Foster
814	Knox, James
814	Lancashire & Yorkshire Bank
814	Leader, Robert Eadon
814	Leader, Robert Eadon
814	Leighton-Boyce, John Alfred Stuart
814	Lewis, C M
814	Lloyd, Humphrey
814	Lloyd, Samuel
814	London & South Western Bank
814	Mackenzie, Edward Montague Compton
814	Macmillan, David S
814	MacRae, R J
814	Malcolm, Charles Alexander
814	Malcolm, Charles Alexander
814	Manning, Peter
814	Martin, John Biddulph
814	Martins Bank
814	Mathew, William M
814	Matthews, Philip W & Tuke, Anthony W
814	Maude, Wilfred
814	McBurnie, John M
814	McCulloch, John Herries & Stirling, Kenneth James
814	McKay, J A
814	Miln, John
814	Morgan Grenfell & Co
814	Morton, Frederic
814	Moss, D J
814	Munn, Charles W
814	Munn, Charles W
814	Munn, Charles W
814	Munn, Charles W
814	Munro, Neil
814	North of Scotland Bank
814	O'Hagan, Henry Osborne
814	O'Sullivan, Timothy
814	Ollerenshaw, P G
814	Orbell, M John
814	Overend, Gurney & Co
814	Page, Donald T
814	Payne, Peter Lester
814	Payne, Peter Lester (ed)
814	Pena, R O & Duhalde, E L
814	Perkins, Edwin Judson
814	Perkins, Edwin Judson
814	Peterhead Savings Bank
814	Prescott's Bank

815	Bellman, Charles Harold
815	Boatmens' Building Society
815	Boddy, Martin
815	Broadbridge, Seymour Albert
815	Brooks, William Collin
815	Brooks, William Collin
815	Cameron, Rondo
815	Cassell, Michael
815	Cassis, Youssef
815	Central Mining
815	Cleary, Esmond John
815	Collins, Michael
815	Coventry Building Society
815	Coventry Provident Building Society
815	Crow, Duncan
815	Davenport-Hines, Richard P T (ed)
815	Davies, Glyn
815	Davies, Peter Neville
815	Davies, Peter Neville
815	Davis, Martyn
815	Dormer, Ernest W
815	Elkington, George
815	Fort, George Seymour
815	Fort, George Seymour
815	Halifax Building Society
815	Halifax Building Society
815	Halifax Building Society
815	Henriques, Robert David Quixano
815	Henriques, Robert David Quixano
815	Hicks, Agnes Hedvig
815	Hicks, Agnes Hedvig
815	Hobson, Oscar Rudolf
815	Hughes, Fielden
815	Jessup, Edward
815	Jessup, Edward
815	Lambert, Richard Stanton
815	Lambeth Building Society
815	Last, Donald
815	Lowe, C J
815	Mansbridge, Albert
815	Martin, P W
815	McGrandle, Leith
815	Mee, F
815	Michie, Ranald C
815	Noakes, Aubrey
815	O'Hagan, Henry Osborne
815	Parry, T V

815	Peterborough Provincial Benefit Building Society
815	Phillips, R J
815	Price, Seymour J
815	Price, Seymour James
815	Raw, Charles
815	Redden, Richard
815	Reid, Margaret Isabel
815	Scottish Amicable
815	Spender, John Alfred
815	Tozer Kemsley and Millbourn
815	Wainwright, David
815	Weir, Ronald B
815	Williams, N
820	Allen, Walter Gore
820	Alliance Assurance
820	Anderson, B L
820	Anderson, James Gibson
820	Ashmead, John
820	Barnard, R W
820	Baumer, Edward
820	Beaver, Patrick
820	Beresford, M W
820	Besant, Arthur Digby
820	Bignold, Charles Robert
820	Blake, Robert Norman William
820	British and Foreign Marine Insurance
820	Brown, Antony
820	Brown, Antony
820	Bruce, George
820	Butt, John
820	Catchpole, William L & Elverston, E
820	Chaloner, William Henry
820	Chaloner, William Henry
820	Champness, A
820	Chapman, Stanley David
820	Clark, G
820	Clegg, Cyril
820	Cockerell, Hugh Anthony Lewis
820	Colvin, C J L
820	Commercial Union Assurance Co: Exeter Branch
820	Conder, William S
820	Cox, F Hayter
820	Davies, Edward Andrew
820	Dickson, Peter George Muir
820	Dinsdale, Walter Arnold
820	Drew, Bernard
820	Drew, Bernard

820	Drew, Bernard
820	Eagle Star Insurance Co
820	Edwards, Norman
820	Felce, Ernest
820	Finch, Robert J & Roberts, Alfred
820	Francis, Eric Vernon
820	Friends' Provident & Century Insurance Office
820	Friends' Provident & Century Insurance Office
820	Fry, Richard
820	Garnett, Ronald G
820	General Accident, Fire & Life
820	General Accident, Fire & Life
820	General Life Assurance
820	Gibb, David Eric Watson
820	Golding, Cecil F & Page, Douglas K
820	Gray, Imrie E
820	Gray, William Forbes
820	Gresham Life Assurance Society
820	Grey, Henry M
820	Guardian Assurance Co
820	Hand-in-Hand Fire & Life
820	Hand-in-Hand Fire & Life
820	Hazell, Stanley
820	Head, Victor
820	Hodge Group
820	Hodge Group
820	Hodgson, Geoffrey
820	Howard, R B
820	Humpherson, L H
820	Hurren, George
820	Insurance Institute of London
820	Janes, Hurford
820	Jones, Charles A
820	Kent Insurance Co
820	Knapman, Geoffrey J
820	Leigh-Bennett, Ernest Pendarves
820	Liveing, Edward George Downing
820	London and Lancashire Insurance Co
820	Magnusson, Mamie
820	Mainland, J F & Howard, E H
820	Marine Insurance Co
820	Marriner, Sheila (ed)
820	Martin, Frederick W
820	Mason, Alfred Edward Woodley
820	Matthews, Wrightson Group
820	Maude, Evelyn John (ed)
820	Maxwell, Herbert Eustace

820	Minnitt, Jack
820	Morrah, Dermot MacGregor
820	National Bank of Scotland
820	Newman, Tom Seth
820	Noakes, Aubrey
820	North British & Mercantile Insurance Co
820	O'Sullivan, Timothy
820	Ogborn, Maurice Edward
820	Palmer, Sarah Rosalind
820	Phoenix Assurance Co
820	Phoenix Assurance Co
820	Plaisted, H
820	Price, Forbes
820	Prudential Assurance
820	Prudential Assurance
820	Ralfe, Pilcher G
820	Recknell, George Hugh
820	Robinson, Harry Perry
820	Rock Life Assurance Co
820	Rock Life Assurance Co
820	Roper, D H & Harrison, John
820	Ryan, Roger J
820	Ryan, Roger J
820	Ryan, Roger J
820	Schooling, William
820	Schooling, William
820	Scott, Samuel H & Scott, F C
820	Scottish Equitable Life Office
820	Scottish Widows' Fund
820	Shearer, W Russell
820	Shepherd, A F
820	Sherriff, Francis Henry
820	Siepmann, Harry Arthur (ed)
820	Simpson, James Dyer
820	Spater, E
820	Steuart, Mary D
820	Straus, Ralph
820	Street, Eric & Glenn, R
820	Street, George Slythe
820	Supple, Barry Emanuel
820	Supple, Barry Emanuel
820	Tarn, A W & Byles, C E
820	Thames & Mersey Marine Insurance Co
820	Toulson, Norman
820	Trebilcock, Ronald Clive
820	Treble, J H
820	Treble, J H

837	Brown, Antony
837	Byatt, Ian Charles Rayner
837	Cameron, A & Farndon, R
837	Carter, Alan
837	Dale, Rodney
837	Dale, Rodney
837	Fayle, Charles Ernest
837	Hall, Philip J
837	Herring, Daw & Manners
837	Herring, Daw & Manners
837	Johnson, J H & Randell, W L
837	Johnson, J H & Randell, W L
837	Lloyd's List and Shipping Gazette
837	Lloyd's Register of Shipping
837	Marsh, J
837	Potts, J D
837	Rowland, John Herbert Shelley
837	Snow, Frederick
837	Swindin, Norman
837	Wake, Joan
837	Wilson, Elena
838	Ashworth, A H
838	Dempsey, Mike (ed)
838	Dempsey, Mike (ed)
838	Dempsey, Mike (ed)
838	Dempsey, Mike (ed)
838	Gould, Roger
838	Hadley, Peter
838	Hadley, Peter
838	Jackson, Lionel George
838	Jones, Albert Everett
838	Littler, Eric Raymond
838	Mills, Godfrey Hope Saxon
838	Nevett, Terry R
838	Ogilvy, David Mackenzie
838	Pasold, Eric W
838	Pigott, Stanley
838	Sharpe, Len
838	Treasure, John A P
838	Williams, Edmund
839	Allen, G C & Donnithorne, A G
839	Allen, George C & Donnithorne, Audrey G
839	Allingham, E C
839	Anglo-South American Bank
839	Antrobus, Hinson Allan
839	Antrobus, Hinson Allan
839	Avery, David

839	Greenhill, Robert G
839	Griffiths, Percival
839	Griffiths, Percival
839	Harrisons & Crosfield
839	Harvey, Charles E
839	Harvey, Charles E
839	Henry, James Archibald
839	Henry, James Archibald
839	Herrmann, Frank
839	Hicks, Agnes Hedvig
839	Hill, N K
839	Hill, N K
839	Hollowood, Albert Bernard
839	Hollowood, Albert Bernard
839	Holt, Cecil R (ed)
839	Holt, Cecil R (ed)
839	Holt, John
839	Holt, John
839	Holt, John Alphonse
839	Hook, Elizabeth
839	Hunt, Wallis
839	Hurst, Margery
839	Imperial Continental Gas
839	Janes, Hurford
839	Janes, Hurford
839	Janes, Hurford & Sayers, H J
839	Jardine, Matheson
839	Jardine, Matheson
839	Jardine, Matheson
839	Jardine, Matheson & Co (Japan)
839	Jennings, Eric
839	Jessup, Edward
839	Jones, Charles A
839	Jones, Geoffrey
839	Jones, Geoffrey
839	Jones, Geoffrey
839	Jones, Geoffrey
839	Jones, Roderick
839	Jones, Stephanie
839	Joslin, David Maelgwyn
839	Joslin, David Maelgwyn
839	Keswick, Maggie (ed)
839	King, Frank Henry Haviland
839	Knowles & Foster
839	Le Fevour, Edward
839	Leubuscher, Charlotte
839	Lewis, C M

839	Liu, Kwang-Ching
839	Longhurst, Henry Carpenter
839	Macaulay, R H
839	Macmillan, David S
839	Malcolm, D O
839	Marillier, H C
839	Marriner, Sheila & Hyde, Francis E
839	McFarlane, Larry A
839	Melrose, Andrew & Co
839	Mui, Hoh-Cheung & Lorna H
839	Mui, Hoh-Cheung & Lorna H
839	Muir, Augustus
839	Orchard, Vincent Robert
839	Owen Organisation
839	Owen Organisation
839	Pedler, Frederick Johnson
839	Pena, R O & Duhalde, E L
839	Pointon, Arnold Cecil
839	Pointon, Arnold Cecil
839	Ralli Trading Group
839	Randall, Robert W
839	Redford, Arthur (ed)
839	Rutter, Owen
839	Scott, George Edwin
839	Sewell, V
839	Siepmann, Harry Arthur (ed)
839	Smith, Bell
839	Storey, Graham
839	Sugiyama, Shinya
839	Swire, John & Sons
839	Teetgen & Co
839	Tennant
839	Terry, C
839	Travers, Frank
839	Travers, Joseph & Sons
839	Tregonning, Kennedy Gordon Philip
839	Tuke Mennell & Co
839	Tyson, Geoffrey
839	Vaughan-Thomas, Wynford
839	Vere-Hodge, Edmund Reginald
839	Warde, Edmund (ed)
839	Weir, Ronald B
839	West, Richard
839	Williams, David M
839	Wilson, Sons & Co
839	Wise and Co
839	Xenos, Stefanos

841   Greysmith, Brenda
841   Hudson, Kenneth
842   Mingay, G E
842   Whitehead, Robert Arthur
846   Tute, Warren Stanley
850   Artizans
850   Associated Owners of City Properties
850   Brennan, John
850   British Land Company
850   Burnand, I B
850   City of London Real Property Co
850   Faulkner, Ewart
850   Fenter, Frances Margaret
850   Gordon, Charles
850   Gresham House Estate Company
850   Griffiths, A J
850   Hicks, Agnes Hedvig
850   McFarlane, Larry A
850   Reader, William Joseph
850   Slough Estates
850   Weir, Ronald B
911   Abbott, Arthur William
933   Nichols, Philip Peter Ross
940   Dale, Rodney
940   Dale, Rodney
940   De Barr, A E & Sharman, S M
963   B E A M A
963   Bankers, Institute of
963   Barty-King, Hugh
963   Greysmith, Brenda
963   Harris, Leonard
963   Howitt, Harold Gibson
963   Hudson, Kenneth
963   Kemp's Mercantile Offices
963   Kingsford, Reginald John Lethbridge
963   Liverpool Corn Trade
963   Musson, Albert Edward
963   Nixon, St John Cousins
963   Wigham, Eric Leonard
969   Barty-King, Hugh
969   Jones, S G
969   Keir, David E & Morgan, Bryan (eds)
971   Disher, Maurice W & Bruce, Michael W S
971   P E P (Political and Economic Planning)
971   Perry, G
971   Wood, Alan
974   Allen, William Edward David

974	Booth, John
974	Briggs, Asa
974	Briggs, Asa
974	Disher, Maurice W & Bruce, Michael W S
974	Donohue, Joseph Walter (ed)
974	Fulford, Roger Thomas Baldwin
974	Jenkin, Roger
974	Lukens, John
974	Mason, Alfred Edward Woodley
974	Nathan, Archie John
974	Roberts, Peter
974	Sanger, George
976	Austin, F Earle
976	Bourlet, James & Sons
977	Agnew, Geoffrey
977	Colnaghi, Paul & Dominic
977	Parker, Thomas H
979	Fairfax-Blakeborough, John Freeman
979	Finn, Ralph Leslie
979	Jones, S G
979	Lukens, John
979	Mills, Cyril Bertram
979	Nathan, Archie John
979	Sanger, George
981	Beaver, Patrick
981	Bird, Leslie
981	Clay, Ewart Waide
981	Dobson, Eric B
981	Elson, C H & Sons
981	Fraser, John Foster
981	Fulford, Roger Thomas Baldwin
981	Fulford, Roger Thomas Baldwin
981	Imperial & Queen Laundries
981	Johnson, Leslie
981	Macnab, A & J
981	Mingay, G E
981	Roberts, Cecil R J
982	Trumper, George F
989	Fletcher, R S